Comparative Politics

Fourth Edition

This fourth edition of *Comparative Politics: Interests, Identities, and Institutions in a Changing Global Order* provides a comprehensive introduction to the diverse historical pathways that key countries around the world have taken in their quests to adapt to the competitive pressures of twenty-first-century globalization. The authors are leading figures in comparative politics, and their combined expertise ranges across the political economies, ideologies, and histories of societies from every continent. Combining insights from cutting-edge institutional analysis with deep study of specific national histories, the case studies presented in this textbook will inspire thought-provoking debates among students and specialists alike. With rewritten chapters on theory and twelve updated and rewritten case study chapters, this book offers a creative and flexible framework for thinking about the field. The book proposes a new view of social science, shows through application boxes how theories relate to real-world applications, features completely rewritten country chapters, utilizes a new and transparent theoretical framework that corresponds with the concrete country examples, includes tables that illustrate key moments and terms in each country's political development, and features a new study on the European Union.

Jeffrey Kopstein is Professor of Political Science at the University of Toronto.

Mark Lichbach is Professor of Political Science at the University of Maryland, College Park.

Stephen E. Hanson is Professor of Government at the College of William and Mary.

For Simone, Barbara, and Jen

Comparative Politics

Interests, Identities, and Institutions in a
Changing Global Order

FOURTH EDITION

EDITED BY

JEFFREY KOPSTEIN
University of Toronto

MARK LICHBACH
University of Maryland

STEPHEN E. HANSON
College of William and Mary

CAMBRIDGE
UNIVERSITY PRESS

CAMBRIDGE
UNIVERSITY PRESS

32 Avenue of the Americas, New York, NY 10013-2473, USA

Cambridge University Press is part of the University of Cambridge.

It furthers the University's mission by disseminating knowledge in the pursuit of
education, learning, and research at the highest international levels of excellence.

www.cambridge.org
Information on this title: www.cambridge.org/9780521135740

First edition published 2000
Second edition published 2005
Third edition published 2008
Fourth edition published 2014

Printed in the United States of America

A catalog record for this publication is available from the British Library.

Library of Congress Cataloging in Publication data
Comparative politics : interests, identities, and institutions in a changing global order / edited by
Jeffrey Kopstein, Mark Lichbach, Stephen E. Hanson. – Fourth edition.
    pages   cm
Includes bibliographical references and index.
ISBN 978-0-521-13574-0 (paperback)
1. Comparative government.   I. Kopstein, Jeffrey.
JF51.C6235   2014
320.3–dc23   2014002454

ISBN 978-0-521-13574-0 Paperback

Contents

Tables

Maps

Contributors

Anthony Gill is a professor in the Department of Political Science at the University of Washington and a Distinguished Senior Fellow at Baylor University's Institute for Studies of Religion.

Andrew C. Gould is associate professor in the Department of Political Science at the University of Notre Dame.

Antoinette Handley is associate professor in the Department of Political Science at the University of Toronto.

Stephen E. Hanson is a professor in the Department of Government and Vice Provost for International Affairs at the College of William and Mary.

Okechukwu C. Iheduru is a professor in the School of Politics and Global Studies at Arizona State University.

Jeffrey Kopstein is a professor in the Department of Political Science and Director of the Centre for Jewish Studies at the University of Toronto.

Paulette Kurzer is a professor in the School of Government and Public Policy at the University of Arizona.

Mark Lichbach is a professor in the Department of Government and Politics at the University of Maryland.

Laurence McFalls is a professor in the Department of Political Science at the Université de Montréal.

Vali Nasr is a professor of international relations and Dean of the School of Advanced International Studies at Johns Hopkins University.

Peter Rutland is professor in the Department of Government at Wesleyan University.

Miranda A. Schreurs is a professor in the Department of Political and Social Sciences and Director of the Environmental Policy Research Center at the Free University of Berlin.

Rudra Sil is a professor in the Department of Political Science at the University of Pennsylvania.

Yu-Shan Wu is a professor in the Department of Political Science at National Taiwan University and Director of the Institute of Political Science at the Academia Sinica.

1 What Is Comparative Politics?

Jeffrey Kopstein, Mark Lichbach, and Stephen E. Hanson

Introduction

Imagine that you could design the political order for a country of your choosing. Where would you start? Who would get to rule? What rules for political life would you choose? Could you make rules that would be fair to everyone? If not, whom would these rules favor and whom would they disadvantage? Would they be rules that even those at the bottom of the social order, the poorest and least powerful people, would agree to? What would be the procedures for changing the rules? These are difficult questions because to answer them in a meaningful way requires an understanding of why and how different countries of the world are governed differently. With so many choices to make, it is easy to see why the job of designing a constitution would be such a difficult one.

It could, however, be made easier. One might start by evaluating the existing possibilities as exemplified by the various forms of government in the states of the world. The state is an organization that possesses sovereignty over a territory and its people. Yet, within our world of states, no two are ruled in exactly the same way. Why should this be the case? Why are societies run, and political orders designed, in so many different ways? What consequences do these differences hold for a people's well-being?

Comparativists (i.e., political scientists who study and compare the politics of different countries) believe it is possible to provide answers to these questions. In this book students will begin to understand the craft of comparative politics. Even if it is not possible to design a country as one sees fit, it is possible to understand why countries develop the way they do and why they are ruled as they are. By comparing the range of possible political responses to global opportunities and constraints, we can begin to account for the emergence of various political orders and evaluate the trade-offs involved in constructing each type. Understanding and evaluating the differences among the politics of countries are really the core concerns of comparative politics.

Comparative Politics and Political Science

Within political science, comparative politics is considered one of the major "subfields." How is it situated in relation to other subfields? Let us consider two that are among the most closely related: political theory and international relations.

In some ways, the first comparativists were political theorists. More than two thousand years ago, the ancient Greek political theorists Plato and Aristotle identified different kinds of political orders – such as aristocracy (literally "the rule of the best"), oligarchy ("the rule of the few"), democracy ("the rule of the people"), and tyranny ("the rule of the tyrant") – and wrote carefully argued treatises and dialogues on which form of government is the best. Although they offered basic explanations for why one type of government changed into another, they were more interested in justifying their judgments about the right kind of government than in telling us systematically why we get the kind of government that we do. Contemporary political theorists within political science continue this venerable tradition. They continue to write about different kinds of political orders and analyze the structure of ideas about those orders primarily to help us form judgments about them. They continue to teach us what democracy and its rivals are about.

Comparativists, by contrast, tend to suspend their normative evaluation of the world in favor of describing the political world and explaining why it is the way it is. It is important to remember that comparativists do this not because they lack preferences or are unwilling to make normative judgments but rather because as social scientists they are committed first to offering systematic explanations for the world as it is. A comparativist may not like fascism or communism (or even democracy!) but nevertheless considers it important to answer the question of why some countries become fascist, communist, or democratic in the first place. Comparativists may disagree about whether the knowledge they acquire may help make the world a better place or help us make better moral judgments about politics, but they usually agree that the job of describing and explaining is big enough, and perhaps some of the deeper philosophical meanings of our findings can be left to the political theorists. So, for example, rather than evaluating whether democracy is good or not, comparativists spend a great deal of time trying to understand and identify the general conditions – social, economic, ideological, institutional, and international – under which democracies initially appear, become unstable, collapse into dictatorship, and sometimes reemerge as democracies.

What is the relationship between comparative politics and international relations? Like comparativists, most students of international relations consider themselves to be social scientists. In addition, like comparative politics the subfield of international relations can also trace its roots to ancient Greek political theory. In this case, the person of interest is Thucydides, who attempted to understand the origins and consequences of the Peloponnesian Wars (431 BCE to 404 BCE) between the Greek city-states. War, as we know, is unfortunately an important part of the human condition. Modern scholars of international relations understandably devote a great deal of time and energy to explaining why states go to war with each other. Of course, peoples of different states do not only fight with each other. They also trade goods and services with each other and interact in many different ways. It is not surprising then that scholars of international relations also study trade between countries.

Comparativists, although acknowledging the importance of war and international trade, concentrate on politics within countries rather than the politics that occurs between them. The intellectual division of labor between comparativists, who study "domestic politics," and international relations specialists, who study the "foreign politics" of states, has long-characterized political science. With so much to learn, it seemed a sensible way of dividing up the discipline.

In the last quarter of the twentieth century, this division began to change. For one thing, most scholars of international relations now recognize that what happens within a country may determine whether it wages war or makes peace. Would there have been a Second World War without the electoral success of Hitler's Nazi Party in Germany in 1932? It is difficult to say for certain, but there is no doubt that politics *between* the European states during the 1930s would have been very different than they were if politics *within* one of them, Germany, had not led to Hitler's rise to power.

Comparativists have also come to understand the huge impact that international relations has upon the politics of almost every country in the world. War and preparing for war have always influenced domestic politics. So has international trade. Today, the ease with which goods and services, people and the ideas they espouse, move around the world have made our planet a much smaller place. Clearly, what transpires between countries influences what happens within them.

Rather than sustain an artificial division between comparative politics and international relations, in this book we explicitly take account of the global context in which the politics of a country takes shape. The international environment often provides a political challenge to which countries have no choice but to respond. In responding as they do, however, they may introduce a new kind of domestic political order that other countries find appealing or threatening and to which they in turn also feel compelled to respond. There is an intimate connection between international and domestic politics, and in the next chapter we offer a framework for thinking about this connection.

How Comparativists Practice Their Craft: Concepts and Methods

Regime Types

Although comparativists think about a broad range of questions, they are most frequently interested in the origins and impact of different kinds of government, or what they refer to as "regime types." That is, if we accept that there are different kinds of political orders in the world, what are the main characteristics of those orders, and why do they appear where and when they do? For example, all of the chapters in this book consider why democracy took root or did not take root in the country in question.

Before inquiring into the origins of democracy, however, one must have a fairly clear concept of what democracy is and what it is not. The classification of countries into regime types is tricky. Most comparativists do not simply accept the word of the rulers of a country that its political institutions are democratic. Instead, they operate with a definition of democracy that contains certain traits: competitive, multiparty elections, freedom of speech and assembly, and the rule of law are the minimum that most comparativists require for a country to be classified as a democracy.

Similarly, when comparativists classify a country as communist, they usually mean that it is ruled by a communist party that seeks to transform the society it rules according to the tenets of an ideology, Marxism-Leninism. Real countries, of course, never practice perfectly all the traits of any regime type. They are never perfectly democratic, communist, fascist, or Islamist. Democracies sometimes violate their own laws or conduct elections that are not perfectly free and fair. Beyond a certain point, however, it makes little sense to categorize a country as democratic if it prohibits free speech or falsifies election results. Was the United States a democracy before the era of civil rights? Or, to take an example from this book, if a communist country, such as China today, allows markets to determine much of economic life, at what point do we cease categorizing it as communist? Comparativists do not agree on the answer to these questions, but clearly they are important ones because before we can understand why certain regime types exist in one place and not in another, we have to agree on what that regime type looks like.

Tools of Analysis: Interests, Identities, and Institutions

Even when they agree on the important differences among democratic, communist, fascist, and Islamist states, comparativists frequently disagree on how best to evaluate the conditions that produce political regime types. This is also a very tricky question. Let us say that you were parachuted into a country and had to figure out quickly what the most important facts about that country were for determining its politics. On what would you choose to concentrate? Comparativists do not always agree on this either.

In general, we can divide comparative politics into three basic schools of thought. A first group of comparativists maintains that what matters most is material interests. People are rational calculators. They organize politically when it serves their interests and support political regime types that maximize their life chances. They are rational in the sense that they minimize their losses and maximize their gains. If you accept this assumption, then, to get a handle on the politics of a given country, what you should be studying is the structure of material interests in its society and how people with those particular interests organize themselves to gain power.

In democratic states, interest groups are usually mobilized by formal organizations such as trade unions, social movements, and political parties. In nondemocratic states, it may be illegal for individuals to come together in interest groups or competing political parties, but even in communist and fascist states, political scientists have identified many ways in which people pursue their interests to the kinds of public policies that benefit them the most.

A second group of comparativists maintain that there is no such thing as "objective" interests outside some set of ideals and ideas that defines the interests in the first place.

Who you think you are – your identity – determines what you really want. Yes, all people require food and shelter, but beyond this minimum what people value most in this world may have very little to do with maximizing their material lot. Compelling ideas on their own may influence politics in profound ways. It is all too easy to find people who are willing to die for what they believe in (that is, to act against the most important material interest of all – physical survival). Instead, what people demand out of their rulers and what rulers do is pursue the ideals that they most cherish and enact policies that are consistent with their identities. So, rather than focusing on material interests, to understand politics, you are much better off concentrating on the dominant ideas and identities of a given society.

Religion and ethnicity are two of the most common forms of identity. In democracies, political scientists have consistently shown that religion and ethnicity are very good (although not perfect) predictors of how people vote and what kinds of policies they favor. In the United States, for example, most Jews vote for the Democratic Party and most Southern Baptists vote Republican because these respective parties are considered by both groups as having ideas similar to their own on important issues. In India, a state that consists of a multitude of nationalities and religions, parties based primarily on particular ethnic and religious groups have successfully competed against parties that run on a nonethnic platform. And it is not only ethnic and religious minority groups that engage in identity politics. The success of anti-immigrant parties throughout Europe and also the importance of the Hindu nationalist party in India show that majorities engage in identity politics too.

Modern societies constantly generate new identities based not only on religion and ethnicity but also on gender, sexual orientation, and care for the environment. Democratic societies now have strong and important women's rights, gay rights, and environmental movements. And, of course, identity politics matters not only in democratic settings but also in nondemocratic ones. Communist revolutionaries hoped that if they built a better society, people would begin to define themselves and their interests in new ways and that a new "socialist man" would appear who would subordinate his selfish desires to the greater needs of society as a whole. Part of what makes the study of politics so interesting is the constant proliferation of new identities and ideals and the myriad ways in which these new ideals are either accommodated or rejected by the political order or can undermine the existing order.

A third set of comparativists maintains that neither material interests nor identities really determine on their own how a country's politics works. What matters most are institutions, that is, the long-term, authoritative rules and procedures that structure how power flows. People may deeply desire a certain kind of policy (a new health-care system, for example) and have an identity that would support this (say, a widespread ethic of care that reflects the simple maxim "I am my brother's keeper"), but the rules of the political game may be structured in such a way that numerical minorities can easily block all attempts to change this policy. So, if you want to get a quick analysis of a country's politics, what you should concentrate on are the authoritative rules for organizing human behavior: the institutions.

Political life is teeming with institutions. Democracies have institutions for electing their leaders, for channeling the flow of legislation, and for determining whether the laws are just or "constitutional." Some of these institutions are so important, such as regularly held free and fair elections, that they are part of what we mean by democracy. Other institutions, such as the rules for electing leaders, have a great impact on the politics of a country but no single set of electoral rules can be held to be more "democratic" than another. In Great Britain, parliamentary leaders are elected much as in the United States, in local electoral districts in which the leading vote getter wins the election – in other words, "first past the post" elections. In Germany, members of the Parliament, the Bundestag, are elected primarily in a multimember district, "proportional representation" contest in which parties are represented in the legislature according to their share of the popular vote. Both systems have strengths and weaknesses but are equally democratic.

Of course, nondemocratic countries have institutions, too. The most important institution in a communist state is the Communist Party, which has small party cells at all political levels spread throughout the society. Communist states also have elaborate institutions for economic planning and administration. And, of course, there is the institution of the secret police. Iran, as an Islamic republic, not only has an elected parliament but standing over this parliament is an unelected Supreme Revolutionary Council of religious leaders that possesses the right to declare invalid legislation that contradicts its interpretation of Islamic law. As in democratic countries, the institutions of nondemocratic countries shape the political arena and influence what kinds of policies are enacted.

In this textbook, we combine the three major approaches to studying why political regimes work as they do. These three ways of studying the determinants of politics – interests, identities, and institutions – represent the dominant modes of inquiry in comparative politics, and some admixture of them is present in virtually all studies, including the chapters of this book. They give us a powerful set of tools for grappling with some of the most important things that comparativists think about.

Consider again the question of why some countries (or "cases," as comparativists often refer to them) are democratic and others are not. Scholars who stress the importance of interests often argue that democracy depends on the size of a country's middle class, and hold that poorer countries have diminished chances for sustaining democracy. Comparativists who study ideals and identities explain the presence or absence of democracy by the strength of the commitment to representative government and democratic participation of the leadership and the population. Institutionalists, by contrast, focus on which kinds of political arrangements (U.S.-style presidentialism or British-style parliamentary government, for example) best ensure that elections, freedom of speech, and the rule of law will continue to be practiced. All of these approaches contribute to our understanding of democracy in the modern world.

Comparativists apply the tools of interests, identities, and institutions not only to the determinants of regime type but also use these concepts to understand why countries have the kinds of public policies they do. Even among democracies, one finds important differences. For example, some have large and extensive welfare states – systems to reduce people's material inequality. Others have much smaller welfare states. Consider the issue of publicly financed health insurance. It is generally acknowledged that most wealthy democratic countries have universal systems of government-funded health insurance and tightly controlled regulations for the provision of medical services. The big exception to this rule historically has been the United States, where health insurance and service provision remain mostly private and largely unregulated, even after new legislation in 2010. Why is this the case? What accounts for this American exceptionalism? An analysis based on interests might point to the influence of powerful groups, such as insurance companies and physicians, who oppose government interference in the market for health care because it would reduce their profits and incomes. An analysis based on identities and ideas would stress the value most Americans place on individual responsibility and the suspicion they generally harbor toward governmental intervention in the market. An institutional analysis of this question would point to the structure of political institutions in the United States in order to show how health insurance legislation can be blocked relatively easily by a determined minority of legislators at several points along its way to passage. Which of these different approaches to the question yields the most powerful insights is, of course a matter of debate. What comparativists believe is that the answer to the question of U.S. exceptionalism can only be found by comparing U.S. interests, identities, and institutions with those of other countries.

In fact, the concepts of interests, identities, and institutions can be used to assess a broad range of themes that comparativists study. Why do some democratic countries have only two parties, whereas others have three, four, or more? Why do minority ethnic groups mobilize politically in some countries and during some eras but not in others? Why do some people enter politics using parties and elections, whereas others turn to street demonstrations, protest, or even terrorism?

A question that many comparativists have studied using interests, identities, and institutions is that of when revolutions occur. Of course addressing the issue means having a clear notion of what a revolution is. Did Egypt experience a revolution in the spring of 2011 when thousands of ordinary Egyptians came out into the street to overthrow their dictator, or was it something else? Even if we can agree on what a revolution is, however, explaining when one occurs is especially fascinating for students of comparative politics because political change does not always occur peacefully or gradually. Some of the truly momentous changes in political life of countries throughout the world occur quickly and entail a great deal of violence. Notice, for example, that most of the countries in this book have experienced political revolutions at some time in their histories. Their political orders, especially in those countries that became democratic early in their history, were born as much through violent revolutionary conflict as through peaceful compromise. Comparativists frequently deploy the concepts of interests, identities, and institutions in order to identify the conditions under which revolutions occur.

Using these tools and the cases they study, comparativists often establish explanations for general families of events such as revolutions, elections, and the onset of democracy itself. When the explanations works so well (that is, when they can account for the same phenomenon across a sufficiently large range of cases) and the family of events is general enough, comparativists will use the term "theory" to describe what they are talking about. Theories are important because they help us discover new facts about new cases, and cases are important because they help us build new and more powerful theories.

Comparative Politics and Developmental Paths

A Changing Field

Comparative politics grew as a subdiscipline in the United States after World War II. At that time, Americans suddenly found themselves in a position of leadership, with a need for deep knowledge about a huge number of countries. The Cold War between the United States and the Soviet Union raised the question of whether countries around the world would become increasingly democratic and capitalist or whether some version of communism would be more appealing. A few prominent comparativists initially provided an answer to this question by maintaining that over time most countries would look more and more alike; they would "converge" with each other. Others, while rejecting "convergence theory," nevertheless argued that as countries became wealthier, industrialized, educated, and less bound by unquestioned tradition, states throughout the world would become more democratic. In other words, as societies changed, "political development" would occur. This approach to comparative politics was called modernization theory.

Even though it yielded important insights and inspired a great deal of research throughout the world, by the late 1960s modernization theory confronted withering criticism on a number of fronts. First, it universalized the particular experience of the West into a model that all countries, independent of time or place, would also follow. Political scientists doing field research in other areas of the world maintained that this was simply not happening. In poorer countries, in particular, democracies often collapsed into dictatorships. Second, and more important, political scientists working in poorer regions of the world argued that even if the history of Europe and North America (the "West") did represent a shift from traditional to modern society, the fact of the West's existence changed the context in which poorer countries had to develop. Some political scientists maintained that the poorer nations of the world lived in a condition of "dependence" on the West. Large Western corporations, so the argument of the dependency theorists ran, supported by their governments at home and by the regimes they controlled in the poorer countries of the world, economically exploited these countries. As long as this relationship existed, the people of these poorer countries (called the "developing world") would remain poor and would live in undemocratic conditions. Even those who did not share this view came to believe that the notion of a unilinear path to the modern world was not supported by the facts and that the West's existence at a minimum changed the context in which the poorer countries of the world had to live. In the face of these trenchant criticisms, most comparativists backed away from thinking in such broad terms and began to concentrate on "smaller" and more tractable questions such as public policy, taxation, political parties, and health care.

During the 1970s, however, a new wave of democratization began and dozens of countries that had been dictatorships for decades or that had never known democracy at all became democratic. Rather than return to modernization theory, with its sweeping generalizations about the intimate tie between industrial and capitalist society on the one hand and democracy on the other, comparativists have attempted to develop theories that are more sensitive to historical and geographic contexts. That is the point of departure in our book. Although we share the long-held interest of comparativists in the conditions that produce and sustain democracy, our approach acknowledges the uniqueness of the experience of the West and the huge impact that this experience has had and continues to exercise on the political development of the rest of the world.

Our approach is thus "developmental" in that we place the analysis of each country within the context not only of its own history but also within a broader global history of political development. The initial breakthrough of the West into industrial capitalism and political democracy in the eighteenth and nineteenth centuries set out a challenge for the rest of the world. The responses to this challenge sometimes took a democratic form, as in the case of France's response to Great Britain's power in the nineteenth century, but sometimes they did not, as in the cases of Nazi Germany and the Soviet Union. In fact, all of the nondemocratic regime types examined in this book were responses to the challenge posed by the most powerful capitalist and democratic countries. The international context provides the impetus through which domestic interests and identities create new institutions.

Not every comparativist will agree with our approach. Some maintain that the perspective emphasizing the Western developmental challenge to the rest of the world is too focused on the "West" and ignores indigenous developments that have little to do with the West. Others contend that it is best to leave these large questions aside altogether because they are basically unanswerable and that the purpose of comparative politics is to approach matters of the "middle range" (that is, questions amenable to neat generalizations). Although we acknowledge the hazards of starting with the West and proceeding to the frequently poorer and less democratic areas of the world – the "East" and the "South" – the West's impact is too important to ignore. It is entirely possible that some time in the future political scientists will start this kind of book with the more "advanced" East and analyze the East's decisive impact on the development of the West but that day has not yet arrived. Even when it does, however, it will still be necessary to account for the East's rise to power as a response to the initial breakthrough made by the West.

Equally, although we understand that theorizing about such large questions as why countries have the political orders they do is asking a great deal, comparativists have never shied away from asking big questions about the origins of regime types and their impact on world history. Furthermore, as the country chapters make clear, there is no reason smaller and more tractable questions cannot be pursued within our framework of interests, identities, and institutions.

Paths of Development

We divide our country chapters into four groups. Each group represents a distinct developmental path. The first group we term "early developers," and we use the examples of Great Britain and France to illustrate what is distinctive about this group. We could also have chosen other Northern and Western European cases such as the Netherlands, Sweden, and Switzerland, as well as the United States and Canada. Great Britain and France, however, offer important features that make them worth studying. In both cases, long-term economic changes created urban middle classes who used their new social power to demand a great say in the affairs of government. In Great Britain the economic growth that produced the new middle class was so rapid and decisive that it has been termed by economic historians an "industrial revolution" and caused Britain to become the most powerful country in the world and remain so for over a century. France, too, became very powerful and created an overseas empire that competed with Great Britain's. In both cases, however, democracy became firmly rooted. In Great Britain, it was never questioned, even if it took a long time to encompass all of society. In France, where the struggle for democracy was much more intense, the proponents of democratic government time and again gained the upper hand.

A second group of countries took a different developmental path. We term them "middle developers." We include in this group Germany and Japan, although we could also have included Italy, Spain, Austria, and several other countries of Central Europe. The key feature of this pattern of development is that these countries all got a "late start" in economic development and had to catch up with the early developers if they were to compete militarily and satisfy the material desires of their people. In all cases, the state played a much larger role in fostering economic development, the traditional agrarian nobility did not really leave the political scene until well into the twentieth century, the military wielded a great deal of influence, and the middle classes were socially far weaker and politically more timid than in the early developers. The combination of external pressure to develop, the dominance of traditional social classes in the modern world, and the relative weakness of the middle classes laid the groundwork for episodes of uncertain democratic politics and authoritarian rule. In the twentieth century, both Germany and Japan developed indigenous responses to the early developers that political scientists have termed "fascist." Fascism offered an alternative way of looking at the world compared with the liberal democracy of the early developers. It stressed ethnic and racial hierarchy over liberal democracy's legal equality, dictatorship over representative government, and military conquest over international trade. Although the fascist response to the challenge of the West was largely defeated in World War II, and both Germany and Japan subsequently entered the family of democratic states, fascist ideology continues to attract support in parts of Europe and Asia.

Our third group of countries we term "late developers." We include here Russia and China, although we could also have included other countries in Eastern Europe and Southeast Asia. In both Russia and China, economic development occurred so late after its initial breakthrough in the West that the state was forced to play the dominant role. As both societies entered the twentieth century, the middle class was relatively small and weak. The industrial working class was also small, deeply disaffected, and lived in horrible conditions. The majority of both societies consisted of illiterate and landless peasants. The response in both cases was a communist revolution based on an intellectual elite leading the mass peasantry in the name of a yet-to-be-created industrial working class. Communism promised a world based on material equality and a nonmarket planned economy under the leadership of a communist party that supposedly understood the scientific "laws" of historical development. At the beginning of the twenty-first century, the late developers cast off their communist economies. China, and, after a decade of serious economic crisis, Russia as well experienced rapid economic growth. Both, however, remained less than democratic – China continues to be formally ruled by a communist one-party dictatorship and Russia had significantly backslid on earlier democratic reforms – and both were still attempting to close the economic gap between their own countries and the more advanced West.

The countries in our fourth developmental path we term "experimental developers." We have chosen as our cases Mexico, India, Iran, South Africa, Nigeria, and the European Union. These cases are confronted with unique developmental uncertainties. Mexico's grand experiment is independence. Is it possible for a country to be autonomous when its northern neighbor happens to be the most powerful country in the world? Until the 1990s, Mexico's postrevolutionary political development was characterized by a one-party state and an autarkic economy (meaning a preference for economic independence over trade). These features have changed dramatically since the mid-1990s. India's grand experiment is non-revolutionary democracy. Is it possible for a large postcolonial country to be a democracy when it has had a major independence movement but still remains burdened by significant widespread poverty? It is interesting to note that India's one-party dominance and autarkic development have also been strongly challenged by both domestic and international pressures for change. Iran's grand experiment is Islamist governance. Is it possible for a country to be economically and politically powerful and thrive in the modern word after an avowedly "traditionalist" revolution? Is there a distinct Islamist path into the modern world? Iran seeks a distinctive path of development that combines political participation and markets in ways that accommodate local religious traditions. South Africa's grand experiment is multiracial democracy. Is it possible for ethnoconstitutional democracy in which power is shared along ethnic lines to survive in a country that made a relatively peaceful transition from colonialism and apartheid? Nigeria in some ways combines the developmental challenges of Mexico, India, Iran, and South Africa. It is poor, multiethnic, religiously and linguistically diverse, dependent on revenues from oil exports, and only sporadically democratic. The results have sometimes been heartening but mostly they have been sobering and even depressing. Is there a way forward for a country confronting all of the challenges of development at once? Although much wealthier than Nigeria, the European Union's experiment is perhaps the most ambitious of all, for it is essentially an attempt by multiple states in Europe to ensure peace and prosperity over the long term by yielding the most precious resource that states have: their independence and their sovereignty. The crisis surrounding Europe's single currency, the euro, that began in 2010–2011 and stretched out over many months illustrates how hard it is for democracies to form a new kind of polity beyond the nation-state.

These six grand experiments remind us that political development is open-ended. It is by no means inevitable that countries will become democracies. Undiscovered paths may still emerge. It is true during the 1990s the end of the Cold War and the demise of communism diminished the pride of being part of the "developing world" and hence encouraged the search for alternative paths to development. Many countries formerly considered part of the developing world began to redefine their interests, identities, and institutions to compete globally via democracy and markets. This redefinition was not always easy or genuine, and some countries did not stay democratic for long or were democratic only on paper. Still, there is no doubt that during the 1990s, the global hegemony of democracy and capitalism seemed unchallengeable.

The terrorist attacks of September 11, 2001, the wars in Afghanistan and Iraq in the subsequent decade, and the destabilization and severe downturn of the global economy as the second decade of the twenty-first century began, brought much of this into question. Liberal democracy, again, no longer seemed to be the default condition for much of the world. But what was the alternative? The intention of Osama bin Laden's Al Qaeda network was to launch a global holy war against the world's democracies in the hope of creating Islamist revolutions throughout the Muslim world. Bin Laden's death at the hands of the U.S. military and the events of the "Arab Spring" of 2012 seemed to suggest the failure of this project. At the same time, China's remarkable economic rise had yet to be matched by its articulation of an appealing ideology that others might follow or imitate. Perhaps even more important, China as the world's newest leading power had yet to translate its economic might into military prowess. Challengers to liberal democracy have not disappeared but they did not appear poised to threaten the global order in the same way they did in the twentieth century.

Why Study Comparative Politics?

Even once we have agreed on the questions we care about and the main concepts used in our analysis, there remains the question of how exactly we should go about studying politics. Comparativists, as the name indicates, are deeply committed to comparing and believe that a great deal can be learned by comparison of just about anything. Not only can we compare but we must compare in order to get an accurate picture of political life. Just think about why we snap pictures of giant redwood trees with people or automobiles in the background. We do this because it is impossible to understand the size of these majestic trees in the absence of something of known magnitude against which we can compare it. So, too, for political life. We compare political orders and policies so that we can understand what we are looking at in each one. It is easier, for example, to understand what a democracy is by learning something about a dictatorship.

All governments grapple with complex global issues: the need to accommodate diverse ethnic and religious identities, the struggle to increase economic security and growth, the quest to provide a strong basis for national citizenship, and the effort to cope with demands for democracy and participation. The world is a laboratory in which countries engage in grand experiments in development. There are a variety of such experiments: many different forms of culture, civil society (informal networks of citizens), economic markets, political democracy, state bureaucracies, and public policies. The comparativist compares and contrasts how two or more countries conduct these experiments. Much of this book involves describing and explaining the similarities and differences among countries.

Why, for example, are political parties different in Britain, France, and Germany? Perhaps they are different because of institutions. As noted previously Britain and Germany have very different electoral rules. Perhaps, however, the differences in parties can be attributed to differences in identities: France's tradition as one of radical revolution and Great Britain's one of slow evolutionary change. To take another example, why did Britain and

Germany react so differently to the oil shocks and budget crises of the 1970s, the highly competitive international economy of the 1990s, and the global economic downturn after 2008? Perhaps they reacted differently because of the configuration of interests. Interest groups work more closely with government in Germany than in Britain. On the other hand, perhaps the differences can be attributed to identities: German workers value more highly the protections offered by the state against the ups and downs of the market and were therefore less willing to accept cuts in their benefits (employment security, duration, and size of pay from the state in case of unemployment, health, and disability insurance) than were their British counterparts. We try, in other words, to construct plausible explanations for the variations we observe. Comparison thus allows us to test our ideas about political life. When done well, this sort of comparison provides us with a powerful set of explanations and theories that can help us understand not only the countries from which we developed them but also new countries that we have yet to consider.

The purpose of this book is therefore not to cram your head with information about politics in faraway places and times long ago (though there is nothing wrong with this). Comparing cases and explanations helps us to study politics because it forces us to think in a rigorous way. It forces us to think theoretically. It also forces us to confront in a particularly acute way the problem of applying theories to reality. Recall our example of the absence of universal public health insurance in the United States. It is quite common to read about the role of powerful interest groups in preventing this policy outcome. But did not powerful interest groups oppose its introduction in other countries? It will not surprise you to learn that Canadian doctors and insurance companies were just as opposed to universal public health insurance as their U.S. counterparts. Yet Canada enacted universal publicly funded health insurance as far back as 1963. So clearly, interest group politics alone does not determine the fate of health-care policy. By helping us to eliminate wrong answers, this small comparison of two cases illustrates how powerful a tool comparison is for helping us zero in on the correct answer to an important question.

You are not likely to become a social scientist, however. As policy makers and advisors, or as citizens wishing to participate in politics, we have two reasons for comparing countries. First, comparison encourages us to broaden our knowledge of political alternatives and possibilities and allows us to recognize diversity. Such knowledge permits us to make informed judgments about our leaders and political life. Second, the laboratory of political experience may be transferable. Countries can learn from one another. They can borrow foreign models or adapt acquired knowledge to perfect their own institutions. In short comparison allows us to draw positive (and negative) lessons from successful (or failed) experiments.

Comparison, in sum, allows social scientists to describe and explain and allows citizens to understand and choose. There are, however, many obstacles to comparing countries that differ in language, size, culture, and organization. The end result of our comparisons might be to recognize the differences rather than the similarities of various countries' experiences and experiments. Comparing the problems of two or more countries may lead us to conclude that each country is unique. The dimensions of this uniqueness, however – the precise way in which each country is unique – can only be discovered through comparison.

2 The Framework of Analysis

Stephen E. Hanson, Jeffrey Kopstein, and Mark Lichbach

Introduction

In the previous chapter, we outlined our basic approach to comparative politics. In short, we see the world as made up of competing "regime types," such as democracy, authoritarianism, fascism, and communism, which emerged in specific global and historical contexts and which shape domestic interests, identities, and institutions in particular ways. The success or failure of a given regime in one part of the world, in turn, can have dramatic effects on the global environment, influencing the domestic politics of other countries in powerful and sometimes surprising ways.

Any global order thus involves competition in world-historical space and time that affects the evolution of states. Here are the questions comparativists ask: What was the competitive international situation in which a state found itself when it attempted to modernize and industrialize? Who were its principal rivals and competitors among sovereign states? In other words, who developed first, had a head start, and could serve as a benchmark? And who developed later, had to play catch-up in order not to be left behind, and hence looked for negative and positive role models?

In order to answer these crucial questions, we deploy a standard analytic framework that will be utilized throughout this book. The core organizing principle is simple: we will explore the three most important aspects of domestic politics – interests, identities, and institutions – in a set of country studies that are explicitly set in world-historical and developmental perspective. We teach, in short, the following framework (see Table 2.1).

This diagram will be used to structure our discussions of individual countries throughout this book, so it is worth going over it carefully. Essentially, this framework allows us to analyze politics in any part of the world through a five-step process:

(1) We assess the global context facing a given country. Is the country facing serious threats or is the global situation relatively peaceful? Is economic competition severe or is the country's economy reasonably self-sufficient? Are the principles and values upheld by a

Table 2.1   The Framework of Analysis

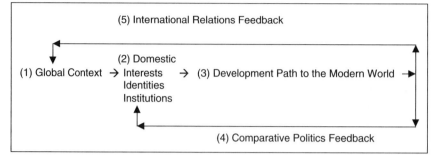

given government ones considered legitimate by people in other countries, or are they shunned as immoral or outmoded?

(2) We then explore how politicians and ordinary citizens have adopted domestic inter-ests, identities, and institutions in response to the global challenges they face. To assess people's interests, we ask: What are the major goals of politicians, businesses, civic associations, and ordinary citizens, and what strategies have they adopted to achieve them? To assess people's identities, we ask: What values, norms, ideological beliefs, and emotions shape their worldviews most profoundly? Finally, we analyze institutions by asking: What are the authoritative rules of the political order, whether written down or informal, that reward or punish particular sorts of behavior?

(3) The particular configuration of interests, identities, and institutions in each country then produces particular developmental paths to the modern world – in other words, the course by which each country tries to maintain its political, economic, military, and cultural standing within an ever-more technologically advanced and interconnected world. Some of these developmental paths allow a country to achieve significant power over rival nations; others end in failure – and still other developmental paths succeed for a time, only to fail at a later point.

(4) Each country's developmental path to the modern world has feedback effects on its domestic interests, identities, and institutions. If a developmental strategy produces positive outcomes, those who benefit from it and who identify with it most strongly will likely fight to maintain it. If a strategy leads to political unrest, economic crisis, and/or military defeat, by contrast, calls for radical change to domestic interests, identities, and institutions may emerge.

(5) Finally, each country's developmental path to the modern world has feedback effects on the global context as well. If a country becomes a model for emulation around the world, if it produces goods exported internationally, or if it conquers its neighbors, such results will shape the environment in which other countries seek to advance their own interests, identities, and institutions. The failure of a particular developmental strategy, however, can have equally profound effects on the global context – as in the case of the defeat of fascism in World War II or the collapse of the communist Soviet Union in 1991.

Our approach allows us to raise important empirical questions about comparing governments and to refine our ideas about how to evaluate good and bad governments. Let us turn to each of the five parts of our framework.

Global Context

Our world has always been interconnected. People have always migrated over long distances in search of economic benefits or to flee disease, poverty, and oppression. Ideas and innovations in one part of the world have always spread to other cultures over time. In the modern era, however, as new technologies for communication and transportation have enveloped practically the entire planet, the world has become increasingly small. Our book therefore has a "globalist" slant. The global context for comparative politics involves tensions between nations and states, contradictions between global homogenization and local diversity, and conflict among states at particular points in history.

Nations and States

A quick glance at a map of the world shows that it is divided into around 200 separate political entities called "states." At least in principle, most states appear to represent a particular people who feel that they share a common origin, or "nation." Thus political scientists frequently describe our contemporary global context as a "world of nation-states," in which each nation is represented by a particular independent government.

Yet an equally quick glance at any contemporary newspaper shows that the claim of most states to represent a single dominant nation is usually contested. To take but a few examples: the Kurds in Northern Iraq hope to establish a separate state of their own, Tibetans demand increased autonomy from the Chinese government in Beijing, and the nations that make up the United Kingdom have pressed for greater political decentralization. Some states, including the United States in the nineteenth century, have experienced civil wars because of bitter debates about just how to align national identities and state boundaries. Thus an important fact about the world is that nations and states are often in tension with one another.

When we speak of modern states, we mean first that states are externally independent. Political scientists call this external independence sovereignty. Governments have armies, navies, and air forces to maintain their external security. They send and receive ambassadors to other states, and the vast majority belong to the global club of states, the United Nations. Sovereignty also has a second, internal dimension. The international community of states generally recognizes and accepts the right and power of the government to make laws and monopolize force within its boundaries. This means that states have internal control over their populations. They maintain domestic order, collect taxes, regulate economic life, confine people in prisons, and conscript or recruit citizens into the armed forces. States vary, however, in how much external independence and internal control they in fact exert.

Some states, such as the United States and Great Britain, possess independence that is widely accepted externally, and they also exercise significant control over their populations. Other states, such as Afghanistan or Somalia, enjoy much less external independence and exercise so little control over their populations that political scientists argue about whether they actually constitute states.

The meaning of the word "nation" is even more subjective. The origins of nations and their defining characteristic may be linguistic, religious, or racial, or the perception of a common history or shared fate. But many people who consider themselves to be one nation share all of these characteristics – including the United States, whose citizens are highly diverse in all of these ways. Put simply, then, if a person considers oneself to be a nation, then we must at least begin to think of him as a nation.

Global society is thus divided into states that are defined organizationally and nations that are defined culturally. Because a state is a set of governing institutions and a nation a community of people, some – especially nationalists – argue that the two should always coincide in a nation-state. Nationalists maintain that the only proper form of government is one in which the boundaries of the state correspond with the boundaries of the nation. They claim that only in a nation-state, where people identify with the state because the rulers of the state are also members of the nation, will people accept the government as the legitimate representative of their community that is entitled to make laws on their behalf.

Although nationalists believe that national identity should coincide with state boundaries, when we look at a map of the world we quickly discover that the relationship between state and nation is highly imperfect. In fact, they rarely coincide. Very few states are composed of a single national group. Some states, such as Russia and India, are composed of dozens or even hundreds of ethnic groups, many of which consider themselves to be nations. Some nations, such as the Kurds, are spread out over many states and have never governed themselves. Finally, there are some nations, such as the Jews and the Armenians, that are spread out over many states, but that also have one central governing state – Israel and Armenia, respectively – more or less serving as a focal point for their nationalist aspirations.

State and nation often do not coincide because of history. "State-building" (the formation of a state) frequently did not coincide with "nation-building" (the formation of a sense of national unity). It may surprise you to learn, for example, that late into the nineteenth century, many people in large parts of France did not even speak French as their first language. These people had to be "made" into French men and women through the expansion of French-language public education and the official designation of standard French state symbols and holidays. It may also surprise you to learn that more than two centuries ago, when the United States gained its independence, there were fewer than twenty governments in the world that we would designate today as states. Most political entities were principalities, city-states, empires, and tribal areas without fixed and legally recognized boundaries. Today, nearly the entire surface of the globe is divided into independent states that make claims to control national territories and their populations.

Globalization and Local Diversity

A second important thing to understand about the political world is that countries all experience simultaneous and contradictory pressures for standardization and for preserving their distinct interests, identities, and institutions. Political elites want to model their counties after the example of the leading great powers of the day, yet they also wish to maintain a sense of historic continuity with past traditions and to satisfy the demands of entrenched interest groups. What is often called "globalization" – that is, the increasing interconnection of global politics, economics, and culture – thus does not necessarily produce uniform outcomes across the planet.

Clearly, interests, identities, and institutions have all become global. Trade, finance, and production are now global activities. Global markets exist not only for land and capital but also, increasingly, for labor. Economic problems are consequently global problems. Growth and prosperity are global problems. Inequality and poverty are global problems. The gap in political and social equality and economic prosperity between those living in the Northern and Southern hemispheres is a global problem. Diseases and epidemics are global problems. Environmental problems are also now global. And, of course, so is terrorism. In sum, it is not possible for a country to isolate itself from global economic trends, cycles, and shocks.

Examples abound of the ways in which Western values dominate and define social and cultural identities throughout the world. For instance, English is the international language used in business, politics, the arts, and the sciences. Innumerable technical standards derived from the West define the global business culture. The notion of universal human rights derives from Western ideas of justice. At a more mundane level, consumer culture itself has become global. People throughout the world increasingly wear the same kinds of clothing, eat many of the same kinds of food, listen to the same music, and watch the same television programs. The global masses who consume Coca-Cola and McDonald's hamburgers, wear sneakers and blue jeans, and watch Harry Potter films attempt to move up the material and status hierarchy and enter the world of Armani apparel, Chanel perfume, and Dom Perignon champagne. Much of the upwardly mobile global middle class, in turn, strives to acquire the lifestyle of Lear Jets, Porsche cars, and Prada bags. These aspirations, at each level, are the same around the world.

Not only have interests and identities become global, but institutions have, too. Examples of regional or continent-wide institutions include the European Union and the North American Free Trade Agreement or NAFTA (the comprehensive regional trade agreement signed by the United States, Canada, and Mexico in 1994). Global actors such as the United Nations, the World Bank, the International Monetary Fund, and the World Trade Organization issue extensive supranational regulations and exert an extraordinary amount of influence. International nongovernmental organizations such as the Roman Catholic Church, the International Red Cross, Greenpeace, and Amnesty International affect the lives of ordinary people in large and small ways.

Global markets, Western values, and international institutions exercise an important common, one might even say homogenizing, influence across borders. In some ways, the world has partially converged, and the result is diminished diversity of political and economic institutions. And the more states and societies begin to resemble each other, the more pressure there is on nonconforming states to change their ways to fit in.

Despite these pressures toward standardization, however, the worldwide movement toward variations on a common theme of democracy and markets – a theme originally developed in the West – has generated its own antithesis. Notwithstanding global trends, there persist important and interesting differences. States attempt to develop distinctive national policies to deal with the global economy and invent institutional variations of democracies and markets. In some market economies such as those in Great Britain and the United States, the state plays a primarily regulatory role, setting out the rules of the game in which people and companies compete. In Germany and Japan, by contrast, the state has a much stronger hand in guiding the market, frequently involving itself in such areas as finance and wage negotiations. Despite some global convergence, the idea of different paths to the modern world – for example, variations on democracy, authoritarianism, fascism, and communism – is still relevant.

For example, since the 1980s, political scientists have debated whether global economic competition will force all advanced industrial economies to adopt similar social policies and levels of taxation. So far, there is little evidence in the twenty-first century that this is actually occurring, and in fact the pressures of economic competition have intensified the search within different countries for ways to adapt that preserve their national identities, unique structures of domestic interests, and distinctive institutional orders. Since 2000, for example, Russia's leaders have pushed to restore the role of the central state in managing much of the country's key industries; at the same time, in the United States, a growing libertarian movement argues for the full deregulation of markets, the privatization of state services, and severe cutbacks in welfare-state expenditures and public-sector taxes.

Similarly, some political scientists have argued that globalization will lead to an increasingly secular world in which traditional religious loyalties begin to fade. Yet there is much evidence of the continuing power of religious identity in shaping political action, in countries as different as Iran, Israel, the United States and even in the European Union. At the same time, demands for the full political equality of women, gays, lesbians, and the transgendered have been met with vastly different responses in different parts of the world.

Comparativists often study challenges to the state "from below" under the rubric of social movements and revolutions. These, too, are profoundly affected by the global context. Student revolts, terrorism, and fascist, Marxist, and democratic revolutions have come in waves that affect many countries at the same time. Yet the outcomes of social movements and revolutions in different countries often diverge dramatically. Herein lies another paradox of globalization: the increasing interdependence of the world also generates heterogeneity, as different countries with different domestic interests, identities, and institutions confront the same global forces in different ways.

In your reading you will find contradictory global and local forces that characterize the current community of nations and states. Although since the 1800s there has been a consolidation of the world into nation-states, there has also been a set of challenges to the state: those from below, which challenge the state through the growing independence of civil society; and those from above, which challenge the state through the growth of regional and supranational forces.

Developmental Paths and Conflicts among States

A third important fact about the world is that because of their different developmental paths, different countries' strategies come into conflict with one another with remarkable frequency. Thus in addition to the tensions between states and nations and the contradictory pressures faced by governments toward standardization and preserving their distinctiveness, the global political world is marked by nearly perpetual competition among states themselves.

Our historical point of departure in this book is the profound and irreversible change that occurred in the northwest part of Europe, and especially Great Britain, approximately 250 years ago. This most important critical juncture in modern history is often subsumed under the rubric of the Industrial Revolution, which ran its course roughly from 1780 to 1850. In a very short period, new technologies of mass production, the creation of large urban areas containing a growing proportion of the population, the commercialization of agriculture, the increasing ability to manipulate nature because of rapid advances in scientific knowledge, and new methods of organizing people in administrative bureaucracies combined in Great Britain and a few other countries to generate a new society of unprecedented power that succeeded during the nineteenth century in conquering much of the rest of the planet.

Like it or not, the rest of the world had to respond to the British challenge. Comparativists have spent much time documenting and explaining these responses. To take just one example, once Great Britain became *the* major power in the world, Germany felt pressure to catch up. In responding, however, Germany could not simply repeat the British experience because that would have taken, many Germans believed, far too long. Instead, Germany developed its own set of political and economic institutions that exercised an important impact on its subsequent political and economic history. In fact, as we will see later, Germany still lives with the institutional legacies of its initial response to the British "challenge."

The developmental logic of countries differs partly because countries began their development during different world-historical eras. As mentioned previously, for example, Great Britain embarked on the path to modern capitalist development before any of the other states and thus laid down the political, economic, and military challenge to which other states responded. In Europe, France, Germany, and Russia responded to the British challenge out of fear of being considered backward and fear of military invasion and/or political humiliation, but they did so in their own ways, and hence their developmental histories differ from Britain's and from each other's. Japan, China, Mexico, India, Iran, Nigeria, and South Africa – the other countries studied in this book – attempted to find their own ways into the modern world of competitive sovereign states. Each used the resources – human, institutional, and economic – available at the time it responded to the challenges that came from the outside world.

To understand the politics of states today, it is crucial to look at the strategic and defensive modernization that these states undertook historically to preserve their national interests, identities, and institutions. Global political competition affects all countries of the world. Late development brought challenges in the form of malevolent Western colonialism and imperialism. It also brought opportunities in the form of support for establishing liberal democracy by the United States and its allies after World War II. In short, positive and negative models of development permitted the late and experimental developers to learn from the positive experiences and avoid the negative experiences of countries that preceded them historically.

In sum, we stress that domestic politics must be understood in world-historical perspective; that our descriptions and explanations must take into account particular historical situations; and that domestic economies, cultures, and politics are invariably affected by the competitive international environment of states.

Domestic Interests, Identities, and Institutions

What aspects of domestic politics are affected by the global context of development? We advance three concepts that are relatively simple but very powerful. First, people are rational beings who pursue their interests. Second, people are meaning-seeking beings who are defined by their identities. Third, people's interests and identities are shaped by and pursued within institutions. Interests, identities, and institutions are all, in turn, shaped, as shown in our country chapters, by the global context of development. The global context of development, therefore, matters to comparativists because it produces certain patterns of interests, identities, and institutions that persist over time and shape the countries in which we live.

Interests

Politics is partly about the pursuit of interests. One reason that people become involved in politics is to get the things they want from the government and to ensure that the state enacts laws and policies that advance their interests. Of course, what people want varies greatly. Still, there is no denying that a large part of politics in any society revolves around the question of who gets what. I may want a higher economic standard of living and you may want a cleaner environment. How these differences in interests are resolved tells us much about a country's politics.

We therefore assume that individuals have preferences, goals, and objectives. They also face temporally fixed constraints, limitations, and resources. People are problem solvers who try to optimize their gains and minimize their losses. They therefore make choices among available alternatives in order to reach their goals. In politics, what this means is that material interests often determine policy preferences. People react to the incentives they face and devise strategies and tactics to pick the alternative that best enables them to satisfy their material self-interest.

Material interests are pursued not only by individuals but also collectively. People who share an interest often attempt to act as if they were a single individual. It is not easy to do this because of what political scientists call the collective-action problem: people who want to act as a unified group often find that individuals are narrowly focused on their own personal situation and see no rational reason to contribute their time or resources to collective causes. Yet, people do band together in pursuit of their common concerns and join political parties, interest groups, and social movements that become important bodies. Professional associations, trade unions, health lobbies, and environmental organizations are but a few of the many kinds of interest groups that people join in order to pursue their interests.

Comparativists frequently focus on a particular category of collective interest that they term "class." For example, when they write of the "working class," they are referring to the large group of people who make their living by selling their labor. Of course, with such a large group it is unlikely that they will speak with a single voice or act as if they all had the same interest. The concept of class therefore can be a very tricky one to use.

Comparativists also note that interest groups are more powerful in some countries than in others. Well over a century ago, Alexis de Tocqueville observed the propensity among the inhabitants of the United States to join groups and participate in associational life. Since then, other comparativists have painted a more complex picture. In some countries, such as Germany and Japan, large numbers of people join trade unions. In others, such as the United States and Canada, this number is much smaller. In dictatorial countries such as the USSR under Joseph Stalin or China under Mao Zedong, it may be very difficult for interest groups to form because the leaders have the power and will to prevent them from coming into existence. One measure of whether a country is becoming more democratic is whether the people have the right to form interest groups and through these groups to influence political decisions. The kinds of interest groups and their strength determine much about the politics of a country.

So many interest groups are often at work in a country that its politics become gridlocked. All too often such is the case in the United States. In countries such as India and South Africa, ethnic interest groups frequently alter the legislative agendas of ruling coalitions and presidents. Another focus for comparativists therefore is how conflict and cooperation among interest groups get worked out in different societies. In Great Britain, as in the United States, politics revolves around the intense competition among interest groups that comparativists call "pluralism." In Japan and Germany, on the other hand, social groups often seek to cooperate and avoid conflict, even of the peaceful kind, through institutionalized bargaining arrangements called "corporatism."

Comparativists doing interest-based analyses typically ask: What is the distribution of resources in society? What are the major interest groups in a society? What are their political preferences? What are the obstacles to collective action, and which groups have managed to overcome the obstacles to acting collectively? Are there coalitions between well-endowed or poorly endowed groups that can tilt the balance in the case of conflict? Who are the winners and losers of conflicts?

In sum, the pursuit of material interests through interest-group politics is affected by the global context and, in turn, interest groups battle over alternative paths of development. The pursuit of material interests thereby affects the distribution of economic rewards in society and consequently represents one important way of approaching comparative politics.

Identities

Politics is also about identity. Although evidence shows that people all over the world often pursue similar goals, and thus can be said to share certain interests, people also frequently define what is in their interest differently. Based on particular sets of beliefs and values that we often refer to as culture, they will even define their material interests differently. What people are willing to give their life for, how much hardship they will bear during war, or how many hours on weekends they are willing to work varies across societies. Likewise, the kinds of ideas, political language, and even physical demeanor that people expect from their politicians also vary greatly across nations and states.

Think, for example, how religion and ethnicity influence politics. If people define their identity in religious terms – that is, if they say to themselves, "We are primarily Jewish, Christian, or Muslim, and not German, French, or Iranian" – they will define their interests differently from people who do not tend to define their identity on the basis of religion. In turn, they will support different kinds of governmental policies toward religion, schooling, and popular culture. Ethnicity and national sentiments have a similar kind of influence on how people define themselves. If someone defines herself primarily in ethnic terms, she will tend to care most about how many people of her own ethnic group or nation are in positions of political power. She will tend to define her interests in ethnic terms. It is common, for example, for people of an ethnic group to want a state that will defend its rights to schooling in their language and cultural traditions and to want politics and administration to be controlled by people of their ethnic group.

Just as people with different economic or material interests can clash over their differences, people with different identities also frequently disagree on politics. Although the Soviet Union was a single country, it consisted of many different ethnic groups that were never fully subordinated to a single "Soviet" identity. Indeed, this lack of a common Soviet identity was an important contributing factor to the breakup of the Soviet Union. Often, however, the results of identity politics can be tragic. During the Yugoslav civil wars of the 1990s, people who speak basically the same language began to define their identities so differently (often in terms of religious and "ethnic" differences) that they were willing to kill one another in order to live in areas that were ethnically "pure." In the aftermath of the U.S. invasion of Iraq in 2003, many Sunni and Shiite Muslims who had lived side by side for several centuries no longer felt they could live in the same neighborhood, or even the same country, as each other.

Of course, people may possess not simply one identity but several competing ones, and it is not obvious which one will dominate or how people will ultimately act based on their identities. Someone might be, for example, a woman and black and feel equally strongly about both of these identities. Political leaders often play an important role in mobilizing some identities and neutralizing others. In France, for example, right-wing politicians have tried since the 1990s to persuade the French that their traditional notions of who is

French – someone born on French soil – should be changed and that the true French are those who have been born into the French culture. The idea here is to exclude as many immigrants from citizenship and public life as possible. On the other hand, at the same time, German politicians have been working to alter the notion of who is a German, an idea that to this day remains primarily based on blood ties to other Germans, in order to make German identity more inclusive. Similarly, successive Indian governments have worked very hard at catering to the various subnational identities within the country while simultaneously carving out a distinctive "Indian" national identity that will be more important to people than all of their other identities.

Religion and ethnicity are only two of the more important kinds of identities. One can easily point to a politics of gender, environmental, and regional identities. Each of these identities informs what people want out of politics, what they are willing to do, and how they define their interests.

The subject can be made even broader, however. Comparativists frequently study attitudes in society toward such issues as the role of government, the kinds of institutions that people want, and the degree of their commitment to democracy. Such studies may take the form of quantitative public-opinion surveys about attitudes and opinions or may be microlevel ethnographic studies of civic associations, such as Greenpeace, the National Rifle Association, or local Parent-Teacher Associations.

Material interests frequently trump social identities. In 1992, for example, Bill Clinton won the U.S. presidential election with the slogan "It's the economy, stupid." But it is easy to be cynical and think that people care only about money. In fact, many types of social identities can trump material interests, allowing identity politics to prevail. For example, in Iran, Ayatollah Khomeini thought that "economics is for donkeys." The world has seen a revival of traditional communities, religious fundamentalism, ethnic and racial identities, and gender identifications that have not been washed away by (and have actually been strengthened as a reaction against) Western materialism.

In fact, social identities can even influence what people think their material interests are. The great German social scientist Max Weber showed how the early Protestants' concern about the fate of their immortal souls caused them to work as efficiently as they could and consume as little as possible in the hope that their worldly success would be a sign that they were members of the "elect" and not the "damned." This work ethic, the Protestant ethic, as Weber termed it, created a huge increase in productivity and savings and laid the foundation for modern capitalism. The impact of identities on material life, however, extends well beyond the West. Because identity can discipline a labor force for economic development, authoritarian states often try to impose ideas on societies in order to promote economic growth. Stalin in the Soviet Union and Mao in China were ideologically committed to Leninism. They sought to create a dedicated population of true believers who would suspend their own material desires in the present in order to build utopian, egalitarian societies in the future. In Iran at the beginning of the twentieth century, secular nationalism replaced Islam in part to encourage economic development. After Iran's secular nationalism was replaced by an Islamic Republic in 1979, many hoped that Islam, too, would encourage economic development.

Comparativists doing identity-based analyses of politics ask: What are the dominant ideas of a society? What do people value most? How do these values shape political behavior? What ideals do people expect their leaders to share? Why do some identity groups conflict and others live in relative harmony? How do leaders use identities to mobilize their populations for projects they deem important? What ideological principles do leaders hold that may influence their policies and decisions?

Institutions

We now turn from interests and identities to institutions. Institutions provide an important arena in which politics takes place. When comparativists speak of institutions, they usually mean the authoritative rules that structure political life. We first explore how the global context influences domestic institutions and how these institutions, in turn, affect developmental paths by influencing identities and interests. We then explain why many comparativists consider the study of politics to be synonymous with the study of institutions.

Comparativists often start their analysis by examining the state. As described previously, the state is an organization that maintains external sovereignty and internal control over a particular territorial jurisdiction. It is important to note, however, that this control may be stronger or weaker depending upon a great number of circumstances. An important factor affecting how societal interests and identities influence politics and public policy is whether the state is strong or weak. But what do we mean by a "strong" or "weak" state? Comparativists usually think of state strength as being determined by two factors: autonomy and capacity.

Consider autonomy. The state may be autonomous from the interests and identities of society. This means that state leaders and officials cannot be easily influenced by specific groups in society – business associations, working-class unions, or religious identity groups, for example – that try to penetrate and capture the state to use it to pursue their narrow concerns rather than the broader public good. The state's political and administrative leaders in a strong state are capable of formulating and defining their own preferences for what they would like to see the state do. Hence, the state can be autonomous in the sense of making its own decisions free from outside interference.

Now consider capacity. The state might also have great power and capacity in relation to the interests and identities of society. That is, a strong state will have the resources and the ability to use those resources effectively to implement its decisions and strategies in order to address the problems, challenges, and crises of development, in spite of what class interests and religious identities might prefer.

Many comparativists believe that a strong – that is, autonomous and capable – state is good for economic development. Certainly those states that fail to provide for the minimum of public safety and services, such as Iraq and Afghanistan, are usually considered to be failed states. By contrast, a strong state can pursue the general good of all society. It does not have to follow the narrow interests or identities of a single subnational group that has selfish reasons for not contributing to the public welfare. A strong state does not have to accept the notion that the public good is the sum of the interests and identities that emerge from voting and lobbying. Rather, a strong state can pursue the "true" public good of the entire nation. In other words, some argue that a strong state can rectify the selfishness found in society. The Japanese state, for example, embodied in the persons of its bureaucrats and civil servants, has often operated autonomously of business and labor interests and has had the capacity to implement its choices over the opposition of both groups.

Many leaders of the late developing states thus avoided emulating common democratic institutions such as divided government, checks and balances, and federalism because they were thought to decrease state power and promote political fragmentation, instability, and gridlock. On the basis of recent experience, however, many comparativists have come to believe that a strong state *hinders* economic development because it burdens society with high taxes and other policies that are designed to feather the beds of the bureaucrats rather than foster economic growth for the population as a whole. Ironically, former totalitarian states such as the Soviet Union proved weaker than the supposedly weak-state democracies, such as the United States. Democracies, especially those with a powerful president or prime minister, can be strong because the state power they wield is considered legitimate by most people. Under these circumstances, democratic states may even reinforce national unity and provide the key to resolving political conflicts over interests and identities.

To summarize: we have maintained that the competitive geopolitical context generates the demand for economic development that, in turn, generates individuals and groups with material interests and social identities. Interest groups and identity groups with different preferences about development then come into conflict with each other. We have also argued that political institutions empower some groups and constrain others, thereby transforming interests and identities into public policies. Bureaucratic and democratic institutions thus influence the formation of interests and identities, restrict and promote their expression, and finally mold them into policies associated with paths of development.

Interest groups and identity groups realize that institutions influence the outcome of their policy struggles over a path of development and therefore seek to retain or change institutions in order to gain the political power needed to satisfy their own interests and identities. An important part of politics thus involves generally unequal groups fighting over the making and remaking of political institutions. As we will see in the chapter on Russia, for example, the struggle over the rules of the game after the collapse of communism was especially intense. But this is, in fact, an age-old part of politics. In Britain during the eighteenth and nineteenth centuries, middle-class interests fought against monarchs and aristocrats. They sought a parliament to limit the king and enhance their own status and power. In Germany during the nineteenth and early twentieth centuries, urban industrial and rural landowning elites fought against lower-class workers' and peasants' interests. They sought a strong state that would preserve their influence. In both cases, democratic and bureaucratic institutions were the outcomes of interest- and identity-driven political struggles. Hard bargains were struck. In some cases, elections were introduced, but the right to vote was extended to the lower classes only gradually. In other cases, landowning and urban elites enjoyed disproportional representation in Parliament. Although some believed that the bargains made everyone in the country better off by permitting economic development, others believed that the bargains bestowed much greater advantages on some than others.

Because institutions are so central to politics, they stand at a pivotal point in our framework. Although the global context influences domestic interests, identities, and institutions alike, ultimately it is institutions that filter interests and identities into distinct developmental paths.

Developmental Paths to the Modern World

Global competition forces countries to adopt a developmental path. States and societies choose domestic and foreign policies in politics and economics to compete in the global order. What do such policies, paths, and regime types entail?

With respect to domestic policy, states do many things. Governments pursue extractive policies. They take goods and services from their citizens in the form of money (taxes) and time (military service). Governments also pursue distributive policies in which they return goods and services to their citizens, for example, roads and social security payments. Governments organize and pay for systems of public education. Governments also pursue regulatory policies in which they set the rules for property rights, human rights, and occupational safety. Finally, governments sometimes attempt to shape the equality of opportunity and/or the equality of results.

Governments also pursue foreign policies. Some states expend a great deal of energy on preserving the global status quo. Others are "revolutionary" and attempt to change the global order. Some states pursue war as a tool of statecraft. Others remain relatively peaceful, except under the most extreme circumstances.

Different world-historical circumstances favor certain grand strategies over others. Take, for example, economic policy. During the Cold War, Japan developed its export-oriented consumer goods industries and India chose to develop its nascent industries by protecting them from foreign competition. The global trading system may influence whether nations adopt import-substitution industrialization, as in India's case during the Cold War, or export-led industrialization, as in Japan's attempt to compete in the world automobile market. World markets might influence whether states are free traders or protectionist, whether they institute a laissez-faire market economy or a statist one, and whether they pursue peaceful or aggressive foreign policies.

A major theme of this book is therefore that there are, and have always been, many alternatives to Western-style democratic capitalism. *There is no single developmental path to the modern world.* States can and do make their own developmental choices and often evolve local institutional variations of globally or regionally dominant political economies. Theories suggesting that all states move through common stages and converge in the end, such as some versions of modernization theory, are wrong. Looked at historically, there have been multiple paths to the modern world. There has been no inevitable triumph of democracy, markets, and peace. Domestic interests, identities, and institutions have combined in the past and continue to combine today with the global context to support undemocratic, anticapitalist, economically closed, and militaristic paths. And a key source of local variation in institutions today is the existence of alternatives to and variations on democracy, markets, and peace.

We therefore need to develop a comparative and historical understanding of the alternative paths to the modern world adopted in different international environments. We offer four sets of country studies that have been chosen to exemplify the different developmental logics of countries that began their journey into the modern world during different world-historical eras.

1. Early Developers: Britain and France
2. Middle Developers: Germany and Japan
3. Late Developers: Russia and China
4. Experimental Developers: Mexico, India, Iran, South Africa, the European Union, and Nigeria

These cases should remind us that development is open-ended. Because new challenges to development exist in today's small world, undiscovered paths may still emerge.

You should note three things about our choice of cases. First, our global and developmental perspective allows us to compare states on theoretical and substantive grounds and thus to set contemporary issues of policy and performance in a larger setting. Second, we have chosen cases that are among today's engines of development for the Western, Middle Eastern, Asian, African, and Latin American regions of the world. Third, all of our cases have had revolutions of one type or another rooted in world-historical problems of development, which, in turn, have influenced country-specific patterns of development.

You should also note two features of developmental paths. First, paths are competing political alternatives. People always debate the choice of a developmental path, and these debates inevitably involve a power struggle among competing interests and identities. In early twentieth-century China, for example, some people within the urban intelligentsia advocated a liberal path based on urban middle-class interests, Western liberal values, and democratic institutions. The nationalists pushed an authoritarian path rooted in conservative rural elite interests, a strong nationalist ideology, and statist institutions. The communists advocated a communist path based on peasant interests, Marxist ideology, and totalitarian institutions controlling civil society. Similar debates among liberals, conservatives, and socialists can be located in every Western country during the 1930s. Fascist, communist, and liberal movements that vied for political power also can be found in Russia during the late nineteenth, the entire twentieth, and early twenty-first centuries.

Second, the choice among various developmental paths leads to governing or developmental coalitions, combining state and societal actors, that form behind grand strategies of development, and these coalitions attempt to implement their development strategies using institutions designed for that purpose. Under fascism, aristocrats, fascist party leaders, and military elites used the state to repress workers, peasants, and groups defined as ethnically "alien." Under post–World War II "corporatist" systems in Europe, business, labor, and government worked together. During the 1990s, and in many parts of the world at the beginning of the twenty-first century, market-oriented (or what are sometimes called neoliberal) development coalitions became dominant in many countries. Such policy coalitions, however, face formidable problems. They are vulnerable to shifts in global context and can be quite unstable. Some members leave voluntarily and others are purged. Many, for example, have traced the failure of democracy in Weimar Germany to government instability, and others have traced government instability to the failure of the democrats to put together a viable developmental coalition. Hitler and the Nazi Party then seized power and proposed a new grand strategy of conquest and genocide for Germany and Europe. This example teaches us that although state-society coalitions are difficult to construct, their success defines development – for better or worse.

In sum, comparativists believe that the world-historical time in which countries modernized or industrialized has influenced their development strategy. This book therefore chooses its cases based on the international situation within which states found themselves when they first attempted to develop.

Comparative Politics Feedback

A particular developmental policy backed by a specific regime coalition may or may not be successful. Based on the rule of thumb, "If it ain't broke, don't fix it," one would expect that when development is working well for everyone in the country, regimes would want to consolidate their developmental path.

Often, a developmental path performs poorly everywhere and for nearly everyone except a very small group of beneficiaries. A path such as the creation of a predatory, non-developmental state could produce little economic growth, wasteful and inefficient allocation of resources, crime and violence, corruption, worker absenteeism, and alcoholism. Moreover, developmental strategies can produce misdevelopment, uneven development, or exploitative development. For example, the British approach to colonial development in India involved a divide-and-rule strategy that produced distorted development: interests, identities, and institutions were constructed to favor Britain and not India. And, more generally, developmental experiments can fail and result in either stagnant or collapsed states. Although some regimes are by definition interim, transitional, and provisional, there are dead-end developmental paths that did not look so dead-end at the time they were adopted. The dustbin of history is littered with colonial administrations, occupation governments, world empires, principalities, city-states, tribal areas without fixed territorial boundaries, bureaucratic authoritarianism, feudalism, slave states, apartheid systems, weak democracies, and fascist and communist regimes.

Poor economic performance in failed and misshapen development experiments leads to uncertainty, poverty, and social tensions: civil disorder and political anarchy, leadership succession crises, illegitimacy, and alienation. Developmental models are thus constantly being rethought. For example, until 1990, countries throughout the world sought to emulate the Japanese economic "miracle"; when Japan sank into a prolonged recession, it was no longer considered a "model." The result of such new thinking can be evolutionary or revolutionary change of domestic interests, identities, and institutions in order to pursue new developmental paths.

Failed developmental paths also can be altered by revolutionary changes of interests, identities, and institutions from above. National elites can coalesce into a new regime whose purpose is to resist the global order. For example, German and Japanese "revolutions from above" during the nineteenth century and the first half of the twentieth century remade social classes, solidified national identities, and created militant and strong states that sought to reshape the global order rather than adapt to it.

Of equal importance, failed developmental paths are sometimes changed by revolution from below, often after failed attempts at revolution from above. For example, economic and political liberalization under Soviet leader Mikhail Gorbachev in the 1980s created new interests, identities, and institutions that soon brought about the collapse of the Soviet Union. It appears that certain developmental paths and the coalitions behind them produce the same bad results wherever and whenever they are tried and therefore contain the seeds of their own revolutionary demise. Not long ago, for example, many academics and policy makers believed that late-developing countries needed strong states to mobilize resources for industrialization, assure territorial integrity, collect taxes, and staff bureaucracies. As resistance movements began to think otherwise and toppled many such states, global thought shifted. It is now widely argued that strong populist authoritarian regimes, patrimonial states that concentrate power in rulers and their families, and state-led industrialization generate typical problems, such as bloated public sectors, mismanagement, corruption, waste, and inefficiency. At the same time, however, some comparativists now believe that "neo-liberal" policies of rapid marketization, advocated for many states by the major international financial institutions, can also produce instability and the possibility of revolution. If strong states provide too much control, weak states provide no framework at all for capitalist development. Different developmental regimes, in short, contain different flaws that eventually lead to the appearance of resistance movements in a set of similarly situated countries.

International Relations Feedback

National development also influences the global context within which a regime finds itself. Consider some examples. British power helped define the eighteenth- and nineteenth-century worlds. In the aftermath of World War II, the United States imposed its own vision on the global economic order. The decision by the U.S. Federal Reserve Bank to raise interest rates from 1979 to 1982 contributed to the world debt crisis by increasing the amount that debtor states in poorer regions of the world had to pay for borrowed money. German authoritarianism and fascism plunged the world into global war. Japanese authoritarianism had the same result. The Soviet Union's and China's internal patterns of development led them to try to export communist regimes to the rest of the world. During the Cold War, Mexico and India legitimized and encouraged a third way of development for a large number of states. Iran's decision, along with the rest of the major oil-producing states, to raise oil prices in the 1970s shook the developed world. Its Islamic Revolution shook regimes throughout the Arab and Muslim worlds. And, finally, South Africa's bold experiment in multiracial democracy has important implications for other deeply divided states.

In sum, developmental paths may contribute to global peace and prosperity. They also contribute to global war and poverty. A nation's development can thus have an impact far beyond a single nation's borders.

The two feedback loops of our framework – comparative-politics feedback and international-relations feedback – yield a path-dependent view of history. Once a state starts down a developmental path, where it goes next is affected by where it has been. Choices made at critical junctures in a state's history not only set a state down a certain path but also preclude alternative paths. A state's contemporary problems thus originate in the historical crises and challenges it has faced. The developmental choices a country makes today are partly a result of the choices that were put in place when it began to develop in a particular world-historical context.

For example, interests, identities, and institutions can persist even through revolutions. First, economic markets and the interests they define show continuity. Today's close connection between interest groups and government in Germany, for example, can be traced to the developmental choices of Germany's nineteenth-century rulers. Second, cultural identities and the values and beliefs that people cherish are resilient. Religion and ethnicity often reemerge after a revolution and affect developmental priorities and choices. Fundamentalist Islam in today's Iran, for example, survived the Shah's regime and was in many ways a response to his industrialization policies; similarly, the middle class identity that emerged under the Shah remains important in the opposition to Iran's current Islamist regime. Finally, institutions that define and resolve conflicts among different interests and identities in a country can also survive revolution. Contemporary Russia's interests, identities, and institutions are part of the historical legacy of communism.

The two feedback loops also offer a "punctuated-equilibrium" view of how the present is shaped by the past. What comparativists mean by "punctuated equilibrium" is that countries have developmental regimes, supported by developmental coalitions, that are separated by identifiable political crises or critical junctures that produce break points and turning points in a country's history. In other words, a country's global context; its domestic interests, identities, and institutions; and, most significant, its developmental path to the modern world can change and lead to a new developmental regime. Germany, for example, made the transition from empire, to the democratic Weimar Republic, to two states divided by capitalism and communism, and finally to a new united and democratic Germany. Regime changes are often closely identified with leadership changes. Thus, the change of leadership from Gorbachev to that of Boris Yeltsin in Moscow in 1991 involved a redefinition of Russian state institutions and national identity, as did the change from Yeltsin to Vladimir Putin in 2000. Our country chapters are chronologically organized to take account of the historical changes in regimes associated with changing global contexts; domestic interests, identities, and institutions; and developmental paths.

Our Approach to Comparison

Comparison is essential to comparative politics, and we have made it central to this book. Our approach to comparison involves, first, a common set of tools with which we fashion country studies that reveal distinctive paths of development, and second, explicit comparisons among two or more cases designed to establish the causes and consequences of the significant differences among countries.

First, we have provided a set of tools to study substantive problems rather than a blueprint to develop a theory of comparative politics. Because politics in Britain is interestingly different from politics in France, which is interestingly different from politics in Germany, we have not forced the chapters into a common, encyclopedia-like framework. Rather, we have allowed our authors to use our common tools to bring out what is unique and significant about each country. This approach gives students a better sense of British politics, French politics, and South African politics than would be possible if every country's politics were forced through a homogenizing boilerplate framework that drains the countries of their uniqueness. Our framework permits authors to tell the story of their own country in their own way and hence makes for more interesting reading.

Second, after each part of the book – divided into early developers, middle developers, late developers, and experimental developers – we include a section called "stop and compare." These sections should really be called "stop and think" because we ask students to use the comparative method to draw empirical and moral lessons from the country studies by establishing the similarities and differences within and between each of our four sets of cases.

Here are the sorts of questions we ask: How are Britain and France variations of early development, and how are they different from the United States? How are Germany and Japan variations of middle development, which are different from the early developers? How do our two late developers, Russia and China, differ from one another, and how are they different from the early and middle developers? Finally, what are the similarities and differences among contemporary experimental developers – Mexico, India, Iran, South Africa, and the European Union – and what sorts of contrasts do they make with the early, middle, and late developers we have studied?

By alternating country studies with explicit sections on comparison, we demonstrate how comparativists think. Comparativists mix the specific and the general. They begin with cases, turn to theory, and then return to the cases in a never-ending sequence of induction and deduction.

CONCLUSION

This book guides the beginning political science student through the master concepts, dominant theories, and substantive problems of comparative politics. The country chapters that you are about to read take you on a journey through space and time. Why would you, a college student, be interested in joining this tour through the countries of today's small world?

Our global framework implies that what happens in other countries is important to you, no matter where you live. Take the United States, for example. Although the United States is large, important, and rich, and spans a continent separated from the rest of the world by oceans, Americans are dependent on the economics and the politics of countries around the world. Our political and economic security, our material welfare, and the well-being of our environment are wrapped up with political change and development in the rest of the world. The transportation and communication revolutions that have contracted time and space have created global interdependence. The process is accelerating: It is only since the 1960s that we have had pictures of the globe as a "whole" world, and it is only since the 1990s that the Internet has provided instant multimedia communication to people around the world. In short, a state – even a powerful one such as the United States – that seeks to be isolated, autonomous, and sheltered from global forces is doomed to fail. A state that accepts the inevitability of contacts between different societies, and hence attempts to integrate itself into today's small and interdependent world, can potentially succeed. Americans thus need to know and understand what is going on elsewhere. Citizens in the United States and in other countries must be aware of the world in which they live. They need to be cognizant of the potential dangers and challenges, as well as the possible opportunities, which will confront them in the decades ahead. The same would apply to any student reading this book in any country of the world.

Our approach allows you to be exposed to the theoretically and substantively important currents in contemporary comparative politics. Moreover, we do not expect you to be interested in names and dates for their own sake but because understanding the contemporary world is made easier by knowing some of the more important ones.

At critical points along our journey, we will stop and make comparisons in order to explain and evaluate what we see. Let us repeat our framework: (1) the global context influences (2) domestic interests, identities, and in situations that produce (3) developmental paths to the modern world, that in turn, generate (4) comparative-politics feedback effects on domestic interests, identities, and institutions, and (5) international-relations feedback effects on the global context. Let us begin.

PART I
Early Developers

BRITAIN

MAP 3.1. Map of Great Britain.

3 Britain

Peter Rutland

Introduction

Britain is widely regarded as having a political system that is a model for the rest of the world. It is a vigorously competitive democracy in which the rule of law is firmly established and individual freedoms are well protected. The constitutional order has been functioning for centuries, undisturbed by wars or revolutions. The experience of countries in the "third wave" of democratization, during the 1970s and 1980s, seems to confirm that parliamentary systems are more successful than presidential systems in reconciling conflicting interests in society and, hence, promoting less violence and greater stability.

However, the British system entered into a profound crisis in the 1970s, from which it has not yet emerged. Social changes have eroded the class structure that was the foundation of the two-party system. No party won a clear majority in the 2010 general election, resulting in the first coalition government in sixty-five years. Parliamentary sovereignty has been weakened by the need to conform to the laws of the European Union (EU), which Britain joined in 1973. Other important constitutional developments since the 1990s include a stronger role for the judiciary as a check on executive power, and the introduction of parliaments for Scotland and Wales for the first time in three hundred years. However, successive governments have been unable to come up with a viable plan to reform the unelected upper chamber of Parliament, the House of Lords. Britain finds itself headed into the twenty-first century with a system whose basic features were laid down in the nineteenth century.

The sense of crisis goes beyond tinkering with political institutions. The July 2005 terrorist bombings on public transport in London raised doubts about the viability of Britain's multiculturalist approach to assimilating immigrants. Memories of empire and World War II, and the "special relationship" with the United States, make it psychologically difficult for many Britons to see themselves as active and committed citizens of the European Union. British national identity is still very much a work in progress.

Moving from identity to interests, we see that Britain's entrenched social hierarchy led to a period of class warfare among capital, the state, and organized labor that lasted from the early 1800s to the 1990s. This struggle polarized the political system, paralyzed public policy making, and hampered Britain's ability to adapt to a changing global economy. Only since Prime Minister Tony Blair's Labour Party gave up its struggle to transform market capitalism in the mid-1990s has the country managed to shake off this legacy of social confrontation. In contrast with most of continental Europe, Britain has now embraced U.S.-style capitalism, with a lower level of social protection from the state. But prosperity remains elusive for a large and growing underclass.

The British Model

Britain pioneered the system of liberal democracy that has now spread in some form or other to most of the world's countries. Its political institutions – especially its legal tradition – had a very strong influence on the political system that was created in the United States.

The United States sees itself as the most pristine model of democracy because it introduced the first written constitution in 1787 and has lived under that same constitution for more than two hundred years. Britain, in contrast, lacks a formal written constitution, so it is hard to put a date on the introduction of liberal democracy to that country. The story usually begins with the **Magna Carta** of 1215, when powerful regional lords forced King John to sign a charter respecting their feudal rights in return for the taxes and troops they provided to the king. Parliament emerged as the institution through which the lords, and later common citizens, could negotiate their rights with the king. Under the leadership of Oliver Cromwell, the parliament fought a civil war with the king in defense of these rights from 1642 to 1648, culminating in the execution of King Charles I. But the monarchy was subsequently restored. In the **Glorious Revolution** of 1688, the Protestant William of Orange deposed the Catholic king James II and took office as a constitutional monarch who accepted that ultimate sovereignty rested with the parliament. Since then, there have been no violent political upheavals in Britain.

One of the main virtues of the British model is its capacity to adapt gradually over time. The British model is based on an evolving set of social conventions, and not on a set of ideas captured in a single document. Many of these practices, such as the system of common law (a legal system based on judicial decision rather than legislation), jury trials, freedom of speech, a bill of rights, and the notion of popular sovereignty – were already established by the seventeenth century and formed the bedrock on which the U.S. Constitution itself was based. But many of the features of the contemporary British model cannot be found in the United States, such as **parliamentary sovereignty** (the idea that ultimate political authority rests with the parliament) and constitutional monarchy (a monarch who is the formal head of state, but with very limited political powers).

The British political system is a product of that country's unique history. There is an old story about the Oxford college gardener who, when asked how he kept the lawn so immaculate, replied: "That's easy, you just roll it every day … for 300 years." This raises the question of whether Britain's **Westminster model** of parliamentary sovereignty can ever be successfully "exported" elsewhere.

The U.S. model of democracy comes more ready for export. Its essence is captured in a short document, based on a fairly simple set of principles: the equality of all men, the rule of law, and the separation of powers. This has enabled the United States to play the leading role in the spread of democracy around the world since the end of World War II. It was U.S. – and not British – advisers who oversaw the writing of new constitutions in postwar Germany and Japan.

But the British model is no less important than the U.S. model in understanding the global spread of democracy. As the British Empire shrank after 1945, it left in its former colonies a series of democratic political systems modeled along British lines. Cross-national analysis shows that countries that were formerly British colonies are more likely to be stable democracies than are former French or Spanish colonies. India, for example, has remained a democracy for more than sixty years despite a very low level of economic development. The British ex-colonies in Africa do not fit this pattern, however. With the exception of Botswana, they have all slipped into periods of military or one-party rule since independence.

The Long Road from Empire to Europe

An Island Nation

If you ask someone from England the most important date in English history, they will almost certainly say 1066. That was when the invading Norman army of William the Conqueror defeated the Anglo-Saxon forces of King Harold at the Battle of Hastings. Britain has not been invaded since. The Spanish Armada was repulsed in 1588, as were Hitler's forces in 1940. Britons are proud of having preserved their sovereignty against foreign invasion for more than nine hundred years.

The fact that Britain is an island meant that it relied on the Royal Navy for its security and did not need a large standing army to protect itself from its neighbors. This meant that, unlike the absolutist monarchs of Europe, Britain's rulers did not have a large army that they could also use to put down social unrest. Instead, they had to meet popular discontent with compromise. (The United States, like Britain, also had no need of a standing army.) Whereas the European powers introduced compulsory military service during the nineteenth century, Britain did not implement a military draft until World War I. It was dropped in 1919, reintroduced in 1940, and finally abolished in 1960. Most other European countries still had compulsory military service until the 1990s.

The End of Empire

By the nineteenth century, Britain had become the dominant imperial power, and British colonies covered one-quarter of the planet in an empire on which "the sun never set." After World War I, Britain lost its position as global economic leader to the United States. Britain lacked the resources and ultimately the political will to fight the growing independence movements in its colonies. After 1945, Britain granted independence to India and Palestine, then Malaya, and then its possessions in East and West Africa. As U.S. Secretary of State Dean Acheson observed in 1963, Britain "had lost an empire but not yet found a role." Most former British colonies joined the **British Commonwealth** (now called the Commonwealth of Nations), a loose association of fifty-three countries with a largely ceremonial role.

With the British Empire a receding memory, in 1982, Argentina's military rulers decided to seize the Falkland Islands, a British territory a few hundred miles off the Argentine coast. Prime Minister Margaret Thatcher sent a naval task force to liberate the islands, which was accomplished at the cost of 5,000 Argentine and 125 British lives. The **Falklands War** boosted Thatcher's waning popularity ratings and helped her win a second term as prime minister in 1983. The British Empire achieved symbolic closure in July 1997 when Britain returned Hong Kong to the People's Republic of China on the expiration of its ninety-nine-year lease on the territory.

Most older Britons look back at the empire with nostalgia, believing that British rule brought civilization in the form of railways and the rule of law to the more primitive corners of the globe. The uglier side of imperial rule was edited out of collective memory. There was no guilt over Britain's role in the transatlantic slave trade, the brutal suppression of the Kenyan "Mau Mau" revolt in the 1950s, or the 1842 war with China, whose goal was to force China's rulers to allow the import of opium.

Although Britain was no longer a global power, as one of the "big three" allied nations that won World War II, it was given one of the five permanent seats on the United Nations Security Council in 1945. It acquired nuclear weapons in the 1950s. The Labour Party advocated unilateral nuclear disarmament in the 1980s, a policy that it dropped in the 1990s. Despite fierce opposition from within his own Labour Party, Prime Minister Tony Blair decided to commission a new generation of submarine-launched missiles to replace the existent Trident system. The proposal passed the House of Commons in March 2007 thanks to support from the Conservative Party.

Britain owes its prominent role in world affairs since 1945 to its "special relationship" with the United States. This began with Franklin D. Roosevelt and Winston Churchill during World War II and was carried over into the Cold War. As part of the U.S.-led North Atlantic Treaty Organization (NATO) alliance, Britain kept fifty thousand troops in West Germany until the end of the Cold War. Britain sent troops to support U.S.-led military actions in Korea in 1950 and Iraq in 1990 and 2003. There were some rocky periods in the relationship, however. The United States blocked the Anglo-French seizure of the Suez Canal in 1956, and Britain refused the U.S. request to send troops to Vietnam in 1965. The close partnership between Britain and the United States continued under Prime Minister Margaret Thatcher and U.S. President Ronald Reagan in the 1980s, when they were united in opposition to the Soviet "evil empire."

Britain often put the special relationship with Washington ahead of deeper integration with Europe. In 2003, France and Germany refused to support the U.S.-led war in Iraq, but Tony Blair persuaded Parliament to send forty-five thousand British troops to take part in the invasion. As the war dragged on, Blair's resolute support of the United States became increasingly unpopular with the British public and within the Labour Party itself. Roughly one-third of the Labour Members of Parliament opposed the war from the outset.

The Reluctant European

Although Britain was one of the victors in World War II, it was economically drained by the struggle, and was neither able nor willing to become involved in building a new political structure on the shattered continent. In 1952, it refused to join the European Coal and Steel Community, an early forerunner of the European Union, fearing that plans for a common industrial policy would infringe on its national sovereignty. The European Economic Community (EEC, a broader European economic regional alliance launched in 1957) emerged as Britain's major trading partner, and its economic growth outpaced that of Britain. Twice during the 1960s, Britain tried to join the EEC but was rejected, mainly because Paris feared that British entry would weaken France's influence.

It was not until 1973 that Britain entered the renamed European Community. Much of the next decade was spent haggling over the terms of Britain's membership. In 1984, the Euroskeptic Margaret Thatcher won a reduction in Britain's high contribution to the common budget, half of which went to subsidies to inefficient European farmers. Thatcher warily signed the Single European Act (1986), which promoted the free flow of goods, labor, and capital but also introduced qualified majority voting in place of the veto that the larger countries formerly enjoyed. Thatcher favored free trade but opposed EU-mandated labor and welfare programs. She wanted a Europe of nation-states rather than a federal Europe ruled by supranational institutions that lacked democratic accountability. Many conservatives objected to the fact that the European Court of Justice had the power to invalidate British laws that contradict EU law. Thatcher's resistance to European integration caused splits within the Conservative Party and led to her removal as prime minister in 1990.

Britain, together with the Scandinavian EU member countries, declined to enter the economic and monetary union that was agreed to at Maastricht in 1991, when the EC renamed itself the European Union. Britain reluctantly incorporated EU regulations (the *acquis communautaire*) into British law, but refused to adopt the single European currency (the euro), which was introduced in stages beginning in 1999. Britain's links to Europe grew closer with the opening of the Eurotunnel for trains under the English Channel in 1995. In the next decade Britain's strong economic growth drew in millions of young job-seekers from Europe. By 2006, London was home to an estimated three hundred thousand Poles and three hundred thousand French.

Even as economic ties between Britain and the Continent continued to deepen, Britain was reluctant to pursue political integration with Europe. Britain was a strong supporter of "widening" the European Union to include the former communist countries of Eastern Europe, in part because it was thought this might delay a political "deepening" of the union. (Ten more countries joined the European Union in 2004, Romania and Bulgaria joined in 2007 and Croatia joined in 2013, raising the number of members to twenty-eight.) But closer political union would undermine Britain's ability to run an independent, liberal economic policy and weaken its strategic alliance with the United States. A "federal Europe" would challenge the principle of parliamentary sovereignty, which lies at the very heart of the British political tradition.

Who Are the British? Contested Identities

We all have an image of who the British are: Lady Diana, the Beatles, Austin Powers, the Queen. The British seem to be confident and self-assured, even complacent. But this image of comfortable homogeneity is an illusion. Britain was always riven by deep social-class divisions at home and doubts over the viability and morality of its empire abroad. Britain's political identity as the country enters the twenty-first century is more fragile than outsiders usually suppose.

Despite nine hundred years of continuous self-rule, Britain's national identity remains contested and ill-defined. The political identity of many older Britons is tied to the empire that disappeared from the world atlas more than sixty years ago. Britain's reluctance to join its neighbors in European integration stems from the fear that such a step would undermine British identity. The Scots, Irish, and Welsh are still there to remind us that "British" should not be conflated with "English." Finally, the influx of immigrants from South Asia and elsewhere over the past forty years has changed the face of many British cities.

Forging a British Nation

"Britain" and "Great Britain" are synonyms, referring to the main island that includes England, Scotland, and Wales. The United Kingdom is the political unit that includes Great Britain and Northern Ireland. The 63 million inhabitants of the United Kingdom have a complex and shifting hierarchy of identities. They identify themselves as English, Scots, Welsh, or Irish, and at the same time they are aware of themselves as British subjects. Regional identities within each of the countries are also quite strong, with many counties and cities having distinct dialects and proud traditions. While the empire existed, the peoples of the British Isles were united in a common endeavor of mutual enrichment through global conquest. With the end of the empire, that powerful practical and ideological cohesive force is now lacking.

From the sixth to ninth centuries, England was settled by Anglo-Saxons, and Vikings from northern Europe. The French-speaking Normans displaced the Anglo-Saxon rulers in 1066 and set about creating a unified kingdom. By the end of the sixteenth century, a notion of the English people was quite firmly established – as reflected in the patriotic plays of William Shakespeare. Through the stick of conquest and the carrot of commerce, the English absorbed the Celtic peoples of Wales (1535), Ireland (1649), and Scotland (1707). Local parliaments were dissolved, and a unitary state was created and run from London.

The process of absorption was different in each of the three Celtic regions. English lords moved into Wales and took over the land, but the peasantry maintained their distinct Welsh identity. Today, about one-fifth of the three million residents of Wales still speak the distinctive Welsh language at home. In Scotland, while most of the lowland lords sided with London, the Highlanders put up a fierce resistance, culminating in their defeat at Culloden in 1745, the last battle fought on British soil. Most of the rebellious clans were deported to America. The Scottish elite played a leading role in the forging of the British nation and the expansion of its empire. During the eighteenth century, Edinburgh, the Scottish capital, rivaled London as an intellectual center. It was there that Adam Smith developed the conceptual framework of liberal capitalism.

Like the Welsh, the five million Scots still maintain a strong sense of national identity, although the Gaelic language has almost disappeared. Scotland preserved its own legal and educational systems, independent from the English model. The Scottish National Party (SNP) believes that Scotland's identity would be best preserved through the creation of an independent Scottish state. Their cause was boosted during the 1960s by the discovery of oil and gas in the North Sea off eastern Scotland. Also during the 1960s, a nationalist movement, **Plaid Cymru,** arose in Wales. The nationalists won concessions from London in language policy: Welsh road signs, a Welsh TV station, and the teaching of the Welsh language in schools. Plaid Cymru routinely wins around 10 percent of the vote in Wales in elections.

Whereas the focus of Welsh nationalism is culture, the Scottish movement is primarily political. As a result, its support fluctuates, depending on the level of voter disaffection with the mainstream parties. The SNP managed to garner 30 percent of the vote in 1974. This led the Labour government (1974–1979) to steer more public spending into the Celtic regions. The Labour Party also promised to create regional assemblies in each country with the power to pass laws and raise taxes, a reform known as **devolution**. Scots were split on the idea because the SNP still wanted outright independence. A referendum was held in 1979, and only 12 percent of Welsh and 33 percent of Scots voted in favor of a regional assembly.

The idea of devolution was dropped, but then it was revived during the 1990s by the Labour Party under its new leader, Tony Blair. In a 1997 referendum, 74 percent of Scots voted for a new Scottish parliament. In their referendum, the Welsh backed a Welsh parliament only by the slimmest of margins (50.3 percent to 49.7 percent), on voter turnout of only 50 percent. A proposal in a 2004 referendum to create a new elected regional assembly in North-East England was decisively rejected.

Many Britons fear (or hope) that the creation of the Scottish parliament will lead ineluctably to full independence for Scotland. Despite a number of scandals since they started work in 1999, the two new regional parliaments have been moderately successful, broadening the range of political participation and leading to more diversity in public policy. For example, in Wales (but not England), medical prescriptions are free, and in Scotland, students pay no tuition – while since 2012, English universities can charge students up to £9,000 per year. In elections to the Scottish parliament in May 2011, the SNP won a majority of seats for the first time. With 45 percent of the vote they earned sixty-nine seats, ahead of Labour with 32 percent (thirty-seven seats) and the Conservatives with 14 percent (fifteen seats). A referendum on full independence for Scotland will be held in 2014 – although polls show only a minority of Scots favor full separation. The U.K. government spends $1,600 ($2,500) per head more in Scotland than in England, which means that independence would come with a hefty price tag. It is unclear whether an independent Scotland would be able to keep the pound sterling as its currency, or would have to re-apply in order to join the EU as a new member.

The Irish Question

Catholic Ireland was brought under British control only after brutal military campaigns by Oliver Cromwell (1649) and William of Orange (1689). English lords took over the land, while Scottish Protestants established a colony in Ulster (present-day Northern Ireland). The English banned the Irish language, which survived only in the more remote regions. Unscrupulous landlords, cheap food imports from the United States, and the failure of the potato crop resulted in famine in the 1840s and a mass exodus. A growing movement for Irish independence was met with proposals for autonomy ("home rule") from London. These plans foundered initially over land reform and later because of opposition from the Ulster Protestants.

There was an abortive nationalist uprising in Dublin in 1916. After World War I, Ireland erupted into civil war. London granted independence to the southern Republic of Ireland in 1921, while maintaining Northern Ireland as part of the United Kingdom. Northern Ireland was granted its own parliament (Stormont), which was controlled by the 1.6-million-strong Protestant majority. The eight hundred thousand Catholics of the province lived in segregated housing estates and went to separate schools. The Protestants controlled the police force and steered jobs and public spending to their own community.

In 1968, a civil rights movement sprang up, demanding equal treatment for the Catholics and borrowing the tactics of the U.S. civil rights movement. Its peaceful protests were brutally dispersed by the Protestant police. The Irish Republican Army (IRA), a long-dormant terrorist group, mobilized to defend the Catholics, but their goal was for Northern Ireland to leave the United Kingdom and join a united Ireland. In 1969, sixteen thousand British troops were sent in to police the province. Over the next three decades, Northern Ireland was wracked by a three-way "low-intensity" conflict among the British army, the IRA, and sundry Protestant paramilitaries. Riots, bombings, and assassinations became part of everyday life. The British government fought back with special courts and internment without trial. From time to time, the IRA planted bombs on the British mainland. All told, the conflict caused more than thirty-six hundred deaths and forty thousand injuries.

The British abolished the Stormont parliament in 1972, but efforts to introduce power sharing between Catholics and Protestants were blocked by Protestant **Unionists,** who staunchly defended remaining part of the United Kingdom. The Protestants feared exchanging their majority status in Ulster for minority status in a united Ireland.

Britain and Ireland drew closer as they both became further integrated into the European Union, and in 1985 London agreed to grant Dublin a direct role in any future peace settlement for the North. London promised the Unionists that Ulster would join a united Ireland only if a majority in the North voted in favor of it. Peace talks resumed in 1993, under the chairmanship of former U.S. senator George Mitchell. The IRA and Protestant paramilitaries promised to disarm, and in return their convicted comrades would be released from prison. Protestant and Catholic politicians in the North agreed to share power in an assembly elected by proportional representation. The "Good Friday" accord was approved in a referendum in 1998, winning 71 percent support in the North. Prisoner releases began, but the IRA refused to disarm and Protestant leaders balked at sharing power with their Catholic counterparts.

After the September 11, 2001, terrorist attacks in the United States, the IRA sensed that world opinion was turning against terrorism, and they started to "decommission" some of their weapons under the supervision of an independent commission headed by a retired Canadian general. However, low-level sectarian violence continued, and in 2002 the London government suspended the Northern Ireland Assembly and Executive for the fourth time since 1998 as relations between the leaders of the two communities broke down. Elections to the Assembly in 2003 saw further losses for the moderate parties that had championed the peace process (the Ulster Unionists and the mainly Catholic Social Democratic and Labour Party) at the expense of the intransigent Democratic Unionist Party and republican Sinn Fein. In 2005 the monitoring commission finally certified that the IRA had put all its weapons "beyond use." In March 2007 the hard-line leaders of both sides (Ian Paisley for the Democratic Unionists and Gerry Adams for Sinn Fein) agreed to form a united coalition government after the elections scheduled for May 2007, and sealed the deal with a historic handshake. Although clashes continue – especially around the Orange marches organized by Unionist groups – the peace seems to be holding.

Ireland was the first – and last – British colony. The Northern Ireland "Troubles" are a blot on British democracy and the most painful reminder of the legacy of empire.

A Multicultural Britain

Another important echo of empire was the appearance in the 1960s of a community of immigrants from Asia and the West Indies. These Asians and blacks broke the image of social and ethnic homogeneity that had prevailed in Britain for decades.

Facing a labor squeeze, as early as 1948 Britain started to recruit workers from Jamaica and Trinidad, former British colonies in the West Indies. These black workers were joined by a flow of migrants from India and Pakistan, a process accelerated by the expulsion of Asians from Kenya and Uganda in 1965. More restrictive immigration laws were introduced, which slowed but did not halt the flow. Between 1993 and 2011 the foreign-born residents in the United Kingdom rose from 3.8 million to 7.5 million, or 13 percent of the total population. Following Poland's entry to the EU in 2004, Poles emerged as the second largest group of immigrants after Indians, with 600,000 recorded in the 2011 census. Four out of ten immigrants live in London, where in 2011 they made up 42 percent of the city's population. In 2011, one in four babies in the United Kingdom was born to an immigrant mother. Including community members born in Britain, the 2011 census recorded 1.9 million blacks (half African, and half from the Caribbean); 1.6 million Pakistanis and Bangladeshis, and 1.5 million Indians.

Race and ethnic diversity is not the only issue. The South Asian migrants are Hindus and Muslims, and their arrival posed a challenge to Britain's avowed status as a Christian nation. The Church of England is the established state religion, with the Queen as its official head, even though less than 10 percent of the British population are regular churchgoers. With the appearance of Muslim and Hindu pupils in the 1970s, most state schools stopped their compulsory Bible classes, and new "faith schools" were opened for those religions. The new immigrants forced Britain to acknowledge the fact that it was in reality a secular, urban, individualist culture, and that its old self-images of queen, church, and empire were sorely outdated.

Immigration was also a political challenge. Many older Britons harbored racist attitudes from the days of empire, and some young workers saw the immigrants as a threat to their jobs and state housing. The racist National Front Party arose in the late 1960s, and there were occasional street battles between racist skinheads and immigrant youths from the 1970s to the present. The situation began to change as the first cohort of British-born blacks and Asians passed through the educational system and entered the professions. Whereas their parents had kept a low social and political profile, the second generation was more assertive in demanding a full and equal place in British society. But it took several decades before the new immigrant communities achieved political representation. In 1987, four minority candidates won seats in Parliament, rising to ten in 1997 and twenty-six in 2010 (4 percent of the total). Tony Blair appointed the first black minister in 1997, and he named a black woman to head the House of Lords.

In contrast to the policy of rapid assimilation of immigrants pursued in France, Tony Blair's Labour government adopted a policy of **multiculturalism,** encouraging immigrant groups to retain their own traditions and identities through separate educational, religious, and social institutions. London is now a vibrant, multicultural city. Intermarriage rates across racial lines are high (in comparison with the United States): around 50 percent for both blacks and Asians. The media deserve much of the credit for helping to redefine Britain as a multiracial community. However, accusations of racism in the police force were highlighted by the failure to prosecute the skinheads who killed a black youth, Stephen Lawrence, in London in 1997. In May 2001, race riots broke out in several northern cities, highlighting the tension in poor white and immigrant communities competing for scarce jobs and housing. During the 1990s, attention focused on the problems posed by an influx of asylum seekers, mainly from Eastern Europe but also from countries as far-flung as Afghanistan and Somalia. More than five hundred thousand entered the United Kingdom from 1991 to 2001, with ninety thousand arriving in 2002 alone. Four out of five applicants were rejected, but housing and processing them caused public outrage. The government responded by tightening border controls. To reduce regular immigration, a points system favoring highly-skilled immigrants was introduced in 2006.

After September 11, attention focused on the activities of radical imams who were recruiting potential terrorists from young men who attended their mosques in England. These fears turned into horrible reality on July 7, 2005, when four young Moslem men set off bombs on three subway trains and a London bus, killing 52 and injuring 700. This was the first suicide bombing in Europe. There was a second attempted attack on July 21, but the three bombers failed to detonate their charges.

Three of the July bombers were born in Britain to families from Pakistan, the fourth had been born in Jamaica. The fact that the bombers were born and raised in England was a profound shock to the British public. Radical Islamists felt alienated from British society and were opposed to U.K. involvement in the war in Iraq. Moslem community leaders mobilized to try to reach out to the disaffected youth, while Prime Minister Blair pledged to "pull up this evil ideology by its roots." The government stepped up state funding to Muslim schools, and tried to liaise with "moderate" Muslims while marginalizing their "extremist" counterparts.

In an echo of the veil controversies in France, in 2006 an English teacher was suspended for wearing a full-face veil (*niqab*). Prime Minister Blair supported the school's decision, arguing that the veil was a "mark of separation." But while France and several other countries went on to ban wearing the *niqab* in public, it remains legal in Britain. There was also growing concerns about the practice of forcibly arranged marriages for young girls in South Asian immigrant communities.

Unfortunately, the July 2005 bombings could not be treated as an isolated incident. In a November 2006 speech Dame Eliza Buller, Director of the Security Service (MI5), said there were some 200 groups in Britain, with 1,600 members, intent on committing acts of political violence, while polls suggested that "over 100,000 of our citizens consider that the July 2005 attacks in London were justified." According to a Pew Global Attitudes Project survey released in June 2006, only 7 percent of Muslims in Britain saw themselves as British citizens first, while for 81 percent their primary identity was Muslim. Fifteen percent even believed violence against civilian targets could "sometimes" be justified.

The government pushed through bills increasing police powers to meet the terrorist challenge, which critics claimed amounted to an attack on civil liberties. The strict 2006 Terrorism Act made it a criminal offense to encourage others to commit acts of terrorism, including the glorification of terrorism, the circulation of terrorist publications, or training in terrorist techniques. Suspects can be held without charge for up to twenty-eight days. In November 2005 the Commons rejected the government's proposal to extend the detention for up to ninety days – the first time Blair's government was defeated in the House. Forty-nine Labour MPs (Members of Parliament) voted against the government. Also in 2005 the government introduced a bill to introduce compulsory national identity cards for all residents, including biometric information. The House of Lords rejected various versions of the bill twelve times before it was finally passed in 2006. In the 2010 election the Conservatives campaigned on a promise to cancel the scheme. A law was introduced abolishing the cards, and the data files of the National Identity Registry were destroyed in February 2011.

As public debates over the nature of British identity continued, 2005 saw the introduction of a new "Life in the U.K." test for citizenship, which included some fairly obscure questions about British institutions and cultural traditions (what date is St. George's Day?). The test was criticized for including some factual errors and for being too difficult. About one in three applicants failed – as did many native-born British who tried out the test online (including the present author).

In July 2012 London hosted the **Olympic Games**, which much to everyone's surprise were a resounding success. The feared transport logjams, airport workers' strikes, and terrorist attacks failed to materialize. Britain turned in its best performance since 1908, finishing in third place in the gold medals table. "Team GB" was a triumph of multiculturalism, with star performances from the Somalia-born runner Mo Farrah and heptathlete Jessica Ennis (whose father is Jamaican). **Danny Boyle's** stunning opening ceremony won accolades for its wit and creativity. Boyle showed Britain's transformation from rural idyll to industrial hell to hip information society, linked together by what he described as the country's two main achievements – pop music and children's literature. Boyle's spectacle single-handedly turned around the debate on British national identity – at least for a while.

British Political Institutions

The British political system was traditionally seen as characterized by a high level of stability. Institutions evolved in order to defuse the deep conflicts in British society before they turn violent. The core features of what is known as the Westminster model – parliamentary sovereignty, prime ministerial government, and two parties alternating in power – have indeed remained basically unchanged for more than a hundred years. But the model has seen some important but uncoordinated reforms over the past two decades, in a process of profound structural change that is still unfolding.

The Path to Parliamentary Democracy

The U.S. political system is based on a written constitution, whereas the linchpin of the British system is the notion of parliamentary sovereignty. The parliament, representing the people, has the power to enact any law it chooses, unrestrained by a written constitution. Another difference is that the U.S. system strives for a separation of powers among the executive, legislative, and judicial branches. In contrast, the British tradition of parliamentary sovereignty fused the executive with the legislature, while the House of Lords also served as the nation's highest court.

Parliamentary sovereignty rests on the notion of popular sovereignty, where voters get to choose their leaders through frequent direct elections. At first, in the eighteenth century, the number of voters who got to participate was very small, perhaps 2 percent of the population. It took two hundred years of social conflict before the franchise spread to the majority of citizens. The parliament was an institution originally designed to protect the interests of medieval nobles, but it subsequently came to be accepted by industrial workers as a useful instrument for the protection of their interests.

Regional *parlements* ("talking places") emerged in France as a forum for nobles to resolve disputes. The institution spread to England in the thirteenth century, providing a place for the king to bargain with his nobles. The monarch grew more powerful and came to be seen as the divinely chosen ruler of the kingdom (whose right to rule was subject to approval by the pope). In 1534, King Henry VIII broke with the Church of Rome and established a separate Church of England, with himself as head. The rhetoric of king and Parliament gradually shifted from divine right to that of serving the interests of the people and nation.

The upper chamber of Parliament (the House of Lords) was made up of **hereditary peers,** lords appointed by the monarch, whose title automatically passed down to their eldest sons. The lower chamber (the House of Commons) consisted of representatives elected by property owners in the public at large. Conflict between king and the parliament over the right to raise taxes erupted into civil war (1642–1648). After a brief period of military-theocratic rule by Oliver Cromwell, in the **Glorious Revolution** of 1688, the parliament installed William of Orange as a constitutional monarch with limited powers. In the eighteenth century, the parliament's role developed into what has come to be known as the **Westminster model** (named after Westminster, the London district where the Houses of Parliament are located.). One of its most important features is the emergence of two distinct parties – Her Majesty's Government on one side and **Her Majesty's Opposition** on the other. The idea that one can disagree with the government without being considered a traitor was novel, and is still a rarity in many authoritarian regimes. The two-party system came be seen as integral to the Westminster model.

In his classic 1971 book *Polyarchy,* Robert Dahl argued that liberal democracy develops along two dimensions: contestation and participation. "Contestation" means that rival groups of leaders compete for the top state positions; "participation" refers to the proportion of the adult population who play an active role in this process through elections. Over the course of the twentieth century, many countries have made an abrupt transition from closed authoritarian regimes to competitive, democratic ones. In these cases, contestation and participation expanded simultaneously. In the British situation, however, the politics of contestation were firmly established long before mass participation appeared on the scene.

The House of Commons

The centerpiece of the British political system is the House of Commons, which consists of 650 MPs elected from single-member constituencies. The winner is the candidate who scores the largest number of votes, the same "first past the post" system as in the United States. Although a handful of members sit as Independents, the vast majority of MPs run for election as members of a political party. The Commons must submit itself for election at least once every five years in what is called a General Election. (If an MP dies or resigns between elections, an individual by-election is held for that seat.) After a general election, the leader of the party with a majority of MPs is invited by the Queen to form a government. If no single party has an absolute majority, party leaders negotiate and the monarch appoints a coalition government. That is what happened in 2010 – for the first time since 1935.

The best example of British democracy in action is **Prime Minister's Questions.** For thirty minutes once a week, the prime minister stands before the Commons and answers questions, largely unscripted, from MPs of both parties. The ritual often strikes foreign observers as rather silly. The questions are not really intended to solicit information but to score political points and make the other side look foolish. Members of Parliament from both parties shout, whistle, and laugh to express their encouragement or displeasure. The drama is enhanced by the fact that the two main parties sit on ranked benches facing each other, just yards apart. (Since 1989, question time has been televised.)

The spectacle seems juvenile, more akin to a college debate than a legislative assembly. However, the game has a serious purpose: public accountability. Week after week, the members of the government have to take the stand and defend their policies. It is a kind of collective lie-detector test in which the failings of government policy are ruthlessly exposed to ridicule by the opposition. In the United States, in contrast, the separation of powers means that a sitting U.S. president never has to confront his political adversaries face to face. Once a year he goes to Congress to give a State of the Union address, with no questions allowed.

From Cabinet to Prime Ministerial Government

The head of the government is known as the prime minister (PM). The PM nominates a cabinet of about twenty ministers, who are appointed by the Queen to form Her Majesty's Government. There are another seventy to ninety ministers and deputy ministers without cabinet rank. Whereas U.S. cabinet members work for the president, their British counterparts are accountable to Parliament. All ministers are drawn from members of either the Commons or the Lords, and they must account for their actions to that body. On the other hand, individual ministerial appointees are not subject to confirmation by the legislature as in the United States.

The cabinet meets weekly in the PM's residence, **No. 10 Downing Street.** The PM chairs cabinet meetings, and votes are usually not taken. The most senior ministers are those heading the foreign office, the treasury, and the home office (dealing with police, prisons, etc.). The ministers rely on the permanent civil service to run their departments, with only a handful of personal advisers brought in from outside. The total number of outside appointees when a new government takes power is fewer than a hundred, compared with more than two thousand political appointees in the United States.

There is no clear separation of powers between the executive and legislative branches under the British system. On the contrary, the two are fused together. The public elects the House of Commons knowing that the majority party will form the executive branch. The PM comes from the party with a majority in the Commons, and this majority always votes according to party instructions. This means that the legislative program of the ruling party is almost always implemented. The government rules as long as it can sustain its majority in the Commons. A government will resign after defeat in the Commons on what it deems to be a vote of confidence.

This system gives the PM tremendous power, in what Lord Hailsham, a leading Conservative, called "an elective dictatorship." The power of the PM is augmented by the fact that he or she chooses when to call an election. The Commons can vote to dissolve itself at any time, leading to a general election just six weeks later. Thanks to having control over the majority party in the Commons, the prime minister can choose when to face the electorate. This gives a tremendous political advantage to the incumbent government. The PM carefully monitors opinion polls and economic data, and calls an election when support is at a peak (although an election must be called no later than five years after the previous election).

If the U.S. Congress is a *policy-making* legislature, Westminster is at best a *policy-influencing* legislature. In Britain, the government is responsible for introducing virtually all legislation: It is extremely rare for a bill proposed by an individual MP to make it into law. Members of Parliament are expected to vote in accordance with party instructions (the party "whip"), except when a vote is declared a matter of personal conscience. An MP who defies the whip may be expelled from the party and denied its endorsement at the next election, which will usually prevent her or his reelection. Even so, in about 10 to 20 percent of votes in the Commons, a small number of rebels defy the party whip. The parliaments of 1974–1979 and 1992–1997 saw frequent revolts by dissident MPs from the ruling party, but they had only a marginal effect on the government's capacity to enact its program.

During the 1980s, when Margaret Thatcher was PM, there were complaints that the PM was becoming too powerful, even "presidential," in her ability to dictate policy to her ministers. In particular, Thatcher took over direct control of foreign policy, at the expense of the foreign secretary. These complaints returned after Tony Blair became PM in 1997. After his re-election in 2001, Blair created special units for European and foreign/defense affairs inside the prime minister's office, further undercutting the role of the foreign office and defense ministry.

The upper chamber of Parliament, the House of Lords, has only limited capacity to block or delay government legislation. Any act that is passed in three readings by the Commons and Lords and signed into law by the Queen supersedes all preceding laws and precedents and traditionally was not subject to judicial review, since there was no written constitution to which they could appeal to declare a law invalid. The lack of a bill of rights troubled many liberal observers.

For centuries Britain had a unitary system of government: there was no federal structure that could block the powers of the Westminster parliament. There were separate ministries for Scotland, Wales, and Northern Ireland, whose main task was spending regional development funds. Eighty percent of the funding for local councils comes from the national government, and there are strict rules over how it can be spent. Margaret Thatcher was so annoyed by the policies of the Labour-controlled Greater London Council that she had parliament abolish the council in 1986. (It had been created only in 1964.) The New Labour government of Tony Blair set about reversing the centralization of the Thatcher years, creating a new Greater London Authority in 1999 and moving ahead with plans for the introduction of new parliaments in Wales and Scotland.

The Electoral System

Britain operates a first-past-the-post, or winner-take-all, electoral system, similar to that in the United States. Until recently this produced clear winners and strong alternating majority parties in the House of Commons. However, it is criticized for offering voters an exceptionally narrow range of alternatives (two) and denying third parties adequate representation.

Each of the 650 MPs is elected from a single-member constituency in which the candidate with the highest number of votes wins. This system works to the advantage of the two leading parties, which tend to finish first and second in every race. Britain's third-largest party, the Liberal Democrats, has 15 to 25 percent support in nearly every constituency in the country, but this is not enough to displace a Labour or Tory incumbent with 40 to 60 percent support. Hence, the Liberal Democrats win very few parliamentary seats.

Another problem is that the winner may well have only a plurality and not an absolute majority of the votes cast, because there are usually more than two candidates competing for each seat. At the national level, there is no guarantee that the party that wins the most seats will have won a majority of the popular vote. In fact, no government since 1935 has gained more than 50 percent of the votes cast in a British election – yet this did not prevent those governments from having absolute control of the Commons and pursuing an aggressive legislative program.

The first-past-the-post system is unpredictable in translating voter preferences into parliamentary seats. Small differences in the votes gained by the rival parties can produce huge differences in the number of seats won. As a result some advocate the introduction of a system of proportional representation (PR), in which seats are allocated in proportion to each party's share of the national vote. In 1992, both Labour and Tories won more seats than they would have had under a PR system, whereas the Liberal Democrats got only one-fifth of the seats they would have had under PR. In 1997, the Liberal Democrats won twice as many seats as they did in 1992, even though they actually garnered fewer votes than in the previous election. The Conservatives (Tories) did worse in 1997 than they would have under PR, whereas Labour scooped up two-thirds of the seats with only 44 percent of the national vote.

In June 2001, Labour scored a second consecutive victory in national elections. They won 413 seats (6 fewer than in 1997), while their share of the vote slipped by 2.5 percent to 40.7 percent. The Conservatives polled 31.7 percent of the vote but garnered only 166 seats In May 2005 Tony Blair won an unprecedented third term. Even though he only narrowly led the conservatives, by 35.2 percent to 32.3 percent of the popular vote, this translated into 355 seats for Labour and only 197 for the Tories. The Liberal Democrats, with 22.0 percent of the vote, picked up a mere 62 seats.

The unequal relationship between votes and seats is exacerbated by the unequal geographical concentration of voters and the economic divide between the prosperous Southeast and the depressed North and West. Labour does well in London and in northern cities but usually wins few seats in the southern suburbs and rural areas. The gap in regional voting patterns actually increased during the 1970s and 1980s. As a result of this pattern, four out of five constituencies are "safe seats" that rarely change hands between parties in an election. Despite this, voter turnout was relatively high, usually 80 percent, although it slipped to 69 percent in 1997 and 57 percent in 2001, recovering to 65 percent in 2010.

Under the first-past-the-post system, minor parties with a regional concentration, such as the Scottish and Welsh nationalists, can win seats on their home turf. The third-largest party in Britain, formerly the Liberals and now called the Liberal Democrats, wins seats mainly in the alienated periphery where their supporters are concentrated: Scotland, Wales, and the southwest of England.

There have been growing calls for a reform of the British electoral system in order to make the results more representative of voter opinion. The Liberal Democrats have the most to gain from the introduction of European-style proportional representation. Britain now has some experience with the PR system. Elections to the European Parliament using the PR system have taken place in Britain since 1999. And the two new parliaments in Scotland and Wales are elected by PR (single-seat constituencies, topped up by additional members from a national party list to ensure proportionality).

Defenders of the existing British system argue that it produces a strong government with the power to implement its legislative program. Proportional representation would spread power among three or more parties, which would require coalition governments of more than one party. This may be undemocratic because in most countries coalition governments are usually formed in backroom deals that take place after the election.

In its 1997 election manifesto, Labour promised to hold a referendum on electoral reform, but it dropped the idea after the election. In the 2010 election neither Labour nor Tories won a clear majority, so the Tories formed a coalition government with the Liberal Democrats. As a condition for joining the government, the Lib-Dems insisted on holding a referendum on electoral reform. They proposed a semi-proportional system called the Alternative Vote. This preserves single-member constituencies, but allows voters to rank order the candidates. The votes of losing candidates are redistributed according to their second preferences. The system is rather cumbersome: only three countries in the world currently use it (Australia, Fiji, and Papua New Guinea). The referendum took place in 2011, with both the Labour and Conservative parties campaigning for the status quo. Voters rejected the reform by 68 percent to 32 percent, with a turnout of 41 percent. Britain seems stuck with its archaic electoral system for the foreseeable future.

Political Behavior

In postwar Britain, the Labour Party was seen as representing industrial workers and Conservatives the rural community and middle classes. In the decades after 1945 Labour lost the loyalty of the majority of workers at the same time as the working class itself was shrinking in size. In 1970, 56 percent of manual workers had voted Labour, but this was down to 33 percent by 2010. In 1970 manual workers made up 66 percent of the population, but a 2011 survey found 70 percent of respondents self-identifying as middle class, and only 24 percent as working class.

The decline of class politics led to the weakening of the two-party system of Labour versus Conservatives. The protracted economic crisis of the 1960s and 1970s eroded party loyalties as voters started to shop around for new ideas. In 1950, 40 percent of those polled "strongly identified" with a single party, but this figure had halved by 1992. Between 1970 and 2010 the combined vote share of the Labour and Tory parties shrank from 90 percent to 65 percent. Voting became less a matter of habit and more a matter of choice. Voter behavior became more volatile, harder to predict, and more likely to be swayed by party campaigns and media influence. Voter turnout fell, especially among young people.

Given the large number of "safe" seats, the parties focus their efforts on winning the "marginal" seats, those that may change hands at every election. In **marginal seats,** the parties canvas every household and record the voting intentions of each family member. On election day, party volunteers stand outside polling stations to record voters' registration numbers. The data are collated at party headquarters, and supporters who have not voted are reminded to go to the polls.

Tight limits on campaign spending have mostly prevented the spread of U.S.-style money politics in Britain. There are no limits on donations to national parties, however, which has fueled repeated scandals. But it is the role of the media, rather than money, that has been the main source of controversy in British politics. The British are avid newspaper readers (average daily circulation is 14 million). In contrast with those in the United States, most British papers are not politically neutral but actively campaign for one of the parties. The papers are not controlled by political parties, as in much of Europe, but are owned by quixotic business magnates who enjoy playing politics. The Australian media magnate **Rupert Murdoch** owns 40 percent of Britain's newspapers through the News International corporation. Most of the British papers, including those owned by Murdoch, usually back the Tories. In 1995 Labour leader Tony Blair traveled all the way to Australia to plea for Murdoch's support in the 1997 election. He was successful: Murdoch switched his paper's allegiance to Labour, helping Blair secure a landslide victory in 1997. (In 2010 Blair became godfather to Murdoch's daughter.)

Unlike the press, radio and television stations are required to be politically neutral and there is a ban on paid political advertising on broadcast media. The BBC is state-financed, whereas the three other broadcast stations are commercially owned and depend on advertising for their financing. Murdoch owns a large stake in the leading satellite TV station, British Sky Broadcasting (BSkyB).

A huge scandal erupted around Murdoch's newspapers in 2011, exposing serious corruption and abuse of office in the corridors of power. In 2007 it was discovered that journalists at ruthlessly competitive tabloid newspapers owned by Murdoch were routinely hacking into the voice mail of celebrities in the search for gossip. Two arrests were made in 2007, but neither the police nor the media followed up on the story. It was only after the liberal *Guardian* newspaper took the story to the *New York Times* in 2009 that the British press started to cover the scandal. Public outrage was ignited in 2011 by the revelation that the *News of the World* had hacked the voice mail of a child who had been abducted and killed – leading her parents to believe that she was still alive. Murdoch took the extraordinary step of closing down the paper, but it was too late. A parliamentary enquiry grilled the Murdochs, father and son, and turned up evidence of collusion of some police officials in the hacking and the cover-up. The head of London's Metropolitan Police was forced to resign, as was Andy Coulson, press secretary to Prime Minister David Cameron, who had been editor of the *New of the World* until 2007. By 2012, forty arrests had been made in the case, and News International had paid tens of millions of dollars in civil damages. Murdoch was forced to abandon his bid to take full ownership of BSkyB.

The Dignified Constitution: Lords and Monarch

Queen Elizabeth II ascended to the throne in 1953. She is the head of state but has only limited influence over the affairs of government: she "reigns but does not rule." The Queen meets the PM each week for a private chat over tea. The most important function of the monarch is to invite a potential prime minister to form a government, usually after a general election. If that government wins majority support in the Commons, the monarch's effective role is at an end.

The last time the monarch played a significant role in British politics was in 1910. The House of Lords blocked a high-spending welfare budget passed by the House of Commons. Liberal prime minister Herbert Henry Asquith called an election, which he won, and he asked the king to create enough new peers to tip the voting in the upper chamber. The Lords gave in and accepted a new law abolishing its right to delay bills involving public spending. They retained the right to return non-spending bills to the Commons, although if passed a second time by the Commons, such bills become law after a two-year delay (reduced to one year in 1949). A second chamber can be useful in scrutinizing laws passed on party lines in the Commons. For example, the Lords introduced substantial amendments to the 2001 Anti-Terrorism Crime and Security Bill. Most democracies have a second chamber, usually elected to represent regional interests, as is the U.S. Senate. In addition to its legislative functions, the House of Lords also served as the highest court of appeal, with twelve specially appointed Law Lords.

However, the House of Lords is a bizarre anachronism. In a democracy, it does not make sense to give a legislative role to the descendants of medieval knights. The Lords consisted of 800 hereditary peers and 600 life peers. Hereditary peers are exclusively male, and they pass their title to their first sons. The system of life peers was introduced in 1958. They are mostly retired politicians, men and women, who are nominated by the PM and appointed by the Queen. Their heirs do not inherit their seat in the House of Lords. The average age of the Lords is sixty-nine.

The ultraconservative hereditary peers gave the Tories a guaranteed majority in the upper chamber, so the new Labour government elected in 1997 made reforming the House of Lords a priority. As a first step, in 1999 the number of hereditary peers able to sit in the Lords was limited to ninety-two. However, reform proved difficult because the House of Commons did not want to create a new elected second chamber that could rival its power. Blair was unable to come up with an acceptable plan: some in his party wanted to abolish the second chamber altogether. The prospect of an upper chamber that was appointed rather than elected raised fears of cronyism – and the sense that such a chamber would be redundant, a duplicate of the Commons. In 2003 the Commons voted down all the reform options on the table. In 2007 they voted in favor of a fully elected second chamber – but this was rejected by the House of Lords. The 2005 Constitutional Reform Act did remove the Law Lords from the House of Lords and created a new Supreme Court as the ultimate appeals tribunal.

In the coalition government that came to power in 2010, the Lib-Dems made Lords reform a top priority, favoring a fully elected upper house. A large group of Conservative MPs were resolutely opposed to any changes, however. The coalition government came up with a compromise proposal for an upper chamber of 300 hereditary peers (down from 800) with 240 elected (for a period of 15 years), and 60 appointed. However, in a procedural vote on the draft bill in July 2012, ninety-one Conservative MPs voted with the Labour Party to block an accelerated timetable for discussion of the bill. Prime Minister David Cameron shelved the bill. Despite fifteen years of effort, Lords reform remains a chimera.

The idea of reforming the **monarchy** is not on the agenda. Having a ceremonial, nonpolitical head of state does not challenge the authority of Parliament, and few people advocate abolishing the monarchy in favor of an elected or appointed president. The main argument is over money. Each year, the Commons votes a budget for the Queen and her extended family in recognition of their public duties. During the 1990s, as the royal family fell prey to divorce and scandal, the public began to wonder whether they were getting value for their money. Defenders of the monarchy argue that royal pageantry is good for the tourism industry.

The life of the royals is a reality TV soap opera that provides endless copy for the tabloid press in Britain and throughout the world. Princess Diana, the wife of Prince Charles, was probably the most well-known woman on the planet even before her dramatic divorce and untimely death in a 1997 car accident. Diana's death was a blow to the public image of the House of Windsor. However, Queen Elizabeth II soldiered on, marking her 60th Jubilee in July 2012. Shortly thereafter the eighty-five-year old queen attended the opening of the London Olympics, gamely taking part in a video sequence that culminated in her appearing to parachute into the stadium with James Bond. The monarchy had won back its public support.

Rival Interests and the Evolution of British Democracy

Political institutions in Britain evolved as a result of the competition between strong, well-organized social groups seeking to defend their respective economic and political interests. By the seventeenth century, British thinkers were describing the emergence of a "civil society" consisting of a dense network of independent social actors linked through mutual respect, accepted social norms, and the rule of law.

In class terms, British history was dominated by the powerful landowning aristocracy, which was later joined by a rapacious commercial bourgeoisie. This rising capitalist class, along with elements of the landed aristocracy, went to war against the king and his aristocratic supporters in the middle of the seventeenth century to decide which institution would rule – the monarch or the elected parliament. The institutions that emerged as a compromise in the wake of the civil war (parliamentary sovereignty and constitutional monarchy) have persisted to the present day. These institutions were embedded in a broad consensus of political values – respect for individual rights combined with loyalty to king and country.

Many social groups, such as peasants, religious minorities, and women, were shut out from civil society and struggled to find a political voice. In the nineteenth century, industrial workers forged a powerful trade-union movement and later a parliamentary political party to defend its interests. Each of these social classes (lords, peasants, capitalists, and workers) lived a different life, went to different schools, and even spoke different dialects. Everyone was fully aware of the existence of the class system and his or her family's location within it. They all "knew their place."

Despite this highly stratified social system, Britain emerged as a peaceful, stable democracy. The general level of social unrest and political violence (except Northern Ireland) has been quite low. Britain has functioned with the same set of political institutions, without coups or revolutions, since 1689. There are few nations in continental Europe that can make such a claim. Germany has gone through four regimes since its formation in 1871, and France is on its fifth republic since 1815.

The Rights Tradition

An important part of Britain's consensus values was the recognition of individual rights and the notion of limited government. Over centuries, medieval England built up a body of common law, which is based on the precedents set by previous court cases rather than statute law. The rights protected by common law included the right to trial by jury and habeas corpus, which means protection against arrest without a court hearing (literally, the right to one's own body). Such rights to personal liberty and private property were spelled out in the Magna Carta, a contract that was presented to King John in 1215 by a few dozen leading nobles. The Magna Carta was designed to protect the privileges of a narrow and oppressive aristocracy, but it set the precedent for the sovereign's power being negotiated and conditional on services rendered. Over the ensuing centuries, the same rights were slowly extended to broader sections of the population. Even in the British system, statute law has priority over common law: laws passed by Parliament are not subject to judicial review.

The rights to personal liberty did not initially extend to religion. Although the 1689 Act of Toleration granted freedom of worship to those outside the Church of England, it was not until the 1820s that bans on Catholics and Jews serving in the military or in public office were lifted.

Unlike in the United States, the right to bear arms is not part of the British tradition. Restrictions on personal gun ownership are very tight. British police usually patrol unarmed, and guns are used in fewer than 100 murders per year in Britain (compared with some 10,000 in the United States). After the massacre of sixteen children by a deranged gunman in Dunblane, Scotland, in 1996, private possession of handguns was completely banned.

In recent decades Britain has introduced elements of a written constitution, because of its growing ties with Europe. In 1951, Britain ratified the European Convention on Human Rights, which created a supranational European Court of Human Rights in Strasbourg, France. Since 1966, British citizens have been able to appeal to that court (and the court has reversed British legal decisions in some fifty cases). In 1998, the Blair government introduced the Human Rights Act, which formally incorporated the European Convention on Human Rights into domestic law. This moved the United Kingdom closer to U.S.-style judicial review. Although the 1998 act gives judges the right to challenge laws, their decision has no force unless Parliament chooses to act on it. For example, the Law Lords declared the 2001 Anti-Terrorism Crime and Security Act, on the detention of terrorism suspects, in violation of the European Convention. But the law continued in force until it was replaced by the 2005 Prevention of Terrorism Act. The same thing holds true for decisions of the European Court of Human Rights. For example, in 2005 the court ruled that Britain must give prisoners the right to vote. The House of Commons voted in 2011 to defy the court and refused to pass enabling legislation. In May 2012 the European Court reaffirmed its decision, and it assumed that eventually parliament will amend the law to give some prisoners the right to vote.

Perhaps the most important constitutional innovation of the Blair years was the creation of a new Supreme Court, which replaced the House of Lords as the court of final appeal. The court, which began working in 2009, consists of twelve judges appointed for life by an independent commission. It monitors the compliance of U.K. legislation with European law and ensures that ministerial regulations conform to the laws passed by Parliament. The Supreme Court has been much more willing to challenge decisions of the executive branch than were the Law Lords. For example, in July 2012 the court ordered the Home Office to present all its regulations regarding deportation of illegal immigrants to Parliament before they can be implemented. The court's defenders insist that it serves to bolster and not undermine the tradition of parliamentary sovereignty, in the face of an excessively powerful executive branch.

The Impact of Industrialization

In the seventeenth century Britain began to emerge as the preeminent maritime power, pulling ahead of Holland, Spain, and finally France Napoleon described England as a "nation of merchants" (often mistranslated as "a nation of shopkeepers").

Britain was the first country to experience the agricultural revolution. Peasants were driven from their subsistence plots to make way for extensive farming methods. Many of the peasants forced away from the land opted for emigration. About one-quarter of the population left the British Isles (some unwillingly, as convicts) for America, Canada, Australia, and other outposts of the empire. This provided a safety valve, reducing the surplus population and easing social discontent. In a TV interview, the Rolling Stones' Mick Jagger was asked why there had never been a revolution in England. He replied that it was because all the people who did not like the place had left. Whereas the United States was formed as a nation of immigrants, Britain was a nation of emigrants.

Britain was also the first country to experience the Industrial Revolution, in the first decades of the nineteenth century. Industry and empire grew together. Britain became "the workshop of the world," selling its manufactured goods through its global trading network. However, British workers found themselves crowded into Dickensian slums and laboring long hours in the "dark satanic mills" evoked by Danny Boyle's Olympics opening ceremony. Britain's ruling elite feared that the example of the 1789 French Revolution could be replicated in Britain. Growing protests from the expanding working class were met with a mixture of repression and reform. The 1832 Reform Act loosened the property requirements for voting, but even then only 5 percent of the adult population was enfranchised. A two-party system emerged in the House of Commons, with reformist and reactionary elements grouping themselves into the parties of Liberals and Conservatives (also known as **Tories**). Further Reform Acts in 1867 and 1884 gave the vote to 20 percent and then 40 percent of the population. By giving most adult men the right to vote, Britain's ruling elite provided an outlet for workers' political frustrations and turned them away from political violence.

Trade unions started to form among craftsmen in the 1840s, and by the 1880s they were expanding to the masses of unskilled workers. In 1900, the unions formed the Labour Representation Committee (LRC) to advance their interests in Parliament. They realized that they needed legislative protection after a court case had threatened severe civil penalties for strike action. The LRC renamed itself the Labour Party and won fifty seats in the 1906 parliamentary election in alliance with the Liberal Party.

The Liberal government that ruled from 1906 to 1914 introduced the elements of a **welfare state,** such as rudimentary public health care, school meals, and public pensions. These measures were not merely a response to the rise of labor. They were also prompted by the shocking discovery that one-third of the recruits for the British army in the Boer War in South Africa (1899–1902) were medically unfit to serve. To match the mass armies of Germany and Russia, Britain would have to start looking after its workers. Joseph Chamberlain, the reform-minded cabinet minister who served as Colonial Secretary during the Boer War, advanced the philosophy of "social imperialism" – welfare spending in return for the workers' political loyalty in imperial ventures. This was clearly an echo of Otto von Bismarck's model of welfare capitalism in Germany. However, the program did not include equal rights for women. The Liberal government resisted a vigorous protest movement for a woman's right to vote (the Suffragettes). It would take the shock of World War I to change public opinion on the issue.

The British elite came through the Industrial Revolution with its medieval institutions remarkably intact. The aristocracy went from country house to London club, educating their sons at Oxford and Cambridge and sending them off to fight in the colonies in the family regiment. There were a few innovations during the nineteenth century. The new Harry Potter–style "public" schools (they were called "public" because in theory they were open to anyone who could pay the stiff fees) forged a new elite of like-minded young men through a rigid regimen of sport and Latin. In 1854, officials in government service were organized into a politically neutral career civil service, in which recruitment and promotion were to be based on merit rather than political connections.

Labour's Rise to Power

The bloodbath of World War I was a major challenge to the integrity of the British state. Britain would have lost the war had the United States not intervened. The conflict killed one in ten of the adult male population and drained the economy. Still, the British Empire survived, while the war caused the complete collapse of the German, Russian, Austro-Hungarian, and Ottoman empires.

In recognition of the people's sacrifices in the war, in 1918 all adult males were given the vote, irrespective of their property holdings, as were women over the age of twenty-eight. (The "flappers" – eighteen-to twenty-eight-year-old women – were enfranchised ten years later.) Thus, it was not until 1929 that "one person, one vote" was established in Britain, showing that democracy is a quite recent historical development.

The Labour Party came out of the 1924 election as the largest single party. Although they did not control a majority of seats in the House of Commons, they formed a minority government. It had taken the trade unions only two decades to ascend from the political wilderness to the pinnacle of power. The euphoria was not to last, however. The 1924 government fell within a year, and economic recession triggered a decade of poverty and industrial conflict.

It was not until World War II that a major shift could be seen in the distribution of power within the British political system. British patriotism blossomed in 1939–1941, when the nation fought alone against Nazi-occupied Europe under a coalition government headed by Conservative prime minister Winston Churchill. In return, the people demanded a brighter future once the war was won. In 1942, the government released the Beveridge Report, promising full employment and state-provided health care, insurance, and pensions. This was not enough to satisfy the voters. In 1945, they turned out Churchill and for the first time in history elected a majority Labour government, although Labour won only 48 percent of the vote.

That government introduced a radical socialist program. Health care, jobs, and housing were seen as social rights to which everyone was entitled. The government introduced a comprehensive "welfare state" including a National Health Service, state pensions, state-funded higher education, and state-subsidized housing provided by local councils. (In 1945, one-third of Britons were still living in houses without bathrooms.) The government also had radical socialist goals that went beyond a welfare state, to challenge the very foundations of capitalism. One-quarter of private industry was taken into public ownership (or "nationalized"), including all coal mines, electric and gas utilities, steel mills, docks, railways, and long-distance trucking. The expropriated private owners, who were paid modest compensation, were powerless in the face of Labour's parliamentary majority. There was no constitution to protect their property rights.

The postwar government granted independence to India and Palestine, recognizing that Britain had neither the will nor the resources to fight to retain these colonies. Despite its socialist agenda the Labour government was not sympathetic to the Soviet Union, and supported the United States in forming NATO to oppose Soviet expansionism. They reintroduced the draft to help fight the Cold War. The new commitment to socialism at home and the Cold War abroad provided a new sense of purpose in the face of loss of empire.

The Postwar Consensus

During the 1950s, British politics slipped into a familiar pattern that would last until 1979. The Labour and Conservative parties alternated in power, and both accepted the basic institutions of postwar Britain. The Tories acquiesced in the retreat from empire and realized that it would be political suicide to try to dismantle the welfare state. Labour knew that the British public did not want more nationalization, not least because problems soon emerged in the management of state-owned industry. Both parties accepted Keynesianism, the economic analysis of John Maynard Keynes, who argued that state intervention with public spending could have prevented the Great Depression of the 1930s.

This consensus left little for the two parties to debate. Anthony Downs in his 1957 book *An Economic Theory of Democracy* offered one powerful explanation for the convergence of the parties over time. In a two-party system, Downs reasoned, leaders will compete for the "median voter" in the middle of the policy spectrum. Hence, both party programs will tend to converge on the center.

During the 1950s and 1960s, successive governments managed to avoid another depression. However, it proved difficult to "fine-tune" the economy by adjusting interest rates and the money supply to ensure economic growth, low inflation, and full employment. These efforts produced a debilitating "political business cycle." Conservative governments tried to lower inflation, triggering a recession and causing voters to switch their support to Labour. The succeeding Labour government would try to inflate the economy through public spending, causing inflation and eventually a debt crisis, when international investors deserted the British pound sterling (as happened in 1967 and 1976).

Despite the introduction of the welfare state, relations between workers and employers were tense and confrontational. Unlike in Germany or Scandinavia, after the war there was no attempt to introduce corporatist institutions, such as works councils, to give labor a say in the management of private industry. With unemployment held at 3 to 4 percent, workers were able to threaten strike action to push for better wages and conditions. The economy was plagued by waves of strikes, which came to be known as the **"British disease."** British industry was slow to adopt the latest technology, and Britain was overtaken in industrial output by Germany, France, Japan, and even Italy. London was still a major center of international banking, however, and the British economy became increasingly dependent on the financial sector. The easy profits from banking, or the prestige of a career in the civil service, tended to draw the "brightest and best" away from careers in industry.

The 1960s were not all gloom and doom. A new youth subculture was invented in Britain and exported to the rest of the world. Music and the arts flourished in "swinging" London, putting Britain back on the world map as a cultural superpower. By the end of the 1970s, Britain was earning more from exports of rock music than it was from steel.

The 1964–1970 Labour government tried to address the problem of industrial stagnation by promoting tripartite negotiations among the state, employers, and unions to set prices and incomes. But Labour could not challenge the power of the unions. The unions financed the Labour Party, and their 10 million to 12 million members dominated the 250,000 individual party members in elections to choose parliamentary candidates and the party's National Executive Committee. Industrial unrest led to the Labour Party's defeat in 1970, and a prolonged strike by coal miners brought down the Tory government in 1974. The 1974–1979 Labour government was undermined by a wave of strikes by garbage collectors, railway workers, and nurses that culminated in the 1978 "winter of discontent."

Exasperated by the dominant role of unionists and left-wing radicals in their party, a group of centrist Labour leaders broke away to form a new **Social Democratic Party (SDP).** Their centrist program appeared to reflect the views of the majority of voters. However, the winner-take-all party system makes it very difficult for third parties to gain a foothold in Parliament. In the 1983 election, the SDP-Liberal alliance won 26 percent of the votes (only 2 percent less than Labour) but won only 23 of the 635 seats in the House of Commons at that time. The SDP eventually merged with the Liberal Party to form the Liberal Democrats.

By the end of the 1970s, the British model seemed to be in irreversible decline. The economy stagnated, while inflation hit double figures. Journalists began to write about the "ungovernability" of Britain and a system "overloaded" with the demands of competing interest groups.

Thatcher to the Rescue?

At this point, change came from an unexpected source – the Conservative Party. In 1975, the Conservatives selected Margaret Thatcher as their new leader. Thatcher was an aggressive intellectual with an iron will and razor-sharp debating skills. Unusual for a Tory leader, she came from humble social origins – her father was a grocer. She worked as a research chemist before switching to a legal career to have more time to raise her children.

Thatcher was influenced by the writings of the libertarian Friedrich Hayek and the monetarist Milton Friedman. Her philosophy of popular capitalism drew heavily upon U.S. ideas of rugged individualism and free-market economics. Her aim was to minimize state interference in the economy and society. "Thatcherism" had a profound impact on British society, shattering the postwar consensus on the welfare state and locking Labour out of power for eighteen years.

Thatcher's new approach caught the attention of the British public and gave the Conservatives a clear victory in the 1979 election. She had ambitious plans to deregulate the economy, to privatize state-owned industry, and to follow a tight monetary policy in order to control inflation, whatever the effect on unemployment. Unlike in the United States, the New Right in Britain did not have a social agenda (abortion had been legal since 1967).

Thatcher's first task was to break the power of the trade unions. She introduced new legislation to make it more difficult to call strikes (requiring pre-strike ballots and cooling-off periods). She doubled spending on police and equipped them with riot gear so that they could take on rock-throwing strikers. Thatcher used the courts to seize the assets of the coal miners' union when they mounted an **illegal strike in 1984,** and she went on to shut down most of the state-owned coal mines. By 1990, the number of coal miners had fallen from 300,000 to 50,000. Thatcher broke the back of organized labor, and labor unrest shrank to historically unprecedented levels.

Economic growth was sluggish during Thatcher's first term, and it was probably only her victory in the 1982 Falklands War that won her re-election in 1984. One of her most successful policies was allowing tenants to buy public housing with low-cost mortgages. From 1979 to 1989, home ownership leapt from 52 percent to 66 percent of all households. She privatized the leading state-owned industries: British Telecom, British Gas, and the electric and water utilities. The top personal income tax rate was cut from 90 percent to 40 percent. Workers were encouraged to opt out of the state pension system and invest in a private retirement account. A deregulatory program for the financial markets in 1983–1986, called the "Big Bang," enabled London to reinforce its position as the world's leading international financial center.

By the late 1980s, the economy was growing, living standards were rising, and productivity and profits were booming. However, inequality was rising. Average incomes rose 37 percent during 1979–1993, but the earnings of the top 10 percent of the population leaped by 61 percent while those of the bottom decile fell 18 percent. Unemployment climbed to 10 percent from a level of 5 percent in the 1970s, but fell again to 5 percent by 1989. Still, one-third of the population lived in poverty, and there arose a large underclass of jobless youth, which led to a surge in drug use and crime. Ironically, demographic changes and the rise in unemployment caused state welfare spending to rise during the Thatcher years despite her intention to cut public spending.

In 1988, Thatcher introduced an ambitious "New Steps" program to change the way state services were delivered. State agencies had to introduce cost accounting for each stage of their operations. State services were contracted out to private companies or voluntary agencies through competitive tendering. Local governments, the National Health Service, and the education system were forced to adopt these reforms. Individual schools were encouraged to opt out of local-authority financing and receive direct grant funding. From 1979 to 1993, the number of civil servants was slashed by 30 percent, and about 150 new semi-independent government agencies were created. The reforms increased efficiency and cut costs but led to increased corruption. They triggered widespread protests, especially over the unpopular "poll tax," introduced in 1988, that replaced the former local property tax with a flat per capita tax.

The Fall of Thatcher

Thatcher secured re-election to an unprecedented third successive term in 1989. However, after ten years in power strains were beginning to show in the upper ranks of the Conservative Party. Many traditional conservatives disliked Thatcher's radical reforms, and her authoritarian style alienated many colleagues. Her vocal opposition to further European integration, such as the introduction of a single currency, lost her the support of the internationalist wing of the party. Between 1979 and 1992, membership in the Conservative Party slumped from 1.5 million to 500,000. Her popularity steadily eroded, dipping to 29 percent in 1990, and she came to be seen as an electoral liability.

Thatcher's departure came not with a bang but with an uncharacteristic whimper. At that time, the Conservative leader was selected by an annual ballot of MPs. Usually, no candidates ran against the incumbent. In 1990 ex-defense minister Michael Heseltine ran against her. Thatcher beat Heseltine in the first round by 204 votes to 152 (with 16 abstentions). Under party rules, a candidate winning less than two-thirds of the vote has to face a second round. Even though she would almost certainly have won, Thatcher chose to resign, partly in order to clear the way for her chosen successor, **John Major.**

Major, like Thatcher, came from humble origins. His father was a circus trapeze artist turned garden-gnome manufacturer. Major left school at sixteen to be a bus-ticket collector, and later worked his way up from bank teller to bank director before entering politics. Major was a wooden figure who lacked Thatcher's charisma. Despite a deep recession that began in 1990, Major won the 1992 election, thanks mainly to the inept Labour campaign.

Major pressed ahead with privatization of British Rail and the nuclear power and coal industries. But the Conservative Party was badly split over Europe, with a hard-core right-wing opposing further integration. The British public was skeptical about the Brussels bureaucracy but generally favored EU membership. In 1990, Britain joined the **Exchange Rate Mechanism (ERM),** the precursor to the single European currency. But in 1991 Britain opted out of the "social chapter" of the Maastricht treaty on European integration. This would have introduced the EU's generous labor legislation to Britain (longer vacations, shorter working hours) and was opposed by employers.

The key turning point in the Major administration was September 1992, when the British pound came under attack from international speculators. Despite desperate government efforts, the pound was forced to leave the ERM. This left the government's financial strategy in ruins, and Major's approval rating plummeted from 49 percent to 25 percent. Conservative Party credibility was further battered by a series of sex and corruption scandals. The biggest policy disaster came with the 1996 discovery that "mad cow" disease (BSE), an incurable disease that attacks the brain stem, had spread from cattle to humans, killing fourteen people. The government initially downplayed the problem and delayed ordering the mass slaughter of cattle. (A government minister even appeared on TV feeding hamburgers to his daughter.) Eventually all of Britain's cattle had to be killed and burned.

Clearly, the Tories had been in power for too long. But was Labour in a fit state to replace them?

The Rise of New Labour

After the 1992 election, the Labour Party feared that it would never be able to defeat the Tories and might even be overtaken by the Liberal Democrats as the main opposition party. In 1994, the party selected the young, charismatic Tony Blair as its new leader. Blair set about fashioning a new Labour Party that would recapture the voters who had defected to the Tories.

Following their defeat in 1979, the Labour Party was split between parliamentary leaders anxious to improve the party's electoral chances and trade-union bosses keen to retain their control over the party. The party's 1918 constitution had given Labour MPs the right to choose the party leader, but in 1981 an electoral college was introduced, with 40 percent of the votes in the hands of the trade unions. In 1983, **Neil Kinnock** became the Labour leader, and he waged a vigorous campaign to diminish union power and expel left-wing militants from the party.

After their defeat in 1987, the Labour leadership started to expunge leftist policies from the party program, dropping their commitment to reverse Thatcher's privatizations, to strengthen union power, and to give up Britain's nuclear weapons. Intraparty reforms shifted the balance of power away from union bosses toward the parliamentary leadership. The union vote at the annual party conference was cut from 90 percent to 50 percent, while the share of union contributions in the party budget fell from 80 percent to 40 percent thanks in part to an influx of cash from sympathetic business interests. The unions had been weakened by Thatcher's defeat of the miners and by changes in the economy. The share of manufacturing in total employment fell from 38 percent in 1956 to 19 percent in 1990, and the proportion of the workforce in unions fell from a peak of 53 percent in 1978 to 30 percent in 1995.

Kinnock resigned following the humiliating 1992 electoral defeat. In 1994 Tony Blair took over as party leader. Blair, a deeply religious, forty-one-year-old lawyer from a middle-class background, sought to turn Labour into a modern European social-democratic party of the center. Britain had become a society of "two-thirds haves and one-third have-nots," and Labour would never get back into power by appealing to the "have nots" alone.

But what would "New Labour" stand for? New Labour agreed with Margaret Thatcher that free markets are the best way to create prosperity, and they even accepted her reforms of public-sector management. In 1995, the Labour Party finally removed from its constitution Clause IV (put there in 1918), which called for state ownership of industry. But it would not be enough simply to steal Thatcher's reform agenda. Blair used American-style focus groups to try out new ideas, before hitting on the formula of the **"Third Way."** As Andrew Marr explained (*The Observer,* August 9, 1998): "The Third Way can be described by what it is not. It isn't messianic, high spending old socialism and it isn't ideologically driven, individualist conservatism. What is it? It's mostly an isn't." The state should stay out of economic management while providing moral leadership, investing in education and welfare, and devolving power to the regions. The centrist Third Way was encapsulated in the Labour slogan "Tough on crime, tough on the causes of crime."

Tony Blair described New Labour as a "pro-business, pro-enterprise" party, albeit one with a compassionate face. He stressed the values of community and moral responsibility in contrast with Thatcher's brazen individualism. (Famously, the "Iron Lady" had once said, "There is no such thing as society.") Blair also appealed to British patriotism. He even said in May 1998: "I know it is not very PC [politically correct] to say this, but I am really proud of the British Empire."

New Labour was also more open to women. In 1993, the party decided that half of the new candidates selected by local parties for the next parliamentary election must be chosen from women-only short lists. (In 1996, a court struck down this rule as discriminatory.) As a result of these efforts, in the 1997 election 102 women were elected as Labour MPs. The total number of woman MPs from all parties rose from 60 in 1992 to 120 in 1997, dropping to 118 in 2001 and rising to 141 in 2010 (22 percent of the total).

Blair used an expensive and sophisticated U.S.-style media campaign to sell the party to the public. Along with a New Labour, there was to be a New Britain: sophisticated, multicultural, and hip (from "Rule Britannia" to "Cool Britannia"). Labour's main slogan was the patriotic "Britain Deserves Better." Campaign innovations included posters above urinals in pubs, saying "Now wash your hands of the Tories." In a bid to reassure the voters that their tax-and-spend policies were behind them, Labour pledged to maintain the Conservative government's spending limits for at least two years after the election. No new welfare initiatives were planned beyond a new scheme to make 250,000 unemployed youths take up government-sponsored jobs as a condition to qualifying for welfare benefits.

Labour won a landslide victory in the May 1997 election. The Conservatives lost half their seats, and 10 percent of voters switched from Tory to Labour – the largest swing in the past century. Major went down to defeat despite a strong economic recovery, scotching the widely held notion that British election results are driven by economic performance. In June 1997, he was replaced as party leader by the thirty-six-year-old William Hague.

Voters did not choose Labour because they preferred Labour's program to that of the Tories, as the parties' policies were nearly identical. Rather, the Tories were seen as divided, corrupt, and inept, whereas New Labour was trusted to do a more competent job of governing the country.

The only significant policy difference between the two parties was over Europe. Most Tory MPs were skeptical about European integration. As recently as 1983, the Labour Party had called for Britain's withdrawal from the European Union, which it saw as a capitalist plot. But Blair was adamantly pro-Europe, although he promised to hold a referendum before taking Britain into the single European currency.

One of the first acts of the new Labour government was the granting of independence to the Bank of England, a striking example of their rejection of the old policies of Keynesian demand management. Since its founding in 1694, the Bank of England had followed government advice in setting interest rates. From now on, like the U.S. Federal Reserve, the independent board of directors could fix rates as they pleased in order to prevent a rise in inflation. The head of the treasury, Gordon Brown, followed a tight monetary and fiscal policy, although he borrowed heavily to fund higher spending on health, education, and welfare.

Blair at the Helm

On June 7, 2001, the Labour government won a second consecutive landslide victory, while the Conservative Party scrambled to hold onto second place. People started to wonder whether the Conservatives, once the "natural party of government," would ever manage to win an election again. William Hague resigned as Conservative Party leader in the wake of the electoral defeat. Previously, Tory leaders had been elected by Tory MPs. In 2001, for the first time, the MPs picked the two leading contenders, and the party's 320,000 members selected the final winner. The pro-European Kenneth Clarke lost to Iain Duncan Smith.

In September 2003, Labour lost the Brent by-election, the first such loss since Tony Blair became party leader in 1994, but the Conservatives finished third behind the Liberal Democrats. In October 2003, the Conservative Party congress removed the ineffective Duncan Smith as leader and replaced him with the centrist Michael Howard.

Tony Blair proved to be a skilful political leader, asserting strong control over the Labour Party and steering public opinion in what David Goodhart has called a "media driven popular democracy." Blair used this power to pursue an ambitious agenda of domestic and foreign reform, with mixed results.

On the home front, Blair's New Labour forged ahead with the most ambitious **constitutional reforms** that Britain has seen in the past hundred years. First, there was the decentralization of power through the creation of Scottish and Welsh parliaments. Second was the plan to reform the House of Lords, which resulted in a deadlock over whether to have an elected or appointed upper chamber. The third major reform was the introduction of a bill of rights and judicial review through the European Court of Human Rights. Finally, in 2003, a new department for constitutional affairs was introduced that will take over the judicial appointment process. This meant the abolition of the post of Lord Chancellor, who formerly served as head judge, speaker of the House of Lords, and member of the cabinet, fusing all three branches of government in a single individual.

Blair introduced these reforms in a top-down manner, without extensive public comment and without a clear conception of how the new system would work. Constitutional expert Vernon Bogdanor noted (in *Prospect,* April 20, 2004): "We are transforming an uncodified constitution into a codified one, but in a piecemeal and pragmatic way." Lord Neuberger, the second president of the new Supreme Court, joked that it had been created "as a result of what appears to have been a last-minute decision over a glass of whisky."

On the **foreign policy** front, Blair developed a close partnership with U.S. president Bill Clinton, whose views matched Blair's own, and he had ambitious goals for Britain in helping to shape a new, more just world order at America's side. Blair supported NATO's war to force Yugoslav troops out of Kosovo in 1999. Blair continued with this strategy when Clinton was replaced as U.S. president by the conservative George W. Bush. Blair even supported Bush's plan to build a missile-defense system, which led to the United States withdrawing from the 1972 treaty with Russia barring such a system's deployment. After the September 11, 2001, terrorist attacks in the United States, Blair expressed unequivocal support for the war on terror, sending British troops to take part in the war in Afghanistan. In return, Blair hoped to persuade Bush to tackle the roots of terror by restarting the peace process between Israelis and Palestinians

Things came to a head with the **Iraq war**. Blair persuaded the British Parliament that Iraq was in possession of weapons of mass destruction that could be launched on forty-five minutes notice, according to an intelligence report released in September 2002 (later known as the "dodgy dossier"). Blair encouraged Bush to go through the United Nations, first sending U.N. weapons inspectors into Iraq in August 2002 and then going back to the U.N. for endorsement of military action in February 2003. Blair failed to foresee the strong Franco-German resistance, which forced the United States to go ahead with the invasion without U.N. support. British public opinion was against going to war without U.N. approval. In February 2003, 750,000 people marched through London in opposition to the war, the largest protest gathering in British history. Parliament approved military action on March 18, 2003, although one-third of Labour MPs voted against.

Criticism focused on the "45 minutes" chemical weapons claim contained in the "dodgy dossier." The BBC reported that Blair's advisers had "sexed up" the intelligence claims in the dossier. A defense-ministry weapons expert, David Kelly, admitted that he was the BBC's source and committed suicide on July 17, 2003. The subsequent **inquiry by Lord Hutton,** a senior judge, exonerated the government of any wrongdoing but led to the resignation of the two top BBC executives. The subsequent insurgency in Iraq, and obviously inadequate planning for postwar reconstruction, added to the criticism heaped on Blair. But he had managed to survive the biggest political crisis of his career.

Meanwhile, relations between the United Kingdom and Europe were in the doldrums. Tony Blair welcomed the draft EU constitution in July 2003, having successfully resisted attempts by some EU members to extend majority voting to foreign affairs and taxation, which would have threatened Britain's capacity to pursue independent policies in these areas. The rejection of the new draft constitution by French and Dutch voters in 2005 was something of a relief to Blair, as it meant he did not have to put the measure before the British public. Back in 1997, Blair had promised to hold a referendum to take Britain into the euro-zone. Public skepticism about abandoning the pound sterling for the euro caused Blair to postpone the vote. Thanks to vigorous lobbying, Blair managed to beat out Paris and win London the right to host the 2012 Olympics.

New Labour had only limited success in delivering the promised improvements in public services through decentralization and increased competition. The public remained very dissatisfied over the quality of the health and education services, not to mention the accident-prone railways. (In 2001, the privatized Railtrack collapsed and was taken back into public ownership.) British society saw a surge in petty crime, causing Blair to introduce tough measures to crack down on "anti-social behavior." The 2004 Civil Partnership Act legalized civic unions for gay couples, and by the end of 2006 fifteen thousand couples had registered. In 2003, Blair introduced legislation allowing universities to charge fees of up to £3,000 per year. Previously, not only were universities free, but all students also received state grants to cover living expenses. The economy grew at a steady 2.7 percent 1997–2006, while unemployment was held to 5.5 percent, below the EU average. Pensioner poverty fell by one-third and child poverty by one-sixth, but the Gini coefficient, a measure of overall income inequality, did not budge during Labour's decade in power. Labour ramped up public spending on health and education, increasing government spending from 39 percent of GDP in 1997 to 42 percent in 2006. Globalization of the economy meant that the British state, like all states, had less discretion in national economic policy than it did during the 1950s and 1960s. Increasingly, British policy was driven by informal networks of transnational corporate elites not represented in the institutional structures of the Westminster model.

As voters became disillusioned with the mainstream political parties and turned toward "postmaterialist" values, there was an increase in political activism outside the traditional channels. The environmentalist group **Greenpeace** saw its membership swell tenfold to more than four hundred thousand, in part thanks to media coverage of their spectacular protests. Groups protesting new road construction and defending animal rights continued to be active throughout the 1990s. However, environmental issues did not really transform the agendas of the mainstream political parties, and no viable Green Party emerged. Conservative rural interests opposed to a proposed ban on fox hunting managed to draw more than four hundred thousand people to a rally in 2004.

New Labour itself also moved away from the collective interest politics of previous decades toward identity politics and a focus on the individual citizen and consumer. Labour Party membership fell from 405,000 in 1997 to 280,000 in 2002, and 190,000 in 2013. Having abandoned its traditional working-class ideology, it became increasingly difficult to say what exactly Labour stood for. Blair's government swung between cynical populism and lofty idealism, argued David Goodhart, editor of *Prospect* magazine (June 19, 2003).

Despite discontent with the war in Iraq and poor public services, Blair was able to win a third term in the May 2005 election, but Labour squeaked home with 35 percent support, the lowest share of the vote of any government in British history. Tory leader Michael Howard closed the gap with Labour by campaigning for tougher immigration rules, but the divisions in his party prevented him from attacking Blair's pro-European policies.

The Blair government was dogged by a series of scandals. The most serious was the legal investigation that was launched in 2006 over the possible "sale" of peerages by Blair's top fund-raiser, Lord Levy, in return for loans to the Labour Party. Increasingly, Blair came to be seen as a liability rather than an asset for the Labour Party. In 2004 Blair stated he would not be running for a fourth term, and in September 2006 he announced that he would resign within a year. (The declaration came after a letter signed by sixty-seven Labour MPs calling on him to resign.)

The obvious successor was **Gordon Brown**, a dour Scottish academic who had headed the Treasury since 1997 and who took much of the credit for Britain's steady economic performance. Back in 1994 the two men had met at the Granita restaurant in Islington and struck a deal. Brown agreed not to run against Blair for the post of party leader, in return for a promise that Blair would step down and hand the leadership to Brown at some future point. Whatever the precise terms of the "**Granita pact**," once in office the two men feuded bitterly behind the scenes. As Treasury Secretary, Brown jealously guarded control over the government's social and economic policies, severely limiting the power of Blair as prime minister.

In June 2007 Blair resigned, and the Queen invited Gordon Brown to form a government. Power passed from one prime minister to another without the voters being consulted. Brown was under pressure to call a snap election in the fall of 2007 to legitimate his rule, but he declined, as opinion polls showed the Conservatives with a clear lead over Labour, for the first time in a decade. The financial crisis that struck in 2008 further eroded the government's popularity. Brown took a leading role in international efforts to stem the global financial breakdown, coordinating the bank bailouts and subsequent stimulus spending.

The scandals continued. In May 2009, the *Daily Telegraph* newspaper exposed fraud in the expense claims filed by MPs. Taxpayers found themselves billed for everything from fictional second homes to moat cleaning. Four former Labour MPs and two Tory peers were jailed for falsifying their expenses. It was the 2000 Freedom of Information Act that made possible the disclosure of MP expenses. The act was intended to restrain the executive branch, but it ended up dealing a serious blow to the reputation of the House of Commons.

Coalition Government

By 2005 the Conservative Party was anxious to return to power after thirteen long years in opposition. Deeply divided over ties to the European Union, the party feared being overtaken as the main opposition party by the Liberal Democrats.

In the wake of the 2005 election, Howard was replaced as leader of the Conservative Party by the thirty-nine-year old **David Cameron**. For the first time, the Conservative leader was chosen by a ballot of the entire party membership. Cameron promised to make people "feel good about being Conservative again." After graduating from Eton and Oxford,

Cameron went straight to work for the Conservative Party, and spent his entire career in politics. Despite his traditionalist origins (at Oxford he joined one of the more reactionary dining clubs), Cameron projected a modern image. Charismatic and gregarious, he admitted to having smoked pot, sometimes cycled to work, and took paternity leave when his wife gave birth. He was a self-styled "compassionate conservative" who nevertheless took a traditional stance on many issues: he supported the war in Iraq and opposed further European integration. Cameron promised to reverse the government's ban on foxhunting and the introduction of identity cards. In many respects, he was the Conservative equivalent of Tony Blair, a determined centrist. Critics argued that the emphasis on Cameron's charisma came at the expense of programmatic coherence, in a party deeply divided between liberal centrists and Thatcherite hardliners. The May 2010 general election resulted in a divided or **"hung" parliament** where no single party had a majority of the seats (see Table 3.1). One wag described the result as a "three-way car crash." The Tories won a mere 36 percent of the popular vote, against 31 percent for Labour and 23 percent for the Liberal Democrats. The Tories had 306 seats, 20 short of what they needed to form a majority government. The Liberal-Democrats, with 57 seats, were the kingmakers. Their natural ideological ally was Labour, but their personable young leader, Nick Clegg, disliked Gordon Brown, and people were tired of seeing Labour in power. (Also, a coalition of Labour and Lib-Dems would have been ten seats short of a majority, and would have needed support from some of the smaller parties.) After five days of feverish talks, Cameron persuaded Clegg to join a coalition government with the Tories. Clegg became deputy prime minister and about half of all the Lib-Dem parliamentarians were rewarded with government positions. Cameron promised Clegg that the government would reform the House of Lords and hold a referendum on changing the electoral system. The Lib-Dems pointed to the unfairness of a system that gave them only 8 percent of the seats despite having won 23 percent of the votes.

At forty-three, Cameron was the youngest British prime minister since 1812. He positioned himself as the "heir to Blair," forging a modernization coalition with the Lib-Dems that would restore the Tories to their rightful place as "the natural party of government." (Between 1886 and 1997 the party was in power for 77 of 111 years.) More sober observers noted that the coalition gave the Tories the majority they had been denied them by the electorate, and was needed by Cameron to balance against the hard right of his own party who were opposed to his modernization agenda.

This was the first time that Britain had seen a coalition government since World War II. No one quite knew what to expect. Many Lib-Dem voters, who included many disillusioned Labour supporters, were aghast at seeing their party enter power with the Conservatives.

One of the most important actions of the coalition was a new law introducing fixed-term elections at five-year intervals. The Liberal Democrats insisted on this reform as a way of removing the power of PM Cameron to terminate the coalition and call an election at any time. In the future, 55 percent of MPs would have to support a motion to dissolve parliament.

At first the coalition was presented as a meeting of minds, but over time it became clear that it was essentially transactional in nature – and the Tories failed to deliver on their side of the bargain. As described previously, the government held a referendum on

Table 3.1   May 2010 United Kingdom General Election

	Seats	% seats	% votes
Conservatives	306	47.1	36.1
Labour	258	39.7	29.0
Liberal-Democrats	57	8.8	23.0
Democratic Unionist	8	1.2	0.6
Scottish Nationalist	6	0.9	1.7
Sinn Fein	5	0.8	0.6
Plaid Cymru	3	0.5	0.6
UK Independence	0	0	3.1
British National	0	0	1.9

electoral reform in 2011, in which voters rejected the alternative vote system favored by the Lib-Dems (and opposed by both Conservatives and Labour). A backbench revolt caused the government to abandon plans to reform the House of Lords in 2012. The Lib-Dems retaliated by refusing to support boundary changes – which may have been worth twenty seats to the Tories in the next election. Polls indicated a drastic drop in support for the Lib-Dems, so it is likely that the next election will see the return of the two-party system.

Soon after taking office the coalition government launched an unpopular **austerity program** in a bid to trim the fiscal deficit, which had caused government debt to balloon from 30 to 70 percent of GDP since 2000. However, this looked increasingly unwise in the face of the persisting economic recession. In 2012 Britain entered a double-dip recession, and the cumulative loss in GDP exceeded that experienced during the 1930s. In December 2010 the government pushed through an unpopular hike in student tuition– something the Lib-Dems had campaigned against in the election. The fees were tripled to £9,000 per year. Cameron set out to shrink the bureaucratic state that had been expanded by the Blair government to balance the workings of the market economy. He launched an ambitious reform of the welfare system, seeking to fix a cap of £26,000 annual benefits per family, and introduced elected commissioners to oversee police operations, but he lost his way over health-care reform and green policies.

Senior military figures complained that cuts in defense spending would make it impossible for Britain to repeat operations such as its participation in enforcing the Libyan no-fly zone in 2011. In August 2013, Cameron lost a vote in the House of Commons on the question of using force to punish Syrian President Assad for having used chemical weapons against his own population. Thirty Conservatives and nine Liberal Democrats joined the opposition in voting against the government's motion.

Managing the coalition was no easy task. Cameron and Clegg had to negotiate a common position for their two parties while staving off revolts from their respective backbenchers. The government was forced to retreat over several issues in the 2012 budget, from a tax on take-out food to a proposed fuel tax increase. Much of the trouble has come from truculent Tory backbenchers. For example, MP Nadine Dorries called the prime minister and chancellor "two posh boys who don't know the price of a pint of milk." There were growing complaints that Cameron was ineffective as a manager. Given that voters were increasingly judging governments by their competence rather than their ideology, these were serious concerns. Revelations continued to surface in the ongoing Murdoch phone hacking scandal, and regarding misbehavior by banks that contributed to the 2008 crash. Most notably, in July 2012 it was revealed that Barclays and other banks had been rigging the LIBOR interbank lending rate.

August 2011 saw the most serious unrest in London since the Brixton riots of 1981. The trouble began in Tottenham after the shooting by police of a black resident during a routine arrest. Mayhem spread to two-thirds of London's boroughs and half a dozen other cities, with unprecedented scenes of arson and looting of neighborhood shops. The riots were facilitated by social media that enabled flash mobs to congregate in areas where there was no police presence. The police were criticized for being slow to deploy in adequate numbers and for their reluctance to use force. Thanks to Britain's extensive network of public security cameras, more than four thousand rioters were subsequently arrested, and sentenced to long jail terms. The rioters were predominantly young, nonwhite males from areas of high poverty. The emergence of such a criminal underclass was taken as evidence of what Cameron called a "broken society" in the inner cities. Thankfully, the national mood was revived by the success of the 2012 London Olympics.

Cameron distanced himself from EU efforts to save the euro in the face of the insolvency of the Greek and Spanish governments. At an acrimonious summit in Brussels in December 2011, Cameron cast the sole negative vote, blocking a bailout deal and forcing euro managers to find a workaround. Cameron was opposed to a proposed financial transaction tax that could have harmed London's banks. The veto dismayed Cameron's Lib-Dem partners, who were pro-Europe. Polls show a majority of voters favor leaving the European Union. Cameron bowed to pressure from his own right-wing and pledged to renegotiate Britain's terms of membership and hold a referendum on whether Britain should stay in the EU. European leaders told Cameron that there was no chance of renegotiating Britain's EU treaty, while Liberal Democrats blocked the government's efforts to introduce a bill mandating a referendum by 2017. One of the main issues was a demand to end unrestricted movement of labor within the EU, since the flood of workers from Poland, Bulgaria and Romania was blamed for driving down wages and driving up unemployment.

The Conservative Party found itself under increasing pressure from the UK Independence Party (Ukip), a right-wing populist party founded in 1993, that David Cameron described in 2006 as a party of "fruitcakes, loonies and closet racists." Ukip's main demand was immediate withdrawal from the EU, a stance that attracted increasing numbers of Tory voters. In the 1999 elections to the European Parliament Ukip won 7 percent of the vote and was awarded three seats, rising to 16.5 percent of the vote and 12 seats in 2009. In the 2010 general election the party polled just 3.1 percent, but in local elections in May 2013 it took 23 percent of the vote – ahead of the Liberal Democrats with 14 percent, and close behind the Tories with 25 percent and Labour at 29 percent. After that shocking result, right-wing Tories were proposing an electoral pact with Ukip in the 2015 general election in order to avoid splitting the anti-EU vote. It looks increasingly unlikely that British politics will return to its classic pattern of two strong parties alternating in government any time soon,

CONCLUSION

Britain has a robust and successful political system that seemed to have recovered, under the government of Tony Blair (1997–2007), from the economic stagnation and class warfare of the 1970s and 1980s. But the lasting impact of the 2008 recession, and the instability of policy making under the 2010 coalition government, once again raises questions about the viability of Britain's adversarial political system. The Westminster model is no longer the "envy of the world," as was complacently assumed by many Britons during the nineteenth century.

The major challenge facing Britain is the same one that confronts the other European countries: crafting transnational institutions to manage the global economy while maintaining the capacity to tackle social problems that arise at the national level, and also preserving a sense of national unity and common purpose. Britain has been a follower rather than a leader in the process of international institution-building (such as the European Union), which is a reflection of its diminished role in the international system since the end of its empire. Its bold embrace of a multicultural national identity was challenged, but not dislodged, by the terrorist attacks of July 2005. For all of the stumbles and setbacks, the British model of tolerance and reasoned debate can still serve as an example for the rest of the world.

Table 3.2 Key Phases in Britain's Development

Time Period	Regime	Global Context	Interests/ Identities/ Institutions	Developmental Path
1688–1832	Constitutional monarchy, Parliamentary Sovereignty	Imperial expansion	Elite consensus on values, interests	Capitalism, limited state
1832–1914	Parliamentary sovereignty, Electoral Democracy	Global hegemony based on naval power	Extension of franchise	Industrialization, free trade, gold standard

(continued)

Table 3.2 *(cont.)*

Time Period	Regime	Global Context	Interests/ Identities/ Institutions	Developmental Path
1918–1945	Rise of Labour Party, three-party system, Coalition Governments	Hegemony weakened, struggling to retain empire	Intense social conflict	Defensive
1945–1973	Two-party Competition	Retreat from Empire, Cold War, U.S. alliance, exclusion from Europe	Keynesianism, welfare-state consensus	Slow growth
1973–1979	Two-party Deadlock	Entry into European Union, global recession	Severe labor unrest, N. Ireland conflict	Crisis
1979–1987	Margaret Thatcher Dominant	Economic globalization, second Cold War	Organized labor crushed	Neoliberalism: deregulation, privatization
1987–2010	Tony Blair's New Labour dominant, Constitutional Reform	Economic globalization, European integration, war on terror	Economic boom, Scottish devolution, Lords reform, worries over immigration	Neoliberalism, reformed welfare state, multiculturalism, citizens' rights
2010–2012	Coalition of Tories and Lib-Dems	Economic crisis	Political deadlock, Murdoch media scandal	Politics of austerity, search for new model

BIBLIOGRAPHY

Beech, Matthew, and Simon Lee, eds. *The Cameron-Clegg Government: Coalition Politics in an Age of Austerity*. New York: Palgrave Macmillan, 2011.

Bogdanor, Vernon. *The Coalition and the Constitution*. London: Hart Publishing, 2011.

Bogdanor, Vernon. *The New British Constitution*. London: Hart Publishing, 2009.

Butler, David, and Philip Cowley. *The British General Election of 2010*. New York: Palgrave Macmillan, 2010.

Foley, Michael. *The British Presidency: Tony Blair and the Politics of Public Leadership*. New York: Manchester University Press, 2001.

Hannan, Patrick. *A Useful Fiction: Adventures in British Democracy*. London: Sede, 2009.

Heffernan, Richard, Philip Cowley, and Colin Hay, eds. *Developments in British Politics 9*. New York: Palgrave Macmillan, 2011.

Hennessy, Peter. *The Prime Minister. The Office and Its Holders since 1945*. London: Palgrave Macmillan, 2001.

Heppell, Timothy, and David Seawright, eds. *Cameron and the Conservatives: The Transition to Coalition Government*. London: Palgrave Macmillan, 2011.

Hutton, Will. *The State We're In*. London: Jonathan Cape, 1995.

Kavanagh, Denis. *Thatcherism and British Politics: The End of Consensus?* New York: Oxford University Press, 1990.

King, Anthony. *The British Constitution*. New York: Oxford University Press, 2008.

Loughlin, Martin. *The British Constitution. A Very Short Introduction*, New York: Oxford University Press, 2013.

Marquand, David, and Anthony Seldon. *The Ideas That Shaped Modern Britain*. London: Fontana Press, 1996.

Riddell, Peter. *The Unfulfilled Prime Minister: Tony Blair's Quest for a Legacy*. London: Politicos, 2006.

Seldon, Anthony. *Blair's Britain 1997–2008*. New York: Cambridge University Press, 2008.

Seldon, Anthony, and Guy Lodge. *Brown at Ten*. London: Biteback Publishing, 2011.

Stephens, Philip. *Tony Blair: The Making of a World Leader*. New York: Viking, 2004.

Thatcher, Margaret. *The Downing Street Years*. New York: HarperCollins, 1993.

IMPORTANT TERMS

Danny Boyle – film director (*Slumdog Millionaire*) and producer of the opening ceremony at the 2012 London Olympic Games.

British Commonwealth – cultural association linking fifty-three former colonies of Britain.

"British disease" – a high level of strike activity caused by powerful trade unions taking advantage of low unemployment to push for higher wages.

Devolution – the creation of regional assemblies in Wales and Scotland, debated since the 1970s and introduced in 1999.

Euro – currency unit introduced in January 1999 for Germany and the ten other members of the European Monetary Union. The German mark is now officially just a denomination of the euro, which fully replaced all national member currencies except for the British pound, in July 2002.

European Union (EU) – now an organization of twenty-seven European countries. It originated as the six-member European Coal and Steel Community in 1951 and became the European Economic Community in 1958, gradually enlarging its membership and becoming known as the European Community (EC) until the Maastricht treaty of 1991 came into effect in 1993 and enlarged its authority and changed its name to the European Union.

Exchange Rate Mechanism (ERM) – the common currency band of European Union currencies, which Britain joined in 1990 and was forced to leave in 1992.

Falklands War – the 1982 conflict that resulted after Argentina had seized the British-owned Falkland Islands and a British naval task force was sent to recapture them.

Glorious Revolution – the 1688 removal of the Catholic king James II by Protestant William of Orange, who accepted the principle of parliamentary sovereignty.

Granita Pact – a 2004 deal in which Gordon Brown promised to support Tony Blair as leader of the Labour Party.

Greenpeace – an environmental action group that saw its membership expand during the 1980s.

David Cameron – the leader of the Conservative Party since 2006 and prime minister since 2010.

Hereditary peers – members of the House of Lords appointed by the monarch and whose title automatically passes down to their sons.

Her Majesty's Opposition – the second-largest party in the House of Commons, which is critical of the government but loyal to the British state as symbolized by the monarch.

"Hung parliament" – one in which no single party has an absolute majority of the seats in the House of Commons.

Hutton inquiry – investigation into the government's actions leading Britain into the 2003 war with Iraq.

Keynesianism – a philosophy of state intervention in the economy derived from the work of John Maynard Keynes, who argued that the Great Depression could have been avoided by increasing state spending.

Magna Carta – the contract guaranteeing the rights of noble families that King John agreed to sign in 1215.

John Major – Conservative Party leader who replaced Margaret Thatcher as prime minister in 1990 and resigned after losing the 1997 election.

"Marginal" seats – those seats in the House of Commons that are closely contested and are likely to change hands between parties in an election (the opposite of "safe" seats).

Multiculturalism – a policy of encouraging immigrant groups to retain their own traditions and identities through separate educational, religious, and social institutions.

Rupert Murdoch – the Australian-born magnate who owns one-third of Britain's newspapers and has considerable political influence.

1984 miners' strike – the coal miners' strike that was defeated by Margaret Thatcher, clearing the way for legislation limiting the power of trade unions.

No. 10 Downing Street – the prime minister's residence and the place where the cabinet meets.

Parliamentary sovereignty – the power of Parliament, representing the people, to enact any law it chooses, unrestrained by a written constitution or the separation of powers.

Plaid Cymru – the nationalist party in Wales that advocates more rights for the Welsh people, including use of the Welsh language.

Prime Minister's Questions – the thirty-minute period once a week during which the prime minister stands before the House of Commons and answers questions from MPs.

Social Democratic Party (SDP) – a group of moderate socialists who broke away from the Labour Party in the early 1980s.

"Third Way" – the new, moderate philosophy introduced by Tony Blair after he became Labour Party leader in 1994.

Tory – the colloquial name for a member of the Conservative Party.

Unionists – the Protestant majority in Northern Ireland, who want to keep the province part of the United Kingdom.

Welfare state – the program of state-provided social benefits introduced by the Labour Government of 1945–1951, including the National Health Service, state pensions, and state-funded higher education.

Westminster model – the British system of parliamentary sovereignty, prime ministerial government, and two parties alternating in power.

STUDY QUESTIONS

1. What were the main features of the bipartisan consensus in British politics that lasted from the 1950s to the late 1970s?
2. Why did some observers argue that Britain was "ungovernable" in the 1970s?
3. Which aspects of British society were the targets of Margaret Thatcher's reforms?
4. What did Tony Blair mean by the "third way"?
5. What factors have been holding Britain back from greater participation in the European Union?
6. When did most British citizens get the right to vote, and why?
7. Does the lack of a written constitution make it easier, or harder, for Britain to introduce political reform?
8. How does the power of the prime minister compare with that of the U.S. president?
10. What are the strengths and weaknesses of the first-past-the-post electoral system compared with proportional representation? Is Britain likely to introduce PR in the near future?

FRANCE

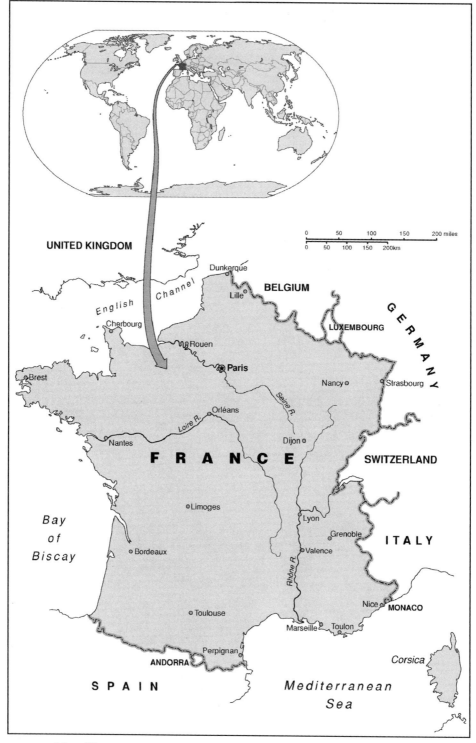

MAP 4.1. Map of France.

4 France

Laurence McFalls

Introduction

The United States and France have a long-standing love-hate relationship of mutual respect, envy, and suspicion. The French came to the rescue of the American revolutionaries in their War of Independence from Britain, and twice in the twentieth century, American soldiers proclaiming "Lafayette, we are here" helped France repel German invaders. Despite – or perhaps because of – their ancient alliance, France and the United States have suspected and accused one another of disloyalty and imperial ambitions. Eager to assert its autonomy after having become a nuclear power, France in 1966, for example, withdrew from the North Atlantic Treaty Organization's U.S.-led integrated command structure. The day after September 11, France's left-liberal newspaper of reference *Le Monde* headlined " We are all Americans," but in early 2003, when France failed to back the U.S.-led invasion of Iraq, the United States retaliated not only by renaming some favorite foods "freedom fries" and "freedom toast" but by trying to drive a wedge between the "old" and "new" Europe.

Ambivalence and occasional animosity have been not only diplomatic but cultural and popular as well. In American minds, France represents elegance and sophistication, but also snobbery, frivolity, and cowardice (during the Iraq War, Google responded to the search request "French military victories" with "Do you mean 'French military defeats'?"). In French minds, Americans are naïve "big children," whom they nonetheless admire for their dynamism and entrepreneurial spirit. While France in trade talks has fought the United States in favor of *l'exception culturelle* in order to protect French and world culture from "hollywoodization," the French have lionized lowbrow comedian Jerry Lewis and adored kitsch-television series such as *Starsky and Hutch*.

To be sure, the United States occupies a greater space in the French *imaginaire* than France does in the American. With a population of 60 million and a landmass the size of Texas, France is no longer the powerhouse that dominated the European continent from the Middle Ages well into the nineteenth century and that controlled a worldwide empire well into the twentieth. From a contemporary American perspective, France is an intermediate, "has-been" power, whose continuing pretensions to *grandeur* are a misplaced irritant at best. No doubt, the tensions that characterize Franco-American relations owe something to France's relative decline and to the United States' ascendancy to superpower status since World War II, but in fact it is possible, and necessary, to trace them back to fundamental differences in interests, identities, and institutions that have distinguished French and American societies for at least four centuries. No one has offered a finer analysis of these differences than the French nobleman **Alexis de Tocqueville**, who already some 175 years ago expressed France's ambivalent appreciation of the United States in his two-volume study of *Democracy in America*. Americans tend to read Tocqueville's masterpiece, which won him election to the *Académie française*, as a celebration of the vibrancy of their civil society, of the participatory dynamism of their local governments, and of the wisdom of their federalist constitutional order, among other elements of a successful American recipe for reconciling the competing values of personal liberty and social equality. By contrast, American readers like to overlook the less endearing, but unfortunately enduring, American traits such as racism, conformism, vulgar materialism, and anti-intellectualism that Tocqueville observed in the United States of the 1830s. As a French patriot who devoted his life to public service and scholarly analysis, Tocqueville was not interested in the United States for its own sake, but as a comparative foil for France. Indeed, for Tocqueville, the United States constituted a natural experiment, a unique case of a new society founded on the democratic principle of social equality, free from a hereditary nobility with its claims to privileges and leadership. He also feared that America's egalitarianism made it susceptible to tyranny when a mass of socially leveled individuals faced a powerful, increasingly centralized state. Indeed, Tocqueville looked to America as an example of both the dangers and opportunities that France faced after the revolutions of 1789, 1830, and 1848 had destroyed the aristocratic principle and had sent France, as we shall shortly see, down its long, tortuous path to modern democratic stability.

Although Tocqueville's ambivalence about American democracy reflected and anticipated long-standing and contemporary tensions in Franco-American relations, the French nobleman was paradoxically an unequivocal admirer of France's ancient Anglo-Saxon nemesis, Great Britain. But Britain, too, was for Tocqueville an exceptional case, a fortuitous land that had avoided the two interrelated forces of modernity: social equalization and political centralization. In England, as we saw in the last chapter, the aristocracy had, during the Civil War of 1642–1649 and the Glorious Revolution of 1688, succeeded in resisting the centralization of power in the monarchy and had retained its social and political preeminence. For Tocqueville, Britain thus did not stand at the avant-garde of political development. Indeed, its insular position, like that of the United States, allowed Britain, as well as its former colony, to avoid the full onslaught of democratic modernity that hit continental Europe. As Tocqueville wrote in his second masterpiece, *The Old Regime and the Revolution*, France, for better but mostly for worse, represented the ideal-typical, or most "normal," path to political modernity, at least within the western European context.

The Medieval Origins of the French State

One of, if not *the*, classic questions of comparative politics is: Why did the modern bureaucratic state first emerge in Western Europe (and we might add: And why with such a vengeance in France)? Debate still rages, but a crucial explanatory factor lies paradoxically in the fragmented, competitive nature of political authority in the age of feudalism that followed the collapse of the Roman Empire in the West in the wake of the "barbarian" invasions of the fifth to tenth centuries. Various Germanic tribal leaders, including the Franks, coveted the title and power of the Roman emperor. Between them, they succeeded in destroying all of the major social, economic, political, and cultural institutions of the late empire, except for one: the Roman Catholic Church. For over one thousand years, Western Europe was thus characterized by political division and religious unity. The upshot was a constant power struggle not only between political authorities but between them and the Church hierarchy under the secular as well as spiritual leadership of the pope in Rome. In the year 800, Charlemagne, the king of the Franks, succeeded in uniting into the Holy Roman Empire most of the territories that would one day become France, Germany, Italy, and the Benelux countries, the founders in 1957 of what would become today's European Union. Divided by his grandsons, Charlemagne's empire had had little chance of survival as even its heroic founder's authority depended on his coronation by the pope. In other words, the division of authority between the spiritual leadership of the pope and the political leadership of the emperor meant that even a successful conqueror of Western Europe would have to come up with sources of legitimacy beyond religious benediction to consolidate his or her power. In any case, the remnants of Charlemagne's empire did not survive the next round of barbarian invasions of the tenth century, including that of the Normans, who settled in the northern part of the Frankish kingdom, whence they successfully invaded England in 1066.

The constant rivalry between feudal leaders on the one hand and between them and the Church on the other proved to be the developmental dynamic from which the modern state emerged on the European continent. The consolidation of the French state in fact owed much to the Norman conquest of England. As no one repeated William the Conqueror's exploit of 1066, unrivalled Norman rule of the island kingdom allowed it to project power back onto the European mainland, where under the complexities of cross-cutting feudal obligations the English royalty was in some areas the subordinate of Frankish kings and in others their superiors. These confusions came to a head in a succession crisis and series of armed struggles known as the Hundred Years War spanning the fourteenth and fifteenth centuries. Whereas the English succeeded in projecting power across the Channel thanks to the coherence of king and nobility after the Conquest and the compromise of the Magna Carta, the French monarchy suffered the typical weakness of feudal devolution of authority, whereby the nobility exercised local authority nominally by grace of the king but where in fact the latter could count on the support of his nobles only by their goodwill. Finally, only in 1431, when the French king's sister disguised as the peasant girl Jeanne d'Arc heroically rallied the troops, did the French manage to drive the English from the continent. Having learned his lesson, Charles VII persuaded his nobility in 1439 to allow him to establish a permanent standing army in exchange, fatally, for the aristocracy's exemption from royal taxes to fund it. This unholy compromise sowed the seeds, as we shall see, for the Revolution that shook France and the world 350 years later, but at the same time it also marked the conception, if not birth, of the European state system.

Even before they began the long struggle to monopolize the control of the means of force on the territories nominally under their rule, the monarchs of Western Europe had begun to develop other crucial means of social control. Although they continued their struggle with the Church to guide their subjects' spiritual beliefs – the French king even went so far as to hold the pope captive in a palace in Avignon during the fourteenth century – Europe's secular leaders began willy-nilly to develop techniques for more effectively governing their subjects' and their own material affairs. Starting in the twelfth and thirteenth centuries, they granted charters to universities, a new institution that not only competed with monasteries as centers of learning in their faculties of theology but trained experts of applicable knowledge in their faculties of law, arts, and sciences. Deprived of religious authority, Western Europe's monarchies necessarily acquired a comparative advantage in the codification of law and the rationalization of taxes and other fiscal obligations. As the laws and obligations they rendered more effective were those that maintained the feudal order and the interests of the dominant class, the aristocracy hardly contested this aggrandizement of monarchical power. Yet as with the concession of a permanent royal army, the feudal nobility would learn to regret the convenience of an effective crown.

Whereas in insular England the aristocracy prevented the monarchy from establishing an army and seizing control of the goverment of local daily affairs, on the continent the more constant, immediate threat of war and invasion favored territorial rulers in their bids to raise armies and to monopolize the control of social resources. In fits and starts, this process gave rise to a new political order called **absolutism**, with suzerains, the nominal holders of ultimate authority over a given territory in the feudal order, becoming sovereigns, the effective final arbiters of authority within their lands. The absolutist monarchs of continental Western Europe did not, of course, exercise absolute authority; they lacked the technical means of modern dictatorships, for example. What was absolute – and novel – about their rule was their claim *potentially* to control all aspects of life within their realms. Historians generally tend to describe Ferdinand and Isabella of Spain as the first absolute monarchs, but France usually occupies the rank of the prototypical absolute monarchy, attaining its highpoint under the long reign of Louis XIV (1642 – 1710), the *roi soleil* whose memorable "L'État, c'est moi" embodied the absolutist principle.

Absolutism and the Origins of Contemporary French Institutions, Interests, and Identity

Two centuries, however, separated Charles VII's establishment of a standing royal army from Louis XIV's glorious reign – two centuries that laid the foundations for the institutions, interests, and identities of contemporary France. With the close of the Hundred Years War, the French monarchy consolidated its rule, notably under Louis XI, whose reign ushered in the French Renaissance, characterized by the construction of the celebrated chateaux along the Loire River and the incorporation into court life of geniuses the likes of Leonardo da Vinci. The French kings did not yet rule unilaterally, though. They still depended, especially in matters of taxation, on the collaboration of the late feudal representative institution of the Estates General, created in 1302. Similar to the two houses of the English Parliament, the Estates separately represented the three orders of feudal society: the nobility, the clergy, and the remaining Third Estate of commoners. In addition, a panoply of local and regional courts and deliberative bodies such as the *Parlements* of Paris and of Languedoc vied with the kings for legislative and judicial authority. In the late sixteenth century, moreover, the monarchy nearly collapsed in the face of the succession crisis and civil war provoked by the death of Henri II, last of the Valois line. Heightened by the conversion of a significant portion of the southern aristocracy, the Huguenots, to Protestantism, this political and religious struggle within the nobility ceased only when popular uprisings in the late 1580s threatened the aristocratic principle per se. A double compromise saved the kingdom in 1589: the Protestant pretender to the throne, Henri IV, founder of the Bourbon dynasty, converted to Catholicism but in turn introduced official religious tolerance through the Edict of Nantes of 1598.

Beginning under Henri IV's reign, seventeenth-century France witnessed the consolidation and institutionalization of the absolutist monarchy through the successive efforts of four particularly capable royal administrators: Sully, Richelieu, Mazarin, and Colbert. Sully's preoccupation was the securing of an independent financial base for the monarchy. By developing indirect forms of taxation and the sale of state offices, Sully and the monarchy netted the short-term windfalls of privatization of public goods and rendered the Estates General obsolete: the last time they convened before 1789 was in 1614. The long-term effect of Sully's initiative of farming out tax collection and other state functions to private entrepreneurs was: a loss of control over tax receipts, two-thirds of which remained in private hands; growing popular frustration with tax inequities and poor public services; and the emergence of a new class of financiers with a strong identification with the state and an interest in maintaining its structural deficits. Following Sully as de facto ruler of France, Cardinal Richelieu attacked the administrative fragmentation and inconsistencies of what was still largely a feudal monarchy. His method, too, was indirect in that he simply added a new, more rational layer of administration – a reform that initiated the centralized structure of the contemporary French state. Dividing the kingdom into thirty-two relatively equal *generalités*, he placed them under the supervision of royal *intendants* loyal and responsible to no one but the monarch.

The administrative and fiscal structures of the bourgeoning absolutist state faced a critical test under Richelieu's successor, Cardinal Mazarin, who governed France from 1642 to 1661, during Louis XIV's minority. France's interventions into the Thirty Years War, which ravaged Central Europe from 1618 to 1648, put such a strain on the tax system that the *Parlement* of Paris finally refused Mazarin's unilateral tax measures. Thus, at the very moment that the Peace of Westphalia in 1648 consecrated the modern concept of the territorial state, Europe's largest state descended into a five-year civil war. Unlike the contemporaneous English Civil War, the so-called Fronde in France resulted not in the breaking of royal power and absolutist ambition but in a figurative decapitation of the aristocracy. Traumatized by his near loss of power, the young Louis XIV, first with the help of Mazarin, then largely on his own, systematically constructed an absolutist state that became the explicit model emulated by monarchs elsewhere on the continent (and in restoration Britain as well until the Glorious Revolution of 1688 definitively established parliamentary supremacy). Louis XIV's methods were military, political, social, and economic: he expanded the army by a factor of ten to three hundred thousand men (out of a total population under twenty million) and founded a royal police force to maintain order in the growing towns. He did not eliminate the representative bodies inherited from the feudal age but failed to convene them and withdrew their right to criticize royal decrees. His most famous measure, though, was the construction of the enormous palace at Versailles, but not as a megalomaniac end in itself. From 1682 on, he required that the upper nobility take up residence at his court in Versailles. Thereby Louis XIV could not only keep an eye on potential rivals but keep them occupied with court intrigues, drain their purses with frivolous expenses for social prestige, and most importantly distract them from their local interests and power bases. Cut off from the countryside and the peasants who sustained them, the upper nobility became a truly parasitic class serving no economic, judicial, military, or social function. At the same time, however, the absolutist state upheld their feudal rights and privileges, inevitably to the growing frustration of commoners in town and country.

Beyond the clever political manipulation and expansion of existing structures and resources, Louis XIV also sought to create new sources of state power. He charged his minister Colbert with the development of state-owned enterprises not only in such strategic sectors as armaments but also in the production of luxury goods such as the huge wall-hangings produced by the state firm Gobelins. With this proactive economic policy, Colbert introduced a historically new function and tool for the state: the promotion of economic growth and innovation. Generally called mercantilism, the state-led pursuit of prosperity and trade surpluses in order to better fill the sovereign's coffers is to this day called **colbertisme** in France. A product of seventeenth-century absolutism, *colbertisme* provides a telling example of the interlocking character of institutions, interests, and identities. In France, the state's long-standing institutional capacity to steer economic development through public ownership of key economic sectors and through the training of qualified experts in public service has shaped private interests, notably with higher civil servants and upper management regularly moving back and forth between public and private sectors in industry and finance. French national identity also derives in part from the *colbertiste* tradition, drawing pride in state-inspired accomplishments from Gobelins tapestries to the nationwide high-speed rail network of *trains de grande vitesse* (TGV).

Louis XIV's long reign (1642–1710) sowed the seeds of not only modern day economic nationalism but also those of absolutism's self-destruction. Having drained the kingdom's capacities with excessive territorial and dynastic ambitions and having outlived his sons and grandsons, the *roi soleil* left France in the hands of five-year-old Louis XV. The occasion was rife for the aristocracy to avenge itself of lost power and prestige. The nobility did not, however, dismantle the absolutist state. Instead, in a process known as the feudal reaction, they transformed it into their private reserve, restricting access to high offices of army and administration to those who could prove birth from four aristocratic grandparents. The repressive capacities of the absolutist state firmly under their control, the aristocracy quite rationally used them not to develop new commercial or industrial activities, as did the British aristocracy of the eighteenth century, but rather to reinforce the feudal obligations of the peasantry and other taxable commoners. This strategy was in fact the only one open to the nobility, for under the absolutist state and the absentee landlordism of Louis XIV's reign, the peasantry had acquired de facto control of much of the land whereas the commercial, financial, and bourgeoning industrial resources of the realm were under the control of the townsmen, or bourgeoisie (from the French "bourg," fortified town). What is more, as the French aristocracy drew its material revenues from its legal control of the land and as the products of French agriculture that lent themselves to profitable commercialization were the labor-intensive production of wine and wheat, the aristocracy had every interest in seeing peasants tied to the land by feudal obligation. As Tocqueville observed in *The Old Regime and the Revolution*, the feudal reaction of the eighteenth century did not mean that the peasantry and other commoners in France were objectively worse off than elsewhere in Europe. *Au contraire*, French absolutism had given them relative autonomy, which was precisely what made them subjectively more resentful of aristocratic power and privilege than was the case elsewhere.

The French Revolution

In hindsight, the great Revolution of 1789 was a foregone conclusion. To get there, however, the absolutist state had to lose control of the repressive social order it had come to sustain. History's great revolutions erupt not from social, economic, and political injustices alone – these are omnipresent – but from their convergence with a breakdown of the political and institutional mechanisms for imposing them. To survive, a state must be able to face down any internal or external challenges to its authority within its territorial boundaries. In eighteenth-century France, the challenges were great but not insurmountable. Indeed, historians still debate whether Louis XVI, with better decisions or advice, might not have been able to ward off the worst – from his own point of view, that is – or at least have saved his head in a constitutional compromise. Fortunately, we need not engage in such counterfactual speculation here as the immediate precipitants of the revolution point to two obvious causes: budget deficits and under-taxing of the wealthy. To be sure, the causes of the French Revolution were manifold. Tocqueville, for example, analyses not only the legitimate frustrations of the peasantry but also the lack of communication between the social classes, the complicity of the Church in maintaining inequalities, the utopian idealism of the *philosophes*' critiques of the absolutist state, and the bad timing of Louis XVI's reform efforts, among many others.

All of these grievances and mistakes came to a head, though, when the monarchy found itself in a grave fiscal crisis resulting, externally, from war and, internally, from the aristocracy's centuries-old exemption from taxation. Indeed, since 1774, the monarchy had found itself in a budget crisis that grew even worse when the French crown decided to intervene in favor of the rebellious colonies in the American War for Independence in order to avenge France for its losses in the previous, costly Seven Years War (experienced as the French and Indian War in America). In a futile attempt to bring order into its affairs, the monarchy in 1788 for the first and last time actually took the trouble to calculate its budget, finding itself to be in a 20 percent budget overrun, with half of the deficit arising from service of the debt. The king's treasury minister Calonne proposed a solution that included a new property tax to which the aristocracy would be subjected alongside the commoners. In a bid to secure some form of approval for this radical measure, Calonne revived a supposedly representative institution unused since 1626, a handpicked Assembly of Notables. But even Calonne's men refused to acquiesce to a principle as repugnant as the taxation of nobles! When in May 1788 the *Parlement* of Paris refused approval as well, Louis XVI ordered the arrest of its leaders, kicking off the Revolution's first phase of aristocratic revolt against the very state that maintained aristocratic privilege. Still, the king needed some sort of legislative approval for his new tax, so he decided to convene the Estates General for the first time since 1614. This institutional mechanism introduced two new dangers: it represented, theoretically at least, the interest of all society, and it mobilized expectations as it entailed the public designation of delegates and the drawing up of lists of grievances. These *cahiers de doléances* have proven to be an invaluable source for historians such as Tocqueville who could read the state of opinion and the interests of all classes of French society straight from the grievances they addressed to their "good king."

On the eve of the Revolution, French society was fragmented into numerous classes and strata whose divergent interests would not only drive the Revolution forward to catastrophe but shape French politics, society, and the state for centuries to come. The peasantry, for example, was divided between those who owned or controlled little or no land, equipment, or animals; those who had enough to engage in subsistence agriculture; and those who generated enough surplus to acquire other goods and even more land. These wealthier peasants, although perhaps still nominally subjected to feudal obligations such as the forced labor of the *corvée*, shaded into the bourgeoisie. Originally a political label to describe town dwellers who enjoyed personal exemptions and collective rights within the feudal order, the bourgeoisie, under absolutism, had become an economic class with a panoply of potentially conflicting interests. Including intellectuals, liberal professionals such as doctors and lawyers, artisans and craftsmen, merchants, bankers, rentiers, and – increasingly since the mid-eighteenth century – industrialists, the bourgeoisie had many competing interests, but one common enemy: the aristocracy, whose social prestige and political privileges frustrated bourgeois ambitions. One of these ambitions, perhaps hypocritical, was to accede to the status of noble through the purchase of feudal estates, titles, and royal offices. Indeed, the frontier between *roturiers* (commoners) and nobles had grown confused under absolutism with the rise of the *noblesse de robe*, royal officeholders of non-noble origin who over time succeeded in acquiring hereditary title. Even the traditional feudal-military *noblesse d'épée*, though, was rife with divisions: some of the enlightened elites close to the monarchy recognized the necessity of rational reform of the cumbersome feudal-absolutist state whereas their poorer, disempowered cousins in the provinces clung to feudal privileges in a rearguard effort to ward off bourgeois ascension. Finally, on top of the schisms among and between commoners and nobles, social and political conflict under the old regime was further confused by the cross-cutting material, institutional and ideal interests of the Second Estate, namely the clergy, divided between noble officials and common priests, between monastic orders with huge property holdings and poor parishes, and between regions with differences in religious practices and loyalties.

We cannot here trace out the infinitely complex interplay of interests, institutions, and identities that convulsed France between the convening of the Estates General in 1789 and the final defeat of Napoleon Bonaparte's revolutionary armies in 1815. The history of the French Revolution fills thousands of volumes and debate still rages as to whether it contributed positively to the emergence of the modern democratic state. More radically and universally than the earlier English or American revolutions, the French Revolution established the principles of popular sovereignty and equal rights, but it did so at the cost of ideological terror and massive warfare. In its initial, peaceful phase, the Revolution of 1789 looked like an attempt to adjust the rickety institutions of the absolutist state to the interests of a society breaking out of feudal agrarian stagnancy. After aristocratic refusal of the king's tax reforms prompted the convening of the Estates General in May 1789, the Third Estate, with delegates representing over 95 percent of the population, became the focal point for contesting royal authority. Having obtained a number of representatives equal to the sum of those representing the First and Second Estates, the Third Estate, emboldened by pamphleteers such as the Abbé Sieyès (who answered his pamphlet's title "What Is the Third Estate?" resoundingly with "the entire nation"), proclaimed itself the constituent National Assembly on June 17. Finding their meeting hall closed by royal order on June 20, the representatives of the Third Estate/National Assembly met on a tennis court and swore in the "Serment du jeu de paume" to continue to assemble until they had drafted a constitution for the kingdom. Louis XVI hesitated to disperse the delegates by force, and a week later all three orders convened together.

Had the Revolution ended there, with the proclamation of a constitutional monarchy, it would have remained, like its English and American antecedents, a political affair settled largely between elites with more or less internecine violence. The strategic blunders of the king, however, propelled events toward popular upheaval and profound social revolution. In a context of famine and rapidly rising bread prices in Paris in particular, the king ordered mercenary troops to mobilize around the city, and on July 12, 1789, fired his popular reformist finance minister Necker. With rumors circulating about a counterrevolutionary coup against the National Assembly and a plan to starve the city, the Parisian masses, the celebrated *sans-culottes*, stormed the royal *Invalides* armory and liberated the prisoners, albeit only seven, of the Bastille fortress in the first great popular *journée* of the Revolution, July 14. Over the months and years to come, the *sans-culottes* would push the Revolution radically forward in a sequence of *grandes journées*, culminating notably on September 21, 1792, in the proclamation of the Republic. Still, the Revolution would not have had a transformative effect on French society as a whole if the overwhelming mass of the population, the peasantry, had not taken part immediately after the storming of the Bastille. Again, in a context of famine, fear of brigandage, real threats of counterrevolutionary plots, disinformation and disorder, a vast movement known as the Great Fear spread across the French countryside between July 20 and August 6. Fully aware of the legal and political underpinnings of the feudal order that left them beholden to parasitic aristocratic landlords and unfair taxes, the peasants stormed aristocratic manors and castles, carefully identifying and destroying the feudal documents codifying their servitude and obligations. As the peasants in many cases were already landowners themselves they did not, however, attack property rights. Indeed, throughout the Revolution, only nobles who emigrated and fought against the Revolution had their land confiscated. Faced with peasant revolt, to recover control of the situation, the National Assembly on the night of August 4, 1789, solemnly proclaimed, with full noble participation, the end of feudalism.

Within a few months and with minimum bloodshed, France had de facto become a constitutional monarchy with a sovereign, popularly representative parliament, equal political and social rights, and an economic order founded on the principle of private property – in short, all the essential ingredients of a liberal representative democracy and a capitalist socioeconomic order. As we know, the Revolution did not end there and instead bequeathed France with a political order that lacked stability or legitimacy or both well into the twentieth century. It also left the French hungry for both radical equality and powerful central authority, the complementary but contradictory characteristics typical of modern democratic societies, according to Alexis de Tocqueville. Before exploring the enduring legacy of the Revolution for French politics down to the present, however, we must briefly suggest why the Revolution could not stop with the dramatic events of 1789. Two factors, which, following Tocqueville, we can link to the institutional dynamics of the absolutist state, drove the Revolution on to death and destruction: namely, the treasonous behavior of the crown and the powerful conflicts of interest within French society. It is perhaps understandable, if not forgivable, that Louis XVI, his queen Marie-Antoinette, their courtiers, and aristocratic allies consistently tried to turn back the constitutional and democratic advances of the Revolution. After all, centuries of absolutism had trained them to disregard representative bodies and decentralized sources of authority, and the remaining absolutist monarchs on the continent actively plotted with them to restore absolutism. Events such as the king and queen's "Flight to Varennes" in June 1791, when they tried to rejoin counterrevolutionary forces near the Belgian border, and the king's subsequent connivance in provoking a proclamation of war against Austria pushed the revolutionary regime to more and more radical measures as it struggled for survival against external and internal enemies.

The counterrevolutionary forces could indeed count on divisions and conflicts of interest within French society to push the Revolution towards collapse or toward ever more authoritarian means. As Tocqueville observed in *The Old Regime and the Revolution*, the absolutist centralization of authority had left Frenchmen equal in their political impotence but isolated from one another in their frustrations. Revolutionary leaders thus inherited a society torn by narrow sectarian interests, and so reverted to the absolutist impulse to centralize power and atomize citizens. These structural tendencies toward divisiveness and authoritarianism of French politics and society were, however, exacerbated by a more immediate, conjunctural legacy of French absolutism: its fiscal crisis, which, as the revolution's immediate cause, still required resolution. In November 1789, the constituent assembly nationalized Church property and issued a new currency, the *assignat*, backed by these nationalized goods. What seemed like a good idea at the time not only prompted a hyperinflationary cycle provoking ongoing food shortages and riots but antagonized much of the Church hierarchy and the faithful in soon-to-be-counterrevolutionary regions such as the Vendée. A year later, the introduction of the Civil Constitution of the Clergy, requiring that priests swear allegiance to the state as religious functionaries, created an enduring cleavage in French politics: well into the twentieth century, the single best predictor of a region's left-right voting behavior was its clergymen's refusal (right) or acceptance (left) of the oath.

Through such immediate conflicts, the Revolution in the long run forged and solidified political identities that characterize the French polity down to the present. In the short run, however, revolutionary politics intensified social conflict. Perhaps the most important tension of the Revolution was that between the popular classes in town and country. The food shortages that preceded the Revolution only grew worse in the periods of disruption and of civil and international war that followed 1789. The Parisian *sans-culottes* in particular were sensitive to the price of bread and exercised direct pressure on the National Assembly, which responded with the *maximum*, a price ceiling on grains. For the peasantry, the revolutionary regime's price controls and wartime requisitions of foodstuff and livestock became as onerous as their previous feudal obligations. Described by Barrington Moore as "the arbiters of the Revolution," who had pushed through the abolition of feudalism but sanctified the non-egalitarian principle of private property, the peasantry remained the arbiters of French politics right through the nineteenth century. Fearful that the revolutionary republican regime might violate their recently acquired equal right to own property, the better-off peasants in particular provided a conservative ballast to French society, while poorer peasants and landless laborers remained socially, economically, and hence politically dependent on large landowners, including monarchist former nobles, of course. In the western region of the Vendée, peasants turned to active counterrevolutionary insurgency, but everywhere in France they jealously guarded their holdings, however small, ultimately throwing the weight of their numbers in support of **Napoleon Bonaparte**. Military hero of the revolutionary wars turned dictator in 1799, Napoleon offered France price stability with the introduction of a new currency, the *franc*, legal security (including title to land) through a new civil code, and relative social cohesion through the redirection of conflict towards imperial wars of conquest. In 1804, Napoleon declared himself emperor, pursuing his exportation of both revolutionary ideals and the centralized bureaucratic structure of the French state across Europe, at least until his disastrous decision to invade Russia in 1812 finally undid his empire and spelt defeat of the revolutionary armies and the restoration of the Bourbon monarchy in 1815.

The Revolution would of course never have come to such a dénouement if the political elites who brought about the constitutional revolution of 1789 had maintained some cohesion. Unlike in eighteenth-century Britain, where the commercial interests of the landed and urban elites represented in Parliament fortuitously converged around the growing trade in wool and textiles, in revolutionary France the bourgeoisie in particular were sharply divided in their interests and ideologies. Indeed, most of the political drama of the

Revolution revolved not around the conflict between the Third Estate, on the one hand, and the clergy and the nobility, on the other, but around rivalries within the Third Estate's bourgeois leadership. Introducing for the first time the spatial, left-right image of the political spectrum, the revolutionary leaders quickly organized themselves into, and sat as, factions in the National Assembly and subsequently in the Convention, France's first representative legislature elected by universal manhood suffrage, which deposed the king and proclaimed the Republic. Drawing names from their seating location (the "Montagnards"), their geographical origins (the "Girondins"), or their meeting places (the "Jacobins" and the "Feuillants"), these proto-parties engaged in a bloody soap opera – too complex to summarize here – of maneuvering, infighting, and ultimately mutual and self-destruction in the Terror and Thermidorian reaction of the mid-1790s. The most famous of these political clubs were the Jacobins, who organized mass membership across the country, came under the infamous leadership of Maximilien Robespierre, and introduced the most radical phase of the Revolution featuring a new calendar and the civic religion of the Cult of the Supreme Being. Paradoxically for such a virulent faction, the Jacobins subscribed to the *philosophe* Jean-Jacques Rousseau's doctrine that no intermediate associations should come between the citizen and the state, understood as the legitimate embodiment of the general will. To this day the term *Jacobinisme* describes policies and opinions that favor the centralized, unitary character of the French state, a character, as Tocqueville argued, inherited from absolutism and only reinforced through the violence and upheaval of the Revolution.

Nineteenth Century France in Search of Stable Institutions and Identity

In short, France entered the nineteenth century with a modernized, rationalized, highly centralized bureaucratic state, the fruit of an absolutist monarchy, a revolutionary Republic, and a militaristic empire. The question that would occupy French politics over the course of the century was what regime form the state would take. With the defeat of Napoleon at Waterloo in 1815, the question was settled from without: the international Congress of Vienna redrew Europe's map to keep France in check and attempted to reintroduce absolutist regimes across the continent and in France. Still, the revolutionary principles of equal rights and constitutionalism once unleashed could be repealed only with difficulty if at all. Thus, in France, the restored Bourbon monarch, Louis XVIII, had to grant a constitutional Charter and governed with a bicameral Parliament including a hereditary Chamber of Peers and a Chamber of Deputies elected with an extremely restrictive wealth-based suffrage for which only 90,000 Frenchmen qualified. Even such feeble constitutionalism proved too much for Louis's successor, Charles X, who in response to the election of a relatively liberal Chamber of Deputies decreed the dissolution of parliament and the suspension of civil liberties on July 26, 1830. The bourgeois liberal press protested, but so too did the Parisian masses. In the face of riots, the king, fearing for his head, fled to England, while the hero of the American and French Revolutions and leader of the parliamentary opposition, the aged general Lafayette, embraced Louis-Philippe, Duke of Orléans, on the balcony of Paris's city hall and proclaimed him "King of the French."

Cousin once-removed of Louis XVI, Louis-Philippe thus established the "July Monarchy" and introduced an enduring schism in the monarchist camp between the more bourgeois *orléanistes* and the more reactionary, aristocratic *légitimistes*. Embracing the legacy of the constitutionalist first phase of 1789 as well as the tricolor flag of the Republic, Louis-Philippe claimed to represent the "juste milieu" (or fine balance) between monarchism and republicanism. Also called the "bourgeois monarchy," Louis-Philippe's eighteen-year reign did indeed liberalize the monarchy: education was secularized, civil liberties restored, and suffrage extended to more than twice as many younger, somewhat less plutocratic men. A time of growing wealth, corruption, and revolving-door parliamentary governments, the July monarchy was a golden age of hypocrisy – and of social criticism as articulated in the brilliant novels of Victor Hugo, Gustave Flaubert, and Honoré Balzac. Hugo's *Les Misérables* well describes the revolutionary ferment and popular dissatisfactions of industrializing France in the 1830s and 1840s. Finally, in early 1848 in a context of economic downturn, a protest movement initiated by bourgeois liberal nationalists in a series of political dinner banquets gave way to popular protests in the streets of Paris. Fearing the worst of the *grandes journées* of the Revolution, Louis-Philippe, too, abdicated and fled, leaving a provisional revolutionary government including representatives of the new Parisian proletariat to organize France's Second Republic.

Part of a revolutionary current that swept all of Europe in 1848, the Second Republic is one of the most fascinating, if briefest interludes in France's political development. Like the Revolution of 1789, the Second Republic has been seen as prototypical for the difficulties of the emergence of liberal democracy in industrializing societies. A keen, firsthand observer of this dramatic phase of French history, the German exile Karl Marx developed his historical materialist theory of economic and political development on the basis of what he observed there and described in still-insight-rich journalistic texts such as *The Class Struggle in France* and *The 18th Brumaire of Louis Bonaparte*. For Marx, the Parisian working class's uprising of February 1848 was a premature proletarian revolution, as the results of the universal manhood suffrage elections of the Republic's constituent assembly proved. These produced a democratic and republican majority, but the peasant and petty bourgeois majority of French society, not to mention the upper classes, feared the egalitarian excesses of the Parisian "mob." When the new government consequently reversed the provisional government's anti-unemployment program, the Parisian workers revolted again in June 1848. This time, however, they were brutally repressed. This unrest played into the hands of the reactionary "party of order," a coalition of conservative bourgeois republicans and monarchists, who won the first regular legislative elections of May 1849. When the petty bourgeois democrats protested the following month, their leaders were arrested, and the following year, the party of order abolished universal suffrage and returned education to the hands of the Church. Their power uncontested and seemingly uncontestable, the conservative and reactionary upper classes quarreled among themselves in parliament, providing the pretext for the democratically elected president of the Republic, Louis Bonaparte, to carry out with the support of the army an anti-parliamentary coup d'état on December 2,

1851. As Marx lucidly analyzed in his *18th Brumaire* (the title alluding to the date in the revolutionary calendar of Napoleon's coup d'état of 1799), Louis Bonaparte, the nephew of Napoleon, had acceded to the presidency thanks to the massive support of the peasantry, who in the face of their own economic decline with industrialization had harkened back to the myth of their imperial savior Napoleon.

In what Marx called a farcical repetition of the tragic collapse of the First Republic into dictatorship, Louis Bonaparte followed in his uncle's footsteps and proclaimed himself emperor Napoleon III on the first anniversary of his coup. The Second Empire, however, represented a new form of authoritarian regime that anticipated the mass-based, populist dictatorships of the twentieth century. Elected to the presidency before the abolition of universal suffrage, Louis Bonaparte presented himself as an enemy of the traditional elite and defender of the democratic masses. Thus, he had both his coup and his proclamation of the empire approved by popular plebiscite, and during his eighteen-year reign he preserved at least the formal trappings of representative democratic institutions, even introducing liberal reforms towards the end of his reign, suggesting that he might have allowed a transition to democratic rule as happened with some late twentieth-century authoritarian regimes. Indeed, his mode of government presaged the developmentalist bureaucratic authoritarian regimes of modern southern Europe and Latin America. **Bonapartism** thus describes not only an ideological current in France favorable to modernizing authoritative, if not authoritarian rulers but, more generally, a developmental strategy whereby a powerful state bureaucracy supplants a divided or weak bourgeoisie to propel capitalist industrial development forward. Along with ambitious public works programs, including the reconstruction of Paris with its famous grand boulevards designed to prevent the erection of revolutionary barricades, Napoleon III provided state subsidies for railroad construction, and organized a concentrated financial banking sector in order to provide long-term credit for large-scale industrial development. In keeping with the *colbertiste* tradition, Napoleon III's industrial policies reinforced the enduring symbiosis between the state bureaucracy and the private economic sector in France.

Because Napoleon's popular dictatorship rested on his ability to offer something to everyone, like modern authoritarian regimes elsewhere, the Second Empire tried to defuse social conflict with appeals to nationalism and expansionist foreign policies. The latter proved to be Bonaparte's undoing when the authoritarian Prussian Chancellor, Otto von Bismarck, outmaneuvered Napoleon into declaring war in 1870. The ensuing Franco-Prussian War allowed Bismarck to unify Germany, to seize Alsace and much of Lorraine from France, and to take Napoleon prisoner at Sedan by the beginning of September of the same year. The revolutionary cycle begun in 1848 thus ended much like that started in 1789. Bismarck, however, did not dictate the form that the new French regime would take. Instead, he insisted the French elect a new government with whom he could negotiate a peace treaty, while German troops surrounded Paris. Whereas the Parisian masses had forced the imperial legislature to proclaim a Republic and to pursue the war effort, the rest of the war-weary country returned a pacifist monarchist majority in the elections of February 1871. Meeting in Bordeaux, the Chamber elected the *orléaniste* Adolphe Thiers, elderly protagonist of the 1830 revolution, to preside over the new government. Installed in the suburb of Versailles, the new government ordered the disarming of the National Guard in Paris. The city rebelled and proclaimed itself a revolutionary Commune under a radical democratic and socialist government. This new political experiment did not last long as the Communards and the Versaillais engaged in a bloody civil war while bemused German troops looked on. In the end, 20,000 Parisians were dead, including the radical and working class leadership, shot by firing squad at the famous Père-Lachaise cemetery. This bloodbath gave birth surprisingly to France's longest lasting, most stable, and perhaps most successful regime since the *ancien regime*.

France's Third Republic and Social Stalemate

The child of military defeat, civil war, and antirepublican electoral results, the Third Republic emerged from a long, uncertain gestation period. Republicanism's fortunes began to change with the first postwar by-elections of June 1871. Now that the pursuit of the war was no longer an issue, republican candidates swept 99 of the 114 seats at stake. Sensing a shift of political winds, Thiers anticipated a new ideological current within republicanism, called "opportunisme," when he came out in favor of a Republic as the regime that "divides the least." He added that the Republic would be a conservative one or there would be no Republic at all. With these remarks, Thiers succinctly evoked the interplay of interests, institutions, and identities at work in the emergence of the Third Republic. To overcome nearly a century of political instability because of conflicting class interests and competing ideas about what constituted the French political community and about what legitimated rule, the founders of the Third Republic had to come up with a compromise: a regime form that minimized social and political divisions by maximizing immobility. As the Franco-American political scientist Stanley Hoffmann wrote of the Third Republic, it was a regime "with plenty of brakes and no motor."

Building such a static political machine, however, required huge efforts on the part of both monarchist and republican politicians. In the case of the monarchists, it would be only a slightly sarcastic exaggeration to say that they had to dig deep into their pockets of political stupidity to snatch defeat from the jaws of victory. In the face of Thiers's opportunistic defection to the republican camp, the *orléanistes* and *légitimistes* in the Chamber of Deputies conspired against him in 1873 to topple his government and to form a new one under the Duke de Broglie with the mandate to restore the Bourbon pretender, the Count of Chambord, to the throne. The Count, however, placed *légitimiste* principle ahead of expediency and refused to accept the *orléanistes*' symbolic demand that the monarchy accept the tricolor flag. The monarchist majority thus found itself with no monarch to embody the political community. Almost despite itself, and by a one-vote majority, the Chamber grudgingly adopted the constitutional laws and the name of the Republic in January 1875. In the meantime, however, an electoral college of parliamentarians (the Chamber of Deputies and the Senate convened simultaneously as the National Assembly) had elected the monarchist General Mac-Mahon, "hero" of the bloody repression of the Paris Commune, to the seven-year presidency of the still-indeterminate regime form. In the so-called May 16 crisis of

1877, Mac-Mahon staged the monarchists' last stand against the nascent Third Republic, exercising his constitutional prerogative to dissolve the Chamber. When the republicans won a slim majority in the ensuing elections fought around the religious and constitutional differences between president and parliament, strong presidentialism and monarchism lost their attraction: the presidents of the Third Republic never again dared to use their power to dissolve the Chamber, preferring instead to play the figurehead role in a resolutely parliamentarian regime.

The republicans' relative electoral success, first in the by-elections of 1871 and then in 1877, was not due to the monarchists' strategic blunders alone. Like the conservative republican Thiers, the "opportuniste" republican leaders, notably Léon Gambetta, understood the need to portray the Republic as a socially conservative option. They also understood the importance of what would today be called "identity politics" for shaping interests and forging stable institutions. Gambetta in particular realized that the republicans could win and sustain parliamentary majorities only if the peasantry, still the majority of the French population after a century of slow but steady industrialization, could not only trust the Republic but identify with it as well. A powerful orator, Gambetta took the then-radical initiative of going out to campaign in the *campagne* (countryside) to persuade peasants that the republicans were not the dangerous *partageux* (literally "sharers") who had confiscated their goods during the most radical phases of the Revolution. In the longer run, though, the peasants had to be liberated from the conservative clutches of the clergy and large landowners. The Third Republic's strategy for turning "peasant into Frenchmen" (to cite the title of a well-known study of the period), and more importantly Frenchmen loyal to the republican ideal of the nation, was primarily educational. The education minister Jules Ferry, in 1881–1882, thus introduced a trinity that is almost as sacred to French republicanism as the revolutionary motto "Liberté-Égalité-Fraternité," namely "l'enseignement gratuit, laïc et obligatoire" (free, secular, and mandatory education for all). To this day, the principle of **laïcité** (a commitment to secular, humanist education as a source of common political values and identity) remains the major legacy of the Third Republic and a lightning rod for French political debate (as witnessed in recent debates on the banning of "ostentatious" religious symbols such as head scarves in French public schools).

Uniform education across the country along with other "nation-building" policies such as universal male military conscription, imperialist expansion in Africa, and propaganda to recover the "lost" territories of Alsace and Lorraine succeeded in forging modern French national identity. From Celtic Brittany to Italian Nice, from French Flanders to the French Basque lands, French citizens did not even speak the same language or celebrate the same history until the Third Republic sent its *instituteurs* to every last village to stamp out obscurantism, local languages and dialects, and the power of priests. The Republic's mission of *laïcité* of course rekindled the anger and opposition of devout Catholics to anything that smacked of the Revolution. What is more, the positive project of *laïcité* often descended into knee-jerk anticlericalism, a Church and priest-bashing that helped conceal the diverging interests and opinions within the republican camp. Although a papal encyclical of 1891 allowed a certain reconciliation of practicing Catholics with the republican regime, the fundamental cleavage between clericalism and anticlericalism defined politics in the

Third Republic right up until World War One (and beyond). The **Dreyfus Affair** of the late 1890s dramatically illustrated this virulent dividing line within French political culture: Catholics, monarchists, and reactionaries blindly defended the army's false, anti-Semitic accusations of treason leveled against the Jewish officer Alfred Dreyfus while republicans, notably the novelist Émile Zola, fought many years to have Dreyfus's conviction and sentence to Devil's Island overturned, a conviction for which the French army only in 1995 offered a full apology!

While anti-clericalism may have been the ideological decoy that distracted French republicans from their divergences, protectionism consolidated the regime's social basis. Legislated in 1892, the Méline tariffs provided protection to both industry and agriculture, thereby preserving many small-scale family firms and peasant farming. Thus, on the eve of the First World War, France's economy and population remained 56 percent rural and 40 percent agrarian, at a time when Britain and Germany had become overwhelmingly urban and industrial. This relative underdevelopment had a long-term silver lining for France: the survival well into the late twentieth century of vibrant small-town and country life preserved the local charms (and cheeses!) that make France the world's current number one tourist destination. At the beginning of the twentieth century, however, France's social, economic, and political stagnation generated fatalism and defeatism. Although the Third Republic could muster the resources and popular support to slowly roll back, with last-minute American help, the German invaders of 1914, the regime enjoyed only "obedience without love" in the words of the cynical republican philosopher Alain. Although the Republic did produce some remarkable popular and democratic leaders such as Gambetta and Ferry, the socialist Jean Jaurès, and the victor of World War I, Georges Clemenceau, the rise and fall of governments at the rate of almost one per year and with little connection to the outcome of elections left the general public largely estranged from politics while significant minorities continued to yearn for the arrival of a Bonapartist strongman on horseback.

Although France's "blocked society" (in Stanley Hoffmann's words) may have gotten the government it deserved, it would be a mistake to write off the Third Republic as a dead-end route to political and socioeconomic modernity. After all, the regime established universal manhood suffrage and guaranteed democratic citizenship rights not only before Germany but before Britain as well. For better and for worse, it built a colonial empire, and it survived and won a world war. After the war, it weathered the economic crises of the 1920s and 1930s that destroyed the fragile new democracies of Germany, Italy, Spain, and Eastern Europe, and even in the face of the Great Depression it succeeded in integrating the working classes into the political order.

From the *Front populaire* to the Vichy State

Indeed, since the bloody repression of the Paris Commune of 1871, the industrial working classes had been by and large excluded from political life in the Third Republic. Their political weakness was because of not only their defeat and decapitation in 1871 as in 1848 but their structural fragmentation in an industrial economy characterized by a few heavy industrial firms (in the coal and steel sector of the northeast) and a plethora of small-scale, specialized, relatively high-skill industries. As elsewhere in continental Europe, various socialist movements and parties embracing revolutionary or electoral strategies sought to organize the working classes, with growing success in the 1890s. In France, Karl Marx's son-in-law Jules Guesdes, for example, took a radical stance in opposition to Jean Jaurès's reformist collaboration with bourgeois democrats. In 1905, the socialist left nonetheless succeeded in uniting within a single party, the SFIO (or the French Section of the Workers' International), forerunner to today's *Parti socialiste* (PS). This unity did not survive the 1920 party congress of Tours, at which the radical left, loyal to Moscow's new Communist International, broke away to become the French Communist Party (PCF). In addition to this schism between communists and socialists, the working class movement in France included another major, resolutely anti-electoral current: anarcho-syndicalism. Inspired by the direct action of the *grandes journées* of the Revolution, the anarcho-syndicalist movement in France cultivated the myth of the general strike as a heroic tool for bringing about immediate, radical social change. This idea has taken deep root in the French labor movement. Divided and relatively disorganized outside of the public sector, French unions to this day do not function as collective bargaining agents but put on strikes seemingly at random but with maximal public disturbance in order to generate a "social climate" favorable to their interests.

To the credit of both the French left and the Third Republic, France in the 1930s did not succumb to the temptation of fascism, at least not immediately. In February 1934, in a context of a political corruption scandal and growing economic hardship, French fascist leagues inspired by the successes of Hitler and Mussolini staged a violent march on the National Assembly building. In a dramatic last minute show of unity, in part because of the Communist International's change of strategy after Hitler's consolidation of power in Germany, the left-wing parties organized a counterdemonstration against the fascist threat and in defense of the Republic. With the Left united and the Communists willing to support if not participate in a coalition between the SFIO and the parties of the center-left, a "Popular Front" government swept into power under the premiership of the socialist millionaire Léon Blum in the elections of 1936. With their first taste of power since 1871 and their aspirations high, the French working classes immediately launched a general strike, which the Blum government defused with the introduction of important, still-celebrated social reforms such as the forty-hour work week and paid vacations. To combat the financial crisis and kick-start the economy, the Popular Front also nationalized the Bank of France and the railroads. As usual under left-wing governments, the resistance of business interests and petty bourgeois anxiety over property rights put a break on reforms as the centrist Radicals withdrew their support for Blum and the far left denounced his timidity. Meanwhile the Catholic bourgeoisie rallied to the fascist leagues' anti-Semitism, embracing the slogan "Sooner Hitler than Blum." As the centrists vacillated, toppling and rejoining Popular Front governments in response to internal and external crises, the Third Republic lost its will to survive even before the *Blitzkrieg* brought the reputedly world's-strongest army to its knees by June 1940. On July 11, the same Chamber that had brought Blum to power four years earlier abdicated full powers to the increasingly senile hero of World

War I, Field Marshall Philippe Pétain. The collaborationist and rabidly anti-Semitic regime, based in the spa town of Vichy, took on the name of the "French State" and abandoned the republican slogan of "Liberté-Égalité-Fraternité" for the authoritarian motto "Family-Work-Fatherland."

Blame for France's darkest hour can be spread across the political spectrum. The Right was of course still rife with monarchism, Bonapartism, and authoritarian impulses, always ready to dismantle the Republic. On the far left, the Communists were beholden to Moscow and had withdrawn support for the Popular Front with the Hitler-Stalin pact of 1939; they would become heroes of the Resistance only after Hitler invaded the Soviet Union in 1941. The centrist and center-left defenders of democracy and republicanism were so concerned with preserving the petty bourgeois and peasant basis of the "blocked society" that they feared the social democratic reforms that Britain and even the United States embraced to weather the economic crises of the 1930s. Finally, even members of the resolutely democratic SFIO, such as the future socialist president **François Mitterrand**, were willing at least initially to work under the Vichy regime to preserve some semblance of French national autonomy. In June 1940, only an obscure if visionary general, **Charles De Gaulle**, speaking by radio from London, called on the "Free French" to fight on against the Nazis. After the Second World War, almost everyone in France claimed to have heard De Gaulle's speech and to have supported the Resistance, but the truth is that most went about their business as usual and many went beyond the call of "duty" to the Nazis, denouncing Jewish neighbors and participating in their deportation to death camps. Only in the 1980s and 1990s did the French begin seriously to confront their collaborationist past, the case of Maurice Papon being particularly illustrative of the complexity, complicity, and cover-ups characterizing collaboration and resistance. Officially recognized "resistant," close political ally of De Gaulle, commander in the Legion of Honor, center-right parliamentarian and member of the government, Papon was first accused of participating in the deportation of Bordeaux Jews in 1981. He came to trial and conviction only in 1997, and even at his death in 2007, Papon caused controversy in the French presidential election campaign, when his family and lawyer insisted he be buried with his revoked Cross of the Legion of Honor.

From Liberation to the Brink of Civil War

The myths of Resistance and Liberation in 1944 by De Gaulle's Free French Forces alongside the Anglo-American Allies of course had foundational qualities for postwar French national identity. France could claim the status of a victorious power and blame initial defeat and the Vichy interlude on the institutional defects of the Third Republic. Thus, when De Gaulle's provisional republican government called elections in October 1945, 96 percent of the voters, who for the first time included all adult women, chose, in a referendum parallel to the parliamentary vote, to make the new assembly constituent. Virtually no one wanted a return to the institutions of the Third Republic, and the centrist republican Radicals, who had carried the former Republic and around whom power had always pivoted, were practically eliminated from France's partisan landscape. With 26 percent of the vote, the communists (PCF), pumped up by their leadership role in the Resistance and by the Red Army's victory over Nazi Germany, were the big winners, but they were closely followed by the SFIO, whose democratic credentials were relatively untarnished by Vichy, and by the new but short-lived center-left Christian democratic *Mouvement républicain populaire* (MRP). Representing three-quarters of the electorate, these parties formed a grand coalition labeled "tripartism" under the nonpartisan leadership of General De Gaulle, as they had already in the provisional government. Almost immediately, however, De Gaulle resigned the premiership, his personal presidentialist, if not neo-Bonapartist ambitions conflicting with the partisan parliamentarians of the tripartist government. The three governing parties were divided among themselves on constitutional questions, with the PCF favoring a unicameral parliamentary regime and the socialists and the MRP preferring various bicameral or presidential checks on parliament precisely in order to prevent the communists from taking advantage of their power as the largest party. The PCF prevailed in the constitutional negotiations, but in the subsequent referendum of May 1946, a narrow majority of voters, more on anticommunist than constitutional grounds, rejected the new Republic's proposed foundational laws. Ensuing elections for a new constituent assembly reproduced the tripartist majority, although now with the MRP narrowly as leading party, and constitutional haggling continued. De Gaulle briefly returned from his first of three political "retirements" to plead in favor of a presidential regime and to encourage voters to reject the tripartists' new proposal of a bicameral parliamentary regime in which they promised to establish proportional representation. In the constitutional referendum of October 1946, only 36 percent of voters approved, 31 percent disapproved, and 31 percent abstained. Thus France again ingloriously gave birth to another Republic, the Fourth.

Also called "la mal aimée" (the unloved), the Fourth Republic was in many senses a remake of the immobility and instability of the massively (96 percent) rejected Third, only worse. The regime did retain the office of the president of the Republic, elected by the members of the National Assembly and the Council of the Republic (the upper chamber of parliament, itself elected by a complex, partly indirect proportional system), and ultimately the president would put an end to the Republic in a semi-constitutional coup d'état. During the Fourth Republic's short existence, however, power resolutely resided in the National Assembly, which made and broke councils of ministers with alarming regularity. One historian has calculated that the Fourth Republic suffered a ministerial crisis that threatened or toppled the government on average once every nine days of its 11 1/2–year existence. It is, however, all too easy and too common to dismiss the Fourth Republic as a failure from birth, as yet another aborted attempt to install a left-leaning if not revolutionary regime in a fundamentally conservative society, or as a proof that a highly democratic, proportionally representative parliamentary regime cannot govern a country as fractious as France.

The Fourth Republic, in fact, succeeded in radically modernizing France, although to be sure within the institutional framework of Jacobinism and *colbertisme* inherited from the past. The two new major institutions associated with the Fourth Republic were actually immediate responses to the postwar crisis of reconstruction, initiated even before the Republic's constitutional foundation. General De Gaulle's tripartist governments established the ***École nationale d'administration*** (ENA) to train civil servants untainted by

Vichy before the first postwar elections, and shortly thereafter created the *Commissariat general du Plan*, an indicative economic planning agency under the future architect of what would become the European Union, **Jean Monnet**, as first commissioner. The ENA quickly produced a technocratic elite, the so-called *énarques*, who to this day dominate not only public administration in France but the leadership of all political parties from the center-left to the center-right as well as much of the private business sector. The *énarques* embody the *colbertiste* tradition of coziness between state and economic interests, with the state assumed, in Jacobin fashion, to take the leading role as purveyor of the general will and the common good. Among the modernizing initiatives of the bureaucratic/technocratic Fourth Republic were the mechanization of agriculture, which spelled the beginning of the end of French peasant society; the introduction of a Social Security system including universal health care; and the massive development of publicly owned nuclear power stations.

Despite the French *dirigiste* tradition, it would be a mistake to overemphasize the specificity of state planning of the economy in France. The more liberal British state had introduced it to combat the Depression, and massive state intervention proved necessary everywhere to reconstruct war-ravaged Europe. The United States' introduction of the Marshall Plan in 1947 helped not only to fund European economic recovery, to subsidize American exports, and to combat Soviet/communist influence, but also to encourage economic planning and international cooperation. Paradoxically, the experience of wartime economic integration, albeit under Nazi hegemony, had also strengthened the idea that Europe's economic and political salvation might lie in collaboration rather than competition between nations, especially the dominant powers, France and Germany. Thus in 1950, Jean Monnet persuaded French Foreign Minister Robert Schuman to present to German Chancellor Konrad Adenauer a plan, which in 1951 led to the creation of the European Coal and Steel Community, the first formal institutional forerunner of today's European Union. By the end of the Fourth Republic, French politicians, diplomats, and bureaucrats had lain much of the groundwork for the Treaty of Rome, founding the European Economic Community on March 25, 1957.

While France was thus moving toward European integration, its colonial empire was disintegrating. Following military defeat at Diên Biên Phu in 1954, the Fourth Republic abandoned French Indochina and in 1956 granted independence to Tunisia and Morocco, thus laying the groundwork for the dismantling of its remaining African empire in the early 1960s. The political instability of the Fourth Republic, however, prevented it from weathering the most sensitive case of decolonization, namely that of Algeria, considered an integral part of the Republic by over a million European settlers since French conquest in 1830. When a National Liberation Front began an armed struggle to assert the sovereignty of the disenfranchised indigenous majority, a civil war erupted and almost engulfed metropolitan France. The ensuing struggle, which in many respects presaged the tragedy of America's intervention in Iraq, would merit lengthy excursus on terrorism, counterterrorism, and civilian-military relations, but for the purposes of a synopsis of French political development, it will have to suffice to suggest that a politically divided parliamentary Republic confronted by an army whose republican loyalties were hardly guaranteed and by a retired popular, heroic general who had been campaigning against the Republic's constitutional order since its inception had little chance to survive the threat of civil war. When French settlers rioted in Algiers on May 13, 1958, with the connivance of parts of the army and of leading supporters of General De Gaulle, the last government of the Fourth Republic fell. To avoid threatened violence and army-supported insurrection in France proper, the president of the Republic asked De Gaulle, who had announced that he was willing to take control without specifying whether he meant constitutionally or not, to form a government. To the credit of De Gaulle's democratic credentials, he scrupulously respected legal procedure and obtained a parliamentary majority for his nonpartisan government on June 1. The following day parliament honored his request to confer constituent powers to the government, thereby bringing a formal end to France's Fourth Republic. In a referendum held on September 28, 1958, the French electorate approved a new constitution tailored to De Gaulle's principles and ambitions.

France's Fifth Republic: A Stable Democratic Institutional Order?

Over half a century later, France's Fifth Republic has apparently withstood the test of time, but its implantation and consolidation depended on the personal authority and Machiavellian genius of its founder. Once elected to the Presidency by a college of parliamentarians and local officials, De Gaulle had to quell the crisis that had brought him to power in the first place: the Algerian war and army insurrection. Again to De Gaulle's credit as a democrat and a republican, he recognized the untenability of French Algeria and did not hesitate to betray those in the army and the die-hard French Algerians who had precipitated his return to power. De Gaulle's "betrayal" provoked terrorist attacks and his attempted assassination, but ultimately he had read French opinion right. With 400,000 French troops unable to secure order in Algeria, De Gaulle negotiated the Évian agreements of 1962, which granted Algeria independence after more than 90 percent of French voters approved them in a referendum. Exercising a form of authority reminiscent of the plebiscitarian Bonapartist Second Empire, De Gaulle understood that his ability to exercise power in the Fifth Republic depended on his demonstration of popular approval. Thus, in a second 1962 referendum, which he called unilaterally, provoking constitutional protest, he asked the French electorate to approve the direct, universal-suffrage election of the president for the traditional seven-year term. The socialist leader François Mitterrand denounced De Gaulle's populist, Bonapartist practices as a "permanent coup d'État," but his opposition to the emergent constitutional order did not keep Mitterrand from running for the presidency in the first direct election of 1965. Paradoxically, Mitterrand's strong showing – he forced De Gaulle into a second, run-off round – helped to consolidate the regime's democratic character: as the winner of a closely contested election, De Gaulle was brought down from the mythical level of charismatic hero to the mundane level of the ordinary politician.

   With the popular election of the president, the Fifth Republic became a hybrid presidential-parliamentary regime form, unique in French history and among other Western democracies. As in the American presidential system, the president of the Fifth Republic is head of state and assumes effective responsibility for the executive branch of government, but he also designates a head of government, the prime minister and, on the latter's recommendation, appoints the remaining cabinet ministers. The president chairs the council of ministers and exercises considerable influence over its agenda. Unlike in the American system, but as in the British parliamentary regime, the government, that is the prime minister and council, are subject to the confidence of the lower chamber of the legislative branch, the National Assembly. The president must therefore appoint a prime minister and a government from the party or, given the fragmentation of the French party system, the coalition of parties that holds the majority of the 577 seats in the National Assembly. Until 1986, the president was always able to appoint a government drawn from the same family of parties that had brought him to power, but when the left-wing alliance that had finally brought François Mitterrand to the presidency in 1981 lost its majority in the legislative elections of 1986, Mitterrand had to appoint the Gaullist leader Jacques Chirac to the premiership, introducing what the French call **cohabitation**. Contrary to expectations of constitutional gridlock and crisis, the first experience of cohabitation proved the institutional resilience of the Fifth Republic. Mitterrand refused to become a figurehead, preserved his prerogatives and initiative in the "high politics" areas of defense and foreign policy, and exercised a certain moderating influence on the right-wing government without blocking its policy orientations. Since then, both left- and right-wing presidents have well survived cohabitations, and the French electorate seems to have acquired a taste for the centrist consensus that the unusual constitutional arrangement favors.

The relative weakness of parliament vis-à-vis both the president and the government might explain the success of cohabitation. The president can dissolve the National Assembly, but usually does so only immediately after entering office, in order to obtain a favorable majority. In addition to enjoying considerable latitude to govern by issuing rules and regulations by executive order, the prime minister and the government can force legislation through parliament by declaring it an issue of confidence that can be overturned only if the opposition can cobble together a majority to censure and topple the government. Designed to combat the governmental instability of the Fourth Republic, the powers of the Assembly are restricted to approval of the budget and the elaboration of legislative texts, of which fewer than 20 percent emanate from private members (as opposed to the government). Divided into only six unwieldy permanent committees, the 577 deputies of the National Assembly can exercise little oversight or investigative power over the government. As for the upper chamber, the 321-seat Senate, a third of whose members are renewed every three years by an electoral college of deputies and local elected officials, it "enjoys" the same powers as the Assembly, except that of censuring the government. Given its more conservative composition and its being out of synch with other electoral cycles, the Senate theoretically can have a moderating influence on legislation, but being elected to the Senate is a more of a sinecure than a legislative responsibility. Since 1974, however, members of parliament, and of the opposition in particular, have at least acquired the ability to contest the constitutionality of legislation: sixty senators or sixty deputies, as well as the presidents of the Republic and of each chamber, can demand a judicial review of legislation, decrees, and treaties by the nine-member Constitutional Council. Also responsible for settling contested election results, the

Constitutional Council, on the basis of one of its own decisions in 1971, has become the self-proclaimed guardian of fundamental civil rights and republican principles.

A certain consolation for the relative powerlessness of the members of parliament is the fact that virtually all of them occupy other political positions at the local and regional levels. Most famously, Jacques Chirac, for example, when he was not prime minister or president, was simultaneously deputy for a rural part of central France and mayor of Paris! Known – and denounced – as the *cumul des mandats* (the accumulation of offices), this practice allows politicians, particularly those in the opposition, to develop a power base, to gain administrative experience, and to forge a public profile. Since decentralization legislation in 1982 introduced a new level of regional government that organizes metropolitan France's 36,000 *communes* (municipalities) and 96 *départements* into 22 regions, most with prerevolutionary historical roots, the presidency of a Regional Council has become a new political springboard. For example, Ségolène Royal, the socialist candidate for the presidency of the Republic in 2007, could campaign on, among other things, her experience in education, economic development, and transport as president of the Poitou-Charentes region. Since decentralization has largely freed the *départements* from the powerful tutelage of central government's prefects (the postrevolutionary successors to the absolutist *intendants*), the presidencies of departmental General Councils, like the position of mayor in a larger city, also provide meaningful outlets for ambitious parliamentarians. Finally, the proof that municipal offices offer tangible power and other benefits (as well as encouraging ground-level political recruitment) lies in the fact that France's countless *communes* jealously guard their autonomy, refusing attempts at consolidation into more rational administrative units: villages and hamlets with a few dozen residents may have long lost their primary school but still insist on electing a mayor and council and on maintaining a community hall.

This plethora of local public officeholders has a no-doubt unintentional institutional feedback effect on France's presidency and party system: as a candidate need gather only 500 signatures from among these numerous and often cantankerous or nonpartisan officeholders in order to appear on the national ballot for the first-round of the presidential election, French electors have found themselves with a choice of up to 16 candidates in the first round of presidential voting, with candidates representing the interests of everyone from hunting and fishing sportsmen to the most radical spokespersons of the Marxist-Leninist fringe. This embarrassment of choice contributed, as we shall shortly see, to the electoral fiasco of 2002, but more generally it has reinforced both the fragmentation and the polarization of the French political party system within a constitutional order where, as in the United States, the primacy of the presidency has a structuring effect on all other electoral contests. No presidential candidate, not even the Republic's founder De Gaulle, has been able to win a majority of votes in the first round of elections, and only a handful of deputies well-entrenched in their districts ever enter the National Assembly after only one round (with the exception of the 1986 elections held with proportional representation). After the free-for-all of the first round, usually only the top two contenders (though sometimes even three or four contenders, if they have won 12.5 percent of votes in the first round) face one another in the second, decisive ballot one week later. This sequence allows a multiplicity of parties to test their luck or to act as spoilers but then forces an alignment or coalescence around two candidates, usually but not always one from the left and one from the right of the ideological spectrum.

The particular case of the Fifth Republic fuels the general debate among institutionalist analysts of party systems as to whether electoral rules cause or, alternatively, reflect the relative fragmentation of party systems. As under the Third Republic, the two-round majoritarian electoral system has, under the Fifth Republic, tended to produce a relatively stable left-right cleavage in electoral politics while fostering recurrent divisions and fusions within the partisan camps of the Left and the Right. In light of France's fractious political and social history, it is not clear, however, whether this polarized fragmentation results from the strategic logic of partisan competition or from deep-seated sociological cleavages in interests and political identities. On the Right, political parties under the Fifth Republic have continued to be either loose electoral coalitions around powerful personalities or ideological nuances such as those that caused *orléanistes* and *légitimistes* as well as monarchists and conservative republicans to converge or diverge in the nineteenth century or, in the case of the different organizational manifestations of the Gaullist movement, to be mass-based fronts uniting the disparate interests of bourgeois nationalists, peasants, and populist petty bourgeois and working class elements as under Bonapartism. On the left, the parties have tended to be sociologically and organizationally anchored in the interests of civil servants, school teachers, and unionized workers but to continue to be ideologically fractured. Perhaps the most significant political development under the Fifth Republic, however, has been the decline and, today, virtual disappearance of the PCF, with a drop in communist support from a solid 20 percent in the 1960s to below 1 percent today. This erosion of the PCF has followed not only from the relative socioeconomic decline of the industrial sector and the ensuing further disorganization of the working class (union membership has dropped to less than 10 percent of the French labor force) and from the discredit and collapse of Soviet communism but also from the effective strategic manoeuvring of the *Parti socialiste* (PS). Founded under the leadership of François Mitterrand in 1971, after the divisions between the old SFIO and other leftist and centre-left parties of different ideological persuasion had allowed two right-wing candidates to face each other in the second round of the 1969 presidential election, the PS succeeded in luring the PCF first into a common platform and electoral alliance and then, from 1981 to 1984, into government, thus sapping the PCF of its revolutionary raison d'être.

The electoral success of the united left in 1981 marked, as we shall shortly see, the most important political, social, and economic challenge that the Fifth Republic has faced to date. Designed by and for a right-wing leader, the Fifth Republic, like the Third up until the Popular Front election of 1936, had largely rested on the exclusion of the working classes and the Left. Unlike the conservative caretakers of the "blocked society" of the Third Republic, though, De Gaulle was a modernizer who did not hesitate to use the statist levers inherited from the Fourth Republic and the *colbertiste* tradition vigorously to pursue economic development, notably around "national champion" firms, both private and public. Indeed, during the "trente glorieuses," that is, the thirty glorious years following the Liberation, France enjoyed the highest economic growth rates in Western Europe at over 5 percent per year. Relative undervaluation of the French franc, high investment rates thanks to state participation in the industrial and financial sectors, inflationary policies to diminish debts and deficits, and low wages because of the feeble organization of labor all contributed to French competitiveness and high growth rates, but economic inequality also increased with growth. De Gaulle was of course not indifferent to working class interests: his government initiated the construction of low-cost high-rise housing estates in France's suburbs, a policy that would of course come to haunt France in recent years. Substituting national pride for social solidarity, De Gaulle's foreign policies defended "une certaine idée de la France" from what he railed against as Anglo-American hegemony. In addition to withdrawing from NATO's American-led command structure and denouncing U.S. domination of the international financial system (the Breton-Woods fixed exchange rate system that allowed the United States to accumulate deficits at no expense), De Gaulle twice vetoed Britain's entry into the European common market. Although he pushed European integration as a means to France's historic reconciliation with Germany, De Gaulle jealously guarded French sovereignty within the European Economic Community and steered its policies in France's favor, notably the Common Agricultural Policy, which to this day disproportionately subsidizes French farmers.

De Gaulle's heavy-handed policies antagonized intellectuals as well as workers. In 1968, traditional May Day demonstrations sparked an antiauthoritarian and what has come to be called "postmaterialist" student protest movement in Paris, which in turn encouraged spontaneous strikes in firms around the country. At the height of the unrest, in a climate echoing past revolutions, army trucks had to transport essential goods, and President De Gaulle mysteriously disappeared for several hours (he had flown to Germany by helicopter to consult a general to assure himself of army backing). De Gaulle knew, however, that he could count on the conservatism of the provinces once again to quell the revolutionary élan concentrated in the capital. He dissolved the National Assembly and organized counterdemonstrations, while the Prime Minister Georges Pompidou charged a young secretary of state, Jacques Chirac, to negotiate generous concessions to the labor unions: a 35 percent increase in the minimum wage and a 10 percent raise for the rest, albeit gains that were quickly wiped out by inflation. The Gaullists won a clear majority in the ensuing June elections, but feeling the need to renew his own mandate, De Gaulle called a referendum on decentralization in April 1969. When his proposal narrowly failed to pass, De Gaulle, as promised, resigned, dying the following year. The proof that May 1968 and its aftermath had not really constituted a serious left-wing challenge to the Gaullist Fifth Republic, however, came with the election of De Gaulle's successor: his prime minister, Pompidou, rode easily into office over a divided left and another lackluster conservative candidate in the second round.

France without De Gaulle: Democratic Consolidation or Lack of Leadership?

With President Pompidou's death in April 1974, the Fifth Republic faced new challenges as the Left was now united behind François Mitterrand, the Right was divided with no clear Gaullist successor, and the theretofore booming economy suddenly faced the stagnation and inflation ("stagflation") of the first oil crisis. Pompidou's easy election in 1969 had postponed the Right's reckoning with a future without De Gaulle. Minister of Finance and Economy under both De Gaulle and Pompidou, Valéry Giscard d'Estaing, none-theless succeeded in profiling himself as a critic and a more centrist, liberal alternative to Gaullist nationalism and dirigisme. He owed his narrow victory over Mitterrand in the second round of the 1974 presidential election, however, to the backing of Jacques Chirac, who had positioned himself as heir to the Gaullist nationalist and populist mantle. Giscard appointed Chirac to the premiership, but their alliance was uneasy as Chirac, in 1976, refounded the Gaullist movement into a powerful electoral machine for himself, the Rassemblement pour la République (RPR). Giscard in turn created a federation of inde-pendent centre-right parties in 1978, the Union pour la Démocratie Française (UDF), to back his aspirations for re-election. Given this re-creation of the Right's traditional divi-sions and the fact that the economy was mired in *la crise* (the somewhat oxymoronic term the French have come, over the past three decades, to use to describe the enduring situa-tion of relative decline that followed the exceptional boom of the "trente glorieuses"), the only surprise of the 1981 presidential election should have been that Giscard even came close to holding onto power.

In conservative France, however, François Mitterrand's victory in May 1981 and the united left's convincing victory in the following month's National Assembly elections came as a political earthquake. In polemical exaggeration of the PCF's minor ministerial role in the government of Pierre Mauroy, the right-wing press railed against the "socialo-com-munist" regime while rumors circulated that the army would not tolerate a left-wing gov-ernment. Meanwhile, on the Left, utopian expectations of a revolutionary transformation of daily life were ripe for disappointment. Although the new government did nationalize the "commanding heights" of the economy, notably the banking sector, where the state had been heavily involved since 1945, Mitterrand and Mauroy's strategy for pulling France out of *la crise* was classic Keynesian reinflation of the economy through increased consumer spending and state investment by way of wage increases and budget deficits. Described later as "Keynesianism in one country" (in allusion to Stalin's strategy of "socialism in one country"), the socialist-led government's economic policy exposed France's integration into the European and global economies as France's reflationary policies ran counter to the neoliberal monetarist policies adopted at the time not only in Thatcher's Britain and Reagan's America but also, albeit less dogmatically, in France's largest trade partner, tra-ditionally inflation-shy Germany. As prices and budget and trade deficits rose, the value of the franc collapsed, forcing three major devaluations in two years. As early as March 1983, the Mauroy government had to reverse policies, tying the franc to the deflationary strong D-Mark policies of the German Bundesbank. Mitterrand appointed a new govern-ment with PCF support, but no ministerial participation, under Laurent Fabius in 1984. Although the economy stabilized and the government changed the electoral law to a system of proportional representation to save as many seats in the National Assembly as possible, the 1986 elections gave the Right a solid majority, leaving the socialist president no choice but to appoint the Gaullist leader Jacques Chirac to the premiership of a government that not only continued monetarist policies but reversed the strategic nationalizations of 1981.

Despite the disappointments and reversals of Mitterrand's first *septennat* (seven-year term), his presidency proved the resilience of the institutions of the Fifth Republic and their adaptability to the conflicting interests and identities of the French Left and Right. Initially critical of the "permanent coup d'État" of the presidential republic, Mitterrand must be credited for his careful, strategic defense of institutional continuity in a context first of radical policy initiatives in 1981–1983 and then of policy reversals. He demonstrated that **alternance** was possible under the Fifth Republic, that is, not only that the Left of revolutionary tradition could come to power without changing the regime form but also that the Right could overturn the Left by peaceful means and that the Left and Right could cohabit within the two-headed executive. In short, competitive democracy had finally become banal in France two centuries after the Revolution! Thanks to his mastery and defense of the democratic institutions of the Republic, Mitterrand did not become a lame duck after his party's defeat in 1986. Instead, he devoted himself to the cause of European integration, committing France to the Single European Act of 1987 and then negotiating economic and monetary union in what would become the **Maastricht Treaty** of 1992, establishing the European Union and initiating the move to a single European currency, the euro. Both dignified and avuncular (his nickname in the popular press was "Tonton," the familiar diminutive for uncle), Mitterrand profited from the Right's habitual clash of personalities and from its propensity for questionable business dealings and presented himself as the centrist, unifying embodiment of the nation to handily win the 1988 presidential election over "his" prime minister Jacques Chirac. Consistent with their re-endorsement of Mitterrand, who had promptly dissolved the National Assembly, French voters returned a socialist majority under the premiership of Mitterrand's intra-partisan rival Michel Rocard.

The end of the first cohabitation did not, however, mark a return to the status quo ante of Fifth Republic politics, for the presidential election of 1988 also brought the electoral breakthrough of Jean-Marie Le Pen, leader of the extreme right Front National (FN). Thanks to the proportional representation of the 1986 National Assembly elections, Le Pen and thirty-four other FN-members had acceded to parliament, gaining more visibility for their xenophobic, anti-immigration, and anti-European platform. Le Pen had actually won a seat with the right-wing populist Poujadist movement exactly thirty years earlier as the youngest deputy of the Fourth Republic. He quit his seat, however, to fight as a volunteer in French Algeria, later admitting to have tortured "terrorists." In 1974, his presidential bid as leader of the recently founded FN garnered only 0.75 percent of the vote, and in 1981 he failed to secure the 500 signatures necessary to appear on the ballot. In the context of *la crise*, growing political disenchantment, and the collapse of the PCF as an outlet for anti-system protest during the early 1980s, though, the Front National became a lightning rod for dissatisfaction, gaining seats and publicity in municipal elections in 1983 and then tying the PCF with 6 percent of the 1986 National Assembly vote. Two years later, the full measure of racist, reactionary, populist, and/or simply enraged opinion among French voters – ironically often in rural areas with little or no experience with immigration – became clear when Le Pen received over 14 percent of the vote in the first round of the presidential election. Despite (or perhaps because of?) countless court convictions for hateful inflammatory speech, Holocaust-denial, and defamation, Le Pen and, since she succeeded him as head of the party in 2011, his daughter Marine Le Pen have remained a fixture and an embarrassment on the French political landscape, their consistent support among a significant minority of voters always calling into question the strength of France's liberal democratic and republican values.

Le Pen (*père et fille*) and the FN owe a good part of their success, of course, to the failings of the democratic Left and Right, in particular to their inability, within a context of European integration and global competition, to defend numerous interests within French society and to articulate a convincing image of France's identity and place in the world. *La crise* has prevented France from growing its way out of problems of inequality and social exclusion. Instead, a *fracture sociale* widened as those, often but not exclusively in the civil service and public sector, with protected, well-paid jobs and generous social security benefits resisted – rightly or wrongly – any reforms aimed at greater flexibility and efficiency as neoliberal ploys of Anglo-Saxon inspiration, whereas others, typically the young, women, and immigrants, had to make do with low-wage, low-benefit, short-term contract jobs or join the ranks of the unemployed (about 10 percent of the working population for the past twenty-five years). France's relative economic and political decline pushed Mitterrand and his successors to pursue European integration as a means for disciplining and redressing the economy as well as for giving France a stronger voice within a larger political community, but this strategy also left the French with a keen sense of lost sovereignty and diminished national pride as France found itself increasingly a smaller fish in the bigger pond of an expanding European Union.

Thus, Mitterrand's second term and both terms of his successor Jacques Chirac came under the shadow of decadence. Although the government of Prime Minister Michel Rocard between 1988 and 1991 succeeded with the help of four UDF ministers in forging a centrist consensus on social welfare reform and in making a dent in unemployment, Rocard's personal animosity with Mitterrand finally ended with Rocard's forced resignation. Mitterrand appointed France's first female prime minister, Édith Cresson, but her scandal-plagued administration lasted less than a year, as did that of her successor, Pierre Bérégovoy. Indeed, at the time, it seemed that Mitterrand was more concerned with the completion of monuments to his "reign" such as the new National Library that bears his name. In a referendum held on September 1992, Mitterrand did still manage to convince French voters to approve the Maastricht Treaty on European Union and, by extension, in De Gaulle's tradition, to renew their support for the president – but only by the narrowest of margins. A few months later, the legislative elections of 1993 disavowed the socialist government, giving a landslide majority of 472 out of 577 seats to the RPR and the UDF. As Jacques Chirac refused to assume the premiership again in cohabitation with Mitterrand, his former Finance Minister, Edouard Balladur, took on the job and, to Chirac's chagrin, became highly popular and a leading contender for the 1995 presidential election. Ever the clever campaigner, however, Chirac positioned himself as an "outsider" and to the left of Balladur, promising to heal the *fracture sociale*. (The "Balladurians" were subsequently marginalized in Chirac's first administration, a fact that could explain the animosity between Chirac and his party's candidate to succeed him in 2007, Nicolas Sarkozy.)

In principle, Chirac should have enjoyed smooth sailing at the start of his term. His prime minister, Alain Juppé, had a huge majority in parliament, and he himself a fresh mandate to take on *la crise*. But France was also committed to meeting the financial and budgetary criteria set by the European Union for the introduction of the single currency, so when Juppé proposed budget tightening measures in the autumn of 1995, a wave of strikes and demonstrations reminiscent of May 1968 brought France to a standstill by mid-December. Despite the disruption, the strikes enjoyed widespread popular support and sowed the seeds for a renaissance of the French left in the libertarian, anarcho-syndicalist tradition. The strikes generated a new form of social and political activism outside the partisan arena, with local action being tied to a critical discourse on globalization and the neoliberal orientation of the world economy. Among the "children" of 1995 is the group ATTAC, founded in France with chapters around the world pursuing an alternative globalization or "altermondialisation." Its spontaneity and use of new media (Internet and social networking) anticipated the even more inchoate movements such as "Occupy" that have arisen since the global banking, financial, fiscal crisis erupted in 2008.

With his government's reform efforts stalled in the face of popular opposition, President Chirac took the risk of dissolving the National Assembly with a huge centre-right majority a year before its term expired. His move backfired horribly and from 1997 to 2002 he was forced to cohabit with a socialist prime minister, Lionel Jospin, leading a comfortable left-wing majority of the PS, the PCF, and, represented for the first time in France, the Green Party. Thanks to a favorable international economic climate, Jospin's government presided over a reduction in unemployment from 12.2 percent to 8.6 percent, but his concrete economic policies – the reduction of the work week to thirty-five hours, a new youth employment contract scheme, and his (partial) privatization of national standard-bearers such as France Telecom and Air France – raised controversy among his political allies as well as opponents. His introduction of civil unions for homosexual partners and the discovery of his Trotskyist activism in his youth, however, incensed conservative opinion. In September 2000, he persuaded President Chirac to back a constitutional referendum to reduce the presidential term of office to five years in synch with the legislative period: both men shared an interest in preventing future cohabitations – and in making their presidential candidacies more palatable to voters who might not be able to stomach the prospective of seven more years of either Chirac or Jospin. Almost 84 percent of voters approved the change, but barely 30 percent of electors bothered to vote, thereby signaling their lack of support for either the president or the prime minister. Nineteen months later, the fiasco of the 2002 presidential election proved the unpopularity of both men and, more importantly, called into question the entire political order of the Fifth Republic.

On April 21, 2002, the incumbent president faced the humiliation of receiving only 19.9 percent of votes in the first round of the election. Even worse, Jospin, who with 23.3 percent had outpolled Chirac in the first round of the 1995 election, won only 16.2 percent while, ironically, the Trotskyist fringe candidate Arlette Laguiller scored an astonishing fifth-place finish of 5.7 percent. Meanwhile on the Far Right, Jean-Marie Le Pen had improved his support from 15 percent in 1995 to almost 16.9 percent and beyond all expectations found himself in the second round to be held two weeks later. The result sent shockwaves through France as tens of thousands of left-wing voters took to the streets to "defend the Republic" but also in an act of contrition. Explanations and excuses for the disaster abounded: a record number of voters (28.4 percent) had stayed away from the polls in the first round, many expecting a repeat of the Chirac-Jospin confrontation of 1995. For the same reason, numerous critical PS members and supporters had voted for "Arlette," the sympathetic self-educated bank clerk who had been on every presidential ballot since 1974. On the Right, the decision to make security a central campaign issue with veiled undertones of anti-immigrant, anti-Muslim racism had played to the advantage of the aging, contested FN leader, Le Pen, who after all represented the real thing. Virtually the entire political spectrum from the respectable Right to the Far Left rallied around Chirac, who handily trounced Le Pen with 82.2 percent of the vote.

Chirac's victory was hardly one for liberal democracy, but he took it as an occasion to do that at which he best excelled: constructing a new electoral machine. For the June legislative elections, his backers created the Union pour la Majorité Présidentielle (UMP), unifying the RPR with smaller centre-right formations and most of the UDF (the rump organization remaining under François Bayrou, who made a remarkable comeback in the first round of the 2007 presidential election). Subsequently renamed Union pour un Mouvement Populaire, the UMP easily carried the National Assembly vote as the PS fought without a leader since Jospin's immediate resignation from office following the April 21 debacle. After five years of cohabitation, Chirac again enjoyed a majority tailored to his person, but his second term proved as fruitless as his first. He appointed a fairly obscure provincial politician, Jean-Pierre Raffarin, to be his entirely subordinate prime minister, and the latter initially enjoyed popularity because of his distance from the corrupt Parisian political elite. Indeed, Chirac's previous prime minister, the president of the UMP, and the Gaullist leader's heir apparent, Alain Juppé, had been under investigation for nepotistic abuse of office while working as Chirac's right-hand man while the latter was mayor of Paris. Convicted in 2004 and disqualified from public office until 2006, Juppé was symptomatic of the sleaze surrounding the Gaullist machine as investigators circled like vultures waiting for Chirac's presidential immunity from potential prosecution to end. In such a climate, Raffarin's timid reform efforts, including tax cuts for the rich, could hardly remain popular especially as European Union convergence criteria required France, now fully integrated into the single-currency euro-zone, to squeeze its budget deficit to under 3 percent of GDP.

With European integration and globalization taking the blame for France's laggard economic and budgetary performance in the discourses not only of the Far Left and of the Far Right but also of the president of the Republic, Chirac and Raffarin seemed to be headed for political suicide when the president announced on the national holiday, July 14, 2004, that he would submit approval of the new European Union Constitution (drafted under the leadership of former president Giscard d'Estaing) to a referendum to be held the following May 29. A classic Gaullist/Bonapartist tactic to plebiscite his personal authority and to divide the opposition, Chirac's referendum initiative did the latter but royally failed to accomplish the former. Socialist voters were split down the middle, torn between their loyalties to the European ideals and their distrust of a complex constitutional text that seemed to place economic liberalism ahead of social solidarity. In the end, fear of competition from eastern Europe and, perhaps a few years down the road, from Turkey pushed economically precarious middle- and working-class voters to bring the referendum to a 54.7 percent rejection. Unlike his hero De Gaulle, who had resigned thirty-five years earlier when his referendum failed, Chirac stayed in office and sacked his prime minister. Henceforth, however, he was a lame duck president, apparently primarily interested in frustrating the efforts of the Interior Minister and president of the UMP, Nicolas Sarkozy, to succeed him in 2007. He thus appointed to the premiership the Foreign Minister, Dominique de Villepin, who had acquired presidential stature with a remarkable speech at the United Nations in early 2003 in opposition to the Iraq war. De Villepin's bubble quickly burst, though, when police brutality sparked rioting in the Parisian suburb of Clichy-sous-Bois on October 27, 2005. Over the next eighteen days, violence spread to the depressed, low-cost housing estates that have become the ghettos for unemployed immigrants and minorities around all of France's major cities. De Villepin allegedly delayed declaring a state of emergency and stemming the violence in order to make his rival but his own Interior Minister Sarkozy look bad, although in fact the prolongation of the crisis merely played into the heavy-handed law-and-order discourse of Sarkozy, who, himself the son of a Hungarian immigrant, described the rioting children of immigrants as "rabble." Any remaining hope that de Villepin could displace Sarkozy as the Right's pretender to the presidency quickly disappeared a few months later when he tried to force a flexible hire-and-fire scheme for first-time employees through parliament. After hundreds of thousands of students and trade unionists took to the streets and closed schools and universities for several weeks in a movement again reminiscent of May 1968, Chirac disavowed the controversial legislation and, in the process, his prime minister. His presidency was washed out.

With Chirac's departure from office in 2007, the Gaullist phase of the Fifth Republic truly came to an end, for the candidates to succeed Chirac, with the exception of the aging Jean-Marie Le Pen, no longer had any personal or historical connection to De Gaulle either as fellow-travelers, adversaries, or enemies. To be sure, "Arlette" was still among the twelve candidates in the first round, though with less than 1.3 percent of the vote (even less than the 1.9 percent for the candidate of the once formidable PCF) she failed to be a spoiler for the Left. On the Far Right, Le Pen's drop in support to a "mere" 10.4 percent signaled less a decline in extremism than the UMP candidate Nicolas Sarkozy's not-always-so-subtle ability to appeal to authoritarian and anti-immigrant sentiments. Probably the most significant result of the election's first round, however, was the strong showing (18.6 percent) of the centrist UDF candidate François Bayrou as it suggested a potential breakdown of France's traditional left-right polarization as well as a disenchantment with the machine politics of the (post-)Gaullist UMP. Although Bayrou made it clear before the second round of voting that he preferred the Socialist candidate Ségolène Royal, his supporters nonetheless confirmed the French centrists' penchant to plump for the Right in a clinch and handed Sarkozy a comfortable 53 percent to 47 percent victory over Royal. In the campaign, however, both Sarkozy and Royal tried to break out of the old left-right mold, highly personalizing the campaign and crossing partisan divides with Royal, for example, developing conservative themes of national pride and Sarkozy promising to include leftists among his cabinet ministers.

Indeed, Sarkozy's first government, under Prime Minister François Fillon, suggested a new style of government with a strong representation of women, of minorities, and of personalities from across the political spectrum. Most notably, Bernard Kouchner, cofounder of *Médecins sans frontières* and twice previously Health Minister under Socialist governments, took on the job of Foreign Minister until 2010, when he was sidelined in a cabinet shuffle. Styling himself as a hands-on man of action and in a break with the Fifth Republic tradition according to which the president left the management of legislative details and daily affairs to his prime minister, Sarkozy the "hyper-president" promised to shake up France's top-heavy administration, to liberalize the economy, and to facilitate individual entrepreneurship. His government's first major legislation, a law on the "Freedoms and Responsibilities of Universities," proved emblematic. It sought to revitalize France's moribund public university system by granting universities more administrative and budgetary autonomy and encouraging competition among them, albeit for dwindling resources, but it did so by increasing the power of university presidents and business interests represented on councils at the expense of student and faculty participation. Passed during the 2007 summer holidays, the legislation sparked, with the autumn return to classes, massive student protests against an alleged neoliberal privatization of a public good. Only the concession of new funds for universities and scholarships could buy the peace in a reform process that quickly became one of giving with one hand what the other took. Similarly, the "Grenelle of the environment" (named for the multipartite negotiations that had resolved the May 1968 crisis) sought, in the fall of 2007, to introduce consensual decision making in the fields of environmental protection and sustainable development, but it quickly came under fire as more show than substance, in particular when the government failed to follow through on its promise to establish a carbon tax.

It is of course difficult to assess Sarkozy's will and strategy to reform France's political economy as most of his *quinquennat* fell under the shadow of the global financial crisis that began in 2008 and prompted huge state deficits that led to Europe's sovereign debt crisis and shook confidence in Europe's common currency, the euro, and in the entire project of European integration. By the end of his first – and last – term in office, however, it was less the substance than the style of Sarkozy's political and economic reform efforts that cost him the presidency in the May 2012 elections. Refreshing to some at the beginning of his term, Sarkozy's hyperactive, energetic style ultimately threatened the institution of the presidency as his extreme personalization of power recalled nineteenth-century Bonapartism. In an age of 24/7 real-time media exposure and image consultants, Sarkozy lived and died by the sword of his personalized politics of self-styling as the antidote to the stalemate and stagnation induced by the Fifth Republic's established *énarque* elite of Left and Right. In the end, Sarkozy alienated the mass of French people who "get up early to go to work" to whom he had promised in 2007 that the more they worked, the more they would take home. With the lack of any substantial economic, political, or social reforms under his hyperpresidency, the French were ready after five years to abandon the man they called the "bling-bling" president and blamed for "*People*-izing" politics.

Nonetheless, Sarkozy left his mark on the French presidency, for his successor, the Socialist François Hollande, campaigned in the 2012 election as the anti-Sarkozy, cultivating

Table 4.1   Key Phases in France's Development

Time Period	Regime	Global Context	Interests/Identities/ Institutions	Developmental Path
800–1589	Feudal monarchy	Competing claims to political and Religious authority	Three Estates: nobility, clergy, commoners (peasants, townsmen)	Territorial consolidation
1589–1715	Absolutism	Emergent international state system	Bureaucratization, disempowerment of landed nobility	Centralization of political authority, mercantilism
1715–1789	Feudal reaction	Growing international competition, emergent capitalism	Polarization between landed aristocracy and commoners (3rd Estate)	Labor-repressive agriculture, authoritarianism
1789–1804	Revolution	War, intervention	Heightened conflict, terror, ideology	Preconditions for capitalism, liberal democracy
1804–1875	Postrevolu-tionary instability	Birth of contemporary state system, global capitalism	Unresolved conflicts among classes, ideologies	Liberalism, Bonapartism
1875–1940	Third Republic	Imperialism, world wars	Repression and rebirth of working class movements	Conservative modernization
1940–1944	Vichy	Occupation	Collaboration, resistance, liberation	Reactionary authoritarianism
1946–1958	Fourth Republic	Economic cooperation/ integration	Rise of technocratic elites	Technocratic modernization
1958–1981	Fifth Republic	Cold War, struggle for autonomy	Prosperity versus rise of "postmaterialist" interests	From (Gaullist) neo- Bonapartism to neoliberalism
1981–present	Fifth Republic (post-Gaullist)	Deepening, widening, and crisis of European integration	Dualist split between protected and marginalized social strata	Ongoing crisis of the French model of capitalism

his image as the "normal" and modest negation of his incumbent opponent's flamboyance. Hollande thus also relied more on his personality than on his program, which, aside from his promise to withdraw combat troops from Afghanistan by the end of 2012 and to raise marginal tax rates on millionaires, read more like a technocrat's recipe for fine-tuning than a platform to change the world as the Fifth Republic's first Socialist president had promised thirty-one years earlier. Hollande had indeed led a rather unremarkable, conventional political career, rising from the *École nationale d'administration* to the post of general secretary of the *Parti socialiste*. His previous claim to fame was to have been the common-law husband of the unfortunate PS presidential candidate of 2007, Ségolène Royal. Hollande's blandness, however, had served him well as a party manager and became his trump card in the PS's primary election. A long-shot candidate against the favorite but undeclared candidate Dominique Strauss-Kahn, former Minister of Finance, Economy, and Industry and Managing Director of the International Monetary Fund, Hollande's placid style made him unbeatable when "DSK" was arrested in New York City for a sex scandal that many in the PS suspected President Sarkozy of having orchestrated. Once elected to the presidency with 51.6 percent of the vote (a relatively weak showing in light of Sarkozy's rock-bottom popularity), Hollande continued cultivating his image of normalcy and modesty, imposing a 30 percent salary cut on his government ministers and on himself. After a hundred days in office, the traditional "honeymoon" period, Hollande had "succeeded" in keeping expectations low, with most commentators underscoring his legislative inaction. By the second year of his presidency, Hollande's inability to turn around the economy or to introduce substantial reforms with any future promise brought him to rock-bottom popularity rankings. As we shall shortly see, however, the question is not whether Hollande's presidency is more of a failure than those of his two ignominious predecessors, but rather whether any French president can any longer aspire boldly to defend France's interests, to revitalize its institutions, and to recast its identity.

CONCLUSION: FRENCH INTERESTS, INSTITUTIONS, AND IDENTITY IN THE FACE OF EUROPEAN (DIS)INTEGRATION AND GLOBALIZATION

On the evening of his inauguration on May 15, 2012, François Hollande boarded an airplane to fly to Berlin to visit German Chancellor Angela Merkel. On takeoff his place was struck by lightning and he was obliged to return to Paris to change planes. The incident was as ironic as it was symbolic. The immediate visit to Berlin was almost a ritual obligation, for ever since Charles De Gaulle and German Chancellor Konrad Adenauer's historic postwar reconciliation mass at the cathedral of Reims fifty years earlier, the Franco-German rapprochement had become the veritable motor of European political and economic integration. While the lightning strike signaled that serious trouble was brewing in the Franco-German partnership, Hollande's symbolically significant insistence on restarting the journey was all the more ironic for the fact that he had just campaigned against "Merkozy," that is, against the tight personal and policy bond between Merkel and Sarkozy, where the

German chancellor was seen to be calling the shots, imposing austerity as the only admissible solution to Europe's deepening debt crisis in the wake of the 2008 banking crisis. In a pale echo of François Mitterrand's attempt through Keynesian demand stimulation to buck the monetarist orthodoxy of his time three decades earlier, François Hollande had given hope to Europe's center-left with his campaign promises to promote growth at the expense of delaying the imposition of budget deficit targets such as those that had brought Ireland, Portugal, Spain, Italy, and Greece to their economic knees and to political paralysis by late 2011. Once in office, however, Hollande found his hands perhaps even more tightly bound than those of his predecessors' had been.

Indeed, Hollande's limited margins for action followed from policy choices dating back to the beginning of the ongoing *crise* in the 1970s. In the wake of the collapse of the Breton-Woods international monetary system's fixed exchange rate mechanism and in response to the stagnation and inflation associated with the oil crisis of 1974, French leaders began to look for alternatives to France's traditional *colbertiste*, inflationary state-led industrial policy, turning toward the German or "Rhenan" model of capitalism, namely one of monetarist fiscal conservatism geared toward promoting specialized small and medium-sized firms as opposed to "national champions" but also giving a collaborative role to organized labor in micro- and macroeconomic management. Personified in the close collaboration between President Valéry Giscard d'Estaing and Chancellor Helmut Schmidt and their first moves towards a common currency with the creation in 1979 of a European Monetary System, this shift from political to economic rapprochement between France and Germany was, as we have seen, only briefly interrupted by Mitterrand's first government's attempt at "Keynesianism in one country." In fact, Socialist reforms introduced at the same time, from decentralization to worker participation in firm management, more or less explicitly sought to reproduce Germany's localized market flexibility in the French context. Typically for such attempts at institutional transfer, these French reforms produced unintended consequences that political economist Jonah Levy has dubbed the effects of "Tocqueville's revenge." In light of the weakness of civil society and of local authorities, weaknesses inherited from the *ancien regime* and reinforced by the Jacobin state, such reforms drawn from Germany's more decentralized and diverse economic and political systems could hardly bear fruit.

Still, in a classic illustration of path dependency, France's policy option of ever-closer economic ties with Germany within the framework of European integration became more constraining with the end of the Cold War. Once in place, a policy orientation such as monetary union crowds out other possibilities. Thus, less than a month after the fall of the Berlin Wall, when German reunification suddenly looked inevitable, François Mitterrand, at the European summit in Strasbourg on December 8, 1989, proposed the creation of a European Union coupled with a common currency as the best institutional solution for preserving France's economic interests and political identity in the face of a united Germany. Less than ten years later, on January 1, 1999, France abandoned a key element of its sovereignty, its power to issue and control its own currency, to the European Union and the European Central Bank. Today, despite the costs of France's inability to orientate its economic destiny as it had, for example, through devaluations and inflation during the *trente glorieuses* (its thirty postwar boom years), the costs of leaving the euro would be greater than the benefits, so that a left-wing president such as Hollande finds himself as beholden to the German chancellor as was Sarkozy.

The French use an expression that they rarely need to complete. It starts, "*Plus ça change* [the more things change]," and everyone knows without saying that it ends, "*plus c'est la meme chose* [the more they stay the same]." It applies particularly well to French politics. The Fifth Republic has indeed demonstrated remarkable continuity over the course of its five-decade history and also with respect to a millennium of French history. These continuities are not just rhetorical or symbolic but sociologically profound as well. The Fifth Republic has, for example, had a tiresomely unchanging cast of characters: France's longest-serving president, François Mitterrand, began political service under Vichy, while Fourth-Republic *énarque* Jacques Chirac was minister, premier, president, or mayor of Paris for over forty years; and Jean-Marie Le Pen, the star of the Extreme Right for over fifty years, still looms behind his daughter Marine, who actually surpassed her father's upsetting 16.9 percent in 2002 by capturing 17.9 percent of the vote in the first round of the 2012 presidential elections. Even though the other leading candidates in 2012, Sarkozy and Hollande, also represented a new generation, they, too, slipped into character roles of the past: Sarkozy, the Mac-Mahon of the 2005 suburban riots, dipped into the Bonapartist repertoire of being all things to all people, whereas François Hollande, like Jacques Chirac, against whom he lost his first election to the National Assembly, made his electoral career in the rural *département* of Corrèze while pulling strings in the party machine and living in Paris. These recurrent character roles do not, however, simply reflect a lack of political imagination or the institutional difficulties of acquiring and maintaining power in the hybrid presidential-parliamentary regime and the fragmented, polarized party system reinforced by the two-round electoral system. They are also the product of deep-rooted conflicting interests in French society and of challenges to French identity in the context of a changing global order.

Ever since the prerevolutionary age of monarchical absolutism, material interests in France have been divided between economic actors dependent on the state (at the time: aristocrats, financiers, monopoly holders), those in new private commerce and industry (the burgeoning bourgeoisie), and those in local, subsistence activities (peasants, artisans). For reasons we have seen in this chapter, the monarchist, republican, or Bonapartist state in France has intervened to accelerate, to slow down, to direct, or to redistribute economic development in order to maintain internal social order or to face external competition. From an Anglo-American perspective, this prominent economic role of the French state is a developmental aberration, a brake on liberalism, on capitalism, and purportedly on democracy. Although France has certainly suffered authoritarian interludes over the centuries since the Revolution, their causes have had little to do with state constraints on economic competition and much to do with the virulence of political competition. Despite postwar planning and the strength of the PCF in the two decades following the Liberation, France has had a capitalist market economy ever since the Revolution established the principles of private property and formal individual equality. But it is a variety of capitalism peculiar to France, just as Britain, the United States, Germany, Italy, and – today – China, among other societies, have their own historically grounded models of capitalism.

Political debate in and about France today centers largely on the virtues and vices of the "French model" of contemporary capitalism, though mostly on its purported vices. France has indeed been mired in *la crise* since the mid-1970s, and virtually every leader since then has dashed the electorate's hopes of recovery. France has of course previously experienced long periods of relative decline, the entire Third Republic, for example, and other countries have as well – once stellar Japan since 1990 and Britain throughout France's "trente glorieuse," to name but two. It would be a mistake, of course, to overstate France's deep-seated structural economic difficulties. French (and Franco-European multinational) firms, from Airbus to Alstom, from Dassault to Danone (Dannon), from Renault to Ricard, remain world leaders in their sectors; the country remains an export leader and even ran a foreign trade surplus throughout the crisis years of the 1990s; and in recent years has led the European and world market in developing fuel-efficient cars. Although British per capita GDP, pumped up until recently by its banking sector, has nominally surpassed France, any visitor to the two countries will recognize that France's standard of living and infrastructure (transport, housing, health, commerce) remains superior. Still, France has some serious problems, particularly in the effectiveness of its large public sector, which François Hollande, like his predecessors has promised to pare down. As historian Timothy Smith has neatly summarized, France has succeeded in matching Scandinavian levels of social spending while maintaining (not quite) American levels of socioeconomic inequality. France offers generous social services in health, education, and child-care, yet clearly not enough to keep young people, immigrants, and women from merely scraping by. As even the best-intended politicians of the Fifth Republic have learned, they cannot provide more without straining French capital and competitiveness, nor provide less without provoking revolt among civil servants, students, and the underprivileged.

Since at least 1992 and the adoption of the Maastricht Treaty creating the European Union, France has pursued the strategy of European integration for revitalizing its economy, disciplining its institutions, and redefining its identity as part of a greater whole. The financial and sovereign debt crisis of the second decade of the new millennium, however, has shown the limits and constraints of such a strategy as France and its European partners realize the impossibility of simultaneously bringing their budget deficits under control, stimulating their economies, keeping the banking and financial system afloat, and avoiding the worst effects of social exclusion. Stuck between their obligations to their European partners, within the single currency euro-zone in particular, and their responsibility to the French electorate, French leaders face the additional challenge of rearticulating and rallying their divided and divisive countrymen around a coherent vision of France's place in the world either as part of the European Union or not. The notion that "la France éternelle" has long had a powerful, unified sense of identity is a myth, of course. In medieval times, the heroism of Jeanne d'Arc, appropriated as patron saint by the Front National, was more a symptom of divisions between the aristocracy and the crown than of a budding national consensus. The Third Estate, as we saw, proclaimed itself to embody the nation during the Revolution, but nineteenth-century vacillations among popular Empire, monarchisms, and republicanisms proved that France's universalist values and "mission civilisatrice" were a fig leaf for a fractured political community. The Third Republic educated peasants into Frenchmen and propounded the doctrine of France's "natural" hexagonal borders, the better to recover lost territories on the Rhine, while De Gaulle's defense of "une certaine idée de la France" from the Liberation through the founding years of the Fifth Republic was decidedly vague in its certitude! The point, of course, is that any society requires a foundational or aspirational myth to maintain a minimum of coherence. Since De Gaulle's departure and the end of the postwar boom, the Fifth Republic has been in quest of such a myth. Presidents Giscard, Mitterrand, Chirac, and Sarkozy all embraced the noble project of European integration as a myth of salvation, but the near-miss of the 1992 Maastricht Treaty referendum, the crash-and-burn of the European constitutional referendum of 2005, and the serious questioning of the pro-European partnership with Germany across the political spectrum in 2012 have proven that the European ideal has opened division, wounds, and fears as well as hopes that France might find its role within a larger, more powerful political community. Whether the European Union can fulfill that mission in a world of global flows of goods, capital, people, and ideas remains a question to be addressed in Chapter 13 of this book.

BIBLIOGRAPHY

Agulhon, Maurice. *The French Republic, 1879–1992*. Oxford: Blackwell, 1995.

Anderson, Perry. *Lineages of the Absolutist State*. London: Verso, 1974.

Bell, David S. *François Mitterrand: A Political Biography*. Cambridge: Polity Press, 2005.

Bloch, Marc. *Strange Defeat*. New York: W. W. Norton, 1999.

Debray, Régis. *Charles De Gaulle: Futurist of the Nation*. Translated by John Howe. London: Verso, 1994.

Hoffmann, Stanley et al. *In Search of France: The Economy, Society and Political System in the 20th Century*. New York: Harper Torchbooks, 1963.

Larkin, Maurice. *France since the Popular Front: Government and People, 1936–1996*. New York: Oxford University Press, 1997.

Lefebvre, Georges. *The Coming of the French Revolution*. Princeton, NJ: Pronceton University Press, 1989.

Marx, Karl. *The 18th Brumaire of Louis Bonaparte*. New York: International Publishers, 1963.

Mendras, Henri. *La seconde révolution française (1965–1984)*. Paris: Gallimard, 1994.

Moore, Barrington. *Social Origins of Dictatorship and Democracy*. Boston: Beacon Press, 1966.

Paxton, Robert O. *Vichy France, 1940–1944*. New York: Columbia University Press, 2001.

Rousso, Henry. *The Vichy Syndrome: History and Memory in France since 1944*. Translated by Arthur Goldhammer. Cambridge, MA: Harvard University Press, 2006.

Skocpol, Theda. *States and Social Revolutions*. Cambridge: Cambridge University Press, 1979.

Smith, Timothy B. *France in Crisis: Welfare, Inequality and Globalization since 1980*. Cambridge: Cambridge University Press, 2004.

Strayer, Joseph R. *On the Medieval Origins of the Modern State*. Princeton, NJ: Princeton University Press, 1970.

Tocqueville, Alexis de. *The Old Regime and the French Revolution*. Translated by Stuart Gilbert. New York: Anchor Books, 1983.

Todd, Emmanuel. *La nouvelle France*. Paris: Seuil, 1990.

Weber, Eugen. *Peasants into Frenchmen: The Modernization of Rural France, 1870–1914*. Palo Alto, CA: Stanford University Press, 1976.

IMPORTANT TERMS

Absolutism – historically linked to the emergence of the sovereign state, absolutism describes a form of rule in which a monarch claims, and more or less effectively exercises, a monopoly of political authority on a delimited territory. Absolutism centralizes political functions (justice, defense, taxation) previously fragmented and devolved to the aristocracy under feudalism but maintains the nobility's social and economic privileges.

Alternance – literally "alternation," this term describes a change of government between the right and left ends of the political spectrum. Under the Fifth Republic, the predominance of right-wing parties until 1981 made the question of *alternance* a test of the regime's democratic character and viability. Successive *alternances* and experiences of *cohabitation* since 1981 have proven the Gaullist Constitution's success.

Bonaparte, Napoleon – born on the island of Corsica in 1769, Napoleon Bonaparte died in British captivity on the island of St. Helena in 1821. At the age of twenty-six he was already a general and hero of revolutionary army campaigns in Italy and Egypt. He took power in France through a coup d'état in 1799 before proclaiming himself Emperor of the French in 1804. His expansionary foreign policy rallied the nation but ended in disaster in 1815.

Bonapartism – derived from the periods of imperial rule of Napoleon I and his nephew Louis Bonaparte (Napoleon III), this term describes both an ideological current in French politics that favors the authoritative, even authoritarian, leadership of a charismatic politician and a socioeconomic development strategy whereby the state, under a powerful leader, assumes responsibility for modernization and industrialization.

Cohabitation – originally seen as a possible defect in the Fifth Republic's constitutional order, cohabitation describes the situation where the president must nominate a prime minister who does not hold the same partisan allegiances because the president does not command a majority in the lower house of parliament, the National Assembly. Since 1984, France has experienced three periods of cohabitation.

Colbertisme – initiated by and retrospectively named for Louis XIV's minister Jean-Baptiste Colbert (1619–1683), this economic doctrine was the French version of mercantilism. The label still applies generally to the prominent role of the French state in directing economic development.

(la) crise – following three "glorious" decades of record economic growth since 1945 ("les trente glorieuses"), France has been bogged in three decades of relative stagnation commonly called "la crise." Shorthand for a complex of phenomena ranging from high unemployment to poor integration of immigrants, the expression describes more a national mood of self-doubt than a concrete economic crisis as France remains a world leader in many sectors.

De Gaulle, Charles – born in 1890, De Gaulle was wounded and taken German prisoner as an officer in World War I. He rose to the rank of general at the beginning of World War II, subsequently refusing to accept the Vichy government's capitulation and calling for resistance by radio from London. He led the provisional government upon Liberation in 1944 but opposed the parliamentary constitutional order of the nascent Fourth Republic. In 1958 he founded and became the first president of the Fifth Republic, resigning office in 1969, the year before his death.

Dreyfus Affair – the false accusation and condemnation for espionage of the Jewish officer Alfred Dreyfus in 1894 became a political crisis revealing the cleavages of the Third Republic when the novelist Émile Zola publicly denounced the scandal in his celebrated newspaper article "J'accuse" in 1898.

École nationale d'administration – one of France's elite "grandes écoles" the ENA was founded in 1945 to train administrators for government and business in the wake of collaboration and the Vichy government. Known as "énarques," its graduates are often denounced as a coterie of technocrats with undue power and influence. They practice "pantouflage," literally "house-slippering," that is, an all-too-comfortable moving back and forth between government and business.

Feudalism – this social order predominated in Europe for over a millennium from the fall of the Roman Empire until the French Revolution. Feudal society was divided into three orders: the nobility, the clergy, and the rest – or respectively those who fought, those who prayed, and those who worked. The third order, or estate, of commoners consisted overwhelmingly of peasants tied to the land and under obligation to their lords but also included townspeople (the "bourgeoisie") collectively exempt from many feudal obligations.

Jacobinism – derived from the radical revolutionary faction known as the Jacobins, this term describes the tendency toward the centralization of political authority and the ideological valorization of the state as the embodiment and articulator of the general will and collective well-being of society.

Laïcité – roughly translatable as secularism, this term in French political discourse describes the Republican principle not only of separation of Church and state but also of relegation of religion to the private sphere. The principle of *laïcité* has recently and controversially been invoked to justify the prohibition of "ostentatious" religious symbols (such as the Muslim headscarf) from public places such as schools.

Maastricht Treaty – signed in February 1992 in the Dutch city of Maastricht, this treaty founded the European Union and initiated the movement toward the single European currency, the euro. Submitted for approval referendum in France in September 1992, the treaty sharply divided opinion, passing by a narrow margin of 51 percent.

Mitterrand, François – France's longest-serving president (1981–1995), Mitterrand won election only at his third candidacy and after having had a long political career under Vichy, the Fourth Republic, and the Fifth Republic. He succeeded in bringing the Left to power by refounding the Socialist Party in 1971 and making an electoral alliance with the Communist Party, ultimately undermining its postwar stranglehold on 20 percent of the electorate. Born in 1916, Mitterrand concealed and battled cancer outliving his second term by one year until 1996.

Monnet, Jean – born in 1888, Monnet was one of the architects of the Allied victory in World War II, having persuaded U.S. President Franklin D. Roosevelt to begin rearmament before the American entry into the war. His wartime planning skills qualified him to organize France's postwar reconstruction as planning commissioner. Recognizing the benefits of closer cooperation and integration for economic and political reconstruction, Monnet became the instigator for the European Economic Community and today's European Union. He died in 1979.

Tocqueville, Alexis de – born in 1805, this French nobleman became one of the most astute observers of *Democracy in America* and a brilliant historian of *The Old Regime and the Revolution* in France. A statesman as well as a literary giant, Tocqueville died in 1859 in self-imposed internal exile under the Second Empire before he could finish his history of the revolutionary period and aftermath.

STUDY QUESTIONS

1. How did international competition on the European continent shape France's early political development during feudalism and absolutism in distinction from that of England?
2. How did absolutism shape social classes and interests and how, in turn, did those interests exacerbate the tensions inherent to absolutist rule?
3. How did competing interests during the revolutionary period prevent the consolidation of stable political institutions?
4. What interests and institutions favored the emergence of representative democracy in nineteenth-century France? Which ones militated against it?
5. What were the competing conceptions of the French political community and identity in the postrevolutionary period?
6. To what degree and how did the Third Republic succeed in reconciling competing interests, identities, and institutional models?
7. Would the Third Republic have survived if Nazi Germany had not invaded in 1940?
8. Is it fair to describe the Fourth Republic as a failure?
9. Why did François Mitterrand denounce the institutions of the Fifth Republic as a "permanent coup d'état"?
10. Did the *alternance* of 1981 normalize French democracy?
11. What are the current challenges to the French political system? Which ones are new, and which ones can be traced back through the millennial history of the country?

Early Developers: Britain and France

An important part of democracy is the role of parliaments. Much of Great Britain's history has been a constant refinement of the principle of representative parliamentary government. Through a long series of struggles and reforms, British parliamentary government emerged triumphant over the rule of kings and queens. In the course of these changes, the monarchy remained a symbol of national integration and historical continuity, but the real political power came to reside in the prime minister and his or her cabinet of ministers. Of course, even in Britain, parliamentary and cabinet government did not necessarily mean the same thing as democracy: the right to vote – the franchise – was only gradually extended to the lower classes and women, and the final reforms came about during the twentieth century.

Despite the important upheavals in British history, political scientists continue to view the British experience as one of successful gradualism, of a gradual extension of the freedoms of liberal democracy to ever-larger groups of people. In the creation of liberal democracy, the British were undoubtedly aided by the simultaneous and successful rise of a commercial and capitalist economy during the eighteenth and nineteenth centuries. This was the age of the Industrial Revolution. Although the transition to a new kind of economy was not easy, for the first time in history an economy generated large amounts of goods that could be consumed by a large number of people. To be sure, at first these goods were enjoyed only by the new "middle" classes, but over time the new lifestyle spread to the working class as well. Accompanying these changes in material living standards came changes in the way people thought about their place in the world. One's position and life chances were no longer set in stone from birth. Upward mobility was now a possibility for people who never would have thought such a world possible a mere century earlier. It was in this context that common people could begin to demand a political voice commensurate with their contribution to the public good. The argument was a powerful one, and gradually the old feudal/aristocratic oligarchy gave way to wider sections of society in search of political representation.

Of course, a further important feature of the British experience was the creation of a global empire between the seventeenth and the nineteenth centuries. Industrialization both contributed to and was assisted by the military, economic, and political conquest of large parts of Africa and Asia. The empire provided raw materials for manufacture, markets for export, a "playground" for military elites, and a source of national pride that made it easier for the British to try to universalize their particular experience. As other countries in Europe began to compete economically and militarily, however, and as locally subjected peoples from Ghana to India recognized the incongruity of British ideals of parliamentary democracy and law with continued imperial domination, the costs of empire began to rise. By the beginning of the twentieth century, Britain had clearly fallen from the imperial heights it had once occupied, and domestic discussion began to focus on issues of economic decline and how to extricate the country from costly imperial commitments. With Britain divested of its empire, its economy continued to decline throughout the twentieth century relative to other European countries, and much of contemporary British politics has concerned ways to reverse this decline. In Britain's (mostly) two-party system, both parties have proposed cures for what ails the economy, but neither has been able to offer recipes for regaining the national confidence (indeed, some say arrogance) that was once taken for granted.

Notwithstanding such troubles, the British experience continues to be the benchmark against which comparativists think about the developmental experience of other countries. The British (or what is sometimes called the Westminster) model of government became the standard against which other countries measure their own progress.

Britain's experience could not be duplicated, however. Even France, the country whose experience we pair with Britain's, initially developed in Britain's shadow and bridged early and late developmental paths. The logic of pairing France and Britain is, nevertheless, compelling. Like Britain, France's history is largely one of the people emerging victorious over kings. The difference is that, in France, the monarchy and the old feudal oligarchy were displaced not through a long series of conflicts and compromises but largely through a major revolution in 1789 in which the monarch was executed and the aristocracy hounded out of political life. Over the course of the next century, French political history was tumultuous, the political pendulum swinging back and forth between democratic development and periods of authoritarian or populist regimes. Despite these changes, what remained a constant in French political life was the notion that power ultimately resided with the people. Even such populist demagogues as Napoleon and, later, his nephew Louis Bonaparte (Louis-Napoleon) never managed to depart fully from the notion of popular sovereignty. Indeed, they could not, if only because postrevolutionary France depended on its people to serve in its armies and mobilize for war.

If the British political experience is one of subjugating monarchical power to representative institutions, the French democratic experience is one of regulating a strong centralized state through plebiscitary mandate. War was a staple of political life on the European continent and preparing for it an important part of what states did. The French state was no exception; in fact, it became a model for others to emulate (and eventually surpass). Even before the French Revolution, French monarchs and their states played an important part in encouraging economic development and collecting taxes for the purposes of military preparation. The revolution did little to change this and in many ways intensified the power of the French state. In fact, one way of thinking about the revolution is in terms of a rebellion against the taxing power of the French monarchy and its resurrection in the form of more or less democratically elected heads of state who, because of their popular mandate, had more power to draw on private resources for public goals than ever before. Given its pattern of development, it is perhaps not surprising for us to learn that after much experimentation with various forms of representative government in the latter part of the nineteenth century and first part of the twentieth, France has settled on a strong, popularly elected presidency with a five-year term of office.

This contrast between parliamentary rule in Britain and presidential rule in France has become a model one for political scientists. Such differences in democratic institutions have important long-term effects on politics and policies. Given the importance and centralized nature of the French state, it is natural that the state became highly involved in economic development during the twentieth century. French economic planning, a subtle and highly developed system of state guidelines and state-induced market incentives, has often been contrasted with the heavy-handed Soviet communist model, not merely in the differences in style but also because for a very long time the French model seemed to work so well. More recently, however, the impacts of European integration and increased global trade have brought the feasibility of the model under question and led to a debate in France on the future of French-style economic planning and whether it will have to adapt to the competing model of Anglo-American capitalism. Britain has also experienced a debate between Euroskeptics and Europhiles.

Finally, globalization has also meant that both Britain and France are now home to large numbers of people born in other countries. Right-wing sentiment against "foreigners" has emerged, and politicians have raised questions about national identity. Questions of identity are nothing new to Britain and France. British identity has always been contested – the Celtic periphery of Scots, Irish, and Welsh has frequently challenged the hegemony of the English. French identity has long been split between a Catholic and conservative France rooted in the rural peasantry and a secular and progressive France rooted in the urban classes. Yet, for both Britain and France, the presence of so many "non-Europeans" in their midst is something quite new. How democracies, especially two of the oldest and most stable ones, manage the tensions among multiculturalism, national unity, and democratic politics is a topic that will capture the interest of comparativists for years to come.

PART II

Middle Developers

GERMANY

MAP 5.1. Map of Germany.

5 Germany

Andrew C. Gould

Introduction

In October 1990, the East German state (the German Democratic Republic – GDR) collapsed and its territory and people were absorbed by West Germany (the Federal Republic of Germany – FRG), even though just months before almost no one had expected this to happen. Western troops did not fire a single shot; easterners were fleeing to the West. Yet, the strange fate of East Germany makes sense as part of Germany's path through the modern world, which has been influenced strongly by external political and economic challenges. A precarious military-strategic position in Europe made it difficult for one German polity to rule over everyone who is in one way or another conceivably German. Even today, millions of German-speaking people and considerable territories that were formerly governed by German rulers remain outside of the unified state. Germany's economic success as a middle-developer means that the country still has powerful influence beyond its own borders: in the wake of the recession of 2008–2010, other European governments called for more German assistance and cooperation even as they feared heavy-handed intervention and criticized Germany's reluctance to provide more resources.

The challenges that Germans faced and their responses were characteristic of what happens when a major power takes a middle path through political and economic development. Germany was at a disadvantage with respect to the early developers. In politics, German rulers could not match France in establishing strong central authority over a vast territory. In economics, German industrial development lagged behind Britain's. Along with these military and economic disadvantages, however, the rapid diffusion of new ideas into Germany offered certain opportunities. Germany's newer bureaucracies skipped over incremental improvements to traditional practices and instead adopted only the latest and best organizational techniques. German industries, unimpeded by false starts, implemented advanced technology on a massive scale. In the struggle with the early developers, Germany developed powerful political institutions (a professional army and an authoritarian monarchy), mobilizing identities (ethnic conceptions of nation), and significant economic interests (heavy industry and labor-repressive agriculture), all of which imperiled liberalism and democracy.

The German experience demonstrates that responding to political and economic backwardness has powerful and wide-ranging effects. When Germany was attempting to catch up to Britain and France, its industries modernized, its state engineered massive social and economic changes, and its leading political ideologies emphasized power, obedience, and material well-being rather than political freedom. The culmination of this approach, the fascist regime of Adolf Hitler's Nazi Party, ultimately failed to deliver social order, prosperity, and global leadership atop a new world order. In the wake of World War II, when two new superpowers emerged in virtually unassailable positions, German elites no longer sought to challenge for predominance. Instead, postwar Germany was divided into two states, and one of them, the FRG, became a medium-size state almost entirely dependent upon the United States for its security, with no offensive military capability of its own. During the Cold War, the FRG took the strategy of military alliance and trade with other Western powers. Its economy grew to become one of the world's most successful, and democracy, freedom, and the rule of law began to flourish in the heart of the European continent. Meanwhile, the economy of East Germany languished by comparison, as the DDR and its Soviet sponsor invested in military preparedness and domestic repression.

Contemporary interests, identities, and institutions in Germany derive from Germany's path through the modern world. With regard to interests, the reliance of major German industrialists on the state and big banks for funding during the nineteenth and twentieth centuries, and the struggles of many small- and medium-sized firms to stay afloat, stemmed from Germany's economic position and attempts to catch up with France and Britain. In the early twenty-first century, German firms, unions, banks, and educational institutions coordinate directly with each other (in addition to using price signals in markets) to align their plans for economic development – much more so than in the United Kingdom and the United States. The almost bewildering variety of contemporary German identities – from right-wing nationalism, to ecological activism, to recent immigrants seeking greater status and recognition – also flows from previous episodes of identity formation and reformulation. Some key institutional features of the contemporary German state, including the post-unification relocation of the capital from **Bonn** back to **Berlin**, show the pull of past practice. Other political institutions, notably the **Basic Law** (**Grundgesetz**) of 1949, were explicitly crafted to prevent any reemergence of authoritarianism. In this chapter, we explore how Germany's particular developmental sequence created domestic and international legacies that strongly influence the country today.

Origins of a Middle Developer, 100 BCE–AD 1800

If you place key moments in history, even familiar ones, in the analytic framework of this text, then you can see just how much influence the global context has on the development of a given country. To start the analysis, and in contrast with nationalist myths of a pure beginning, the origins of modern Germany did not lie uniquely within German lands but instead in the contact between two societies. Early German and Roman cultures blended and grew together during the expansions and contractions of the Roman Empire across Europe. Roman influence, starting in the first century BCE, brought a common culture of Christianity, a common elite language of Latin, and a common experience of the Roman legal code. As the Roman Empire declined during the fifth century, Germanic warriors reinvigorated their practice of honor-based pacts of loyalty that provided a political foundation for new feudal kingdoms.

Germany at this time resembled the rest of Europe. As in the rest of Europe from the eighth through the twelfth centuries, aspiring German kings were usually at war with one another. As in other parts of Europe, strong cities emerged during the thirteenth through sixteenth centuries, especially along the Rhine River and the Baltic Sea. In contrast to the personalistic and custom-bound rule in feudal kingdoms, cities governed themselves through written laws and representative institutions. Also during the sixteenth century, a wave of religious revival swept across Germany and Europe; the Protestant Reformation and Catholic Counter-Reformation left German territories religiously divided.

Germany became a middle developer during the seventeenth and eighteenth centuries because this is when German rulers could not match the successes of monarchs in France and England. Whereas each of the early developers became unified under absolutist or would-be absolutist rulers, Germany remained politically divided. For instance, starting in 1618, the Thirty Years' War devastated the population and economy of many German states; it ended with the 1648 Peace of Westphalia, which signaled the ascendancy of France under Louis XIV as a European power and which highlighted the inability of Germany's nominal imperial ruler (Ferdinand III, Holy Roman Emperor) to stem the growing sovereignty of the many different and competing German states and principalities. The weakness of pan-German political institutions and the persistence of political divisions accentuated other differences within the German lands, such as the cleavage between Protestants and Catholics and the contrast between economically advanced regions in western and southern Germany and the backward agricultural economies and social structures east of the Elbe River.

Competing Modern States, 1800–1871

German polities were middle developers in building a modern state, that is, in building a political organization that could successfully claim to be the only organization with the right to use violence over the German territory and its people. The two most powerful political units were the Austrian Empire in the southeast and Prussia in the northeast. They competed with each other and with dozens of other would-be states in what is now modern Germany. The winnowing down of German states accelerated under the renewed military conquests of an early developer. In 1806, the French emperor Napoleon Bonaparte invaded, consolidated many German states into larger units, and imposed a common legal code. German leaders sought both to imitate and resist Napoleon by rationalizing their own bureaucracies and building stronger armies. It is characteristic of these changes that Francis II dissolved his virtually moribund Holy Roman Empire, which ineffectively claimed to organize political rulers throughout German lands, and instead focused on ruling with his hereditary name and title as Francis I, Emperor of Austria. When the armies of Francis I (Austria), Frederick William III (Prussia), George III (Great Britain), Alexander I (Russia), and the other allies finally defeated Napoleon in 1815, Austria and Prussia emerged even stronger than before compared to the other German states. As an eastern power, Prussian military might was centered on its capital in Berlin, but the peace treaty agreed to at the Congress of Vienna awarded Prussia control over many economically advanced territories in the west along the Rhine River.

Two main social and political groups contended for influence in Germany during the nineteenth century. The first group included many people energized by the broader European liberal movements for nationalism and constitutionalism. They were liberals in the nineteenth-century meaning of the term: they favored large and free markets, the separation of church and state, and constitutional representative government. German liberals sought to build a German nation that encompassed all of the people then divided into various polities; they wanted a national market unhindered by internal boundaries; and they wanted to limit monarchical power by building new political institutions, such as a national electoral system, a parliament, and a written constitution. Leading intellectuals, professors, government officials, industrialists, professionals, and various members of the middle classes played key roles in the liberal movement.

The second group contending for influence was the landed elite (**Junkers**) of eastern Prussia. These owners of large tracts of land employed agricultural labor in conditions of near servitude to produce grain for world markets. They were deeply conservative politically and sought to forestall any political change that threatened their control over land and people, including any changes in the system of German states, in the ways the various states were governed internally, and in the harsh conditions of life for their agricultural workers. Their estates produced grain for the world market at very competitive prices, but their approval of market economics did not extend to the conditions of production for their workers. In fact, their economic success rested on political repression and economic exploitation.

German monarchs successfully resisted most of the political demands of the liberal group and allied themselves with the landed elite. For example, in 1830, liberal revolutions took place in France, Belgium, and Switzerland. Liberalism was strong in the Rhineland as well, but the Prussian king in Berlin avoided changes by taking advantage of his government's physical separation from most of the revolutionary action and his additional military resources based in the east. Even less change occurred in Austria than in Prussia.

Next, in 1848, important political reforms again engulfed many countries of Europe. In Germany, widespread revolutionary activity in the Rhineland, Berlin, and Vienna led to a call for the election of a national assembly of delegates. Elections were held in all of the German states, from Prussia to Austria and the many other states. The delegates met in Frankfurt to draw up a new constitution for a unified German state, but the Prussian and Austrian monarchs used force to preserve their rule, and the **Frankfurt Parliament** proved unable to reform, overthrow, or even unify the conservative states; the parliament disbanded without achieving any of its intended aims.

The rejection of liberalism not only signaled a nondemocratic development strategy, but it also had the unintended consequence of setting in motion future revolutionary movements. In the spring of 1841, **Karl Marx** was a twenty-three-year-old student whose dissertation was accepted by the University of Jena. Marx had planned for a career as an academic philosopher, but the Prussian government's imposition of strict controls on university appointments meant that he had to write for a different audience. His new job as the editor of a newspaper financed by liberals and run by radicals, the *Rheinische Zeitung*, ended abruptly when the Prussian censor closed the paper for being too critical. Unable to find work in Germany, Marx left for France in 1843, where he met his lifelong collaborator, Friedrich Engels. In 1848, he and Engels wrote the *Communist Manifesto*, closing with the statement: "The proletarians have nothing to lose but their chains. They have a world to win. Working men of all countries, unite!" Marx returned to Germany during the revolutionary movements of 1848 and advocated an alliance with liberal reformers, but the failure of this revolution finally convinced him and many other activists and supporters that real reform was impossible without more fundamental changes in the economy and society.

In the battle for supremacy among the German powers, the Prussian monarchy adopted the economic dimension of the liberal program but relied on military strength both to dominate the smaller German states and to reject the political dimensions of liberalism. Prussia sponsored a growing free-trade zone among the German states; the size of its own market made it costly for other states to avoid joining. Prussia defeated Austria in war in 1866, paving the way for the formation of the North German Confederation under Prussian leadership in 1867. The final steps in Germany's first modern unification required that France be forced to accept the change in the German situation. The Franco-Prussian War of 1870 matched two nondemocratic rulers – France's emperor Louis-Napoleon (Napoleon Bonaparte's nephew) against the King of Prussia, Wilhelm I. The war had widely divergent consequences. Louis-Napoleon lost the war and was replaced by a democratic regime, the Third Republic (1870–1940); Prussia won the war and used its victory to consolidate a larger German state under continuing authoritarian rule.

The Prussian king – advised by his chancellor, Otto von Bismarck – had himself crowned the emperor of Germany while at the French palace of Versailles in 1871. The title of emperor was chosen to evoke memories of the Holy Roman Empire that had been disbanded in 1806; the new regime became known as the Second Empire. The new borders were fixed by military victory. Unified Germany encompassed Prussia (including eastern territories along the Baltic in what is now Poland and Russia) and virtually all of the non-Austrian German states. It also included territory taken from France: the economically advanced provinces of Alsace and Lorraine. Austria and Switzerland remained outside of the new German empire as independent countries.

Unification under Authoritarian Leadership, 1871–1919

Germany's late unification gave its newly constructed state institutions a great deal of influence over society. The state's initiative played a crucial role in changing Germany, even if the state was not always successful in its efforts. In other words, the developmental path of relatively late state-building in Germany gave the German state, compared with early state-building in Britain and France, an opportunity to attempt to reshape society, the economy, and politics.

The leaders of the German state planned to recast institutions and reformulate identities. First, the mainly Protestant leaders attacked Catholicism. In the early 1870s, the state leaders pursued a **cultural struggle** (**Kulturkampf**) with laws and regulations to make it difficult for Catholic priests to carry out their work. Political activists responded by founding a political party, the **Center Party** (**Zentrumspartei**). The party's top decision makers were Catholic lay leaders, and Center Party candidates received the implicit and explicit aid of the Church. The long-term effects of the Kulturkampf, however, were neither what the German political elite wanted nor what the Catholic Church expected. Instead of a retreat from politics, the struggle against Catholicism induced Catholics to mobilize in their own political party. Instead of increasing the power of the Catholic Church in politics and society, as the Catholic hierarchy would have preferred, the Catholic resistance to the Kulturkampf brought about the emergence of professional party leaders – lay leaders, not priests – who could claim to speak for the Catholic community. The state reconciled with the church during the 1870s, but the Center Party remained to represent German Catholics, and it went on to become one of the country's largest political parties.

As the regime made its peace with a newly politicized Catholic community, the leaders next turned their attention to the emerging political movements among the working classes. The Socialist Worker's Party was formed in 1875 from various radical groups. Although it won only 9 percent of the vote in 1877, Bismarck blamed the party for Germany's economic situation: "As long as we fail to stamp on this communist ant-hill with domestic legislation," he said, "we shall not see any revival in the economy." In 1878, Bismarck won majority support in the Reichstag (parliament) for severe antisocialist legislation. The government closed Socialist Party offices and publications, prohibited its meetings, and generally harassed its organizers. Many left-wing activists fled from Germany, especially to Switzerland, and sought to keep their efforts alive in exile.

Despite the repression, many workers and other supporters continued to identify themselves as working class and to support the Socialist Party. Most of the antisocialist laws lapsed in 1890, and the party reemerged under a new name as the **Social Democratic Party** (Sozialdemokratische Partei Deutschlands, SPD). The Socialists climbed at the polls in 1898 with 27 percent of the vote. In the final elections under the empire in 1912, the Social Democratic Party won even more – 35 percent of the vote. The typical Socialist voter was a young, urban worker who was Protestant but did not go to church, and who was German rather than Polish or other national minority. The party attracted little support from Catholics or people living in rural areas. Still, the Social Democrats had almost a million members in 1912, a substantial accomplishment, as its members were expected to pay regular dues (as in many other European mass-based parties). Like other big parties in Europe, the Social Democrats reached beyond the purely political realm to organize potential followers in myriad other ways: funeral societies, buying cooperatives, book-lending libraries, gymnastic societies, choral clubs, bicycling clubs, soccer teams, and dance courses, for example.

The new German state had to foster economic development in difficult circumstances. Most important, from 1873 to 1896 there was a Europe-wide depression. Agricultural prices fell with the introduction of inexpensive Russian and Midwestern American grain on world markets; industrial prices also fell, employment figures were unstable, production rose, and profits decreased. One response to these difficult conditions lay beyond state control: many Germans emigrated from Europe to North and South America.

German firms enjoyed some "advantages of backwardness." They could adopt advanced machinery and industrial organization from British examples without having to devise the innovations themselves. But there were also disadvantages of backwardness. In order to acquire expensive technology and survive early competition with established businesses, many German firms relied on large banks and the state for the necessary capital funds. From 1875 to 1890, both the eastern German grain growers (the Junkers) and the big industrialists sought and won state protection from imports in the form of high tariffs; Germany's relatively large working class would have preferred freer trade and cheaper food.

One can argue that the institutions of the Second Empire were on their way to becoming more democratic during the early twentieth century. The Social Democratic Party and the Center Party were gaining in strength, and liberal industrialists were gaining in influence over the old Junker elite. As the success of industrialization began to materialize in the 1890s, for example, many leading industrialists saw that they could compete on the world market and broke with the Junkers to seek lower tariff barriers. Industrialists, like workers, now favored low tariffs and the resulting lower prices on food. Several shifts in cabinet formation resulted, followed by a victory for low-tariff delegates in the Reichstag election of 1912.

For all of the democratic gains at the ballot box under the empire, however, Germany's position within the global context made a transition to democracy problematic. German leaders ruled over a middle developer and felt threatened by the early developers. Facing Britain and France as leading imperial powers, the German elite responded to a crisis in southeastern Europe by opting for war in 1914. Their basic hope was for a quick victory, which would expand Germany's base and allow them to challenge the established powers more effectively. But the quick German victory did not materialize. Instead, the forces of Germany and its ally in this war, Austria-Hungary, bogged down in trench warfare against those of the Triple Entente (Britain, France, and Russia). The German high command's next gamble to win the war quickly – by introducing submarine warfare in the Atlantic – did not weaken Britain and France sufficiently before the feared and ultimately decisive intervention of American troops and resources.

As in other countries affected by the Great War, as World War I was called, massive mobilization had political consequences for Germany. Eleven million men, amounting to

18 percent of the population, were in uniform. Workers and families scrambled to support the war effort. Massive propaganda campaigns encouraged a strong national feeling and the sense that every German person was a valuable member of the nation. Similar campaigns in the other great powers boosted the feelings of national belonging in every state and increased the pressure for political reform to give every member of the nation an equal set of citizenship rights.

Although there was a gradual democratization of political life under the Second Empire, the transition to a full democracy came abruptly. As it became clear that Germany was losing the war, several navy and army units mutinied. This was followed by uprisings in Berlin and William II's abdication as emperor of Germany in 1918. As in France at the end of Emperor Louis-Napoleon's rule, loss in war combined with military defections and domestic uprising sparked a transition from authoritarianism to democracy.

Democracy and Competitive Capitalism, 1919–1933

A democratic and constitutional regime now took command of the German state. Under the Weimar Republic, all adult men and women had the right to vote in elections to the Reichstag. Elections were also held to select a president. In turn, the president usually requested the leader of the strongest parliamentary party to serve as the chancellor, form a cabinet, and lead the government. If the chancellor's party could not form a majority on its own, the chancellor had to put together a coalition of parties in the Reichstag in order to govern. Given the absence of a single party that could command a majority, most governments were coalition governments composed of several parties. Not all coalition governments are weak, but in the case of Weimar Germany many were.

Former adherents of the authoritarian empire retained considerable influence even under the new regime. The new democratic leaders never purged reactionary officers from the army or police. Instead, the democrats relied on the old authoritarians. For example, the Social Democratic leaders of the new German government called on the army to suppress demonstrations, in a bid to restore order to rioting cities, quell the threat of a communist revolution, and prevent the spread of the recently successful 1917 revolution in Russia. In addition, most judges had received their legal training under the empire and continued to interpret the law in an antidemocratic fashion. Many highly trained and well-placed civil servants were holdovers from the previous era. Whereas the first president was a leading Socialist, **Friedrich Ebert**, the second and only other president, **Otto von Hindenburg**, was a Junker and former army officer. It was Hindenburg who appointed Hitler as chancellor in 1933.

The Weimar Republic depended on strong parties in the middle of the political spectrum. The leading parties in the regime during the 1920s were the center-left Social Democratic Party, which usually received about 25 percent of the vote, and the Center Party, which usually received about 15 percent of the vote. On the center-right, various bourgeois, liberal, and traditional-nationalist parties accounted for most of the remaining 45 percent of the vote. The governments worked reasonably well, as long as the far-left Communist

Party did not expand its support beyond the 15 percent range and until a new extreme-right nationalist party attracted substantial support.

Important aspects of the Weimar Republic's demise were the increasing strength of extreme left-wing and right-wing parties committed to the destruction of the republic, and the failure of the center-right parties to retain their constituencies. Beginning with the election of 1930, the new **National Socialist German Workers' Party (Nazi Party)** started to capture a substantial share of the vote, mostly from the old center-right, bourgeois, and liberal parties. In 1933, the last democratic election, the Socialists still received almost their typical amount at 20 percent, and the Center Party won its usual 15 percent. The Communists received a somewhat higher than normal 17 percent. It was the collapsing center-right and right-wing parties that provided the Nazis with a plurality of 33 percent of the vote, paving the way for Hitler to be named chancellor.

Our perspective on global contexts and paths to development illuminates important causes of the democratic collapse and fascist takeover that stand up to comparative analysis. First, Germany's size and middle-developer status interacted in ways dangerous for peaceful relations with other countries. Germany was a big country, and many of its leaders had seemingly reasonable expectations that Germany would become the next great power. Yet, years of competition with the early developers, especially Britain and its ex-colony, the United States, and even added competition with a late developer, the Soviet Union, seemed to leave Germany lagging behind. For many people in Germany and in other populous middle developers (such as Japan and Italy), one temptation was to embark on a military strategy to remake the world order with their nation on top. This tendency had already faded in the countries that had suffered serious defeats in attempts to use force and authoritarianism to improve their global position (Sweden in 1648; France in 1815 and 1870); the appeal was also weak in smaller countries with no realistic hope of a military path to greatness. Thus, one can see World War I, World War II, and the authoritarian regimes that pushed them forward as part of a common tendency among large middle developers to seek to improve their global position by military means. It is interesting to note that this tendency remains even today in several other large countries with frustrated developmental ambitions.

Second, Germany's middle-developer status allowed antidemocratic groups at the top of its social structure to exercise considerable influence. Although Germany's rapid industrial development helped to produce a substantial middle class and working class, both of which can be important supporters of democratic regimes, there also remained a small but powerful class of landed elites who employed labor-repressive modes of agriculture on their estates. These Junkers were also highly placed in the German state and used their political position to maintain their social and economic status. As we have noted, it was Hindenburg – Junker and president of the Weimar Republic – who appointed Hitler as chancellor. Although most Junkers certainly preferred more traditional conservatism, the Nazis successfully mobilized mass support and were seen as useful tools in the larger struggle against communism. Other landed elites using labor-repressive modes of agriculture (such as plantation owners in the southern United States) also fought against full democracy; in these and similar cases, only a major military defeat forced them to relinquish key aspects of their authority.

Third, Germany's path to development set up political institutions that made it more difficult to reach agreements among social and political forces. Other middle-developing democratic regimes (in Sweden, Norway, Denmark, and Czechoslovakia) survived the difficult economic period of the 1920s and 1930s without succumbing to domestic fascist movements. These liberal democracies survived at least in part because their democratic regimes were supported by strong coalitions between socialist and agrarian parties. Such urban-rural coalitions of pro-democratic groups did not form in Germany or in the two other Western European countries that succumbed to home-grown fascist movements (Italy and Spain). Thus, it may be that the inability of predominantly urban socialists and predominantly rural agrarian parties to cooperate fatally weakened the German, Italian, and Spanish democracies during the interwar years. Taken together, the recourse to conquest, the survival of authoritarian groups, and the failure of pro-democratic coalitions, all implied that Germany's responses to its global position undermined democracy and competitive capitalism through the middle of the twentieth century.

Nazism in Power, 1933–1945

Germany's Nazi regime was similar to other fascist regimes in several key organizational aspects. Hitler used his legal appointment as chancellor of the Weimar Republic to consolidate his command of the Nazi Party and put his party in control of the state. Within weeks, Hitler took advantage of communist resistance as a pretext to prohibit and suppress the Communist Party. During the rest of 1933, other parties were strongly encouraged to dissolve and allow their members to join the Nazi Party; for the remainder of the regime's rule, the Nazi Party was the only legal party in Germany. In principle, Nazis sought to enroll all Germans from every social class in various party-affiliated organizations. With these steps toward constructing a one-party, mobilizing, authoritarian regime, German Nazism can be seen as similar to the fascism in Italy under Benito Mussolini and, to a lesser degree, Spain under Francisco Franco.

What separates Nazi Germany from other cases of fascism, however, is the world war it initiated and the genocide it committed. Widespread support for militarism and expansionism, especially to the east, were part of Hitler's initial program and appeal. Hitler prepared for war from the start and successfully annexed Austria in 1938 and the Sudetenland in Czechoslovakia in 1939 without provoking a military response from other countries. There is evidence that Hitler hoped to avoid having to fight until the middle 1940s, and many Germans believed that war, when it did come, would be short. Nevertheless, the German invasion of Poland in September 1939 led the British and French to declare war. When German forces entered Paris in 1940, many Germans hoped for both victory and peace, but as the fighting dragged on over Britain and deep into Soviet Russia, this combined outcome became unlikely. From 1939 until the Nazi regime's fall in 1945, Germany, Europe, and the rest of the world's major powers were at war.

The Nazi regime undertook a brutal and virtually unique policy, the mass murder of civilians based on beliefs about their racial background, an outcome that both demands and evades explanation. The **Holocaust**, as the Nazi destruction of European Jewry is called, could not have gone forward without a combination of four factors: racist beliefs, the organizational capabilities of a modern state, a fascist political regime, and a leader who favored killing a whole people as a major policy objective in its own right, not just as a means to another end. Of the major fascist regimes of the period, only the Nazi regime carried out a campaign to exterminate all European Jews and people belonging to many other groups (Sinti and Roma, homosexuals, psychiatric patients, and the handicapped). In Italy, for example, the early fascist leadership openly included some people of Jewish descent, and Mussolini did not seek a campaign against Jews. Prior to the Holocaust, traditional forms of anti-Semitism were influential in Germany (but also throughout much of predominantly Christian Europe), as were modern, scientific forms of racism and population theories (these, too, were present elsewhere in Europe and in the United States). Other demagogues sought power in all of the major Western countries, but these potential leaders were less successful than Hitler. Taken alone or in various partial combinations, racist ideologies, modern states, authoritarian regimes, and murderous leaders have contributed to terrible outcomes throughout history and around the world, but the full combination of all four has so far come together only under Hitler's regime.

The choices made in the 1930s and early 1940s carried unintended consequences. Whereas many Junkers welcomed Hitler, although at arm's length, in a bid to maintain order in their rapidly changing society, the result of Nazism and its failure was the Junkers' elimination from a role in German politics. Germany lost its eastern territories to Poland and the Soviet Union, and the landed elite lost their grip on military and political power. World War II weakened all of the European powers, including Germany, and left two other powers at the top of the global military system: the Soviet Union and the United States. The global context of a bipolar, Cold War world was thus ushered into being by the developmental path and choices taken by Germany's political leaders.

Occupation (1945–1949), Division (1949–1990), and Unification (1990–)

Germany today is strongly democratic, capitalist, and internationally cooperative with other democratic, capitalist states. The radical transformation from its past took place in three basic steps. The victorious Allied powers occupied and administered Germany in four zones with virtually no central state apparatus from 1945 to 1949. Two new German states then emerged from the occupation: the Federal Republic of Germany (FRG), based on the American, British, and French zones in western Germany, and the German Democratic Republic (GDR), based on the Soviet zone in the east. The two-Germanies situation seemed destined to last for generations, yet a third period began with the fall of Soviet communism in Central Europe in 1989, the rapid collapse of the GDR, and the unification of the German states in 1990.

Germany's place in the global arena changed decisively. During the Cold War, each of the German states was tied to one of the major powers. The FRG became one of the world's leading economic developers, albeit without its own offensive military capabilities. The economy of the GDR languished and remained tied to the less successful command economies of the Soviet bloc. The collapse of the Soviet Union sparked the final decay of the GDR. Reunited Germany now occupies a leading position within Europe – and its economy is a world-leader, but it still lacks a population comparable to that of the United States or China. Like all other major powers in the early twenty-first century, Germany lags far behind the United States in military power, especially in the ability to conduct large-scale military operations outside of its home territory. As we shall see, these changes in the global context influence the makeup of Germany's current interests, identities, and institutions, as well as its overall development path.

Interests in Contemporary Germany

Germany's economy ranks at the very top of the world's large, industrialized economies. According to the World Bank, Germany had the world's fifth-largest economy overall in 2013, as measured by its 3.2 trillion Gross Domestic Product (GDP-PPP); only the United States, China, India, and Japan had larger economies. The economy yielded a per capita GDP of $39,500. This average income per person is impressive, especially considering Germany's population of 81 million people. Only one country in the world has both a higher per capita GDP and a larger population, the United States ($52,800 per person, 319 million people).

Germany today benefits greatly from competing economically within the current system rather than attempting to subvert it through military force as it attempted to do earlier. Germany is a top-three exporter of goods and services. German exports in 2011 were valued at $1.4 trillion (surpassed only by the United States' $1.5 billion and China's $1.9 trillion). Whereas, prior to World War II, Germany had achieved impressive economic growth but still lacked the imperial success of Great Britain, now German economic and political ambitions seem well served by the current distribution of power. Germany is a member of the Organization for Economic Cooperation and Development (OECD) and a leader in the Group of Seven (G7), which is composed of the leaders from the world's eight largest economies. Several constraints on German sovereignty have been lifted since 1990 as a result of unification. The German-Polish border was finally settled at the **Oder-Neisse line**; the old Allies from World War II no longer occupy Berlin. Although Germany is a member of the United Nations, it still lacks a seat on the powerful Security Council, which includes, by contrast, Great Britain and France. A persistent constraint is that Germany does not govern a large internal market and needs to develop its reach through the European Union, through which it has created a large common market but not a unified system for taxing and government spending.

Within Europe, Germany was, along with France, one of the key states that pushed for greater economic and political cooperation in the European Union. In contrast with its own past, Germany adopted a radically new stance toward other European states. In order to avoid future military conflicts and to guide growing intra-European trade, West

German leaders supported the drive for closer economic and political cooperation among European countries. The FRG was one of the six founding members of the European Coal and Steel Community in 1951, and it was a major supporter of the Rome Treaties of 1957 that built the European Economic Community and related institutions of cooperation. During the 1970s and 1980s, the United States and Japanese economies put severe pressure on European industries. In response, West Germany took the lead, along with France, in pushing for a stronger European cooperation, notably in the Single European Act, which went into effect in 1987 and significantly reduced barriers to trade and institutional obstacles to Europe-wide political cooperation. Unified Germany in the 1990s supported the Treaty on European Union of 1992, which strengthened the EEC and other institutions, transforming them into the European Union. Germany also supported integrating new EU members during the 1990s and 2000s, so that the European Union now includes twenty-eight member countries, including most of the former communist countries in Central Europe.

As a whole, Germany's material interests lie in maintaining and working within the current world economic system. But that does not mean that all Germans have exactly the same interests. What are the various interests in Germany? Which interests emerged as dominant, and how do they seek to position Germany in the world economy?

One way to see the different interests in a society is to look at the major factors of production in the economy: labor, capital, and land. As you might expect, these factors have distinct interests. Owners of labor – that is, workers – favor low food prices and high wages. Owners of capital – factory owners – favor low food prices, low wages, and high prices for their own products. Owners of land favor low costs for labor and industrial products – the inputs for agricultural production – and high prices for agricultural products.

Since the end of World War II, the impact of the generally expanding world trade on these different interests has helped to sustain democratic and capitalist institutions in Germany. Productive labor and capital are both relatively abundant in Germany. The German workforce is highly skilled and productive. Germany imported more workers as immigrants, especially during the 1960s, and the German workforce remains one of the world's most technically adept. One problem was relatively high unemployment; it reached 10 percent in 1997, remained at 8 or 9 percent through 2003, hit 11 percent in 2005, but fell to just over 7 percent in 2010 – Germany has kept its unemployment lower than in most of its European neighbors. With regard to capital, Germany possesses a massive industrial base, some of which survived from before World War II but much of which was built after the war along highly efficient lines. To take one measure of Germany's capital abundance, in 1953 West Germany was the seventh most industrialized country in the world, measured by industrialization per capita, and by 1980 it was the third most industrialized country (behind only the United States and Sweden). German industry relies on being able to sell its goods in European and other foreign markets.

Germany, however, has a relatively scarce supply of agriculturally productive land; there are too many people and too small a territory. In West Germany, there were fully 414 people per square kilometer of arable land. By contrast, for example, in the land-abundant United States, there are only about 41 people per square kilometer of arable land. Agriculture adds just 1 percent to German GDP (whereas it adds 2 percent to the U.S. GDP and 3 percent to that of France); agriculture produces just 1 percent of Germany's merchandise exports (compared with 2 percent of U.S. merchandise exports). Thus, unlike industry and labor, most of German agriculture was not in a position to produce on a global scale at competitive prices; Germany could not meet its demand for agricultural products from domestic sources.

One can see the practical political effects of these economic interests in at least two ways. First, industry and labor have won the fight with agriculture to put Germany in the free-trade camp. German industry and labor now have strong interests in an open international trading system in which they use their strength to compete in a world market and avoid flooding their own market with too many goods. Given the size of these two sectors in Germany, their joint interests overrode those of the opposing agriculturalists, who would have preferred trade restrictions and higher food prices. As a result, the main political parties agree on the basic outlines of economic policy. The center-left Social Democratic Party, with a stronghold in the working class, favors free-trade industrialization. The center-right **Christian Democrats** (composed of the allied parties of the Christian Democratic Union and the Christian Social Union), with strong support from industrialists, also favor free-trade industrialization. Both have pushed for the reduction of trade barriers on a global scale and within Europe.

The second political impact of interests is that the main parties advocate even greater economic free trade and are willing to compensate the losers under this policy. Even during the late 1990s and late 2000s, when world financial crises unsettled global markets, the major political parties remained strongly in favor of the continued economic integration of Europe, including monetary union with other European countries. A major concession that the government regularly has to make in order to deepen European integration is to its farmers. As compensation to landowners and farmers for the losses caused by economic integration and free trade, to this day the European Union spends the bulk of its budget on support for farmers. Both of Germany's two main political parties have supported the relatively generous welfare provisions of the German state that cushion the blows of international economic competition and allow the employed workforce to maintain its high level of technical skills, albeit at the cost of relatively high rates of exit from the labor force and pension costs.

The social classes that make up German society come out of a tradition of stark class distinctions. However, the experiences of fascism, the post–World War II economic success, and now the transition to a service-oriented economy have dulled long-standing divisions. One can take the occupational composition of the workforce as a measure of changes in Germany's class structure. In 1950, 28 percent of workers were in agriculture or self-employed, 51 percent were manual workers (mostly in industry), and 21 percent were salaried, nonmanual workers (so-called white-collar and service workers). By 1994, only 10 percent were in agriculture or self-employed and only 38 percent were manual workers, whereas fully 52 percent were salaried, nonmanual workers. Thus, as in the rest of the industrialized world, Germany has developed a combined industrial and postindustrial social structure.

Identities in Contemporary Germany

Gradually, after World War II, antidemocratic values weakened. The failure to win world domination shook many people's faith in the fascist alternative to democracy. After the war, many Germans avoided overt politics and turned inward – toward family, work, and the pursuit of personal well-being – and abandoned a belief in grander political ends. The relative economic success of the West German economy during the 1950s and 1960s reinforced the value placed on the pursuit of prosperity.

Support for democracy has grown. In a 1950 survey, German respondents were asked about political competition. Fully 25 percent said that it is better for a country to have only one political party, and another 22 percent were undecided about this question or gave no response. A bare majority, just 53 percent, said that it is better for a country to have several parties. It would be hard to say that a political culture is democratic if such a slight majority of people believe that political competition among parties is a good idea. Things have changed, however. In a 1990 survey, just 3 percent of respondents said that it is better to have only one party, and only 8 percent were undecided or gave no response. The overwhelming preponderance of respondents, 89 percent, stated that it is better for a country to have several political parties.

A strong faith in democracy developed at the elite and mass levels. The German political philosopher Jürgen Habermas has described "constitutional patriotism" as the ultimate political value. Support for democracy is also reflected in public-opinion polls. In a survey carried out in the 1990s, 50 percent of respondents in Germany stated that they were "very satisfied" or "fairly satisfied" with the way democracy worked in Germany, 37 percent stated they were "not very satisfied," and only 11 percent were "not at all satisfied." Although this measure of support for democracy was not as high as in the United Kingdom – where 61 percent reported that they were "very" or "fairly satisfied" – the distribution of responses to this question in Germany was about average among EU countries. There were important differences between the former East Germany and West Germany: only 30 percent of respondents in the former East stated that they were "very" or "fairly satisfied," compared with 55 percent in the former West. The indicators of public opinion suggest that there is widespread support for human rights as a basic value and broad support for the current version of democratic institutions in Germany.

Still, the 81 million people living in Germany do not share a single identity. One dimension on which Germans differ is how they situate themselves with respect to the rest of Europe and the possibility of a European identification that transcends national identifications. In a survey conducted in the late 1990s, 49 percent of respondents said that they consider themselves to be "German only." Another 35 percent of respondents said that they considered themselves to be "German and European." Seven percent said that they considered themselves "European and German," and 5 percent chose "European only." The distribution of national versus European identity in Germany was about average for the EU countries. Among the bigger countries, German national identity is located halfway between the weak national identity in France (where just 31 percent chose

"French only") and the strong national identity in the United Kingdom (where 60 percent chose "British only").

Many Germans are relatively new residents of the German state, and this also leads to varied identities. In the post–World War II period from 1949 to 1989, while Germany was divided, approximately 13 million refugees whom the FRG identified as ethnically German arrived from Poland, the Soviet Union, and the GDR. The territory of the GDR in 1948 was home to about 19 million people. The GDR's population shrank during the decades of division, mostly because of legal and illegal migration to the FRG. In 1989 alone, some 344,000 people from the GDR left for the FRG, along with 376,000 ethnic-background Germans from the Soviet Union and elsewhere in Eastern Europe. As mentioned earlier, what was left of the GDR's population, 16 million people, came under FRG control in 1990. The nearly automatic right of ethnic-background Germans to immigrate and acquire German citizenship was curbed partially in the 1990s and early 2000s with requirements to prove German language abilities and cultural assimilation.

Many people who live in Germany are considered by the German state to be foreigners; indeed, there are more foreigners in Germany than in any other European country. In the mid-2000s, over 10 million people living in Germany were born elsewhere (12.5 percent of Germany's total population, comparable to the 12.3 percent figure for the United States and above the median 9 percent for other European countries, according to OECD data). About 7.3 million people were citizens of other countries (8.9 percent of the population, the largest percentage for any big OECD country and above the OECD median of 5 percent). Many people from Turkey and southern Europe (the former Yugoslavia, Greece, and Italy) arrived during the 1960s under the government's policy of encouraging the temporary migration of foreigners to work in German industries that needed more labor. Almost a million people left Germany during the 1970s when the government provided incentives for foreign workers and their families to leave Germany, yet most of the immigrants did not leave. The single largest group of foreign citizens in Germany is from Turkey; other large groups of foreign nationals are from Italy, Greece, and Poland.

Although there are signs of change toward a more permanent official status, the conventional term for foreign workers in the 1950s and 1960s, "**guest workers**" (***Gastarbeiter***), underscored the state's attempt to emphasize the temporary nature of their stay in Germany, despite their growing and deep involvement in the German economy and society. Many of the hardships faced by these immigrant groups are common to the experience of immigrant laborers in other industrialized countries: low wages, dangerous employment, few opportunities for advancement, racism, victimization by crime, discrimination in housing and employment, and the near-constant threat of legal deportation. The difficult situation of many immigrants considered nonethnic Germans is exacerbated by their exclusion from political rights. It was virtually impossible for foreign workers, or even their children, to earn the right to vote, become a citizen, or run for public office. The *jus sanguinus* legal tradition of defining citizenship by descent, rather than by place of birth, remains strong. A child born in Germany to two non-German parents does not automatically have German citizenship. A 1999 reform allowed a child of non-German parents to apply for and acquire German citizenship if at least one parent has held a permanent resident permit for three years and has actually resided in Germany for eight years.

Religious identities among the Christian and formerly Christian population are roughly evenly divided among Protestants, Catholics, and those who declare themselves unaffiliated, with about 26 million people in each group (in addition there are 900,000 Orthodox Christians, mainly immigrants from Greece and Serbia). Protestants are predominant in the old East (where Protestantism had long prevailed); the nonreligious are more prevalent there as well (in the aftermath of a secularizing, Communist regime).

There are growing groups of Jews and Muslims. A 1925 census recorded almost 565,000 Jews in the Weimar Republic. Just several thousand German Jews survived the Holocaust, and only about thirty thousand Jewish people lived in Germany in the 1980s, predominantly in Berlin. With the collapse of Communism in the east, many Jews from the Baltic countries and the former Soviet Union moved to Germany and the Jewish population has grown to just over a hundred thousand people by the mid-2000s (according to German government statistics). There were fewer than 7,000 Muslims in the FRG in 1961; by the second decade of the twenty-first century, Germany had over 4 million Muslim residents, constituting about 5 percent of the population.

Muslims constitute an exceptionally heterogeneous and diverse group. A majority of Muslims in Germany are Sunni, around 65 percent, and there are also Alevites, Imamites, and some Turkish Shiites. Most of the approximately 2.4 million Turkish-origin residents of Germany, including several hundred thousand Kurds, are Muslim. There are approximately 600,000 Muslims from Bosnia-Herzegovina and Albania, North Africa, and the Arab Middle East. Around 100,000 are Iranian, stemming from the flight of more secular Muslims from Iran beginning in the 1980s. Around 2 percent of Muslims are German converts to Islam. Germany's Muslims hold diverse views and values. In a 2006 Pew Global Attitudes survey, the greatest concern of Germany's Muslims was unemployment – 56 percent said they were very worried about this; other religious and cultural matters ranked much lower – 23 percent of Muslim respondents were very worried about extremism and only 18 percent were very worried about the decline of religion. Half of the Muslim respondents said that there was a struggle between extremist and moderate Muslims in Germany; among those who saw a struggle, 14 percent said they identified with the extremists.

The identities of men and women with respect to gender roles are changing, too. Germany emerged from World War II with gender identities rooted in the past. In the FRG, the law still reflected greater rights for men than for women, especially in regard to marriage and property. In the GDR, strict legal equality was undermined by pervasive informal occupational segregation by gender. Nearly 90 percent of women in the communist East had worked outside of the home, whereas not even half of women did in the West. Pay and working conditions were better in the West, but the advancement of women into the higher ranks of important professions remained slow. A movement for women's rights developed during the 1970s in the FRG, as in virtually all Western democracies. By force of example, this movement has changed how men and women think of themselves. Institutional changes have reinforced these new conditions, although not as dramatically as in some other countries. Abortion laws were almost liberalized in the 1970s but were turned back by a conservative majority on the Constitutional Court, which cited right-to-life provisions in the Basic Law. After unification, the differences in abortion laws between West and East proved to be a difficult political issue and negotiators agreed to allow temporarily different laws in the former East and West. The liberal abortion law for the East finally expired in 1992, and a moderately pro-choice, all-German law was declared unconstitutional in 1993, again by a more conservative Constitutional Court. The parliament crafted a new compromise law in 1995 that fits the court's ruling; most abortions are technically illegal, but no one can be prosecuted, and public funds may be used if the woman falls below an income threshold. There is substantial variation in the practical availability of abortion services from state to state. Many women seeking abortions travel within Germany or to neighboring countries such as the Netherlands.

Institutions in Contemporary Germany

The founding document of the Federal Republic of Germany is the 1949 Basic Law (*Grundgesetz*), which officially became the Constitution of the United German People in October 1990. Between 1949 and 1990, although political actors used it much like a constitution, the Basic Law was usually not called a constitution, given the prominent role that the occupying Western powers had in its formulation and the reluctance to recognize as permanent the division of Germany into two parts. Under the Western occupation, political life began to reemerge mainly at the regional rather than the national level. In September 1948, the Allied military governors and provincial leaders convened a constituent assembly of sixty-five delegates to draft a provisional constitution. The aims of the framers were to avoid the perceived weaknesses of the Weimar system, to prevent a renewed fascist movement, and to lock western Germany into the Western alliance. The resulting document strengthened the chancellor and the legislature over the bureaucracy and army, and it decentralized power to the various regional governments. The framers placed the rule of law and basic liberal institutions at the very heart of the system. Their proposed Basic Law was ratified by regional parliaments in May 1949. It has been amended several times, and its provisional character has faded; it was not replaced during unification, but rather its terms were used to incorporate the former East Germany into the FRG.

The two largest political parties in post–World War II West Germany grew out of the Christian Democratic and Socialist camps from the Weimar era in radically new ways. The Christian Democratic Union (Christlich-Demokratische Union, CDU) and the Christian Social Union (Christlich-Soziale Union, CSU) comprise the Christian Democratic camp. Although officially two parties, most political scientists consider them to function as one party for they do not nominate candidates to compete in the same district; the CSU contests elections in predominantly Catholic Bavaria, whereas the CDU contests them in the rest of the FRG. The two parties are often referred to collectively as the CDU/CSU. A major transformation is that the CDU explicitly sought support from Protestants as well as Catholics. Various Christian Democratic parties won local elections in the occupied zones after World War II, and many of them came together once CDU leader Konrad Adenauer became chancellor with the support of the CSU. The CDU/CSU supporters were not just former Center Party voters but also those who had supported liberal and socialist parties in the past. A second major transformation was that the party, especially Economics Minister Ludwig Erhard, who later became chancellor himself, strongly championed free-market economics. The CDU/CSU has been a center-right party, advocating capitalism with strong social protections, close ties to the United States and other Western powers, and strong anticommunism. It formed every government, in coalition with other parties, from 1949 to 1966, from 1982 to 1998, and from 2005.

The Social Democratic Party (Sozialdemokratische Partei Deutschlands, SPD) was reshaped by the unexpected post–World War II successes of the CDU/CSU and the SPD's long years in opposition until 1966. The party emerged from the Nazi-era ban on its activities as the best-organized party in occupied Germany. Yet its failure to win elections during the 1950s convinced its leading figures, such as future chancellors Willy Brandt and Helmut Schmidt, of the need to break from its reliance on orthodox Marxist rhetoric and almost exclusively working-class support. With major reforms at the 1959 Bad Godesberg party conference, the SPD officially stated a new policy of reaching out to religious believers and to middle-class voters, changes that gradually began to have their effect on voters, who gave the SPD increasing support in the early 1960s. The successful participation of the SPD in the Grand Coalition government with the CDU from 1966 to 1969 demonstrated the ability of its leading figures to manage the economy and politics in pro-democratic and pro-capitalist ways and paved the way for its electoral success in 1969 and the formation of its own governing coalition with the Free Democratic Party through 1982. It returned to power in coalition with the Green party from 1998 to 2005.

Two medium-sized parties have played pivotal roles in modern German politics as well. The Free Democratic Party (Freie Demokratische Partei, FDP) stands for individualism and free economic competition. In the immediate post–World War II years, the party was formed by Weimar-era liberals, although the anticlerical emphasis of German liberalism was pared away to leave the focus on free-market economics. Although the FDP has never polled more than 15 percent of the vote in national elections, it has frequently been able to give one of the two larger parties the necessary support to form a government. With roots in the environmentalist and antinuclear social movements in the 1970s, another party, the Greens, first won parliamentary representation in the 1983 elections. For much of the 1980s, the party was divided into a fundamentalist faction that advocated far-reaching reforms to reject capitalist development and to protect the environment, and a realist faction advocating less drastic reform while working within the system. After reunification in 1990, the Greens joined with Bundnis90, former East German counterparts who had been leading dissidents under the GDR, but the alliance between the wealthier and poorer partners has not been smooth. The Greens served in government as a junior coalition partner with the SPD following the 1998 and 2002 elections.

Some other parties have won seats in the **Bundestag** (the lower house of parliament), although not participation in the formation of a government. The Party of Democratic Socialism (PDS) attained thirty-six seats in 1998; it had been formed by leading figures from the former Communist Party of the GDR such as Gregor Gysi, and won in districts of the former East Germany, mainly with support from older voters dissatisfied with the rapid pace of postunification change. The PDS performed poorly in the 2002 elections, winning just two seats, and merged with other left groups in the former West Germany to form the new Left Party, which went on to win fifty-four seats in 2005. The far-right National Democratic Party of Germany – The People's Union (NPD) won less than 2 percent of the vote in 2009 and no seats in parliament, although it has performed better in some regional elections. The closest it came to surpassing the 5 percent threshold for winning seats in the Bundestag was in 1969, when it won 4.6 percent.

In part because of the Basic Law's well-crafted institutional design, Germany has sustained its political democracy since 1949. At the most basic level, Germany qualifies as a political democracy because all of the major actors in German society expect that elections for the highest offices in the state will be held on a regular basis into the foreseeable future. This situation contrasts with the Weimar Republic, where many leading political actors either sought to end the practice of elections or at least reasonably expected that elections would be suspended at some point. According to the Basic Law of 1949, elections to the national legislature are held every four years. (The Basic Law's exceptions to this rule occur when the legislature is deadlocked. If this happens, it provides for the **federal president** [**Bundespräsident**] to call early elections. So far, this has happened only twice, in 1972 and 1982.) The intervals between German national elections are not quite as regularly spaced as election intervals in presidential systems, such as the United States, but they are more regular than in other parliamentary systems, such as that of the United Kingdom.

For the most part, the powers of the president are severely restricted compared with the relatively powerful role for the president under the Weimar system. Although the president is the official head of state, the president's powers are mainly restricted to the calling of elections and ceremonial functions, and one person can serve for no more than two terms as president. The president can pardon criminals and receives and visits other heads of state. The president promulgates all federal laws with a signature (the authority to refuse to sign is disputed, and presidents have signed all but perhaps five laws). The president is not popularly elected. According to the Basic Law, every five years a special federal convention convenes for the sole purpose of selecting the president; it is composed of the delegates to the legislature, an equal number of representatives from the state assemblies, and several other prominent persons. The selection by the federal convention has so far led to presidents with moderate views, at the end of distinguished careers and well respected by the political elite. Johannes Rau began serving his presidential term in July 1999 at the age of sixty-eight; he had previously served as the deputy national chairman of the Socialist Party and as prime minister of Germany's largest state, North-Rhine-Westphalia. His 2004 successor, sixty-one-year-old Horst Kohler, was chosen by the majority in the federal convention held by parties in opposition to the SPD-Green government – the CDU/CSU and the FDP. Trained as an economist and political scientist, Kohler served in the economics and finance ministries of CDU governments, rising to deputy minister of finance from 1990 to 1993, during which time he helped to negotiate the Maastricht treaty on European Economic and Monetary Union and undertook major responsibilities for the process of German unification. Some presidents have been able to influence national debates by means of skillful speech making,

Table 5.1   German Chancellors since World War II

1949–1963	Konrad Adenauer (CDU)
1963–1966	Ludwig Erhard (CDU)
1966–1969	Kurt Georg Kiesinger (CDU)
1969–1974	Willy Brandt (SPD)
1974–1982	Helmut Schmidt (SPD)
1982–1998	Helmut Kohl (CDU)
1998–2005	Gerhard Schröder (SPD)
2005–	Angela Merkel (CDU)

as when Richard von Weizsacker (president 1984–1994; CDU) gave a 1985 speech commemorating the fortieth anniversary of the end of World War II that cautioned Germans not to forget the nation's past and to guard against a revival of nationalist sentiment. Kohler, however, resigned just months into his second term when he faced criticism for advocating more vigorous use of military force to protect German trade interests abroad, and his successor, Christian Wulff, resigned in his second year over allegations of corruption in his previous government position.

The **federal chancellor** (**Bundeskanzler**) is the real executive power in the German system. Although the chancellor is responsible to the legislature, as in other parliamentary systems, he or she may appoint and dismiss other cabinet ministers at will, rather like U.S. presidents. The relatively regular interval between elections gives the chancellor a somewhat firm idea about the political struggles that lie ahead and enhances the authority of the legislature and the chancellor over that of the president. Another source of the chancellor's authority is Article 67 of the Basic Law, the so-called **constructive vote of no confidence**, which states that the legislature may dismiss the chancellor only when a majority of the members simultaneously elects a successor. This brake on the authority of the legislature helps prevent weak chancellors from emerging. For example, the only time that a constructive vote of no confidence succeeded was in 1982, when the Free Democratic Party (FDP) withdrew from the ruling coalition and went along with a vote of no confidence regarding Social Democratic Party (SPD) Chancellor Helmut Schmidt (Table 5.1). A new FDP and CDU/CSU coalition in the legislature selected Helmut Kohl as chancellor. With a majority behind him from the beginning and with several election victories thereafter, Kohl served as chancellor from 1982 until 1998. In other parliamentary governments, legislatures can agree to dismiss a sitting government but then may fail to agree on a strong successor, agreeing instead only to select weak figures unable to take real initiatives on their own.

The lower house (Bundestag) of the bicameral legislature produces the executive. The lower house is directly elected, whereas the upper house (**Bundesrat**) is composed of delegates chosen by the sixteen federal states (*Länder*). The leader of the largest party in the lower house usually puts together a two-party coalition (neither of the two largest parties controls a majority of seats alone); the coalition in turn supports the party leader as chancellor. The chancellor must maintain a legislative majority in order to stay in power. With majority support, however, the chancellor has a relatively free hand in appointing and dismissing members of the cabinet. For example, the Social Democratic Party won the single largest block of seats in the 1998 and 2002 elections; after each election, its leader, Gerhard Schröder, formed a coalition with the Green Party to control a majority of seats. His cabinets were dominated by SPD politicians, but some key posts were given to Green Party politicians, notably the post of foreign minister to Joschka Fischer. After the 2005 elections, neither of the two big parties could form a majority alone or in coalition with one of the smaller parties; the government was formed by a new grand coalition of the SPD and the CDU/CSU with Angela Merkel (CDU) as chancellor. After the 2009 elections, The CDU/CSU kept Merkel in power by dropping the declining SPD and forming a new coalition with the rising FDP.

The rules for translating votes into seats comprise a crucial institution in any democracy. Germany employs a mixed-member proportional formula (a subtype of proportional representation). Each voter makes **two ballot choices** in a national German election for representatives in the lower house. One choice is for a candidate to represent the voter's district. The winning candidates in each district take half the seats in the lower house. A voter's second choice is for a national party overall in the lower house. The other half of the seats are awarded such that the proportion of seats per party matches the votes per party on the second ballot choice. The two types of representatives give the system its mixed-member label; once in place, however, the two types of members behave the same and have identical powers in the legislature.

Germany's mixed-member proportional system preserves the influence of medium-sized and large parties and minimizes the impact of small parties with widely dispersed supporters. Germany's medium-sized parties gain national representation via the second ballot choice more easily than under a plurality electoral system, in which the voter makes only one choice for a given office and the top vote-getter in a district wins the office (as is the case in the United States and United Kingdom). Most notably, two German parties have won seats in the legislature by securing a national vote of more than 5 percent on the second ballot choice, even though their candidates did not win any districts on the first ballot choice. The Free Democrats have been a crucial player in legislative politics since 1949, while typically winning about 10 percent of the popular vote. Similarly, the Greens have become almost as influential since the 1980s although securing only around 5 to 10 percent of the popular vote. Grand-coalition governments of the SPD and the CDU/CSU ruled from 1966 to 1969 and from 2005 to 2009, but every other coalition government has involved one of the big parties with one of the medium-sized parties.

The big winners in the electoral system are the two largest parties. Germany's electoral system includes several special rules, two of which aid the largest parties. One is the "5 percent rule": a party must win at least 5 percent of the national vote on the second ballot choice in order to get a matching share of seats. Thus, small parties with support distributed across many districts are eliminated from gaining representation (for instance, the extreme right-wing Republican Party won 3 percent of the national second-choice vote but no seats in 1994; similar results emerged in 1998 and 2002). Even the medium-sized parties, the Free Democrats and the Greens, are perennially concerned about falling below the 5 per-cent threshold; their coalition partners in government have periodically advocated strate-gic voting in order to ensure that the medium-sized parties do not fall below that mark. During the SPD-FDP coalition of 1969–1982, SPD supporters offered crucial support to the FDP on their second ballot choice; in 1998, the FDP relied upon second ballot choices of CDU supporters, while the Greens relied upon second ballot choices of SPD supporters. The 5 percent threshold thus increases the reliance of the medium-sized parties on their larger partners.

A second important rule is the "three-district waiver" exception to the 5 percent rule: if a party wins a seat in at least three districts, then the national 5 percent rule is waived, and the party is also awarded seats according to its share of the total vote on the second ballot choice. This second modification permitted the former East German Communist Party, campaigning as the Party of Democratic Socialism, to win national representation after unification in the elections of the 1990s, based on its victories in the former East Berlin, despite its very small national vote share. This second modification is the only one that aids very small parties, and it comes into play only if the small party's supporters are concen-trated in a few districts. In 2002, the PDS won only two districts and thus did not qualify for additional seats by the three-district waiver. By the 2005 election, the PDS had formed an alliance with a small extreme-left party in former West Germany and together they won 8.7 percent of the vote and fifty-four seats. In 2009, the alliance had reformed as The Left Party (*Die Linke*) and won 11.9 percent and seventy-six seats.

Finally, the "excess mandate provision" holds that if a party wins more district man-dates than the proportion of the popular vote on the second choice would otherwise award the party, then the party gets to retain any extra seats, and the size of the legislature is increased accordingly. Although of relatively little consequence for most of the Federal Republic's electoral history, the excess mandate provision during the 1990s began to help the big parties that win seats in many districts. It gave the CDU six extra seats in 1990, and then in 1994 gave the CDU twelve extra seats and the SPD four. In 2005, the CDU received nine and the SPD received seven so-called overhang seats. In 2009, the CDU/CSU won all twenty-two overhang seats.

All of these rules, combined with the way voters actually cast their ballots, produce gov-ernments. To take a specific example, the 2002 elections gave five parties seats in the lower house: Social Democratic Party (SPD), 251 seats; Christian Democratic Union (CDU)/ Christian Social Union (CSU), 248 seats; Bundnis90/Greens, 55 seats; Free Democratic Party (FDP), 47 seats; Party of Democratic Socialism (PDS) – socialist, former communist – 2 seats. Over a dozen other parties were on ballots in one or more states but did not qualify for national representation. As in previous elections, the extreme right-wing parties were fragmented and ineffectual at the national level. These seat totals for the five parties in the legislature produced an eleven-seat majority for the SPD-Green alliance, so SPD Chancellor Schröder remained in power, although he shuffled some individual cabinet posts.

Voter support for the SPD has mostly been falling since the 1980s and especially since 2002. In 2005, the SPD came in second, receiving 34.2 percent of the vote compared to 35.2 percent for the CDU/CSU. It had to enter into coalition as the junior partner in a grand-coalition government, giving the chancellorship to CDU-leader Angela Merkel. In the 2009 elections, support for the SPD collapsed to just 23 percent, the lowest level in post–World War II history. Support for the CDU/CSU declined only slightly, to 33.8 percent; it formed a new coalition with the FDP, allowing Merkel to remain in power. The three medium-size parties all achieved their best-ever results in 2009: 14.6 percent for the FDP, 11.9 percent for the Left Party (successor to the PDS and a break-away faction from the SPD), and 10.6 percent for the Greens. A critical issue is which parties voters will support as Germany copes with the great recession and its aftermath.

The elections of 2013 provided the first indications of how the parties are faring in the new economic situation. The SPD maintained its hold on second place, gaining 25.7 percent. Angela Merkel's CDU/CSU won a stunning 41.5 percent, which brought her within five seats of a majority. Merkel formed a new grand coalition of the CDU/CSU with the SPD to support a new government. The medium-size parties fared poorly, especially the FDP, which received only 4.8 percent and thus no seats at all. Vote shares for the Left and the Bundnis90/Greens were between eight and nine percent, still enough to secure seats in the Bundestag, although fewer than in 2009. The strongly anti-EU party, Alternative for Germany (AfD), climbed to 4.7 percent, almost overtaking the FDP. The coming years will test the ability of the main parties to govern in difficult economic times and keep anti-EU sentiment in check.

As we have seen, Germany's bicameral system can provide other opportunities for the opposition and their supporters despite a government's majority in the lower house. The opposition was able to play a strong role in influencing Schröder's sweeping economic reform plans in 2003 after elections in the states of Hesse and Lower Saxony in February of that year gave victories to the CDU; with the CDU in power in those states, their delegates to the Bundesrat gave a majority to opposition parties. The final legislation agreed to in December 2003 required the government to compromise from its original proposals.

Germany's federal structure gives the republic's constituent units a great deal of power. Sixteen states make up the republic. The combination of federalism in the state and bicameralism in the legislature gives Germany a substantial amount of institutional overlap that differs both from unitary systems (such as in the United Kingdom and France) and from other federal systems that have sharper federal-state distinctions (such as in the United States). Compared with regional governments in Europe, the states possess a good deal of power in relation to the central government. Each state has a premier and a legislature. The state legislatures send delegates to the assembly that elects the president and also send delegates to the national legislature's upper house (the Bundesrat). The Basic Law reserves certain powers for the states, including education, police and internal security, administration of justice, and the regulation of mass media. The states are also responsible for administering federal laws and collecting most taxes. Changes since the Basic Law of 1949 have been designed to enhance or at least preserve the states' powers. They now have at least a joint role in higher education, regional economic development, and agricultural reform.

Reforms in 1994 were designed to give the various states a voice in policy making at the European level; until then, the federal government had a larger role to play.

The Basic Law recognizes freedom of religion, but Article 140 grants important public authority to religious institutions that had exercised such authority under the Weimar Republic. Most notably, Lutheran and Catholic churches are granted "public corporation" status that includes, among its key features, a provision that the government directs a percentage of the tax payments from persons who identify with these religions to their respective churches (the amounts are substantial – about 8–10 percent of what individuals owe in taxes). Individual states make decisions on granting public corporation status to other religions, and they have done so for several Christian sects and Jews. In contrast, no Muslim organization has been awarded public corporation status.

There are hundreds of Muslim organizations in Germany, many with strongly competing goals and values. Several high-profile efforts to form single, umbrella organizations for Muslims have failed to incorporate key groups and/or have splintered soon after their formation. In the 1970s and 1980s, the federal government relied mainly upon organizations associated with the Turkish state to manage the affairs of Muslims in Germany, notably the Turkish State Directorate for Religious Affairs. The competing organizational network of political Islam in Germany was the Islamic Community Milli Görüs, organized by Turkish Muslims who opposed the secularizing character of the official organization. Beginning in the 1990s, however, German governments have sought to co-opt and to incorporate both types of organizations into German-centered institutions. Several states have established special councils for state-Islam relations and the federal government – especially through the Ministry of the Interior, the courts, and the Federal Office for the Protection of the Constitution (Bundesamt für Verfassungsschutz) – has attempted to nationalize the political and religious organization of Muslims in Germany. In November 2006, the Interior Ministry launched the German Conference on Islam (*Deutsche Islam Konferenz, DIK*), a formal venue for negotiation and communication between the federal government and officials in organizations of Muslims living in Germany. The government dropped members linked to Milli Görüs from the *DIK* and undertook a second term of activities in 2010. The process is slow, but the German government is forging stronger official partnerships with Muslim organizations.

The economy itself can be seen as an institution, especially because its key actors are linked in stable relationships that go beyond mere monetary exchange. Many terms have been used to describe the economy of the Federal Republic of Germany: neo-corporatism, social democracy, and coordinated market economy, to name three important ones. These terms seek to capture Germany's blend of social and market institutions in a single economy. In fact, a term that Germans commonly use to describe their economic order is a "**social market economy.**" A social market economy rests not only on market principles of supply and demand but also on extensive involvement by the state and societal institutions. Germany has institutions that are designed to ensure the smooth functioning of free economic exchange. Prior to the European Monetary Union, Germany's central bank, for example, was for a long time one of the most independent and powerful central banks in the world. In fact, Germany's central bank was the main model for the European Central Bank.

Germany's bank sought to keep interest rates and inflation low and the currency stable. There is no purer example of a firm commitment to market principles than a central bank free of political influence. On the social side of the equation, the German state guarantees a free university education for all who qualify academically, and basic health care and adequate income for all its citizens. In addition, the state supports organized representation in the workplace and vocational training for workers, rather than letting these matters be handled by firms or unions alone.

At the heart of Germany's social market economy is the "social partnership" of business and labor. According to the political scientist Lowell Turner, social partnership is defined as "the nexus – and central political and economic importance – of bargaining relationships between strongly organized employers (in employer associations) and employees (in unions and works councils) that range from comprehensive collective bargaining and plant-level co-determination to vocational training and federal, state and local economic policy discussions." In addition to labor and business, there are also important "framing and negotiating roles" for two other actors: large banks and the government. In this kind of system, negotiated agreements between the social partners of business and labor shape politics and economics at all levels: national, regional, and local. As an example of national peak agreements, one could point to the Concerted Action of 1967 or the Solidarity Pact in 1993. There are also industry-wide or simply firm-level agreements regarding, for example, vocational training and industrial policy.

The Solidarity Pact of 1993 nicely illustrates a peak bargain under social partnership. The federal government agreed not to let old industries in the former East Germany simply wither away. Instead, it sought an active role for itself in industrial restructuring. Eastern industries benefited from temporary assistance, as did labor, because employment was protected. Western industrialists were also given opportunities for developing infrastructure (such as roads, railroads, and government offices), while they promised to invest in the old eastern industrial core rather than simply dismantling it and confining their production to the already developed western regions. Unions, in return, promised to hold back wage demands in both the East and West and promised to support the program of adjustment in the East rather than adopt a posture of militant opposition. Although this bargain worked to the benefit of all sides, it was the product of institutionalized negotiation, not simple economic logic.

Scholars and policy makers do not agree on the future of German social partnership. In the view of many, the Solidarity Pact of 1993 was just an isolated episode in a period more noted for conflicting interests. The early 1990s witnessed a new phase of economic globalization: Would the institutions of social partnership survive the neoliberal economic policy atmosphere? Would they hold up against rapid financial movements across international borders? Could they be maintained in the face of widening international economic competition as the costs of communication and transportation continued to fall? During the early 1990s, it was plausible that Germany's more moderate social partnership would succumb to the new conditions. Unemployment rose to over 10 percent in late 1995 and grew to over 12 percent in early 1997. Because unions typically find it difficult to maintain their bargaining position in the face of persistent joblessness among workers, German unions will likely find it hard to sustain their influential role. Furthermore, the integration of European economies weakens the position of national-level actors, especially labor unions.

Others are more optimistic that German social partnership may be resilient after all. Although recognizing the difficulties facing partnership, especially the challenges facing organized labor, one can point to more positive signs. In the first place, the eastern decay has not spread to the West; instead Western institutions have spread to the former East Germany. Employer associations, industrial unions, comprehensive collective-bargaining arrangements, elected works councils, and legally mandated codetermination have all taken root in the old East. The economic integration of the East, although not complete and not as painless as Chancellor Helmut Kohl argued it would be in 1990, certainly has not led to an economic collapse. According to these optimists, few companies actually relocated to low-wage countries during the 1980s. They further maintain that there will likely be little relocation to the East during the next few decades. Investment in the East, moreover, may serve to stimulate demand for exports from Germany and may also open up even more markets for German goods. In addition to these favorable trends, the international financial crises of the late 1990s – first in Asia, then in Russia, and then in Latin America – dampened enthusiasm for unregulated free markets, even among global investors. In times of uncertainty, many international financial decision makers sought the greater security provided by more institutionalized forms of industrial organization. European Union institutions leave a great deal of leeway to national-level institutions, by the principle of "subsidiarity" (the notion that decisions should be made at the most local level possible), and because each individual government, especially governments of big countries such as Germany, has a major say in what happens at the European level. Finally, Germany's major firms have actually sought to preserve key elements of its social market economy, such as their successful efforts to maintain policies of generously supported early retirement for workers.

Unemployment above 11 percent and poor economic performance were cited by the Schröder government as the reasons for major cuts in social spending and labor-market reforms in 2003. Although key reforms did pass, making it easier for firms to hire workers without providing them protections against firing, for example, two key features of the German labor market did not change: sectorwide wage agreements and workers' codetermination. Both of these institutions involve businesses, labor unions, workers' elected representatives, and the state in managing change on the shop floors of Germany's leading industries. Thus, even as Germany's Social Democratic and Green coalition governing parties attempted to put forward major changes in the state and the economy, the core features of social partnership continued to play key roles.

The new German judiciary and the legal philosophy of the state is the product of a deliberate attempt by post–Nazi era political actors to transform radically an institution that had not protected basic civil and human rights. On the side of institutional redesign, the Basic Law created a Federal Constitutional Court with the power of judicial review. The practice of judges reviewing state actions for conformity with a higher law – in this case, the Basic Law – was completely foreign to the German legal tradition before 1949. The change was strongly championed by the U.S. occupiers, who had at their disposal the model of the U.S. Supreme Court and who were clearly thinking of the old German judiciary that did not strike down any of the Nazi government's decrees.

A distinctive and controversial aspect of German law and legal institutions, however, concerns what Americans would call freedom of speech. Unlike in the United States, "hate speech" is unconstitutional in Germany, and the organizations that promote it are banned after being investigated by the Federal Office for the Protection of the Constitution. It is illegal, for example, to organize a Nazi party, to deny publicly the historical fact of the Holocaust, or to sell or distribute Nazi propaganda. How does the German state justify actions and policies that Americans would consider unacceptable, and even unconstitutional, departures from liberal democratic practices? Germans view their democracy as a "militant democracy" that is unwilling to permit antidemocratic forces to use the protections of the liberal state to help undermine it. These ideas and the institutions that are in place to back them up are one obvious reaction to Germany's authoritarian past.

The German judiciary nevertheless also shows some continuity in its institutional practices. On the side of persistence, German judges are closely integrated with the state bureaucracy, and their posts are like those of high bureaucrats. They are rarely former politicians, prosecutors, or other types of attorneys, as is often the case in the United States. Instead, aspiring jurists begin their careers as apprentices to sitting judges; they then rise through the hierarchy and, if they are successful, never leave the judicial branch. The dominant institutional philosophy of judging puts the judge in the role of actively applying the law to individual cases in a deliberate pursuit of the truth, unlike U.S. judges, who more commonly see themselves as impartial arbiters between two conflicting parties. German judges do not set precedents as do their Anglo-American counterparts; the job of German judges is simply to apply the law correctly, not interpret it or adapt it to circumstances unforeseen by the framers of a statute. Despite the otherwise federal structure of the judiciary, the German legal code is uniform across all of the various state governments.

Germany's Post–World War II Developmental Path

Whereas Germany had relied upon state-led development for most of its unified history, the post–World War II German state acted as a cooperative partner in social and economic development. The FRG itself led much of the world's post–World War II economic growth, partly financed internationally by the U.S. Marshall Plan for European recovery. Germany's economic development was grounded domestically in close cooperation among top businesses, organized labor unions, and the state. The state still influences Germany's society and economy through institutions similar to those found in many other European countries. The economic slowdown and persistent unemployment in the early twenty-first century present challenges for governments that are seeking to streamline the state and energize economic growth, yet Germany today is still a model for those seeking to strike a new balance between the strengths of the free market and the support of significant social protections. In its foreign economic policy, Germany promotes deep economic integration with world markets and especially within an expanded European Union. In foreign security policy, Cold War Germany was the forward base of U.S. power in Europe. Germany remains a key U.S. ally in the early twenty-first century, although it advocates greater multilateralism when confronting terrorists and rogue states around the world.

Germany's path of political development was profoundly shaped by its long period as a middle developer (see Table 5.2 at the end of the chapter). Germany began much like the rest of Europe. Yet, compared with England and France, Germany's lateness in developing a single territorial state and a strong industrial base, and then new challenges from even later developers, such as Russia, put Germany in a difficult position. Germany was also a relatively large middle developer, like Japan, and thus it acquired domestic interests, identities, and institutions different from smaller middle developers, such as Sweden and Denmark. The temptation to use a massive state apparatus for military conquest in a bid to improve its global position did not disappear in Germany until after World War II. Germany's persistent reliance on the state to address many important tasks fostered a distinctive set of interests, identities, and institutions that made it hard to develop or sustain democratic political institutions. As a result, for much of its history, Germany's economic development was state-led, and its political order was authoritarian.

Germany's global context predisposed it to adopt the state-led path to development. The Second Empire was the prize Prussia won by defeating its military rivals, notably France. With a heavy reliance on its army and bureaucracy, the state aided the growth of heavy industry in a bid to catch up with leading industries in Britain. In politics, the state strongly discouraged dissent and refused to permit elections to the highest public offices. The Second Empire never became a democracy. The Weimar Republic departed from the imperial pattern to adopt competitive capitalism and democratic, constitutional government. In stark contrast with the preceding regime, the two political parties at the core of most of Weimar's coalition governments were the Socialist Party and the Catholic Center Party. The global context, however, remained unfavorable for capitalist democracy in Germany. In addition to the burden of reparations payments to France and Britain after World War I, Germany still faced stiff industrial competition from the Western economies. After the establishment of communist rule in Russia during the 1920s, Germany felt threatened and discriminated against, now from both the West and the East. The economic crisis brought on by the Great Depression was the final blow to the Weimar Republic. In the end, the Nazi Party offered Germans a chance to take a new version of antiliberal, state-led development. Thus, the durability of the Second Empire, the difficult experiment with democracy under Weimar, and the reversion to state-led development under Nazi rule all point to the importance of the state for much of Germany's existence.

The path of state-led development was difficult to change because of the feedback effect through domestic institutions. The legacies of the Second Empire, including strong authoritarian enclaves in the army, bureaucracy, and presidency, made the survival of the Weimar Republic precarious. The Second Empire's support for Protestant nationalism against Catholicism and class-based sentiments left contradictory legacies. On the one hand, Catholic and working-class identities and institutions developed in opposition to the regime and then went on to be bulwarks of the Weimar Republic. On the other hand, the legacy of strong nationalism and the experience of stigmatizing various groups as

Table 5.2 Key Phases in Germany's Political Development

Time Period	Regime	Global Context	Interests/Identities/ Institutions	Developmental Path
1800–1870	Competing monarchies (authoritarian)	Industrial and political revolutions	Strong landed elite Protestant nationalism and Catholic resistance authoritarian institutions evade reform	State-building
1871–1918	Second Empire (authoritarian)	European imperialism	Industry and landed elite strong nationalism and working-class and Catholic subcultures authoritarian with elections	State-building
1919–1933	Weimar Republic (democratic)	Rise of U.S. economic power; communist revolution in Russia	Strong industry socialism, Catholicism, nationalism, weak democratic values, and fear of communism democracy with powerful reserved domains for authoritarian office-holders in army and bureaucracy	Competitive capitalism
1933–1945	Third Empire (authoritarian)	Great power rivalry and global depression	Strong industry, fascism and anti-Semitism authoritarian	Totalitarian overthrow of world order
1945–1949	Foreign occupation (military)	U.S. and Soviet military dominance	Reindustrialization, fascism discredited parties, unions, and local governments rebuild	International aid

Time Period	Regime	Global Context	Interests/Identities/ Institutions	Developmental Path
1949– 1990	Federal Republic of	Cold War and economic growth in capitalist countries	Automobiles and high-technology industry democratic values grow, new immigrants, feminism, and environmentalism parties, unions, federal state	Embedded liberalism
	Germany (democratic) German Democratic Republic (authoritarian)		heavy industry, communist indoctrination but increasing disaffection one-party state	Leninism
1990–	Federal Republic of Germany (democratic)	United States as sole superpower and globalization	Advanced industry and services, strong democratic values, cultural nationalism, feminism, environmentalism parties, unions, federal state, European Union	Embedded liberalism

unpatriotic and non-German fed into support for the Nazi Party and the overthrow of the democratic system.

Germany's state-led development also fed back into the international system itself. German militarism provoked Soviet defensive action and the fortress mentality of communist regimes, and it also provoked the established Western powers to use force in defense of the liberal international order. The defeat of Nazi Germany in World War II laid the groundwork for a new global rivalry between the United States and the Soviet Union. These two main powers occupied and divided Germany. The U.S. and international support for West Germany's reindustrialization and reintegration into the world economic and political systems helped to set Germany down a new path.

Germany's new global position as one of the world's leading economic powers supports a revised set of interests, identities, and institutions and a kind of democratic capitalism that can be described as embedded liberalism. Germany stands for strongly liberal economic policies, and its industries are fiercely competitive in the international marketplace. Its institutions sustain a firmly democratic regime with a constitutional framework. The market is combined with the social partnership of strong labor unions, business leaders, and key administrative agencies. Germany's political parties, labor unions, and federal institutions all consistently support the basic practices of constitutional, parliamentary democracy. As for political values, most political scientists agree that Germany is as solidly democratic today as any country in Europe.

The continuing globalization of the economy presents a new set of challenges and opportunities for Germany. With the collapse of the Soviet Union, a unified Germany is exercising even greater influence in European and world politics, especially through its leading role in the European Union. In the wake of the economic recession of 2008–2010, Germany pressed austerity conditions five on other economies that use the euro (Ireland, Greece, Portugal, Spain, and Italy) in exchange for bailouts; aid to these countries was unpopular with German voters, yet Germany's overall economic strategy and high-tech manufacturing exports depend on continuing trade with its EU partners. The German social welfare system so far remains more or less intact, despite some cuts in recent years. Germany also maintains a high level of wage equality and keeps government budgets largely in balance, but at the cost of relatively high unemployment. Germany has attracted labor immigrants and political refugees, many of whom are Muslim, but there are few political or religious institutions that successfully facilitate integration into German society; moreover, current efforts at improved integration are frequently confounded by internal diversity among Muslims, by competition between Muslim organizations, and by debates among Germans about whether and how to recognize their society's new ethnic and religious heterogeneity. The question of how Germany's distinctive set of interests, identities, and institutions will respond to new global challenges remains an exciting issue to follow in the coming years.

BIBLIOGRAPHY

Bairoch, Paul. "International Industrialization Levels from 1750 to 1980." *Journal of Economic History* 11, no. 2 (Fall 1982): 269–333.

Dahrendorf, Ralf. *Society and Democracy in Germany.* New York: Norton, 1967.

Ertman, Thomas. *Birth of the Leviathan: Building States and Regimes in Medieval and Early Modern Europe.* Cambridge: Cambridge University Press, 1997.

Eurobarometer Surveys. Public Opinion Analysis Section of the European Commission. Accessed at http://ec.europa.eu/public_opinion/index_en.htm.

Federal Statistical Office, Germany. Official statistics and reports accessed at https://www.destatis.de/DE/Startseite.html.

Gerschenkron, Alexander. *Economic Backwardness in Historical Perspective: A Book of Essays.* Cambridge, MA: Harvard University Press, 1962.

Gould, Andrew C. *Origins of Liberal Dominance: State, Church, and Party in Nineteenth Century Europe.* Ann Arbor: University of Michigan Press, 1999.

Janos, Andrew C. "The Politics of Backwardness in Continental Europe, 1780–1945." *World Politics* 41, no. 3 (April 1989): 325–358.

Klausen, Jytte. *The Islamic Challenge: Politics and Religion in Western Europe*. Oxford: Oxford University Press, 2005.

Laurence, Jonathan. *The Emancipation of Europe's Muslims: The State's Role in Minority Integration*. Princeton, NJ: Princeton University Press, 2012.

Luebbert, Gregory M. *Liberalism, Fascism, or Social Democracy: Social Classes and the Political Origins of Regimes in Interwar Europe*. New York: Oxford University Press, 1991.

Moore, Barrington. *The Social Origins of Dictatorship and Democracy: Lord and Peasant in the Making of the Modern World*. Boston: Beacon, 1966.

Organization for Economic Cooperation and Development (OECD). Statistics accessed at http://www.oecd.org/statistics/.

Rogowski, Ronald. *Commerce and Coalitions: How Trade Affects Domestic Political Alignments*. Princeton, NJ: Princeton University Press, 1989.

Suval, Stanley. *Electoral Politics in Wilhelmine Germany*. Chapel Hill: University of North Carolina Press, 1985.

Turner, Lowell, ed. *Negotiating the New Germany: Can Social Partnership Survive?* Ithaca, NY: Cornell University Press, 1997.

Wehler, Hans-Ulrich. *The German Empire, 1871–1918*. Leamington Spa: Berg Publishers, 1985.

World Bank. World Development Indicators. Accessed at http://databank.worldbank.org/data/home.aspx.

IMPORTANT TERMS

Austrian Empire – the south-east German polity governed from Vienna by the Habsburg dynasty and the main rival to Prussia for control over German territory. It was officially founded in 1804 by the Habsburgs in response to Napoleon; it was succeeded by the Austro-Hungarian Empire in 1867, which was then dissolved in 1918. Formerly Habsburg lands became the states of Austria, Hungary, Czechoslovakia, and portions of Poland, Rumania, Italy, and Balkan states.

Basic Law (Grundgesetz) – founding 1949 document of the Federal Republic of Germany that serves as its constitution. Originally designed to be replaced by "a constitution adopted by a free decision of the German people," it has never been replaced but has been amended several times, including incorporating the new states from the East in 1990.

Berlin – city in northeastern Germany, capital of reunified Germany since 1990. It was earlier the capital of the kingdom of Prussia, the Second Empire, the Weimar Republic, and the Third Reich. It was occupied and divided after World War II. The support of the United States during the Berlin airlift (1948–1949) kept Soviet forces from taking the western sector. The Berlin wall (1961–1989) kept easterners from leaving for the West. Berlin's eastern half was the capital of the German Democratic Republic.

Bonn – city on the Rhine River in western Germany, from 1949 to 1990 the provisional capital of West Germany. After 1990, it continued to house many federal offices during the move back to Berlin. It was occupied by French revolutionary forces in 1794 and was awarded to Prussia in 1815.

Bundesrat (Federal Council) – the second, or upper, house of the Parliament in which each state (*Land*) receives at least three votes and larger states receive up to three additional votes based on population; there are sixty-nine votes total. A state's delegation must cast all of its votes together as the state government instructs, and no split votes can be registered, even from states governed by coalitions of parties. The Bundesrat's approval is required in about two-thirds of legislation, where the states' powers are involved. The Bundesrat is secondary in power to the Bundestag but important when different parties control the two houses.

Bundestag (Federal Diet) – the primary, or lower, house of the Parliament. Its delegates are chosen by popular vote, with all seats up for election normally every four years. The exact number of seats can vary slightly from one election to another because of the "excess mandate provision" and the "three-district waiver" electoral rules (603 delegates were seated after the 2002 election; 614 after the 2005 election). The Bundestag's approval is required for all legislation, as in most parliamentary systems, and it exercises more oversight of cabinets than do most parliaments. Its majority party or a coalition selects the chancellor.

Center Party (Zentrumspartei) – the political party that emerged in defense of Catholic interests in the 1870s under the Second Empire. It was the second-largest party for much of the Weimar Republic (with 15 percent to 20 percent of the vote), and it frequently was in the governing coalition. Its predominantly Catholic supporters for the most part did not defect to the Nazi Party during the early 1930s, but its deputies voted for the Enabling Act that gave Hitler dictatorial powers in 1933.

Christian Democrats – the Christian Democratic Union (CDU) and the Christian Social Union (CSU), allied parties on the center-right. The CDU campaigns in all states except Bavaria, where it is allied with the more conservative CSU. The CDU's founding in the post–World War II era broke from the tradition of the Catholic Center Party by including Protestants as well as Catholics. Since 1949, it is one of Germany's two main political party groupings.

Congress of Vienna – the 1815 great-powers conference after the defeat of French Emperor Napoleon Bonaparte. The powers agreed to give Prussia control over most of the Rhine territories in order to keep France in check, greatly expanding Prussia's role in Germany overall.

constructive vote of no confidence – requirement in the Basic Law that the Bundestag, in order to dismiss the chancellor, must simultaneously agree on a new chancellor. It was designed to limit the power of the parliament and strengthen the chancellor. Attempted twice but successful only once, it has generally had the intended effect.

Friedrich Ebert – leader of the moderate wing of the Social Democratic Party and first president of the Weimar Republic.

federal chancellor (Bundeskanzler) – head of the government, usually the head of the leading political party. Once the chancellor is selected by the Bundestag, he or she can count on majority support most of the time. The chancellor has more authority than prime ministers in most parliamentary systems.

federal president (Bundesprasident) – head of state with largely ceremonial authority. The president is selected by a federal convention of all Bundestag deputies and an equal number of delegates selected by the state legislatures. The position has a five-year term and is usually filled by senior politicians; activist presidents can use the office to influence public opinion.

Federal Republic of Germany (FRG) – Bundesrepublikdeutschland (BRD), the current German state. Founded in 1949 and based on the U.S., British, and French zones of occupation, it was often known as West Germany until 1990. It acquired the German Democratic Republic (GDR) in the unification of 1990.

Frankfurt Parliament (1848–1849) – the all-German Parliament elected in 1848 that met in the city of Frankfurt and attempted to unify and reform the many German states along more liberal or democratic principles. Its inability to do so began a long period of authoritarian predominance in German states.

German Democratic Republic (GDR) – Deutsche Demokratische Republik (DDR), the German state based on the Soviet zone of occupation from 1949 until 1990, often known as East Germany.

guest workers (*Gastarbeiter*) – frequently used term for immigrant workers in the 1950s and 1960s that underscored their temporary status in Germany.

Otto von Hindenburg – the Junker former army officer who became the second president of the Weimar Republic and appointed Hitler as chancellor in 1933.

Holocaust – the Nazi attempt to kill all European Jews during World War II. During it, 5.7 million Jewish people were killed. Other so-called undesirable people – including Roma, homosexuals, psychiatric patients, the handicapped, and political opponents, especially Communists – were also targeted for destruction. A total of between six and seven million people lost their lives. Auschwitz and Treblinka were two major death camps.

Junkers – the landed nobility of eastern Prussia. Their vast estates east of the Elbe River produced grain for Germany and the world market but only by keeping agricultural laborers in near slavery. They formed the core of the Prussian state administration and the Second Empire's administration, and never fully accepted the legitimacy of the Weimar Republic.

Kulturkampf (cultural struggle) – the attempt by the Second Empire to break the authority of the Catholic Church in unified Germany by means of legislation, regulation, and the harassment of priests, mainly between 1871 and 1878. It reduced the church's authority in some areas but generally sparked a revival of political Catholicism and popular religiosity.

Karl Marx – founding thinker of modern socialism and communism. Born in 1818 in Trier, in the Rhine province of Prussia, he became involved in various German and French radical movements during the 1830s and 1840s. He wrote *The Communist Manifesto* (in 1848, with Friedrich Engels) and many other polemical and analytical works. The guiding personality in the Socialist International movement in the 1860s, he died in London in 1883.

National Socialist German Workers' Party (Nazi Party) – the fascist party taken over by Adolph Hitler in 1920–1921. It became the largest political party in the Weimar Republic in the early 1930s, winning 38 percent of the vote in July 1932 and 33 percent in November. Hitler's appointment as chancellor in 1933 was followed by the end of the republic and the beginning of one-party Nazi rule until 1945.

Oder-Neisse line– the contemporary eastern border of Germany with Poland along these two rivers.

Prussia – the North German state governed from Berlin by the Hohenzollern dynasty beginning in 1701 that grew in military strength and gained control of most of what is now Germany and western Poland during the eighteenth and nineteenth centuries. It formed the core of the Second Empire in 1871. Subsequently a state within Germany, it was disbanded during the Allied occupation in 1947.

Social Democratic Party – Germany's oldest political party, generally on the center-left. It emerged in the 1870s as a working-class protest party, and its main wing helped to found and frequently govern the Weimar Republic. Since 1949, one of Germany's two main political parties.

social market economy – a term for tempering the free market with concern for social consequences. It is based on a "social partnership" of business and labor, along with the state and banks, to shape politics and economics at the national, regional, and local levels in order to cushion and guide economic change.

two-vote ballot procedure – the voting method to select delegates in the Bundestag that is a form of proportional representation. The first vote is for a candidate to represent the voter's district. Half of the seats are awarded as a result. The second vote is for a party overall. The remaining seats are distributed so that the overall share of seats for each party matches the second ballot choices.

Weimar Republic – the German state and democratic regime that was formed after the fall of the Second Empire in 1919 and lasted until 1933. It was named for the city where its constitution was written. Bitter and polarized partisan competition from the communist Left and the extreme nationalist right wing made it difficult for the moderate and mostly Social Democratic and Center Party governments to operate.

STUDY QUESTIONS

1. Consider Germany in 1815. In what ways was it like the rest of Europe? How was it different?
2. Why were Germany's political institutions under the Second Empire authoritarian rather than democratic?
3. Why did the Weimar Republic fail to survive as a democracy?
4. What were the main features and policies of the Nazi regime?

5. How did the Allies reshape interests, identities, and institutions in occupied Germany from 1945 through 1949?

6. What were the major differences between the FRG and the GDR between 1949 and 1989?

7. How did Germany's interests, identities, and institutions change as a result of reunification in 1990?

8. What are the major political parties in the FRG?

9. What impact has the FRG had on Europe and the world since World War II?

10. How is the global context after 1990 affecting Germany's developmental path?

JAPAN

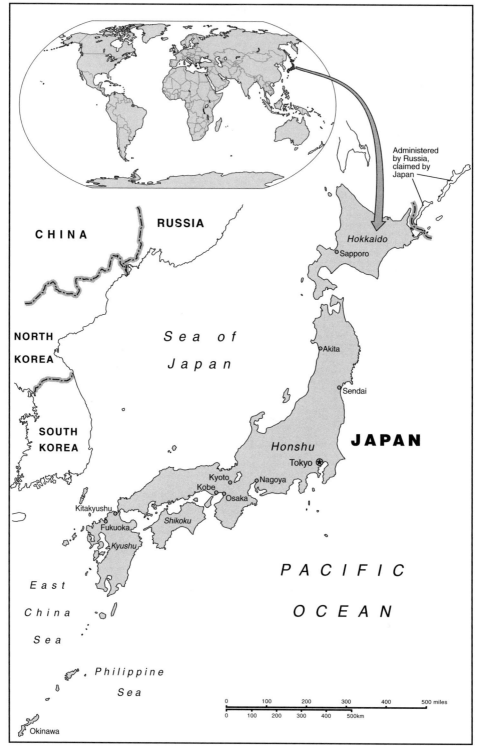

MAP 6.1. Map of Japan.

6 Japan

Miranda A. Schreurs

Introduction

Japan is a fascinating country for political scientists to study. Japan's interests, identities, and institutions have both been shaped by and played a significant role in shaping the global order.

Within a little more than a century from its opening to the West in 1853, Japan went from being an isolated feudal society to one of the world's richest economies and most stable democracies. In the transition, Japan experienced a wide range of political forms, including a shogunate, imperial rule with an emperor supported (or controlled) by oligarchs, a kind of imperial democracy, military (some argue fascist) rule, and empire.

From 1945 until 1952, Japan was occupied by the U.S.-led Allied forces. The postwar Japanese Constitution, which was heavily influenced by the occupying forces, renounces war as a sovereign right of the nation and places sovereignty in the hands of the people. Japan's subsequent political transition to democracy is among one of the most successful cases in the world of democratic consolidation. It is also a case of where democracy was largely imposed from outside. By the end of the Occupation, Japan was viewed as an important U.S. ally in the Pacific. Japan's security has been guaranteed by the U.S.-Japan Security Treaty ever since. Because Japan does not function as a "normal" state in the realpolitik sense of the word (that is, as a state that wields power through military strength), Japan has had to rely on economic and "soft" power in its foreign relations. Some in Japan are eager to rewrite the constitution while others wish to retain its pacifist core.

Despite much Western influence over Japanese institutions and interests, Japan retained and developed many unique institutions. These include the close neo-corporatist–style working relationship between the government and industry and a strong emphasis on the importance of societal and workplace relationships. Japan developed a form of economics that includes a far greater degree of governmental intervention and planning than exists in the United States. Loyalties to family and firm are also very strong. For many years, these institutions were viewed as important factors in Japan's rise as an economic power.

As we will see, many of the same interests, identities, and institutions that shaped Japan in the second half of the twentieth century as the country focused its energies on catching up with the West have been under pressure. Ever since Japan caught up with Europe and North America economically, it has struggled to adapt its political, social, and economic institutions to a changing global context. Japan's economy has been mired in a recession or near-recession that has continued for close to two decades. The rise of China has added new economic and political dimensions to regional politics and created a sense of unease regarding Japan's position in the region. Problematic governmental responses to the government's burgeoning debt (measuring over 200 percent of GDP) as well as to crises, such as the Kobe Earthquake in 1995 and the March 11, 2011, triple disaster – the massive earthquake, tsunami, and nuclear meltdown at the **Fukushima** nuclear power plant – have added to a public sense of unease and distrust in the government.

The relative stability that defined postwar Japanese party politics has been replaced by instability. During its long period of postwar economic growth, a single political party maintained a hold on government: the conservative, pro-business **Liberal Democratic Party** of Japan (LDP). The LDP was in power from 1955 until 2009 except for nine months during 1993–1994. The party, however, increasingly had to rely on coalition partners to form governments and there were increasingly rapid changes in party leadership. In the twenty-four years between 1989 and 2012, Japan had sixteen prime ministers. Of these, only Prime Ministers Toshiki Kaifu, Ryutaro Hashimoto, and Junichi Koizumi were in office for more than two years. In 2009, the **Democratic Party of Japan** was able to oust the LDP from power, but it failed to develop a new vision for the country or to respond effectively to the country's problems. Its dismal approval ratings in the post-Fukushima period led to its rejection in the December 2012 elections to the House of Representatives. In a landslide victory, the LDP was returned to power under the leadership of Shinzo Abe, who for the second time became prime minister of Japan (his first time was for one year from 2006 to 2007). What this means for Japanese party politics in the years ahead remains to be seen.

The Japanese Nation

Japan is an archipelago made up of over 6,800 islands extending 1300 miles from north to south, the distance from New York City to Miami, Florida. There are five large islands where the majority of the population live: Honshu, the main island, where both the ancient capital of Kyoto and the modern capital of Tokyo are located; Hokkaido, the relatively sparsely populated island to the north; the southern island of Okinawa, which was returned to Japan only in 1972 and is home to the largest U.S. military base in the Pacific; Kyushu; and Shikoku. Japan has territorial disputes with Russia, South Korea, and China regarding the ownership of numerous small islands. These disputes have strained relations between Japan and its neighbors as the ownership of the islands is both a question of historical interpretation and national pride as well as of access to fishing and potential offshore oil and gas resources.

Japan's 127.5 million inhabitants make it the world's tenth most populated country (just ahead of Mexico) and also one of its most densely populated. The population density is exacerbated by Japan's mountainous terrain. The population is heavily concentrated in the area stretching from Kansai to Kantō, which include major cities such as Chiba, Nagoya, Tokyo, Yokohama, Osaka, and Kyoto. Tokyo is the world's largest metropolitan region.

The strong sense of nation may also be tied to the country's relatively harsh natural conditions. The Japanese islands were created through volcanic activity, and there are still many active volcanoes. As a result, the country experiences over a thousand earthquakes each year, most of which are too small to notice, but several hundred of which are large enough to feel. A major earthquake in 1923 led to fires that destroyed much of Tokyo. In 1995 an earthquake hit the Kobe region causing widespread structural damage and loss of life. A series of earthquakes in March 2011 unleashed a tsunami that devastated the northeastern coast of Japan and triggered a disaster at the Fukushima Daiichi Nuclear Facility.

As a group of volcanic islands, Japan lacks fossil fuels and other natural resources. Japan is thus heavily dependent on coal, oil, natural gas, and mineral imports. Some argue that the reason Japan was able to do so well economically is precisely because the Japanese people have had to learn to survive with so little. This contributed to a strong sense of community as well as a politics of resource efficiency. It also has required Japan to import most of its fuel and other resources from countries around the world.

Although most Japanese claim not to have a religion, most follow certain Buddhist and Shintoist traditions. Japan is also relatively open to other religions and beliefs. Indeed, many Japanese may get married in a part Christian, part Shinto wedding ceremony, go to a Shinto shrine to pray for the good health of their newborn child, and have their funeral in a Buddhist temple. This may explain the lack of strong religious tensions in the society.

The Historical Roots of Japanese Political Institutions, Identities, and Interests

To understand Japan today, it is important to have an understanding of the country's historical origins and the role they played in the development of Japan's modern political institutions, identities, and interests.

A Period of Peace, Prosperity, and Isolation: The Tokugawa Era, 1603–1867

In 1600 Ieyasu Tokugawa succeeded in military battles to unify a country that had essentially been divided into 260 feudal fiefdoms, each headed by a **daimyo**, a feudal lord. Although still technically ruled by the imperial family, Japan's emperors had become too weak to keep real power. For the next two-and-a-half centuries (1603–1867) the Tokugawa **shogunate** ruled Japan from Edo (now, Tokyo) while the emperor maintained his residence in Kyoto. By 1720 Edo had a population of well over one million, making it the world's largest city.

Japan was remarkably isolated from the world during the Edo period. In the 1630s, Japan closed its ports to foreigners, except the Dutch and Chinese who were granted permission to trade out of the port of Nagasaki in Kyushu. Japan's isolation was broken in 1853 when **Commodore Matthew Perry** steamed into Edo Bay with four armed ships carrying a letter to the Japanese emperor from U.S. president Millard Fillmore requesting (and in essence demanding) that Japan open its ports to American ships for trade and supplies. Recognizing the superior military power of the Americans, the shogunate acquiesced and a peace and friendship treaty that allowed for limited trade was signed. Perry's voyage was to mark the beginning of similar demands by other countries and Japan's forced acceptance of what are now known as "unequal treaties," trade agreements that gave Westerners extraterritorial rights and trade terms that were less negotiated than imposed.

Catching Up with the West: The Meiji Era, 1868–1912 and Taishō Democracy, 1912–1926

The shogun's acquiescence to American demands was viewed by some as a betrayal of the Japanese nation, and led to national uprisings. In 1868 the period of shogun rule was brought to an end in a process known as the **Meiji Restoration**. The Meiji Era was an immensely important period of institutional and cultural transformation. The emperor moved the imperial capital to Tokyo (the characters for Tokyo are "eastern capital"), and a centralized government was formed. State Shintoism was made the ideology of the country; it reified the emperor as the divine ancestor of the Sun Goddess Amaterasu.

During the Meiji Era, profound changes were made to virtually all sectors of society. With the goal of achieving *fukoku kyohei* ("rich country, strong military") Japan's leaders set out to modernize the nation. They brought in Western advisors and teachers and sent hundreds of Japanese abroad to study Western science, technology, political systems, constitutions, education, medicine, and culture. By the end of the Meiji Era, Japan's reformists had succeeded in containing popular revolts from below while creating a modern state and world power.

Japan was a Confucian, class-based society, with samurai at the top of the hierarchy, followed by peasants, artisans, merchants, and *eta*, the outcasts. During the Meiji period, the samurai class was abolished, partly because of the large financial strain it put on the state and in part to restrain the potential for uprisings. Members of the Imperial court and the *daimyō* became part of a new nobility that maintained certain privileges.

In 1889, a constitution was adopted that was heavily influenced by the Prussian (German) and British models. The U.S. constitution was rejected as being too liberal. The Meiji Constitution created a parliamentary system ruled over by an emperor. Sovereignty rested with the emperor, who was declared "sacred and inviolable." An imperial **Diet** (or parliament) was created, with a popularly elected House of Representatives. Suffrage, however, was limited to propertied males (about 1 percent of the population) until the right to vote was extended to all adult males in 1925. In addition, a House of Peers, modeled on the British House of Lords, was formed. Its members came from members of the nobility.

The emperor appointed cabinet ministers, had legislative supremacy over the Diet, and could issue emergency decrees and enter into treaties. Only the emperor could amend the constitution. The military was directly responsible to the emperor and not to the Diet. This weakness in the constitution was later used by the military to take control of power.

In the ensuing decades, Japan became increasingly strong and wealthy. At the beginning of the Meiji era, Japan's population was 35 million. By the start of World War II it was somewhat over 70 million. Japan developed a major shipping industry and an elaborate rail system, and became a global exporter of silks and textiles. It also gained some experience with *Minpo Shugi*, what in Japanese is called a democracy for the people as opposed to one of the people. Given that the emperor was supreme, the Western-style of democracy in which sovereignty rests with the people (*Minshu shugi*) was considered inappropriate. Already in the Meiji Period and even more so in the Taishō Era (1912–1926) political parties took root, competing with each other in elections. This early experience with democracy is a reason some argue that Japan was able to transition to democracy relatively smoothly in the post–World War II period.

Japan as a Military Power and Colonial Force

Japan's rapid industrialization during the Meiji Era was paralleled by a strengthening of the Japanese military. Japan tested its military strength in the Sino-Japanese War of 1894–1895. Japan's victory was a humiliating blow to China. As a result of the war, Korea was made a protectorate of Japan, and Taiwan, the Liaodung Peninsula, and the Pescadores were ceded to Japan. Concerned about competition from Japan in China, however, Russia, France, and Germany forced Japan to return the Liaodung Peninsula to China. This was but one of many events that were to leave the Japanese feeling that they were not respected as equals by Western powers, which in turn nourished resentful nationalism.

Japan achieved another military victory that surprised the world when it prevailed over Russia in the 1904–1905 Russo-Japanese War. Defeated, Russia recognized Japanese paramount political, military, and economic interests in Korea as well as Japanese control of the railways of Inner Manchuria and Port Author. Russia also was forced to cede to Japan the southern portion of Sakhalin and the adjacent islands. These islands are now known as the Northern Territories or Kurile islands and remain areas that are territorially disputed between Russia (which seized them at the end of World War II) and Japan. Because of this territorial dispute, Russia and Japan have yet to sign a treaty officially ending the Second World War!

Japan formally colonized Korea in 1910. This history is the basis for the strained relationship that still exists between Japan and the two Koreas. The tensions that continue to exist among the states of East Asia have deep historical roots.

During World War I, Japan joined the Entente powers (Britain, France, and Russia), declaring war on Germany in August 1914. It seized German-leased territories in China (the Shandong Peninsula and Tsingtao) and islands in the Pacific (the Mariana, Caroline, and Marshall Islands). At the end of the war, Japan was recognized as one of the "Big Five" at the Treaty of Versailles and obtained a permanent seat in the League of Nations. Thus, within a few decades of being forced to open to the West, Japan had become a major military might in Asia and a global power.

Still, Japan failed to persuade Western powers to include a racial equality clause in the Treaty of Versailles, and resentment about this and other forms of unequal treatment persisted. Domestically, the stage was being set for the rise of militants. In 1925, conservatives pushed through a Peace Preservation Law, which made illegal organizations and movements that had as their goal changing the political system (basically targeting socialists, communists, and anarchists). All political parties were dissolved in 1940 and replaced by the Imperial Rule Assistance Association that was to channel the energy of the people for the sake of the nation. Essentially, a single-party state was established. Ultrarightists and militants had gained the upper hand and the hopes for a democratic Japan faded.

Japan strengthened its grip on Manchuria, forcefully detaching it from China in 1931. In 1937, Japan attacked China, beginning the Pacific War. The United States reacted with an economic embargo on Japan. Japan allied itself with Germany and Italy in 1940 and attacked Pearl Harbor on December 7, 1941. It then extended its sphere of influence into Southeast Asia in a quest to secure oil and to become the dominant power in Asia. Japan's colonization of Korea, China, Taiwan, and its military advance into large parts of Southeast Asia was done in the name of expelling Western imperialists from the region and creating a Greater East Asia Co-Prosperity Sphere. The often brutal Japanese colonization and military rule and the millions of civilian and military casualties of the war left bitter memories and much resentment toward Japan in much of Asia. The Pacific War dragged on until August 14, three months after Germany capitulated, ending only after two atomic bombs were dropped on the cities of Hiroshima and Nagasaki.

The Demilitarization and Democratization of Japan

At the end of World War II, **General Douglas MacArthur** was appointed by President Harry S. Truman to be the Supreme Commander of the Allied Powers (SCAP) and head of the Allied occupation of Japan. Although the officials who were considered the masterminds of the war were purged, imprisoned, and in some cases tried by the Tokyo War Crimes Tribunal, the government was left largely intact; SCAP worked with and through the Japanese bureaucracy and the Diet as it tried to demilitarize and democratize the country.

Two months after the occupation began, MacArthur called for the "liberalization of the constitution" and democratization in five key areas – emancipating women, permitting the unionization of labor, liberalizing education, establishing an effective judicial system to protect human rights, and dismantling of the *zaibatsu*, financial and business conglomerates who controlled much of prewar Japanese business and became closely linked to the military.

In February 1946, six months into the occupation, the Japanese government presented a draft constitution to SCAP headquarters. Unhappy with the Japanese draft, which apparently made only a few modifications to the Meiji Constitution, MacArthur had his staff prepare a more liberal model. Beata Sirota (later, Beata Gordon), one of only a few Americans who could speak, read, and write Japanese, was part of the drafting committee. She inserted a clause guaranteeing legal equality between men and women in relation to marriage, divorce, property rights, inheritance, and other matters pertaining to marriage and the family.

Another major addition was **Article 9**, the peace article:

Aspiring sincerely to an international peace based on justice and order, the Japanese people forever renounce war as a sovereign right of the nation and the threat or use of force as means of settling international disputes. To accomplish the aim of the preceding paragraph, land, sea, and air forces, as well as other war potential, will never be maintained. The right of belligerency of the state will not be recognized.

Although there is some dispute as to this article's author, it was probably Prime Minister Kijūrō Shidehara, who wanted to prevent any kind of military establishment in the country. The draft was then debated in the Diet and the new constitution went into effect in May 1947. It has never been amended despite numerous attempts to have Article 9 revised.

The constitution changed the status of the emperor from head of state to symbol of state; abolished the House of Peers, replacing it with an elected House of Councilors; and greatly strengthened the House of Representatives. The bicameral Diet (parliament) was made the highest organ of state and given sole lawmaking authority. The constitution stipulated that the prime minister and the majority of ministers should be members of the Diet and that the prime minister should be elected by the parliament. The new constitution also emphasized fundamental human rights and individual freedoms. The age of suffrage was changed from twenty-five to twenty.

The occupation of Japan was successful in large part because it was considered legitimate by the Japanese, who were weary of war. When the occupation began, Japan was a demoralized, exhausted, malnourished, and ravaged country. Japan's cities had been heavily bombed and much of its heavy industry destroyed. In this context, it proved relatively easy to blame the military for Japan's ill-fated imperialism. Moreover, when the war ended, it was the emperor, considered sacred by his people, who ordered that the military disarm.

Rather than trying Emperor Hirohito as a war criminal or having him abdicate the throne as some wanted (and was even suggested by his younger brother, Prince Mikasa), MacArthur felt the imperial family should be spared. The emperor's subsequent endorsement of the occupation and its reforms helped to legitimize SCAP's activities. Also important was the support for the reforms received from Japanese prime minister **Shigeru Yoshida**, who was in office from May 1946 to May 1947 and again from October 1948 to December 1954. Yoshida chose to align Japan with the United States politically and economically, focus Japan's political attentions on economic development, and allow the United States to take on the role of protecting Japan. His policies, referred to as the Yoshida Doctrine, became the basic guiding ideologies of the conservative LDP when it formed in 1955.

One of the other remarkable postwar developments is that Japan, which had gone to war against the United States, became one of the most important U.S. allies in the Pacific.

The initial goals of the U.S. occupation were to demilitarize and democratize Japan and help it regain basic economic functions in order to be self-sufficient. The onset of the Cold War and concerns about the spread of communism in East Asia gave Japan new strategic significance in U.S. eyes. It also led SCAP to clamp down on the activities of the Japanese Communist Party, the only party to have spoken out against Japan's military aggression, and labor leaders who were closely aligned with the party. The politics of this period created a deep-seated ideological divide between conservatives, who supported the United States in most of its policy initiatives, and the parties of the Left and, especially, the **Japan Socialist Party** and the JCP, which opposed Japan's strong alignment with the United States.

In 1951, the United States and Japan concluded the San Francisco Peace Treaty, ending the U.S. occupation of Japan, and the U.S.-Japan Security Treaty. The occupation formally ended on April 28, 1952, one month after the U.S. Senate had ratified the agreement. The security treaty engendered considerable opposition both within Japan from left-leaning parties and internationally, as it gave the United States the right to maintain troops in Japan. Today, the United States maintains over fifty thousand troops in Japan, over half of which are in Okinawa. The question of whether U.S. troops should remain in Japan continues to be an important and divisive political issue, and is an especially significant question in Okinawa.

Two years after the Occupation ended and with the blessing of the United States, Japan turned its National Police Reserve into the Japan Self-Defense Forces (JSDF) for the protection of the country. The JSDF are now one of the largest military forces in the world but because of Article 9 they are restricted to national self-defense and since the 1990s also to noncombat roles in UN peacekeeping operations. At least since the time that Yasuhiro Nakasone was prime minister (1982–1987), there has been a debate in the country about whether Japan should assume a larger military role. Such debates engender great consternation among Japan's Asian neighbors.

Understanding Japan's "Economic Miracle"

Few would ever have predicted that Japan would emerge from its war-ravaged state in 1945 to become one of the world's richest nations by the end of the 1960s. The Japanese **"economic miracle"** was manufactured from within, but aided by external circumstances.

When World War II ended, Japan received financial and technical assistance from the United States. The yen-dollar exchange rate was fixed at 360 yen to the dollar; this rate remained in place until the collapse of the Bretton Woods system in 1973. This rate certainly aided Japan's exports. Japan's economic recovery received a major stimulus from the demand for military and other supplies for UN troops fighting in the Korean War (1950–1953). The dollar purchases gave Japanese a means to pay for its imports and reequip its industries. Steel and other heavy industries did especially well. Japan also benefited enormously from being able to concentrate on economic development while leaving its defense largely to the United States. Japan's budgetary expenditures on the SDF remained at less than 1 percent of the national budget until well into the 1980s.

There were important domestic factors at work as well. First was the stabilization of the political party system and the emergence of a single dominant party, the LDP. The LDP formed out of a merger of two parties with prewar roots, the Liberal Party and the Democratic Party. In reaction to the formation of the LDP, the socialist Left also merged to form the Japan Socialist Party (JSP). The socialists, however, had historically been ideologically divided between those supportive of a more radical, Marxist socialism and those supporting a more moderate democratic socialism. The JSP split in 1959 when the more moderate wing of the party, in connection with the JSP's opposition to the U.S.-Japan Security Treaty's renewal, broke off to create the **Democratic Socialist Party** (DSP). In addition, the Communist Party represented a share of the left-leaning vote. As a result of the division of the left-leaning opposition, the LDP was able to maintain a majority in the House of Representatives. The dominance of the pro-business LDP provided for a high degree of political stability. The presence of several parties on the Left meant that the power of the LDP nevertheless remained in check.

In 1960, Prime Minister Hayato Ikeda announced a goal for Japan to double the national income in a decade. Japan expanded its range of export goods from textiles and low-end goods to heavy industry – including steel, chemicals, ship building, and automobiles – and electronic goods, such as radios, televisions, cameras, calculators, and computers. By 1967, Japan's Gross National Product (GNP) had surpassed that of Great Britain, France, and West Germany. So successful was Japan at importing technologies, improving upon them, and then exporting new designs that Japan began to develop trade surpluses with the United States, and trade frictions between the two countries began to grow. For much of the 1970s and 1980s, the United States worked to open Japan's economy more widely to U.S. goods, which were often barred by real and sometimes perceived protectionist policies.

Japan's economic wealth was more evenly distributed than in many developing countries, in part because of land reforms instituted at the end of the war and salary scales that did not distinguish as strongly as in the United States between top management and regular workers. Most Japanese considered themselves to be part of the middle class. In the 1970s, Prime Minister Kakuei Tanaka, one of the more colorful and controversial prime ministers of Japan, decided that it was important to keep rural areas connected to the increasingly economically dominant cities of the Kantō (Tokyo, Chiba, Yokohama) and Kansai (Osaka, Kyoto, Kobe) regions. He initiated a program called Reconstruction of the Japanese Archipelago. It was this program that led to the building of Japan's famous bullet trains, the *shinkansen*. Under Tanaka and subsequent politicians the construction industry benefited enormously from major public works projects – the building of roads, bridges, airports, dams, and tunnels with taxpayer's money.

Ideas, Institutions, and Interests and the Emergence of Japan's Iron Triangle

Not only formal, but also informal institutions played a role in Japan's postwar economic success. Japan's ministries emerged out of the postwar reforms even more powerful than they had been before. Using a system known as administrative guidance, **gyōsei shidō,** Japan's ministries shaped legislation in consultation with industry, steering the direction of Japan's industrial development. Traditionally bureaucrats had considerable moral authority because of their high educational attainments. Entering the bureaucracy was considered a prestige track for graduates of elite universities. Japan has a career civil service, and entrance to the bureaucracy requires passing extremely difficult exams and interviews. Until the Equal Employment Opportunity Law was passed in 1986, women were permitted to take the exams, but were often screened out during the interview process. In the meantime, the doors of the bureaucracy have been opened to more women, and women are also assuming more powerful posts, including as ministers.

Bureaucrats were highly involved in the formulation of legislation. In fact, most bills originated in the bureaucracy rather than in the House of Representatives even though important committees in the Diet, such as the Policy Affairs Research Committee, did influence the shape of bills, and the Diet had ultimate authority to vote on legislation. Bureaucrats had moral authority in a society that respects educational attainment. Entering the bureaucracy was considered a prestige track although the lure of the bureaucracy weakened as more lucrative career options emerged. More recently, politicians have begun to initiate more legislation, but the bureaucracy still remains powerful and heavily involved in policy formulation.

Two of the most powerful ministries are the Ministry of Finance, because of its influence over budgetary issues, and the Ministry of International Trade and Industry (since 2001 renamed the **Ministry of Economy, Trade, and Industry** (METI)). They used administrative guidance to influence the investment decisions of industry and to lend support to industries determined critical to the Japanese economy. Some of the industries to benefit from this close relationship to the bureaucracy were the automobile, electronics, and nuclear industries. The ministries had various tools in their hands to steer industrial directions, including preferential tax treatment, provision of low-interest loans, information, and connections.

Administrative guidance was aided by the close connections that existed among bureaucrats and, especially, the large corporations where lifetime employment was quite common. Japan is a network society. Personal relationships such as those established during high school and in universities as well as through years of working together are immensely important. These networks helped to link bureaucrats with industries. In addition, because Japan's bureaucracy is a career civil service, as one ascends the ladder of hierarchy, the number of available positions diminishes. Bureaucrats who know they have hit the glass ceiling within their ministries typically retire from the ministry and take up positions either in industry or government-created institutions. This process is so well- known that it has a special name, **amakudari**, or literally, "descent from heaven." The idea behind *amakudari* was that it would provide direct communication links between bureaucrats and industrial officials.

Japan's economy was built on a combination of large industries (e.g., Sony, Hitachi, Toyota, Nissan, NTT) and smaller and medium-sized firms. Historically, Japan's large companies offered men lifetime jobs. Firm loyalty was strong and also fostered by various cultural and institutional practices. There was traditionally little movement of workers among firms, and firms were expected to take care of their employees, and by extension their families. Enterprise-based unions linked the interests of workers closely to those of their firm. Thus, although unions did demand pay raises and better working conditions, this was usually done with the long-term well-being of the firm in mind. One of Japan's big challenges in the last decades has been the slow erosion of this system, the higher likelihood employees now face of being laid off, and the lack of a strong welfare system to take up redundant workers.

Japan's firms also benefited from interlocking business relationships known as *keiretsu*. Firms linked to each other through mutual share holding and ties to a common bank. This system was an important mechanism for insulating the companies from stock market fluctuations and takeover grabs and is argued to be one of the factors that has made longer-term planning possible. There are different kinds of *keiretsu*. Horizontal keiretsu, linking firms around a common bank, include such groupings as Sumitomo (with firms such as Sumitomo Chemical, Sumito Heavy Industries, Sumitomo Corporation, etc.), Mitsubishi, Mitsui, Sanwa, and Dai-Ichi Kogyo. Vertical *keiretsu* link suppliers, manufacturers, and distributors in a single industry, such as the automobile industry. The Toyota Group, Japan's largest corporation, directly controls a dozen other firms in such areas as electronics, air filters, real estate, and auto parts, and several hundred primary part suppliers.

Japan's Iron Triangle

As noted previously, the LDP dominated politics in postwar Japan. For a half century it was able to control the reins of government either alone or in coalition with smaller parties, and most often, the **Clean Government Party** (Kōmeito, later renamed the New Kōmeito). The LDP is a conservative party that is pro-business, pro-agriculture, supportive of Japan's military alliance with the United States, and conservative in its value-structure. The party's success was linked to the partnerships that it formed with other actors and interests. These institutional arrangements are sometimes referred to as Japan's **iron triangle** or Japan Inc. Although a simplification of a far more complex reality, the iron triangle refers to the links between the LDP, a supportive bureaucracy, and industrial and agricultural interests. In return for rural votes and financial support for costly campaigns from industry, the LDP, together with the bureaucracy, supported policies that were favorable to industrial actors and protective of agricultural interests. The close collaboration among the LDP; the powerful economic, finance, construction and agricultural ministries; and Japan's big industrial powers was considered one of the factors that made Japan's extraordinary economic rise possible. Major business sectors, such as the electronics, automobile, and pharmaceutical industries, were supported with favorable tax structures and direct and indirect subsidies. With Japan's export surpluses vis-à-vis the United States growing increasingly wide, informal and formal Japanese institutional practices came under fire. Japan was urged to shorten the working hours of employees, promote more leisure activities, and buy more products from abroad. "Japan bashing" at times took on ugly forms, such as when auto workers in

Detroit bashed a Japanese automobile with bats, or books were written with such provocative titles as *The Coming War with Japan*.

Opposition to the Conservative Agenda and Demands for Reforms

Japan's economic success also had a darker side to it. So strongly did the government back the interests of industrial actors that it failed to protect its citizens from industrial abuses. In the 1960s and 1970s, there were widespread consumer movements and environmental movements across Japan. Consumer movements protested policies that favored industrial expansion at the expense of consumers who had to pay exorbitantly high prices for goods and the lack of adequate safety measures to protect food quality. Environmental movements arose because of the severe health-threatening pollution that resulted from the failure to enact any pollution controls. In the fishing community of Minamata, the Chisso Corporation released methyl mercury–laced effluents into the Minamata water system, contaminating the bay and the fish within it. Those who ate too much contaminated fish suffered mercury poisoning. For unborn infants, this often resulted in severe birth defects. For decades the government failed to regulate the company's activities, allowing it to continue its scandalous practices. In rural Toyama Prefecture, residents who ate rice tainted with cadmium that had been released by mining companies into streams that irrigated their rice paddies, suffered from weakening of the bones and kidney failure. So painful was the disease that the locals dubbed it "*itai-itai*" or "it hurts–it hurts" disease. In this case too, the government was slow to act. Many other pollution problems afflicted the country. Air pollution in and around industrial areas was severe and efforts to protect natural areas lax.

Environmental policy change came about because of years of protest activities by grassroots movements, support received from the Communist and Socialist governors of various urban regions, and a small group of sympathetic bureaucrats. Eventually, in the 1970s, the LDP did respond, introducing stringent pollution control policies. After the first oil shock of 1973, these were then supplemented by policies to improve energy efficiency. In reaction to these developments, some referred to the LDP as a catch-all-interests party.

The Japanese economic miracle was also built on the back of a system that disadvantaged women. There are fairly strong gender role divisions in Japan. Throughout most of the postwar period, women could work, but they were expected to retire upon marriage or at least with childbirth, and not to reenter the workforce until their roles as mothers and primary child-care givers were complete. When they did reenter the workforce, it was usually as part-time workers with relatively low pay. Women therefore provided Japanese companies with highly educated, but relatively cheap employees. Lifetime employment was a privilege seldom conferred upon women. Employers could more easily let women go, providing companies with flexibility as well. A male employee's wages increased upon marriage and with the birth of children, and men typically earned more than women. Since the 1986 Equal Employment Law went into effect, such gender discrimination is now illegal, and as a result the position of women has improved somewhat. Still, during the recession that began around 1990, women, who now make up the majority of university graduates, had a much harder time than their male counterparts in finding suitable employment.

Corruption and Scandal

Other issues began to erode public support for the LDP and reduce trust in the bureaucracy. Questions began to be raised about the lack of transparency in decision making and whether regulatory oversight of industrial activities was adequate. In the 1980s, a case in which the Ministry of Health and Welfare permitted hemophiliacs to be given untreated blood transfusions resulted in more than 1,000 cases of hemophiliacs contracting HIV. This caused a national uproar. Numerous food scandals raised concerns about the safety of food products. In 2007, the Minister of Agriculture, Forestry, and Fisheries resigned after just seven weeks in office after rice tainted with mold and pesticides that was intended for industrial uses (such as the manufacture of glue) was allowed to be sold as food grade rice.

Corruption scandals led to numerous resignations and some imprisonments. One of the most riveting examples of corruption was the arrest of Shin Kanemaru, a godfather-type politician who was arguably the most powerful figure in the LDP. In 1993, Kanemaru was arrested for accepting bribes from Sagawa Kyūbin, a delivery company, and asking the company to put him in touch with the *yakuza*, the Japanese mafia, so that they might take care of his detractors. When the police raided his homes and offices they found over 3 billion yen in bond certificates, tens of millions in bank notes, and over two hundred pounds of gold bars! Later investigations discovered that many of the contributions came from construction companies. Former Prime Minister Kakuei Tanaka also was implicated in the scandal but died before ever serving any time. This scandal led to electoral reform and the first electoral defeat of the LDP in 1993–1994.

The Politics of Electoral Reform

In 1989, the Japanese economy was soaring. Japan's remarkable economic growth had some speculating that Japan would someday surpass the United States economically. Land prices had reached astronomical levels. The real estate value of land adjacent to the Imperial Palace grounds in downtown Tokyo was so high that it led to estimates that the palace grounds themselves – an area similar in size to Central Park in New York – were worth more than the entire real estate value of California! The country's wealth had Japanese traveling abroad, buying luxury goods and investing in properties overseas. The Japanese economic model and Japanese language became popular subjects to study at universities around the world.

But then the economic bubble burst. Real estate prices began to tumble, and banks found themselves sitting upon huge sums of nonperforming loans. Many banks and firms went bankrupt. In addition, excessive public spending – because of policies that supported the construction and other key industries – produced a huge government deficit, measured at 130 percent of Gross Domestic Product (GDP) in 2000 and over 220 percent by 2011, the highest ratio of any industrialized country. Reform would be necessary to keep the country stable.

After the many scandals that hit the ruling party in the late 1980s and 1990s and with a declining economic situation, power struggles within the heavily factionalized LDP led to a splintering of the party in 1992. In that year, Morihiro Hosokawa left the LDP with a small group of followers to form the Japan New Party. He promised to pursue economic, political, and social reforms. Ichiro Ozawa, another reformist politician, also abandoned the LDP and formed a new party, Japan Renewal Party (Shinseito). In the 1993 election for the House of Representatives, the LDP received the largest number of votes, but not a majority, and this opened the door for the first non-LDP government since the end of the Occupation. An unwieldy eight-party coalition formed, including all of the old opposition parties except the **Japan Communist Party**, plus the two newly formed parties. Hosokawa became prime minister. Although the coalition government did not survive for long, it marked the beginning of a new era in postwar Japanese politics of coalition governments and the beginning of the unraveling of what is commonly known as the 1955 system – the system where the LDP was in power and the Japan Socialist Party, the Democratic Socialist Party, the Japan Communist Party, and the Clean Government Party (Kōmeitō, a party formed in 1964 with the backing of a Buddhist group, Soka Gakkai) were in perpetual opposition.

One of the real achievements of Hosokawa's government was electoral reform. Japan's electoral system had been based on a complicated medium-sized, multimember direct system in which each electoral district elected, in most cases, between three and five representatives. As each voter had a single nontransferable vote, this meant that the top vote getters, sometimes receiving as little as 10 percent of the vote, took office. This system pitted members of the same party against each other as well as against other parties as there was no restriction as to the number of candidates a party could field. The system was immensely expensive and helped feed factionalism and corruption. Indeed, the LDP became a highly factionalized party with faction leaders vying with each other for senior posts in the party and the prize position of prime minister. Electoral reform was introduced in the hopes of creating a system that would encourage true competition among political parties, possibly along the model of the British or American systems.

In complicated negotiations, a new electoral system was agreed on for the House of Representatives, the more powerful of Japan's two houses of parliament. The new system adopted a combination of proportional representation and a single-member district system. The system was modified again by changes to the Electoral Law in 2000. Under the new system, three hundred seats are elected in single-seat races. In these races, small parties have little chance of winning as it is necessary to bring in a majority of the votes cast. Another 180 votes are determined by a party-list proportional system across eleven multimember constituencies. Here smaller parties have a better chance of winning seats. Each voter gets two votes, one for a candidate and one for a party. Since this time a dizzying array of political parties have presented themselves to the electorate. Few Japanese, even experts, would be able to name all of the political parties that have formed since this time. Although some parties have lasted for several years, many form and then quickly disappear, join with other parties, or are renamed.

The Return of the LDP and the Demise of the JSP

Eight months after becoming prime minister, Hosokawa was forced to resign over allegations of illegal financial transactions. That the reform-minded politician who had called for a cleaning-up of the Japanese government was himself implicated in a banking scandal was a shock to the nation.

After Hosokawa's resignation, Tsutomu Hata, the president of Shinseito (one of the other small parties in the coalition that formed after a group of politicians led by Ichiro Ozawa and Hata broke away from the LDP), became prime minister. He survived in office for only nine weeks because the Japan Socialist Party abandoned the coalition, depriving it of a majority. Hata's resignation, paved the way for the LDP to return to power this time in an unlikely coalition with its long-time rival the JSP and the New Party Sakigake (another breakaway party from the LDP that no longer exists). In negotiations with the LDP, the JSP was able to claim the position of prime minister, but this came at a heavy price for the party that had been the dominant opposition party during the 1955 system.

Although Tomiichi Murayama was able to enjoy a year as prime minister, in the next House of Representatives election the JSP was decimated at the polls. This was in part because of the compromise the party made when it entered the coalition – giving up its stance rejecting the legitimacy of the JSDFs and the U.S.-Japan Security Treaty. This alienated many of the party's left-wing supporters. During Murayama's time in office, several crises also rocked the nation. A religious cult, Aum Shinrikyo, carried out a sarin gas attack on the Tokyo subway, killing several individuals and panicking the nation. The Kobe region was devastated by a major earthquake in which about 6,000 individuals died. The government's handling of rescue efforts was widely criticized. Murayama resigned in 1996 and the LDP appointed Ryūtarō Hashimoto to succeed him. Later that year, Hashimoto dissolved the House of Representatives and called for new elections. In the 1996 House of Representatives election the JSP dropped from its previous 142 seats (1993 election) down to 4. This led to the party's replacement by the newly formed Social Democratic Party of Japan.

For the next decade-and-a-half, the LDP was able to once again be in command albeit it often needed coalition partners to do so. Its hold on the upper house of parliament, the House of Councillors, however, was less firm. It lost the majority in the 1998 election, regained it in 2001 and 2004, but lost it again in 2007 and 2010. Several politicians, including Hashimoto, attempted to initiate reforms. During his close to three years in office, Hashimoto pushed to open Japanese markets to greater competition by easing foreign investment in sectors ranging from automobiles to insurance, banking, and security exchanges; raised the consumption tax to 5 percent to help deal with the country's growing government deficit; and initiated steps to reduce the size of the government, including reducing the number of ministries and agencies from twenty-two to thirteen.

Prime Minister Junichiro Koizumi (2001–2006) took the reforms further. He created a new Council on Economic and Fiscal Policy to advise the prime minister and appointed Harvard-trained Heizo Takenaka as the first minister of financial services, economic and fiscal policy to address reform of the badly indebted banking system (a problem that was linked to the real estate bubble discussed previously). Koizumi also was seen as a reformer interested in modernizing the LDP. This won him public support but considerable opposition from within his own political party.

Koizumi pushed to break up many of Japan's state-backed corporations, such as the Japan Highway Public Corporation that was a source of funding for much of the pork barrel spending that had supported construction firms close to LDP politicians. He also pushed to privatize the Japanese postal service. This was important because Japan Post provided not only postal services: it offered banking and life insurance services as well. As it had one of the largest holdings of personal savings in the world, there was an ample supply of financial capital to support the LDP's many public works projects. It was thus at the heart of the interest-group–driven politics that was corrupting the party and driving the country ever further into debt.

When both the opposition DPJ and several dozen of his own party members failed to vote to support the postal reform bill in the House of Councilors, Koizumi took a gamble and dissolved the House of Representatives, forcing new elections for both Houses. LDP politicians who had not supported him failed to win his backing for re-election and new candidates were brought in. The gamble was successful and the LDP won majorities in both Houses. The postal reform bill was passed.

It is interesting to reflect on why Prime Minister Koizumi backed such radical economic and fiscal reforms, and why he was willing to pit himself so strongly against members of his own party in pushing forward reforms, even though revision of Japan Post, for example, threatened the electability of some LDP politicians in rural areas where post offices might be shut. He took on the LDP, with the goal of reforming the party, breaking the hold that special interests had on the party, and rejuvenating it. The LDP had survived as a ruling party in large part because of the backing the party received from rural voters. Rural voters who had benefited from the party's agricultural policies and public works projects were loyal supporters of the LDP. The urbanization of Japan, however, meant that the rural population was rapidly aging and declining as young people congregated in cities. Koizumi recognized the need for the party to court more urban and neoliberal voters if it were to maintain its dominance in Japanese politics.

Scandal continued, however, to plague the party. Koizumi's successor, Shinzo Abe, lasted only one year in office, resigning because of ill health (he became prime minister for a second time in December 2012). Four of his Cabinet ministers had been forced to resign and his agriculture minister Toshikatsu Matsuoka committed suicide just before he was to face questions before the Diet related to unusual expenditures. The next two Japanese prime ministers, Yasuo Fukuda and Taro Aso, both managed to stay in office for just twelve months.

The Formation of the Democratic Party of Japan

Since the collapse of the 1955 system, Japan's party system has gone through a bewildering set of changes. Keeping track of Japanese political parties is not easy. Throughout the postwar period, but especially in the past couple of decades, a large number of parties have formed, many only to quickly dissolve or merge with other parties. Many are breakaway parties led by politicians who are uneasy about the direction their party is taking, or are formed because of power struggles within parties. Many of the breakaway parties have not lasted for very long. There was some tradition of breakaway parties under the 1955 system. For example, the Democratic Socialist Party broke away from the Japan Socialist Party in 1959. It remained as a small party for the next several decades. The New Liberal Club broke away from the LDP in 1976 until most of its members rejoined the LDP in 1986 after the parties formed a coalition government under Prime Minister Nakasone of the LDP.

More recently, dozens of small political parties have formed, merged with other parties, changed their names, or been dissolved. New Party Sakigake, a conservative, reformist party with ecologist sympathies that formed in 1993, for example, changed its name to the Sakigake Party in 1998. It then changed its name again to Midori no Kaigi (Environmental Green Political Assembly) in 2002, before closing its doors in 2004 when it failed to garner sufficient support to win any seats in the Diet. There are dozens of additional examples. Even specialists of Japanese party politics would be hard-pressed to remember the names of all of the parties that have formed, dissolved, merged, and renamed themselves in the past two decades. Examples include: Your Party (Minna no Tō), Tomorrow Party of Japan (Nippon Mirai no Tō), People's New Party (Kokumin Shintō), New Party Daichi – True Democrats (Shintō Daichi – Shinminshu), Green Wind (Midori no Kaze), New Renaissance Party (Shintō Kaikaku), New Party Nippon (Shintō Nippon), among many others.

In the mid-to-late 1990s, efforts to consolidate some of the opposition political parties into a viable opposition party to the LDP took root. This led to the formation of the Democratic Party of Japan, a center, left political party, in 1998. The party was formed by defectors from the LDP, members of the Sakigake party, the Democratic Socialist Party, and former members of the Japan Socialist Party. In 2003, the party merged with the Liberal Party run by one of Japan's most powerful politicians, Ichiro Ozawa. In 2007, the DPJ won the largest number of seats in the House of Councilors election and in 2009, it had a landslide victory in the House of Representatives. The DPJ won 308 seats compared to just 119 for the LDP. The remainder of the seats went to smaller parties: Kōmeitō won twenty-one, the Japan Communist Party nine, the Social Democratic Party (SDP) seven, the People's New Party (PNP) three, New Party Nippon one, New party Daichi one, Your Party five, and Independents six. The DPJ formed a coalition with the SDP, the PNP, New Party Nippon, and New Party Daiichi.

The party was viewed with high hopes by a population eager to see change. The DPJ set out to weaken the power of the bureaucracy, introducing numerous independent members' bills. They tried to do away with systems that they argued had led to cronyism, including the system of *amakudari*, described previously. It called for various reforms that would lead to the creation of a fairer and more inclusive social environment, such as free tuition for public high schools, monthly allowances to families with children, and a ban on raising the sales tax for several years. Initiating reforms proved difficult, however, because of considerable resistance from the bureaucracy and powerful interest groups and limited leadership skills or sense of a common vision among its members. The party, moreover, was plagued by its own set of scandals and weak policy performance. The government's response to the March 11, 2011, triple disaster (earthquake, tsunami, and nuclear meltdown) was widely criticized.

Table 6.1   Results of the 2012 Japan House of Representatives Election (Seats)

Party	Seats
Liberal Democratic Party, LDP	294
Democratic Party of Japan, DPJ	57
Japan Restoration Party	54
Kōmeitō	31
Your Party (Minna no Tō)	18
Tomorrow Party of Japan (Nippon Mirai no Tō)	9
Japan Communist Party, JCP	8
Independents and others	9

The coalition began to unravel. New Party Nippon withdrew its support for the coalition in April 2012 and the SDP in May of the same year. With dismally low approval ratings, the Yoshihiko Noda government dissolved the House of Representatives and called for new elections. These were held on December 16, 2012.

The LDP won the election with a landslide. The party won 294 seats, meaning that together with its long-time coalition partner, the New Kōmeitō (the Clean Government Party), which won 31 seats, the LDP achieved a supermajority in the House of Representatives. With a supermajority, it can pass bills even over the objections of the House of Councillors. The 2012 elections were a stinging defeat for the DPJ. The DPJ dropped to fifty-seven seats, just three more seats than were won by the newly formed **Japan Restoration Party** (Nippon Ishin no Kai). Whether the party will be able to revitalize itself and remain as a viable challenger to the LDP in coming elections remains to be seen. The strong performance of the newly formed Japan Restoration Party, led by the former Tokyo governor, Shintaro Ishihara and Osaka mayor, Torū Hashimoto, is also of significance. This party is a populist party that is strongly nationalist, open in its criticism of China, and anti-immigrant. An array of other smaller parties won the remaining thirty-nine seats (Table 6.1).

Second and Third Generation Politicians

Despite the many attempts to reform and open up the Japanese party system, a significant percentage of Japanese politicians are the sons (and only very rarely the daughters), grandsons, or great grandsons of politicians. In 2008, approximately one-third of Diet seats were held by the descendants of politicians. Prime Minister Yasuo Fukuda was the son of Prime Minister Takeo Fukuda. Prime Minister Shinzo Abe is the son and grandson of politicians, and his wife was the daughter of Prime Minister Nobusuke Kishi. Prime Minister Junichiro Koizumi's maternal grandfather and his father both served in the House of Representatives. Both were also appointed as cabinet ministers. His son, Shinjiro Koizumi, won his father's seat after his retirement from politics. The list of such examples is long. Bringing new faces into the Diet was a goal of the Democratic Party of Japan, but some practices are difficult to change.

Women and Politics

Japanese women have made inroads into Japanese politics but are still far behind their Western counterparts. After the 2009 House of Representatives election, women held 10.6 percent of the seats, putting them in 113th place in a ranking of nations based on the percentage of women in lower houses of parliament. This is around the same range as is found in many Middle Eastern countries. After the 2012 House of Representatives election, the percentage of women dropped as women won only 38 of 480 seats up for election or 7.9 percent. Women do somewhat better in the House of Councilors, where they hold 18 percent of the seats (44 of 242).

There are a number of female politicians and bureaucrats who have become household names. Fusae Ichikawa, who campaigned for women's political rights, was instrumental in getting women's suffrage included in the postwar Japanese constitution and herself was elected five times to the Diet, the last time when she was in her late eighties! Takako Doi, an advocate for women's rights, became the first woman to lead a Japanese party when she became head of the Japan Socialist Party in 1986. After the 1993 elections, when the opposition parties formed a coalition to oust the LDP from power, Doi became the first woman elected as Speaker of the House of Representatives. She was one of Japan's most popular politicians but failed in her efforts to shift the party in a more centrist direction. After the party's electoral debacle in 1996, she changed the name of the party to the Social Democratic Party of Japan but little was left of the party to save. Akiko Domoto, a journalist turned politician, became president of the New Party Sakigake (Shintosakigake). The 1996 ruling coalition (led by the LDP) for the first time ever included two women: Takako Doi and Akiko Domoto. Domoto is also one of only six women to become governors in the history of Japan.

The Growing Voice of Civil Society

Another important aspect of political change in Japan since the 1990s has been the empowerment of civil society. There were many restrictions that hampered the formation of a vibrant civil society. The devastating 1995 earthquake that struck Kobe and the important role played by voluntary groups in rescuing victims and providing support to ravaged communities helped to make more favorable government attitudes about civil society. After the Kobe earthquake, laws were passed to ease the establishment and functioning of non-governmental groups.

There has also been pressure on Japan to open the way for a greater role for civil society in decision making, as a result of international conferences such as the United Nations Conference on Environment and Development (1992), the United Nations Conference on Women (1995), or the United Nations Conference on Sustainable Development (2012), where nongovernmental organization participation is expected. In the past decade, there have been important changes to laws governing the establishment of nonprofit organizations and the creation of a freedom of information law.

Nongovernmental organizations and citizens groups, having gained much experience from their involvement in the Hanshin earthquake rescue, played a crucial role in helping to address the needs of the communities that were ravaged by the Tohoku earthquake, tsunami, and nuclear crisis. The Red Cross distributed food, clothing, and medicine. Volunteers helped to search for victims and to clear the coastline of debris.

Social movements also began to form and reorganize to express their opposition to Japan's nuclear energy policies. Various groups coordinated meetings, teach-ins, and protest activities. The Friday protests of antinuclear activists around the prime minister's residence have attracted thousands of protesters. Protesters come to express their opposition to maintaining nuclear energy in the country. In no time since the protests against the U.S.-Japan Security Treaty renewal in 1960 have protests been so large as they were in the first year after the Fukushima nuclear crisis. Since this time, protests have continued but they have attracted fewer participants. Thus, along with the changes in Japan's party structure, there has been a pluralization of actors as new interests and identities have emerged.

Current Policy Challenges

Japan is at a difficult time in its history. Internationally, Japan is struggling to shape and define its role in the new global order. The relative strength of the United States, Japan's most important ally, is declining and that of China, a regional rival, is rising. Where for decades the United States was Japan's most important trading partner, China now holds that position. Japan's relative strength in the Asian region is waning as well. This is further problematized by the strained relations Japan has with its neighbors in part because of still unforgiven and unforgotten wartime memories and unresolved territorial disputes, and in part because of a rivalry for regional power and influence.

Domestically, Japan must find a way to reinvigorate its economy that has suffered from two decades of slow growth. Japan needs to consider how to rejuvenate rural areas and smaller cities that have seen little to no investment in the past several decades.

The country's energy future must be decided after the Fukushima nuclear meltdowns turned much of the population more skeptical of nuclear energy. This is a major challenge for a country that is so heavily dependent on fossil fuel imports. And, governmental leaders must plan for a future with one of the most rapidly aging populations in the world. In the late 1980s, Japan was being looked at enviously by other countries eager to learn how it achieved such rapid economic growth, high education levels, longevity, and low crime rates. Today, many wonder why the country's economy continues to stagnate and its political leaders have had such trouble forging a new vision for the future.

An Aging Population

The Japanese have one of the longest life expectancies (81.25 years) but also one of the lowest fertility rates in the world. This has made Japan one of the most rapidly aging societies, which places immense strains on the pension and health-care systems. Japan's population peaked in 2010 and is now beginning to decline. Without a change in immigration policy, Japan's population could decline by 20 to 30 million people by 2050. Government policy and cultural prejudices have limited immigration into the country. Indeed, Japan is a very homogenous society; 98.5 percent of the population is ethnically Japanese. The rest are primarily Chinese or Korean. How Japan will afford to support its increasingly elderly population and maintain a creative and viable workforce are challenges that will have to be addressed. It will either require bringing more women into the workplace, raising the retirement age, or bringing in more immigrants.

Economic Recession and a Burgeoning Government Deficit

Two decades of slow to no to even negative growth have zapped Japan of much vitality. After a decade of large-scale public spending, Japan had the largest government deficit of any country. Considering the fragility of the global economy, Japan's situation is worrisome. Successive governments have failed to improve the economic situation.

When the LDP was swept back into government at the end of 2012, Prime Minister Shinzo Abe introduced a bold and risky policy reform that has come to be known as **Abenomics**. Abenomics is a major shift in economic policy from the conservative monetary policy of the Bank of Japan that was designed to limit inflation. Abe's government has introduced a policy of monetary easing with the hope that pumping more money into the economy will boost consumer confidence and spending even though it risks inflation. A second pillar of Abenomics has focused on fiscal stimulus, including a devaluation of the yen to stimulate exports and quantitative easing. A third pillar focuses on structural reform with the aim of improving efficiency and economic competitiveness (for example, through participation in the Trans-Pacific Partnership and the introduction of special economic zones to encourage investment). The government is further increasing the public debt with large scale public spending projects, including the cleanup of regions contaminated by the nuclear explosion plus more spending for infrastructure projects. The hope is that this will spur economic activity so that businesses will once again hire and be willing to pay out higher wages, which in turn is suppose to stimulate further spending. The government is betting that the 2020 Tokyo Olympics, which will require much new construction and infrastructure development, will be a further spur to the economy. They are also hoping that the Olympics will lift exports. The consumption tax has also been increased to help pay the national debt. If Abenomics works, Japan may be able to grow out of its economic slump, begin to reduce its high debt level, and address its various social problems (such as a rapidly growing share of the population living in poverty). If Abenomics fails, government debt will further balloon and Japan could fall into even more serious economic hard times than in the past. Abenomics is a major reform gamble.

The country's economic dynamism will also be linked to the ability of Japan's corporations and the Keiretsu systems behind them to respond flexibly to rapidly changing market realities and growing international competition. It will also be tied to the quality of the workforce. Japan must do more to prepare young people for the global challenges of the future. This will mean strengthening English, Chinese, and other language skills and having more young people study abroad to be skilled and knowledgeable of other cultures and practices. Opening the doors more widely to leadership positions for women in business and politics and allowing more immigration into the country will also certainly be required.

The Senkaku Islands and Japan's Military Status

Various territorial disputes cast a shadow on relations between Japan and its neighbors. Arguably the most serious of these regards the Senkaku Islands, a group of uninhabited islands claimed by Japan in the nineteenth century, a claim that China began to dispute in more recent decades after offshore oil reserves were discovered in the region. Although China and Japan are major trading partners, relations between the two countries have grown increasingly strained. Japanese economic interests in China have often been the victim of Chinese nationalism, and Japan bashing has become common in China.

Conservative voices have long been interested in revisiting the Japanese Constitution's Article 9 (the peace clause) and in past years were successful in having the article reinterpreted to allow Japan to participate in UN peacekeeping operations and in noncombat roles. As a result, Japan has been involved in UN peacekeeping operations in Afghanistan and Iraq as well as in Africa.

Right-wing conservatives have called on Japan to confront China more forcefully on its claim to the Senkaku Islands and to revise the Constitution. With its super majority, the conservative LDP passed a law in 2013 criminalizing whistle blowing that involves state secrets, a measure strongly criticized by the press. It has been called the "Fuk-hush-ima" law by some.

Energy Politics

Japan's worst disaster in modern times was triggered by the magnitude 9 Tohoku Earthquake on March 11, 2011 (referred to as 3–11 in Japan), which unleashed a series of tsunami waves that caused widespread destruction along the northeastern coast of Japan, washing away entire villages and killing an estimated 19,000. More than one million buildings were destroyed or damaged by the tsunami and earthquake. The tsunami also flooded nuclear reactors at the Fukushima Daiichi Nuclear Facility. Loss of electricity to the cooling systems resulted in partial meltdowns of the reactor cores. Hydrogen explosions carried plumes of radioactive materials out over the Pacific Ocean as well as areas primarily to the northwest of the plant. Evacuations were required, and some areas remain off limits to humans. The nuclear crisis has turned a population that was largely supportive of nuclear energy into one considerably more skeptical of its safety. After the crisis, Japan's nuclear power plants, which supplied about 30 percent of the country's electricity, were shut down for safety checks. Opposition has prevented most from being put back on line. Nevertheless, in the December 2012 elections, the population returned the pronuclear LDP back to power, suggesting that voters care more about economic issues and foreign affairs than about nuclear energy politics. Shinzo Abe's government intends to restart at least some of the nuclear power plants.

Critics argue that the nuclear crisis was not simply a product of a natural disaster but rather the making of the "nuclear village" (*genshiroku mura*) that formed to support and protect the nuclear industry. The "nuclear village" refers to the government, bureaucratic, industrial, media, and academic supporters of nuclear energy that have fought hard to maintain the privileged position of nuclear energy in Japan's electricity mix. Supported and encouraged by the United States, and despite its experiences as a victim of atomic bombings, Japan embarked in the 1950s on the development of a conventional nuclear energy industry. Because Japan is a country with limited fossil fuel resources, nuclear energy was supported by the LDP and favorable conditions were established for nuclear energy research and development and also the building of nuclear power plants. Communities that agreed to accept nuclear power plants were provided large amounts of compensatory investment. The Fukushima nuclear disaster has led to harshly critical examinations of the nuclear industry and the collusive relationships that permitted safety measures to become lax and information distorted. Even with the LDP back in power, it is doubtful that the country will return to its pre-Fukushima energy policy that envisioned the expansion of nuclear energy to about 50 percent of the electricity supply. There is likely to be a long debate about what role nuclear energy should play in the energy mix and a gradual development of greater renewable energy capacity.

It should be noted that the debate about nuclear energy policy goes beyond a simple question of electricity production: it is also linked to a military debate. Japan has one of the world's largest stockpiles of plutonium. Maintaining civilian nuclear energy capacity could enable the country to develop nuclear weapons, as has been argued for by some of Japan's more right-wing politicians.

CONCLUSION

The same combination of interests, ideas, and institutions that were considered to be factors behind Japan's economic successes are seen as partly to blame for Japan's political and economic problems since the early 1990s. The high degree of cooperation among government, the bureaucracy, industry, and the agricultural sector helped Japan to develop into a major economic power. It also, however, created decision-making structures that were intransparent, prone to corruption, and protective of the status quo.

Japan is still one of the largest economies in the world, enjoys a relatively high quality of life, has far lower crime rates than in many other countries, has a highly educated population, and is free of many of the major ethnic and religious divisions that are found in many other societies. Thus, many of the factors that contributed to the country's past success remain. What it now needs is political vision and leadership to deal with the many domestic and foreign relations challenges the country faces. The LDP's landslide electoral victory in the 2012 elections may be a hope on the part of the electorate that the party that had brought it stability and leadership in the past can do so again in the future. Whether the LDP is up to the challenge and can avoid the pitfalls of corruption and scandal that have plagued it in the past is what only time can tell (Table 6.2).

Table 6.2   Japanese Prime Ministers (PMs) in the Postwar Period

Prime Minister	Dates in Office	Party and Coalition Partners
Tetsuya Katayama	(May 24, 1947–Mar. 10, 1948)	JSP-DP-PCP
Hitoshi Ashida	(Mar. 10, 1948–Oct. 15, 1948)	DP-JSP-PCP
Shigeru Yoshida	(Oct. 15, 1948–Feb. 16, 1949)	DLP
	(Feb. 16, 1949 – Oct. 30, 1952)	DLP/Lib-DP
	(Oct. 30, 1952–May 21, 1953)	Liberal
	(May 21, 1953–Dec. 10, 1954)	Liberal
Ichiro Hatoyama	(Dec. 10, 1954–Mar. 19, 1955)	JDP
	(Mar. 19, 1955–Nov. 22, 1955)	JDP
	(Nov. 22, 1955–Dec. 23, 1956)	LDP
Tanzan Ishibashi	(Dec. 23, 1956–Feb. 25, 1957)	LDP
Nobusuke Kishi	(Feb. 25, 1957–June 12, 1958)	LDP
	(June 12, 1958–July 19, 1960)	LDP

Prime Minister	Dates in Office	Party and Coalition Partners
	(July 19, 1960–Dec. 8, 1960)	LDP
Hayato Ikeda	(Dec. 8, 1960–Dec. 9, 1963)	LDP
	(Dec. 9, 1963–Nov. 9, 1964)	LDP
	(Nov. 9, 1964–Feb. 17, 1967)	LDP
Eisaku Satō	(Feb. 17, 1967–Jan. 14, 1970)	LDP
	(Jan. 14, 1970–July 7, 1972)	LDP
Kakuei Tanaka	(July 7, 1972–Dec. 22, 1972)	LDP
	(Dec. 22, 1972–Nov. 9, 1974)	LDP
Takeo Miki	(Dec. 9, 1974–Dec. 24, 1976)	LDP
Takeo Fukuda	(Dec. 24, 1976–Dec. 7, 1978)	LDP
Masayoshi Ōhira	(Dec. 7, 1978–Nov. 9, 1979)	LDP
	(Nov. 9, 1979–June 12, 1980)	LDP
Zenkō Suzuki	(July 17, 1980–Nov. 27, 1982)	LDP
	(Nov. 27, 1982–Dec. 27, 1983)	LDP
Yasuhiro Nakasone	(Dec. 27, 1983–July 22, 1986)	LDP-NLC
	(July 22, 1986–Nov. 6, 1987)	LDP
Noboru Takeshita	(Nov. 6, 1987–June 3, 1989)	LDP
Sōsuke Uno	(June 3, 1989–Aug. 10, 1989)	LDP
Toshiki Kaifu	(Aug. 10, 1989–Feb. 28, 1990)	LDP
	(Feb. 28, 1990–Nov. 5, 1991)	LDP
Kiichi Miyazawa	(Nov. 5, 1991–Aug. 9, 1993)	LDP
Morihiro Hosokawa	(Aug. 9, 1993–Apr. 28, 1994)	JNP-JSP-JRP-Komeitō-NPS-DSP-SDF
Tsutomu Hata	(Apr. 28, 1994–June 30, 1994)	JRP-JNP-JSP-SDP-SDF-Komeitō -NPS
Tomiichi Murayama	(June 30, 1994–Jan. 11, 1996)	JSP –LDP-NPS

(continued)

Table 6.2 (*cont.*)

Prime Minister	Dates in Office	Party and Coalition Partners
Ryutaro Hashimoto	(Jan. 11, 1996 – Nov. 7, 1996)	LDP-JSP-NPS
	(Nov. 7, 1996–July 30, 1998)	LDP-JSP-NPS
Keizō Obuchi	(July 30, 1998–Apr. 5, 2000)	LDP (Lib-Komeitō)
Yoshirō Mori	(Apr. 5, 2000–July 4, 2000)	LDP-Komeitō-NCP
	(July 4, 2000–Apr. 26, 2001)	LDP- Komeitō-NCP
Junichiro Koizumi	(Apr. 26, 2001–Nov. 19, 2003)	LDP- Komeitō-NCP
	(Nov. 19, 2003–Sept 21, 2005)	LDP- Komeitō
	(Sept. 21, 2005–Sept. 28, 2006)	LDP – Komeitō
Shinzō Abe	(Sept. 28, 2006–Feb. 26, 2007)	LDP – Komeitō
Yasuo Fukuda	(Feb. 26, 2007–Sept. 24, 2008)	LDP – Komeitō
Tarō Aso	(Sept. 24, 2008–Sept. 16, 2009)	LDP – Komeitō
Yukio Hatoyama	(Sept. 16, 2009–June 8, 2010)	DPJ-SDP-PNP
Naoto Kan	(June 8, 2010–Sept. 2, 2011)	DPJ-PNP
Yoshihiko Noda	(Sept. 2, 2011–Dec. 26, 2012)	DPJ-PNP
Shinzō Abe	(Dec. 26, 2012–)	LDP – Komeitō

DP = Democratic Party; DLP = Democratic Liberal Party; DSP = Democratic Socialist Party;
JDP = Japan Democratic Party; JNP = Japan New Party; JRP = Japan Renewal Party;
JSP = Japan Socialist Party; Komeitō = Clean Government Party; Liberal = Liberal Party;
LDP = Liberal Democratic Party; NCP = New Conservative Party; NLC = New Liberal Club;
NPS = New Party Sakigake; PCP = People's Cooperative Party; PNP = People's New Party;
SDF = Social Democratic Federation; SDP = Social Democratic Party

BIBLIOGRAPHY

Beasley, W. G. *Rise of Modern Japan. Political, Economic, and Social Change since 1850*. New York: St. Martin's Press. 2000.

Curtis, Gerald. *The Logic of Japanese Politics: Leaders, Institutions and the Limits of Change*. New York: Columbia University Press. 1999.

Dower, John W. *Embracing Defeat: Japan in the Wake of World War II*. New York: Norton. 1999.

Duus, Peter. *The Rise of Modern Japan*. Boston: Houghton-Mifflin. 1976.

Gaunder, Alisa, ed. *The Routledge Handbook of Japanese Politics*. New York: Routledge. 2011.

Gluck, Carol. *Japan's Modern Myths: Ideology in the Late Meiji Period*. Princeton, NJ: Princeton University Press. 1985.

Hook, Glen D., Julie Gilson, Christopher W. Hughes and Hugo Dobson. *Japan's International Relations: Politics, Economics and Security*, third edition. New York: Routledge. 2011.

Inoguchi, Takashi and Purnendra Jain. *Japanese Politics Today: From Karaoke to Kabuki Democracy*. New York: Palgrave MacMillan. 2011.

Johnson, Chalmers. *MITI and the Japanese Miracle: The Growth of Industrial Policy, 1925–1975*. Palo Alto, CA: Stanford University Press. 1982.

Kingston, Jeffrey. *Contemporary Japan: History, Politics, and Society*, second edition. Oxford: Blackwell Publishing. 2013.

Pempel, T. J. *Regime Shift: Comparative Dynamics of the Japanese Political Economy*. Ithaca, NY: Cornell University Press. 1998.

Richardson, Bradley. *Japanese Democracy*. New Haven, CT and London: Yale University Press. 1997.

Schlessinger, Jacob M. *Shadow Shoguns: The Rise and Fall of Japan's Postwar Political Machine*. Palo Alto, CA: Stanford University Press. 1999.

Schreurs, Miranda A. *Environmental Politics in Japan, Germany, and the United States*. Cambridge: Cambridge University Press. 2002.

Schwarz, Frank, and Susan J. Pharr, eds. *The State of Civil Society in Japan*. Cambridge: Cambridge University Press. 2003.

Stockwin, J. A. A. *Governing Japan: Divided Politics in a Resurgent Economy*, fourth edition. Oxford: Blackwell Publishing. 2008.

IMPORTANT TERMS

Abenomics – the economic reform policy introduced by Prime Minister Shinzō Abe in an effort to stimulate the Japanese economy. It focuses on monetary easy, fiscal stimulus, economic restructuring, and public spending.

amakudari – literally "descent from heaven," this term refers to the common practice whereby retiring civil servants take up positions in Japanese corporations and public-interest bodies.

Article 9 – of the Japanese constitution states that "the Japanese people forever renounce was as a sovereign right of the nation and the threat or use of force as a means of settling international disputes." It has been the basis for the maintenance of a pacifist foreign policy, although over the years it has been reinterpreted to allow for the creation of the Japanese Self-Defense Forces and participation in UN peacekeeping operations.

daimyo – the lords of the 260 feudal fiefdoms of Japan.

Democratic Party of Japan (DPJ) – a center, left political party, which was formed in 1998 by defectors from the LDP, members of the Sakigake Party, the Democratic Socialist Party, and former members of the Japan Socialist Party. In 2003, the party merged with the Liberal Party run by one of Japan's most powerful politicians, Ichiro Ozawa.

Democratic Socialist Party (DSP) – formed by a group of politicians who splintered off of the Japan Socialist Party (JSP) in 1960. The party advocated a moderate social-democratic politics and supported the U.S.-Japan security alliance. The party was dissolved in 1994. Many of its members later joined the Democratic Party of Japan.

Diet – the name used for the Japanese parliament. Japan's Diet was created in 1890 on the Prussian model. Under the postwar Constitution, the Diet consists of a House of Representatives and a House of Councillors.

Economic miracle – a widely used term to describe Japan's remarkable economic growth in the first decades after World War II.

fukoku kyohei – literally "rich nation, strong army," this phrase symbolized Meiji Japan's desire to catch up economically and militarily with the West.

Fukushima triple disaster – refers to the major earthquake, tsunami, and nuclear accident that has led to major changes in Japan's energy and policies.

gyōsei shidō – translated as "administrative guidance," this term symbolizes the power of the Japanese bureaucracy and its influence in helping to steer the Japanese economy during its growth years.

Iron triangle – points to the formal and informal institutional ties among the LDP, the bureaucracy, and industry that have favored big business interests in policy making.

Japan Communist Party (JCP) – one of the only parties to oppose Japanese militarism in the prewar period, the postwar JCP opposes the U.S.-Japan Security alliance, defends Article 9 of the Constitution, and advocates a more democratic form of capitalism. For many decades it was referred to as a 10 percent party although in recent years its electoral success has waned.

Japan Restoration Party (Nippon Isshin no Kai) – led by the former Tokyo mayor Shintaro Ishihara and Osaka Mayor, Torū Hashimoto, is also of significance. This party was formed in September 2012 to be a third political force in Japan. It is a populist party that is strongly based on the visibility of its leadership. The positions of the party remain somewhat vague because of differences in the leadership's views on nuclear power, the best approach to a consumption tax, and the way to deal with China.

Japan Socialist Party (JSP) – the largest opposition party in the 1955 system until its near total collapse in 1996. It followed a Marxist-Leninist ideology and opposed the U.S.-Japan Security alliance into the early 1990s when party leaders tried to bring the party more to the center.

keiretsu – the term for the economic conglomerates that are prevalent in postwar Japan

Liberal Democratic Party (LDP) – a conservative, pro-business party that has dominated Japanese politics from its formation in 1955 through the present with only brief intervals in opposition.

General Douglas MacArthur – appointed Supreme Commander of the Allied Powers (SCAP) by President Harry S. Truman, he was in charge of the occupation of Japan. He was a very powerful figure and had a hand in the writing of the Japanese constitution.

Meiji Restoration – the 1868 revolt that led to the downfall of the Tokugawa clan, the revival of the position of the emperor, and the implementation of a crash course in Western politics, law, economics, and culture.

Ministry of Economy, Trade, and Industry (METI) – the ministry that played an important role in the economic development of Japan. The ministry was formerly called the Ministry of International, Trade and Industry (MITI).

New Kōmeitō (Clean Government Party) – formed in 1954 by members of the Nichiren Buddhist organization Sōka Gakkai. It is a center-right party that has frequently joined in coalition with the Liberal Democratic Party.

Commodore Matthew Perry – sailed four "black ships" into Edo Bay in 1853 and demanded the opening of Japanese ports to foreign trade. Perry's voyages to Japan were behind the great political reforms of the Meiji Restoration.

shogunate – the military leaders and the Tokugawa clan that ruled Japan from 1603 to 1868.

Taisho democracy – the brief interlude during the period from 1918 to 1932 when parties gained political influence and a more pluralist democracy began to function.

Shigeru Yoshida – Japanese prime minister from 1946 to 1947 and again from 1949 to 1954, who chose to focus on economic development and allow the United States to guarantee Japan's security. His policies are referred to as the Yoshida Doctrine and became the guiding ideology of the LDP.

STUDY QUESTIONS

1. In what ways did Japan's long-term isolation during the Tokugawa era impact on the country's subsequent political development? How was Japan able to avoid the fate of many other Asian countries that became colonies of the West?
2. Why was the Meiji Restoration so important to Japan's economic and political transformation?
3. How has Japan's military past affected relations with the country's Asian neighbors?
4. How has nationalism influenced Japanese domestic and foreign politics?
5. What lessons can we take from the Allied occupation of Japan? Why was the occupation of Japan so "successful"?
6. Japan's "economic miracle" stunned the world. How can Japan's rise from postwar destitution to economic powerhouse be explained?
7. How does the postwar Japanese constitution differ from the Meiji era constitution?
8. What were the driving factors behind political reform in Japan beginning with Prime Minister Hosokawa?

9. Do you think Japan should maintain a strict interpretation of Article 9? Why, or why not?

10. Are there characteristics of Japanese politics you would consider to be uniquely Japanese?

11. In what ways did the long dominance of the Liberal Democratic Party lead to problems of lack of transparency and corruption?

12. What steps do you think Japan needs to take to revitalize its economy and political party system?

Early Developers and Middle Developers

Once Great Britain and France developed, all other countries were forced to respond. Germany and Japan were among the first to do so. By the middle of the nineteenth century, Germany was not yet unified and Japan faced Western imperialism. German and Japanese variations on the grand strategies of development found in the early developers are the direct result of international competition – military, economic, and cultural – between early and middle developers.

If Great Britain's and France's historical experiences are models of development and revolution from below, Germany and Japan represent instances of development and revolution from above. Compared with their predecessors, the middle and lower classes in Germany and Japan were weaker and the upper classes stronger. The state, in alliance with the upper classes, helped initiate economic development. Above all, what drove the entire process was military competition with more advanced states.

This developmental path had fateful consequences for liberal democracy and ultimately world peace. After abortive attempts at representative democracy, both Germany and Japan thus went through a period of fascism before they could participate in the world economy on an equal basis with the developed West.

Middle Developers: Germany and Japan

French power on the European continent guaranteed throughout the first seventy years of the nineteenth century that Germany remained a fragmented group of kingdoms and principalities. Among these separate states, however, some were more powerful than others. The most militarily capable was Prussia, which, under the leadership of Chancellor Bismarck, succeeded in defeating the French in the Franco-Prussian War of 1870 and unifying the German states under Prussian leadership in 1871. From the outset, German economic and political development reflected the fact that it came in response to French and British advancement. The fact that the need for military power came in anticipation of, rather than in response to, economic development meant that the path taken by Britain and France, which was largely a story of rising middle classes gradually securing power over monarchs and nobilities, would not be a historical possibility for Germany. Unable to rely on an economically ingenious and politically assertive rising middle class, Germany industrialized by allowing capital to concentrate in relatively few large banks, permitting industrialists to reduce risk through the creation of cartels, and creating a modern military officer corps and state apparatus on the basis of premodern agrarian elites. The coalition on which power rested consisted of an alliance of "iron and rye" that had little interest in genuine parliamentary rule. The parliament, known as the Reichstag, was neither fairly elected nor did it have sovereignty over the kaiser, whose governmental ministers continued to be appointed from the ranks of the noble elite.

Although this pattern of development forestalled democracy, it succeeded quite spectacularly in military competition and economic development. By the beginning of the twentieth century, Germany could field land armies superior to those of the French and could float ships on a par with those of the British. German chemical, machine-building, and metal industries were as advanced as those of its competitors. Such rapid development, occurring really in fewer than forty years, had a price. German craftsmen and especially industrial workers, who were often first-generation city dwellers, lived mostly in very difficult circumstances. Radical working-class parties, such as the Social Democrats, could easily recruit the disaffected and the poor into mass politics. The ruling elite responded in two ways: first by banning the Social Democrats, and when that could not be sustained, by relying on a kind of militaristic German nationalist appeal for solidarity among classes against other nations. Unfortunately, this latter strategy worked. Perceiving the balance of forces to be temporarily on their side, and by tradition inclined toward military solutions to social and diplomatic problems, the kaiser and his advisers exploited a crisis in European security relations in 1914 to launch a continent-wide war, which ultimately became known as World War I.

Defeat in this war forced the kaiser to abdicate and led to a fundamental democratization of German politics. This first try at parliamentary democracy, known as the Weimar Republic (1920–1933), suffered from innumerable handicaps. The old elites had not been decisively replaced either in the economy or in the state bureaucracy, the victory of democracy was associated in many people's minds with a humiliating loss in war (in a country that lived by the cult of war) and an equally humiliating peace treaty signed at Versailles, the country was saddled with heavy reparations payments to the victors, and the political institutions led to a fragmented party system and the temptation to rule by emergency presidential decree. This last factor became the fateful one when Adolf Hitler's Nazi Party managed to gain a plurality of seats in the Reichstag in the 1932 elections. Hitler had revived much of the older militaristic thinking of the pre-Weimar era, but he now laced the new ideology with large doses of revenge and racism. After spending the middle of the 1930s preparing for war, in 1939 Germany initiated, for the second time in the twentieth century, a Europe-wide conflict that cost the lives of millions.

Because war emanated from Germany twice during the twentieth century, the Allied victors decided that this would not happen again. The ultimate price that Germany paid for defeat was, in some sense, to return to the situation from which it had started: national division. The Soviet zone of occupation became communist East Germany, or what was called the German Democratic Republic, and the three Western zones of occupation (those of Britain, the United States, and France) became West Germany, or the Federal Republic of Germany.

Apart from division, the Western allies and democratically minded Germans were also determined to remake Germany from the inside in order to ensure that democracy would genuinely take root there. To that end, Germany developed a set of policies, as well as constitutional and institutional innovations, designed to foster democratic stability and prevent extremist politics from ever returning. For example, although Germany continues to have a multiparty system, there are constitutional features to guarantee that it does not become too fragmented, unstable, or gridlocked in indecision. Another such arrangement is corporatism. Most Germans are organized into trade unions or employer associations. The German government through its public offices attempts to ensure that these two groups hammer out agreements that ensure just wages, low unemployment, and high growth rates. In turn, the government attempts to soften many of the rougher edges of capitalist economics through a comprehensive welfare state. The net impact of these policies is designed to ensure that economic downturns do not occur often and, when they do occur, that they do not turn public opinion against democracy. Perhaps more crucially, corporatist policies are supposed to prevent the most rancorous debates over wages, prices, and welfare and move them off the parliamentary floor and out of politics in general.

Such policies helped secure for the Federal Republic quite remarkable growth rates throughout the postwar era and also created a society that, for the first time in Germany's history, genuinely seems to value liberal democracy for its own sake. However, the challenges of reunification, European unity, and global capitalist competition have induced slower growth rates, much higher unemployment, and a new domestic debate on whether the German model can be sustained into the future. In the first years of the twenty-first century, the German government brought the entire German social market model into question by tinkering with such bedrocks of the German model as health care, unemployment insurance, and state employment. Such questioning of the German model and initial moves to alter it are indeed troubling to most Germans precisely because it was this model that brought the country affluence and, after 1989, national unity – two things that had eluded Germany for the previous century.

Although Japan lies thousands of miles away from the European continent, grouping it together with Germany makes a great deal of sense to comparativists. For one thing, like Germany, Japan confronted external challenges to its sovereignty that forced it into rapid economic development in order to compete militarily. For another, the responses to these challenges were remarkably similar. Finally, the long-term path on which these responses set Japan led it to a similar form of militarism that also could only be overcome by fundamental restructuring after World War II.

Japan entered the early modern period a fragmented country dominated by alliances of local feudal lords (called daimyo), several of whom tried for over a century to gain control over the country. Under the leadership of the Tokugawa family (1603–1868), however, Japan at the start of the seventeenth century overcame its feudal fragmentation. Through concentration of power in the hands of the shogun, the institution of a rigid class system in which the warrior samurai nobility were given the lion's share of privileges, and the isolation of the island through a prohibition on foreign travel and a ban on the practice of Christianity, successive Tokugawa rulers succeeded in crafting out a distinctive Japanese identity and a unified Japanese state.

As effective as this system was in solving the problems of political unification – and the fact that it lasted for 250 years suggests that it was effective – the arrival of U.S. Commodore Perry's "black ships" in 1853, with the purpose of forcing Japan to open its borders to trade and foreign influence, posed challenges that the Tokugawa order was not equipped to confront. In the mid-1860s, a series of rebellions among low-level samurai, who incorporated nonprofessional soldiers and even peasants into their army under a nationalist banner of expelling the foreign "barbarians," succeeded in overthrowing the last Tokugawa shogun from office and replaced him in 1868 with an emperor whom they considered to be the true emperor of Japan, the fifteen-year-old Meiji.

The Meiji Restoration, as historians have subsequently dubbed it, set Japan down a course of economic and military modernization with the purpose of securing the country from foreign control. The slogan of the time, "rich country, strong military," captured the essence of what the Meiji Restoration was about. As in Germany, our other middle developer, industrial modernization occurred primarily in the form of a "revolution from above." A modern army and navy were created, feudal-style control over localities was replaced with a modern local government, and class privileges were formally abolished, thus reducing the power of the old samurai class, in theory, to that of the commoners. As in Germany, industrialization was accomplished at breakneck speed under the guidance of a national bureaucracy and with capital controlled by large family-owned industrial conglomerates called *zaibatsu*. Also as in Germany, the Japanese Meiji elite sought a political model that could accommodate the kinds of changes that were taking place. The constitutional model they settled on, not surprisingly, was that of imperial Germany, with its parliamentary electoral rules that favored the landed elite and a government that remained dominated by military institutions and values.

Fundamental democratization occurred in Japan for the first time only in 1925 with a series of electoral reforms. Unfortunately, the old Meiji ruling elites who remained on the political scene, especially within the officer corps, never fully supported democracy. When the political and economic crises of the 1930s hit, consistent pressure from right-wing extremists and the military high command constrained the actions of civilian government. The ideas of the Far Right and the military about what Japan needed were somewhat diffuse, but they can be summarized relatively easily: solve Japan's economic and domestic problems through the colonization and economic domination of continental Asia. To achieve these goals, starting in 1936 Japan engaged in a series of wars in China that yielded even more power to the military. The military viewed the United States as the main obstacle to Japan's plans for Asia, and it finally pushed Japan to attack Pearl Harbor in 1941 as a preemptive strike against U.S. might.

The devastating end of the war was the U.S. decision to drop the atomic bomb twice on Japan, after which the U.S. occupation inaugurated a series of political and economic reforms that changed life in Japan. A new constitution that forbade foreign military involvement, the complete removal of the emperor from political life, and a series of new institutions and political rules designed to bring constitutional democracy all brought about fundamental change. Japan lives with the result to this day.

Despite these changes, the nature of the Japanese political and economic model shows considerable continuities, or at least influences, from the past that remain a constant source of fascination for comparativists. Government and business continue to work closely together (although Japan's government is the "smallest" in the industrialized world), and capital remains far more concentrated than in the Anglo-American model. Japan developed a system where worker loyalty to the firm was highly prized and there was a high degree of income equality. In more recent years, however, the old economic model has started to unravel. Income inequality is on the rise, firms are no longer follow lifetime hiring practices, and the country has experienced two decades of recession. The Fukushima nuclear explosion has further led to a crisis of trust in the government and put Japan's energy policy under scrutiny. Japan is now looking towards the 2020 Olympics as a goal for revitalization. As in Germany, where the fundamental democratization of the postwar period was accompanied by a selective retention of important aspects of the earlier model that seemed to work, the need to rethink the postwar political-economic model has led to considerable unease within Japan.

PART III
Late Developers

RUSSIA

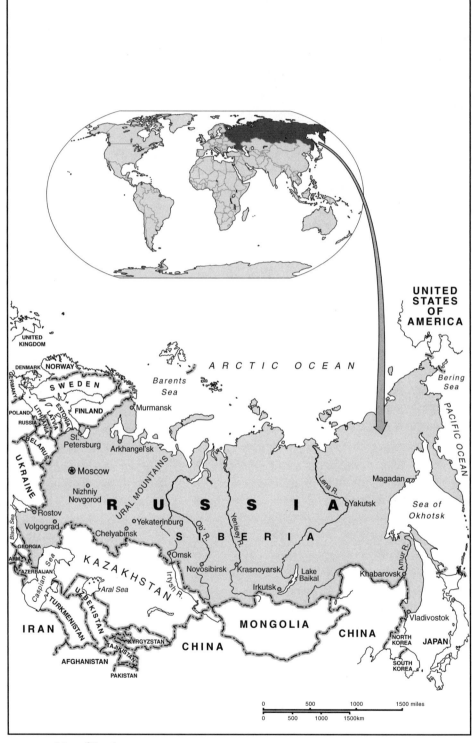

MAP 7.1. Map of Russia.

7 Russia

Stephen E. Hanson

Introduction

Russia has long puzzled and surprised observers of international politics. For seven decades, Russia was at the center of a communist regime – the Union of Soviet Socialist Republics, or USSR – that competed with the United States for global supremacy (see Table 7.1 at the end of the chapter). After the collapse of the USSR in 1991, Russia suffered a prolonged period of political, military, and economic decay. During the first two terms of President Vladimir Putin, the Russian economy rebounded strongly, but this growth was accompanied by a return to political authoritarianism. In 2008, Putin defied many analysts' expectations by stepping down as president to make way for his protégé Dmitry Medvedev and becoming prime minister instead; Putin then turned the tables by returning as president for a third term in 2012. There is no consensus among specialists about how the former communist superpower became so weak so quickly; nor do scholars agree in their evaluations of Putin's efforts to revive the country. Indeed, it seems that Russia simply does not fit conventional analytic categories.

Geographically, Russia is the biggest country in the world. Most of its population is in Europe; most of its territory is in Asia. Although about four-fifths of its population is ethnically Russian, the Russian Federation contains hundreds of other ethnic groups, some of which have engaged in serious struggles for greater autonomy or – in the case of **Chechnya** – battled for full independence during the 1990s. Should we call Russia a European, an Asian, or a "Eurasian" state? Is Russia a nation or an empire? Might Russia eventually break up into smaller regional units? Or is it emerging again as a revitalized great power in world politics?

Economically, Russia is largely industrialized and urbanized, with less than onequarter of its population living in rural areas. Its population is highly educated. Yet many of its factories are inefficient, technologically backward, and environmentally unsafe; its villages still often lack paved roads, sewage systems, and basic services; and its economy remains heavily dependent on exports of oil, natural gas, and minerals. Should we call Russia an advanced,

Table 7.1   Key Phases in Russia's Political Development

Date	Regime	Global Context	Interests/Identities/ Institutions	Developmental Path
1690– 1917	Tsarist empire	Russia as great power on periphery of capitalist West	Landowning aristocracy/"divine right" monarchy/ feudal state	Autocratic modernization
1917– 1928	Soviet Russia/ USSR	World War I, collapse of tsarist empire, civil war, postwar isolation	Revolutionary intellectuals and workers/Marxist ideology/Leninist one-party rule	Party control over key industries, toleration of market production
1929– 1945	USSR	Great Depression, rise of Nazism in Germany, World War II	Stalinist secret police and "heroic" workers/ Marxism- Leninism/ planned economy	Rapid industrialization, brutal collectivization, prison labor, military buildup
1945– 1984	USSR	Cold War with United States, anti-Soviet rebellions in Poland and Afghanistan	Corrupt party and state elites/"superpower" socialism/stagnating planned economy	Enforcement of status quo, military expansion in developing world
1985– 1991	USSR	Military buildup in West, disintegration of Soviet bloc and USSR	Reformist intellectuals/ "socialist renewal"/ institutional disintegration	"Perestroika" (unintended self-destruction of Leninism)
1991– 1999	Russian Federation	Russia as fading power on periphery of triumphant capitalist global system	Former party and state elites and local "mafias"/search for new Russian identity/ weak democracy	"Shock therapy," corrupt capitalism
1999– present	Russian Federation	Russia tries to rebuild its great power status in context of global war on terrorism	Putin loyalists and security services/ pragmatic patriotism/ increasing authoritarianism	Increasing state intervention in economy combined with dependence on energy exports

a developing, or an underdeveloped state? Or does Russia's economy deserve some new theoretical category of its own?

Culturally, Russia has played a key role in European intellectual and artistic history, producing such well-known writers and composers as Lev Tolstoy, Fyodor Dostoevsky, and Pyotr Tchaikovsky. Yet for centuries – and even today – prominent Russian thinkers have claimed that their country can never be truly "Westernized" because of what they claim is the essential mysticism, communalism, and idealism of the Russian "soul." Should we call Russia's culture Western, non-Western, or something else entirely?

Neither Western analysts nor Russians themselves have come up with consistent answers to these questions. Indeed, after the collapse of the communist empire in 1991, life in Russia became even more unpredictable and confusing. As the twenty-first century enters its second decade, Russians are engaged in a seemingly endless debate about their country's future path. Early hopes for a rapid transition to Western-style democracy and capitalism have been dashed, and although the public mood has improved with the stabilization of the economy under Putin, there remains a pervasive anxiety about Russia's future. Russia's sudden annexation of Crimea and its growing conflict with Ukraine in 2014 will only further exacerbate this uncertainty in the long run.

Faced with the paradoxical nature of Russia's geography, economy, politics, and culture, many political scientists have been tempted to agree with Winston Churchill that Russia is "a riddle wrapped in a mystery inside an enigma." Detailed descriptions of Russian institutions seem to become outdated almost as soon as they are written. However, the comparative and theoretical approach to political analysis presented in this book can help us explain Russia's troubled history.

This chapter argues that contemporary Russian interest groups have been decisively shaped by the ideological identity and distinctive institutions imposed on the country by **Vladimir Lenin** and his followers from 1917 to 1991 in an effort to catch up with and overtake the West. In short, the USSR was a failed ideological experiment to design an alternative anticapitalist model of industrial society. Ironically, the collapse of Soviet institutions left Russia once again on the periphery of the global capitalist system, facing challenges of economic backwardness, ethnic conflict, and international insecurity similar to those confronting the country in the early twentieth century. This time, however, there is no consensual or coherent ideology to organize Russia's response to these challenges. Thus, an analysis of the rise and fall of the Soviet Union is crucial for understanding Russian politics today.

The Rise and Fall of the USSR

From Marx to Lenin

What did "communism" mean to the founders of the Soviet regime and their heirs? To answer this question, we must begin with an examination of the Western European theorist who originally invented the idea of communism – Karl Marx. To be clear, Marx himself did not provide a blueprint for the Soviet system. Indeed, he died thirty-four years before the Russian Revolution of 1917. Those who wish to blame Marx for Soviet tyranny forget how little control philosophers and theorists have over the ways in which their ideas are interpreted decades or centuries later. Still, the Soviet leaders all considered themselves Marx's faithful disciples. We therefore need to understand Marx's ideas in order to make sense of the rise and fall of the Soviet Empire.

Karl Marx was born in 1818 in what is now Germany. When Marx was growing up, the vast majority of German-speakers, like the vast majority of human beings elsewhere, lived in small peasant villages ruled by various local lords and princes. The Industrial Revolution that had already transformed England and the United States had yet to reach Germany, where merchant activity was largely confined to the larger cities and towns. Thus, Marx wrote about capitalism as it was first being developed on the European continent.

When Marx was just twenty-nine years old, he and his best friend, Friedrich Engels, composed the most influential revolutionary essay ever written: the *Communist Manifesto*. The starting point for the analysis contained in the *Manifesto* – and indeed for all of Marx's later works – is a theoretical approach that later became known as historical materialism, which asserts that economic forces have ultimately determined the course of human social history. Politicians and philosophers may think that they are battling over principles, but in Marx's view they are really always fighting over the question of which groups get which shares of a society's overall wealth. The ruling ideas in each historical period, according to Marx, are always the ideas of a particular society's ruling class.

Marx argued that every stage of history has been marked by class struggle. Society has always been divided into two main classes: those who own property, and those who are forced to work to survive. The ruling class, Marx claimed, takes all the wealth that is left over once people's basic survival needs are met – what Marx called surplus value. However, the oppressed class always struggles to regain this surplus, which, after all, the workers themselves have produced. Eventually, class struggle ignites a full-scale social revolution against the old order, leading to the emergence of a new and more advanced form of economic organization.

According to Marx, three main types of class society have shaped human history to date: slavery, feudalism, and capitalism. Slavery was the dominant "mode of production" in the earliest human civilizations, such as those of ancient Greece, Egypt, and Rome. After the fall of the Roman Empire, slavery in Europe gave way to feudalism, in which the main class struggle was between the ruling aristocracy and the oppressed peasantry. After 1500 or so, this mode of production also began to weaken and finally disintegrate.

The third and final type of class society, capitalism, emerged in its full-fledged form in England and the United States during the 1700s. In the *Communist Manifesto*, Marx and Engels predicted – correctly, as we now know – that it would eventually encompass the entire globe. Capitalists themselves naturally argue that this new mode of production promotes individual freedom and wealth. In reality, Marx insisted, capitalism is simply another form of class exploitation with its own distinct type of class struggle. The ruling class under capitalism, the bourgeoisie, consists of those who hire workers for wages and/or own the factories, banks, and housing upon which workers are dependent. The oppressed class, the proletariat, consists of all those who own nothing more than their own labor power and are therefore forced to compete for a job in order to survive – that is, the vast majority of people. Surplus value, in the form of capitalist profits, goes straight into the pockets of the ruling class, whereas the proletariat must continually struggle to raise their wages above a very low level.

Marx was convinced that the capitalist system, like slavery and feudalism before it, would eventually be destroyed in a social revolution – this time eliminating class divisions among human beings altogether and ushering in communism, an era of global harmony and abundance. Marx argued that the experience of working together under the dehumanizing conditions of capitalism would serve to strip the proletariat of all forms of identity that had previously divided it. Subjected to the same forms of underpaid, repetitive, mechanized labor, workers would stop caring about one another's race, ethnicity, religion, or nationality and recognize their common humanity. The proletarian revolution, then, would be a revolution of the vast majority of human beings, united as one, to take control over the global economic system. Freed from the tyranny of wage slavery and the terror of unemployment, workers would henceforth work together in conditions of free, creative cooperation. The *Communist Manifesto* concludes: "The proletarians have nothing to lose but their chains! They have a world to win! Working men of all countries, unite!"

Yet there was a central paradox in Marx's thinking. On the one hand, Marx called for workers to unite and struggle for better conditions and wages in order to build proletarian solidarity and learn to exploit the vulnerabilities of the bourgeois system. On the other hand, Marx expected that workers under capitalism would become increasingly miserable over time, making revolution inevitable. What should communists do, then, if every successful workers' struggle against the bosses made workers less miserable and more satisfied with capitalism? Should communists support change within the existing system? Or should they continue to promote global revolution regardless of how capitalism reformed itself? Marx himself never quite resolved this strategic paradox.

In fact, no Marxist revolution has ever taken place in a developed capitalist country. Instead, communist revolution occurred first in 1917 in Russia – a country that had then only barely entered the capitalist age, with over 80 percent of its population consisting of peasants and only around 8 percent industrial workers. Why? Ironically, precisely because of Russia's underdevelopment, Marx's ideas were relatively more consistent with the interests of Russian workers and intellectuals. Although reforms had moderated the worst abuses of Western European capitalism, Russia during the early twentieth century was still suffering through the early period of industrialization, with its characteristic disregard for worker health and safety and its total lack of legal channels for worker representation. The Russian proletariat, small as it was, was thus much more revolutionary than were the better-off workers of the West. Meanwhile, many Russian intellectuals saw in Marxism a way to escape their country's economic and military backwardness without having to adopt the Western capitalist system. By achieving "socialism" – the first stage of communist society – it seemed that Russia could miraculously leap ahead of countries such as England and France in historical development. Finally, Marx's inspiring vision of communism proved especially powerful in a tsarist empire that had become embarrassingly weak, poor, and corrupt. Such factors help to explain the rapid spread of Marxist ideas in a feudal country – and the political evolution of the man who eventually founded a Marxist regime there, Vladimir Il'ich Lenin.

Vladimir Ulyanov – Lenin's real name – was born in the provincial town of Simbirsk, Russia, in 1870. When Lenin was seventeen years old, his older brother, Aleksandr, was arrested for participating in a plot to assassinate the tsar and was later executed. This event placed the entire Ulyanov family under a cloud of suspicion. Lenin was allowed to attend law school in the capital city of St. Petersburg, but shortly after he began his legal studies, he was expelled for participating in student demonstrations against the regime. He began to read radical literature and soon became a convinced Marxist. By 1900, he had become prominent enough within Russian revolutionary circles to be invited to join the leading Russian Marxists in exile in Switzerland, where they lived and worked in order to avoid harassment and arrest by the tsarist police.

In 1902, Lenin published his most famous essay, entitled *What Is to Be Done?* Lenin's ideas on party organization in this work ultimately inspired revolutionaries in China, Vietnam, Cuba, and elsewhere to create one-party regimes modeled on the Leninist example. Lenin's essay contained three main arguments, all of which became quite controversial among Marxists. First, Lenin bluntly insisted that the working class by itself could never make a successful anticapitalist revolution. More than fifty years after the publication of the *Communist Manifesto*, it had become clear that workers would always be satisfied with gains in local wages, benefits, and representation; in this sense, Lenin argued, workers had a kind of "trade-union consciousness" instead of the revolutionary consciousness needed for the successful overthrow of global capitalism. Second, Lenin argued that the movement must be led instead by Marxist intellectuals devoted at all times to revolutionary activity. A special organization of these intellectuals – a "party of professional revolutionaries" – was needed to guide the proletariat toward its eventual and inevitable victory over the bourgeoisie. Finally, Lenin insisted that the party of professional revolutionaries itself be organized as a strictly hierarchical, disciplined, and unified body. Attempts to introduce "bourgeois" forms of voting or legal procedure into the communist camp would only turn it into an ineffective debating society. Instead, the party should practice what Lenin would later term **"democratic centralism"** – meaning that debate within the party should end the moment the party's Central Committee had made a decision on any given issue.

It would be a long time, however, before Lenin and his followers built a party that in reality looked anything like his original institutional proposal. Indeed, Lenin's insistence on his model of organization at a congress of Russian Marxists in 1903 led to a split between two different factions: the Bolsheviks, or majority – so named because of Lenin's success in getting a bare majority of delegates present to vote to prohibit part-time party membership – and the Mensheviks, or minority, who argued for a more decentralized and inclusive organization of Marxists and workers. By 1904, even many of those Russian Marxists who had originally supported Lenin joined the Mensheviks to protest what they saw as his increasingly dictatorial behavior – ironically leaving the Bolsheviks very much a minority among Russian Marxists until 1917.

Indeed, had it not been for dramatic changes in Russia's global environment, Lenin's party might have faded into historical insignificance. However, the outbreak of World War I in 1914 revived the Bolsheviks' fortunes. The tsarist regime found itself hopelessly outgunned by the Germans and began to disintegrate quickly. In addition, the war's unprecedented bloodshed discredited the capitalist system, making Bolshevik ideology appear relatively more attractive. Finally, the war divided the Western European Marxist parties, each of which initially voted to support its own capitalist government in a war against their fellow proletarians – leaving Lenin as one of the few Marxists who could claim to have opposed World War I consistently from the start.

Lenin was outraged by what he saw as the spinelessness of German, French, and other Western socialists. He argued in his essay *Imperialism* that European Marxists had become hopelessly corrupted by payoffs from capitalist imperial expansion. The proletarian revolution, he concluded, was therefore more likely to begin in Russia, in the periphery of the global capitalist system, than in the developed countries of the West. Lenin made it clear, too, that his own Bolshevik Party was ready to lead the Russian proletariat in its revolutionary struggle. Once Russia proved to the workers of the world that socialist revolution was possible, Lenin argued, communism would spread like wildfire throughout the West and beyond.

The opportunity to act on this theory soon arose when the tsar, Nicholas II, suddenly abdicated in March 1917 in response to mounting losses on the battlefield, peasant uprisings in the countryside, and bread riots in the cities. This "February Revolution" – so named because the old Russian calendar was then about two weeks behind the modern Western calendar – left Russia in a state of near anarchy. A **provisional government** made up of former members of the tsarist Parliament tried, with the support of the United States, Britain, and France, to revive the Russian economy and to continue the war against Germany. But this government had very little real authority, and in the cities, actual power devolved to what were called **soviets**, or councils, of workers and soldiers. Meanwhile, in the countryside, peasant revolts spread; many of the old nobility were killed or forced to flee.

Lenin did not, in any way, cause the collapse of tsarism; he had been in Switzerland for most of the war. He returned to the capital city of Petrograd (formerly St. Petersburg) in April 1917, advocating the overthrow of the provisional government, the establishment of a socialist republic based upon the soviets, and the immediate cessation of the war. Although the radicalism of these proposals at first stunned many of his own closest supporters, by the summer, mounting war casualties and the disintegrating economy rapidly turned the tide of public opinion among workers and soldiers in the Bolsheviks' favor.

On November 7 – the so-called October Revolution – Lenin and his supporters successfully seized power in Petrograd. Within a year, they had wiped out all other organized political forces within the territory they controlled. Not only were tsarist and capitalist parties banned, but socialists who opposed the Bolsheviks were also suppressed. A new secret police force, the Cheka – later to become the KGB – was set up to hunt down "enemies of the revolution." Even the soviets, the spontaneous organizations of the workers themselves, were soon reduced to little more than rubber stamps for the party's central decrees. Party cells were set up in every factory, every school, and every public organization to help "guide" the proletariat to communism.

Lenin's theoretical expectation that Bolshevik victory would spark communist revolutions throughout the capitalist world turned out to be unfounded, however. From 1918 to 1920, Lenin and Leon Trotsky, head of the newly formed Red Army, fought an enormously destructive and bloody civil war against various supporters of tsarism, liberalism, anarchism, and anti-Bolshevik socialism. But after having reconquered most of the territory of the former Russian empire, Lenin began to realize that the final global victory of the proletariat might be delayed indefinitely. Global capitalism, apparently, had stabilized.

To survive in power, then, the Bolsheviks had to revive the ruined Russian economy. In March 1921, Lenin introduced the **New Economic Policy**, which freed grain markets and allowed small-scale capitalism in the cities. Trade and agriculture began to recover soon afterward. Simultaneously, however, Lenin further strengthened one-party rule by implementing a "ban on factions" within the party's ranks. In 1922, he promoted a young disciple by the name of **Joseph Stalin** to the new position of general secretary of the Communist Party, entrusting him with the task of ensuring party discipline through control over personnel decisions.

Another vexing problem was that the new Soviet state occupied a territory containing hundreds of different religions and ethnic groups. According to Marx, of course, such identities were supposed to disappear entirely with the victory of communism over capitalism. In reality, such groups as the Ukrainians, the Georgians, and the Muslim peoples of Central Asia tended to perceive the new regime in Moscow as a continuation of the former Russian empire. Lenin appointed Stalin to be the new commissar for nationalities, expecting him to find a reasonable balance between the need for the party's central control and the concerns of non-Russians – after all, Stalin himself was an ethnic Georgian. To Lenin's dismay, Stalin immediately tried to eliminate all forms of national autonomy, even using physical violence to intimidate ethnic leaders who resisted his will. Ultimately, the new "Soviet Union" formed in 1923 did include several "national republics" for the largest and most powerful nationalities of the regime. Real political power, however, was concentrated in the Kremlin in Moscow (to which the Soviet capital had been relocated from Petrograd in 1918).

Shortly after promoting Stalin to these important positions, Lenin suffered a series of strokes that ultimately left him incapacitated. As Lenin lay on his deathbed in 1923, a fierce struggle for power broke out. In the last letter he was able to dictate, Lenin warned that such internecine battles could fatally weaken the party. In particular, his protégé Stalin had concentrated "immense power in his hands" and was "too rude" to occupy the post of general secretary. Lenin's warnings were ignored. Lenin died in January 1924. Within five years, Stalin emerged as the sole leader of the Soviet regime.

From Lenin to Stalin

How did Iosef Djugashvili, the son of a poor cobbler in the small, mountainous country of Georgia, eventually become Joseph Stalin, one of the most powerful and brutal tyrants in history? This question is of immense historical importance because Stalin, even more than Lenin, shaped the playing field upon which Russian and other post-Soviet politicians now struggle for power. Moreover, by forging a communist bloc extending from Asia to Europe, Stalin also helped to create the basic contours of international politics in the second half of the twentieth century.

From the comparative point of view, however, the two main arguments that have been advanced to explain Stalin and Stalinism are rather unsatisfying. Some analysts argue that Stalin defeated his rivals for power and then established a tyranny simply because he was the most power hungry, the most brutal, and the most opportunistic of any of Lenin's heirs.

Although Stalin obviously wanted power and was willing to use violent means to get it, it makes little sense to accuse Stalin of simple opportunism. In order to rise within Lenin's Bolshevik Party in the first place, Stalin had to fight for fourteen years for an illegal organization that until 1917 had few resources, only a few thousand loyal supporters, and a leader who lived in exile in Western Europe. During this period, the tsarist police arrested him a half-dozen times. If this was a strategy to attain future political power, it was one we can recognize as such only in retrospect. Certainly no ordinary rational politician would have chosen Stalin's early career path!

The second argument often made to explain Stalin's behavior is a psychological one: in short, that Stalin was a paranoid schizophrenic who thought that hidden enemies were always plotting against him. Again, this analysis may be clinically accurate. But this hardly explains how Stalin rose to the leadership of the world's largest state. Somehow, Stalin's personal psychology did not prevent him from convincing many intelligent men and women that he was a socialist genius and not a lunatic. How he did so must be explained in terms of the larger political, social, and global environment in which Stalin's personality was situated.

An alternative point of view, which will be defended here, is that Stalin rose to power and remained in control of the USSR until his death because he, like Lenin, was an institutional innovator within the Marxist ideological tradition. In short, Stalin was a convinced communist, as well as a staunch supporter of Lenin's ideas about party organization. Stalin was in a position to gain unprecedented political power at the head of the Leninist party only because he had identified enough with it early in life to have faith in its eventual triumph. This is why Lenin gave Stalin the crucial post of party general secretary: Stalin had proven his loyalty in times of trial, so Lenin thought he could be counted on to defend the party's interests.

Certainly, Stalin did his best to enforce Leninist norms of strict party discipline and control over a potentially hostile society, using his position to attack and purge any party member who dared disagree with the "general line" of the party leadership – within which, of course, he himself was a key figure. In this respect, however – despite Lenin's complaints about Stalin's "rude" behavior – he was only following Lenin's own principles of "democratic centralism." Shortly after Lenin's death, Stalin promoted thousands of young workers to party membership in a mass campaign called the "Lenin levy," creating an even larger base of personal supporters within the Communist Party. None of Stalin's opponents possessed either the institutional levers or the organizational skills of the future dictator – a factor that cannot be ignored in accounting for his rise to power.

Stalin's victory was not only institutional, however; it was also ideological. Stalin, in fact, proposed a very distinct set of answers to the most troubling issue confronting Marxists in the Soviet Union in the wake of their revolutionary victory: namely, how to build socialism in a largely peasant country without the support of proletarian revolutions in more advanced capitalist countries. The policies that flowed from Stalin's analysis ultimately annihilated millions of people and left a burdensome economic legacy for post-Soviet Russia. Yet Stalinism was arguably the most consistent ideological response to the question of what was to be done after Lenin's death.

In order to see this, we must briefly examine the views of Stalin's primary opponents. There were three main positions in the debate: the Left, the Right, and the Center. The Left was led by the famous revolutionary Leon Trotsky, who had played a crucial role in the Bolshevik takeover, almost single-handedly building up the new Red Army and leading it to victory during the civil war. But after Lenin was incapacitated, Trotsky became disillusioned with what he saw as the gradual bureaucratization of the party and the loss of the Soviet Union's revolutionary momentum. Trotsky exhorted Soviet workers to redouble their efforts to build a strong industrial infrastructure as rapidly as possible and argued that the Bolsheviks should strive to foment revolutions throughout Western Europe. Unfortunately for Trotsky, after three years of world war, a year of revolution, and three years of civil war, most party members and ordinary workers were tired of revolutionary appeals. Some thought Trotsky might be harboring designs to take power for himself through a military coup. In the fall of 1923, the Left Opposition was overwhelmingly outvoted in the party's Central Committee, and by 1924 Trotsky's power and influence had begun to decline rapidly.

The Right Opposition in the 1920s was led by Nikolai Bukharin, a well-known Marxist theorist who edited the party's newspaper, *Pravda* (meaning "truth"). After an early alliance with Trotsky, Bukharin became convinced that the Left's proposals for continuous revolutionary advance were not feasible. Instead, Bukharin advocated a slow, evolutionary path to socialism in the USSR. Specifically, he argued that Lenin's New Economic Policy allowing small-scale capitalism should be continued "seriously and for a long time." The peasantry should be encouraged to get rich. Within factories, efficient management should be promoted – even if that meant keeping in place the same capitalist bosses as before the revolution. Eventually, Bukharin claimed, this policy would allow the Soviet people gradually to "grow into socialism." Such a policy was certainly more realistic than Trotsky's romantic leftism. Yet it failed to appeal to those who genuinely believed in the ideals of 1917. Many party members, workers, and intellectuals asked why they had fought for communism if the end result was simply to establish a "New Economic Policy" that looked more like a "New Exploitation of the Proletariat."

The Center Leninist position during the 1920s was advocated by Grigorii Zinoviev, who had been one of Lenin's most loyal supporters during the pre-1917 period. Zinoviev led the Bolshevik Party in the newly renamed city of Leningrad (formerly St. Petersburg and then Petrograd). He also directed the Comintern, a global organization of communist parties loyal to Moscow, which Lenin had founded in 1919. Zinoviev argued that both the Left and the Right had gone too far: the Left called for revolution without rational analysis or professionalism, whereas the Right called for rational economic policies without any revolutionary vision. Surely, true Leninism – as he now began to refer to the regime's ideology – required both revolution and professionalism simultaneously! Unfortunately, Zinoviev himself had little idea of how to bring about a "Leninist" synthesis of these two concepts. His most original idea – enthusiastically supported by Stalin – was to place Lenin's mummified body on display in Moscow's Red Square so that generations of grateful proletarians could line up to see the founder of Soviet communism.

Neither Trotsky, nor Bukharin, nor Zinoviev proposed any practical policies for dealing with Russia's severe economic backwardness in a way that seemed consistent with the

Soviet regime's socialist identity. Stalin did. In December 1924, Stalin proposed an alternative vision that appeared far more realistic in the context of the international isolation of the Soviet regime: "**socialism in one country**." The basic idea behind "socialism in one country" was simple: it was time to stop waiting for revolutions in other capitalist countries and start building socialism at home. This theoretical position contradicted Trotsky's calls for continuous revolutionary advance in Western Europe, as well as Zinoviev's hopes to inspire the world communist movement from Moscow without actually risking revolutionary changes within the USSR itself. Bukharin, assuming that Stalin's idea of "socialism in one country" was identical to his own evolutionary socialism, threw his support behind Stalin in the power struggle against Trotsky and Zinoviev. By 1928, however, having defeated his latter two opponents, Stalin began to attack Bukharin as well, accusing him of being an opportunist who had sold out to the "bourgeois" rich peasants and industrialists. Stalin lined up large majorities to vote against the Right opposition in the Central Committee, and in 1929 he expelled Bukharin and his supporters from the party leadership.

Now the unchallenged leader of the regime, Stalin revealed that his vision of "socialism in one country" required a new revolutionary assault on Soviet society. Like Lenin, Stalin proposed to translate Marxist identity into concrete institutions that would structure the interests and incentives of millions of ordinary people – this time, in the economic and not just the political realm. Marx himself had said very little about how economic institutions should be organized in the postrevolutionary period; certainly, he had provided no guidance concerning how a single socialist state surrounded by capitalist ones could transform a largely peasant economy into an industrial power. However, Marx had indicated that he expected the "dictatorship of the proletariat" to organize state control over both the industrial and agricultural sectors of the economy, to eliminate private property wherever possible, and to organize production according to a common plan. Stalin now expanded on these principles to propose the revolutionary restructuring of the entire Soviet economy on the basis of **five-year plans** drawn up by the state and enforced by the Communist Party. Stalin insisted that although the Soviet economy was a century behind the West in developmental terms, that distance had to be made up in a decade – or the capitalists would "crush us."

The Stalinist planning system contained three key elements: **collectivization** of agriculture, a novel form of "planned heroism" in industry, and the creation of a huge system of prison labor camps known as **gulags**. The first of these, collectivization of agriculture, represented Stalin's "solution" to the dilemma of how to deal with the huge peasant population in forging a socialist Soviet Union: basically, he decided to enslave or kill the entire peasantry. Again, Stalin put his argument in clear Marxist terms. The peasantry as a class, Marx had argued, was a leftover from feudalism. Capitalism was destined to destroy the peasantry and the aristocracy alike; there would be no place for peasant villages in the socialist future. Those who benefited from private property in agricultural production, Stalin reasoned, formed a sort of peasant bourgeoisie – kulaks, meaning "the tight-fisted ones" – while the poor peasants who worked for them were essentially part of the proletariat. Proletarian revolution in the countryside required class struggle against the kulaks and eventually, as Stalin put it, "the liquidation of the kulaks as a class." In place of the old system of private peasant farming, Stalin proposed the creation of new "collective farms" (*kolkhozy*) and "state farms" (*sovkhozy*), where peasants would work for the greater good of the proletariat – under strict party supervision.

In reality, the drive to create collective and state farms amounted to an all-out assault on the countryside by Stalin's party supporters, by the army, and by various thugs and brigands who took advantage of the chaos to loot, steal, and rape. All over the Soviet Union, peasants battled to preserve their autonomy, even killing their own livestock rather than letting their pigs, cows, and chickens fall under party control. By 1932, the collectivization drive had generated a famine throughout the agricultural regions of the USSR during which millions of people starved to death. Even so, Stalin's goal of gaining party control over the production of food was realized. Indeed, even at the height of the famine, Stalin continued to export grain to the West in order to earn hard currency for the regime. By the mid-1930s, most of the land in the country had been collectivized, excluding only tiny private plots where peasants were allowed to work for themselves and their families.

The second key element of Stalin's socioeconomic system was the imposition of centrally planned production targets for every manager and worker within the Soviet Union. The State Committee on Planning, or Gosplan, had been formed in the mid-1920s to provide general projections for future economic development in the USSR; in this respect, the organization acted in ways similar to planning bureaucracies in Western capitalist countries, such as France. But, in 1929, Stalin gave Gosplan officials the unprecedented task of supervising the rapid industrialization of an enormous country. The specific institutional mechanisms used to ensure this result were designed to elicit a sort of "professional revolutionary" economic activity comparable to that expected of good Leninist party members. Specifically, monthly and yearly production targets, calculated in terms of gross output, were issued for workers and state managers of every factory and collective farm in the USSR. However, the party did not promote workers or managers who simply attained these targets – in fact, just "fulfilling" the plan was held to be a "bourgeois," unrevolutionary sort of behavior. Those who consistently overfulfilled their plan targets, thus supposedly demonstrating their superior revolutionary enthusiasm and dedication – the so-called shock workers and heroic managers – were given monetary bonuses, special housing, better food, and even trips to Moscow to visit the dictator himself.

This system of incentives encouraged an atmosphere of constant, chaotic activity, as workers and managers struggled to produce higher and higher volumes of cement, coal, and steel, urged on by the state planners and party leadership. However, Soviet citizens soon learned that overfulfillment of plans by too great an amount could also sometimes get them into trouble. According to a principle known as "planning from the achieved level," Gosplan was instructed to raise plan targets to the point attained in the previous planning period. Thus, if a worker somehow produced double his or her required amount of coal in one year, he or she might be required to attain the same absurd amount of production the next – and failure to do so, again, could lead to arrest and imprisonment. Thus, Stalinist institutions encouraged individuals to overfulfill their plans, but not by too much. Managers and workers were given incentives to be "revolutionary," but in a manner that was simultaneously "disciplined and professional."

During the First Five-Year Plan, an industrial infrastructure was built in the Soviet Union in an incredibly short period of time; this result looked all the more impressive against the backdrop of the Great Depression then enveloping the capitalist West. Over time, however, the constant demands to "fulfill and overfulfill the plan" during the 1930s alienated even those groups who most benefited from Stalin's policies – the proletariat and party officials. A "final-exam economy," in which constant "cramming" to complete plan assignments before the final deadline was followed by the imposition of even greater work demands, could not but produce exhausted and exasperated managers and workers.

Thus, the third key component of Stalin's economic system, the creation of the gulag system, was vital to its overall functioning. The gulags – short for "chief directorate of labor camps" in Russian – were originally set up during the civil war to incarcerate those who opposed Lenin's plans for Communist Party rule. Under Stalin, however, their scope expanded rapidly; tens of millions of people were arrested as "class enemies" of the "proletarian dictatorship." Gulag inmates were put to work building canals, paving roads, digging coal, and constructing monuments to Lenin and Stalin, often under the most brutal conditions imaginable. The contribution of the gulag system to overall Soviet production under Stalin is hard to estimate, but it clearly played a crucial role in the attainment of the ambitious industrialization targets of the 1930s. Moreover, the constant threat of the gulag undoubtedly did much to inspire ordinary people's continued efforts to overfulfill the plan.

However, the types of economic activity encouraged by Stalin's incentive structure were not conducive to the long-run performance of the system. Already during the 1930s, all sorts of dysfunctional behaviors emerged within Soviet enterprises. First, because plan targets were formulated simply in terms of gross quantities of output, the quality of Soviet production often suffered greatly; as a result, the basic infrastructure of Soviet industry began to crumble and decay almost as soon as it was built. The problem of quality control was even more severe in such sectors of economic production as consumer goods and services, which were given low priority by Stalin. Second, the system was poorly equipped to handle technological change. Shutting down assembly lines in order to introduce new, up-to-date machinery meant failing to meet one's monthly and annual production targets, so Soviet managers tended to rely on their existing equipment. Third, Stalinist industrialization was an environmental disaster; to fulfill and overfulfill plans mattered more than long-term concerns with people's health or the preservation of nature. Today, former Soviet factory towns are some of the most polluted places on earth. Fourth, collectivized agriculture was enormously inefficient and wasteful. Indeed, by the late Soviet era, approximately 65 percent of all vegetables and 90 percent of all fresh fruit were produced on the mere 2 to 3 percent of the land given to peasants' private plots!

Finally, the Stalinist system was prone to rampant institutional corruption. The official banning of most forms of private property and markets meant that all kinds of buying, selling, and stealing of state resources went on in black markets and within personal networks. Managers often colluded with local party officials to lower plan targets, falsify production reports, or otherwise protect enterprises from the demands of central planners. Given the absence of both unemployment and bankruptcy procedures, the only way to curtail such behavior was to arrest the perpetrators – but because almost everyone was involved in some form of informal evasion of their official responsibilities, rooting out corruption completely was impossible.

Stalin knew full well that his vision of socioeconomic socialism was, despite its external successes, falling victim to such forms of corrosion from within. But having sacrificed decades of his life – and millions of other people's lives – to establish this system, he was not about to rethink his policies. Instead, he tried to explain the corruption of the planning system as the work of "hidden class enemies" within the USSR and "survivals of capitalist psychology" within people's minds. In 1936, Stalin began a massive blood purge of everyone he thought was conspiring with the global bourgeoisie against socialism. In Stalin's mind, this supposed conspiracy included the Right, Left, and Center oppositions of the 1920s, economists and plant managers, independent artists and intellectuals, and the entire general staff of the Red Army. Between 1936 and 1938 – the period known as the Great Terror – Stalin killed about 75 percent of the Communist Party's Central Committee, including Zinoviev and Bukharin, who were tortured and forced to testify that they were agents of capitalist intelligence services, and then executed. In 1940, one of Stalin's agents assassinated Trotsky, then living in exile in Mexico City. Meanwhile, millions more Soviet citizens were imprisoned or killed.

How did such a coercive system maintain itself? Every institutional order, no matter how oppressive, requires the allegiance of some social group whose interests it advances, and the Stalinist system is no exception. In fact, one small group did quite well within the framework of Stalinist industrialization, namely, blue-collar workers in their twenties and early thirties who had joined the party during Stalin's rise to power. Many of these men (and women, although this group was predominantly male) found themselves promoted extremely rapidly during the period of the First Five-Year Plan to positions of management and within the party hierarchy. They rose even further when their immediate supervisors were killed during the Great Terror. Some of these people ultimately became members of the post-Stalin Soviet Politburo, the highest organ of the Communist Party, including such future leaders as **Nikita Khrushchev** and **Leonid Brezhnev**. For these men, who had started their careers as ordinary workers, the Soviet Union was truly a dictatorship of the proletariat!

Even with the support of the communist worker elite, however, Stalin's system of planned heroism and mass terror might well have disintegrated had it not been for the enormous changes in the international environment wrought by World War II. When Adolf Hitler invaded the USSR in June 1941, Soviet forces were hardly able to resist; within months, the Nazis were at the gates of both Leningrad and Moscow. However, before the conquest of the Soviet Union was complete, the Russian winter began to set in, and the German soldiers found themselves quite unprepared for the extreme cold.

Soon fresh troops from the east came to reinforce Moscow. By December, when the United States entered the war after the Japanese attack on Pearl Harbor, the pressure on the Nazis was increasing. Fighting between Soviet and Nazi troops continued for three more years, and ultimately the USSR lost more than 20 million people in the conflict. However, by the end of 1943, the tide had turned decisively against Hitler, and by 1945, Red Army troops met Allied troops in Berlin in triumph.

After the Soviet victory in World War II, Stalin insisted that his policies of the 1930s had been vindicated. After all, the giant steel mills, cement plants, and weapons factories set up in the First Five-Year Plan had played a crucial role in the Soviet war effort; without this rapid industrialization, the Nazis might actually have conquered Russia. Stalin could now claim – despite his genocidal policies – that he was a great Russian patriot who had defeated an alien invader of the motherland. Finally, at the conclusion of the war, Soviet troops occupied most of Eastern and Central Europe, including the eastern portion of Germany. Within three years, Stalin had imposed both Leninist one-party rule and Stalinist collectivization and planning on these unfortunate nations. If one accepted Stalin's definition of socialism then, it followed that Stalin was the first person who had successfully created an international "socialist commonwealth," one that even included part of Marx's homeland. World War II – or, as the Russians still refer to it, the "Great Fatherland War" – thus greatly solidified the legitimacy of Stalin's regime and led many ordinary citizens to embrace a "Soviet" identity for the first time.

Until his death in 1953, Stalin continued to defend the system he had created – and to use terror to silence his real and imagined opponents. Toward the end of World War II, entire peoples whom Stalin accused of being disloyal, such as the Crimean Tatars, the Volga Germans, and the Chechens, were deported to Siberia and Central Asia. After the war was over, the arrest of supposed capitalist spies continued; even the relatives of prominent Politburo members were sent to the gulag. Meanwhile, Stalin promoted a "cult of personality" in the Soviet media and arts that constantly trumpeted the dictator's supposed genius as an architect, as a poet, as a military commander, as a linguist, and so on. Shortly before his death, Stalin was preparing to launch a new terror campaign against so-called enemies of the people – this time including Politburo doctors, whom he accused of plotting to poison the leadership, and, even more ominously, Soviet Jews, who he claimed were part of a global Zionist conspiracy against him. Fortunately, Stalin died in March 1953, before he could act on these ideas.

From Stalin to Gorbachev

Stalin's successors were faced with a dual legacy. On the one hand, by 1953 the USSR was a global superpower. Its industrial production had become sufficiently large to allow it to compete militarily with the capitalist West; by 1949 it had also built its first nuclear bomb. Newly decolonized and developing countries looked to the Soviet Union as a counterweight to the power of the West and in some cases as an ally whose institutions should be emulated. The Western powers themselves had just emerged from decades of world war and global depression – phenomena Marx had predicted would result from capitalism's "inner contradictions" – and it would be some time before analysts were sure that democratic capitalism in Europe could be revived and sustained.

On the other hand, the fundamental problems of Leninist party politics and Stalinist planned economics remained. Years of dictatorship and terror had killed off much of the popular enthusiasm that had once existed for heroic efforts to build socialism. Bribe taking and black-market activity on the part of Soviet officials had already become a way of life. Problems with economic waste and inefficiency, worker absenteeism and alcoholism, and poor-quality production had become more severe. Clearly, something had to be done to address the growing cracks in the foundation of the Soviet superpower.

Again, the post-Stalin leadership analyzed and responded to these problems in a way they thought was consistent not only with their own personal interests but also with the basic outlines of the Soviet socialist identity. First, every Soviet leader after Stalin's death in 1953 agreed that the days of mass, indiscriminate terror in Soviet society must end. Stalin's last secret-police chief, Lavrentii Beria, was himself executed by the end of the year, millions of people were freed from the gulag, and the most extreme forms of Stalin worship ceased. The post-Stalin leadership also agreed that the next stage in building socialism somehow had to involve the creation of a truly socialist culture that would inspire ordinary workers and peasants to contribute their energies to the further development of Soviet institutions voluntarily. There was, however, no clear consensus on how to do this.

From 1953 until 1985, leadership struggles again centered on debates among what we can now recognize as Right, Left, and Centrist strategies concerning how to create a "socialist way of life" without Stalinist terror. Supporters of the "Right" strategy during this period, such as Georgii Malenkov, the first post-Stalin prime minister, argued that Soviet socialism must abandon revolutionary crusades in economic and foreign policy and instead promote efficiency within enterprises and high-quality production for ordinary consumers. This advice, however sensible from our perspective, struck most party officials and Stalinist planners as a direct attack on their interests and as a departure from the revolutionary ideals of Marxism and Leninism.

By 1954, Malenkov's authority had been eclipsed by Communist Party leader Nikita Khrushchev. Khrushchev advocated the opposite of Malenkov's policies, calling for a revolutionary advance toward communism as rapidly as possible. In a secret speech to the party elite in 1956, Khrushchev sought to inspire mass revolutionary sentiment by exposing the abuses of the Stalin period as "deformations" of socialism that would never be permitted again. This speech was followed by a "de-Stalinization" campaign involving a significant easing of censorship over the media and the arts. Khrushchev called on the Soviet people to participate in a whole series of economic campaigns to set records in corn planting, milk and meat production, and chemical manufacture; he even revised the party program to include a timetable according to which Marx's original vision of "full communism" would be attained in the USSR by 1980! He also pursued a risky and often reckless foreign policy, threatening the West with nuclear missile attacks if it did not agree to Soviet demands. Such "leftist" policies led to administrative chaos at home and military embarrassments, such as the Cuban missile crisis, abroad. In 1964, Khrushchev was ousted in a Politburo coup.

From 1964 until 1982, Leonid Brezhnev presided over an orthodox Marxist-Leninist Politburo that resisted any reform of Soviet institutions – and, besides supporting various pro-Soviet regimes in the developing world, did very little else. Brezhnev and his lieutenants arrested vocal dissidents and tightened censorship to prevent open criticism of the regime, but largely turned a blind eye to private disaffection, corruption, and black-market activity. Party officials and state bureaucrats were rarely fired, and the Soviet elite began to age, and ultimately to die, in office. The planning system, now lacking either mass enthusiasm or fear as incentives for the fulfillment of production targets, sank into stagnation and decline. By the mid-1970s, the Soviet economy became dangerously dependent upon energy exports and sales of vodka. The disastrous Soviet military intervention in Afghanistan in

1979, combined with the declaration of martial law to suppress the independent Solidarity trade union in Poland in 1981, exposed the growing vulnerabilities of the Soviet army and the Warsaw Pact alliance of Leninist regimes in Eastern Europe. Meanwhile, such leaders as Margaret Thatcher in Britain and Ronald Reagan in the United States were calling for a much more aggressive foreign policy to confront the Soviet "evil empire" (to use Reagan's term). Finally, from 1982 until 1985, a veritable parade of dying general secretaries of the Communist Party – Brezhnev, Yuri Andropov, and Konstantin Chernenko – made the USSR an international joke.

It was under these dire global and domestic circumstances that the party elite decided to entrust the key position of general secretary to the fifty-four-year-old **Mikhail Gorbachev**. Upon his promotion to the leadership in March 1985, a furious debate ensued among Western Sovietologists. The "totalitarian" school, which insisted that the Soviet system was still in essence a regime based on terror, tended to see Gorbachev as merely a more polished representative of Soviet tyranny and warned the West to remain vigilant. "Modernization" theorists, who claimed that the USSR had become a developed, modern society not unlike the United States, saw Gorbachev's leadership as a final break with the Stalinist past and hoped for a new era of peace and cooperation between his regime and the West.

In effect, each side assumed that Gorbachev knew what he was doing but did not believe what he was saying. The totalitarian interpretation of Gorbachev assumed that he knew how to revitalize the Soviet economy in order to produce a more technologically advanced and efficient communist challenge to the West but did not believe his own promises of reform and democratization of the Soviet system. The modernization interpretation of Gorbachev assumed that he knew how to eliminate the corruption, mismanagement, and ideological rigidity of the Brezhnev period but did not believe his own constant assurances that he was a Leninist who hoped to revive the ideals of the October Revolution. In fact, Gorbachev believed what he was saying but did not know what he was doing. When he told the world that he was a "Leninist reformer," he meant exactly that. As for what reformed Leninism in the Soviet Union would eventually look like in practice, however, he had no concrete idea.

How could Gorbachev really believe in Leninism as late as the 1980s? Gorbachev had been promoted his whole life for espousing this ideology. He had come of age politically during the successful and painful struggle against the Nazis and had been a teenager during the triumphant emergence of the Soviet Union as a global superpower. As a young man, he was given the Order of the Red Banner of Labor for his "heroic" work as a combine operator on a collective farm. Largely as a result of this award, he was admitted to the prestigious Moscow State University Law School. In his twenties, he became a party official, and by his thirties he had been appointed the first party secretary in Stavropol, an agricultural region in southern Russia. Because of Stavropol's strategic location on the way to various Black Sea and Caucasus mountain resorts, Gorbachev got to know almost every significant Soviet leader, including Brezhnev, Andropov, and Chernenko. By 1978, at the age of forty-seven, he had been promoted to the Politburo as secretary of agriculture, in part because his sincere enthusiasm for Leninism and socialism had impressed his somewhat jaded elders.

Thus, by the time he became general secretary, Gorbachev was one of the few people in the USSR who still truly believed in Leninist ideology. People's enthusiasm for participation in the Communist Party and for heroic plan fulfillment, Gorbachev insisted, could be rekindled – but only if he found some way to eliminate the corrupt, petty bureaucracy that had blocked popular initiative during what he called the "era of stagnation" under Brezhnev. His first step was to purge hundreds of old party bureaucrats. By 1986, Gorbachev had already dismissed or retired almost 40 percent of the Central Committee and felt strong enough to launch his dramatic campaign for perestroika, or restructuring.

Perestroika consisted of three basic elements: glasnost, democratization, and "new thinking" in foreign policy. Glasnost, or openness, meant greater disclosure of people's criticisms of the Soviet past and present in newspapers, television, and films. This campaign got off to a rather ambiguous start when, in April 1986, the Chernobyl nuclear power plant in Ukraine exploded, spewing radioactivity over much of Eastern Europe; the Soviet government hid this information from its citizens for a full three days after the event. However, by the fall of 1986, the quantity and quality of published revelations about Soviet history and current Soviet society began to increase markedly. The release in December 1986 of the famous Soviet nuclear physicist and dissident Andrei Sakharov, who had been sent into internal exile for his public denouncement of the Soviet invasion of Afghanistan, demonstrated the seriousness of Gorbachev's break with Brezhnevite forms of censorship. After 1987, the scope of glasnost widened to include every conceivable topic, including Lenin's terror during the civil war, the horrors of collectivization, and even the dictatorial nature of Communist Party rule itself.

Democratization also began slowly, with vague calls to reinvigorate the system of soviets that had been subordinated to the party hierarchy since the Russian civil war. By 1988, however, at the Nineteenth Party Conference, Gorbachev announced that genuine multicandidate elections would be held for a new Soviet Congress of People's Deputies to replace the old rubber-stamp Supreme Soviet. To be sure, Gorbachev attempted to guarantee the continued leading role of the Communist Party, reserving a third of the seats in the new 2,250 seat congress for "public organizations" under direct party control. Moreover, in many electoral districts, local party bosses still ran unopposed, as in the times of Stalin and Brezhnev. Nevertheless, the national elections held in the spring of 1989 generated many serious, competitive races between reformers and party conservatives that galvanized Soviet society.

Finally, Gorbachev's campaign for new thinking in foreign policy announced a turn away from attempts to build client regimes in the developing world, a campaign to reduce tensions with the capitalist West, and, most significant, an end to the Stalinist subordination of countries in the communist bloc. Since the end of World War II, Soviet leaders had been able to preserve Leninist rule in Eastern Europe only through repeated military interventions, including Khrushchev's invasion of Hungary in 1956, Brezhnev's invasion of Czechoslovakia in 1968, and the Soviet-supported declaration of martial law in Poland in 1981. Now, one of Gorbachev's spokesmen announced that the old "Brezhnev doctrine" of military intervention had been replaced by the "Sinatra doctrine": the former communist satellite states would be allowed to "do it their way." Again, early reaction to this announcement was skeptical, both in the West and in Eastern Europe. In 1989, the seriousness of new thinking was tested when Solidarity candidates won every possible seat but one in new elections for the Polish parliament. When Gorbachev did nothing to prevent the creation of the first non-Leninist government in the communist bloc, liberal democrats and nationalists throughout the region moved to gain their own independence. By the end of the year, revolutions against Communist Party rule had succeeded in every single country of the former Warsaw Pact.

Gorbachev's perestroika, then, was every bit as revolutionary as its author had intended – but not with the results he had expected. Within three years of the launching of the campaign for restructuring, both the identity and the institutions at the core of Leninism had disintegrated. Instead of inspiring a new faith in socialist ideas as Gorbachev had hoped, glasnost made the history of communism appear to be a long and bloody tragedy. Democratization, designed to remove corrupt Brezhnevite bureaucrats in order to make space in the system for more enthusiastic socialists, instead destroyed Lenin's "party of professional revolutionaries" altogether. New thinking, which was supposed to allow the USSR to compete with capitalism more effectively by discarding the coercive methods of past foreign policy, resulted in the rapid disintegration of the Soviet empire.

By 1990, the spiraling loss of party control produced two further unanticipated results: an economic crisis and a nationalist resurgence. Economically, Gorbachev's perestroika had done surprisingly little to change the fundamental elements of the Stalinist planning system other than to permit small-scale cooperatives in the service sector and limited joint ventures with foreign capitalists. The breakdown of party authority by 1990 meant that producers no longer had any reason to obey the orders of the planning bureaucracy. Those who simply hoarded raw materials or manufactured goods, then sold or traded them on the black market, could not be punished in the absence of an effective central-party dictatorship. As soon as some people stopped deliveries of goods to Gosplan, however, other enterprises found themselves without necessary supplies; they were also then forced to hoard whatever they had and barter with their former suppliers. Outright theft of enterprise resources also became commonplace; in some cases, corrupt party officials even shipped valuable minerals out of the country for hard currency and had the proceeds placed in Swiss bank accounts. As a result of the breakdown of the planning system, goods began to disappear from store shelves all over the country.

At the same time, nationalism began to fill the gap left by the discrediting of Marxism-Leninism. In many ways, it is ironic that the system of Soviet republics created by Lenin and Stalin to deal with the multiethnic nature of Soviet territory had actually reinforced national identity in the USSR. Peoples living in the republics had been allowed to preserve schools, museums, and cultural institutes promoting their native traditions and languages but had been ruthlessly subordinated to Moscow politically and economically. The Baltic republics of Estonia, Latvia, and Lithuania had in fact been independent countries until 1940, when Stalin annexed them to the USSR after having made a secret deal with Hitler to divide Eastern Europe. After the revolutions of 1989 in East-Central Europe, people in the republics began to demand greater autonomy and, in the case of the Baltics, outright independence. These trends were further fueled by elections to the Supreme Soviets of the fifteen republics in 1990. In each of these campaigns, advocates of greater republican autonomy outpolled representatives of the Soviet communist center; even those who did not really want full republican independence often voted for "sovereignty" as a way of protesting

Gorbachev's ineffective leadership. By the end of 1990, however, the disintegration of the USSR had become a very real possibility.

That possibility became a reality because of **Boris Yeltsin**'s mobilization of a powerful movement for national independence within Russia itself. Yeltsin had originally been brought to Moscow by Gorbachev in 1986 to be the city's party boss and a candidate member of the Politburo. Yeltsin, born the same year as Gorbachev, shared the latter's belief that Soviet socialism had grown stagnant and corrupt. He won the hearts of Muscovites by criticizing party conservatives, making surprise televised visits to inspect shops suspected of profiting on the black market, and talking with ordinary people on the streets wherever he went. In October 1987, however, Yeltsin made the mistake of attacking conservative Politburo members in a party meeting – thus violating Lenin's decades-old prohibition on "factions" within the party. He was drummed out of the Politburo and given the dead-end job of USSR deputy minister of construction.

The elections for the USSR Congress of People's Deputies in the spring of 1989, however, revitalized Yeltsin's political career. Running on a platform of greater democracy and marketization, Yeltsin gained 90 percent of the votes in his Moscow electoral district. Together with Sakharov, he formed a movement of Congress deputies committed to the end of one-party rule and to reintegration with the West. Such a reintegration, Yeltsin argued, could be achieved only if Russia attained greater autonomy from the Soviet Union and took control over its own political and economic life. Yeltsin's embrace of this distinctive anti-Soviet Russian nationalism attracted even some conservatives to his side, including the Afghan war hero General **Aleksandr Rutskoi**. By the summer of 1990, Yeltsin had quit the Communist Party, and in February 1991 he called on Gorbachev to resign. In June 1991, Yeltsin, with Rutskoi as his vice-presidential candidate, easily won popular election to the new post of president of the Russian Federation – the first time in history that a Russian leader had been democratically elected.

Faced with the potential secession of the Soviet republics, the disintegration of the Soviet economy, and the emergence of a powerful Yeltsin-led opposition in Russia itself, Gorbachev tried desperately to hold the regime together. In May 1991, he negotiated a new "union treaty" with the newly elected leaders of those republics – or at least the nine still willing to talk to him. But on August 19, 1991, the day before the treaty was to take effect, conservative Leninists within the leadership mounted a coup against Gorbachev as he vacationed on the Black Sea. The heads of the KGB, the defense ministry, and the interior ministry announced that Gorbachev was "too sick to continue" in office and proclaimed the formation of a "State Committee for the Emergency Situation" that would lead the country for an unspecified period. However, the coup attempt was ineptly planned and executed. Gorbachev refused to cooperate with the coup plotters, as they had apparently hoped he would. Meanwhile, Yeltsin made his way to the Russian "White House," the building housing the Russian Congress, where over a hundred thousand Muscovites had gathered to protest the coup. He climbed on top of a tank and declared his uncompromising opposition to the coup plotters. At that moment, he became, in essence, the new leader of Russia.

Key units of the KGB and military defected to Yeltsin's camp. The coup unraveled shortly thereafter. Interior Minister Boris Pugo committed suicide; the other leaders of the coup were arrested. Yeltsin announced Russia's recognition of the independence of the Baltic states; he also banned the Communist Party of the Soviet Union, branding it a criminal organization. Gorbachev returned to Moscow on August 22, but he appeared to be totally out of touch with the changed situation in the country, quoting Lenin and defending the Communist Party at a televised press conference. Gorbachev continued to try to preserve what was left of the Soviet Union, but Yeltsin and other leaders of the national republics soon committed themselves to full independence. On December 1, 1991, over 90 percent of the Ukrainian population voted for national independence in a referendum; a few days later, the leaders of Russia, Ukraine, and Belarus announced the formation of a new, decentralized **Commonwealth of Independent States** to replace the USSR. On December 25, 1991, Gorbachev, bowing to the inevitable, resigned as leader of the Soviet Union, thus ending the seventy-four-year history of the Leninist regime.

Interests, Identities, and Institutions in Postcommunist Russia

The Leninist Legacy and Post-Soviet Interests

When the Soviet Union was officially declared dead in December 1991, most Western governments and many analysts understandably greeted the news with euphoria, predicting that Russia would join the prosperous, democratic West in short order. Unfortunately, Westerners tended at the time to underestimate the enormous structural problems that would inevitably face new democratic and market-oriented governments in Russia and other former Soviet republics. As we emphasize throughout this textbook, institutions inherited from the past can exert a powerful influence on politics in the present. This was especially true in the postcommunist world, which was saddled with the legacy of a particularly brutal ideological, political, and socioeconomic tyranny that had endured for decades. Moreover, former communist countries now found themselves exposed to competition from technologically advanced capitalist countries. The economic gap between Russia and the West in 1991 was, if anything, even greater than it had been in 1917.

It was extremely unlikely, then, that a rapid "transition to democracy and markets" in Russia would take place without reversals, inasmuch as the elimination of Soviet institutions often contradicted the interests of the people who had previously lived under them. It is unsurprising that those institutions most costly for individuals to abandon proved the most difficult to destroy. For this reason, Soviet institutions decayed in the same order as they were originally created: first Marxist ideology, then Leninist party politics, and finally, only very slowly, Stalin's planned economy.

Marxist ideology was the easiest to abandon, and it died soon after the collapse of the regime. Indeed, in the immediate aftermath of the August coup, popular disgust with the ideological language of the old regime was so widespread that labeling oneself a Leninist or even a socialist was tantamount to committing political suicide – as Gorbachev soon discovered. Mainstream Russian politicians strove to outdo one another with professions of opposition to communism. Even those who still called themselves communists largely stopped referring to Marx, Engels, and the global proletarian revolution. Even more significant, the sudden disappearance of Marxism-Leninism left in its wake an almost total ideological vacuum; in contrast with the Soviet period, the politics of short-term material interest now blocked all efforts to articulate a new post-Soviet national identity.

In response to this situation, Yeltsin and his advisers became convinced that there was no alternative to adopting liberal capitalist ideology. However, whereas liberals in other postcommunist countries could claim – with some justification – to be returning to national traditions suppressed under Soviet rule, liberalism in post-Soviet Russia appeared to many as a capitulation to the West. As the post-Soviet crisis continued, anti-Western sentiments in Russian society understandably strengthened, and those in search of consistent ideological visions often gravitated toward radically antiliberal figures.

This brings us to the second legacy of Leninism, that of one-party rule. Again, the initial effect of Yeltsin's banning of the Communist Party of the Soviet Union (CPSU) in the days after the August coup was to encourage widespread formal defection from that organization. However, leaving the party was potentially far more costly than disavowing Marxist-Leninist ideology. Because Communist Party officials had monopolized every significant position of power in society, right down to the shop-floor level, membership in alternative political organizations could hardly deliver comparable benefits in the short run. For this reason, formal withdrawal from the CPSU was, in most cases, followed by a scramble to cement key personal ties and to maintain access to economic resources inherited from one's days as a communist functionary.

It was therefore somewhat comical to see early post-Soviet Russian politicians accuse their opponents of being communists, as almost all of them had been members of the CPSU in the recent past. This is not to deny that a very real degree of political pluralism emerged after 1991, especially compared with Soviet times. However, the legacy of one-party rule continues to be a serious obstacle to the formation of genuine, alternative grassroots organizations and mass political parties in the Russian Federation. Indeed, long after the collapse of the USSR, throughout Russia one could still find former party bureaucrats ruling over their local fiefdoms as they did under Leninist rule.

A final political legacy of Leninism was the inheritance of administrative boundaries that tended to worsen, rather than ameliorate, ethnic conflicts. The borders of the Russian Federation, like those of the other Soviet republics, had been drawn up by Stalin with little concern for nationalist sensibilities. More than 20 million ethnic Russians lived outside the new Russian state and were now suddenly inhabitants of foreign countries. Meanwhile, the Russian Federation itself contained dozens of "ethnic republics" and "autonomous districts" formally set aside for regional non-Russian ethnic groups, and although most of these regions seemed content to remain part of Russia, others, in particular Chechnya, mounted their own drives for national independence. As a result, popular acceptance of the existing boundaries of the state was weak, and several prominent opposition figures called for restoration of at least part of the old Soviet empire.

The most burdensome institutional legacy of the Soviet system, however, was the residue of the Stalinist planned economy. All over Russia and the other former Soviet republics – indeed, all over the postcommunist region – an enormous rust belt of outdated factories continued to produce goods that few consumers wanted, to poison the surrounding environment, and to waste scarce energy and other resources. Enterprises that had for decades been judged solely according to their ability to overfulfill plan targets – or at least fake it – were poorly prepared to compete in a market economy, especially in the global high-tech environment of the 1990s. Unfortunately, Stalinist factories employed tens of millions of people and under the Soviet system had distributed a whole range of welfare benefits, including child care, recreational facilities, housing, and even food. The loss of one's factory job meant the disappearance not only of one's salary but also of one's social safety net. Blue-collar workers, former Soviet managers, and the local party officials who had formerly supervised them thus formed a natural lobby against any rapid transition to competitive capitalism.

The legacy of Stalinist collectivization of agriculture reinforced this anti-market lobby. The brutal methods used to create *kolkhozy* and *sovkhozy* during the 1930s had drained the countryside of its most knowledgeable and productive farmers; the poor services and supplies found in rural regions had inspired most young people to leave the villages for the cities. The remaining 30 million Russians living in rural areas at the end of the Soviet era were primarily elderly, poorly skilled, and culturally conservative. They, too, were hardly prepared for the establishment of a capitalist farming system.

Along with the sheer weight of inefficient agricultural and industrial sectors in the post-Soviet Russian economy came a more subtle problem, namely, the absence of most of the market institutions now taken for granted in advanced capitalist societies. The USSR, for example, had never created a functioning real estate market because private ownership of land was banned; a decade after the Soviet collapse, there was still no consistent legal basis for land ownership in Russia. Nor did the Soviet economy possess anything like a capitalist financial system. The Soviet ruble was never freely tradable for currencies such as the U.S. dollar or Japanese yen; its value was set artificially by state bureaucrats. Soviet banks, instead of making careful investment and loan decisions based upon calculations of profit and loss, simply funneled resources to those enterprises the planners directed them to support. Stock and bond markets were also nonexistent under Soviet rule, and those operating in the early years of the Russian Federation were prone to wild speculative swings. Finally, the Soviet judiciary was not trained in the enforcement of legal property rights, and it has been difficult to get post-Soviet Russian courts to uphold business contracts in a consistent manner.

Thus, decades of Leninism had generated huge institutional obstacles to a smooth reentry into the Western capitalist world. Nonetheless, Yeltsin and his supporters chose what might be termed a revolutionary, rather than evolutionary, approach to Westernizing Russia. With the support of Western political leaders and economic advisers, they launched an all-out drive to reintegrate Russia into the global economy. Predictably, the results fell far short of expectations.

Yeltsin and the Design of Post-Soviet Institutions

During the autumn of 1991, Boris Yeltsin fought successfully against conservative nationalists and supporters of Gorbachev who wished to preserve the USSR. In this struggle, he maintained the enthusiastic support of the Russian Congress of People's Deputies that had been elected in 1990. The Congress voted in November to grant Yeltsin special emergency powers for one year in order to deal with the extraordinary political and economic crisis resulting from the Soviet Union's collapse. On New Year's Day, 1992, the Russian Federation became, along with the rest of the former Soviet republics, an internationally recognized independent state; Yeltsin declared himself Russia's first prime minister.

Immediately, Yeltsin used his emergency powers to implement a policy of rapid marketization popularly known as **shock therapy**. To administer this policy, he named a thirty-five-year-old economist, Yegor Gaidar, as his deputy. The theoretical assumption behind shock therapy was that unless Russia made immediate moves toward capitalism, it would remain stuck in a hopeless halfway house between the old Stalinist system and the new global market economy. In theory, shock therapy would be painful in the short run but better for Russian society in the long run. Gaidar's plan, drawn up in close consultation with Western advisers and the International Monetary Fund (IMF), contained three key elements: price liberalization, monetary stabilization, and privatization of state property.

The argument for freeing prices was hard to refute. For decades, the Soviet planners had kept prices for energy, housing, consumer goods, and basic foodstuffs artificially low in order to prevent public protest. Such low prices made it unprofitable for anyone to produce these goods, except on the black market. Letting prices rise was arguably the only way to induce entrepreneurs to deliver food and basic goods to markets in time to prevent starvation during the cold Russian winter. But the end of price controls was bound to cause social unrest.

Price liberalization was announced on January 2, 1992. Within days, prices had doubled and even tripled; by the end of the year, they were over seventeen times higher. The effect was to wipe out most people's savings. An elderly person who had painstakingly saved 10,000 rubles – a significant sum in the Soviet era – by 1993 found that her fortune was worth approximately $10. On the positive side, goods did reappear in shops throughout the country; the old Soviet phenomenon of people lining up for blocks to buy scarce consumer goods was now a thing of the past.

Fighting inflation required attention to the second key element of shock therapy, monetary stabilization – controlling the money supply in order to make the ruble a strong, convertible currency like the U.S. dollar. This turned out to be easier to do in principle than in practice. By the spring of 1992, Soviet factories and collective farms everywhere were struggling to pay for supplies at vastly higher prices than before. Russian managers called up their old friends in the Congress of People's Deputies in Moscow to demand that money be sent to help enterprises pay their bills. By May, the Central Bank of Russia had begun to issue new rubles day and night to subsidize failing enterprises. Instead of achieving monetary stabilization, Russia was flooded with money; as a result, inflation remained extremely high. The alternative, however, was to shut down an enormous number of huge factories and farms and to fire the millions of workers who worked in them.

In theory, of course, unemployed workers should have been able to find new jobs at more efficient start-up companies generated by capitalist competition. But new companies could not easily emerge in a country still owned almost entirely by the state. Thus, the third element of shock therapy, privatization of property, was seen as crucial to the entire reform effort. The privatization drive was led by Gaidar's close ally and friend, Anatoly

Chubais. In late 1992, privatization "vouchers" were issued to every man, woman, and child in Russia; they could either use them to bid on state enterprises put up for sale at privatization auctions or sell them for cash. The idea was to build a mass base of support for the new capitalist economy by giving everyone at least a small share of the proceeds of the sale of Soviet properties. Unfortunately, few ordinary Russians had much of an idea of what to do with their vouchers. Many people invested them in bogus "voucher funds," the organizers of which simply cashed in all their vouchers and fled the country. An even greater problem was that much of Soviet state property was doomed to produce at a loss under market conditions – so why bid on it? After a few showcase privatization auctions, the voucher campaign bogged down.

Chubais now engineered a compromise proposal. According to a "second variant" of privatization worked out with leaders of the Russian Congress, 51 percent of the shares of a company could simply be handed over to its existing management and workers, with the rest being divided between the state and any interested outside investors. More than two-thirds of Russian enterprises chose this form of privatization – which, in effect, amounted to a simple declaration that former Stalinist factories were now private property, although they were run by the same people, and with the same workforce, as before. In this way, Yeltsin, Chubais, and Gaidar could claim that, within two years, two-thirds of the Russian economy had been privatized; underneath the surface, however, inefficient Soviet production methods remained largely in place.

The collapse of the Soviet Union and the inconsistencies and mounting social unrest associated with the shock-therapy program quickly turned a majority of Congress deputies against Yeltsin's Westernization drive. Yeltsin's own vice-president Rutskoi now forged an alliance with the parliament's leader, Ruslan Khasbulatov, in opposition to Yeltsin and Gaidar. At the Sixth Congress of People's Deputies in December 1992, a majority refused to confirm Gaidar's reappointment as prime minister. Yeltsin's emergency powers had by then expired, so he was forced to appoint a compromise candidate, **Viktor Chernomyrdin**. Chernomyrdin was the former head of the state natural gas monopoly, Gazprom, and shared the basic economic views of the factory managers clamoring for an end to shock therapy. At the same time, Chernomyrdin was rumored to have become a multimillionaire through profits from exports of gas to Western Europe. In practice, Chernomyrdin tried to be a centrist, calling for an "end to market romanticism" but not a reversal of market reforms.

Chernomyrdin's appointment as prime minister did not end the growing tensions between Yeltsin and the Congress. Rutskoi and Khasbulatov now openly called for the creation of a new government led by the Congress and its executive body, the Supreme Soviet. In April, Yeltsin turned to the public, sponsoring a nationwide referendum on his leadership and economic policies, and asking whether early elections should be held for the president and/or the parliament. The results showed that Yeltsin's public support remained, at this stage, remarkably strong, with a majority even supporting the basic economic policies of the past year. The opposition in the Congress, however, continued to press for Yeltsin's ouster.

During the summer of 1993, a form of dual power emerged. Both the president and the parliament issued contradictory laws and decrees; both sides had drawn up new constitutions for the Russian state. Given the administrative chaos in Moscow, Russia's eighty-nine regions and ethnic republics began to push for even greater autonomy, withholding taxes and resources and often insisting on the primacy of regional laws over central laws. Fears that Russia would disintegrate like the Soviet Union became increasingly widespread. In September, Yeltsin brought the crisis to a head by announcing the disbanding of the Supreme Soviet and Congress. The parliament responded by declaring Yeltsin's presidency null and void and declaring Rutskoi as the new Russian leader. The possibility of civil war loomed. On October 3, extremist supporters of the Congress tried to take over the main television station and mayor's office in Moscow. Yeltsin then decided to order a military assault on his enemies.

More than 150 people were killed in the attack on the Russian White House in October 1993. There was a sad symbolism in watching Yeltsin order the shelling of the same building where he had courageously defied the Soviet coup plotters just two years earlier. After October 1993, the impression that "democracy" was merely a disguise for naked presidential power became widespread among disaffected groups in Russian society.

The destruction of the Russian Congress did, however, allow Yeltsin to design and implement a new constitution in December 1993 (just barely approved by Russian voters – at least officially). The Russian constitution, like democratic constitutions elsewhere, formally divides political power among the legislative, judicial, and executive branches. The legislature is bicameral. The lower house, the **State Duma**, consists of 450 deputies. From 1993 through 2003, half of them were representatives of national parties selected on the basis of proportional representation (PR) and half were representatives of local electoral districts; beginning in the 2007 Duma election, all deputies are selected through PR. The 178 members of the upper house, the **Federation Council**, represent the governors and regional legislatures of each of Russia's federal regions. The judicial branch is led by the Constitutional Court, empowered to rule on basic constitutional issues, and the Supreme Court, the country's highest court of general appeal. However, the 1993 Russian constitution gives by far the greatest share of political power to the president. The Russian president is the commander in chief of the armed forces, appoints the prime minister, and even has the right to issue presidential decrees with the force of law, as long as they do not contradict existing legislation. Moreover, if the State Duma refuses to confirm the president's choice for prime minister three times or votes no confidence in the government twice, he or she can dissolve the lower house and call new elections.

Notwithstanding the overwhelming powers of the presidency, Russian elections after 1993 have had genuine political significance. Even in the first elections to the State Duma in December 1993, Russian voters were able to express their alienation from those responsible for the shock-therapy reforms of the preceding two years. Despite highly visible state support, Gaidar's political party, Russia's Choice, attained only 15.5 percent of the party-list vote – the parliamentary seats allocated according to proportional representation. Meanwhile, the two other most successful parties were led by antiliberal ideologues. A full 23 percent of the electorate chose the Liberal Democratic Party of Russia (LDPR) farcically named, considering that it was led by **Vladimir Zhirinovsky**, a flamboyant ultranationalist who promised to lower the price of vodka, shoot criminals on the spot, and invade the Baltic states and the Middle East. An additional 12 percent of the voting public chose **Gennady Zyuganov**'s Communist Party of the Russian Federation (CPRF), which called for the resuscitation of the Soviet Union – not because of any lingering faith in Marx's communist workers' utopia but in order to rebuild Russia as a great power. The remainder of the Duma was split among smaller parties that managed to surpass the 5 percent barrier to party-list representation – such as the more moderate promarket party Yabloko (Apple), led by economist **Grigory Yavlinsky**; the Agrarian Party, representing collective farms, and the Women of Russia Party, which emphasized problems of unemployment and abuse facing many Russian women – and independent deputies elected in local electoral districts.

A new constitution and elections did not eliminate Russia's continuing economic problems, however. The government did gradually manage to get inflation under control, primarily by stopping the printing of rubles. But factory managers throughout the country responded to the cutoff of subsidies by resorting to barter and by ceasing to pay their workers for months at a time. Eventually, mounting "wage arrears" to Russian workers, state employees, and soldiers grew into an intractable social problem. Small businesses, meanwhile, were strangled by a combination of arbitrary state taxation, corrupt bureaucrats demanding bribes, and interference by local "mafias" demanding protection money. Foreign and domestic investment remained at a very low level, and the overall gross domestic product (GDP) continued to decline. Taxation to cover government expenditures became increasingly difficult because many people (understandably) did their best to hide their incomes. The government began to rely on revenues from the privatization drive, which continued to favor well-connected elites. By 1995, a handful of billionaires – popularly known as the **oligarchs** – had gained control of most of the country's energy and mineral resources, banks, and mass media.

Moreover, although the new constitution contributed to a temporary stabilization in relations between Moscow and the various regional governments of the Russian Federation, the danger of state disintegration remained. Yeltsin was soon forced to conclude a series of separate treaties with restive regions, such as oil-rich Tatarstan and the diamond-producing republic of Sakha in the Far East. Then, in December 1994, hard-line advisers persuaded Yeltsin to reassert Moscow's authority over the regions by invading the rebellious republic of Chechnya. The invasion quickly escalated into a full-scale war that killed tens of thousands of ordinary citizens – including many elderly ethnic Russians who could not escape the Chechen capital of Grozny in time. But the war only succeeded in further stiffening Chechen resistance to Russian rule. The utter failure of the campaign in Chechnya demonstrated clearly that the Russian military, like the rest of the government, was in a state of near-total demoralization and ineffectiveness.

Given Russia's continuing decline – and Yeltsin's growing health problems and increasingly erratic behavior – it is perhaps unsurprising that parliamentary elections in 1995 once again favored antiliberal forces. That voters were confronted with a long, confusing ballot listing forty-three competing parties did not help matters. This time, Zyuganov's CPRF was the biggest vote-getter, attaining 22 percent of the PR vote. Zhirinovsky's LDPR still polled a disturbing 11 percent. The only two other parties to exceed the 5 percent barrier were Yavlinsky's Yabloko, with 7 percent, and a new pro-government party called Our Home Is

Russia, led by Prime Minister Chernomyrdin, which managed to attain only 10 percent of the party-list vote despite an expensive government-sponsored media campaign. Gaidar's party dropped below the 5 percent barrier and won just a few single-member district seats. Meanwhile, because of the absurdly large number of competitors on the ballot, a majority of Russian voters voted for parties that did not get any Duma seats at all.

The first post-Soviet presidential campaign in Russia, in 1996, thus began with Yeltsin's political future in grave doubt. In February, polls showed that only 6 percent of Russians supported the Russian president, whereas over one-quarter supported his Communist challenger, Zyuganov. With the fate of Russia's weak democratic-capitalist regime hanging in the balance, however, Yeltsin mounted a remarkable comeback. He traveled throughout the country, energetically shaking hands, handing out money to pay late pensions and wages, and even dancing to a rock band. Yeltsin's campaign was financed by a huge infusion of cash from the IMF, which delivered the first installment of a $10 billion loan to Yeltsin's government, and by the oligarchs, who were terrified that their newly privatized companies would be renationalized in the event of a Communist victory. The oligarchs also flooded Russian newspapers and television with political advertising portraying Zyuganov as a tyrant who would reimpose totalitarian rule. Zyuganov, meanwhile, made such fears seem realistic by praising Stalin as a great Russian leader and declaring that the USSR still legally existed.

In the first round of the presidential elections in June 1996, Yeltsin got 35 percent of the vote to Zyuganov's 32 percent. In third place with 15 percent was General **Aleksandr Lebed**, who called himself a "semidemocrat" and promised to restore "truth and order." Yavlinsky managed fourth place with 7 percent of the vote, and Zhirinovsky came in fifth with 5 percent. Five other minor candidates polled less than 2 percent each – including Mikhail Gorbachev, supported by a minuscule 0.5 percent of the electorate.

Russian electoral rules require a runoff between the top two vote-getters in the first round of presidential elections if no candidate attains a majority. Thus, voters now faced a stark choice between Yeltsin and Zyuganov. The oligarchs continued their media campaign, portraying the election as a decision between freedom and totalitarianism. Lebed decided to support Yeltsin in return for an important government post. Zyuganov himself repeated his standard themes, blaming the IMF, the West, and Yeltsin for the ruin of Russia and calling for the restoration of Soviet power. In early July, Yeltsin completed his comeback, gaining 54 percent of the vote versus 40 percent for Zyuganov (with 5 percent of voters declaring themselves "against both").

Yeltsin's re-election meant that the flawed democratic-capitalist institutions he had established after 1991 in Russia would endure at least a while longer. However, powerful postcommunist interest groups, including many blue-collar workers, collective farmers, pensioners, military men, and anti-Western intellectuals, continued to oppose Yeltsin's regime. Moreover, the perpetual crises, violence, and economic decline of the early post-Soviet period had alienated even Yeltsin's own supporters among the urban, educated middle class, most of whom in 1996 had in essence voted against Zyuganov and a return to communism, rather than for the aging and erratic president. Indeed, a few days before his re-election, Yeltsin had suffered a severe heart attack; he was barely able to attend his own inauguration ceremony and was only sporadically active afterward. The president's incapacitation set the government adrift while its political, economic, and regional challenges mounted. Elections for regional governors in 1997 – although marking an important extension of Russian democracy – tended to strengthen further the power of Russia's regions as the capacity of the central government decayed.

In the spring of 1998, during one of his infrequent periods of political activity, Yeltsin made one last effort to rejuvenate market reforms. He unexpectedly fired Chernomyrdin as prime minister, replacing him with Sergei Kiriyenko, a thirty-five-year-old ally of Gaidar, Chubais, and other liberal "young reformers." However, the underlying structural problems in the Russian economy were by this point too severe to fix. Given continued economic stagnation, decreasing confidence on the part of foreign investors, poor tax collection, declining world oil prices, and an increasingly unmanageable debt burden, Russia's budget deficit became unsustainable. The IMF tried to help Kiriyenko's government, delivering almost $5 billion in late July, but within a few weeks this loan had been exhausted in a failed attempt to prop up the weakening ruble.

On August 17, 1998, Kiriyenko suddenly announced a devaluation of the ruble and a ninety-day moratorium on government debt payments. A deep financial crisis ensued. Inflation soared to almost 40 percent for the month of September alone, dozens of banks failed, and foreign investors left Russia in droves. Yeltsin fired Kiriyenko but then inexplicably proposed to replace him once again with Chernomyrdin. Besides Chernomyrdin's own party, no major faction in the Russian Parliament would go along. After tense negotiations, all sides agreed to support the compromise candidacy of Foreign Minister **Yevgeny Primakov**, a Soviet academic specialist on the Middle East and former chief of Russian foreign intelligence. On September 11, 1998, Primakov was overwhelmingly confirmed as Russia's new prime minister. The constitutional order had been preserved.

Unfortunately, the endemic uncertainties of Russian politics continued. Only seven months after Primakov's promotion, another nearly disastrous battle between the president and the parliament erupted when Zyuganov's Communist Party initiated impeachment proceedings against Yeltsin. Although more moderate political forces seemed unlikely to support some of Zyuganov's most extreme claims – for example, that Yeltsin had committed "genocide" against the Russian people by launching the shock-therapy program – the vote to impeach the president for unconstitutional actions in launching the war in Chechnya looked too close to call.

But on May 12, 1999, just three days before the impeachment vote in the Duma, Yeltsin suddenly dismissed Primakov as prime minister, proposing to replace him with Interior Minister Sergei Stepashin. Now a full-scale constitutional crisis loomed. According to the text of the 1993 Russian constitution, the Duma would be disbanded if it failed to confirm Stepashin as the new prime minister on a third vote; yet, at the same time, the constitution also forbade the president from dissolving the Duma if it voted for impeachment.

Faced with the very real possibility that Yeltsin would take advantage of the constitution's ambiguity to declare a state of emergency rule – and worried that they would lose their parliamentary perks and privileges as a result – the Duma majority backed down. The vote to impeach Yeltsin failed, and Stepashin was later easily confirmed as prime minister.

Even this was not sufficient to make the increasingly isolated president feel secure, however. In early August, two new threats to Yeltsin's regime emerged. First, Primakov and the powerful mayor of Moscow, **Yuri Luzhkov**, announced the formation of a new political party supported by many of Russia's most powerful regional governors, the Fatherland–All Russia Bloc, which would compete against parties supported by the Kremlin in the December 1999 Duma elections. Then, Chechen extremists led by Shamil Basaev and the Islamic fundamentalist Khattab invaded the neighboring ethnic republic of Dagestan, proclaiming their goal to be the creation of an Islamic state in southern Russia. Yeltsin fired Stepashin, who appeared to have been taken by surprise by these events, and replaced him with the dour, forty-six-year-old former KGB spy Vladimir Putin, who headed the KGB's successor organization, the Federal Security Service (FSB). Yeltsin also announced that he considered Putin to be his heir and that he hoped that Russians would rally around him as the 2000 presidential elections neared. Remarkably, despite Putin's almost total political obscurity at the time of his appointment, this is exactly what happened.

The key event propelling Putin into the top position in Russian politics was the outbreak of the second war in Chechnya in the fall of 1999. Although rumors of a renewed Russian assault on the breakaway republic had been swirling for some time, the final decision to launch a full-scale invasion was reinforced by shocking events in September: terrorist bombings of apartment buildings in the suburbs of Moscow and in the southern Russian city of Volgodonsk that killed nearly 300 Russian citizens. Putin's government immediately blamed these bombings on the Chechen rebels led by Basaev and Khattab, whipping up an understandable public outcry for revenge – although doubts about who was really responsible for the terrorist attacks remain.

The Russian military counterattack on the Chechen rebels soon escalated into an all-out invasion of the Chechen republic. Putin now declared his intention to wipe out the Chechen "bandits" once and for all. The resulting conflict, like the first Chechen war, led to the deaths of thousands of innocent Russian and Chechen civilians and the near-total destruction of much of the region, including the capital city of Grozny, which was finally taken by Russian troops in February 2000. Once again, the Chechen resistance fighters fled to the mountainous southern part of Chechnya, from which they continued to launch bloody attacks on Russian forces.

The emotionally charged political environment generated by the new Chechen war could not help but affect the outcome of the 1999 Duma elections. A new pro-Putin party known as Unity, made up of various regional leaders and state bureaucrats, was hastily thrown together in October; it ended up gaining 23 percent of the party-list vote. Zyuganov's nationalist CPRF did very well, attaining 24 percent of the party-list vote and forty-six seats in single-member districts. The Union of Rightist Forces, including famous liberal "young reformers" such as Gaidar, Kiriyenko, and Chubais, also received an endorsement on television from Putin; as a result, they, too, did surprisingly well, attaining 8.5 percent of the party vote. Meanwhile, pro-Kremlin television mounted a sustained mudslinging campaign against Primakov and Luzhkov; as a result, the Fatherland–All Russia Party performed well below early expectations, with just over 13 percent of the vote. Finally, Yavlinsky's Yabloko

Party – the one political force publicly critical of the war in Chechnya – barely squeaked past the 5 percent barrier, as did Zhirinovsky's party.

This popular endorsement of Putin and his policies reassured Yeltsin that he could now leave the political stage with no fear that he or his circle of intimates would later be investigated or prosecuted, as had been continually threatened by the communists and their allies. On New Year's Eve 1999, Yeltsin stunned the world with the sudden announcement of his early resignation as Russia's president. As specified in the Russian constitution, Prime Minister Putin now became acting president as well, and early elections for the presidency were scheduled for March 26. Given Putin's war-driven popularity and the limited time available for his opponents to campaign against him, his victory was certain.

The Putin Era

When Vladimir Putin was formally elected as Russia's president in March 2000, he inherited a corrupt government, an imbalanced economy, and a demoralized society. A new defeat in Chechnya, he claimed, might under such circumstances lead to the final disintegration of the country. Thus, the central priority for President Putin was the rebuilding of the Russian state. Pursuit of this goal would involve a reformulation of Russia's political identity and major reforms of its institutions – changes that, inevitably, had important effects on the organization of Russian social interests.

Putin's conception of Russian national identity can be summed up in one of his most frequently used slogans: *gosudarstvennost'*, or loyalty to the state. In Putin's view, a general lack of state-oriented patriotism, and a desire to pursue only short-run selfish interests, played a key role in undermining the global power of the Soviet Union and in weakening the coherence of Russia's post-Soviet institutions. His conception of *gosudarstvennost'*, designed to combat the decline of patriotism, contained three main elements. First, Putin claimed that victory in Chechnya, and the final suppression of "banditry" and "terrorism" emanating from the southern borders of Russia, would lead to the resurrection of Russia as a global great power; he even declared that the stabilization of the Caucasus was his personal mission. Second, Putin called for the restoration of what he termed the "vertical of power" linking Kremlin leaders to state officials throughout Russia's vast territory: Dutiful obedience to one's superiors was supposed to replace the political and social free-for-all of the Yeltsin era. Third, Putin expressed intense suspicion of independent social forces that opposed the Kremlin, arguing that in many cases such forces represented foreign interests trying to weaken Russia from within.

Putin's efforts to rebuild Russians' trust in the state had some positive initial impact. Public-opinion polls during Putin's first term showed that ordinary Russians were more optimistic about the country's future than at any time in the 1990s. At times, however, Putin's efforts to restore loyalty to the state, and to stifle political criticism, recalled the secrecy and political conformity of the Soviet era. In August 2000, for example, the Kursk nuclear submarine sank after a failed test of a new torpedo, killing all 118 men on board; Putin, who was on vacation at the time, remained silent about the crisis for days, while the head of the Russian navy blamed the accident on a collision with an American sub. By December

2000, Putin – over the strenuous objections of liberal lawmakers – had moved to restore the Soviet-era national anthem (with new, noncommunist lyrics) and, for the Russian military, the red flag of the USSR (without the Marxist-Leninist hammer and sickle). A shadowy new youth organization called Moving Together began to organize mass pro-Putin rallies, and to criticize "unpatriotic" authors, in many Russian cities. Still, Putin's calls for state patriotism did not constitute the resurrection of any full-blown political ideology like the Marxism-Leninism of the past; indeed, Putin's political worldview remained in many respects both vague and flexible.

Along with Putin's efforts to resurrect Russian patriotism came a series of reforms designed to rebuild Russian state and economic institutions. To prevent further disintegration of central authority over the regions and republics of the Russian Federation, Putin initiated a series of federal reforms in May 2000: The eighty-nine subjects of the federation were now regrouped into seven new federal districts, headed by appointed "supergovernors" answering directly to the president; regional governors and parliamentary heads were removed from their seats on the Federation Council and replaced with unelected representatives generally more supportive of the Kremlin; and new legislation allowed the Russian president to dismiss regional governors if they acted "unconstitutionally." (Later in his presidency, Putin worked to reduce the number of federal subjects to eighty-three, merging several of the smaller ethnic districts with larger neighboring regions, and expanded the number of federal districts to nine, including a new one for Crimea after its 2014 annexation.) To streamline economic policy, Putin during his first presidential term reduced the income tax to a flat rate of 13 percent and the corporate tax to 24 percent, introduced a new land code allowing – for the first time in Russia's history – the legal buying and selling of both urban and agricultural land, and introduced a new labor code weakening the power of Russia's trade unions and making it easier to hire and fire workers. The judicial system, too, was reformed: trial by jury was introduced on a limited basis; judges' salaries were raised in order to lessen the temptations of corruption; and, in a reversal of both tsarist and Soviet-era practices, defendants were now officially to be considered innocent until proven guilty beyond a reasonable doubt.

Such policies convinced many analysts and business investors that Putin was at heart a Westernizer, continuing in the same basic spirit as the architects of shock therapy but with more decisiveness and competence than his predecessor Yeltsin. However, the antiliberal and authoritarian elements of Putin's *gosudarstvennost'* were also evident early in his presidency. In particular, Putin launched an attack on the oligarchs that seemed to focus solely on those billionaires who had the temerity to oppose the Kremlin; other pro-Putin oligarchs were allowed to keep and even expand their business empires. In June 2000, Vladimir Gusinsky, owner of the main independent television station, NTV, along with several liberal newspapers and magazines, was jailed on embezzlement charges. He was released only after pledging to give up control of NTV to Gazprom, and soon fled the country. Then Putin's government opened up an investigation concerning powerful oligarch Boris Berezovsky, who had been the primary financial backer of both Yeltsin and later Putin himself during the late 1990s. Berezovsky, seeing the writing on the wall, gave up his seat in the Duma and also fled to Great Britain, where he died under mysterious circumstances in 2013. Such attacks on oligarchs were generally quite popular among ordinary Russians, most of whom thought of these "robber barons" as thieves profiting from the poverty of the masses; simultaneously, Putin's policies sent a threatening signal to other businessmen, journalists, and opposition figures. At the same time, FSB agents also began to hassle, detain, and in some cases imprison independent journalists, scholars, and leaders of nongovernmental organizations (NGOs).

For Putin to rebuild the Russian state, however, not just identity and institutions would be important – he would have to appeal to important interest groups in Russian society as well. In this respect, he clearly benefited from his extraordinarily good economic timing. The post-Soviet depression of the 1990s came to an end in 1999, just as Putin entered the political arena, and Russia's GDP grew strongly every year of his presidency, in large part because of profits from oil and gas exports. Putin used this windfall to balance the budget, repay Western debt, and – most importantly for ordinary people – to eliminate most of the wage arrears that had accumulated under Yeltsin. Still, in order to attack the interests of oligarchs, regional governors, and opposition politicians simultaneously, Putin had to promote the interests of a more specific social group willing to back him in tough battles. Here he largely turned to friends and associates within the secret police and, to a lesser extent, the military. Five of the seven new supergovernors, for example, were FSB or military generals. In March 2001, Putin's FSB colleague and close friend Sergei Ivanov was appointed defense minister. By the end of Putin's first term, according to analysts Olga Kryshtanovskaya and Stephen White, at least one-quarter of the Russian government elite had military or security backgrounds, and their number continued to rise steeply after that.

A final factor that was crucial in shaping the contours of Putin's Russia is the new global context generated by the terrorist attacks on the World Trade Center and Pentagon in the United States on September 11, 2001, and the subsequent global war on terrorism launched by U.S. president George W. Bush. Surprisingly for many, 9/11 and its aftermath led initially to much closer relations between the United States and Russia; indeed, Putin was the first foreign leader to telephone the White House to express his condolences after the attacks, and he pledged his full support for the war on terror. In many respects, in fact, the U.S. response to 9/11 only reinforced Putin's general political line: he, after all, had argued all along for a more decisive and forceful response to "Islamic terrorism." Putin's position was reinforced further as Chechen rebels continued to launch major terrorist attacks throughout his first term in office – most spectacularly, the seizure of more than 900 hostages at a downtown Moscow musical theater in October 2002, an event that ended in tragedy when well over a hundred hostages died from the effects of a poison gas used by the Russians to incapacitate the hostage-takers. Given the new global environment, Western official criticism of continuing Russian brutality in Chechnya became significantly more muted. In the end, the U.S.-Russian "strategic partnership" declared after 9/11 failed to live up to initial high expectations, as the two countries began to quarrel over trade issues, U.S. plans to build a missile defense system, the expansion of NATO (the North Atlantic Treaty Organization) to include the Baltic states, and, especially, the U.S. decision to invade Iraq in March 2003. But general Western support for Putin's political approach continued through the end of his first term, helping him maintain the backing of many liberals and Westernizers within the Russian elite.

By the end of 2003, Putin had become so dominant over his political opponents that there was little if any doubt he would win a second term. Indeed, a kind of miniature cult had emerged around the president. In one popular song, a female singer complained that she wished she could find "a man like Putin," who would not lie, drink, or break his promises. A government-sponsored Web site for children, www.uznai-prezidenta.ru, displayed photos of a smiling president Putin and his black dog. In a manner reminiscent of Soviet times, television news began to feature Putin's daily activities, no matter how trivial, as the lead story every evening. And even independent public-opinion polls continued to show Putin's popularity rating in the 70–80 percent range.

Given this political milieu – and the Kremlin's active efforts to ensure political loyalty – it is perhaps not surprising that the elections of 2003–2004 were far less competitive than those of the Yeltsin era. The campaign for the State Duma got off to a troubling start when, in October 2003, oligarch Mikhail Khodorkovsky – then Russia's richest man, and the key funder of the liberal Yabloko Party and the Union of Rightist Forces, as well as a backer of Zyuganov's Communists – was arrested by masked FSB police at an airport in Siberia and charged with embezzlement and tax evasion. Khodorkovsky's imprisonment not only deprived these opposition parties of crucial monetary resources but also made both the liberals and the Communists look like the pawns of an unpopular robber baron. State-run television also did its best to promote the pro-Kremlin United Russia Party; opposition politicians found it extremely difficult to compete for news coverage. In the end, the party of power received 37.6 percent of the party-list vote; counting single-member district seats and defections from other parties and factions, United Russia controlled over 300 seats – that is, a two-thirds majority in the new Duma. Zhirinovsky's LDPR, capitalizing on rising nationalist sentiment, rebounded to 11.5 percent, whereas CPRF support was cut in half compared with 1999, to just 12.6 percent. The new pro-Kremlin nationalist Motherland Party, cobbled together just a few months before the election to draw votes away from the Communists, did surprisingly well, attaining 9 percent of the vote. Meanwhile, both liberal parties failed to break the 5 percent barrier for Duma representation and won only a handful of seats, leaving their political future very much in doubt.

With Putin enjoying near-total dominance over the Parliament, and with no credible political opposition, his re-election in March 2004 was a foregone conclusion. Indeed, even a few weeks before the election itself, Putin moved to replace his primeminister, Mikhail Kasyanov – a holdover from the late Yeltsin era who had been openly critical of the Khodorkovsky arrest – with the more pliable bureaucrat Mikhail Fradkov, saying that he wanted voters to know what sort of government he planned for his second term. Both Zhirinovsky and Zyuganov refused to run against Putin at all and named obscure subordinates to campaign on their parties' behalf. Another presidential candidate even told voters that he himself favored Putin's reelection! In the end, Putin received 71.9 percent of the vote, compared with just 13.8 percent for his closest challenger, Nikolai Mikhailovich Kharitonov of the Communist Party of the Russian Federation.

Despite Putin's increasing personal power, his second term in office got off to a very difficult start. On the first day of the new school year, September 1, 2004, Chechen rebels took hundreds of schoolchildren, parents, and teachers hostage in the southern town of Beslan; more than 340 were killed when terrorist explosives were detonated in advance of a rescue attempt by FSB troops. Putin's response to the Beslan tragedy was once again to strengthen the power vertical: He abolished elections for regional governors, who would henceforth be appointed by the president. Soon afterward, Putin's attempts to help elect the pro-Russian candidate Viktor Yanukovich in Ukraine's November 2004 presidential elections backfired when evidence of serious electoral fraud generated massive popular demonstrations in Kiev. This "Orange Revolution" forced the Ukrainian authorities to hold new elections in December which were won by the pro-Western presidential candidate, Viktor Yushchenko. In January 2005, Putin's efforts to eliminate Soviet-era welfare policies, such as free sub-way rides for World War II veterans and heavily subsidized prescription drug benefits for the elderly, generated large-scale national protests. Meanwhile, the trial of oligarch Mikhail Khodorkovsky dragged on and on; after a year and a half in prison, in May 2005 he was formally convicted and sentenced to a nine-year term for embezzlement. Finally, the situation in Chechnya and the rest of the North Caucasus continued to deteriorate: pro-Putin Chechen president Akhmad Kadyrov was assassinated by Chechen rebels while attending a parade to celebrate the Soviet victory over the Nazis on May 9, and in October, attacks on police stations by Islamist and anti-Putin militants in nearby Kabardino-Balkaria were suppressed at the cost of over a hundred lives. All of these developments caused deep concern in the West about the future direction of Russian politics.

Yet by 2006, many of these troubling trends in Russian politics had seemingly been reversed. Most significant, surging prices for oil and natural gas on world markets, along with the continuing recovery of Russian light industry and services, now fueled a true economic boom in Russia affecting not only Moscow and St. Petersburg, but also most other cities throughout the country. By the end of the year, Russia had paid off its entire debt to foreign countries ahead of schedule and had declared the ruble a convertible currency like the euro and the U.S. dollar. Russian foreign currency reserves, levels of foreign investment, and the Russian stock market index all hit record levels. And while levels of inequality between Russia's new rich and the population of rural areas and poorer cities remained a source of intense social discontent, the organized protests of pensioners against Putin's welfare policies had died down completely. The year 2006 also saw a major shift in the fortunes of Russia's campaign to subdue resistance in Chechnya and the North Caucasus. The young Ramzan Kadyrov, who took over de facto control over Chechnya from his father after the latter's assassination, managed to restore a degree of order in the republic (even if this order depended on widespread fear of Kadyrov's increasingly powerful personal militia). Then in July, Shamil Basaev, the mastermind of the most brutal terrorist attacks on Russia since the initial 1994 Russian invasion of Chechnya, was killed in an explosion, leaving the Chechen rebels without effective leadership.

Given Russia's continuing economic success combined with the stabilization of the situation in Chechnya, Putin's sustained popularity ratings during his second term – approaching or exceeding 80 percent in most reputable polls – were hardly surprising. Paradoxically, however, Putin's increasing support at home was now accompanied by increasingly vocal Western criticism of the authoritarian direction of Russian politics. Signs of renewed authoritarianism in Russia were indeed quite clear by 2006. A new law requiring the reregistration of Russian NGOs approved by Putin in January 2006 appeared to target primarily those NGOs with ties to the West, those focused on preserving democratic freedoms in the

Russian Federation, and those devoted to taboo topics such as promoting Russian-Chechen reconciliation. The state's control over major sectors of the economy, too, was growing rapidly, as the remnants of Khodorkovsky's Yukos, other major energy assets, and even large Russian manufacturing concerns were swallowed up by various Kremlin-controlled conglomerates with strong ties to the FSB. As the parliamentary elections of 2007 and the presidential elections of 2008 approached, a whole series of changes to Russian electoral laws were adopted, seemingly designed to ensure more effective control by the Kremlin over the results – including the abolishing of all single-member district seats in the State Duma, which would henceforth be elected purely by proportional representation; the raising of the threshold for party representation in the Duma from 5 percent to 7 percent of the electorate; the elimination of the previous option to vote "against all" parties on the ballot; and the abolishing of all minimum voter turnout requirements for the election to be considered valid. Such maneuvering raised the inevitable question, both in Russia and in the West, of whether Putin himself would actually step down as Russia's leader as scheduled in March 2008 – as the president had repeatedly promised to do in a variety of public settings – or find some legal or semi-legal way to continue in office after all.

By this point, a disturbing disconnect had emerged between a Russian public that, by and large, approved of Putin's course and had few concerns about the increasing centralization of state power, and Western opinion leaders who wished to punish Putin in some way for his betrayal of democracy. In such an environment, the sense among many Russians that the West was conspiring to bring Russia to its knees – perhaps to counter Russia's economic rebound and renewed international prominence – remained widespread. Western critics of Putin who decried his efforts to rebuild the power vertical seemed to wish a return to the Yeltsin era – one perceived by the vast majority of Russian citizens as a time of chaos, economic disaster, and international humiliation. Precisely when Putin had decided to ignore Western economic advice and recentralize the Russian state, it seemed, Russia's economy began to skyrocket; so why should anyone in Russia listen to Western criticism of Putin now? The gap between Russian and Western perceptions became obvious to everyone in November 2006, when a prominent FSB defector and critic of Putin, Aleksandr Litvinenko, was poisoned at a fancy London hotel after he somehow ingested highly radioactive material at a meeting with two Russian businessmen. While much of the Western media directly blamed the Kremlin for Litvinenko's murder, the Putin administration along with many ordinary Russians claimed the entire affair to be a conspiracy organized by anti-Putin forces to blacken Russia's image.

The widespread feeling among Russians that their country stood entirely alone against the world greatly aided Putin's efforts to manage the problem of leadership succession at the end of his formal second term as Russian president. As the December 2007 parliamentary elections approached, the Kremlin further stepped up its efforts to harass or intimidate independent political groupings of all sorts, portraying them as agents of hostile foreign powers. Both of Russia's liberal parties, the Union of Rightist Forces and Yabloko, now found it nearly impossible to gain access to state-controlled television or even to obtain permits to hold political meetings. An opposition group known as The Other Russia, led by former chess champion Garry Kasparov and novelist and radical activist Eduard Limonov, mobilized anti-Kremlin rallies in several Russian cities, but these were quickly dispersed by police. In the meantime, the pro-Kremlin United Russia party was showered with positive media coverage, and huge advertisements appeared all over the country promoting the party of power as the vehicle for realizing "Putin's Plan." The result of this highly uncompetitive campaign was another triumph for United Russia, which received 64 percent of the vote and more than two-thirds of the seats in the Duma. Zyuganov's Communists received 12 percent, while Zhirinovsky's LDPR attained 8 percent, as did another new pro-Kremlin party, Fair Russia. Once again, liberal parties were shut out of the parliament entirely. Armed with this convincing show of popular support, Putin now formally announced his choice of successor – Dmitry Medvedev, a forty-two-year-old lawyer who had worked with Putin since the 1990s, ultimately rising to the positions of Gazprom chairman and deputy prime minister. Medvedev then announced that if elected president, he in turn would nominate Putin as his own prime minister – a post that Putin soon afterward promised to accept. On March 2, 2008, Medvedev predictably trounced his three nominal opponents for the Russian presidency – Zyuganov, Zhirinovsky, and the little-known Andrei Bogdanov – receiving more than 70 percent of the popular vote.

The Medvedev Presidency, 2008–2012

After Dmitry Medvedev was sworn in as the new Russian president in May 2008, many observers in both Russia and in the West saw signs that a genuine liberalization of the Russian political system might be in the offing. Medvedev, unlike Putin, did not have a background in the security services, and his campaign rhetoric calling for the urgent reform of Russia's hypercentralized and corrupt institutions inspired even some Russians who had been skeptical of his initial candidacy. The subsequent election of Barack Obama as U.S. president in November 2008 kindled hopes in both countries that these two new leaders – both lawyers in their forties with a reputation for reformism – might put U.S.-Russian relations on a more productive and cooperative footing. President Obama's call for a positive "reset" of bilateral relations with Russia was furthered by the evident personal chemistry between Obama and Medvedev at their summit meetings. For the remainder of Medvedev's four-year term in office, the notion that he might somehow engineer a break from Putinism toward a more democratic and decentralized Russian regime continued to inspire liberals in Russia's larger and more cosmopolitan cities. Formally, after all, President Medvedev had the constitutional right to fire Prime Minister Putin at any time, just as Presidents Yeltsin and Putin had dispensed with a whole series of prime ministers in their periods of rule. The idea that Putin's protégé might suddenly turn against him thus seemed at least plausible.

In reality, however, the new Medvedev-Putin "tandem," as it became popularly known, did not represent any deeper shift in the underlying power structure of Russian politics. Behind the scenes, Prime Minister Putin continued to be the dominant figure in Russian decision making – not only in domestic politics, but even in foreign policy, where the president's constitutional role was supposed to be paramount. This already became clear by the summer of 2008, when escalating tensions between Russia and its southern neighbor in the Caucasus, the former Soviet republic of Georgia, threatened to lead to all-out war.

Over the course of the year, a series of escalating threats between pro-U.S. Georgian president Mikhail Saakashvili (who had studied law at Columbia University) and the Medvedev-Putin tandem had led to a genuine crisis in Russian-Georgian relations. Russia repeatedly denounced Saakashvili as an anti-Russian "dictator" and tool of the West, banned the import of Georgian wine and mineral water, and pledged support for the autonomous ethnic regions of Abkhazia and South Ossetia, which remained within Georgia's formal territory but had broken away from Georgian rule de facto in the 1990s. President Saakashvili, meanwhile, accused Russia of harboring ambitions to dismember the Georgian state and to recreate the former Soviet Union's imperial control over the entire South Caucasus, and he worked to cultivate close ties with influential American politicians such as Republican presidential candidate senator John McCain.

On August 7 2008, Saakashvili launched an attempted surprise attack on South Ossetia's separatist government, in the hopes of reestablishing Georgian control over the breakaway region before Russia could fully respond. Not only did Saakashvili's attack fail to subdue the South Ossetians, but it also provoked a large-scale Russian military invasion into South Ossetia, Abkhazia, and the rest of Georgia's northern territory. For a few days, Russian military occupation of Georgia's capital Tbilisi and even Russian annexation of Georgia itself seemed conceivable. And despite the constitutional primacy of the presidency in Russian foreign policy making, Prime Minister Putin publicly took a leading role at several key points in the crisis. Putin, who had been attending the opening of the 2008 Summer Olympics in Beijing and meeting with U.S. president George W. Bush when hostilities broke out, quickly flew back to Russia, and he appeared within days with Russian troops near the front lines. Medvedev, who adopted a bellicose anti-Georgian position essentially identical to that of Putin, appeared to take a back seat to the prime minister in military planning for the duration of the conflict.

In the end, entreaties to both sides by the United States and the European Union, as well as the quick deployment of a U.S. aircraft carrier to the Black Sea, led to a Russian-Georgian cease-fire. Russian troops pulled out of Georgia's uncontested territory, yet Georgia had still suffered a major defeat that resulted in a full loss of political control over South Ossetia and Abkhazia, where Russian troops continue to be stationed. The Russian Federation even recognized both regions as fully independent states, although only a handful of countries – Nicaragua, Venezuela, Tuvalu, and Nauru – followed suit.

Shortly after the cessation of hostilities in Georgia, the Medvedev-Putin "tandem" was hit by another major challenge: the global financial crisis that spread across the world in the fall of 2008. As investors weighed the possible collapse of several major global financial institutions, which threatened a total breakdown of the capitalist banking system as a whole, Russia's raw-material dependent economy looked increasingly vulnerable. The price of Russia's major export commodity, oil, plummeted from its all-time high of $148 per barrel in July to just above $30 a barrel in December 2008. Unemployment, which had been reduced to around 6 percent during Putin's second term, began to rise sharply, reaching nearly 10 percent of the working population by the spring of 2009. Not surprisingly, the Russian stock market, dominated as it was by major Russian energy companies, plunged as well, at one point losing 70 percent of its former value. In response, President Medvedev and

Prime Minister Putin pledged to pump $200 billion – nearly a third of Russia's hard currency reserves – to prop up the weakening Russian ruble, to subsidize industries run by the oligarchs, and even to buy up Russian stocks directly. Like stimulus efforts in other countries at the same time, including the United States, this speedy government action prevented an even deeper economic depression. Still, Russia entered the new year with a substantially weakened economy suffering from depleted foreign currency reserves, a growing budget deficit, higher rates of unemployment and inflation, and a GDP that shrank by 8.1 percent in 2009.

Such a deep economic crisis could not help but affect the popularity of the new Medvedev-Putin government, further increasing speculation about who was really in charge. In his first official State of the Union address to the Russian parliament in October 2008, Medvedev announced significant new changes to the Russian Constitution: henceforth, Russia's presidential term would be extended from four to six full years, while terms for legislators in the Russian Duma would be extended from four to five years. Medvedev hastened to add that such changes would not apply to the current occupant of the presidential office – that is, to Medvedev himself. It escaped few people's attention that such changes would put Putin in a position to return to the Russian presidency in 2012 and, potentially, to run for two new six-year terms that would allow him to rule Russia until 2024, when he would be seventy-two years old.

For the rest of Medvedev's presidency, Putin would periodically emerge to remind ordinary Russians that he was the country's ultimate decision maker – publicly berating Russian oligarchs such as Oleg Deripaska for their failure to pay Russian workers on time, attacking the United States as a hypocritical and hostile country that preferred to criticize Russia rather than remedy its own democratic failings, and appearing in the Russian media as a heroic figure who could single-handedly tranquilize Siberian tigers and retrieve priceless ancient Greek vases on dives in the Black Sea. In interviews with journalists, Putin also began to hint more frequently about his interest in running to regain the Russian presidency when Medvedev's term was over in 2012.

Despite these early signs that the Medvedev-Putin tandem was little more than a fig leaf to provide Putin a "constitutional" mechanism for maintaining control over the Russian state, the mere fact that President Medvedev remained in the formal top position still encouraged the hopes of the Russian opposition that Putin's influence might be weakened over time. Medvedev, for his part, also tried to encourage the notion that he was a force for "liberalization." In 2009, he launched what he termed his "modernization program," designed to propel the Russian state fully into the twenty-first century by eliminating corruption, increasing economic competition, and experimenting with at least small-scale efforts to solicit a broader range of public opinion in political decision making. His public denunciations of the horrors of Soviet totalitarian rule appeared heartfelt and genuine, and contrasted starkly with Putin's evident nostalgia for the Soviet era. Medvedev's 2009 manifesto "Forward Russia!" – published originally on the Internet – criticized Russia's historical reliance on top-down, paternalistic management, and called for a more decentralized politics and economics that might allow for increased innovation from below. His signature economic project, the building of the Skolkovo high-tech research center near Moscow, which was designed to become the "Silicon Valley" of the Russian Federation, appeared to demonstrate Medvedev's resolve to wean Russia away from its overwhelming economic dependence on oil and gas revenues – even if in many ways, the Skolkovo project could itself be seen as a typical example of heavy-handed Kremlin interference in Russian economic development.

Still, by 2010, Medvedev appeared to have regained his public image as a genuine reformer who might someday challenge Putin for political primacy. The Russian economy now began to recover from the depths of the world financial crisis, posting 4 percent GDP growth for the year. Relations with the United States, too, improved markedly, and negotiations between Presidents Medvedev and Obama on arms control, missile defense, and bilateral trade began to produce concrete results. In April 2010, the two leaders signed the "New Start" treaty committing Russia and the United States to cut their nuclear arsenals by about 30 percent. Obama also announced that the United States, after nearly two decades of negotiations, would at last support Russia's entry into the World Trade Organization – a result that became formalized when Russia joined the WTO in August 2012. By October 2010, when Medvedev fired the long-serving and powerful mayor of Moscow, Yuri Luzhkov, replacing him with Kremlin loyalist Sergei Sobyanin, the president's independent political power appeared to be at an all-time high.

Accordingly, Russian opposition figures once again began to speculate that even slight apparent divisions between Medvedev and Putin might generate a larger split that could be utilized to promote major regime change. Such hopes were further encouraged by the outbreak of the "Arab Spring" revolutions in Tunisia and Egypt in early 2011, which raised the prospect that the increasing access of young, opposition-minded Russian citizens to social media technologies such as Facebook and Twitter might be utilized in Russia to generate revolutions against corrupt autocracy, just as in the Middle East. It was no doubt to quell such speculation that Putin and Medvedev announced in separate speeches in September 2011 that Medvedev would in fact step down at the end of his term to make way for the return of Vladimir Putin to the presidency. Remarkably, both men went a step further, informing the Russian citizenry that this decision had been made four years earlier, before Medvedev had been allowed to run in the presidential election in the first place!

This degree of seeming public candor from Russia's leadership, however, proved to be a serious miscalculation. Russian moderates and liberals who had been willing to give Medvedev and his presidency the benefit of the doubt for over three years were now informed that the entire "tandem" experiment had been a charade: as cynics had suspected, Putin had been calling the shots all along. Many Russians felt personally insulted that their political support had been taken so completely for granted in this way. Not only did the announcement of Putin's return to the presidency destroy what remained of Medvedev's legitimacy as president, but it also had a significantly negative effect on Putin's own popularity, which sank from earlier stratospheric levels to just over 60 percent in reputable polls. At one public appearance at a martial arts match in November 2011, Putin's arrival on stage was greeted with loud booing from the audience – an event that, captured on YouTube and replayed countless times by Internet users across Russia, demonstrated to the whole country the growing degree of discontent with the nation's aging leadership.

The approach of the scheduled Duma elections of December 2011 thus seemed to provide a golden opportunity for renewed opposition mobilization. To be clear: no one really expected that the 2011 parliamentary elections would be free and fair. As had been the case with elections since at least 2004, the Kremlin planned to "manage" the electoral process very carefully so as to ensure a pro-regime result. United Russia would surely maintain its electoral dominance; the "acceptable" opposition parties, the CPRF, LDPR, and Fair Russia, would once again gain their relatively small shares of parliamentary representation. But given the growing anger at Putin's stage-managed effort to return to the presidency, the precise percentage of the United Russia vote, as well as the degree of naked fraud necessary to attain it, could be considered crucial signals of just how unpopular Russia's authoritarian regime had really become. This ensured that the degree of public scrutiny of the voting process and ultimate outcome would be higher than at any point since the early Putin era.

Indeed, for a party with the full weight of the state machinery behind it, United Russia fared quite poorly in the election, attaining just over 49 percent of the popular vote, with 19 percent going to the Communists, 14 percent to Fair Russia, and 12 percent to Zhirinovsky's LDPR. As according to Russia's electoral law, votes for parties that did not make the 7 percent barrier to entry in the Duma – including Yabloko, which attained 3.4 percent, along with a handful of smaller parties – would be redistributed to the winners, United Russia still ended up with a strong majority of parliamentary seats: 238 of 450. However, this total was far below the 315 seats held by United Russia in the previous Duma from 2007 to 2011; no longer would the ruling party hold the over two-thirds majority necessary to amend the Constitution at will. More important, opposition leaders and Russian NGOs serving as electoral monitors declared that the vote totals for United Russia had been significantly inflated by fraud. Chechnya, for instance, now entirely under the thumb of strongman Ramzan Kadyrov, reported a 99 percent vote total for United Russia; several other ethnic republics reported similarly unbelievable majorities for the approved Kremlin party. The spread of the Internet in Russian society also now meant that videos showing election officials engaging in ballot-stuffing and other clearly fraudulent activities at election sites were quickly circulated and watched by millions of Russians.

Armed with such evidence, opposition leaders were able to rally tens of thousands of demonstrators on the streets of Moscow to protest the election results. Strikingly, the backgrounds of these protestors were noticeably different than had been the case in previous opposition rallies in the Putin era. Demonstrations now drew a much younger, highly educated, and professional crowd, in addition to the pro-communist pensioners and extreme nationalist groups that had formed the bulk of earlier anti-Putin protests. As the word began to spread among middle-class citizens in cities throughout Russia that a new spirit of opposition had been awakened in the country, these anti-Putin demonstrations grew larger and larger. Over the course of the winter of 2012, several opposition rallies in Moscow attracted crowds nearing or exceeding 100,000 people, according to the estimates of the organizers – posing the biggest threat to Putin's rule since his rise to power in 1999. White ribbons, the symbol of the protest movement, began to appear on people's lapels and handbags throughout the country, and were particularly widespread in the major cities of Moscow and St. Petersburg. Putin seemed at first unsure how to respond, at one point claiming that the protestors were taking orders from U.S. secretary of state Hillary Clinton and saying that the oppositions' white ribbons looked to him like condoms – but then shortly afterward allowing Medvedev to announce significant political reforms, such as a return to the direct election of Russian governors, in an effort to appease the crowds.

Yet in the end, even these mass protests were not enough to dislodge Putin from power. Several factors combined to limit their political impact. First, while opposition sentiment among Russia's educated middle class and youth had obviously deepened considerably, Putin still remained popular with over half of Russia's population, including many elderly Russians, those living in rural areas and small towns, and those with strong beliefs in Russian Orthodoxy, which Putin emphasized more and more frequently in his speeches. Second, the opposition itself was badly divided among several would-be leaders with widely divergent ideologies, including the Yeltsin-era liberal Boris Nemtsov, the radical revolutionary communist Sergei Udaltsov, media figures such as television commentator Ksenia Sobchak, and nationalist anti-corruption crusader **Aleksei Navalny**, who most observers saw as the most charismatic of the group. The leadership issue was further confused by the appearance at opposition rallies of figures close to Putin such as oligarch Mikhail Prokhorov, owner of the Brooklyn Nets basketball team, and liberal former finance minister Aleksei Kudrin, who had quit his government post after the public announcement that Putin and Medvedev would trade places, but who had remained on good terms with Putin personally. Third, Putin's top elite, made up of a few dozen loyal associates primarily with intelligence backgrounds, along with pro-Kremlin oligarchs who had repeatedly demonstrated their loyalty to the regime, showed no signs of splitting under the pressure of the protests – ensuring that when the state finally decided to crack down on the opposition, it would be able to do so in a unified and consistent manner.

Putin Returns to the Presidency

Despite the emergence of mass opposition, Putin was still able to engineer a fairly easy re-election in the 2012 presidential campaign, attaining 64 percent of the vote in the first round of balloting (with Zyuganov once again coming in second with 17 percent). This result, too, was marred by significant electoral fraud, and the opposition once again tried to use this issue to galvanize protest against the newly reinstalled president Putin in May 2012. But turnout at these rallies was significantly less than in the heady days following the December 2011 Duma elections. Moreover, the regime now used a few incidences of street violence during the May protests to justify the detention of dozens of opposition leaders, including Nemtsov, Udaltsov, and Navalny. In June, the homes of Navalny, Udaltsov, Ksenia Sobchak and other opposition figures were raided by masked investigators who confiscated private photographs, computer files, and cash. The crackdown on protest continued in July 2012 with the high-profile trial of three members of the feminist band Pussy Riot, who had been arrested after they had filmed themselves in Moscow's Cathedral of Christ the Savior performing a "punk prayer" that Russia be "delivered from Putin"; in August, they were each sentenced to two years in prison. Ordinary Russians who had flocked to Moscow's major squares in the winter now began to fear incarceration or worse if they continued to protest. Not surprisingly, the numbers of participants in opposition protests dwindled further.

By the autumn of 2012, Putin had clearly triumphed over the opposition movement for the time being. The "tandem" was formally reestablished, this time with Putin serving as president and Medvedev serving as prime minister – although by now, practically no one took Medvedev seriously as an independent figure, and his reform initiatives of the 2008–2012 period were all quietly shelved or scaled back. The proposed return to the popular election of Russia's governors, for example, was watered down with a new requirement that gubernatorial candidates first receive approval from Kremlin-dominated municipal legislative assemblies in their regions before being allowed to run. Newly launched investigations of corruption and mismanagement at the Skolkovo project, meanwhile, signaled a de-emphasis of Medvedev's highest profile economic initiative.

Yet despite his rapid reconsolidation of executive power, President Putin had evidently been scarred by the experience of confronting open opposition on a mass scale for the first time. Putin's public rhetoric became more stridently antiliberal and anti-Western than ever before. Along with the rhetoric, Russian policy changed as well, with a whole series of laws passed in the subservient Duma to restrain the Russian opposition, including a new law requiring NGOs with any foreign funding whatsoever to register with the authorities as "foreign agents" if they engaged in "political activity"; a new law on "treason" authorizing up to twenty years in prison for anyone considered to have weakened Russian "security"; a new law banning so-called homosexual propaganda, which criminalized even the slightest expression of public support for the rights of gays and lesbians; and significant new restrictions on the Internet. U.S.-Russian relations also began to sour. In September 2012, Putin ordered the closing of the U.S. Agency for International Development Moscow office in Moscow. In December, the U.S. Congress passed the Magnitsky Act banning travel to the United States and confiscating the U.S. assets of Russian officials suspected of involvement in the 2009 death in prison of American investor Bill Browder's lawyer Sergei Magnitsky or other human rights abuses. The Russian Duma subsequently responded by passing legislation banning the adoption of Russian children by Americans. In July 2013, former NSA contractor Edward Snowden, hoping to escape prosecution for leaking millions of classified U.S. documents, escaped from Hong Kong to Moscow; he was later granted temporary asylum by the Russian government, provoking deep criticism by President Obama and many members of the U.S. Congress. From this point on, despite continuing efforts at bilateral cooperation in resolving international issues such as the Syrian civil war, U.S.-Russian relations generally were worse than at any time since the end of the Cold War.

During Putin's third presidential term, the Russian political system, despite its residual democratic trappings, could be fairly described as fully authoritarian, built around personal loyalty to the leader and an economy still overwhelmingly dependent on state-controlled energy companies. The Russian opposition continued to hold occasional anti-Putin protests, but the threat of intensified state repression sharply limited mass participation in such activities. Against this background, opposition activist Aleksei Navalny emerged as the single most persistent critic of Putin's regime, continuing to rail against the corrupt enrichment of high state officials and castigating the ruling United Russia party as the "party of swindlers and thieves." In July 2013, Navalny was tried and sentenced to five years in prison on an ostensibly ridiculous charge of embezzlement from a Russian timber company. Although Navalny was subsequently released on bail and allowed to begin campaigning for the post of Moscow mayor, most observers assumed that this was merely a ploy to make the re-election of Putin's protégé Sobyanin look more "democratic." In fact, Navalny's growing national profile and his appeal among both urban youth and ethnic Russian nationalists helped mobilize anti-Putin sentiment in the Moscow mayoral elections of September 2013, and he turned in a surprisingly strong performance, winning 27 percent of the vote to Sobyanin's 51 percent. Navalny immediately appealed the results, which he claimed were due to fraud, but whether he and his supporters could effect genuine regime change remained doubtful.

Indeed, as President Putin presided over the stirring opening ceremony of the Sochi Winter Olympics in February 2014 – one that united themes from tsarist, Soviet, and post-Soviet history – Putin's clear mastery over the Russian political system was hard to dispute. Several weeks before the Olympics, in an apparent effort to dampen criticism of the Russian regime during the games, Putin had even declared amnesty for a number of Russia's most high-profile prisoners. Mikhail Khodorkovsky was released after more than ten years in prison and immediately flew to Germany to be reunited with his family. The two members of Pussy Riot still incarcerated were also amnestied, along with thirty members of the Western environmental NGO Greenpeace, who had been arrested after launching a raid of a Russian Arctic oil rig in September 2013. During the Sochi Olympics themselves, however, little protest activity of any kind was tolerated.

Institutions, Interests, and the Search for a New Russian Identity

By the end of the Medvedev presidency, it was clear to everyone that the dream of a rapid transformation of postcommunist Russia into a liberal capitalist country such as the United States was just that – a dream. From the perspective adopted in this textbook, which emphasizes the long-term impact of institutions created at critical junctures in a country's history and the specific social interests that these institutions generate, the initial failure of market economics in Russia should not have been surprising. After all, the political and economic institutions of the Soviet Union were designed by men committed to destroying global capitalism. The all-powerful Communist Party was supposed to train new "professional revolutionaries" to conquer the world bourgeoisie, but it degenerated into a giant, corrupt bureaucracy entangled with a vast network of secret police. Those who had benefited from their positions in the party hierarchy were thus rarely interested in establishing new institutions that would strictly enforce norms of democratic citizenship and the rule of law. Soviet industrial cities were supposed to be heroic sites for revolutionary production but decayed into polluting, outmoded factory towns. They were thus ill-suited for the task of producing consumer goods according to Western standards of efficiency.

Despite the burdensome legacy of its communist past, the collapse of the Soviet Union in 1991 – like the collapse of tsarism at the beginning of the century – marked another critical juncture in Russia's history during which new institutions promoting new interests could be established (see Table 7.1). Indeed, despite all of the country's well-publicized problems, Russia did manage during the 1990s to establish the first democratic regime in its long history. Even if Russia's democracy remained rife with state corruption, undermined by abysmal economic performance, and threatened by vocal antiliberal movements, this accomplishment should not be dismissed.

The Putin era has seen a return to sustained economic growth, a resurgence of Russia's influence in the international arena, and a partial restoration of the coherence of the state. At the same time, however, Putin has presided over the rollback of most of Russia's early democratic achievements, and the 1993 Russian constitution itself has been rendered essentially irrelevant. Moreover, Russia finds itself in a new global context that remains highly threatening, with continued turbulence and uncertainty on nearly all of its borders. Indeed, during the Sochi Olympics themselves, political tensions building over months of stalemate between the government of President Viktor Yanukovich and street protestors in Kiev, the capital of Ukraine, exploded in violent clashes leading to over a hundred deaths. Yanukovich fled to Russia, denying that his government had given the orders to use violence–and leaving behind evidence of massive state corruption, as ordinary Ukrainian citizens toured the president's palatial personal residences for the first time. Declaring the overthrow of Yanukovich a "coup" backed by the United States and Ukrainian "fascists," Putin unexpectedly sent undercover Russian troops to the Crimean peninsula, who worked with local allies to hold a stage-managed referendum declaring overwhelming Crimean support for reunification with Russia. Putin's formal decision to annex Crimea on March 18, 2014 was initially met with a wave of nationalist rejoicing in Russia, but it also triggered deep concern in the West and elsewhere about the precedent this move could set for other global territorial disputes. Indeed, the Crimean precedent immediately prompted new secessionist claims in the predominantly Russian-speaking regions of eastern Ukraine–prompting fears that Ukraine as a whole might experience civil war or even state disintegration.

Russia's future depends not only on the nature of its institutions and interests and the global environment it faces, but also on the outcome of Russia's search for a new state identity, now that both Marxism-Leninism and "revolutionary" capitalism have failed. Indeed, with the military still largely unreformed, unresolved international tensions not only between Russia and Ukraine but also with many of its other neighbors, continuing bloody terrorist attacks by insurgents in the North Caucasus, and widespread popular distrust of all political parties and movements, the Russian Federation remains an unstable state prone to sudden political shocks – a terrifying prospect given Russia's still substantial stockpiles of chemical and nuclear weapons. Russia's collapse, however, appears highly unlikely, given Putin's success in reversing the institutional chaos of the Yeltsin years and the strong sense among almost all citizens of the Russian Federation that "Russia," in some form, must be preserved and defended.

But which Russia? The liberal capitalist Russia originally envisioned by Gaidar and his allies has been largely discredited by the Yeltsin-era economic crisis. Zyuganov's nostalgic communist version has little appeal for younger, educated Russians, and the CPRF is a fading political force. Zhirinovsky despite the LDPR's continuing presence in the Russian Duma, has long ago ceased to be anything more than a bogeyman cynically manipulated by the Kremlin. More explicitly pro-Nazi and anti-Semitic politicians continue to try to convert disgruntled youth and soldiers to their cause – but ever since Hitler's invasion in World War II, "fascism" has been deeply unpopular in Russia; indeed, in the Ukrainian crisis Putin has actually claimed to be defending Russian-speakers from "fascist" Ukrainian nationalists. Nor, despite the annexation of Crimea and the increasingly imperialist tenor of Russian official foreign policy, do any of Russia's other leading political figures – including Putin himself – have a clearly developed new definition of "Russia." As long as Putin and his team remain popular and the Russian economy continues to grow, the Kremlin's efforts to rebuild the Russian state might appear relatively successful. But Russia's economy still faces enormous challenges in the years ahead; there continue to be serious factional rivalries among the Russian elite; and new domestic or international challenges could quickly erode popular support for the regime. The one thing that can be predicted with confidence, then, is that we have not seen the final chapter in Russia's painful transition from Soviet rule.

BIBLIOGRAPHY

Baker, Peter, and Susan Glasser. *Kremlin Rising: Vladimir Putin's Russia and the End of Revolution*. New York: Scribner, 2005.

Breslauer, George. *Khrushchev and Brezhnev as Leaders: Building Authority in Soviet Politics*. London and Boston: Allen and Unwin, 1982.

Brown, Archie. *The Gorbachev Factor*. Oxford and New York: Oxford University Press, 1997.

Conquest, Robert. *The Great Terror: A Reassessment*. New York: Oxford University Press, 1991.

Conquest, Robert. *The Harvest of Sorrow: Soviet Collectivization and the Terror Famine*. New York: Oxford University Press, 1987.

Dunlop, John B. *The Rise of Russia and the Fall of the Soviet Empire*. Princeton, NJ: Princeton University Press, 1993.

Fish, M. Steven. *Democracy from Scratch: Opposition and Regime in the New Russian Revolution*. Princeton, NJ: Princeton University Press, 1995.

Fitzpatrick, Sheila. *The Russian Revolution*. Second edition. Oxford and New York: Oxford University Press, 1994.

Hanson, Stephen E. *Time and Revolution: Marxism and the Design of Soviet Institutions*. Chapel Hill: University of North Carolina Press, 1997.

Hill, Fiona, and Clifford G. Gaddy. *Mr. Putin: Operative in the Kremlin*. Washington DC: Brookings Institutions Press, 2012.

Hoffmann, David. *The Oligarchs: Wealth and Power in the New Russia*. New York: Public Affairs, 2002.

Jowitt, Ken. *New World Disorder: The Leninist Extinction*. Berkeley: University of California Press, 1992.

Kotkin, Stephen. *Armageddon Averted: The Soviet Collapse, 1970–2000*. Oxford: Oxford University Press, 2001.

Kryshtanovskaya, Olga, and Stephen White. "Putin's Militocracy." *Post-Soviet Affairs* 19, no. 4 (October 2003): 289–306.

McAuley, Mary. *Russia's Politics of Uncertainty*. Cambridge: Cambridge University Press, 1997.

McFaul, Michael. *Russia's Unfinished Revolution: Political Change from Gorbachev to Putin*. Ithaca, NY: Cornell University Press, 2001.

Putin, Vladimir V., with Nataliya Gevorkyan, Natalya Timakova, and Andrei Kolesnikov. *First Person: An Astonishingly Frank Self-Portrait by Russia's President*. New York: Public Affairs, 2000.

Remnick, David. *Resurrection: The Struggle for a New Russia*. New York: Random House, 1998.

Shevtsova, Lilia. *Putin's Russia*. Washington, DC: Carnegie Endowment, 2003.

Solnick, Steven. *Stealing the State: Control and Collapse in Soviet Institutions*. Cambridge, MA: Harvard University Press, 1998.

Taylor, Brian D. *State Building in Putin's Russia: Policing and Coercion after Communism*. Cambridge and New York: Cambridge University Press, 2011.

Triesman, Daniel. *The Return: Russia's Journey from Gorbachev to Medvedev*. New York: Free Press, 2011.

Yeltsin, Boris N. *Midnight Diaries*. New York: Public Affairs, 2000.

Yeltsin, Boris N. *The Struggle for Russia*. New York: Random House, 1994.

Zaslavsky, Viktor. *The Neo-Stalinist State: Class, Ethnicity, and Consensus in Soviet Society*. Armonk, NY: M. E. Sharpe, 1994.

IMPORTANT TERMS

Leonid Brezhnev – leader of the Communist Party of the Soviet Union from 1964 until his death in 1982. He presided over an orthodox Marxist-Leninist regime that became more and more politically corrupt and economically stagnant over time.

Chechnya – an ethnic republic that declared its independence from the Russian Federation in September 1991. In December 1994, Yeltsin launched a disastrous full-scale military attack on Chechnya in which tens of thousands of Chechens and Russians were killed. This first war was settled in the summer of 1996, but the political status of the republic remained unresolved. A second Chechen war broke out in the fall of 1999, which Putin utilized to build popular support. Chechen strongman Ramzan Kadyrov has consolidated a pro-Putin authoritarian regime in the region.

Viktor Chernomyrdin – prime minister of the Russian Federation from December 1992 until March 1998. Chernomyrdin, the former head of the Soviet natural gas ministry, was originally promoted as a compromise candidate after the refusal of the conservative Russian Congress of People's Deputies to reconfirm Yegor Gaidar as prime minister. Later, he became the leader of the pro-regime Our Home Is Russia Party and, under Putin, Russia's ambassador to Ukraine.

collectivization – Stalin's policy of creating "collective farms" (*kolkhozy*) and "state farms" (*sovkhozy*) throughout the Soviet countryside, supposedly in order to build socialist agriculture. This policy led to the deaths of millions of peasants through political violence and famine, and it created an enormously inefficient agricultural system.

Commonwealth of Independent States (CIS) – the loose association of former Soviet republics formed in December 1991 to replace the USSR. It was officially created at the Belovezh Forest meeting of Boris Yeltsin, president of the Russian Federation, and the presidents of Ukraine, Belorussia (Belarus), and Kazakhstan. The CIS has been largely ineffective since the collapse of the Soviet Union.

democratic centralism – the central institutional principle of Leninist political organization. According to this principle, "democratic" debates among party members are allowed only until the party leadership makes a final decision, at which point all members are obliged to implement the orders of their superiors without question.

Federation Council – the upper house of the Federal Assembly. The Federation Council has since 2001 been made up of representatives appointed by the governors and regional legislatures of all of Russia's federal regions and republics.

five-year plan – the basic organizing framework of Stalinist economic institutions. Beginning with the First Five-Year Plan of 1928–1932, all industrial and agricultural production in the USSR was regulated by monthly and yearly output targets given to each manager and worker. Bonuses went to those managers and workers who over-fulfilled their plan targets to demonstrate their revolutionary zeal.

Mikhail Gorbachev – leader of the Communist Party of the Soviet Union from 1985 to 1991. Gorbachev tried to reverse the stagnation of the Brezhnev era by launching a policy of "revolutionary restructuring" (perestroika) that called for open criticism of the past, greater democracy, and "new thinking" in foreign policy. The result was the wholesale disintegration of Leninist political institutions and Stalinist economic organizations, leading to the collapse of the USSR.

gulag – the Russian abbreviation for "chief directorate of labor camps." The gulags were a vast network of labor camps, set up by Lenin and greatly expanded by Stalin, that were used to imprison millions of people who were suspected of opposing the Communist Party and its policies.

Nikita Khrushchev – leader of the Communist Party of the Soviet Union from shortly after Stalin's death in 1953 until 1964. Khrushchev endeavored to reinvigorate Soviet socialism by means of a series of "revolutionary" economic campaigns in agriculture and industry, and also attacked Stalin's terror. This "leftist" strategy, however, only produced general administrative chaos, and Khrushchev was ousted in a Politburo coup.

Aleksandr Lebed – popular general who came in third in the 1996 presidential elections, after which he became the head of the Security Council. After having settled the first war in Chechnya, Lebed was fired by Yeltsin. In 1997, he was elected governor of the vast Krasnoyarsk region in Siberia. In 2002, he was killed in a helicopter crash.

Vladimir Lenin – Russian revolutionary and the author of *What Is to Be Done?*. Lenin insisted on strict "professional revolutionary" discipline among Marxists. In 1917, Lenin led the October Revolution and founded the Soviet regime in Russia.

Yuri Luzhkov – mayor of Moscow and leader of the Fatherland Party, which merged with Putin's Unity Party to form the pro-Kremlin party, United Russia. Luzhkov built a mini-empire through his control over business activities in Russia's capital city and became one of the country's most influential politicians. He was ousted by President Medvedev in 2010.

Karl Marx – nineteenth-century German intellectual, the coauthor (with Friedrich Engels) of the *Communist Manifesto* and the author of *Capital*. Marx provided the main theoretical inspiration for the later movement to create a socialist society in Europe.

Aleksei Navalny – opposition blogger and leader of the anti-Putin Russian opposition. Navalny rose to prominence through his Web site's exposés of Kremlin corruption at the highest levels, and became one of the most vocal protestors against Putin's return to the presidency in 2012. In 2013 he was tried and convicted of embezzlement in a heavily politicized trial, and sentenced to a five-year term in prison that was suspended while he ran for election against Moscow mayor Sobyanin.

New Economic Policy – often abbreviated NEP, the economic program adopted by Lenin in 1921 in the wake of the social devastation caused by the Russian civil war, which he saw as a "strategic retreat" from the ultimate goal of building socialism. The NEP allowed for the reestablishment of markets for agricultural products and legalized small-scale trade in the cities, but the Soviet state retained control over the major industries, and one-party rule was strengthened.

oligarchs – the group of a few dozen bankers and industrialists who took advantage of the rapid privatization of Soviet property to amass huge personal fortunes. During the 1990s, this group controlled most of Russia's most powerful media, banks, and raw-material companies. President Putin launched a crackdown on those oligarchs who openly opposed his regime. Pro-Putin oligarchs, however, continued to prosper from their ties to the Kremlin.

Yevgeny Primakov – former academic adviser to Gorbachev and later head of the Foreign Intelligence Service and foreign minister. Primakov was appointed prime minister in a compromise between Yeltsin and the communist-led Duma after the financial crisis of August 1998; he was then fired as the communists tried to impeach Yeltsin in the spring of 1999.

provisional government – the temporary government of former parliamentarians that ruled Russia after the fall of the tsarist empire in February 1917. This ineffective body failed to stabilize the revolutionary situation in the country and was overthrown by Lenin's Bolshevik Party in October.

Vladimir Putin – first appointed prime minister by Yeltsin in August 1999, he was then elected as Russia's president in 2000 and 2004. Putin attained high popularity among Russians for his prosecution of the war in Chechnya, his restoration of economic and social stability, and his efforts to restore the power of the Russian state. He took the post of prime minister under the 2008–2012 presidency of Dmitry Medvedev, but never relinquished de facto control over Russian politics. Putin was elected to a new six-year presidential term in a controversial election in 2012.

Aleksandr Rutskoi – general during the Soviet war in Afghanistan, and Yeltsin's vice-president from 1991 to 1993. He originally supported Yeltsin's Russian nationalism against Gorbachev's conception of "socialist reform" but later broke with Yeltsin when the president agreed to break up the USSR and tried to implement capitalism in the Russian Federation. Rutskoi was a leader of the opposition in the Russian Congress in 1993.

shock therapy – policy of rapid transition to capitalism officially adopted by Boris Yeltsin in January 1992. In theory, shock therapy was supposed to involve the simultaneous liberalization of all prices, privatization of state property, and stabilization of the Russian currency. In reality, the program was implemented only haphazardly, generating disastrous economic and social results.

socialism in one country – Stalin's slogan advocating the defense of Marxism-Leninism within the USSR alone, despite the absence of a global worker revolution in response to the Bolshevik Revolution of 1917. This phrase was used to denounce opponents such as Trotsky and Zinoviev, and to justify Stalin's policies of rapid industrialization and collectivization of agriculture.

soviets – a word that means "councils" in Russian. It refers to the spontaneous groups of workers and soldiers that formed in the chaotic social situation under the provisional government. Lenin saw these bodies as the seeds of the future communist society, and for this reason he declared the country a "soviet regime" after his party seized power. Until Gorbachev came to power, however, the soviets remained politically powerless and wholly subordinate to the party.

Joseph Stalin – the unrivaled leader of the Communist Party of the Soviet Union from 1928 to 1953. Stalin rose to power in a bitter and prolonged struggle with Trotsky, Bukharin, and Zinoviev after Lenin's death. He then implemented a policy of rapid industrialization and mass terror designed to build "socialism" in peasant Russia as quickly as possible – at the cost of tens of millions of lives.

State Duma – the lower house of the Federal Assembly, the Russian parliament created in the constitution of 1993. The Duma has 450 members. Until 2007, half of them were selected by proportional representation on party lists and half of them were elected in single-member districts. From 2007 forward, the entire Duma has been elected by PR.

Grigory Yavlinsky – leader of the Yabloko (Apple) movement, so named after the initials of its three founders. He argued that capitalism in Russia must be implemented by means of democratic and uncorrupted state institutions rather than via shock therapy.

Boris Yeltsin – the first democratically elected president of Russia. He organized the movement to declare the Russian Federation an independent country and thus to destroy the USSR. In 1993, he violently disbanded the Russian Congress of People's Deputies and introduced the new Russian constitution. After winning re-election in 1996, Yeltsin experienced increasing health problems, and his power gradually diminished. He resigned on December 31, 1999 and died on April 23, 2007.

Vladimir Zhirinovsky – leader of the so-called Liberal Democratic Party of Russia (LDPR). Zhirinovsky and his party argue for an ultranationalist solution to Russia's postcommunist problems, envisioning an eventual expansion of Russia to the Indian Ocean. In practice, however, Zhirinovsky has often voted in support of the government in return for political and financial support.

Gennady Zyuganov – leader of the Communist Party of the Russian Federation (CPRF). Zyuganov and his party argued for the restoration of "Soviet power," including the reconstitution of the USSR. The ideology of the party, however, is much more oriented toward great-power nationalism than toward original Marxism or Leninism.

STUDY QUESTIONS

1. Should Russia today be classified as a developed industrial society comparable to Britain, France, or Germany? Why or why not?
2. Was Lenin's conception of a revolutionary one-party regime consistent with Marx's vision of communism, or was it a betrayal of Marx's dream of worker liberation?
3. What were the main reasons for the rise of Stalin and his policies of mass terror? Would you blame primarily the ideals of communism, the institutions of Leninism, the interests of Stalin and his supporters, or the global context in which the Soviet Union was situated?
4. Does the failure of Gorbachev's perestroika demonstrate that the Soviet system in the 1980s was unreformable? Or could some alternative strategy for reforming communism have succeeded in revitalizing the institutions of the USSR? What is the relevance, if any, of Deng Xiaoping's reforms in China to the Soviet case?
5. Should social scientists have been able to predict the disintegration of the Soviet bloc? What explains the remarkably poor track record of Western scholars in making predictions about the future of the Soviet Union and Russia?
6. Compare and contrast the problem of ethnic conflict in the Soviet Union and in the Russian Federation. Why did the USSR break up into fifteen independent countries, while Russia instead appears to be expanding its geopolitical power beyond its borders?
7. Was Russia's post-Soviet economic crisis caused by the failure of Yeltsin's shock-therapy program or was it simply because of the legacy of Stalinist socioeconomic institutions? Might some alternative strategy for building capitalism in post-Soviet Russia have been more successful?
8. Are capitalism and democracy in conflict in postcommunist Russia, or do they instead reinforce each other?
9. In 1917, the tsarist empire collapsed, and Lenin's radical Bolshevik Party came to power soon after. In 1918, the German empire collapsed, and within fifteen years the Nazi Party came to power. Is there any chance that a radically antiliberal ideology such as Lenin's or Hitler's will eventually triumph in post-Soviet Russia as well? Why or why not?
10. Would you expect the next generation of Russian politicians to be more successful at institution-building than was the generation reared under communism? Why or why not?
11. If you were a Russian voter, would you support or oppose Vladimir Putin? Would you support or oppose Aleksei Navalny? Why?

CHINA

MAP 8.1. Map of China.

8 China

Yu-Shan Wu

Introduction

China has one of the world's most ancient civilizations, dating back more than 3,000 years. It is easy for political scientists studying China to emphasize its uniqueness, as Chinese culture, language, political thought, and history appear quite different from those of any of the major Western countries. Modern Chinese history was obviously punctuated with decisive Western impacts, but the way China responded to those impacts is often considered to be uniquely Chinese. Furthermore, Chinese political leaders themselves frequently stress that they represent movements that carry uniquely Chinese characteristics. China, it seems, can only be understood in its own light.

When put in a global and comparative context, however, China loses many of its unique features. Imperial China, or the **Qing dynasty,** was an agricultural empire when it met the first serious wave of challenges from the West during the middle of the nineteenth century. The emperor and the mandarins (high-ranking Chinese officials) were forced to give up their treasured institutions grudgingly after a series of humiliating defeats at the hands of the Westerners. This pattern resembled what occurred in many traditional political systems when confronted with aggression from the West. From that time on, the momentum for political development in China was driven by global competition and the need for national survival. China differed from other cases in the developing world mainly in the immense dimensions of the country, not in the nature of its response.

As in other developing countries, different political forces in China competed for power as the country faced international challenges since the middle of the nineteenth century. Those different political forces represented distinct interests, developed alternative identities, and proposed competing institutions. The final outcome of their prolonged competition determined the developmental path of China in the middle of the twentieth century. After several decades of treading on that developmental route, however, China found itself lagging behind not only the West, but neighboring countries in East Asia. This realization triggered soul searching by the elites and a shift of developmental path, one that brought

China closer to other East Asian countries. The success of this second developmental path has had a great impact on the international environment as China looms as the second largest economy in the world and wields ever greater influence in international affairs.

As previous chapters have noted, late developers tended to put more emphasis on the state's role in development. Thus, from Britain to France, Germany, and ultimately Russia, one finds an increasingly coercive state accumulating scarce capital to fuel economic growth. British liberalism was translated into strategic investment in France, state sponsorship in Germany, and total state control under the name of communism in Russia. Using this logic, one could safely predict that China would follow a development strategy that puts a much stronger emphasis on a developmental state than would a typical Western liberal model. The short-lived experiment with multiparty democracy in the early years of the **Republic of China (ROC)** that replaced the Qing dynasty in 1911 testified to the weakness of the Western approach, as its supporters were unable to build strong institutions to consolidate democracy and develop the market. China was bound to adopt an approach in which the state would play a dominant developmental role.

Developmental state in the German (and Japanese) or in the Russian sense? This is the major difference between the **Kuomintang (KMT** or nationalist) regime that ruled China from 1928 to 1949 and the communist regime that established the **People's Republic of China (PRC)** in 1949 and has ruled the country since then. The global European and Japanese challenge forced the Chinese to adopt new institutions with greater governing capacity and, at the same time, offered models for the Chinese to emulate. The KMT opted for the German model, whereas the **Chinese Communist Party (CCP)** chose the Soviet model. The KMT and the CCP represented two different interests, upheld nationalism and communism as their respective identities, and established authoritarian and totalitarian regimes, respectively. Although both are undemocratic in nature, a totalitarian regime controls and mobilizes the society to a much greater extent than an authoritarian regime. In short, the international challenge to China brought about two distinctively different developmental models, as represented by the KMT and the CCP, and the interests, identities, and institutions of these two dominant political forces. Their duel ended with the CCP's victory. Communist modernization was to become China's developmental path.

During the post-1949 period, mainland China experienced first **Mao Zedong's** totalitarianism, followed by rapid economic and political reform under **Deng Xiaoping,** and then a consolidation staged by **Jiang Zemin, Hu Jintao, and Xi Jinping.** Through three decades of transition, today's China is characterized by post-totalitarian politics and state capitalism, partly converging to the route of authoritarian modernization that is a far cry from Mao's radical socialism. On the island of Taiwan, to which the KMT and its followers had fled after 1949, the KMT experienced a less turbulent and more linear development toward Western liberal capitalism and an increasing attenuation of its authoritarian model, leading ultimately to the adoption of democratic institutions. Viewed from a historical perspective, irresistible forces have compelled both the CCP and the KMT to adapt to the world market and play by its rules. Global competition first compelled the Chinese to establish a strong state for the initial push of industrialization on both sides of the Taiwan Straits, and then pressured them to tinker with the market when the state proved ineffective at

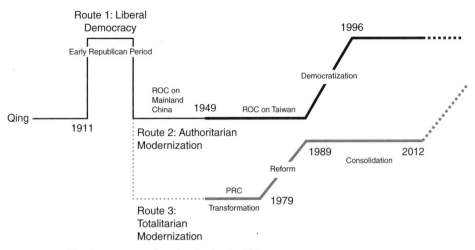

FIGURE 8.1. The three routes of modernization in China

sustaining growth. Markets and private property then nurtured social demands for political tolerance and a cultural shift away from collectivism to individualism, thus undermining authoritarian rule in both mainland China and Taiwan. Taiwan has already conformed to that pressure for democracy, partly because of the strong influence of the United States, on which Taiwan has been totally dependent, whereas mainland China remains opposed to democratic change, but with increasing difficulty.

Figure 8.1 demonstrates the three routes of modernization for China. Route 1 is liberal democracy, which the country attempted to tread but failed during its early years. Route 2 is authoritarian modernization, a developmental path pursued by the KMT both on the mainland (from 1929 to 1949) and on Taiwan (from 1949 to 1987). After democratization, the ROC became a full democracy, marked by its first popular presidential election in 1996. Its development trajectory thus moved up to the level of liberal democracy. Route 3 is totalitarian modernization, pursued by the communists on the mainland from 1949 to 1978. The 1980s witnessed rapid political and economic reform under Deng, only to be abruptly halted after the tragic Tiananmen incident in 1989. From that time on, China entered a protracted period of consolidation in which the paramount goal of the communist regime was maintaining political stability, amid hyper growth and social mobilization. The PRC's trajectory shifted upward and got close to authoritarian modernization, but there remained a gap. This is because there is a plethora of control mechanisms in place that is characteristic of a post-totalitarian system, but absent in an authoritarian regime. The dotted lines after 2012 show possible future development for both China and Taiwan.

In short, global challenges, foreign examples, and reliance on outside sponsors (in the case of Taiwan) shaped the political institutions of China. It is impossible to recognize or understand Chinese political development without first grasping the fundamental forces that influence China from outside its borders. Chinese responses to the world do carry certain characteristics that one does not easily find in other developing countries. However, the impetus and momentum for those responses and the general directions they took are quite understandable in a global and historical context. In the following discussion, we will trace the political development of China during modern times from the Qing dynasty to Deng's reform and subsequent development. Our focus will be on mainland China, but we will also make comparative references to Taiwan, an alternative Chinese society that has taken a different developmental route.

Historical Background

Imperial China was a static system. Dynasties came and went, but the basic outlines of China's patriarchal social structure and absolutist-monarchical political institutions remained unchanged from the Han dynasty (206 BCE to AD 220) until its collapse at the beginning of the twentieth century. Authoritarian control by head of the family in the private realm was mirrored by the absolutist rule of the emperor in the public domain. Confucianism, a way of thought developed by the Chinese philosopher Confucius around 500 BC that emphasized social order, was enshrined as the state ideology, and stressed filial piety and loyalty to the emperor as the ultimate virtues. A sophisticated examination system recruited intellectuals into the government based on their mastery of Confucian classics. Technological innovations and successful human organization made it possible for the Chinese dynasties to expand into great empires that often dominated neighboring tribes and nations in East Asia. Up until the Yuan dynasty (1271–1368), when China had Mongol rulers, the Middle Kingdom, as the Chinese referred to their country, was the envy of many Europeans.

In the mid-nineteenth century, Westerners began their exploitation of China's vast markets on a mass scale, pioneered by British opium dealers who were equipped with guns and steamers. Unequal treaties were signed by the Qing emperors with Western countries after humiliating defeats of the ill-equipped and poorly trained Chinese army in the hands of much superior European military. The Qing rulers could not come up with an effective response to the challenge posed by the West but the dynasty was able to drag on in decline for yet another half-century before it was buried amid lost wars, unequal treaties, depleted national wealth, and a disintegrated social fabric. During this agonizing period of national humiliation and attrition, the deep-rooted sense of superiority of the Chinese elite gradually gave way to a realization that China was actually inferior to the West, not only in military might but also in institutions and even in culture.

The Manchu dynasty was ultimately overthrown in 1912 by a revolutionary movement led by **Sun Yat-sen,** a U.S.-trained doctor from the Guangdong province. The Republic of China (ROC) was then founded. The new nation was faced with the urgent task of choosing its route of modernization. The victory of the Western Allies in defeating the Central Powers in World War I seemed to suggest the supremacy of democratic market capitalism, a model exemplified by Great Britain and the United States. However, the rise of Japan proved a more visible example of the appropriateness of authoritarian state capitalism for a late developer. The emergence of the Soviet Union as a challenge to Western institutions offered yet another model of development, that of totalitarian state socialism, with its full implications for the society yet to unfold while its anti-imperialist rhetoric was highly appealing to

Chinese intellectuals. A decision is to be made among the three routes of modernization: Anglo-American democratic market capitalism, Japanese-style authoritarian state capitalism, and Soviet-type totalitarian state socialism (see Figure 8.1).

Sun's ideal was to transform China into a modern, democratic, and affluent country that could repel foreign invasion and offer the Chinese people a decent life. Sun and his colleagues were at the time mainly inspired by the Anglo-American model and hoped China could evolve into a liberal democracy. However, political turmoil ensued, as no political-military force was able to prevail in China's postimperial era. Yuan Shikai, a Qing general turned president, attempted to restore imperial rule and make himself emperor. He was forced to curtail his ambition when beleaguered by defecting generals and Sun's comrades, who swore to protect the new republic.

After Yuan's death in 1916, China split into warring territories controlled by warlords of various kinds. Foremost were Zhang Zuolin in Manchuria and northern China, Wu Peifu in the Yangtzu area, and Sun Chuanfang in the southeast provinces. For his part, Sun established the KMT in 1919, expecting to relaunch the revolution and save the republic. Unable to receive support from the West, he then sought Soviet help from his base in the southern province of Guangdong and accepted Moscow's advice to establish the Whampoa Military Academy for the training of an officer corps loyal to his ideas, foremost of which were the **"Three Principles of the People"** – nationalism, democracy, and people's livelihood – a kind of democratic socialism with distinct Chinese characteristics. General **Chiang Kai-shek** was then appointed commander of the academy and charged with producing a highly indoctrinated revolutionary army for the KMT. Dr. Sun now envisioned a strong KMT-dominated state to fulfill his ideal. This was the basis of his policy to "ally with Russia and incorporate the communists." Although the KMT turned away from the Anglo-American model, Sun's policy shift was meant to be only temporary and instrumental, and would end with the introduction of the constitutional rule.

With the Western model of development out of the question, the KMT was faced with a choice between a German/Japanese-style statist model or a Soviet communist model. Because a large group of Chinese communists were admitted into the KMT, Sun's disciples found themselves competing with the newcomers for control of the party. Among Sun's disciples, General Chiang succeeded in building a revolutionary army committed to Sun's ideas, but only with heavy infiltration by the communists, who followed an order from Moscow to join Sun's KMT and develop the CCP's influence inside the KMT apparatus and military establishment. Sun died of liver cancer in 1925, leaving a heavily divided KMT. Chiang then launched a northern expedition in 1926 to expand the KMT's territory and shed communist influence. The initial thrust north was successful, and in early 1927 the KMT army was able to control the provinces south of the Yangtze River. Chiang established his power base in Nanjing and Shanghai, on the east coast of China, while the KMT Left and their communist allies set up a separate center in Wuhan in central China. Chiang then purged the communists in territories under his control, while the left-wing elements of the KMT and the communists were finding their relations strained because they could not agree on how to deal with Chiang. Finally, the communists were forced out of the KMT and began organizing peasant riots against Chiang's government in the countryside hitherto dominated by the landowning gentry class. In the end, Chiang was able to suppress the communist uprisings, subjugate the left-wing KMT factions, and complete his conquest of northern China in 1928. He established a nationalist government in Nanjing, the capital of the Republic of China. The country was unified.

The communists became rebels in China's mountainous areas, which they called the "Soviet regions." They tried to find support in China's tenant farmers, who had long been yearning for land through a land-redistribution scheme. Moscow's influence loomed large at the time. A Chinese Soviet Republic was established in Jiangxi province and later became a target for Chiang's "annihilation campaigns." In 1934, the communists' main base in Jiangxi was attacked, and they were chased across the south and southwest provinces of China by the pursuing KMT army. This desperate retreat was what the communists would later call the "**Long March.**" Ultimately, the retreating communist forces founded a new base in Yan'an, a remote town in the north of China. There the KMT offensive was finally thwarted, for the nationalist government faced a much more serious challenge from Japan's military incursions at that time. During the Long March, Mao Zedong was able to grasp first military and then political leadership of the CCP by criticizing and ousting those Chinese communists trained in Moscow. In Yan'an, Mao firmly established his personal leadership.

The period from 1928 through 1936 is considered the golden years of the KMT's rule in China, showing the initial success of authoritarian modernization. Industry grew, commerce expanded, and foreign trade surged. China might have taken a different route from what it actually did had it not been for an all-out Japanese invasion and the ensuing Sino-Japanese War, which totally devastated the country. As it turned out, the communists were able to appeal to nationalism and generate strong support among Chinese intellectuals, who grew increasingly critical of Chiang's concentration on crushing the communist insurgency. In December 1936, Chiang was kidnapped by Zhang Xueliang, a Manchurian warlord and, although he was finally released, the nationalist government was forced to shift its priority from mopping up the communists to preparing for war with Japan.

On July 7, 1937, Japan launched an all-out attack on the Chinese army guarding Peking (Beijing). China and Japan entered into a protracted and devastating eight-year war. The Japanese had built a powerful war machine that dwarfed China's fragmented and poorly equipped army. Chiang's strategy was to "trade space for time," and the KMT troops went into a large-scale retreat and rebuilt their defense line in the inland. As the war dragged on and the Japanese military was spread thin in China's vast territory, the KMT army was able to hold its defense line, while the CCP found great opportunities to expand in rural China, which the KMT vacated and the Japanese failed to penetrate. As it turned out, the Sino-Japanese War decisively altered the balance of power between the KMT and the CCP so that at the end of the war the communists were in control of north China and, with the help of the Soviets, Manchuria.

The nationalist government was ill prepared to fight a civil war with the communists after eight years of fighting with the Japanese. Most people simply wanted peace and were unwilling to support the KMT's war effort. Corruption and inflation cost the nationalists their traditional urban support, whereas communists were successful in mobilizing peasants with their land-reform programs. In the end, the nationalist troops were demolished in several decisive campaigns, and Chiang Kai-shek led millions of KMT loyalists to the island of Taiwan, a territory retroceded to the ROC by the Japanese after World War II. On October 1, 1949, the People's Republic of China (PRC) was formally established in Beijing, while the ROC migrated to Taiwan. There has been no peace treaty between mainland China and Taiwan since then, and the Chinese civil war technically has not ended to this date.

The civil war was significant in shifting China's developmental path. During the republican period, the KMT basically pursued a statist development model, which had technocratic capitalism, authoritarian political control, and exultation of nationalism as its major components. Even though one finds traditional elements and emphasis on Confucian teachings in the KMT's ideology, the system established by Chiang was modeled on those of Germany and Japan. It was not totalitarian, as the KMT lacked the capacity to penetrate deeply into the rural grass roots, and had to share power with the gentry class, urban bourgeoisie, and international capital. Religious leaders, intellectuals, and underworld gangs also exercised great influence. The KMT attempted to monopolize the mass media but was unable to do so. Those weaknesses were fully exploited by the communists. With the defeat of the KMT, China moved into a new developmental stage characterized by Soviet-style institutions and, later on, Maoist frenetic movements, mobilization campaigns of extreme intensity.

The reason that the KMT opted for the German or Japanese model was simple. China was facing a crisis of national survival. It was only natural for the ruling elite to emphasize the importance of concentrating power in the hands of the leadership and guiding national development from the top. However, as the nationalist leaders came primarily from the middle and upper classes of Chinese society, they had no appetite for radical social revolutions as championed by the communists. The nationalists appealed to Chinese nationalism to gain legitimacy and criticized the communist notion of a class struggle. This strategy proved successful in their initial competition with the communists, inasmuch as the latter's radical land-redistribution program antagonized the landowning class while failing to mobilize genuine peasant support. Also, it can be argued that the rise of communist power during the Sino-Japanese War was a direct result of the CCP's shift from blatant class struggle to peasant nationalism. The nationalists' social background further suggests a deep commitment to many traditional values, such as filial piety (abiding respect for parents and ancestors), and the rich cultural legacies of China. For the communists, however, those values were dispensable as long as they stood in the way of rapid modernization.

During the first half of the twentieth century, international competition and national survival forced the Chinese elite to choose an effective modernization model. The liberal, statist, and communist models, as exemplified by Britain, Japan, and the Soviet Union, were particularly appealing to the urban intellectuals, the gentry, and the emergent bourgeoisie (represented by the KMT), and the peasants and workers (represented by the CCP), respectively. These were the interests on which the identities of liberalism, nationalism, and communism were formed. Three distinctively different institutions would flow naturally from the three interests and identities. The triumph of the urban intellectuals would bring about a Western-style democracy. The victory of the KMT would install a modernizing authoritarian regime. The success of the CCP would establish a totalitarian party-state. As it turned out, the liberal intellectuals lacked the organizational means to realize their ideas. The British model never had a real chance.

China's choice, then, was narrowed down to two models: authoritarian statist or communist. When the CCP won the civil war in 1949, China's fate was sealed. There was going to be a series of stormy movements aimed at thoroughly transforming the society based on the communist model. The CCP's interest was reflected in the communist identity and a totalitarian institution – the communist party-state. On the separate island of Taiwan, however, the KMT kept the authoritarian model alive and managed to produce an economic miracle based on private enterprise and government control of the market. The main identity on Taiwan was nationalism, and the key institution was an authoritarian state. In later years, Taiwan's statist model was attenuated by the rise of an affluent middle-class society and the dominant influence exercised by the United States, which preferred the liberal-democratic model.

As Taiwan gradually moved to liberalism, mainland China experienced a partial shift from the communist model to the statist model that Taiwan had exemplified in the past. The driving force for such a fundamental change stemmed from the inherent defects of the communist, and particularly the Maoist, developmental model, which proved inadequate in the face of economic and military competition. As we will see, the destructive Cultural Revolution transformed the minds of the party cadres and turned them into modernizing technocrats. They became keenly aware of the deficiencies and atrocities of the old model. A feedback process is evident here. The CCP regime began moving toward the KMT's statist model. Communism was gradually being replaced by nationalism as the national identity, and the totalitarian regime was being transformed into an authoritarian state, although specific totalitarian mechanisms (such as deeply penetrating party cells and functionaries in all work units) remain in place. With the relaxation of political control, the adoption of an "open-door policy" to the outside world, and the introduction of the market and private property, reform in China has even rekindled a liberal-democratic tendency rooted in the republican period, as demonstrated in the **Tiananmen** Square protests in June 1989 when Beijing's college students allied themselves with workers and citizens in order to stage a massive, one-and-a-half-month sit-in for political freedoms in the heart of the capital. During that period, there were several massive demonstrations that involved more than a million participants, an unprecedented phenomenon in communist China. However, the ease with which this pro-democracy movement was suppressed shows that liberal roots had not been thoroughly established in China. The current economic reform, however, may ultimately bring about an affluent middle-class society heavily influenced by international liberalism and eventually turn China institutionally toward liberalism, as happened earlier in Taiwan. However, because of the rapid growth of China's economic power and international influence, which the CCP naturally takes credit for, the current model of post-totalitarian politics cum state capitalism may be sustained into the future. The post-totalitarian control mechanisms helped in providing resilience for the regime. In all, economic growth provides legitimacy to the regime, while social development brings about challenge to it, as modernization theory posits. The democratic prospects in China thus hinge on these two variables.

Some words on mainland China's relations with Taiwan are in order here. Since 1949, several armed conflicts have erupted in the Taiwan Strait, and the United States has acted as Taiwan's guardian, thwarting invasion from the mainland with a strong commitment to the security of Taiwan. In 1979, changing strategic calculations by the United States caused a shift of Washington's formal diplomatic recognition from the ROC to the PRC as the legitimate government of China. However, Taiwan still received a security guarantee from the United States through the Taiwan Relations Act, which helped the island wade through the political turbulence of the 1980s. **Chiang Ching-kuo,** Chiang Kai-shek's son, lifted martial law and allowed the formation of the opposition party, the Democratic Progressive Party, before his death in 1988. Ching-kuo was succeeded by Lee Teng-hui, who further democratized Taiwan's political system by holding a full-scale parliamentary election in 1992 and a direct presidential election in 1996. As it turned out, democratization in Taiwan produced a strong tendency toward independence (as demonstrated by an attempt to replace the name Republic of China with Republic of Taiwan and permanently separating Taiwan from mainland China) that since the mid-1990s has challenged the "one China" commitment held dearly by both the KMT and the CCP in the past. Tension ran high and threatened to engulf the United States in a cross-Strait war on several occasions, most noticeably during the 1995–1996 missile crisis, making the Taiwan Strait one of the most volatile hotspots in international politics at the turn of the twenty-first century. The election of the blatantly pro-independence Chen Shui-bian from the Democratic Progressive Party as the ROC's tenth president in 2000 further fueled the cross-Strait tension. The core of the conflict resides in Chen's professed plan to rewrite Taiwan's constitution, and to apply for UN membership under the name of Taiwan, acts widely understood as hallmarks of declaring permanent legal separation of the island from the Chinese mainland. Such a possibility prompted Beijing to seek help from Washington to rein in Chen's ambition and to comanage the crisis in the Taiwan Strait. In 2008, the KMT's presidential candidate Ma Ying-jeou won the election and his colleagues maintained control of the Legislative Yuan (parliament). Because the KMT was willing to adhere to the "one China" principle, although emphasizing that one China is for them the Republic of China, it reached a compromise with the CCP and greatly improved cross-Strait relations. A flurry of agreements was signed, including an FTA framework, and mainland tourists poured into Taiwan. Although cross-Strait relations are much calmer than they used to be, there remains underlying strategic tension as Beijing and Taipei still cannot solve the most thorny sovereignty issue. In this context the strategic interaction among the United States, mainland China, and Taiwan is critical to the stability of the region, and to whether Washington can successfully handle the rise and challenge of China on a global scale.

Developmental Stages of the Communist Regime

Because political power in the PRC has been highly concentrated in the hands of a small group of communist leaders, and particularly in the hands of the paramount leader (Mao Zedong from 1949 to 1976 and Deng Xiaoping from 1978 to 1997), China's post-1949 political development can best be understood in terms of the ideas and policies of its top leaders. However, this does not mean that individuals determined China's political development by dint of their personalities and particular political inclinations. As strong as Mao's and Deng's influence on the political process may have been, they nevertheless reflected underlying forces that propelled the Chinese communist regime through different developmental stages. In this sense, both Mao and Deng (as well as Jiang, Hu and Xi who succeeded them) were more representative of the underlying trend than they were creators of such a trend. The developmental stages of a communist regime can be characterized as (1) the initial transformation aimed at remaking the society, (2) the reform backlash, and (3) the conservative consolidation. The logic behind these stages is simple. The communists, as true believers in their utopian ideas, tend to act on the ideology when they seize political power. This is the period of great transformation and revolutionary politics: private property is confiscated, markets are abolished, a centrally planned economy is erected, and a forced-draft industrialization drive is launched. At this stage, one usually finds a tyrannical despot concentrating all political power in his hands and terrorizing his subjects into total subservience. In China this was Mao's era. Elaborate party networks, an all-powerful secret police apparatus, and gigantic state enterprises are created, and a totalitarian party-state comes into existence. However, after years of traumatic totalitarian rule, a reform period is bound to emerge. Totalitarianism traumatizes not only ordinary people but also a ruling elite whose fate is tied to the whim of the totalitarian despot, who launches repeated political campaigns to "purify" the party. The whole nation yearns for relief from economic deprivation and treacherous politics. The reform era is ushered in. A more benign ruler succeeds the despot, but usually not until the despot dies a natural death. In China this happened after Mao died in 1976, and Deng rose to political dominance after 1979, with Hua Guofeng acting as a transitional leader in the interlude. The party-state then comes to a truce with the society. One finds a relaxation of state control over the economy in the form of "perfecting the planning system" or "market socialism," a withdrawal of secret police from their most blatant intrusion into citizens' private lives, and a diminution of the party's omnipresent control of cultural expressions of the society.

The reform backlash does not last long, however, as the very liberal policies characterizing this period breed further social expectations and threaten to undermine the communist regime. What follows then is usually a conservative technocratic regime that does not embark on any major political reform but clings to the status quo and gives it a conservative twist. The mission is no longer radical transformation of the society or desperate redressing of the excesses of totalitarianism but rather entrenchment and consolidation. The leaders at this consolidation stage might keep or even deepen certain aspects of the reform stage, particularly on the economic side, but their overall mentality is conservative and their paramount goal is stability. The elite maintained political stability, through economic performance and an all-embracing coercive apparatus. In the following analysis, we see that China moved into the consolidation stage with the death of Deng Xiaoping and the political ascendancy of the technocrat par excellence, Jiang Zemin, as the new top leader of the CCP in 1997. The succession of Jiang by Hu in 2002, and Hu by Xi ten years later further consolidated this trend, for all three are pro-stability technocrats, unlike Mao the fervent revolutionary and Deng the daring reformer. Political succession has been significantly institutionalized, adding predictability and stability to elite politics. Top leaders are subject to age and term limits, and are periodically rejuvenated. In all, China has stabilized in the consolidation phase, turning itself into a post-totalitarian regime. During the same period of time, China modernized its economy beyond anyone's expectations. Under Deng, market reform was introduced and private property crept back. People's Communes were broken up and replaced by family farming. Stock markets were also set up. China became open to the outside world, inviting foreign investment and launching an export drive. Under Jiang, Hu and Xi, economic reform was deepened, state enterprises were sold, and private entrepreneurship was exalted. Those radical economic measures transformed China's economy, making it a huge newly industrializing country (NIC). In many respects, China resembles the preceding NICs such as South Korea and Taiwan, only it is much larger. By putting the political and economic pictures together, we find China becoming a post-totalitarian, capitalist developmental state, combining features from the Soviet and East European experience, and developmental traits of the East Asian NICs. The combination of constituent elements from these two highly divergent models and regions would make the Chinese developmental case unique, were it not for a similar development in Vietnam.

The Maoist Period: Transformation

We begin our analysis with Mao Zedong, the totalitarian leader who transformed China. Mao rose to power when he assumed command of the Red Army at the Zunyi conference in 1935 on the Long March. Prior to that meeting, Mao had been dominated by a group of Moscow-trained communists. Mao understood that there was no hope for the communists to establish power bases in China's cities. The size of the working class there was too small and their revolutionary consciousness too underdeveloped. Instead, the Chinese communists had to rely on the peasants. This meant that the CCP had to adopt a strategy of "encircling the cities from the countryside" and tailor its programs to the needs of the peasants; that is, redistributing land instead of creating socialist communes. Mao's idea was in serious conflict with the Soviet experience, which relied heavily on the workers in the cities for vital support. It was not until the KMT's fifth annihilation campaign, which swept the communists from their Jiangxi base, that Mao grasped a golden opportunity to unseat his Moscow-trained rivals and assume military leadership. He then put his strategy into practice. This realistic shift of strategy, when combined with the Japanese invasion, contributed greatly to the CCP's resurgence as a serious contender for power during the post–World War II period.

Mao's greatest contribution to the communist movement was, of course, leading the party to the defeat of Chiang Kai-shek in the civil war and establishing the People's Republic of China in 1949. The 1950s witnessed a great transformation of Chinese society. The traditional gentry elite was purged. Social hierarchy in the rural areas was smashed. The business class in the cities was deprived of its properties. A Soviet-style command economy characterized by state economic units under the control of the central bureaucracy was installed with the help of Soviet advisers. The end of the civil war brought about a golden opportunity for national reconstruction. Women were given equal status with men and emancipated from their traditional subjugation in the family. One witnessed great social mobility. Although the nationalist government initiated many social reforms before 1949, its inability to penetrate into the depths of Chinese society limited the effectiveness of its reforms. Under the communists, traditional society was turned upside down for the first time in China's multithousand-year history. All of this happened under heavy Soviet influence. In 1950, Mao paid a tribute to Stalin in Moscow when he made his first visit to a foreign country and signed a treaty of friendship between the PRC and the Soviet Union. To the outside observer, especially to politicians in the United States, it appeared as if there was now one large, unified communist bloc that extended from Berlin to Beijing.

It was only a matter of time, however, before the Chinese and the Soviets would compete for influence in the world communist movement. Mao was, after all, the leader of China, the world's most populous nation, and a country proud of its ancient civilization. It would be difficult to imagine a subservient China bowing to the interests of the Soviet Union in the name of a world communist movement. During the 1950s, Mao developed his own ideas about how to govern China and conduct Beijing's relations with other countries in the world.

This struggle for dominance in the world communist movement led to an outright acrimonious split after Stalin's death and the criticism of Stalin in the Soviet Union under Khrushchev's rule. Mao launched a series of verbal attacks on Soviet "revisionism," seeing in Nikita Khrushchev a weak, willing traitor who flirted with the world's arch-capitalist nation, the United States. Determined to shed Soviet influence, Mao in the late 1950s urged the party to adopt a uniquely Chinese modernization strategy, which would prove disastrous for the nation.

Mao's experience with the Chinese civil war, in which the ill-equipped communist fighters had overpowered the KMT's huge army, convinced him that spiritual mobilization was the key to success. As China was short of capital, Mao found the abundant Chinese labor a ready substitute. Mao believed that people could be mobilized through political campaigns modeled on revolutionary action. This idea was a natural extension of Mao's wartime strategy, which had relied on China's huge peasantry. The result was a policy that Mao called the "**Great Leap Forward.**" The apex of the campaign was the creation of the gigantic People's Communes, which presumably embodied the communist ideal. Communes were large in scale, collectively owned, and were composed of several production brigades, which were subdivided into production teams. They organized production activities, distributed revenues, performed governmental functions, and took care of social welfare. In the heyday of communization, rural markets were abolished, prices were set by the state, and private property was eliminated in the countryside. The commune experience had little economic rationality and was imposed on the country at the whim of Chairman Mao. The result of this experience was a total disruption of agricultural production that ended in an unprecedented man-made famine during which some 30 million Chinese people died. Mao was forced to the second line by his pragmatic colleagues, such as Liu Shaoqi, Deng Xiaoping, and **Chen Yun,** but the "great helmsman" refused to accept his political downfall and made a revengeful comeback by launching the Great Proletarian **Cultural Revolution** that ravaged the nation for a whole decade (1966–1976).

Mao's comeback tilted the balance between the party and the state. Prior to 1949, the CCP had an extensive party organization that performed regular government functions in the communist-controlled areas. The party was initially led by a **general secretary,** then by a chairman. The CCP practiced the "democratic centralism" of a typical Leninist party, which meant, in practice, the concentration of power in the hands of a supreme party leader. After the establishment of the People's Republic, the communists began to build a set of state institutions and gradually shifted administrative power to the newly founded government bureaucracies. This process of "normalization" coincided with Beijing's "leaning toward the Soviet Union" and demonstrated, at the time, China's earnest effort to build a society modeled on the well-established Soviet system.

In September 1949, the party began to set up a Central People's Government as the highest organ of state power. Mao was elected its chairman. Under it was the Government Administrative Council headed by **Zhou Enlai.** After the 1954 constitution was promulgated, a National People's Congress was created to serve as the Parliament. The Government Administrative Council became the **State Council** and was responsible to the people's deputies. Zhou Enlai continued to serve as the premier. This arrangement resembled the governing structure of a typical communist country. The Communist Party remained the ultimate source of power and legitimacy. The leader of the party, Chairman Mao in the Chinese case, ruled supreme. The head of government was usually the second most powerful figure in the party-state as long as that position was not taken by the party leader himself.

There was an ill-defined division of labor between the party and the government, with the party initiating policies and guaranteeing their political correctness, and the government implementing those policies. The military also played an important role at this initial stage of the People's Republic. From 1949 to 1952, military administrative committees directly controlled twenty provinces. The power of the generals, however, was curbed by Mao when the political and economic situation of China stabilized. Mao himself headed the party's Central Military Commission (CMC) and directed the People's Liberation Army in that capacity. The government's control of the military (both the People's Revolutionary Military Commission and the National Defense Council) was totally overwhelmed by the party CMC. A firmly established tradition in the PRC is for the party to "command the guns" and for the leader of the party to head the party CMC. The party's control over the military was also guaranteed by recruitment into the party of all officers above the rank of platoon commander, setting up political commissars and political departments in the army, and establishing party committees at the regiment level and above.

The party, the government, and the army are the three power pillars in the PRC. In Table 8.1, we see that it is not always easy to figure out the real top leader simply by looking at the official positions held by China's top politicians. The general rule is that the top leader always controls the party CMC. This held true until Deng formally gave that position to Jiang at the end of 1989 while still running the show from behind the scenes. That anomaly did not occur during Mao's reign from 1949 to 1976, however, when he was both **chairman of the Central Committee of the Chinese Communist Party** and chairman of

Table 8.1 China's Top Leaders and Their Positions

	President[a]	Prime Minister	Communist Party Leader	Chairman of Party CMC	Top Leader
1949 Oct.	Mao Zedong	Zhou Enlai	Mao Zedong	Mao Zedong	Mao Zedong
1959 Apr.	Liu Shaoqi				
1968 Oct.	Dong Biwu				
1975 Jan.	ZhuDe				
1976 Feb.		Hua Guofeng (acting Feb.–Apr., 1976)			
1976 July	Song Qinglin (acting)				
1976 Oct.			Hua Guofeng	Hua Guofeng	Hua Guofeng
1978 Mar.	Ye Jianyig				
1978 Dec.					Deng Xiaoping
1980 Sept.		Zhao Ziyang			
1981 June			Hu Yaobang (Party Chairman)	Deng Xiaoping	
1982 Sept.			Hu Yaobang (General Secretary)		
1983 June	Li Xiannian				
1987 Jan.			Zhao Ziyang		
1987 Nov.		Li Peng			
1988 Apr.	Yang Shangkun				

	President[a]	Prime Minister	Communist Party Leader	Chairman of Party CMC	Top Leader
1989 June			Jiang Zemin		
1989 Nov.				Jiang Zemin	
1993 Mar.	Jiang Zemin				
1997 Feb.					Jiang Zemin
1998 Mar.		Zhu Rongji			
2002 Nov.			Hu Jintao		
2003 Mar.	Hu Jintao	Wen Jiabao			
2004 Sept.				Hu Jintao	Hu Jintao
2012 Nov.			Xi Jinping	Xi Jinping	Xi Jinping
2013 Mar.	Xi Jinping	Li Keqiang			

[a] The PRC's president is the state chairman when that position exists (i.e., from 1954 to 1975 and from 1983 on). In the absence of a state chairman, it was the chairman of the National People's Congress who took on the function of the head of state.

its Central Military Commission. That is to say, Mao directly controlled the party and the military. The government was left in the hands of Zhou Enlai, who had risen to the CCP's top leadership earlier than Mao. The 1959 promotion of Liu Shaoqi to state chairman was not an insignificant move, for even though the PRC's head of state was a titular position, Liu's advancement was widely considered to be a sign that Liu, as a moderate, was in line to be Mao's successor, which would have been consistent with the de-Stalinization campaign unfolding in the Soviet Union. However, Liu's assumption of the state chairmanship proved ominous in view of Mao's vengeful rearguard actions that followed his blunders in the Great Leap Forward. These kinds of power struggles, inherent in communist leadership succession, became entangled with international competition and ideological dispute within China.

Mao's rupture with Khrushchev proved fatal to China's state-building efforts, as he began to whip up local support for his Great Leap Forward and People's Communes. Mao abhorred Soviet-style technocratism and overconcentrated state planning. In 1958, Mao began to delegate very significant power to party officials (cadres) in running the economy;

this set China apart from the Soviet Union and Eastern European countries, which had a more centrally controlled economy under communist rule. Even though China underwent several rounds of "decentralization-recentralization" in the following years, it never went back to the original planned-economy model that the Soviet advisers had helped China to build during the 1950s. This historical legacy of a decentralized system was later hailed as a unique Chinese advantage for implementing market reform during the 1980s. However, institutionally, the most important development during the 1958 decentralization was the shift of power from state technocrats to party cadres, which was reminiscent of the revolutionary years when they had had an important mission.

Mao's experiment proved disastrous and temporarily diminished his power. As a result, the short interlude between the Great Leap Forward and the launching of the Cultural Revolution saw a temporary revival of state institutions. The stormy politics of the Cultural Revolution, however, again dampened the vitality of government agencies and returned power to party cadres. Mao launched campaigns against the "small clique of capitalist-roaders in power" who were often found in government institutions. Revolutionary committees took the place of the local governments, and direct military control was instituted to curb the excessive infighting among Red Guard zealots, militaristic groups of students who had been sent to monitor and brutalize government critics and "class enemies," who Mao himself had unleashed. The normal politics of the 1950s was replaced by the stormy movements of the 1960s. State institutions were attacked, government officials were purged and sent to reeducation camps in China's remote provinces, and millions of intellectuals were humiliated and condemned to forced labor. For Mao, this was a "class struggle." The simple fact remained that Mao did his best to undermine the very institutions that he helped establish during the first decade of the People's Republic.

Even though Mao vehemently attacked the Soviet Union in the ideological battle between the two communist giants, his basic position and policies did not deviate from orthodox Stalinism. As a matter of fact, he based his attacks on Khrushchev's leadership on its betrayal of the original ideals of communism. During the decade of the Cultural Revolution, the personality cult of Mao was carried to absurd lengths. The chairman was hailed as a great hero in all walks of life. He was the greatest military genius, a brilliant and accomplished poet, and a swimmer who broke the world's record. Bountiful harvests could be assured simply by reading the "little red book" that recorded the chairman's words. Children were taught not to love their parents but to love Chairman Mao. The whole world was said to admire this great leader of China. Mao actually ruled by terror, exercising it even against his chief lieutenants (most notably State Chairman Liu Shaoqi and Party General Secretary Deng Xiaoping). Public denunciations and beatings at mass rallies were substituted for Soviet-style show trials, with equally fatal consequences for the accused. The Red Guards were Mao's invention, for he lacked organizational means to defeat his opponents in the party-state hierarchy. As a result, the chairman was able to unleash abundant social anger at the regime after the traumatic Great Leap Forward campaign and the resulting famine, directing it toward his intraparty enemies. The devastation was greater than in the Soviet Union, where purges and power struggles were conducted in a more "orderly" manner. On the economic front, Mao mercilessly mobilized China's resources to

Table 8.2 Share of Investment by Industries in China, 1953–1978

Years	Agriculture	Light Industry	Heavy Industry	Other Industries
First Five-Year Plan (1953–1957)	7.1	6.4	36.2	50.3
Second Five-Year Plan (1958–1962)	11.3	6.4	54.0	28.3
1963–1965	17.6	3.9	45.9	32.6
Third Five-Year Plan (1966–1970)	10.7	4.4	51.1	33.8
Fourth Five-Year Plan (1971–1975)	9.8	5.8	49.6	34.8
1976–1978	10.8	5.9	49.6	33.7

Source: Lin Yifu, Cai Fang, and Li Zhou, *Zhongguo de qiji: fazhan zhanlue yu jingji gaige* (China's Miracle: Developmental Strategy and Economic Reform) (Hong Kong: Chinese University Press, 1995) p. 56.

pursue heavy industrialization, and both agriculture and light industry that directly affected the livelihood of the population were severely neglected (Table 8.2). The developmental priorities were thus the same as in the Soviet Union, although Mao's strategy of spiritual mobilization and absolute egalitarianism were quite counterproductive in the long run. In short, Mao's rule in China was a classical case of totalitarianism, characterized by massive ideological indoctrination, the personality cult of the leader, rule by terror, a state-run economy geared toward heavy industrialization, and disregard of consumers' needs in economic planning. In many respects, Mao's practices were even more excessive than Stalin's. From 1949, when the People's Republic was established, to 1976 when Mao died, China experienced a turbulent and protracted period of transformation.

Deng Unleashes Reform

The conflict between Mao and his political enemies in the leadership was a fight between the leftist radicals and the pro-stability technocrats, between the movement-oriented party and order-conscious state. Here one finds the conflict between two interests (cadres versus technocrats), two identities (revolution versus development), and two institutions (party versus state). With the death of Mao and the political demise of the ultraleftists, a new force emerged that advocated market reform and political relaxation. Those reformers then competed with the technocrats for supremacy.

The pro-stability technocrats constituted a significant political force in the PRC after the 1950s. However, throughout the Maoist era, they were suppressed by the leftists. Their early leader was Liu Shaoqi, Mao's designated successor. Liu was an organizational man who favored orderly development of the country's economy in the manner of Soviet-style five-year plans. He abhorred the anarchy that Mao's endless campaigns brought about. With regard to basic economic policy, Mao's "red" line insisted on breathtaking growth through ideological movements, whereas the "expert" line of Liu's technocrats emphasized the need for balanced development and allowed modifications of the system in order to improve performance. This "line struggle" was elevated by Mao to the height of "class struggle," and repeated movements were launched from above to ensure that Mao's line was in command.

As the Soviet and Eastern European experiences demonstrate, totalitarianism is but a stage in the development of communist regimes. Stabilization of the political process and turning to economic reform to improve performance seem to be a natural tendency. In the PRC, however, Mao's political genius and his overwhelming prestige in the party-state artificially delayed the end of totalitarianism. In the 1960s and 1970s, Mao mustered all his vigilance to guard against having the CCP slip into Soviet-style revisionism as in the Khrushchev and Brezhnev eras. As a result, the Chinese communist regime delayed its reform stage until the death of its despotic ruler.

Reform was inevitable, however. Mao's revolutionary politics and stormy economic campaigns provided few benefits to either the population at large or to the ruling elite, who were in constant fear of being Mao's next target and were forbidden to enjoy a decent material life. China's economy was on the brink of collapse by the time of Mao's death in 1976, suffering from the inefficiencies and rigidities of a socialist planned economy and the irregularities of Mao's unpredictable ideological campaigns. Persistent poverty seriously undermined the regime's legitimacy, particularly when the population compared China's economic plight with the high-speed growth of neighboring countries in East Asia. On the international front, Mao's radical politics at home antagonized the Soviet Union while forestalling a genuine rapprochement with the United States. Being at odds with both superpowers put the country in a dangerous position internationally. In these circumstances, Beijing's leaders were acutely aware of the fact that a backward economy and a predominantly rural society could not support China's ambition to compete on the world stage. The discrimination against students from the propertied classes, the absolute demand for equality but not quality, the disdain for intellectuals, and the glorification of manual labor at the expense of formal education devastated the school system and left a whole generation of Chinese youth uneducated. Even the military was indoctrinated in the virtue of the people's war, exulting in ideological correctness and willpower at the expense of absolutely necessary military modernization. China's immense potential to become a great nation in the world was suffocated by Mao's ideology and the endless internal strife perpetuated by it. It became obvious to all but the most radical faction in the CCP elite that things had to change and that reform was necessary to save both the country and the leaders themselves. In order to survive both domestically and internationally, China had to restructure its system and shed the debilitating aspects of Mao's totalitarianism.

The fact that China resisted the advent of reform longer than most other socialist countries foretold the vengeance with which reform would ultimately come. In terms of politics, the personality cult and ruthless persecution of comrades were denounced in reform-era China, much as they had been during periods of reform in the Soviet Union and Eastern Europe. Obviously, this is not democratization but relaxation in a post-totalitarian society, as witnessed by Deng's continued insistence on the leading role of the Communist Party. Stability now hinged on material benefits that the communist regime delivered and on a widespread sense of improvement on the previous decades of impoverishment and rule by terror.

Mao's legacy was dismantled bit by bit. One month after Mao's death in September 1976, the **Gang of Four** (including Mao's wife, Jiang Qing, and three other ultraleftist leaders) were arrested. Two years later, at the historic **Third Plenum of the CCP's Eleventh Central Committee** held in December 1978, the interregnum leader Hua Guofeng was defeated by Deng Xiaoping, and the reform era was ushered in (see Table 8.3 at the end of the chapter). With the ultraleftists dislodged from power, a schism developed in the anti-Hua coalition. The radical economic reformers, led by Deng and his handpicked lieutenants **Hu Yaobang** (general secretary of the party) and **Zhao Ziyang** (premier), did not see eye to eye with the technocrats, led by Chen Yun. Although Deng's reform project was a reaction to totalitarian excesses, one can nevertheless find a similar mentality between the ultraleftists and the radical reformers. They all took a pro-growth stance as opposed to the technocrats' pro-stability line. Mao, Hua, and Deng were all proponents of high growth, although they resorted to different means for achieving that same goal: Mao with his Great Leap Forward, Hua with his Great Leap Westward, and Deng with his market reform. The determination of those Chinese communist leaders to achieve supergrowth had a lot to do with their realization that China was backward and that extraordinary means were necessary for the country to compete effectively in the world. It was under this "surpassing mentality" that the strategic goal of doubling the PRC's industrial and agricultural production by the year 2000 was set at the Twelfth Party Congress in 1982, when the era of reform formally began.

The technocrats thought otherwise. For them, stability of the system was a paramount consideration. Led by Chen Yun in the post-Mao era, the technocrats stressed the need for balanced development, limited spending, and measured growth. After the death of Mao and the short interlude of Hua Guofeng, the technocrats' line temporarily gained dominance in Chen Yun's "adjustment" policy, designed to curb the rash and unbalanced investment surge under Hua's Ten-Year Plan. But Chen's line was in command for only five years (1979–1983). It was then swiftly replaced by Deng's pro-growth marketization drive, implemented by the new prime minister, Zhao Ziyang. With the country on the road to reform – that is, with Deng in command – the technocrats found themselves circumvented, although continuing struggles between the reformers and technocrats testified to the resilience of the latter. Vested interests were also involved in this factional conflict, as inland provinces, production ministries, planning agencies, state enterprises, and other heavily subsidized sectors of the economy naturally loathed radical market reforms, whereas coastal areas, light industries, local governments, and those sectors benefiting from reform measures supported expansion and deepening of the reforms.

Several economic cycles during the 1980s shaped the balance of power between the pro-growth reformers and the pro-stability technocrats. As a rule, the reformers fueled the economy with expansionary policies and liberalization. High growth was pursued at the expense of macrostability. Under Deng, one saw the failed People's Communes farming system abolished and a realistic household-responsibility system instituted that combined compulsory state procurements with peasant discretion over above-quota produce. Prices of agricultural products increased. Rural markets revived. Township and village enterprises mushroomed. In the cities, one first saw the emergence of millions of small individual businesses *(getihu)* and then the rapid development of hitherto unthinkable private enterprises. The state enterprises were also reformed, first by raising the profit-retention ratio and then by a contract scheme that resembled the household-responsibility system in the countryside. A tax-for-profit reform was launched in 1983–1984 that was designed to provide level ground for healthy competition. Various kinds of ownership reforms were tested after 1986, culminating in the introduction of stock shares and their free trade in newly opened stock markets. An open-door policy invited a huge inflow of foreign capital that provided timely funding for the rapid growth of the Chinese economy. Indirect foreign investment also surged as international lenders designated China as a promising market. According to the World Bank, China's annual per capita GDP (gross domestic product) growth reached an average of 8 percent between 1978 and 1995. Only South Korea and Taiwan grew at comparable rates.

It is not surprising that high growth brought about inflation and a trade imbalance, as happened in 1985, 1988, and 1993–1994. With wide fluctuations of the economy came episodes of political unrest, the most serious of which was the Beijing Spring of 1986–1987 and the Tiananmen pro-democracy movement of 1989. The first incident brought down the then General Secretary Hu Yaobang and the second one, Hu's successor, Zhao Ziyang. The **Tiananmen incident** was a tragic confrontation between student demonstrators demanding political liberties and a communist regime heavily divided between reformers and hard-liners. It showed the destabilizing effect of Deng's reforms, the limits of which were not clearly defined by Deng himself. In an atmosphere of increasing economic liberties and political relaxation, it was only natural that young students would grow impatient with the regime's authoritarian style and demand structural political reforms. Deng's own advocacy of political reform added to the momentum for structural change. Economic mismanagement of the time provided an immediate impetus, while the signs of intraregime schism further emboldened the student activists. The Tiananmen incident was started when students memorialized the death of Hu Yaobang, a bona fide reformer in the regime, and refused to leave the Tiananmen Square in front of Beijing's Forbidden City. The stalemate between the pro-democracy students, whose numbers on the square surged, and the regime continued until Deng ordered a ruthless crackdown and soldiers fired at the unarmed demonstrators on June 4, killing hundreds or thousands of them. The picture of a brave lone man standing in front of an approaching tank column, daring them to run him over, was broadcast around the world and has become the single most powerful image of the Tiananmen suppression. It became clear that once the regime was able to mend its internal division (ousting Zhao, the sympathizer in this instance), the post-totalitarian state found it easy to quell whatever resistance and protest that the young dissidents of China were able to mount against it. However, the fact that the Tiananmen protest did happen and that tanks had to roar and shots be fired in the center of the capital city to quell it demonstrates how Deng's reforms had disturbed political stability in China. From the regime's point of view, obviously reform had gone too far, and something had to be done to prevent the recurrence of another Tiananmen protest.

In the aftermath of Tiananmen, General Secretary Zhao was replaced by Jiang Zemin, a technocrat from Shanghai. In an overall environment of regimentation, the technocrats regained some power, silencing the society with mass arrests and show trials, reimposing strict control over mass media, and launching ideological war against China's peaceful evolution into a "bourgeois democracy." Economically, they reduced investment and tightened the monetary supply, particularly against the nascent private sector. Further reform measures were put on hold. In this way, stability was restored but only at the expense of growth. Seeing his economic reform in a quagmire, Deng made a breakthrough tour to the south, from where he relaunched a reform drive. With Deng's active intervention, the reformers resurged and snatched power from the technocrats. The economy entered a high-growth phase again, starting a new cycle. However, on the political front, there has not been any relaxation of control or even discussion of political reform comparable to the 1980s. China entered a period of protracted political regimentation.

During the course of relaunching the economic reform, Premier Li Peng was reprimanded by Deng for his overconservative goal of 6 percent annual growth for the Eighth Five-Year Plan period (1991–1995). After Deng's southern tour, the Chinese economy registered double-digit growth rates for five consecutive years. Soon, however, the economy overheated and a new policy of "macroadjustment" came into vogue. The person in charge of this limited austerity program was **Zhu Rongji**. Zhu was widely considered Deng's favorite to succeed Li Peng as the prime minister. This should not blur the fact that there was no substantial difference between him and Li or Jiang. Jiang, Li, and Zhu were all technocrats with a good educational background, and they all considered stability a paramount goal at the PRC's current stage of development. They might belong to different power blocs and might compete vehemently for ascendancy in the post-Deng period, but they were not pro-growth zealots in the mold of the old patriarch. The desperate pursuit of supergrowth had come to an end with the phasing out and, ultimately, the death of Deng. To summarize, Deng's rule in China has left a legacy of unprecedented growth that lifted the largest number of people out of poverty in human history. It also brought about economic volatility and political instability. Unparalleled openness to the outside world and increasing influence from the West were accompanied by the creeping return of many traditional aspects of Chinese society, such as the unequal treatment of women in rural areas. Economic reform also enhanced regional disparities and inequalities between the cities and the countryside. In short, growth and openness were gained at the expense of equality and stability.

Jiang, Hu, Xi, and Consolidation

In post-Tiananmen China, political regimentation went hand in hand with deepened economic reform. This dual-track policy was designed to address the inadequacies perceived by the regime of the reform in the 1980s: not enough economic relaxation and too much flirting with political liberalism, with the former failing to deliver enough economic benefits and satisfy the demand of the masses, while the latter was inviting further pressure for opening up the system. The turbulence in Tiananmen was the direct result of these two defects, so observed the party leaders. They would need to tighten political control and deepen economic reform, so as to render bigger sticks and more carrots. "Stability in command" became the regime's motto.

On the political front, the CCP further penetrated into the society, cracked down on dissent, and tightly controlled media (including the Internet). After the Tiananmen crackdown, Jiang raised the issue of "anti-peaceful evolution" against the West's attempt of regime change in China. The downfall of the European communist regimes highly alerted the Chinese leaders to the vulnerability of their system. In 2005 Jiang launched a "mindful of politics" campaign, embraced first by an ardent People's Liberation Army and spreading to the whole nation. Its purpose was to raise political consciousness against forces hostile to socialism. In this context, Jiang ordered a suppression of the Falungong religious cult, which had been attracting great numbers of practitioners within China and many believers around the world. The cult was originally approved and applauded by the communist regime for its combination of apparently innocuous religious beliefs, spiritual and body exercises, and healing techniques. Soon the ability of Falungong to recruit members from party, government, and military organizations, and to mobilize supporters to stage protests against the regime, terrified Jiang and led to a large-scale suppression that shocked the West. The underlying cause of the regime's overreaction was its obsession with absolute political control of the society.

On the economic front, Deng relaunched economic reform against the resistance of the conservatives in the early 1990s with his famous "southern tour" in the winter of 1991–1992. This new wave of reform burst asunder the insistence on public ownership in the 1980s and boldly moved into the realm of state-sponsored capitalism. The property rights structure in China underwent a fundamental change. The state would maintain only the commanding heights (such as finance), while letting private capital expand into all the other realms. Foreign capital was also introduced on a scale larger than in the 1980s. The country has decisively shifted from market socialism in which the reform concentrates on introducing market to replace socialist planning, to state-driven capitalism in which private enterprises are nurtured to grow strategic sectors of the economy.

After thirteen years in power, Jiang officially retired as general secretary at the Sixteenth Party Congress, held in 2002. He was succeeded by Hu Jintao who had been promoted to the Politburo's Standing Committee (PSC) in 1992 by Deng to be Jiang's heir apparent. Despite Deng's death in 1997, this succession plan was dutifully implemented five years later, testifying to Deng's lasting influence in the party, but also creating tension between Hu and Jiang for the latter could not appoint his own successor. In 2003, Wen Jiabao replaced Zhu Rongji as premier. Jiang still held chairmanship of the party's Central Military Commission and exercised great influence from behind the scenes until September 2004, when he handed over the military command to Hu. The ineptitude with which Jiang handled the SARS pandemic was one of the major reasons for his final bow-out. The new Hu-Wen regime was not significantly different from the Jiang-Zhu regime in that both were dominated by technocrats with stability on the top of their agendas. Specifically, the new fourth-generation leadership was keenly aware of the danger of an overheated economy, increasing social stratification and unrest, ecological crisis, rampant corruption, rising unemployment, and was determined to crush any political opposition. They differed from Jiang's third-generation leaders only in their younger age, higher educational credentials, and still lower prestige.

As disparities and inequalities grew, Hu and Wen stressed the need to build a "harmonious society" based on better social security, more equitable distribution, and widespread health care. They abolished the agricultural tax on farmers, and showed greater lenience toward migrant workers. Hu built his power base in the Chinese Communist Youth League (CCYL) and served as party secretary in several inland provinces before advancing to the center. When he took over from Jiang, according to Deng's will, he found his predecessor placed powerful figures around him and exercised influence from behind the scene. This Jiang faction, or Shanghai gang, gradually lost influence as time passed, and Hu was able to promote a group of Youth League cadres to high positions. Under Hu, those Leaguers constituted a faction (*tuanpai*) and advocated policies to address the country's increasing social inequalities and distributional injustices. Although the effect of such policies was in question, the fact that they were promoted pointed out the Leaguers' priority concerns. Opposite to Hu and his followers rose a new grouping: the princelings, or children of revolutionary veterans and high party cadres. They typically advanced to the power center by way of leadership positions in the well-developed coastal provinces, and allied themselves with China's new rich. This tendency was in line with Jiang's Shanghai gang, and the two supported each other. The Leaguers and the princelings represent two tendencies in the CCP's high power echelon: the former stress distributional issues, while the latter emphasize continued growth. The strengths of the Leaguers are in organization, propaganda, and rural administration, but they lack the ability to manage trade, investment, and finance – areas in which the princelings excel. Family background, work experience, geographic distribution, and priority policy thus set these two factions apart.

The result of the factional competition was revealed in the Seventeenth Party Congress held in October 2007, when one witnessed the appointment of the fifth-generation leaders Xi Jinping, a princeling, and Li Keqiang, a Leaguer, to the ruling PSC, apparently for succeeding the current leadership when they phase out in 2012. Compared with their predecessors, Xi and Li are even younger (both in their early fifties, ten years younger than the senior members on the PSC), less experienced, better educated, and less prestigious. Xi received a PhD in law from Tsinghua University. The son of a revolutionary veteran, Xi was promoted to the party's chief of Shanghai in 2007 after serving in the coastal provinces of Fujian and Zhejiang for a total of twenty-two years. He is a princeling par excellence. Li headed Liaoning, a northeastern province of China after rising within the hierarchy of the Youth League. Li holds a BA in law and a PhD in economics, both from the prestigious Peking University. Xi and Li are the first top leaders of China who received PhDs. The standard profile of the fifth-generation leaders suggests that China remained entrenched in the stage of technocratic consolidation. On the other hand, the announcement of a princeling and a Leaguer to be China's top future leaders suggested an even distribution of power between the two factions, and the two tendencies that they represented.

The succession went smoothly as planned. In the Eighteenth Party Congress of November 2012, Xi assumed the position of general secretary and chairman of the party's central military commission. Hu made a full bow-out, unlike his predecessor Jiang who held to military power after relinquishing control of the party. For his part, Li took Wen's position as premier in the National People's Congress held in early 2013. The cohabitation of the princelings and the Leaguers thus began. Among the seven Eighteenth PSC members, five were princelings or closely associated with Jiang. There were only two Leaguers. However, among the twenty-five Politburo members, the Leaguers were the majority, posing to become the dominant force in the Nineteenth Party Congress to be held in 2017. The Eighteenth Party Congress thus brought about equilibrium between the two rival coalitions. They competed for influence, but they also understood the need to keep cohesion of the party, and they compromised on personnel and policy decisions. The ease with which the factions could play by the rules and preserve solidarity in the regime, unlike their predecessors up to the 1980s, was because of much less ideological difference among them, and the shared values of the technocratic elite as a whole.

Jiang, Hu, and Xi should be viewed less as unique personalities than as representatives of three generations of technocrats who rose to positions of leadership after the rule of revolutionaries (the Maoists) and radical reformers (the Dengists). The new technocratic rulers wielded much less power than their predecessors. Deng was certainly less powerful than Mao, but in many respects these two men were still comparable. The difference between Deng and his successors was much more striking. Except in the area of education, the third- to fifth-echelon leaders led by Jiang, Hu, and Xi are dwarfed by Deng in all forms of power resources, such as experience, military support, charisma, will to power, vision, self-confidence, and contribution to the establishment and maintenance of the regime. As a result, the personal imprint of Jiang and his successors on Chinese politics and society is markedly lighter than that of Mao or Deng.

Declining personal authority and increasingly technocratic rule seem to be an evolutionary regularity for communist regimes. From a comparative point of view, communist regimes naturally evolved from the stage of totalitarianism, through reform, to technocratic rule. The totalitarian ruler launched political and economic campaigns to transform the society. The horrendous human costs that such transformation entailed forced the second-generation rulers to seek a truce with the society and terminate the rule of terror. Material improvements and political relaxation ensued. However, the reformers, in their zeal to redress the excesses of totalitarianism, often went too far, creating instability with constant institutional restructuring and risking the regime's political control over the society. The cadres' huge vested interest was also undermined. All of this prompted reactions from the technocrats.

Just as the reformers naturally acted against the extremes of revolutionary enthusiasm, the technocrats by their nature sought to bring about stability (on both the individual and regime levels and in both political and economic senses), which had been undermined by radical reform measures. In form, this seemed like a partial return to totalitarianism, but in essence the emergent technocratic rule was a conservative backlash against both revolution (the first stage) and reform (the second stage). The purpose of the regime was no longer to remold the society, or to redress the atrocities of the past and catch up with the world, but simply to keep things as they stood, particularly to keep the communist regime in power. In China, the death of Deng Xiaoping and the political ascendancy of Jiang Zemin signified the advent of the technocratic era. Jiang and his colleagues of the third-generation leadership had more formal and technical education than their predecessors. Hu, Xi, and the fourth- and fifth-generation leadership in turn received even higher education than Jiang and his associates. All of those people were products of an established technocratic system and not its creators or builders. Their experience was typically concentrated on one functional area, and that usually was not military affairs. As technocrats, Jiang, Hu, Xi, and their comrades sitting on the CCP's Politburo were intrinsically more interested in preserving the status quo and pursuing stability than exploring new reform frontiers. In this sense, whether it was Jiang or any other technocrat to succeed Deng is not really important, as communist technocratic rulers basically behave in similar ways. They have a realistic understanding of the popular desire for material betterment, they loathe destruction in the name of revolution and the institutional flux brought about by radical reform, and they want to absorb Western technology and capital, but they abhor pluralistic ideas and democracy. In the history of the PRC, the technocrats were suppressed in both the revolutionary and reform periods, for Mao and Deng were committed to transformation of the society, albeit in opposite directions. With Jiang and his successors at the helm, pro-stability technocrats in the PRC finally have their way.

Despite the conservative mentality of the post-Deng technocrats, they realized the need to satisfy the material demand of the masses – hence the overall importance of the regime's economic performance. The Chinese reform model was particularly influenced by the East Asian NICs (South Korea, Taiwan, Hong Kong, and Singapore) surrounding China. These countries practice developmental capitalism characterized by a growth-oriented authoritarian system, autonomous economic bureaucracy, cooperation between the public and private sectors, and export expansion strategy. When China started its reform in the late 1970s, the gap between its command economy and developmental capitalism appeared unbridgeable. In the 1980s, Deng spearheaded the introduction of market without endorsing the revival of private enterprises – hence socialist market economy. After Tiananmen, however, the communist regime realized the utter importance of economic performance for its political survival, and began tearing down the last ideological defense against capitalism. Private enterprises were openly encouraged and legally protected. At the same time, one still saw the state's visible hand behind the rise of new industries and enterprises. The communist state designates strategic industries, manipulates resource allocation, and practices industrial policy. In this way, China has grown more and more like its NIC neighbors by adopting developmental capitalism. Socialism as an ideal has been closeted, although still paid lip service, while the mechanism of total political control has been maintained and refined. In this sense, one can characterize China as a post-totalitarian capitalist developmental state. This model is similar to the Soviet experience only on its post-totalitarian side. Developmental capitalism is derived from the East Asian NIC experience and has little to do with the trajectory of a Leninist regime. In short, one finds in the Chinese case a blending of two distinctive models: post-totalitarianism from the Soviet Union and Eastern Europe, and developmental capitalism from East Asia; this model has proved resilient in the face of rapid social change, severe international financial crises (such as the 1997 Asian Financial Crisis and the post-2008 international financial tsunami), and waves of global democratization (such as the Arab Spring since 2011).

Xi's governance package testifies to China's resilience as a post-totalitarian capitalist developmental state. At a plenary meeting of the Central Committee in November 2013, an important resolution was passed that, among other proposed reforms, laid out a bold economic reform plan that aims to establish clearer property rights in the rural areas. However, the initiative was taken in a more regimented political atmosphere, as discussion of constitutionalism was stifled and foreign journalists from major international mass media found it more difficult to get permits to enter and report in China. The gap between political and economic reforms in China became ever wider, showing the insistence of the new Chinese leaders to adhere to the route the regime has trodden thus far. In sum, the Chinese technocratic rule that emerged from Mao's stormy revolutionary politics and Deng's precarious reformism is open and adaptable to changing domestic and international environments – hence its resilience. Like a two-faced Janus, the post-Deng regime tames the Chinese people with post-totalitarian shackles, and lures them with high growth from capitalist development. These two aspects complement each other. Without the deeply ingrained control mechanisms that hail from its totalitarian past, the CCP cannot nip social dissent in the bud and maintain monopoly of power. This is how China has thus far defied the logic of modernization – namely economic development begets political liberalization and democratization, as witnessed by China's East Asian neighbors, such as Taiwan and South Korea. On the other hand, without the rapid growth that can only be achieved by adopting a capitalist development model, China cannot satisfy the basic needs of its huge population. This is why the CCP has been able to escape the fate of European communist regimes that fell amid economic crisis. In short, China's post-totalitarian capitalist developmental model offers the regime an optimal institution to wade through the unprecedented challenges that it faced in the late twentieth and early twenty-first centuries. This model also gives China a unique, bewildering feature: the world's second-largest capitalist economy run by the largest communist party that professes to abolish private property, and the fastest growing economy accompanied by the most thorough political control. A natural question arises: Can this hybrid system last for long?

Will China Become Democratic?

This is a one-billion-dollar question in the study of comparative politics today. The PRC is one of the very few communist countries that survived the third wave of democratization in the end of the 1990s. As we have mentioned, China's system is a hybrid of post-totalitarianism that hailed from the Soviet Union and state-driven capitalism practiced by its East Asian neighbors. Both predecessors have experienced major political transition that ended the original authoritarian regime (although in the case of post-Soviet development many successor states have adopted new forms of authoritarianism). However, the unique amalgamation of these two types of institutions provided the Chinese communist regime with sufficient capabilities to withstand domestic and international pressure. Is this system capable of developing into a stable model of its own, or is it bound to succumb to insurmountable pressure and crack, converging to the liberal model, as Taiwan did? Put in other words, will China bear out the predictions of the modernization theory and become democratic eventually?

Discussion of China's political future after the Tiananmen Square protests of 1989 has shifted focus with the apparent increased stability of the communist regime. Although in the immediate wake of the Tiananmen crisis a complete breakdown of the system was predicted, with the consolidation of the post-1989 power structure, less dramatic scenarios have been presented. Among the latter one finds a revival of the neoauthoritarianism theme, which depicts China's future in the light of the East Asian capitalist-authoritarian model, Taiwan and South Korea in particular. Some scholars argue that, although direct democratization is unlikely and even undesirable, a two-step transition through an intermediary phase of enlightened authoritarianism toward the ultimate destination of democracy should be welcomed. China's introduction of competitive (although not multiparty) elections at the village level is seen, from this perspective, as a particularly encouraging sign, which shows mainland China gradually evolving toward political pluralism following Taiwan's trajectory. Since 1949, local economic and political experiments have been used as the basis from which to reorganize China. The introduction of directly elected villagers' committees and other democratic experiments thus carry significance far beyond its immediate impact in the rural areas. A dual power structure has been created in which the villagers' committee is developing into a democratic executive apparatus to manage day-to-day politics, while the party branch has come to be responsible for general policy, and it intervenes if "necessary" by using its ties to township or county governments. Optimists predict that power would gradually migrate from the party branch to the villagers' committee and bring the countryside closer to genuine grassroots democracy. Experiments have been conducted that extend competitive elections up to the township level, a sign for further optimism. Besides leadership selection, there are also innovative measures in the area of participatory budget deliberation. Finally, there are experiments with democratic election of local party bosses, so that democracy can be pursued without undermining the party's power base. These optimistic opinions are a variant on the theme of the time-honored modernization theory, which predicts a universal pluralistic outcome for authoritarian systems undergoing rapid economic development.

Among the less dramatic scenarios is a reprise of the neoconservatism theme that popped up during the retrenchment period in the early 1990s. In the more rigid political and economic atmosphere after the Tiananmen protests, especially in light of the difficulties facing Russia after its democratic transition, this neoconservative theme emphasizes order and stability and harkens back to traditional values, as opposed to the radical reforms of the previous decade. Neoconservatism argues that social progress is best accomplished through a gradual reform of society. It eschews revolution and the sudden overthrow of government. It is asserted that historically in China progress was always made gradually. Revolutionary ruptures from the past without exception begot disasters, as shown in Mao's Great Leap Forward, the Cultural Revolution, and the Tiananmen protests. Neoconservatives generally support the regime and predict long-term stability under the current system. Supporting the theme that China will remain authoritarian, but casting it in a different light, are those who deplore China's trapped transition, which is characterized by a lack of government accountability, weak administrative institutions, and widespread corruption and repression. There are also those who criticize the system from a "New Left" perspective, advocating greater state intervention to address the grievances that market has brought about. The New Left gradually developed into neo-statism and populist nationalism, urging the regime to hark back to its leftist ideals. Their goal is to strengthen the party-state and tilt it to the left. Finally, there are those who shy away from passing any value judgment, but simply point out that the Chinese system is able to adapt and survive because of political institutionalization – hence its authoritarian resilience. Which scenario of the three (regime breakdown, convergence to democracy, or authoritarian resilience) is most likely to be China's future? In order to answer this question, we have to move back to the big picture and read again the country's historical trajectory.

China's political development has always been heavily influenced by the global context in which the country found itself. The emergence of the nationalists and communists as the competing political forces in China was embedded in the country's desire to regain its power and rightful place in a challenging international environment. The KMT and the CCP adopted different developmental models from abroad to revive China. Because the KMT regime lost the civil war and has been highly dependent on the United States, its development on Taiwan witnessed a gradual shedding of the statist system and an adoption of liberal-democratic institutions. The mainland moved into a comparable point in Taiwan's past when it realized that the Soviet/Maoist system was totally ineffective for China to compete in the world and for the communist regime to hold onto power. It has decisively shifted to a statist model, with post-totalitarian authoritarian politics and developmental economic policies, and this new model has specific implications that favor the growth of liberalism (see Figure 8.1).

Global competition will force China to maintain its openness to the world and sustain its market reforms. But China will not soon become a democracy. In the short run, the legitimacy of the regime will be buttressed by superb economic performance. There is even talk about the "China Model" and "Beijing Consensus" that treats the Chinese case of rapid economic development as a model worthy of emulation by other developing countries. In the long run, rapid economic development will nurture social forces that are difficult to contain in an authoritarian political environment, even with the regime keeping post-totalitarian control mechanisms. When China reaches a stage at which economic growth inevitably slows down while at the same time the structural changes go deep enough to arouse strong political participation for liberalization, then the pressure for democracy will greatly increase. Situated in intense international economic competition, China needs to sustain high economic growth, but growth produces a mature society and the pressure to open up the system. As China is not as dependent on a liberal hegemony as Taiwan is, and with all the control mechanisms of post-totalitarianism in place, the route toward democratization will take much longer and will encounter greater difficulties. Nevertheless, the possibility of China's becoming a liberal, democratic system should not be dismissed under its current image of a successful, post-totalitarian, developmental state.

For the democratic scenario to materialize, reformers in the regime need to come to the fore and challenge the system. Intense elite competition and introduction of social forces into intraparty strife was one of the major reasons for the Soviet and East European communist systems (such as the one in Hungary) to tumble. Political succession is the single most important reason for elite to collide, so the rules governing succession are of paramount importance for regime survival. The PRC had arguably the worst record among communist countries in terms of orderly succession under Mao and Deng, but it has significantly improved on that record. In order to invigorate all levels of political leadership, the Chinese designed a system of generational replacement whereby senior leaders were retired when they reached a certain age set for specific levels of posts in the party-state hierarchy. Also officials are not permitted to serve for more than two terms and a total of ten years in one position. Thus, for example, the retirement age for the provincial and ministerial cadres is set at sixty-five, and the age limit for top party leadership is seventy. There are exceptions, of course, to those rigid retirement rules, including Jiang's continued presence at the party's Central Military Commission until September 2004. However, forced rejuvenation of the ruling apparatus with the generational replacement principle has become a hallmark of Chinese technocratic rule and sets it apart from the petrification of leadership in the former Soviet and Eastern European communist regimes.

However, rigid age limits have created problems of their own. For those who were born in the "wrong" years, namely those disqualified from top positions because they would be too old after serving two terms in those positions, the system denies them for an ascriptive reason the opportunity to move upward. Bo Xilai, an ambitious party secretary of Chongqing, a major city in Western China and a hopeful for the PSC of the Eighteenth Party Congress before the scandals involving him and his wife were exposed, could serve only one term in that ruling body had he been given the chance, which means he could not be considered as a candidate for either general secretary or prime minister. His flamboyant advocacy of leftist policies (singing the revolutionary songs and cracking down on corrupt officials to appeal to the masses) and alliances with current PSC members were widely seen as moves to strengthen his position as a PSC hopeful. Bo's popularity in the society, the princeling network in which he is a prominent member, and his bold moves to flirt with

Maoist-style leftism made him a natural challenger to the rigid system that denied him chances to become one of China's top leaders. About 60 percent of China's elite are automatically excluded from the top power game because they are of the wrong age. It can be expected that sooner or later another Bo will rise and challenge the rigid system, especially if that leader appeals to the disgruntled masses. If this happens, the elite solidarity would crack at the top, and authoritarian resilience would be undermined.

China (including Taiwan) made a historical detour away from the original pursuit of liberal democracy in the early days of the Republic of China, through the choice of statist authoritarianism (from the founding of the ROC to the mid-1980s) or communist totalitarianism (post-1949 PRC) as the major development strategy, and finally to the adoption of the liberal formula (Taiwan) or a gradual approach to it (mainland China). China's developmental trajectory has been, to a large extent, determined by a challenging international environment that forces different political actors representing different interests to respond. Urban intellectuals, the KMT, and the CCP spoke for different class interests, opted for different identities, and developed different institutional preferences. The lack of organization and power by the urban intellectuals doomed their effort to bring about a liberal democracy in China in the early years of the republican period. The authoritarian model that the KMT chose was imposed on the country before 1949 but was then transplanted to Taiwan when the KMT lost the civil war to the communists. American pressure and international competition later persuaded the KMT to embrace liberal democracy and abandon its authoritarian past. The Democratic Progressive Party's political ascendancy and the election of its presidential candidate, Chen Shui-bian, in 2000 and 2004 ended the KMT's half-century rule and testifies to the democratic maturity of the ROC. On the Chinese mainland, the CCP's 1949 victory foretold the inauguration of a communist-totalitarian regime modeled on the Soviet Union. Ensuing economic disasters and the pressure of international competition prompted the leadership to embrace the authoritarian model (the post-totalitarian variant), but not until the death of Mao Zedong. The natural tendency toward pluralism inherent in market reforms has already planted seeds of political liberalization in China, even though that tendency is now being resisted by a technocratic regime that treasures stability more than anything else and holds fast to its vested interests.

In short, as in other developing countries, different political forces in China competed for ascendancy as the country faced international challenges. Those different political forces represented distinct interests, developed alternative identities, and proposed competing institutions. The outcome of their competition shaped the developmental route of China, and that outcome was, in turn, contingent on the international environment in which China found itself. The momentum for political development in China has derived from its quest for national survival and the rigors of global competition. China differed from other cases in the developing world mainly in the immense dimensions of the country, not in the nature of its response. As such, China's political development can be best understood from a global and comparative perspective, and it is also from this perspective that one can evaluate the possibility of China becoming a democracy in the future.

BIBLIOGRAPHY

Dickson, Bruce. *Democratization in China and Taiwan: The Adaptability of Leninist Parties*. Oxford: Clarendon Press, 1997.

Dittmer, Lowell, and Yu-Shan Wu. "The Modernization of Factionalism in Chinese Politics." *World Politics* 47, no. 4 (1995): 467–494.

Fewsmith, Joseph. *Dilemmas of Reform in China*. Armonk, NY: M. E. Sharpe, 1994.

Friedrich, Carl J., and Zbigniew K. Brzezinski. *Totalitarian Dictatorship and Autocracy*. New York: Praeger, 1963.

Gerschenkron, Alexander. *Economic Backwardness in Historical Perspective*. Cambridge, MA: The Belknap Press of Harvard University Press, 1962.

Gilley, Bruce. *China's Democratic Future: How It Will Happen and Where It Will Lead*. New York: Columbia University Press, 2004.

Gold, Thomas. *State and Society in the Taiwan Miracle*. Armonk, NY: M. E. Sharpe, 1986.

Hsu, S. Philip, Yu-Shan Wu, and Suisheng Zhao, eds. *In Search of China's Development Model: Beyond the Beijing Consensus*. New York: Routledge, 2011.

Johnson, Chalmers. *Peasant Nationalism and Communist Power*. Palo Alto, CA: Stanford University Press, 1962.

Jowitt, Ken. "Soviet Neotraditionalism: The Political Corruption of a Leninist Regime." *Soviet Studies* 35, no. 3 (1983): 275–297.

Kissinger, Henry. *On China*. New York: Penguin Press, 2011.

Lee, Hong Yung. *From Revolutionary Cadres to Party Technocrats in Socialist China*. Berkeley: University of California Press, 1991.

Lowenthal, Richard. "The Post-Revolutionary Phase in China and Russia." *Studies in Comparative Communism* 14, no. 3 (1983): 191–201.

Meaney, Constance Squires. "Is the Soviet Present China's Future?" *World Politics* 39, no. 2 (1987): 203–230.

Nathan, Andrew J. "Authoritarian Resilience." *Journal of Democracy* 14, no. 1 (2003): 6–17.

Pei, Minxin. *China's Trapped Transition: The Limits of Developmental Autocracy*. Cambridge, MA: Harvard University Press, 2006.

Shirk, Susan. *The Political Logic of Economic Reform in China*. Berkeley: University of California Press, 1993.

White, Gordon. *Riding the Tiger: The Politics of Economic Reform in Post-Mao China*. Palo Alto, CA: Stanford University Press, 1993.

Wu, Yu-Shan. *Comparative Economic Transformations: Mainland China, Hungary, the Soviet Union, and Taiwan*. Palo Alto, CA: Stanford University Press, 1994.

Zheng, Shiping. *Party vs. State in Post-1949 China: The Institutional Dilemma*. Cambridge: Cambridge University Press, 1997.

Table 8.3 Key Phases in China's Political Development

Time Period	Regime	Global Context	Interests/Identities/ Institutions	Mode of Development
1644–1911	Qing dynasty	expansion of Western imperialism	imperial rulers vs. modernizers/ Confucianism/ traditional authoritarian institutions	sporadic reform
1912–1928	Republic of China (rise and fall of warlordism)	rising Japanese imperialism	warlords, KMT, CCP/traditionalism, nationalism, communism/ warlord regimes	country in disunity
1929–1949	Republic of China (KMT authoritarianism)	rising Japanese imperialism and outright invasion	KMT vs. CCP/nationalism vs. communism/ authoritarian developmental state	authoritarian development
1949–1978	People's Republic of China (Maoism)	Cold War	CCP/revolutionary Marxism-Leninism-Maoism/totalitarian state	totalitarianism
1978–1989	People's Republic of China (Dengism)	end of Cold War and globalization	reforming CCP/ socialism with Chinese characteristics/ post-totalitarian party-state, provinces	reform
1989-present	People's Republic of China (post-Deng)	globalization	neoconservative CCP/ Chinese nationalism/ nationalist party-state, provinces	authoritarian capitalist development, consolidation
1949–1987	Republic of China (on Taiwan, party-state)	Cold War	KMT and business interests/Chinese nationalism/authoritarian development state	authoritarian capitalist development
1987–present	Republic of China (on Taiwan, democratic)	globalization	pro-unification and pro-independence interests / liberal-democratic values Taiwanese nativism/state and parties	liberalism and growing Taiwanese nationalism

Note: Rule Separates Mainland China from Taiwan.

IMPORTANT TERMS

Chairman of the Central Committee of the Chinese Communist Party – the paramount leader of the CCP from the Seventh Party Congress of April 1945, when that position was instituted, to September 1982, when that position was abolished. Three persons have assumed that position: Mao Zedong, from April 1945 until his death in September 1976; Hua Guofeng, from October 1976 to June 1981, when he resigned at the Sixth Plenum of the Eleventh Central Committee; and Hu Yaobang, from June 1981 to September 1982, when the Twelfth Party Congress abolished the chairmanship.

Chen Yun – an important leader in the Chinese Communist Party who was particularly powerful during the First Five-Year Plan period (1953–1957) and during the adjustment period that followed Mao's disastrous Great Leap Forward. Chen was a worker with no formal education when he joined the communist movement. After the founding of the People's Republic of China, Chen became the most important cadre in charge of economic construction. He was purged during the Cultural Revolution but was rehabilitated when Deng Xiaoping came to power in 1979. He then resumed the leading role in directing China's economic reconstruction during 1979–1983. After 1983, he quarreled seriously with Deng and the radical market reformers, insisting on a "birdcage economy," by which he meant that the market should be given somewhat of a free hand, but still within broad parameters set by the state. Chen represented the pro-stability technocrats.

Chiang Ching-kuo – son of Chiang Kai-shek, and his successor. He was sympathetic to the communist cause when he was young and spent twelve years in the Soviet Union. Because of his father's anticommunist policy, Ching-kuo was kept as a hostage by Stalin and prevented from returning to China. After his eventual return in 1937, Ching-kuo became an able lieutenant to his father. After the ROC's displacement to Taiwan, Ching-kuo headed the China Youth Corps, the political department in the national army, and the defense ministry. He finally became premier in 1972 and succeeded his father as the KMT chairman in 1975 and ROC president in 1978. Ching-kuo led Taiwan through the turbulent 1970s, when the ROC faced international isolation and global economic recession. Toward the end of his rule, Ching-kuo initiated political reforms and lifted martial law in 1987. He died in 1988.

Chiang Kai-shek – the KMT's supreme leader, who succeeded Dr. Sun Yat-sen in 1926. Chiang led the Northern Expedition to unify China in 1928 and purged the communists from the KMT. He was forced to stop his annihilation campaign against the communists after the Xi'an incident of December 25, 1936, when Chiang Kai-shek was kidnapped. Chiang then led China's resistance war against the Japanese to victory but was defeated by the communists in the civil war that followed. He then led the Nationalist government to Taiwan and ruled the displaced ROC in the island country until his death in 1975.

Chinese Communist Party (CCP) – founded in 1921 as a part of the international communist movement. From the very beginning, the CCP was heavily influenced by the Communist International, the international organization of Communist Parties founded by Lenin in 1919. Its organization, guidelines, and leadership were to a great extent determined by Moscow. In 1922, the CCP members were instructed by the Soviets to join Dr. Sun Yat-sen's KMT to form a united front against the warlords, powerful military leaders who had seized control of land through military might. This KMT-CCP collaboration was short-lived, as the death of Sun and the launch of the Northern Expedition, the military campaign led by Chiang Kai-shek in 1927 intended to unify China under KMT rule, caused an open split between Chiang Kai-shek and the communists over leadership in the revolutionary movement. The communists then organized riots in the rural areas and saw their bases annihilated by the KMT army one by one. The incoming Japanese invasion saved the CCP, as Chiang was not able to concentrate on mopping up the communists. Under the leadership of Mao Zedong, the CCP was able to mobilize peasant nationalism, and it defeated the KMT after the surrender of Japan. The CCP then founded the People's Republic of China in 1949 and it remains the ruling party in China.

Cultural Revolution – Great Proletarian Cultural Revolution, the great political upheaval in the PRC that lasted for a decade (1966–1976). Touched off by Mao's effort to regain political influence after the disastrous Great Leap Forward, the Cultural Revolution was ostensibly aimed at uprooting the traditional Chinese culture that was accused of undermining the communist revolution. The concrete targets were party cadres, state officials, and intellectuals whom Mao and the radicals found threatening to their power. Liu Shaoqi, Mao's designated heir and state chairman; Deng Xiaoping, the CCP's general secretary; and many other prominent leaders were purged. During the revolution, the state was paralyzed, the educational system destroyed, and production seriously disrupted. Young students were recruited into the Red Guard brigades and dubbed "rightful rebels" by Chairman Mao. They finally came into serious conflict with the army and were expelled to the countryside for correction. The Cultural Revolution brought unimaginable damage to China, but, paradoxically, it also laid a solid groundwork for the post-Mao reforms, as the disrupted planned economy of China proved much more conducive to market reforms than the more rigid economic system in the Soviet Union and Eastern European socialist countries.

Deng Xiaoping – paramount leader of the Chinese Communist Party from 1979 to 1997. Deng was originally a lieutenant to Mao and was appointed the CCP's general secretary in 1956. He was purged during the Cultural Revolution but rehabilitated in 1973, purged again in 1976, and rehabilitated again in 1977. Deng was a pragmatist; thus, he opposed Mao's ultraleft line, which caused Deng's downfalls. However, with the death of Mao, Deng was able to gain political ascendancy and directed China toward a structural economic reform. The inefficient People's Communes were abolished, a limited market economy was introduced, foreign capital was invited, stock markets were opened, special economic zones were set up, industrial ownership rights were restructured, and people's living standards were significantly improved. Deng's economic liberalism, however, does not mean that he was pro-democracy, as witnessed by his order to crush the pro-democracy movement in Tiananmen Square in 1989. Deng died in 1997.

Gang of Four – four ultraleftist leaders who were most prominent under Mao Zedong during the Cultural Revolution period. The four were Jiang Qing, Mao's wife and a Politburo member; Yao Wenyuan, propaganda chief and a Politburo member; Vice Chairman of the CCP Wang Hongwen; and Vice Premier Zhang Chunqiao. They formed a faction against the old cadres, such as Liu Shaoqi, Zhou Enlai, Deng Xiaoping, and Chen Yun. After Mao's death in September 1976, the Gang of Four attempted to seize party leadership but was thwarted by Hua Guofeng. They were arrested in October and put on trial for high treason.

general secretary – the top leader of the Chinese Communist Party. From the Fourth (January 1925) to the Fifth Party Congress (April 1927), Chen Duxiu was the general secretary of the CCP. After the KMT purged the communists, Qu Qiubai, Xiang Zhongfa, Chin Bangxian, and Zhang Wentian assumed that position successively before Mao Zedong discarded it at the Seventh Party Congress in 1945 and led the CCP as chairman of its Central Committee. However, the Eighth Party Congress reinstituted the title of general secretary and elected Deng Xiaoping to fill the position, which was reduced to that of chief lieutenant to the party chairman and the one in charge of the secretariat, rather than that of the party's paramount leader. After Deng's purge during the Cultural Revolution, the position was again abolished. At the Twelfth Party Congress of 1982, Hu Yaobang was elected general secretary, ostensibly the top job in the CCP, as the chairmanship had been abolished, but Hu was still beholden to Deng, who was then the paramount leader of the party. Finally, Zhao Ziyang (October 1987) and Jiang Zemin (June 1989) were elected general secretary under Deng's auspices. With the death of Deng, general secretary again became the most important position in the party, a situation that changed when Jiang retired at the Sixteenth Party Congress in 2002 but managed to keep the post of chairman of the party's military commission. The new general secretary, Hu Jintao, had been designated Jiang's successor by Deng when the old patriarch was still alive. With the partial succession of Jiang by Hu in 2002, the new general secretary was nevertheless still beholden to his predecessor, until Jiang's full retirement in 2004. Hu was re-elected general secretary at the Seventeenth Party Congress in 2007. In November 2012, Xi Jinping succeeded Hu by assuming the positions of both general secretary and chairman of the central military commission at the Eighteenth Party Congress, and became the unquestionable leader of the CCP.

Great Leap Forward – Mao's greatest economic adventure. During the First Five-Year Plan period (1953–1957), the PRC adopted the Soviet model and built a centrally planned economy to boost economic growth. Toward the end of that period, serious bottlenecks developed and Mao was impatient. His solution was to mobilize human labor through ideological agitation and plunge the whole population into production campaigns. The goal was to surpass Britain and the United States in industrial production. The Great Leap Forward brought unprecedented famine and the death of 30 million Chinese people.

Hu Jintao – general secretary of the CCP from the Sixteenth Party Congress of November 2002 to the Eighteenth Party Congress of November 2012. He was also president of the People's Republic of China since the Tenth National People's Congress of March 2003, a position taken by Xi Jinping in 2013. Hu assumed the post of chairman of the powerful Central Military Commission of the party in September 2004, succeeded by Xi at the Eighteenth Party Congress. Hu was designated Jiang's successor by Deng and promoted to the all-powerful Politburo Standing Committee at the Fourteenth Party Congress in 1992 as its youngest member. Hu was a graduate of the prestigious Tsinghua University and trained as a water-conservancy engineer. He spent a great amount of time serving in China's remote provinces of Gansu, Guizhou, and Tibet, and he headed the Communist Youth League of China. He is the core of the fourth-generation leadership and a quintessential technocrat.

Hu Yaobang – one of Deng Xiaoping's major lieutenants during the reform era, whose death in 1989 touched off unprecedented massive demonstrations for political reform in Tiananmen Square. Hu first succeeded Hua Guofeng as the CCP's chairman in 1981; then, at the Twelfth Party Congress in 1982, he was elected general secretary of the party. From 1982 to 1986, Hu faithfully executed Deng's reform policies and earned himself a liberal reputation. However, Deng considered Hu too soft toward dissident intellectuals, and in January 1987 he was removed from the position of general secretary.

Jiang Zemin – former general secretary of the CCP and successor to Zhao Ziyang. Jiang was the CCP's Shanghai party secretary when the Tiananmen incident broke out in June 1989. He was chosen at that time to replace Zhao Ziyang because he had been successful in combining economic reform with a tough political stance against "bourgeois liberalism" in both December 1986 and June 1989 without resorting to force. Jiang's strengths also included his being an outsider and not beholden to any of Beijing's entrenched factions. He took the position of chairman of the party's military commission in November 1989, and he was elected president of the PRC in 1993. After the death of Deng Xiaoping in February 1997, Jiang's leading position in the CCP became indisputable. He was replaced by Hu Jintao as general secretary at the Sixteenth Party Congress of November 2002. His other positions in the government and in the army were also taken over by Hu in the next two years.

Kuomintang (KMT) – or Chinese Nationalist Party, the ruling party in the Republic of China till now, except for the 2000–2008 period. The KMT had its precedents in *Xingzhonghui* (Society for Regenerating China) and *Tongmenghui* (Society of Common Cause), the two revolutionary organizations aimed at overthrowing the Qing dynasty. After the founding of the ROC, Dr. Sun Yat-sen first transformed *Tongmenghui* into a parliamentary party, the Nationalist Party, and then remade it into the Chinese Revolutionary Party when he saw no hope of practicing democracy in a China plagued by warlord politics. In 1919, Dr. Sun again transformed the Chinese Revolutionary Party into the Chinese Nationalist Party (Kuomintang, KMT) and then in 1924 reorganized it on the Soviet model. The new KMT was equipped with a centralized party organization, special departments targeting specific groups in the population, and the National Revolutionary Army. After the death of Dr. Sun, Chiang Kai-shek became the paramount leader of the KMT and, in that capacity, dictated politics in the ROC. When the ROC was displaced to Taiwan in 1949, Chiang continued to lead the KMT-ROC party-state until his death in 1975, after which his son Ching-kuo assumed the party's leadership. In 1988, Ching-kuo died and Lee Teng-hui took over. Lee Taiwanized the KMT and led the party to victory in all of the major elections on the national level after having successfully democratized the ROC. The March 2000 presidential election defeat by the KMT's candidate, Lien Chan, threw the party into disarray. That debacle was repeated in the March 2004 presidential election in which Lien was for a second time defeated by his DPP (Democratic Progressive Party) opponent, Chen Shui-bian. The KMT was able to make a political comeback with the victory of its presidential candidate Ma Ying-jeou in 2008. In 2012 Ma was re-elected as the ROC's president.

Long March – the retreat of the communist forces of Mao Zedong from the nationalist army after the annihilation campaign of 1934. After the communists had been purged from the KMT in 1925, the CCP organized riots and set up many "Soviet regions." The KMT then launched five annihilation campaigns against them. In 1934, the largest Soviet region in Jiangxi was overrun by the KMT troops, and the communists were forced to flee from their base with the nationalist army in hot pursuit across southwest China over the most difficult terrain with the most hostile environment. After the Long March, Mao's forces ultimately settled in Yan'an of Shan'xi Province.

Mao Zedong – leader of the Chinese Communist Party from 1935 until his death in 1976. Mao espoused an unorthodox strategy of revolution in China that emphasized the importance of the peasants and land reform and the need to "encircle the cities from the countryside." That strategy at first found no favor with the party leaders, but after the Moscow-sponsored leadership had failed to thwart the KMT's onslaught in 1934 and the whole party had been forced to flee, Mao captured the military leadership at the Zunyi Conference in 1935. Mao's strategy ultimately brought about the CCP's victory over the KMT, and he became the party chairman at the Seventh Party Congress in 1945. After the founding of the People's Republic of China, Mao continued to apply his guerrilla-warfare strategy to economic development, causing the famine and destruction of the Great Leap Forward. His refusal to give up power was followed by his launch of the Cultural Revolution, which threw China into a decade of political chaos. Mao died in 1976.

People's Republic of China (PRC) – the socialist country founded in 1949 and ruled by the Chinese Communist Party. The PRC has had six paramount leaders of the country and the CCP since its founding: Mao Zedong (1949–1976), Hua Guofeng (1976–1978), Deng Xiaoping (1979–1997), Jiang Zemin (1997–2004), Hu Jintao (2004–2012), and Xi Jinping (2012–). During Mao's rule, the PRC had a totalitarian regime. Since Deng, however, the country has gradually shifted to a post-totalitarian authoritarian system.

Politburo – the organ in the Chinese Communist Party where the real power resides. The CCP follows the Soviet model in its power structure. Ostensibly, the Party Congress is the source of ultimate power in the party. However, under the practice of Lenin's "democratic centralism," the real power migrates to the Central Committee, which the Congress elects, and then to the Politburo, which the Central Committee elects. The Politburo is headed by the general secretary and is composed of the highest-ranking officials from the party and the government. The Politburo has a Standing Committee, which assumes the power of the Politburo when it is not in session. The current (Eighteenth Party Congress) Standing Committee of the Politburo is composed of seven members: Xi Jinping, Li Keqiang, Zhang Dejiang, Yu Zhengsheng, Liu Yunshan, Wang Qishan, and Zhang Gaoli. These people are the most powerful leaders in the PRC.

Qing dynasty – the last imperial dynasty in China (1644–1911). The Qing dynasty was founded by the Manchus, who originally lived in the northeastern part of China outside the Great Wall (Manchuria). In the middle of the seventeenth century, they invaded the Ming Empire to the south, captured the capital city of Beijing, and established their own rule all over China. The original emperors of the Qing dynasty – Kangxi, Yongzheng, and Qianlong – were able rulers who contributed greatly to the consolidation of the Manchu reign in China. When the Western powers arrived, however, the Qing dynasty was already showing signs of decline but was able to survive military defeats at the hands of foreigners, unequal treaties, domestic rebellions, and a bankrupting economy for the next eighty years. In 1911, the Qing dynasty was overthrown by a revolutionary movement led by Dr. Sun Yat-sen.

Republic of China (ROC) – the country founded in 1912 by Dr. Sun Yat-sen. The ROC suffered from warlord politics and did not reach genuine political unification until after the Northern Expedition (1925–1928) led by Chiang Kai-shek. After the communists defeated the nationalists in the Chinese civil war, the ROC retreated to Taiwan, an island province off the eastern coast of China. From the 1950s to the 1980s, Taiwan was an authoritarian country with a thriving market economy. Since the late 1980s, its political system has been democratized.

State Council – the central government of the People's Republic of China. The State Council's predecessor was the Government Administrative Council, headed by Zhou Enlai, which was set up in 1949. After the 1954 constitution was promulgated, the Government Administrative Council became the State Council, and Zhou remained the premier until his death in 1976. The State Council is headed by the premier, who is usually the second most important person in the PRC.

Sun Yat-sen – the founding father of the Republic of China, who led a revolutionary movement to overthrow the Manchu (Qing) dynasty in 1912. When the ROC disintegrated into warring regions, Dr. Sun founded the Kuomintang (KMT), built a power base in the southern province of Guangdong, and began inviting Soviet advisers to his camp. He died in 1925 before China was unified under the KMT.

Third Plenum of the CCP's Eleventh Central Committee – the historic party meeting held in December 1978 that ushered in the reform era in post-Mao China. At the meeting, Deng Xiaoping saw his political influence greatly expand as his lieutenants were elected to the Central Committee, and his line, the "four modernizations," was substituted for Mao's "treating class struggle as the major link." Hua Guofeng's authority as paramount leader was undermined with the institution of a collective leadership. The CCP's historians treat the Third Plenum as the turning point in the party's development. It signifies the shift from the totalitarian stage to the reform stage in China's post-1949 political development.

Three Principles of the People – Dr. Sun Yat-sen's political philosophy of nationalism, democracy, and people's livelihood, with the last principle denoting a pragmatic program that emphasizes the combination of private entrepreneurship and active state involvement in economic development. This doctrine is by nature a liberal program for reconstructing China. It is enshrined in the constitution of the Republic of China.

Tiananmen incident – the massive student pro-democracy movement of June 1989 and its brutal suppression. Deng Xiaoping's reforms during the 1980s opened up China to the world, but rapid economic growth was accompanied by omnipresent corruption and rising expectations for greater political liberties. Fluctuations in the economy fueled public dissatisfaction, and students became inspired by Western, especially U.S., democracy. Hu Yaobang's death and the visits to China by U.S. president George Bush and the Soviet communist party leader Mikhail Gorbachev also came into play. The convergence of these factors in the summer of 1989 brought Beijing's college students to the streets and to Tiananmen Square, demanding fundamental political reforms. After a protracted stalemate between the students and the authorities that lasted for a month, martial law was declared and the troops moved in on June 4. Great casualties running in the thousands were reported.

Xi Jinping – general secretary of the Chinese Communist Party since its Eighteenth Congress in November 2012. He is also the Chairman of the CCP's Central Military Commission and replaced Hu Jintao as the president of the PRC in 2013. Xi was born in a high cadre family but suffered during the Cultural Revolution. He advanced rapidly during the reform period, serving as party secretary in the coastal provinces of Fujian and Zejiang, and then in Shanghai, before he was promoted to the center to become a member in the Politburo's Standing Committee and vice president of the PRC in 2007 and 2008. He became the "heir apparent" of Hu and smoothly succeeded the latter in 2012. Xi is the core of China's fifth-generation leadership. He is expected to be the paramount leader of the party and the country till 2022.

Zhao Ziyang – one of Deng Xiaoping's major lieutenants, who from 1983 to 1987 was mainly in charge of economic reform. Zhao succeeded Hua Guofeng as premier in 1980. After the purge of Hu Yaobang in 1987, he was promoted to general secretary of the CCP. His sympathetic attitude toward the students in the summer of 1989 cost him his job. After the June 4 suppression of the pro-democracy movement, Zhao was replaced by Jiang Zemin.

Zhou Enlai – China's prime minister from 1949 to January 1976. Zhou was a senior CCP leader who directed the political department at Whampoa Military Academy in 1924–1925; that is, during the first KMT-CCP collaboration. Zhou was very close to the Communist International but was wise enough to side with Mao Zedong at the Zunyi Conference in 1935, at which Mao took military leadership of the party. After 1949, Zhou became prime minister of the new government, a position he held until his death in 1976. Zhou is remembered for his restraining influence on Mao during the Cultural Revolution period and for his diplomatic sophistication outside China. In 1973, Zhou rehabilitated Deng Xiaoping, a move that later proved critical in bringing the totalitarian phase of China to an end after the death of Mao.

Zhu Rongji – Chinese prime minister from 1998 to 2003. Zhu was a technocrat by training who rose in Beijing's state hierarchy until his critical tendency got him into trouble during the 1957 antirightist campaign, after which he was purged. Deng Xiaoping's political ascendancy brought Zhu back to the official arena, and he advanced rapidly until he was mayor of Shanghai. There he executed Deng's plan to build China's most important window to the world. He was promoted to vice premier during Deng's famous Tour to the South that relaunched economic reform following the conservative retrenchment period of 1988–1991. In March 1988, he was elected premier to replace Li Peng.

STUDY QUESTIONS

1. What kind of developmental strategy did the Kuomintang take on the Chinese mainland? Was it an effective response to the international challenge that China faced at that time?
2. Dr. Sun Yat-sen originally attempted to build China on the liberal model. Why and how did he abandon that model?
3. How was the first KMT-CCP collaboration formed and dissolved?
4. How did the Japanese invasion and the Chinese civil war alter China's developmental strategy?
5. Explain China's post-1949 political turbulence in terms of the conflict between the party and the state and in terms of the shift from transformation to reform.
6. How did Deng Xiaoping's reform agenda conflict with Chen Yun's emphasis on stability in the post-Mao period?
7. How do you place Taiwan's democratization in the general framework of China's political development?
8. How did the CCP amalgamate the post-totalitarian model and state-driven capitalism, and what has been the effect of this hybrid system?
9. Discuss the possibility of China's democratization. Is the current system resilient?
10. Was China unique in its response to international challenges during the twentieth and twenty-first century?

Early Developers, Middle Developers, and Late Developers

If it makes sense to group Britain and France as early developers and Japan and Germany together as middle developers, comparativists feel that it makes even more sense to group Russia and China together as late developers. Not only did both countries industrialize only in the twentieth century, but both also experienced communist revolutions and have lived with the long-term burdens of communist economic and institutional development. Although Russia cast off its communist political institutions and ideology in 1991, it continues to search for a viable path into the capitalist world. Moreover, after initially moving in the direction of democracy after 1991, over the past decade Russia's rulers have become increasingly authoritarian. China, on the other hand, has retained its communist political structures but has done so while rapidly introducing capitalist economic institutions in important parts of the economy. These are the ironies that we examine in the case of the late developers.

Late Developers: Russia and China

Compared with its European neighbors, Russia entered the twentieth century as a politically and economically backward country. As the core region of the tsarist empire, Russia had neither a constitution nor a working national parliament. Instead, Russia's tsar, Nicholas II, ruled as his father and grandfather had – as an autocrat unchecked by the power of law or political opposition. The privileged nobility served the tsar and lived in a moral and political universe separate from that of the masses of powerless and impoverished peasants. Nor did Russia have a consolidated sense of its own nationhood; one look at a map was enough to see that the empire consisted of well over a hundred different ethnic groups and languages. Its economy was still primarily agricultural, despite some serious efforts to modernize agriculture and initiate industrialization in the latter part of the nineteenth century.

In fact, several of Russia's earlier rulers had attempted modernizing reforms. Peter the Great (1680–1725) had introduced modern technologies acquired in the West and had even built a new capital city, St. Petersburg, on the Gulf of Finland, replete with the best Italian and French architecture of the day, as a tangible symbol of Russia's Western orientation. Catherine the Great (1762–1796) had welcomed significant elements of Enlightenment rationalism and European thinking into imperial administration. Alexander II had freed the peasant serfs in 1861 with the intention of unleashing the social energies of ordinary Russians in order to harness them for economic development and military competitiveness.

The problem with all of these reforms, however, was the deep ambivalence Russia's rulers felt toward them. The tsars wanted the military and technological advances that reforms and economic development might bring, but they feared the kinds of social and psychological changes in the population that occurred in France and ultimately led to revolution. Over time, as the rest of Europe was democratizing, this contradiction grew more intense: Military competitiveness required economic development; economic development entailed adopting Western technologies, methods, and ideas; but Westernization appeared to lead inexorably toward some kind of political liberalization – something that all tsars resisted until the very end.

Even within Russian society, there was ambivalence about embracing the experience of the West. During the nineteenth century, some parts of the intelligentsia wanted to preserve distinctive Slavic traditions and were thus dubbed "Slavophiles." Others looked to the West and were thus labeled "Westernizers." The Westernizers themselves were split between those who wanted liberal democracy and those who wanted a distinctively socialist form of industrial modernity. Later on, in the early twentieth century, there were further splits among the socialists dividing those who saw the Russian peasant village as the foundation of socialist society and Marxists who emphasized the socialist potential of the industrial proletariat. Even among the Marxists, there were further splits: the Mensheviks wanted to come to power democratically, and the Bolsheviks wanted a revolution to construct a communist society. Which path Russia would ultimately take became the burning question of the nineteenth and early twentieth centuries.

The Russian Revolution of November 1917, led by Lenin and his Bolsheviks, answered this question for the better part of the twentieth century. Although the Bolsheviks wanted to build a new kind of society, they still had to build this society in a world of hostile countries, and they were thus confronted with some of the same challenges that faced their tsarist predecessors. How could a first-rate military and industry be built on the resources of a less-than-second-rate economy? Unlike their tsarist forebears, however, the Bolsheviks faced a further dilemma. How could all of this be done without capitalist markets and be made into something called "socialism" or "communism"? Lenin died too early to deal with these questions, but his successors were forced to deal with little else.

Lenin's successor, Stalin, undertook what some comparativists have called a second revolution and created distinctive communist economic and political institutions in the successor to the Russian empire, the Soviet Union. The Communist Party became the sole ruler of the country, agriculture was collectivized, and the economy was transformed into a command economy, planned and administered from Moscow (which, perhaps tellingly, had become the new capital after the revolution). The net result of the revolution was to create a totalitarian dictatorship that succeeded in rapidly industrializing the country and creating a huge military-industrial complex. As we now know, this could only be accomplished at a tremendous price in terms of lost lives and wasted resources. After Stalin's death, successive Soviet leaders sought ways to improve the economy and compete with the West without dismantling the distinctive communist political and social order.

The last Soviet leader, Mikhail Gorbachev, undertook what was perhaps the most important set of communist reforms. He too failed, but implemented important political changes (his economic programs were utter nonstarters) that permitted society to mobilize against the Communist Party. In 1991 the Soviet Union broke up and Russia emerged as a smaller but formally democratic state. Once again, however, in some respects Russia found itself in the position it was in before it embarked on the failed communist experiment – a country that is trying to catch up to the West using institutions, methods, and ideas not of its own design. The added burden, however, is that the legacy of the Lenin-Stalin system has made democratic and capitalist transformation exceedingly difficult for Russia's postcommunist leaders. With so many obstacles to successful transformation, Russian politicians have been tempted to cast aside democratic institutions altogether in favor of a return to more familiar hierarchical and authoritarian forms of political rule.

Like Russia, China also experienced a communist revolution. But China continues to be ruled by a Communist Party that has overseen a stop-and-go series of economic reforms over the last fifteen years that have led to spectacular rates of economic growth, accompanied by new social tensions. The reasons for the divergence in experience between the two countries are to be found in the very different legacies of the global past.

Comparativists are quick to point out that unlike Russia, which had always viewed itself as embedded within the broader European culture, China has always understood itself as culturally distinct from Europe. And for good reason, too: Chinese culture is far older than Europe's, and for centuries China remained isolated from the outside world. Under successive Confucian rulers, China had managed to create an impressive form of bureaucratic rule based on the educated elite. These rulers were not subject to democratic control, but they did face the threat of overthrow if the mandarin and gentry felt that the rulers had lost the "mandate of heaven" to govern their country.

The imperial order lasted for centuries but was ultimately destabilized by its encounters with the industrialized West. Over the course of the nineteenth century, the Western powers forced China to open a number of its port cities to foreign merchants and trade. Chinese imperial bureaucrats brought this access into question in 1842, when the British were forbidden to market opium to the Chinese population. In response, the British successfully waged war and secured for the next century foreign domination of China's economically important coastal regions. British imperialism in the region ultimately paved the way for Japanese imperialism, which culminated in the Japanese invasions and atrocities of the 1930s and 1940s.

Military pressures and internal fragmentation brought down the last Chinese emperor in 1911. Initially, after the emperor's departure, China was united under an alliance of the Nationalist Party (the Kuomintang) and the Chinese Communist Party (CCP), but the alliance collapsed in 1927 in a bloody rupture between the two partners. The CCP, although it was nominally a Marxist party and thus could be expected to look for support among the urban proletariat, fled to the countryside where it worked closely with the peasant masses and perfected its unique contribution to revolutionary theory: the conduct of a guerilla war. The leader of the CCP, Mao Zedong, established his base in the countryside among the disaffected and the outlawed. Faced with increased military pressure from the Kuomintang, in 1934 thousands of Communists abandoned their base in Jiangxi to begin their Long March of 7,000 miles, a forced retreat that decimated the ranks of the party (only 8,000 of the original 100,000 arrived at the end) but also provided a formative, steeling experience for the Communist elite.

At the end of World War II in 1945, the Japanese fled the country and the civil war between the Nationalists and the Communists resumed. With the support of the majority of the peasants, who in fact constituted the vast majority of all Chinese, the CCP won the war in 1949 and the Nationalists were forced to flee to the island of Taiwan. The People's Republic of China was proclaimed on October 1, 1949. The CCP could look to the Soviet Union for a model to emulate, but they could easily look to their own "heroic" past to justify carving out their own path. Although important aspects of the Soviet model were adopted, the CCP under Mao's leadership pursued policies that were at times much more radical than in the Soviet Union (the Great Leap Forward and the Cultural Revolution). After Mao's death in 1976, the reformist-direction branch of the party emerged dominant, and under Deng Xiaoping's leadership the CCP ushered in several waves of successful marketizing economic reforms and a broad opening to international market forces. At the same time, the party has retained tight control over political life and has forestalled any move toward democracy. The comparison with the Soviet communist experience is highly instructive. Whereas the Soviet Communist Party fell because it democratized before it marketized, part of the secret of the Chinese Communists' capacity to retain control has been their willingness to marketize their economy without democratizing their politics.

Yet, after much dissatisfaction with the democratic politics in the 1990s, Russia's political elite under President Vladimir Putin turned back to its much older and more embedded traditions of top-down rule. Communism has not returned; but Russia is much more of an authoritarian country than a democratic one. As long as energy prices remain high and export earnings can subsidize living standards, much of Russia's population seems content to revert to some form of state-led market economic development. In short, by the second decade of the twenty-first century, the Chinese model combining political autocracy with economic markets seems to have won out, and in this sense the two great countries of the Eurasian landmass have ended up at basically the same place despite having taken different initial paths after the demise of communist central planning.

PART IV
Experimental Developers

MEXICO

MAP 9.1. Map of Mexico.

9 Mexico

Anthony Gill

Introduction

Mexico provides an interesting case study of a transition between the late industrializers such as Russia and China, on the one hand, and the recently developing nations such as India and Nigeria on the other. Whereas the former experienced decolonization in the middle of the twentieth century, Mexico's independence from Spain was achieved more than a century earlier. Nonetheless, the process of industrialization for Mexico did not begin in earnest until about the 1930s, not much before when the countries discussed later in this text began their jump from predominantly agrarian economies into the industrial age.

The other interesting pattern to note is that Mexico experienced a major political and economic revolution at roughly the same time that Russia did. Indeed, the date in which Mexico's revolution was enshrined in constitutional form was 1917, the same year the Bolsheviks took over Russia. Although not as extreme in terms of confiscating the factors of production as Russia, the Mexican system that was established following its revolution had a socialist flavor to it; communal farms were created and several industries were eventually nationalized or put under close regulatory management of the state. What is more surprising, at least to the comparative political scientists, is that the political and economic system that was created during the Mexican revolution also began unraveling at the same time the Soviet Union began its process of collapse. However, unlike the USSR, Mexico's transition to a more democratic polity was more gradual, with the dominant party that emerged from the earlier revolution – the **Institutional Revolutionary Party** – remaining a significant political player in the new liberalized order.

Besides the interesting comparison with the late developers, particularly Russia, Mexico's trajectory also offers useful comparative lessons to the other experimental developers. Although not fully embracing a socialist order the way that Russia or China did, the Mexican state was extensively involved in guiding the industrialization process through most of the latter half of the twentieth century. The reliance upon import-substitution industrialization led to rapid industrial growth initially as resources were transferred from the agriculture to the urban sector, but this growth in turn produced a series of dislocating economic consequences that had profound political consequences. The rise of an urban middle class that initially benefited from that rapid growth led to later cries for political representation and democratization when those industrial policies started to impose a heavy cost on that same socioeconomic sector. How Mexico negotiated the political turmoil caused by rapid industrialization has many commonalities with the transitions many other nations have recently experienced. But, as with all case studies, Mexico maintains its share of unique circumstances that also provide interesting lessons for students of comparative political development.

Pre-Twentieth Century Politics

The roots of the contemporary Mexican political system date back to the sixteenth-century invasion by Spanish conquistador Hernan Cortes. With his defeat of Aztec emperor Montezuma in 1521, Spain's distinct style of colonial governance prevailed over the territory of New Spain for exactly three centuries. The colonial period had three important effects on modern Mexican political life. First, it laid the ideological bedrock of **corporatism**, the core philosophical framework guiding Mexican political life. Corporatism refers to a system of government wherein the state officials are viewed as being responsible for closely regulating and coordinating various economic and social groups within society, including businesses, labor unions, agrarian co-operatives and even cultural groups. Second, the centralized and top-heavy political structures established by the Spanish monarchy provided comparatively little opportunity for self-governance in the colonies, resulting in political instability and an all-out war for power following independence in 1821. Third, labor relations and land-holding patterns established during the colonial era set the stage for future economic and political problems.

The cultural framework that came to dominate Mexico's national political identity emanated from the intersection of a strong religious tradition (Catholicism) and a political philosophy (corporatism). This line of thinking viewed society as an organic whole: Individuals belonged naturally to a variety of functional social groups (for example, craft guilds, clergy, aristocracy). Although each of these groups may have dissimilar interests, all are needed for the harmonious operation of society. It stands to reason that the interests of the entire body politic should come before the interests of any particular component. The institutional impact of this worldview was a statist, patrimonial style of government. For the body politic to function properly, so the argument ran, a centralized entity needed to mediate any potential conflict between social groups. The most effective way to do this is to have the state determine which interest groups are socially vital and then regulate their operation. Rather than allowing for the autonomous, grassroots organization of individuals with distinct interests, the state itself organizes, grants legitimacy to, and absorbs these groups into the decision-making apparatus of society. It also has a tendency to promote rigid class distinctions while downplaying the possibility of social mobility.

In terms of social interests, the primary motivation driving colonization was the enrichment of Spain, particularly in relation to its European rivals. Although mineral wealth (for example, silver) was highly prized, the Spanish crown also taxed other economic production (for example, cotton and sugar), with the goal of increasing royal wealth. The colonies were thus governed with an eye toward ensuring that local officials remained strictly loyal to the crown. Only individuals born in Spain were appointed to the highest levels of colonial government, served a specified term, and then returned to Spain. Inasmuch as poor administration was punished on return, the rotation of colonial officials in this manner ensured a high degree of loyalty. To enhance it further, the monarchy conducted regular audits of colonial administrators. The Catholic Church was also under the control of the king and was used to keep watch over both colonial officials and citizens (specifically by the Holy Office of the Inquisition). Although relatively complex in nature, the system of colonial administration was far from perfect. The social structure of the community often dictated that even high-ranking officials court the favor of the colonists. Because it was difficult to supervise the behavior of colonial officials completely, corruption was common and, up to a point, even tolerated by Spain.

Despite tight control by Spain, colonists were granted a limited degree of self-governance. Municipal councils (**cabildos**), staffed primarily by individuals born in the colonies, administered the day-to-day activities of town life (for example, issuing building permits). These local councils later became the locus for the independence movement. However, it is important to note that the *cabildos* were relatively isolated from one another and were in no position to provide unified national leadership. Therefore, when Spain eventually did withdraw from Mexico, no strong centralized institutions existed to replace the colonial administration. The inevitable result was that the post-independence period would be one of substantial political uncertainty and instability.

The final consequence of the colonial period for the contemporary era relates to the pattern of land tenure and the resulting social-class relations. To encourage the conquest and settlement of New Spain in the mid-1500s, the Spanish monarchy had granted large tracts of land to conquistadors and the Catholic Church. These land grants typically included access to the labor and tribute of indigenous communities. The result of this pattern of land tenure and labor relations was the creation of a rigid class structure and a serious maldistribution of wealth that closely paralleled racial cleavages: **criollos** (individuals of pure-blooded Spanish descent) typically occupied the upper classes, *indigena* the lowest classes, and **mestizos** (mixed blood) in between. As the indigenous population has tended to be concentrated in southern Mexico, economic and political tension has had a strong geographic component to it. Under such conditions, trying to construct a fair and just governmental system that represents the interests of all Mexicans and creates a common national identity has proven to be an enormous challenge. With criollos claiming higher economic status than the indigena, interest-based conflict has frequently inspired clashes over cultural identity.

Comparative political scientists understand that seemingly distant international events can have very important effects on domestic political arrangements. Mexican independence is a prime example. Both material interests and ideological influences emanating from abroad provoked the separation of Mexico from Spain. The seeds of Mexican independence were sown during the seventeenth-century decline of Spain. Facing a declining economy at home, and increasing pressure from an ascendant Britain and France, Spain attempted to extract more revenue from its colonies by encouraging intra-regional trade while reorganizing and tightening its political control so as to prevent tax evasion. Although the economy boomed, local Mexicans who had never set foot in Spain took the opportunity of Napoleon's invasion of France in 1808 to initiate an independence movement that created divided loyalties and bloody conflict over the next decade and a half. Wealthier landed elites tended to remain loyal to the crown fearing that their estates would be confiscated under a liberal Mexico, a belief that was not unrealistic considering that two Catholic priests led a major peasant insurrection from 1809 to 1814. Although forces loyal to the Spanish crown were able to win victories early in this conflict, King Ferdinand VII's endorsement of a liberal constitutional monarchy in 1820 weakened the conservative forces in Mexico and allowed the more urban and liberal faction to claim victory in 1821.

Mexico's initial government under independence was structured as a monarchy under Augustin de Iturbide. His reign only lasted for three short, tumultuous years and ended in his assassination. Iturbide's death marked the beginning of a cycle of political instability known as the "era of the **caudillos**." (Caudillos were independent military leaders who commanded localized armies.) The most famous (perhaps notorious) was **Antonio López de Santa Anna**, who ruled Mexico directly nine times and manipulated the choice of the presidency on numerous other occasions. The pattern of political instability during this period followed a typical cycle: a sitting president would discover the government was bankrupt and be forced to cut back on military salaries and troop levels. With a stagnant economy thanks to two decades of civil war, unemployed soldiers and officers were unable to find work. Discontent spread rapidly among the military, provoking a coup d'état. The new president would find himself in the same situation as the previous one, and the cycle would be repeated.

All told, there were roughly fifty separate administrations from 1821 to 1860. This was hardly the environment for any single model of government, let alone democracy, to flourish. Nor was this a suitable context for the forging of a national identity, although the long-term effect of this chaos was a preference for more corporatist (in contrast with liberal) forms of government. The anarchic nature of this period allowed for the rise of local political bosses (**caciques**), who firmly resisted attempts to centralize national authority in any meaningful sense. To this day, the "culture" of the caciques persists, as current administrations have difficulty implementing policies without first considering the interests of local power brokers, including the growing power of autonomous drug cartels.

International pressures aggravated Mexico's political chaos. Foreign powers could easily take advantage of the country's weakened domestic position. Primary among these foreign interlopers was a young, expansionist United States. Settlers from the United States began occupying the Texas region in 1821, the year of Mexico's independence. Although Texans were technically citizens of Mexico, efforts by Mexican authorities to make them accountable to central rule led the settlers to call for secession. Tensions escalated as U.S. settlers quickly outnumbered native Mexicans. Domestic U.S. pressure to annex Texas eventually provoked a war in 1846. With Mexico in political disorder, the United States won the war and roughly half of Mexico's national territory (extending from present-day Texas to California and Washington State).

Foreign occupation and war were not the only international influences to shape the Mexican polity. An ideological "invasion" also proved decisive in Mexico's political history as new ideas began to filter into the region. Increased contact with Britain, France, and the United States following independence further exposed many Mexican elite to new streams of political thought. The philosophies of the English Enlightenment and French Revolution, with their emphasis on citizens' liberties and rights, contrasted with conservative, corporatist thought that gave primacy to the state over the individual. Throughout the nineteenth century and for the first several decades of the twentieth, the struggle for a national political identity involved the efforts of liberals to graft their ideological beliefs onto a culture heavily influenced by medieval Catholicism. This resulted in an ongoing conflict between **Liberals** (who favored more middle-class, urban interests) and **Conservatives** (representing the traditional landed elite) for most of the nineteenth century.

Although the political instability of the 1800s took on the veneer of a great battle between competing worldviews, the ideological basis for conflict during this period should not be overestimated. Interest-based struggles over personal power prompted constant turnover in presidential administrations. Politics became a "winner-take-all" game; daily survival in office took precedence over achieving long-term philosophical goals. Over time, Liberals and Conservatives became virtually indistinguishable in their economic policy preferences, with both favoring export-oriented growth and trade relations with Europe and the United States. Politically, Liberals abandoned their federalist pretensions and opted for centralized government, which allowed them to rule a large territory more effectively. This was most evident during **La Reforma** (1855–1876) when Liberals under the leadership of **Benito Juárez** (a pure-blooded Zapotec) finally dominated their Conservative rivals and he became the first president to complete a constitutionally prescribed term in office (1867–1871). Under Juárez's presidency, business investment became a reasonably safe activity and the economy began to show signs of growth.

President Juárez's next term in office ended prematurely with his natural death. The resulting succession crisis gave way to a harsh dictatorship under Porfirio Díaz from 1876 to 1911, a period known as the Porfiriato. Although ruthless, the dictatorship did have a beneficial side. For thirty-five years, Mexico experienced unprecedented political stability and economic growth, bolstered by a favorable global context. Industrial growth in Europe and the United States fueled demand for raw materials. Rising commodity prices boosted Mexico's domestic economy and helped fill state coffers. Government tax revenue, along with U.S. and British foreign investment, was used to build Mexico's infrastructure. Railroads were constructed, ports modernized, and the national bureaucracy expanded.

Porfirio Díaz also left his mark on Mexico's political landscape. He was the first of Mexico's rulers to unify Mexico effectively under central authority for any extended period. He accomplished this by means of shrewd manipulation of military appointments, the buying off of local political bosses (**caciques**), and the creation of a separate police force directly loyal to his authority. Despite ideological loyalty to the liberal constitution of 1857, which provided for a strong legislative branch, Díaz further concentrated institutional power in the executive branch. Since that time, the Mexican president has enjoyed political power above and beyond what is legally prescribed. The Porfiriato's final legacy was to establish a style of rule that has been used to guarantee political stability to the present day – ***pan o palo***, the rule by "bread or club" – meaning the dual use of patronage and coercion. With increased revenues flowing into the treasury during the economic boom, Díaz bought the loyalty of various towns and constituencies. Important members of the elite received lucrative positions in the governmental bureaucracy in exchange for their support. Those who opposed this arrangement were dealt with harshly. Although autocratic in nature, the regime did guarantee a climate of stability that enhanced long-term economic growth, and as the nineteenth century came to an end, Mexico appeared ready to make the transition to an industrial society. However, such transitions in the modern era rarely come without turbulence.

Politics in the Twentieth Century: Revolution and Institutionalized Rule

The Mexican Revolution

The **Mexican Revolution** began as another conflict over presidential succession, something to which Mexicans had grown accustomed. Although generally pleased with the economic management of the country, middle-class professionals began demanding greater political participation, something that their brethren in other Latin American countries were enjoying at that time. The ideological rhetoric of the initial rebellion mirrored the liberal leanings of the 1800s, with a call for representative democracy coupled with checks and balances on executive power. Early on, revolutionary leaders attempted to institutionalize the classic liberal tenets contained in the 1857 constitution. However, the Mexico of 1910 was very different from what it was just thirty years earlier. New social classes, such as urban labor, had arisen, and existing ones (especially the rural peasantry) had grown politicized. These groups brought to the political arena a new set of interests – a desire for higher wages, better working conditions, social welfare, and access to arable farmland – that political institutions needed to capture. A new global ideological climate also shaped the course of the revolution; in Europe, socialist ideals began to challenge the underlying logic of liberal capitalism. The Russian revolutions of 1905 and 1917 provided further examples that the peasantry and urban labor were becoming a major force for social change and could not be ignored in any new political arrangements. Many of those participating in the revolution wanted not only liberal political institutions but also major social reforms aimed at bringing the lower classes into a ruling coalition. Such demands radicalized the revolution and gave form to the resulting **Constitution of 1917** and the corporatist institutions it would spawn.

With the disappearance of Díaz's effective system for holding the country together, internal chaos again reigned. The initial coalition that brought Madero to power began unraveling. Accusing Madero of failing to carry out his promised social reforms, a rebel from southern-central Mexico, **Emiliano Zapata**, declared war on the Liberal administration.

An attempt to suppress this rebellion by relying on one of Díaz's former generals backfired, and Madero was overthrown in a counterrevolution supported by the Catholic Church and the U.S. government. Another faction, led by Venustiano Carranza (northern Mexico's governor and a landholder), toppled this counterrevolutionary regime with the help of Zapata. Unhappy with Carranza's reluctance to implement progressive policies, Zapata's forces marched on Mexico City and forced a number of radical reforms that resulted in the drafting of a constitution in 1917. This new constitution included provisions for workers' rights to unionize, exclusive national ownership of mineral wealth, and communal land redistribution. These provisions represented a step beyond classical liberalism's preference for individual rights and established a basis for a modern corporatist system that gave the state enhanced powers in regulating social conflict. Much of the contemporary political strife in Mexico relates to efforts by recent presidents to rescind these social duties and move the country back to a more liberal framework.

The consolidation of the modern Mexican state began in 1920, the year typically viewed as the end of the revolutionary era. That year marked the beginning of the peaceful transfer of power between presidential administrations and the return of political stability. The decade from 1924 to 1934 saw the emergence of another presidential strongman, Plutarco Calles, the first president to implement the revolution's most radical promises, including the distribution of nearly eight million acres of land to communal farms (**ejidos**) and the organization of labor into government-sponsored unions. Other social policies, including increased wages, better sanitation, and health programs, were also implemented. All of this was made possible by a relatively strong global economy that allowed Mexico to increase its exports of raw materials and attract foreign investment.

Despite the progressive social policies undertaken by Calles, the actual political working order that emerged was far from the liberal-democratic ideals contained in the 1917 constitution. Dissidents were jailed and the press censored. Calles's governing strategy closely resembled the *pan o palo* methods of Porfirio Díaz. Indeed, the heavy reliance on patronage networks by a centralized presidency to win social support and legitimacy is one of the main reasons Mexico's political system remained stable and free from military intervention from the 1920s to the present. Coercion (*palo*) became less needed as time wore on because rapid economic growth guaranteed that the patronage strategy (*pan*) would work effectively. In effect, the legacy of the revolutionary era was the forging of a new mode of governance for Mexico – one that synthesized the basic political elements of liberalism (for example, elections, popular sovereignty) with the corporatist mode of operation (that is, top-down social organization, increased political centralization). Although corporatism came to dominate liberalism, the blend of these two forms of government represented a political system that was uniquely Mexican.

The Revolution Institutionalized

The figure most credited with shaping the Mexican political system into what it is today is **Lázaro Cárdenas**. As president from 1934 to 1940, he institutionalized the corporatist philosophy of government. However, the revolutionary process had radically transformed the philosophic basis of corporatism. The corporatism of the nineteenth century was inherently conservative and exclusionary, seeking to preserve the socioeconomic organization of a bygone colonial era. Political participation by those other than the landed elite was strictly forbidden, and class relations remained static. The corporatist philosophy underlying Cárdenas's political arrangements, on the other hand, was progressive and inclusionary. It sought to transform Mexico into a modern industrial nation by organizing, coordinating, and controlling the social groups that would build the nation. Government would be pro-worker and pro-peasant. The state would try to tame the ravaging effects of "raw capitalism" and build a nation free from foreign influence. Under Cárdenas, Mexico had finally achieved a strong national identity based on a unique blend of liberalism, corporatism, and socialist ideas.

Economically, Mexico's international position prescribed a more state-centric approach to development than the Anglo-American model of capitalism. Being an industrial late-comer placed several constraints on the country's ability to achieve a modern economy. Most of what Mexico wanted to produce domestically was already being produced more efficiently in the United States and Europe. Mexican entrepreneurs were at an inherent disadvantage because domestic consumers would invariably prefer less costly, higher-quality goods manufactured abroad. No incentive existed to engage in entrepreneurial activity unless the state stepped in to guarantee businessmen domestic markets (via protective tariffs) or to subsidize their production costs. It is ironic that providing business with domestic markets meant creating a consumer base for manufactured goods because this, in turn, meant promoting higher wages for urban and rural workers, a situation that businesses try to avoid in order to protect their profits.

The political tumult that ravaged the country for nearly a century meant that there was little private capital to provide the impetus to build factories. Given the high start-up costs of building heavy industry in the mid-twentieth century, few Mexican citizens had the financial capacity to invest in large-scale industry. As in other cases of late development, such as Russia and China, the state would become the main vehicle for raising and investing capital. Mexico's industrialization was promoted extensively by a combination of state-owned enterprises and state subsidization of preferred industries. Overall, this general economic strategy was known as import-substitution industrialization (**ISI**). The component parts of ISI included high import tariffs on manufactured consumer goods, financial subsidies to private business, overvalued exchange rates (to reduce the costs of producer imports), and state ownership of industries with high capital costs (for example, electrical power and steel). Unionization and higher wages were promoted and a welfare system created to provide a consumer base for domestically produced goods. Import-substitution industrialization was common throughout Latin America and other parts of the developing world (for example, Iran) during the mid-twentieth century and was largely a reaction to the Great Depression and World War II, when these countries were cut off from the manufactured goods traditionally provided by Europe and the United States. Although ISI policies were designed essentially to promote autarkic development, the lack of domestic capital inevitably meant courting foreign investment.

The Revolutionary Party, created under President Calles, became Cárdenas's institutional vehicle for achieving political stability and industrialization. The Mexican Revolutionary

Party – later renamed the Institutional Revolutionary Party (Partido Revolucionario Institucional, known by its Spanish acronym, PRI) – was created as an autonomous entity to mobilize the population in support of Cárdenas's reformist agenda. Cárdenas structured the party around three organizational pillars, each representing an important social sector: (1) the Mexican Workers' Confederation (CTM), representing urban industrial labor; (2) the National Peasant Confederation (CNC), representing rural workers and the *ejidos*; and (3) the National Confederation of Popular Organizations (CNOP), composed of white-collar professionals, government bureaucrats, and small entrepreneurs. Each of these organizations was given representation in the policy-making apparatus of the party and, hence, the government. (The PRI was the only party to hold national office from 1934 to 2000.) However, because the party's top leaders chose the officials of these organizations, the PRI became the epitome of inclusionary corporatism. The ruling party organized societal interest groups from the top down, and political loyalties were based on "corporate," not geographic, identities. Autonomous groups that arose over the years were absorbed into the corporatist structure, ensuring that the government maintained tight regulatory control over popular interests.

A fourth organizational body, representing the armed forces, was also created. Cárdenas's early incorporation of the military into the party proved crucial to ensuring his immediate political survival. By currying the favor of officers and troops with substantial pay raises, educational opportunities, and other benefits, he prevented his rivals from using the army to plot against him. More important, these actions institutionalized civilian control over the armed forces, something historically rare in Latin America. In large part, Cárdenas's actions during the 1930s prevented Mexico from falling prey to the intermittent coups and military dictatorships that plagued South America for most of the 1960s and 1970s. The military reforms proved so successful that when the PRI disbanded the official organization representing the military in 1940, no military revolt ensued.

The institutionalization of labor, the peasantry, and the middle class into the ruling party became the crucial defining feature of Mexican politics for the next six decades. By connecting each social sector to the party, Cárdenas ensured enormous popular support for the PRI and set the stage for a single-party state. Relying more on *pan* (patronage) than *palo* (coercion), Cárdenas won the long-term loyalty of the Mexican lower classes. He dramatically improved urban working conditions and promoted the unionization of more than a million workers. During his presidency, roughly one in three Mexicans benefited from land reform involving nearly 50 million acres. The majority of land went to communal *ejidos*, which received privileged loans and technology from the government, further ensuring their political support. Finally, the incorporation of government bureaucrats, teachers, and lawyers into the PRI meant that the state and the Revolutionary Party would become virtually indistinguishable.

Cárdenas also instituted many of the political practices that became standard fare over the next several decades: He extended the presidential term to six years. The president, as head of the PRI, would nominate his successor (a process known as *dedazo*, or "big finger"). Patronage benefits to privileged groups, controlled almost exclusively by PRI officials, increased in the months preceding a national election. Government-organized labor received higher wages, business groups were granted subsidies, and public works projects sprang up in rural communities. This increased spending prompted a period of inflation leading up to the election. Following national elections, the outgoing president would undertake deflationary policies so that the new president could begin his term with the task of rebuilding the economy. In many respects, this pattern represented a classic "political business cycle" of inflation and recession, determined by the electoral calendar.

Cárdenas also institutionalized a number of other political practices that made the Mexican system uniquely stable. Retiring presidents left office quietly and avoided interference in political matters. Power continued to be concentrated in the presidency; the Senate and Chamber of Deputies served as a rubber stamp for the policies of the executive. Although the CNOP, CTM, and CNC were supposed to be involved in the policy-making process, they fell under the increasing dictate of party leaders. Government and party officials decided when and where labor could strike or make demands on employers. Assistance to rural communities was conditioned on unswerving support of the PRI. Reasonably fair elections were held, but real political competition was minimized. All of this combined to ensure the electoral dominance of the PRI and gave the state a quasi-authoritarian flavor. Although outsiders may be quick to criticize the lack of effective democracy in Mexico, it should be remembered that the institutionalization of one-party rule in Mexico gave the country something it had long lacked – political stability. This in turn provided the basis for rapid and sustained economic growth until the 1980s.

The final legacy of the Cárdenas era was his reaction to the international political and economic environment. Mexico had always been at the mercy of foreign powers, either militarily or economically. This changed during the 1930s. The 1938 nationalization of twelve foreign-owned oil companies not only signaled a country seeking to control its own economic development but also was a high point in the creation of a Mexican national identity. Antiforeign sentiment increased noticeably. The economic policies of ISI were a natural extension of this growing nationalism as Mexico sought to become industrially self-sufficient. Despite being located adjacent to the world's foremost superpower, the Mexican government exercised a substantial degree of autonomy in its economic and foreign policy.

The reforms of the Cárdenas era were politically and economically successful, and they benefited from a favorable international climate. When manufactured imports from Europe and the United States slowed to a trickle during the Great Depression and World War II, Mexican industry developed to fill the supply gap. The war also created a high demand for oil and other primary commodities in the world market. Political stability further boosted the domestic economy, and the country entered an era of unprecedented growth known as the "**Mexican Miracle**" (circa 1940–1980). Gross domestic product grew at an average annual rate of over 6 percent, an unprecedented feat in Latin America. Accounting for population growth, per capita income increased approximately 3 percent per year. Within two short decades (1950–1970), living standards doubled.

Presidential succession continued peacefully for the next six decades, and the PRI held onto the major institutions of power. Although much of the PRI's dominance can be attributed to its control over important government resources and manipulation of patronage to loyal constituents, the party's popularity was also attributable to the nation's strong economic performance. The Mexican single-party system maintained a high degree of popular legitimacy. This is not to say that economic gains were distributed evenly. Over time, the actual policies of the government began to deviate from its revolutionary rhetoric and the redistributive legacy of Cárdenas. Large private industries not included in the 1930s corporatist arrangement gained an increasingly privileged position among policy makers. Contrary to the nationalist intentions of ISI, Mexico increasingly depended on foreign investment to fuel economic growth. Nonetheless, economic growth and political stability became mutually reinforcing. As long as the economy stayed healthy, the PRI was able to "buy" the support of most major social groups, and a politically dominant PRI ensured a stable social environment that was attractive to domestic and foreign investors. Despite outward appearances of durability, however, the corporatist system built under Cárdenas was fragile. If either the economy or the PRI faltered, the political system as a whole would become vulnerable to crisis. This is exactly what happened during the 1980s and 1990s. Fortunately, unlike the collapse of other civilian regimes throughout Latin America that ended in military dictatorships from the 1960s to the 1980s, Mexico managed to deal with its political and economic crises with a peaceful transition to an opposition party in the year 2000.

The Formal Institutional Structure of Mexican Politics

At this point, it is worthwhile to review the general institutional structure of Mexican politics in the late twentieth century. These institutions were largely laid down in the 1917 constitution, although they have undergone some modifications since the 1970s. As noted earlier, Mexican politics between the 1920s and the late 1990s was determined by the informal politicking that went on within the dominant PRI. With single-party rule and the president and his close advisers controlling the party, most of the formal constitutional rules of politics held little sway. The Mexican Congress was largely a rubber stamp for presidential decrees, and the judiciary served to bolster executive dominance by posing little challenge. However, with the breakdown of the corporatist control of the PRI and the rise of real electoral competition, the rules establishing these governing institutions will undoubtedly take on greater importance.

The 1917 constitution provided Mexico with a federalist and presidential form of government similar in structure to the U.S. Constitution, although with important procedural differences. First, in keeping with the historical regional fragmentation of the country, Mexico is divided into thirty-one states, and each state has a relative degree of autonomy in setting policy relevant to regional interests. Second, political power was divided among three branches – executive, legislative, and judicial – each of which was to retain institutional autonomy from the others. The president initially was to be elected by popular vote every four years, although this provision was modified under President Lázaro Cárdenas to extend to a six-year term. The memory of Porfirio Díaz dominating the presidency for an extended period of time created a strong desire to impose a strict one-term limit on the president. Unlike the case in the United States, the Mexican political system does not have a provision for a vice president. In the event that the president is unable to fulfill his term in office, the national legislature (Congress) is empowered to appoint an interim president, with a call for a new general election if the president is incapacitated during the first two years of his term. If the president's incapacitation occurs in the final four years of his tenure, the appointed interim president will serve the remainder of the term.

The national legislature, known as the Congress, is divided into two chambers – the Chamber of Deputies (lower house) and the Senate (upper house). Members of the former are elected for three-year terms via two methods of election. Three hundred members of the Chamber of Deputies are elected via plurality rule (first past the post) in single-member districts. The remaining seats are selected via proportional representation with a provision guaranteeing seats to any party able to garner at least 2.5 percent of the vote. Initially, only 100 seats were to be selected in this manner, but bowing to increased pressure for representation by minority parties, the number of seats allocated by this method was expanded to 200 in 1986. The Senate originally consisted of two senators from each state and an additional two from the federal district of Mexico City. A 1993 constitutional reform doubled the number of senators to 128. This reform again represented a concession to minority parties who were calling for greater representation in a system dominated by the PRI. Currently, three of the senators from each state are elected via plurality rule, and the fourth seat is guaranteed to the minority party receiving the highest number of votes. Both deputies and senators are restricted to serving only one term in office.

Finally, the judicial branch of government was designed originally to be an autonomous check on the legislative and executive branches of government. Twenty-six judges, appointed by the president and confirmed by the Senate, sit on the Supreme Court and serve lifetime terms. Despite this guaranteed tenure, a norm developed wherein all Supreme Court justices would proffer their resignation following a presidential election, allowing the new president to retain the justices he desired and appoint any new people from his political coterie. A series of federal circuit courts exist below the Supreme Court, and judges within these courts are appointed by the Supreme Court. Not surprisingly, the courts did not function according to institutional design; instead of being a check on government abuses, the judicial system only served to strengthen and legitimize a top-heavy presidential system.

The Crisis of Corporatism during the Late Twentieth Century

Mexico's political development since the 1980s, defined by the historical tension between liberalism and corporatism, has been a battle of interests as well as identities. Following decades of social turmoil, top-down corporatist institutions proved best at reducing political conflict and promoting rapid industrialization. In turn, the Mexican Miracle financed the corporatist system. But miracles rarely last forever. Political stability and economic growth gave rise to new social interests and demands for a liberalized political system. Addressing these demands was easy when the economy was strong and government resources plentiful. However, changes in the world economy during the 1970s seriously limited state access to the resources needed to keep patronage-based corporatist arrangements intact. With the PRI finding it financially difficult to fulfill its corporatist obligations, groups that were once loyal constituents began organizing independently and seeking help from new political parties. The ruling party's rule is no longer guaranteed, and corporatism is giving way to demands for political liberalization. How Mexico negotiates its transition from a single-party, corporatist state to a liberal-pluralist democracy, if it does so at all, is the central problem facing the country today.

Origins of the Crisis

Mexico's political foundation began to show cracks during the late 1960s. Just as economic growth during the late 1800s gave rise to new social interests that prompted the Mexican Revolution, the Mexican Miracle created new social interests that demanded reform of the country's corporatist institutions. Among these new demands were greater autonomy for local governments, the ability to organize groups independent of government ties, and alternative (non-PRI) political representation. Such demands appeared first in the wealthy industrial and ranching states of northern Mexico. The central government's corporatist policies worked against northern interests by directing patronage resources away from them and toward the more populous central and southern regions. Defending their economic interests meant promoting electoral competition; if PRI power were challenged in the region, the central government would be required to respond to northern interests. In 1965, candidates from the center-right **National Action Party** (Partido Acción Nacional, PAN) won two mayoral elections in the prosperous state of Baja California, Norte. The ruling PRI, unfamiliar with such a challenge, nullified the elections, marking the first time that fraudulent tactics were used openly to retain power. Political liberalization might favor the industrial north, but it was not in the interests of the ruling party. Corporatism still trumped liberalism.

University students also began to call for political change. A booming economy created an expanding middle class; more youths were attending college and expecting professional careers. However, the closed political and economic system of the time could not adapt to meet these heightened expectations of a rapidly expanding population. Frustration among students ensued. Inspired by campus unrest in the United States and Europe, they began to agitate for expanded civil liberties. The well-organized student protesters eventually mobilized the largest antigovernment rally in Mexican history, involving some 500,000 people. Unfortunately, a two-month series of protests ended with government troops firing on demonstrators in the **Tlatelolco** district of Mexico City, killing more than 100 (and perhaps as many as 400) civilians. The Tlatelolco massacre showed that popular support for the corporatist political system was waning.

By the early 1970s, the economy also began to show signs of stress. Import-substitution industrialization encouraged inflation, currency overvaluation, and a serious balance-of-payments crisis. Inflation ate away at the real wages of most Mexicans. More important, the corporatist institutions designed to give workers and small farmers a voice in government (for example, the CTM and *ejidos*) increasingly became a way to repress their demands. The government discouraged workers from striking and implemented policies favoring business interests. The government also promoted large-scale, capital-intensive farming for export, which markedly slowed the pace of land redistribution between 1940 and 1970. Disaffected peasants responded by invading private lands. Contrary to nationalist rhetoric, foreign investment gained a noticeable presence in the economy, causing resentment among local workers and small businesses.

The social unrest of the late 1960s challenged Mexico's corporatist system but did not break it. President Luis Echeverría (1970–1976) responded to this discontent by increasing wages, distributing more land to the rural poor, and permitting the autonomous organization of labor. His administration also allowed limited civil protests. Bowing to pressure for increased political representation, Echeverría's successor, José López Portillo, enacted legislation in 1977 that guaranteed opposition parties 100 seats in the Chamber of Deputies based on proportional representation. These reforms represented a limited "democratic opening" and raised expectations for future liberalization.

The corporatist system survived in large part because of the oil crisis of the 1970s. Mexico, an oil-exporting nation, benefited from the dramatic rise in petroleum prices beginning in 1973. Revenue from the state-owned petroleum industry flowed into the national treasury, where it was used to alleviate economic hardship caused by a global economic slowdown. Additionally, the flood of Middle East "petrodollars" on world financial markets allowed the Mexican government to borrow abroad. Increased government revenue prompted more state intervention in the economy as the state began to nationalize hundreds of firms. In turn, the expansive economic reach of the government provided more avenues for distributing patronage in the form of jobs, preferential loans for favored businesses, and subsidies to important rural clientele. Because Mexico's political stability was built upon the PRI's extensive patronage networks, oil revenue and foreign loans bolstered the survival of the corporatist system during a time of growing popular discontent.

Political Challenges in the 1980s and 1990s

The same global economic system that provided the financial liquidity to keep corporatism afloat during the 1970s served to undo the system during the 1980s and 1990s. Relying upon oil revenue and foreign loans to buy domestic political support was at best a temporary solution for Mexico's socioeconomic ills. Loans required repayment, and reliance on petroleum for the bulk of government revenue was an inherently risky strategy. Two international events during the late 1970s and early 1980s made this strategy unworkable and sent shock waves through Mexico's political system. First, to combat soaring inflation at home, the U.S. Federal Reserve raised interest rates between 1979 and 1982. Rates on international loans followed suit, dramatically increasing Mexico's debt obligation. Concurrently, the world market experienced an unexpected oil glut and prices dropped precipitously. With roughly two-thirds of Mexico's foreign revenue coming from petroleum exports, government income fell sharply just as international financial obligations increased. Facing a massive outflow of economic resources, Mexico devalued its currency, reducing the value of the peso relative to other currencies; announced it was suspending payment on its international debt; and nationalized the country's banking system.

Business and consumer confidence disintegrated rapidly. International loans dried up and domestic investment slowed to a standstill. Mexico, like many countries in the developing world, entered its worst economic recession in more than a century. Total domestic production declined by 4.2 percent in the year following the devaluation and debt moratorium. Real wages tumbled by over 25 percent between 1980 and 1987. Unemployment and underemployment soared. With the economy in decline, government revenue (collected from taxes as well as oil) shrank noticeably. Although halting payment on international loans would seem a reasonable response to the domestic crisis caused by a shortage of government revenue, this solution was not feasible. Defaulting on its loans would have entailed severe economic sanctions from the world community, including the denial of loans in the future. Over the next several years, Mexico renegotiated repayment of its foreign debt, thus averting a major default and restoring partial confidence in the economy.

Part of the debt-negotiation agreement required the implementation of a series of austerity measures designed to control inflation and reduce the fiscal deficit. A radical reduction in government spending ensued. Jobs and wages in the government bureaucracy were trimmed. The government privatized hundreds of state-owned enterprises, which were used in the past to reward union supporters with high-paying jobs. Making these firms competitive meant slashing salaries and positions. Privatization thus struck at the heart of one of the central institutional pillars of corporatism – industrial labor. The peasantry felt the pinch of austerity as well. In order to generate foreign exchange with which to pay back foreign loans, the PRI began to promote agricultural exports. Government policy favored the most efficient, export-oriented farmers, typically those with large, capital-intensive plantations. *Ejidos* typically did not meet this need, and policy turned against their interests. Again, a traditional clientele of the corporatist system felt the brunt of the international economic crisis. A Mexico that had once tried to gain independence from the vagaries of the world market was now more than ever at its mercy.

The Political Consequences of Economic Crisis

Events in the economy profoundly affected the Mexican political sphere. The loss of government revenue placed severe restrictions on government spending. This undermined the ability of the PRI to manipulate patronage networks to ensure popular support. Discontent that had been brewing since the late 1960s erupted during the mid-1980s. A strong civil society began to emerge at the grass roots, a trend contrary to the corporatist philosophy of top-down organization. The growth of civil society received an unlikely push from a series of major earthquakes in 1985 that killed more than 10,000 residents of Mexico City. The massive destruction left a cash-strapped government paralyzed. Foreign assistance poured in, but what really mattered most was the autonomous creation of thousands of small community organizations that assisted in rescue and cleanup efforts. These organizations sowed the seeds from which independent political-action groups took root. For the first time since the modern corporatist system was constructed, a complex network of nongovernmental social groups emerged to challenge the hegemonic authority of the PRI.

The self-assertion of an autonomous civil society affected electoral politics. In 1983, members of the opposition National Action Party (PAN) won a significant number of municipal posts in the northern states of Chihuahua and Sonora. It is interesting to note that whereas one would expect leftist parties to make the greatest gains from labor discontent, PAN occupied the center-right and advocated an economic platform similar to the PRI's current neoliberal policies. National Action Party candidates won these elections because they were the only opposition party with significant organizational strength to mount an independent attack aimed at loosening the PRI's hold over the government. Most left-wing parties had been previously co-opted by the PRI through links to labor unions. Officials in those parties accepted this situation in exchange for token positions at various levels of administration. In other words, the leftist leadership owed its existence to the PRI and thus had little incentive to challenge the ruling party's authority. Only PAN had sufficient leadership that remained independent of the PRI.

National Action Party's electoral success went beyond organizational strength. It also signaled growing dissatisfaction with the PRI. Because northern Mexico is wealthier and more industrially developed than the central and southern states, PAN's success made it apparent that business interests were becoming increasingly unhappy with a PRI-dominated government. Furthermore, the preference for PAN indicated that there was more to the electoral discontent than strictly pocketbook matters; the electorate wanted real political choice and a greater say in government. The top-heavy corporatist model was facing a serious challenge from the grass roots.

The extent of popular unhappiness became clear during the presidential election of 1988. The handpicked PRI candidate, **Carlos Salinas de Gortari**, won the presidency with only 50.5 percent of the vote, a slimmer margin than for any previous PRI candidate. Cuauhtemoc Cárdenas, son of the former president and the representative of a loose coalition of left-wing parties, came in second with 30.9 percent. The PAN candidate, Manuel Clouthier, finished third with 16.7 percent. This in itself signified a substantial defeat for the one-party state. In reality, Salinas may have actually lost the election. Electoral irregularities marred the election, including a power outage that affected the computerized ballot counts. As political competition grew throughout the 1980s, the PRI increasingly resorted to electoral fraud to retain important seats. Although the true totals from the 1988 election may never be known, it is enough to say that this election had a lasting impact on the Mexican polity. The Mexican corporatist framework that had brought an era of unprecedented political stability for Latin America could no longer be sustained in its present form. The 1990s thus initiated a transitional period for the Mexican state.

Interests, Identities, and Institutions at the End of the Twentieth Century

As the 1990s came to a close, Mexico found itself struggling with one of the central political themes of its past – the tension between liberal and corporatist forms of government. Whereas this conflict was resolved for most of the century in favor of a corporatist one-party state, the crises of the 1980s and the rise of an autonomous civil society made liberal-pluralism (a system of private interest articulation outside of government control) a viable contender as the organizing principle of Mexican political life. Economic globalization and the collapse of the socialist model of development have pushed economic policy in the direction of laissez-faire policies. President Carlos Salinas de Gortari (1988–1994) stepped up the pace of privatization begun by his predecessor, Miguel de la Madrid (1982–1988). Under pressure to attract foreign capital and cultivate new export markets, Salinas also gave the central bank greater autonomy and entered into an expansive free-trade agreement (**NAFTA**) with the United States and Canada. His successor, **Ernesto Zedillo**, continued on the same economic path, although Zedillo was more adventurous when it came to introducing liberalizing political reforms. Salinas's policy of economic liberalization under a one-party state was reminiscent, in some ways, of similar reforms undertaken by Mikhail Gorbachev in the Soviet Union – so much so that the Mexican reforms were given the name "Salinastroika." But, as Gorbachev found out, economic liberalization unleashes powerful forces in society. New interests are created, institutions transformed, and identities reshaped.

The economic crises of the 1980s and the resulting laissez-faire (neoliberal) policies remade political interests in ways not seen since the Mexican Revolution. Definite winners and losers emerged. The most extreme example has been in the southern state of Chiapas, where a guerrilla insurgency burst onto the scene in 1994. With land becoming increasingly concentrated in the hands of a few large-scale farmers, *ejidos* found it exceedingly difficult to sustain a living, and grievances against the government grew. In 1992, President Salinas revised Article 27 of the 1917 constitution, which was the cornerstone for earlier land-redistribution programs. The new article made privatizing *ejido* lands easier. Peasants seeking to have their concerns addressed were frequent targets of violent attacks by the state police and private paramilitary groups supported by large landholders. The implementation of NAFTA in 1994 further threatened the interests of *ejido* farmers, as it favored large-scale agricultural exporters over small-scale communal farms. With their economic livelihood at risk, many peasants found it worthwhile to join the **Zapatista National Liberation Army** (EZLN). As of this writing, the EZLN and the Mexican government remain deadlocked over a variety of issues that affect peasant interests, including land redistribution, human rights, effective political representation, and electoral fraud.

The Zapatista movement is not only about economic interests. Because many of the peasants in Chiapas are of direct Mayan ancestry, the movement has asserted strong indigenous claims. Mexican nationalism plays little, if any, role. In fact, the insurgency in Chiapas has demonstrated the difficulty in forging a single Mexican identity. In societies where economic class divisions map closely onto racial and ethnic cleavages, ethnic identity is bound to be closely associated with interest-based politics. How the central government treats the descendants of pre-Columbian inhabitants has become a central policy issue in a country that has largely ignored such concerns for nearly five centuries. Indigenous communities are now identifying themselves as distinct groups within the Mexican polity and demanding to have their voices heard in the central government. This implies a greater respect for civil liberties (for example, freedom of association) and the ability of indigenous groups to freely elect government officials who represent their interests. The rise of a strong indigenous identity thus creates pressures for political liberalization.

The political legacy of the 1990s has been the emergence of real electoral competition, one of the central features of a liberal-democratic polity. With the PRI losing its ability to deliver patronage to its core constituencies because of fiscal restraints on state spending and an ambitious program of privatization and government downsizing, many of those interests tied tightly to the party in the past have sought new avenues of representation. Nongovernmental organizations have appeared as a new force in society. Political participation also has been channeled into two major opposition parties – the National Action Party (PAN) and the **Democratic Revolutionary Party** (Partido Revolucionario Democrático, PRD). The latter was forged from a coalition of leftist parties and disaffected members of the PRI in the early 1990s. It has attracted mostly members of the urban and rural working class and poor, although significant portions of lower-income voters remain tied to the traditional patronage networks of the PRI. Political infighting has also weakened the PRD. During the 1994 presidential elections, the PRD candidate – Cuauhtemoc Cárdenas (a former member of the PRI) – won only 17 percent of the vote in a reasonably clean election. Nonetheless, by the late 1990s, the PRD had scored a number of important victories at the local level, including winning the mayoral seat of the nation's capital.

The PAN has been the most consistent threat to the PRI's political hegemony. Representing upper-income interests, the PAN has tapped into domestic business disapprobation with many of Salinas's and Zedillo's economic policies. Although it seems odd that domestic businesses would be dissatisfied with laissez-faire policies, it must be remembered that many of these businesses benefited from the high tariffs and government subsidies of the 1960s and 1970s, and these businesses were not prepared to compete internationally. Neoliberal policies took many of these benefits away, although overall they have helped to create a friendlier environment for foreign investment. It is ironic that the PAN champions many of the same neoliberal policies as the PRI. In this respect, much of the support for the PAN can be viewed more as a search for an alternative political voice than as a desire to shift the economic policies of the state. This voice has found a forum, as PAN candidates have won numerous local offices and captured key gubernatorial positions in several northern states.

The increase in electoral competition affected two of the country's primary political institutions – the national legislature and the PRI. Power still remains highly concentrated in the presidency, and the executive branch remains under the control of the PRI. However, in 1997 the PRI lost majority control of the Chamber of Deputies (equivalent to the U.S. House of Representatives). Previously, the PRI had enjoyed majority representation in both the Chamber of Deputies and the Senate, making the Congress a rubber stamp for executive decisions. This pattern was reinforced by the fact that the PRI Party leadership chose each legislator, which meant that the president had a strong influence over the career paths of politicians. In some respects, this resembled parliamentarianism in reverse – the leading party executive chose legislators rather than vice versa. Results from the 1997 midterm elections earned opposition parties a combined majority in the Chamber of Deputies for the first time in the twentieth century. Although the PRI still controls the Senate and can play divide and conquer among the deputies to ensure a winning legislative coalition, the presence of a majority opposition in the lower house has forced the PRI to engage in negotiation and compromise, both steps toward more pluralistic interest representation. With opposition parties in general agreement on the need for further electoral reforms, this environment bodes well for continued political liberalization. Political liberalization, in turn, raises the prospects for greater representation for opposition parties in the Congress and for a stronger legislative branch. Although it is still too early to tell, the classic liberal notion of checks and balances may become a reality in the near future.

Increased political competition and social pluralism have shaken the dominant party itself. Within the party elite, a debate rages over how to manage the economic and political turmoil engulfing Mexico. The faction that emerged as dominant since the 1980s represents a more reformist line of thinking. Known as the *técnicos* (technocrats), they harken from the bureaucratic side of the PRI. Presidents Salinas and Zedillo are members of this faction. Both were educated in U.S. universities and earned their political stripes by working their way through the Mexican bureaucracy rather than by winning seats in local and regional government. The *técnicos* began occupying high-level offices during the 1980s, when the economic crisis called for policy makers with specific expertise in managing domestic and international macroeconomic affairs. The ascendance of *técnicos* gave rise to a competing faction within the PRI called the *dinosaurios* for their hard-line, traditional corporatist stance.

The split within the PRI created an interesting and fluid pattern of alliances. The primary intraparty cleavage related to economic policy. Whereas the *técnicos* favored neoliberal economic reforms to modernize Mexico's economy, the *dinosaurios* preferred the old formula of state-directed growth, and opposed both the privatization of industries and NAFTA. This put the *dinosaurios* in policy agreement with the PRD. The *técnicos* found policy allies in the center-right PAN. Despite their differences, both the *técnicos* and *dinosaurios* strongly desired that the PRI hold onto political power. Political survival tended to take precedence over economic policy disagreements, and both factions were involved significantly in vote tampering during the 1980s. The transparency of electoral fraud, especially at the local level, only fueled further dissatisfaction with the ruling party and intensified public cries for electoral reform.

Whereas President de la Madrid (1982–1988) represented a transition between the hard-line *dinosaurios* and the *técnicos*, Carlos Salinas de Gortari firmly identified himself with the latter. Following his narrow electoral victory in 1988, Salinas surprised many analysts by charting a course independent of the *dinosaurios*. It was believed that this would be a dangerous strategy for a man who needed as much internal party support as he could muster. Nonetheless, his institutional reengineering had a lasting impact on the Mexican polity, and he most likely will be remembered as a pivotal character in Mexico's political history. Salinas was credited with disassembling many of the PRI's traditional patronage networks. Realizing that *dinosaurio* power rested in those channels, he cut funds for favored programs and dismissed important union officials. Still needing social support for his presidency, however, Salinas created the Solidarity Program, a new set of patronage networks that circumvented many of the local political bosses who remained loyal to the *dinosaurios*.

President Zedillo continued this tradition through a similar set of programs. The end result was to destroy almost completely the traditional pillars of support holding up Mexico's corporatist system, which had ensured political stability in the past.

Constitutional reforms undertaken in 1992 further changed Mexico's political landscape by removing some of the most radical elements of the revolutionary constitution. Without recourse to the revolutionary ideals of the past, a new legitimating formula needed to be found. Although Salinas and the *técnicos* hoped that economic growth would boost support for the PRI, they realized that economic restructuring would pay dividends too far off in the future. Discontent with the country's economic situation was increasing, especially among the traditional corporatist allies of the PRI – labor, the peasantry, and middle-class bureaucrats. Both presidents Salinas and Zedillo sought to restore the PRI's legitimacy by championing political reform. Salinas began the process of promoting electoral reforms that would allow opposition parties a fair chance at winning office. Secret balloting was guaranteed to prevent voter intimidation, and ballot counts came under greater scrutiny. Salinas further cracked down on local PRI officials who engaged in electoral fraud, although enforcement of this policy typically favored the PAN, not the PRD. Given that the *técnicos* and PANistas shared a similar economic policy agenda, capitulating to their electoral victories was a more palatable solution than allowing PRD victories. Fraud continued against PRD candidates, leading to violent clashes between protesters and police. Despite ideological disagreements, however, leaders of the PAN and PRD found it in their mutual interest to cooperate and press for more electoral reforms. The PRI still controlled access to state financial resources and public media outlets, giving it a significant electoral advantage.

Political reform was put to the test in 1994. The growing rift within the PRI erupted in violence. In March, Luis Donaldo Colosio, a *técnico* and Salinas's handpicked presidential successor, was assassinated on the campaign trail. Although the crime was pinned on a young garage mechanic, it was widely suspected that members of the PRI's *dinosaurio* faction had masterminded the plot. Several months later, the secretary general of the PRI (and brother-in-law of the president) was gunned down. Salinas's own brother was arrested as the prime suspect. Such high-level political violence had a profound effect on Mexican politics. To ensure free and fair elections and deflect further accusations of fraud, an independent electoral commission was established to monitor voting practices. International observers also were invited to oversee national balloting. As a result, Mexico's 1994 presidential elections were the most honest in nearly two decades, a triumph for liberal-pluralism.

The PRI's Ernesto Zedillo, another young *técnico*, won the election with a plurality of the vote (48.8 percent), and the ruling party hung onto a narrow majority in the Chamber of Deputies. The victory came at a severe cost for the country, however. To win popular support amid growing political turmoil, the PRI inflated the Mexican economy throughout most of 1994, making it easier to pay off needed constituents with government projects and providing a general feeling of economic prosperity in the country. The government also issued a large quantity of short-term government bonds to boost the confidence of foreign investors, who were growing increasingly nervous about the spreading political violence (including the Zapatista uprising). However, faced with rapidly declining foreign currency reserves, the incoming Zedillo administration was forced to devalue the Mexican peso. Traditionally, hard economic choices had been made by the outgoing president, thereby allowing the incoming president to avoid public hostility. Former president Carlos Salinas de Gortari, however, was pursuing a bid to become the president of the newly created World Trade Organization, based on his success in negotiating NAFTA. He refused to devalue the peso, knowing that such action would reveal weakness in his administration's monetary policy. When Zedillo finally attempted a controlled devaluation, speculator pressure pushed the currency into a spiraling free fall. Inflation soared and government actions to stem rising prices plunged the economy into another major recession, just as it had a decade earlier. Salinas further challenged the informal norms of Mexican political life by criticizing the Zedillo administration's handling of the economic crisis. Zedillo countered by investigating the former president's financial dealings. In a unique turn of fate for a former Mexican president, Salinas exiled himself abroad, fearing arrest should he return to Mexico. Such an unprecedented situation clearly signals that the Mexican political system is no longer operating as it has in the past, although the future shape of the polity is still unclear.

Pressured by a severe recession, a stalemated guerrilla insurrection, and growing international skepticism about Mexico's business climate, Zedillo was forced to speed up the political reforms begun under Salinas. The centerpiece of these reforms was an electoral reform package implemented in 1996. Among its many provisions, the new laws provided for greater public financing of campaigns and media access for all parties. The plan also eliminated party membership based upon group ("corporate") affiliation. This measure effectively eliminated the basis for corporatist interest representation that had been the bedrock of Mexico's political system for most of the twentieth century. Perhaps more important was the strengthening of the Federal Electoral Institute and the Federal Electoral Tribunal in 1996. The former institution, composed of an independent citizen advisory board, is charged with the duty of monitoring all federal elections to minimize fraud. The Tribunal serves as a court to investigate all electoral irregularities and prosecute individuals engaged in electoral malfeasance. Initially created in 1990, both entities were given full independence and a permanent footing by President Zedillo in 1996. Since introducing these reforms, most observers of Mexican politics agree that the incidence of fraud, although still present, has been greatly reduced. Finally, President Zedillo departed from the traditional practice of the *dedazo*, the selection by the president of a successor. Instead of the sitting PRI president naming his successor, an open primary would be held to determine the presidential candidate of the party. This move was geared largely toward ensuring that the PRI's candidate would be vetted by the voting public and, hopefully, possess greater popular appeal and legitimacy during the general election.

Implementing these reforms has not been easy. Regional PRI caciques continue to manipulate local politics, subverting the implementation of the new laws. A once hegemonic party facing real political competition for the first time can be expected to bend or break rules in order to stay in power. Nonetheless, the reforms have shown some success in guaranteeing a more open political process. The 1997 midterm elections for the national legislature gave opposition parties their first combined majority in the Chamber of Deputies. Both the PAN and PRD made substantial gains in local elections, culminating in the historic victory of **Vincente Fox** in the 2000 presidential election. Despite his rather unassuming personality, overshadowed by the controversial Carlos Salinas de Gortari before him and the animated Vincente Fox who followed, Ernesto Zedillo should really be remembered as one of the most influential Mexican presidents of the twentieth century, perhaps rivaling Lázaro Cárdenas in importance. Ironically, his being perceived initially as a weak president who was not threatening to entrenched interests in the PRI may have granted him the political space in which to undertake these bold political reforms. And as the tumultuous twentieth century came to a close, he could rest assured that his decisions helped to initiate a new era in Mexican politics.

Competitive Democracy in Twenty-First-Century Mexico

July 2000 marked another important moment in Mexican political history. The heretofore dominant PRI went down to defeat in presidential elections. Polls just weeks before the election showed a dead heat between the PAN's candidate, Vincente Fox Quesada, and the PRI's candidate, Francisco Labastida. Although no one assumed that the PRD's candidate, Cuauhtemoc Cárdenas, would win the election, his presence certainly represented a wild card in the race. Mexican citizens held their breath as election results came in. It was feared that a narrow victory by the PRI would raise doubts about the integrity of the electoral process and might provoke social chaos. Alternatively, some feared that if the PAN (or PRD) won by a slim margin, the military might intervene and declare a coup. Although in hindsight such fears appeared overblown, they were nevertheless real at the time. Fortunately, thanks in large part to the credibility of electoral reforms introduced by Zedillo's administration, Vincente Fox emerged as the clear victor in the contest, winning 42.5 percent of the vote compared with Labastida's 36.1 percent. Power to an opposition party was handed over peacefully.

Fox's success at the ballot box certainly resulted from two decades of growing pressure for political change and the liberalizing political reforms championed by Ernesto Zedillo. But an interesting question still presents itself: Why, with the Mexican economy struggling for more than two decades, did the citizenry decide upon a candidate who represented a continuation of the neoliberal economic policies of the new *técnicos* (such as Salinas and Zedillo) instead of the PRD's candidate, who promised a return to a more statist/corporatist approach to economic policy? If anything, the results of the 2000 election signaled that the Mexican populace was hungrier for political change than economic change, and Vincente Fox, as a dynamic campaigner, represented the most viable option for an opposition victory. Moreover, there is no reason to suspect that greater state intervention will be demanded by a population in times of economic crisis. The economic revolutions of Ronald Reagan and Margaret Thatcher were enormously popular among the working classes in the United States and Britain, and more recently neoliberal reforms in New Zealand have garnered widespread support. Even in Chile, the privatization of the social security system has proven to be a political winner. Although academics have often assumed that the interests of economically distressed populations would naturally favor increased state intervention of the nature that the PRD was promising, the results of the Mexican election proved otherwise.

But the reasons for Fox's victory went beyond the policy preferences of voters. At a time when popular support for the PRI was rapidly eroding, the PAN had the strongest political organization and a historical identity that crossed various socioeconomic barriers. Founded in the 1920s, the original aim of the PAN was not so much to win elections as it was to educate Mexicans about civic engagement. This approach represented a long-term strategy in influencing the political landscape and made perfect sense after it was realized that the PRI was the overwhelmingly dominant player in the electoral arena. The PRI initially appealed to an odd mix of socially conscious Catholics and small- and medium-sized-business owners. Both of these groups were excluded from the corporatist pillars established under the Cárdenas regime. As the Mexican Miracle provided a robust economy wherein even small- and medium-sized businesses thrived, the latter group drifted away from the PAN, leaving a number of Catholic lay intellectuals in charge of the party. Influenced by the socially progressive thinking of Pope Pius IX (1846–1878) and the Second Vatican Council (1962–1965), the PAN had a noticeable leftist identity during the 1950s and 1960s. However, as the economy soured during the 1970s and the more interventionist policies of President Echeverría alienated the business community, small-sized business owners began returning to the PAN, moving the party leadership in a more rightward direction in terms of economic policy. Moreover, with the PRI's support beginning to erode among the middle class, the PAN began to focus on a strategy of winning local elections. Focusing primarily on a platform of greater political liberalization, the PAN managed to create a somewhat broad-based ideological umbrella that was comfortable both for the progressive Catholics and neoliberal business interests. The PAN developed an extensive grassroots campaign network that was rather unified in its purpose and, as noted earlier, paid off during the 1980s and 1990s with some significant electoral victories in local elections.

One could contrast this institutional organization with the PRD, which did not come together as a formal political party until the late 1980s and consisted largely of a splintered coalition of leftist parties, each with its own separate organizations, personalities, and ideologies. Although Cuauhtemoc Cárdenas, as the son of the famous Mexican president and a high-profile defector from the PRI, presented a figure to rally around in the 1988 elections, the organizational inexperience and disparate interests within the PRD did little to help them build national momentum. Granted, the PRD was capable of winning local elections (particularly in the southern states that were home to the poor and the indigenous peoples), where their organization was more cohesive, but translating these successes to a national level proved more elusive.

The PAN also benefited enormously from the vibrant personality of Vincente Fox. His story as a self-made business executive, moving from delivery driver for Coca-Cola through the ranks of the company's sales force, and eventually becoming the CEO of Coca-Cola's Mexican subsidiary, gave him the aura, rightfully deserved, of economic success. His towering height and polished speaking skills also added to his reputation as a strong leader. Finally, and perhaps most ironically, Fox apparently fell victim to electoral fraud at the hands of the PRI while running for the governorship of Guanajuato in 1991. This case made Fox a national celebrity and guaranteed his election as governor of the state in 1996. His national profile, combined with his political ambition, made Fox the ideal candidate for the PAN in the 2000 presidential campaign. His optimistic energy contrasted greatly with the more dour and pessimistic campaign style of Cárdenas and, in a new era where opposition candidates were granted greater access to the popular media, this enhanced the electoral edge of both Fox and the PAN Party in general.

The peaceful transition of power to Vincente Fox certainly represented a major step toward competitive multiparty democracy in Mexico. Most observers would now agree that the 2000 election set the stage for a new era of clean and competitive elections. Indeed, the 2003 midterm elections for the Chamber of Deputies were once again hailed as being reasonably free from corruption. Although the PAN lost a substantial number of seats in the Chamber of Deputies and the PRI and PRD gained seats, all of this represents the normal vagaries of democratic politics. With an economy in recession, it was normal to expect that the party holding the presidency would lose seats. The 2003 elections demonstrated that the electoral process continued to function as it should and the main political parties seemed to be adjusting well to a new political environment.

The next major challenge to emerge during this new era of competitive democracy came in the closely contested presidential elections of 2006. Like the 2000 presidential election in the United States, the Mexican presidential contest was decided by a razor-thin margin of roughly 244,000 votes out of nearly 42 million ballots cast, a difference of less than sixth-tenths of a percentage point. Perhaps more important, the victor – **Felipe Calderón** Hinojosa (of the PAN party) – captured only 35.89 percent of the vote, while his closest challenger – Andrés Manuel López Obrador (of a tripartite coalition of leftist parties led by the PRD) – won 35.31 percent. Third place went to the PRI's candidate, who managed only 22.26 percent of the vote. Ironically, it was not so much the strength of the PAN that led to the PRD's defeat as it was fragmentation among the Left. Patricia Mercado, the candidate from a small leftist Peasant Alternative Party, garnered 2.7 percent of the vote, which probably would have gone to López Obrador and moved him past Calderón. The PAN remained a relatively unified force on the political Right while continued factionalization among the Left limited the effectiveness of the PRD at the national level.

Although elected with only a plurality of the vote, Felipe Calderón managed what could rightfully be called a successful term as president. His economic policies represented the free market policies usually attributed to the center-right PAN, as he sought to expand free trade with new economic partners in South America and East Asia. He also sought to maintain a tight monetary policy that would provide long-term incentives for foreign and domestic investment, earning him a reputation as a business-friendly politician. Despite these liberal economic policies, Calderón also pursued a mix of more interventionist (corporatist) policies including the movement toward a national health care system and price controls. One of the defining moments of his presidency came within months of his election as the price of corn skyrocketed, prompting him to negotiate price controls on tortillas and other staples with some of Mexico's largest food companies. These populist policies, combined with his continued encouragement of a business-friendly investment climate, resulted in Calderón maintaining public opinion favorability ratings above 50 percent for the vast majority of his six-year term.

The biggest challenge to Calderón and the viability of the Mexican political system, however, harkened back to the age-old problem of the center being able to control peripheral territories. Whereas in the past local caciques would control who received what resources in towns distant from Mexico City, the last several decades have witnessed the increased power of autonomous drug cartels that, like their cacique predecessors, were able to assert their own authority over the political operations of local municipalities. Indeed, many of these criminal cartels dictated local policies to the elected officials, controlled the police forces, and provided basic public goods such as road construction. The written rule of law as provided by the Mexican constitution and legislation as enacted in the Congress applied in these towns only to the extent that drug lords allowed them to. It is widely believed that these criminal syndicates have purchased powerful allies within the military and civil bureaucracy of Mexico. President Calderón attempted to address this challenge by increasing the pay of military officers with the intent of increasing their loyalty to elected officials. He also engaged in several high-profile arrests of narco-gang leaders and attempted to purge criminal influences within the police forces in Tijuana and Ciudad Juárez. Nonetheless, the extensive nature and power of these cartels continues to provide a strong challenge to the authority of the Mexican government.

In the summer of 2012, Mexico once again faced another test of its electoral democracy. Similar to the election just six years prior, Enrique Peña Nieto of the PRI won the presidential election with only a plurality of the vote (39.2 percent). His closest rival, Manuel López Obrador of the left-wing PRD, captured roughly 32.4 percent of the vote, with the remainder going to the PAN candidate, Josefina Vásquez Mota (26.1 percent) and a new center-right party that recently emerged (2.3 percent). This election was important in that it once again allowed for a peaceful alternation in power between rival parties despite seeing a fragmented party system. Concern over whether Mexico can withstand presidential elections that give the victor less than 40 percent of the vote has led to calls for electoral reform, including a proposal to have a two-stage runoff system (like France). Although introduced and supported by former president Calderón, this reform has not met with much support from party leaders. The relatively equal tripartite division in popular support for the three main parties – PRI, PAN, and PRD – provide little incentive for party leaders to support such a policy as there is uncertainty as to which two parties would eventually become dominant. The PRD, which has come in second-place twice to the PRI and PAN candidates, holds the cards in any such reform discussion yet worries that it may be the party that would lose the most if such changes were enacted.

In terms of what the past several general elections – both presidential and legislative – have meant for the Mexican polity, several observations can be made. First, electoral democracy in Mexico is proving to be resilient. Despite a series of protests, minor violence, and accusations of ballot box corruption, the past three presidents have been allowed to don the sash of the Mexican presidency with the majority of Mexicans accepting each as the legitimate winner. Although some irregularities and charges of voter fraud were present during all of these elections, the independent Federal Electoral Institute – created in the

1990s – and a number of international observers have rated these elections as reasonably clean and fair. Fears of military intervention that always seem to be rumored around election time continually prove groundless. Civilians successfully determined the shape of the government.

Second, Mexico's party structure appears to be developing toward a relatively stable three-party system. In addition to the presidential election being decided by a close plurality of votes between the three main parties, the national legislature looks similar. In the 2012 legislative elections, the PRI held roughly 40 percent of the seats in the Chamber of Deputies, with the PAN and PRD earning 23 percent and the PRD 21 percent, respectively. The remainder of seats went to a smattering of smaller parties. The situation is similar in the Senate, with the PRI holding a slim plurality over the PAN and PRD. More important, these percentages have oscillated over the past decade, giving each party greater or lesser influence after each election, which is a sign that citizen preferences are being represented in the legislative branch of government and the system is not under the hegemonic control of any one faction.

Despite the encouraging democratic gains made over the past two decades, the political future is not unequivocally promising for Mexico. Several problems remain, many of which are directly related to the institutional structures that were developed during the twentieth century to deal with problems of the nineteenth century. Preeminent among the institutional problems facing Mexico is the term limit placed upon the president and members of Congress. In the past, with one dominant party and a system that gave the greatest power to the president, the president was able to get his legislative agenda passed quickly. Concerns over a single-term limit were ameliorated by the fact that the president would choose his successor and determine the political fortunes of others within the party, making almost all legislators willing to give the president what he wanted. Although one could rightly argue that this system was too dictatorial and could lead to bad policy outcomes, it also allowed for rapid government decision making in times of crisis.

The situation in the early twenty-first century is very different. With a president highly restricted in his ability to name his successor, legislators have less incentive to cooperate on policy making with the president. This problem was exacerbated by the specific relationship that Vincente Fox had with his own PAN Party. Being a relative newcomer to the political arena, only getting involved in politics in the decade before he was elected president, Fox had very few loyal connections to PAN members, and many of his initial policies were not to the liking of PAN legislators. Attempts to negotiate a settlement with the Zapatistas by demilitarizing Chiapas early in his administration were met with resistance not only by the PRI but members of his own party as well. A similar situation arose when Fox tried to reform Mexico's complicated and rather archaic tax structure. Major policy successes during Fox's six-year term were rare and the economy lumbered on at a sluggish pace. With few gains to be made on the domestic front, Fox turned his attention toward foreign policy, with a major goal being an immigration policy with the United States that would allow a greater number of Mexicans to work there temporarily and repatriate needed foreign currency.

The policy gridlock witnessed under the Fox and Calderón administrations also resulted from the mixed electoral system that selects the national legislature. Although plurality voting in single-member districts tends to push the political system to a two-party outcome, the presence of proportional representation in deciding a significant portion of the Chamber of Deputies still encourages minority parties. This has resulted in there being no definitive majority party in the legislature since 2000. As noted previously, the three major parties oscillate in their control over the legislature with no single party ever able to control a full majority of support.

The electoral incentives for a multiparty system at the legislative level invariably have an impact upon presidential elections, as was noted in the 2006 and 2012 elections. With small parties having a chance to pick up a handful of seats in the House of Deputies (or within local governing bodies such as states or municipalities), there are incentives for each of these parties to field a presidential candidate to maintain national visibility. Although any of the three major parties – PAN, PRI, or PRD – could craft a coalition with any of these parties, such coalitions remain unstable over the long term. And as noted the fragmentation of the Left makes coalition formation more important for the PRD and creates a handicap for its candidates at the federal level. How Mexicans will manage their party system in the coming years and decades remains to be seen. At least in the short term, it looks as if the country will continue with three major parties while a series of smaller parties will come and go around the fringes of the electoral spectrum. And irrespective of which party can control the presidency and legislature, the presence of an entrenched bureaucracy that was responsible for running Mexico's state-led economy during the previous century continues to be a difficult obstacle for civilian rulers to overcome. Efforts by Presidents Fox and Calderón to reform the system proved difficult, and without the heavy hand of the PRI to guide the bureaucracy as it had following Lázaro Cárdenas, the problem of corruption remains endemic and difficult to combat.

The problem of corruption is not merely a political conundrum. Bureaucratic corruption also places a significant drag upon the economy as government resources are not used in an economically rational and efficient manner and business entrepreneurs become less willing to invest in the economy. Although NAFTA presented Mexico with a great many opportunities to diversify its economy, global economic competition from countries such as China has placed new pressures on the Mexican economy. The administration of President Calderón showed sensitivity to this challenge, and Mexico has begun to diversify its trade relations with other countries around the world, becoming less dependent upon the United States. The privatization of many industries beginning in the 1980s, including the creation of an autonomous central bank, helped to boost the economy, but the heavy hand of the state combined with corrupt bureaucracies and the challenge of autonomous drug cartels continue to prevent Mexico from reaching its full economic potential.

And although Mexico has moved toward a more diversified economy that is less dependent upon its neighbor to the north, relations with the United States still loom large in the country's political and economic development. The problem with autonomous drug cartels challenging state authority in Mexico is due in no small part to the demand for illicit drugs in the United States. Any solution to reining in these criminal gangs will depend on U.S. drug enforcement policies. Likewise the issue of immigration. As Mexico's economic development and overall standard of living lags behind the United States, there will be Mexican citizens who long to find work in the north. Political pressure to curtail illegal immigration in the southern states of Texas, New Mexico, Arizona, and California have often caused tension with the Mexican government, who sees such immigration as a way of ameliorating problems with unemployment in their own country and as a means of obtaining foreign currency as immigrants repatriate some of their dollar earnings back home. Interestingly, as the United States experienced a significant economic slowdown following the 2008 financial crisis, immigration has tailed off. Mexico has largely avoided some of the economic problems that plagued the United States and Europe. Nonetheless, to the extent that a gulf exists between the living standards in these two countries, and as long as people find creative ways to seek out the best economic opportunities, the policies of one country will invariably affect the politics in the other. Knowing more about our neighbors around the globe will help us design better polices that reduce conflict and encourage greater cooperation.

CONCLUSION

The Mexico that we see today is an artifact of its past. The legacy of political violence during the 1800s and early 1900s paved the way for a quasi-authoritarian, corporatist regime. Foreign intervention in Mexican affairs complicated the country's search for political stability and gave the country's policies a decidedly nationalist and autarkic tone. But the world economy could not be ignored. Despite attempts to free itself from dependency on the world economy, Mexico found itself more dependent upon the good graces of the international financial community by the late 1970s. The economic crisis of the 1980s prompted Mexicans to rethink not only their economic development strategy but also their political system. Grassroots demands for greater political representation prompted a movement away from a one-party corporatist state and toward a multiparty pluralist democracy.

All of this history has shaped the interests and identities found within Mexico today. Moreover, Mexico's position in the international arena has combined with these interests and identities to shape its current political landscape. Mexico's long-standing tradition of corporatism has created strong interests in society that expect government patronage. Unionized labor has come to expect job security and wages that support an increasing standard of living. Rural *campesinos* (farm laborers), particularly in the south, have come to expect a certain level of stability that the constitutionally mandated *ejido* system provided. And both small and big businesses (in both the industrial and agricultural sectors) have demanded subsidies and tariff protection to shield them from international competitors. Meeting these basic economic interests was possible when the Mexican economy was growing by leaps and bounds.

Those days ended in the early 1980s when Mexico became saddled with an expanding international debt and a sharp loss in export revenues. Although the international economy changed, societal interests in Mexico did not. The PRI could no longer meet the societal demands that had become part of the institutional and ideological fabric of Mexican society. With a shrinking economy, the various sectors (labor, agriculture, and industry) found their demands in direct competition with one another. Mexico's corporatist identity – the ability to develop economically based on the harmonious balance of competing social interests – was also torn apart. Recognizing that the PRI could no longer deliver upon past corporatist privileges, citizens began to demand more organizational autonomy from the government and a greater say in political decision making.

This conflict of interests also appeared to tear at another aspect of Mexico's national identity. Whereas Mexican heritage had often been presented as a distinct mix of two cultures – Spanish and indigenous (Aztec and Mayan) – it has become increasingly apparent since the 1980s that economic inequity closely mirrored racial and ethnic divisions within society, which in turn reflected geographic patterns. Criollos maintained their historic position at the top of the socioeconomic ladder, whereas indigenous populations languished at the bottom. As noted at the beginning of this chapter, this long-standing problem became evident to the world on January 1, 1994, when a guerrilla insurgency composed mainly of impoverished indigenous farmers placed a damper on the festivities of a New Year's Eve party attended mostly by criollos and well-to-do mestizos. These insurgents proudly identified themselves as being of Mayan ancestry, and far from simply demanding reintegration into past corporatist arrangements, they announced their desire for greater political independence and the ability to freely choose their political representatives. It is interesting to note that these demands demonstrated that the struggle between corporatism and liberalism was not just a historical artifact but a present reality.

By the second decade of the twenty-first century, Mexico finds itself on the verge of a new era of liberal democracy with competitive multiparty elections. Demands for greater political participation during the early 1800s resulted in independence from Spain, although many among the governing elite sought to keep the top-down political arrangements of the colonial era. Similar cries for political reform were heard during the Mexican Revolution a century later. Although significant changes did result in a general rise in economic well-being, governing structures continued to leave little room for popular participation at the grass roots of society. The changes taking place today are reminiscent of those earlier eras. However, the contemporary world in which Mexico operates is, in many ways, smaller than it was before. With international investors demanding a liberalized economy, and with labor and capital mobility more fluid than ever, the Mexican government has less leeway in determining its economic policy. Yet the urgency to rekindle economic growth will affect the country's social stability. The new neoliberal course pursued since the 1990s will undoubtedly affect the interests of important political players and reshape the national character of Mexican society. As in previous centuries, the new shape of politics will play out over time. Interests and identities are not set in stone. Although it is too early to predict what the political outcomes will be, this ever-shifting global environment offers a wonderful opportunity to understand the complexities of comparative politics (Table 9.1).

Table 9.1   Key Phases in Mexico's Political Development

Time Period	Regime	Global Context	Interests/ Identities/ Institutions	Developmental Path
1521–1821	colonialism-strict control of Spanish America by crown; Spain discourages autonomous government in colonies, although some local control granted	rise and decline of the Spanish Empire; Napoleonic Wars and occupation of Spain, combined with growth of liberalism in Spain, prompt independence movement	strong landed elite (*latifundistas*)/ monopolistic Catholicism and mestizo culture develop (Virgin of Guadalupe represents fusion of European colonial culture and indigenous culture)/colonial authoritarian control	mercantilism – raw material exports from colonies to Spain; finished goods imported to colonies from Spain; tight regulation over domestic colonial economy; colonial manufacturing discouraged
1820s–1876	era of the caudillos – period of political uncertainty, instability, and internecine warfare punctuated by foreign economic and military intervention; battles between Liberals and Conservatives	growth in European economic influence (primarily British and French); U.S. territorial expansion leads to war and loss of Mexican territory	geographically located strongmen seek power/ weak nationalism develops and grows/intermittent authoritarianism at national level; local caudillos rule regionally	economic chaos – political instability discourages economic investment and fosters government fiscal crises; export-led growth based on primary goods in latter period
1876–1911	Porfiriato – "liberal dictatorship" of Porfirio Díaz; expansion of middle class	direct foreign economic and military interference wanes	export agriculture and mining/ growing liberal sentiment/ centralized authoritarian rule	export-led growth – economic stability and growth prompts initial industrialization

Time Period	Regime	Global Context	Interests/ Identities/ Institutions	Developmental Path
1910–1920	Mexican Revolution – begins as succession crisis, but radicalized by lower-class social movements and leftist political ideologies; general political chaos	general non-interference in Mexican affairs, U.S. isolationist, and Britain's presence in Western hemisphere waning	geographic strongmen seek power; rise of peasantry and working class as political force/ growing socialist/ redistributive sentiment/ intermittent dictatorial rule	economic chaos – economic activity severely limited by political chaos
1920–1982	state-led corporatism – one-party rule based on incorporation of social groups into government structure; creation of extensive patronage networks	growing U.S. influence in Latin America; Great Depression and movement toward economic openness among industrialized nations	labor, peasantry, and large business closely integrated with state/ corporatism/highly centralized state and one-party rule	"Mexican Miracle" and import-substitution industrialization; restriction of imports of manufactured finished goods; increasing government intervention in economy
1982–2000	decline of corporatism – movement toward greater political openness and party competition; rise of civil society; new model of governance still uncertain	Third World debt crisis and end of Cold War	rise of bureaucratic *técnicos* and decline of influence of labor and peasantry/ disillusionment with one-party rule and corporatism/ gradual decay of one-party rule; opposition parties begin to win local elections	neoliberalism – promotion of free trade (NAFTA) and less government regulation of economy

(continued)

Table 9.1   *(cont.)*

Time Period	Regime	Global Context	Interests/ Identities/ Institutions	Developmental Path
2000– present	continued growth of multiparty democracy and decline of the once-dominant PRI	increased globalization and competition from Asian countries; immigration to United States becoming a hotly contested issue	non-PRI parties show continued success in local and federal elections	continuation of free market policies although state continues to play large role in economy

BIBLIOGRAPHY

Bulmer-Thomas, Victor. *The Economic History of Latin America since Independence.* Cambridge: Cambridge University Press, 1994.

Camp, Roderic Ai. *Politics in Mexico: The Democratic Transformation.* Fourth edition. New York: Oxford University Press, 2002.

Cardoso, Eliana, and Ann Helwege. *Latin America's Economy: Diversity Trends and Conflicts.* Cambridge, MA: MIT Press, 1992.

Chand, Vikram K. *Mexico's Political Awakening.* Notre Dame, IN: University of Notre Dame Press, 2001.

Cothran, Dan A. *Political Stability and Democracy in Mexico: The "Perfect Dictatorship"?* Westport, CT: Praeger, 1994.

Eckstein, Susan. *The Poverty of Revolution.* Princeton, NJ: Princeton University Press, 1988.

Eisendstadt, Todd A. *Courting Democracy in Mexico: Party Strategies and Electoral Institutions.* Cambridge: Cambridge University Press, 2004.

Fuentes, Carlos. *A New Time for Mexico.* Berkeley: University of California Press, 1997.

Gill, Anthony. "The Politics of Regulating Religion in Mexico: The 1992 Constitutional Reforms in Historical Context." *Journal of Church and State* 41, no. 4 (1999): 761–794.

Gill, Anthony, and Arang Keshavarzian. "State Building and Religious Resources: An Institutional Theory of Church-State Relations in Iran and Mexico." *Politics and Society* 27, no. 3 (1999): 430–464.

Grayson, George W. *Mexico: From Corporatism to Pluralism?* Fort Worth, TX: Harcourt Brace, 1998.

Hamilton, Nora. *The Limits of State Autonomy.* Princeton, NJ: Princeton University Press, 1982.

Hansen, Roger D. *The Politics of Mexican Development*. Baltimore: Johns Hopkins University Press, 1971.

Meyer, Michael C., and William L. Sherman. *The Course of Mexican History*. Fourth edition. New York: Oxford University Press, 1991.

Middlebrook, Kevin J. *The Paradox of Revolution: Labor, the State, and Authoritarianism in Mexico*. Baltimore: Johns Hopkins University Press, 1995.

Morris, Stephen D. *Political Reformism in Mexico: An Overview of Contemporary Mexican Politics*. Boulder, CO: Lynne Rienner, 1995.

Ruvio, Luis, and Susan Kaufman Purcell, eds. *Mexico under Fox*. Boulder, CO: Lynne Rienner, 2004.

Skidmore, Thomas E., and Peter H. Smith. *Modern Latin America*. Fourth edition. Oxford: Oxford University Press, 1995.

Wiarda, Howard J. "Toward a Framework for the Study of Political Change in the Iberic-Latin Tradition: The Corporative Model." *World Politics* 25 (1973): 206–235.

Womack, John, Jr. *Zapata and the Mexican Revolution*. New York: Vintage Books, 1970.

IMPORTANT TERMS

cabildos – town councils established during the colonial period that served as the basis for the independence movement.

caciques – political bosses who control local government and are relatively autonomous from the federal government. Co-opting these individuals has been a main concern in the centralization of political authority in Mexico.

Felipe Calderón Hinojosa – the second non-PRI president elected since the 1920s. Calderón is a member of the PAN (National Action Party) and committed to a pro-business, market-oriented economic platform.

Lázaro Cárdenas – president of Mexico from 1934 to 1940. He was responsible for institutionalizing the corporatist form of government and bringing labor, agricultural workers, and industry under the control of the state.

caudillos – political strongmen during the 1800s who frequently controlled their own armies and dominated local politics. Their presence made centralized political authority difficult to establish during the nineteenth century and led to decades of political instability.

Conservatives – loose-knit political party during the 1800s that represented the interests of the agricultural sector while being opposed to industrialization and democratic reforms.

Constitution of 1917 – constitution of the Mexican Revolution that promoted radical agrarian reform and workers' rights. It would become the legal basis for Lázaro Cárdenas to redistribute land and nationalize Mexico's oil industry.

corporatism (Mexican) – an ideology derived from medieval Catholic thought that sees the polity as an organic whole and seeks to minimize social conflict via central government organization of competing interests in society. In its institutionalized form, the government organizes and directs urban and rural labor unions as well as professional organizations.

criollos – individuals of pure-blooded Spanish heritage born in Mexico. The economic and political elite tend to be from this racial class.

Democratic Revolutionary Party (PRD) – a leftist political party formed after the 1988 presidential election by defectors from the PRI in order to offer an electoral alternative to the dominant party.

dinosaurios – a faction of the ruling PRI Party in the last two decades of the twentieth century. Its members want to maintain corporatist forms of economic and political organization.

ejidos – communal farms that originated in pre-Columbian indigenous societies and were promoted in the 1917 constitution. Lázaro Cárdenas established a number of them during the late 1930s as a way of distributing land among indigenous populations and poor farmers (found mostly in southern Mexico).

Vincente Fox – victor of the 2000 presidential election from the PAN (National Action Party) and a former businessman. The first candidate from an opposition party to win the presidency since the Mexican Revolution.

import-substituting industrialization (ISI) – the dominant economic policy of Mexico from the 1930s to the early 1980s, designed to industrialize the nation. According to this general economic strategy, high import tariffs are imposed to stimulate domestic production of consumer goods.

Institutional Revolutionary Party (PRI) – the dominant ruling party of Mexico since the 1920s. Although it originated as a center-left party, it has drifted toward the center-right since the 1980s.

Benito Juárez – a liberal reformer in the mid-1800s who sought to promote land reform, centralize political authority, and modernize Mexico.

La Reforma – a period in Mexican political history (circa 1855–1876) during which liberal political forces predominated over their conservative rivals and began implementing economic and political reforms designed to bring Mexico closer to the policies and forms of government of the United States and Northern Europe. This represented the first time since the end of colonialism that a consistent governmental plan appeared, even though this era was beset by civil war and a foreign occupation.

Liberals – a loose-knit political party during the 1800s that represented urban interests and promoted increased trade ties with Northern Europe and the United States.

Antonio López de Santa Anna – the most important caudillo in Mexico during the nineteenth century, who intermittently served as president.

Mestizos – individuals of mixed Spanish and indigenous heritage. They represent the mingling of two different cultures into a distinct Mexican identity.

Mexican Miracle – a period from 1940 to the 1980s (with the apogee from 1950 to 1970) wherein rapid industrialization promoted high levels of economic growth and improved living standards. This era gave rise to a new middle class with rising expectations that were restricted by the government's inability to satisfy these demands during the last two decades of the twentieth century.

Mexican Revolution – the period from 1910 to 1920 wherein a major civil war among various factions eventually led to a set of radical social programs, namely labor rights and land reform, being included in the Constitution of 1917 and eventually implemented under Lázaro Cárdenas during the 1930s.

National Action Party (PAN) – a center-right party established in the mid-1900s as a challenge to PRI dominance. It won some critical local elections during the 1980s and 1990s that pushed Mexico toward greater political liberalization.

neoliberalism – a policy that emphasizes free trade, privatization of industry, and a reduction in government intervention in the economy. This strategy was pursued by Presidents Salinas and Zedillo during the 1980s and 1990s.

North American Free Trade Agreement (NAFTA) – an international treaty that lowered trade barriers among Mexico, the United States, and Canada. The centerpiece of President Salinas's neoliberal economic strategy, it was implemented on January 1, 1994, the same day that the Zapatista National Liberation Army initiated its guerrilla insurgency.

pan o palo – literally meaning "bread or club," the phrase that refers to two common forms of political power in Mexico. *Pan* (bread) denotes the use of political patronage to buy political support, whereas *palo* (club) implies the use of coercion.

Porfiriato – the period from 1876 to 1910 during which caudillo and dictatorial President Porfirio Díaz ruled Mexico. This was the first time since colonial days that Mexico was unified under central rule for a significant period; it was also a time of strong economic growth that gave rise to new social classes and, eventually, the Mexican Revolution.

Carlos Salinas de Gortari – Mexican president from 1988 to 1994. He reversed decades of corporatist and ISI policies in favor of a neoliberal economic agenda. His economic liberalization prompted calls for political liberalization at the end of the twentieth century.

técnicos – a faction within the ruling PRI that rose to prominence in the 1980s by promoting neoliberal economic reforms. Typically trained in U.S. and European universities, the members are in conflict with the *dinosaurios,* who favor corporatist policies.

Tlatelolco – site of a massacre in 1968 where more than a hundred protesters were killed by state police. The protest signaled that the long-standing legitimacy of the PRI's corporatist rule was wearing thin, especially among students and the middle class.

Virgin of Guadalupe – a symbol of Mexico's unique national identity that blends European Catholicism with indigenous images. It represents the appearance of the Virgin Mary before an indigenous boy during the colonial period and has since been used as a rallying point for Mexican nationalism.

Emiliano Zapata – the leader of a revolutionary army during the Mexican Revolution. He demanded greater rights for indigenous rural workers in southern Mexico, including a substantial land reform that eventually became a centerpiece of the 1917 constitution.

Zapatista National Liberation Army (EZLN) – a guerrilla army that appeared in the southern Mexican state of Chiapas in 1994 following the implementation of NAFTA. Like their earlier revolutionary namesake, Emiliano Zapata, the Zapatistas, as they are known, demanded land reform, economic justice, and freer political representation for the poor indigenous communities.

Ernesto Zedillo – president of Mexico from 1994 to 2000. He oversaw an extension of neoliberal reforms and promoted greater political liberalization, including the first-ever presidential primary election in Mexican history.

STUDY QUESTIONS

1. Mexico has prided itself on its unique blend of Spanish and indigenous heritages. Not only did the Spanish conquistadors adopt a number of indigenous traditions and symbols, but Spaniards and indigenous people also physically intermingled, forming a mestizo (mixed-blood) ethnic group. Nonetheless, economic and political power remains highly stratified along class lines, with criollos holding the most powerful positions, the indigenous population inhabiting the lowest economic classes, and the mestizos falling in between these two groups. Tensions among these groups spilled over most recently during the Zapatista uprising in southern Mexico, with the guerrillas being composed mostly of indigenous, non-Spanish speaking individuals. How might this ethnic/racial stratification affect the ability of Mexicans to craft a single national identity? As long as this stratification exists, is it possible to speak of "one Mexico"? What actions might the government take to alleviate the problems created by these socioeconomic and ethnic divisions?

2. Political instability was one of the main features of Mexico during the 1800s. What factors led to and exacerbated this political instability? (Consider a comparison with the United States, which won its independence from colonial powers four decades earlier.) What were the short- and long-term consequences of this era of political instability? Consider how this era both shaped the interests of various actors in society and affected the nation's political consciousness.

3. A common problem faced by political rulers during the colonial and postcolonial periods was how to govern distant geographic regions that had incentives not to obey central authority. Even today, the Mexican president has difficulty implementing policies in isolated regions, such as the state of Chiapas. Local political bosses (caciques) retain a great deal of power over local populations. How have political leaders dealt with this problem throughout Mexican history? What types of policies could the current Mexican government develop to bring local caciques in line with national policy?

4. The revolutionary Constitution of 1917 promised radical changes in land tenure and workers' rights. Many of these proposals were implemented by Lázaro Cárdenas during the late 1930s, but enthusiasm for continuing these programs has since waned. Why has this been the case? Is it possible to maintain policies that support communal farms (*ejidos*) and government-sponsored labor unions in an increasingly globalized world economy?

5. Consider the name of the Institutional Revolutionary Party. Looking at Mexico's history, why do you think this name was chosen? To what extent can a revolution be institutionalized? To what extent has the PRI remained a revolutionary force in

Mexican society? Now consider the name of the Democratic Revolutionary Party. Why do you suppose this name was chosen? If the PRD gains power, do you expect to see it evolve similarly to the PRI? Discuss.

6. Mexican corporatism brings various social actors (for example, labor, business professionals) into an officially sanctioned ruling coalition. Although guaranteeing certain privileges for these groups (for example, job security for unionized labor and subsidies for businesses), it also limits such freedoms as choosing when to strike or how to allocate capital. Discuss the advantages and disadvantages of such arrangements. Since the 1980s, there has been a move by some groups to obtain greater autonomy from the government. Why? Consider the role of the economic crisis in the 1980s and its effects on government revenue.

7. Mexico's general economic strategy from the 1930s to the 1980s (known as import-substituting industrialization) was to isolate itself from the world economy by imposing high tariffs on imported consumer goods and limiting foreign investment in the economy. Although it was successful in generating rapid economic growth in the short term, this plan has created some long-term problems. Discuss. To what extent is it possible for Mexico to isolate itself from the world economy today? What possible effects might increased economic integration (e.g., NAFTA) into the global economy have on domestic politics?

8. There is a popular saying in Mexico that describes the country as follows: "So far from God; so close to the United States." What role has the United States (and other foreign countries) played in shaping Mexican politics? How has this role changed over the past 200 years? What does NAFTA have to say about changing relationships among the countries of North America? Is the relationship between the United States and Mexico only a one-way street, or has Mexico influenced the domestic politics of its northern neighbor?

9. Both Presidents Salinas and Zedillo faced the difficult task of promoting economic growth and political democracy while maintaining the PRI in political power. What are some of the difficulties in balancing these competing interests? How has the pursuit of these different goals affected the PRI itself? To what extent does the pursuit of economic liberalization and liberal democracy conflict with Mexico's long-standing identification with a corporatist philosophy?

10. Many observers of Mexican politics argue that Mexico's transition to a liberal democracy will not be complete until there is a new party in charge of the executive branch. Consider the results of the 2000 and 2006 presidential elections. Would you agree that Mexico has made a successful transition to a stable democracy? Was the ability to overcome a controversial election, decided by 0.58 percent of the vote, an encouraging sign for the Mexican polity? Or was the 2006 election indicative of more political turmoil to come in a multiparty democracy where the executive (president) cannot garner a majority of the vote nor secure a legislative majority in the Congress? What possible institutional changes would you suggest, if any, to the Mexican political system to make it more fair, democratic, and/or stable?

INDIA

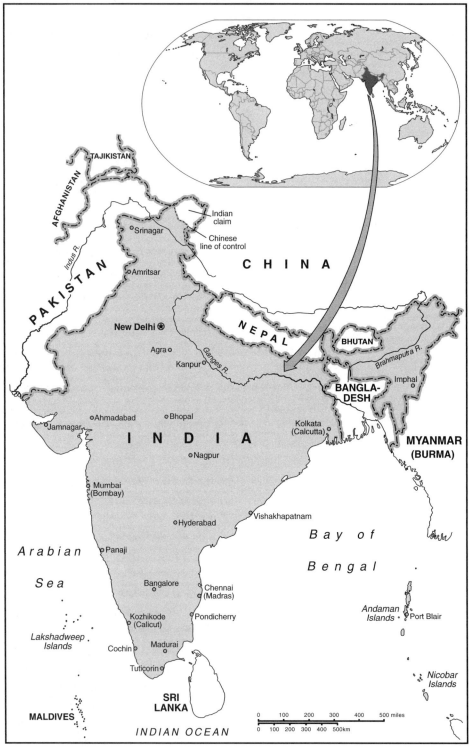

MAP 10.1. Map of India.

10 India

Rudra Sil

Introduction

For most of the period since its independence in 1947, India has been led by the Congress Party. This party, descended from the independence movement once led by Mahatma Gandhi, has been generally committed to a secular, democratic Indian nation in which members of ethnic or religious groups would equally enjoy the benefits of citizenship. Congress's main competitor, the Bharatiya Janata Party (BJP, or the Indian People's Party), descended from political and social organizations committed to redefining Indian national identity in terms of **Hinduttva** (Hindu culture and civilization). Although these parties have been sharply critical of each other and have embraced quite different stances on identity politics, both have been committed to boosting India's economic growth, facilitating India's integration into global markets, and increasing India's military capabilities and geopolitical influence. Although it was the BJP who was in power when India joined the "nuclear club" in 1998, the underground nuclear tests required years of preparation during the years when Congress had been in power. After 9/11, both BJP (until 2004) and Congress (from 2004 to 2014), despite some differences in rhetoric, supported cooperation with the United States in the "war on terror." Although Congress was more attentive to the problems of rural poverty and food security, it was difficult to discern a major shift in economic policy or in the general commitment to liberalization when the Congress-led government took over in 2004. A decade later, mounting frustration over slower growth and persistent corruption helped the BJP and its allies trounce Congress on a platform of better governance and higher efficiency. There is little reason, however, to expect any dramatic changes in policy.

This does not suggest, however, that there is unity and unanimity among India's political elites. A quick glance at India's newspapers reveals fierce battles being fought every day of every year, not only in the capital of New Delhi but also in various states and localities where parties and politicians appeared to be embroiled in unceasing confrontations on issues ranging from corruption and agricultural policy to foreign policy and defense. These battles reveal the power of long-standing identities (such as religion, language, and caste) as well as the evolution of diverse interests (among different classes, regions, and economic sectors) within a well-crafted set of institutions (consisting of federalism and parliamentary democracy) that has so far proven resilient enough to reconcile sharp differences. In part, this is because of the nature of the institutions themselves, but in part, it is because of the nature of the global forces within which all Indians have had to survive and adapt. These include the legacies of colonialism, which provided both supports and obstacles for independent India's development efforts; the geopolitical architecture of the Cold War era during which India sought to cultivate its self-image as a leader of the "Third World" while balancing elements of the market with state-centric development; and the more recent forces of globalization during which we see more fierce political contestation as well as more vigorous social movements in the midst of a push for economic liberalization.

This chapter has three main sections. The first considers the emergence of key social divides as well as a distinct civilization on the Indian subcontinent, and then discusses the establishment of British colonial rule and the rise of Indian nationalism. The second section tracks the developmental path taken by the new Indian nation from independence (1947) to the end of the Cold War (1991), while also reviewing key aspects of India's political institutions and economic approach during this period. The third section follows India into the twenty-first century, capturing the rise of a more fluid pattern of coalitional politics and a more complex interplay of identities and interests in the midst of economic liberalization and growing geopolitical ambition.

The Indian Subcontinent before Independence

The term "India" has its origins in one of the world's great ancient civilizations, the Indus Valley civilization, which reached its peak around 2500–2000 BCE in a region encompassing the northwest parts of present-day India and the southern parts of Pakistan. This civilization developed its own system of culture, language, irrigation, municipal administration, and intercity communications before going into decline by 1500 BCE. A thousand years later, a succession of empires would set out to unify the Indian subcontinent, but none would do nearly as well as the nationalist movement that would arise in response to two centuries of British colonial rule.

Historical Sources of Identity: Diversity and Unity

Following the decline of the Indus Valley civilization, newly arrived Indo-Aryan groups began to settle down across the northern half of the subcontinent. The darker-skinned Dravidians became concentrated in the southern half. Although racial differences between Indo-Aryans and Dravidians were exaggerated by British scholars writing during the period of colonial rule, many in southern India still see themselves as having separate identities and interests. These sometimes provide the basis for ethno-political mobilization in electoral politics and center-periphery relations.

The distinctiveness of Dravidians stems partially from the fact that they speak languages not derived from **Sanskrit,** the ancient language upon which most northern Indian languages are based. Each of the four main Dravidian languages now serves as an official state language in the south (for example, Telegu in Andhra Pradesh and Tamil in Tamil Nadu). The official languages of most other states derive from Sanskrit but are not always mutually intelligible and may not be spoken much outside of those states (for example, Bengali in West Bengal and Punjabi in the Punjab). Of the languages spoken across state borders, the most common is **Hindi,** the main indigenous official language. Constructed by standardizing popular local variants, Hindi is spoken by 36 percent of the population spread over several northern and central states (for example, Bihar, Haryana, and Uttar Pradesh). Another official language is English, which is a legacy of British colonial rule and is regularly used for government documents as well as many newspapers and some television shows. Muslim populations in different states often speak **Urdu,** which combines an Arabic script with vocabulary that is similar to spoken Hindi. Languages have an enduring political salience given that they provide the basis for most state boundaries within India's federal system.

Despite the linguistic diversity on the Indian subcontinent, a common civilization began to take shape in the northern and central plains in conjunction with the formation of a succession of empires. Soon after Alexander the Great's invasion stalled in India, Chandragupta Maurya founded the first major empire in South Asia in 326 BCE. His empire stretched from the Indus Valley region to all but the most southern part of the subcontinent. Subsequent periods of empire-building would consolidate political linkages between various regions to the center through tributary relationships. In the process, a recognizable Hindu culture also began to diffuse across the subcontinent. The philosophical ideas identified with Hinduism can be traced back to such texts as the *Vedas* and the *Upanishads* (written somewhere between the eighth and fifth centuries BCE). But, it is in the course of empire-building that many key Hindu beliefs and practices – including the belief in reincarnation and the rituals of *puja* (the worship of gods and deities) – spread across the Indian subcontinent, even in the south where Dravidian princes, poets, and religious scholars began to embrace Hinduism.

Caste is another key social cleavage that emerged among communities throughout the subcontinent. Although many future Indian leaders such as **Mahatma Gandhi** would reject the caste system, the fusion of religious practice and community organization over the centuries gave rise to the perception that caste is an intrinsic aspect of Hinduism. As a system for solidifying occupational hierarchies, the Indian caste system was not unlike hierarchies that emerged in Japan or Europe during the era of feudalism. What made the Indian caste system distinctive was the fact that specific occupations were ranked in terms of "purity." Priests who read sacred Sanskrit texts and performed Hindu rituals were called **Brahmins,** the "most pure" and highest-ranked caste group. Rulers, court officials, and soldiers constituted the second category in the caste hierarchy. They were followed by merchants and traders; peasants and artisans; and the "untouchables," who performed menial tasks considered most "impure." In everyday life, what really counted was membership in a subdivision (*jati*) of the broader caste categories *within a given region.* One's *jati* marked one's inherited social status, defined the roles and obligations of families, and established the pool of eligible marriage partners within a region. Although the specific rankings and occupations of each *jati* varied across regions, everywhere, there was a recognizable social and occupational hierarchy that marked individuals at birth and precluded any prospect for upward mobility or intermarriage.

Now, we turn to the emergence of the Hindu-Muslim cleavage in India. The Hindu majority accounts for more than 80 percent of the Indian population. Muslims constitute the most significant religious minority, accounting for about 12–13 percent of the population. (The remainder consists of Sikhs, Christians, Buddhists, and members of other religions.) Islam arrived on the Indian subcontinent with invading groups from the Arabian Peninsula and Central Asia. Some of these groups settled down and tried to convert local populations. A more enduring Muslim presence in India came about in conjunction with the last major empire established before British colonialism, the Moghul Empire (1526–1757) founded by Babur. Akbar, Babur's grandson, supported the establishment of new Muslim communities even as he adopted aspects of Hindu political thought, included Hindus in his court in Delhi, treated Hindu scholars with respect, and abolished many policies that discriminated against Hindus. This period of relatively peaceful coexistence between Hindus and Muslims suggests that the relationship between the two groups was not always or inherently a conflictual one.

It is also worth remembering that for all the emphasis placed on social divisions in India, a recognizable set of common experiences and practices came to be shared by many communities in different parts of the Indian subcontinent. The use of Sanskrit as a common language for priests and literati, the spread of beliefs and practices across regions, syncretic cultural forms encompassing Hindu and Muslim communities, and various waves of empire-building all helped to generate a common frame of reference for people in different parts of South Asia. This is quite different from sub-Saharan Africa, where postcolonial leaders would have to weave together new nations from tribes and ethnic groups that had very little in common beyond their shared colonial experiences.

The Period of British Colonial Rule, 1757–1947

The arrival of British traders marked the Indian subcontinent's first sustained encounter with the West. As the Moghul Empire went into decline in the late seventeenth century, the British East India Company, a large trading company backed by the British government, began to negotiate trading concessions in coastal towns such as Bombay (now Mumbai) in the west and Calcutta (now Kolkata) in the east. Local princes in these areas readily signed agreements with the British East India Company, partly to enhance their own positions vis-à-vis other provinces and the court in Delhi. However, they could not foresee the long-term consequences of the rights they were signing away. When a Bengali prince eventually recognized this and tried to push out the British East India Company, it was too late. British troops intervened and won a decisive victory at the Battle of Plassey (1757). Partly because of a lack of unity among India's provincial rulers and partly as a result of superior military technology, the British went on to easily defeat dozens of other regional princes and established military control across the subcontinent.

The result was a British colonial empire based on *indirect* rule. This system functioned through agreements with nobles who kept their titles, lands, and palaces in exchange for supporting British administrators and facilitating their economic activities. A system of *direct* rule emerged after the 1857 Sepoy Mutiny, initiated by British-trained Indian guards who were upset to discover that animal grease from pigs (hated by Muslims) and cows (sacred to Hindus) was being used in their rifles. Many Indian princes took advantage of the unrest and organized a serious campaign to regain political and economic control in their regions. After the mutiny was suppressed, a system of direct rule was established in British India (except in a few provinces that had remained loyal during the mutiny). Queen Victoria was crowned the ruler of India, a viceroy was appointed to rule India on her behalf, and British governors and local officials were appointed to maintain local order. During the next ninety years (1857–1947), the impact of British colonialism became more pronounced, as India became "the jewel in the crown" in the British Empire.

The *political* legacy of British colonialism was twofold. First, there was the establishment of a series of institutions that would be adapted for use by the Indian state following independence. One was the civil service, which assisted in the administration of the colonial state and would later provide the foundation for the Indian Administrative Service (IAS), the bureaucratic core of the modern Indian state. After World War I, the British also proceeded to establish national and regional assemblies consisting of elected representatives in order to create a semblance of legitimacy for colonial policies. Of course, these assemblies had little say over the most important policies and laws introduced by the British, but they would later form the basis for India's parliamentary democracy.

A more problematic political legacy of British colonialism is its differential treatment of various groups. For example, Hindu Brahmins, because of their generally high literacy, were recruited into the colonial bureaucracy in disproportionate numbers. This left the rest of the population – the vast majority – with few opportunities to expand their skills or join the higher echelons of administration. An even more divisive legacy was the manipulation of tensions between the Hindu majority and Muslim minority as part of a deliberate strategy of divide-and-rule. The best example is the 1905 partition of Bengal in eastern India into a predominantly Muslim eastern half (today the nation of Bangladesh) and a predominantly Hindu western half (today the Indian state of West Bengal). Although Hindus constituted 40 percent of the population in eastern Bengal and Muslims constituted 20 percent in western Bengal, the British claimed that the partition was necessary to administer the region more efficiently. Although many Muslims welcomed their new position as a majority in a separate province, most Indians saw the partition as a conscious effort to stifle a nationalist movement that was gathering steam in Bengal. Ironically, the partition would have the unintended effect of giving more impetus to a budding independence movement throughout British India.

British *economic* policies had a more widely felt impact on the interests and identities of different segments of the Indian population. Karl Marx once wrote that British colonialism was a progressive force in India because it helped to dismantle feudalism and pave the way for capitalism (a precondition for socialism). Indeed, colonial economic activities contributed to new mining and construction, the building of new factories and machinery, and the creation of a vast transportation network that included what is today one of the world's largest railroad systems. This led to the first sustained exposure for thousands of Indians to industrial labor and factory life. A small Indian middle class and working class began to expand as a result of the increase in British economic activities in India, setting the stage for class divisions that would cut across cleavages based on caste, region, or religion.

Yet, Marx may have underestimated the negative effects of British colonialism on Indian development. Over two centuries of colonial rule, the original motives that had brought the British East India Company to the subcontinent remained very much in play. Much of the infrastructure set up by the British was designed not to support industrial growth or native entrepreneurship but to facilitate the extraction of valuable resources and the transportation of British-manufactured goods to distant markets. The participation of the Indian merchants in production and distribution was controlled and restricted; for example, limits were imposed on textile production in Indian-owned factories because their products were in competition with the more expensive textiles exported by British factories. Indian workers were severely exploited as the British sought cheap labor to support their own expanding industrial empire. The increased focus on cash crops took away land and labor from subsistence agriculture, intensifying the risk of famine in some rural areas. The British also established monopolies on the sale of key necessities (even salt) in order to make the native population more dependent on the colonial apparatus. In these ways, British colonialism left behind a legacy of "misdevelopment" because its economic policies were intended to exploit local resources and force open local markets rather than to support India's native capacity for industrialization. Overcoming the effects of this legacy would be a key challenge for the postcolonial Indian economy.

The *social* impact of colonialism reached far fewer people but proved to be most relevant to the eventual demise of British rule in India. This impact was most evident among educated, urban, mostly Hindu elites who began attending British schools and universities in increasing numbers. These elites encountered new ways of life and new political ideas such as nationalism, liberalism, and socialism. By the end of the nineteenth century, this exposure had begun to influence debates among Indian intellectuals in response to British social reforms aimed at institutionalizing English common law and eliminating certain local customs (such as the practice in Rajasthan of wives throwing themselves on the funeral pyres of their husbands). Also worth noting is the use of the English language, which not only provided a means of communication among elites from different regions but also enabled these elites to express themselves articulately to foreign audiences. One of the ironies of British colonial rule is that its dependence on an English-speaking Indian elite paved the way for the emergence of a new political class that would lead the movement for Indian independence.

Nationalism and the Movement for Independence

The organization that led India to independence, the Indian National Congress (INC), was established in 1885. The founding members, the majority of whom were educated Brahmins from relatively wealthy families, did not initially challenge British rule. Their original purposes were to expand the representation of Indians *within* the British colonial administration and to debate the merits of various Hindu traditions in light of social reforms initiated by the British. However, the British rejection of even the most moderate demands, together with the outcry over the aforementioned partition of Bengal, spurred the INC to embrace the goal of independence *(swaraj)* in 1906.

The evolution of the INC into a mass movement gained steam with the arrival of Mohandas Karamchand Gandhi (referred to as "Mahatma," or "Great Soul"). Gandhi had gone to Britain to be trained as a lawyer and then spent several years attacking discriminatory British policies in South Africa. Upon his return to India in 1915, Gandhi set out to better connect the INC to the ordinary masses, often dressing like a common villager and traveling by train to document hardships and injustices across rural districts most affected by colonial rule. His philosophy emphasized the power of an inner truth shared by all people, linking this to the more universal aspects of Hinduism (such as its abstract spiritual elements), while attacking those beliefs and practices that served to divide people (such as caste). Some Hindus worried that Gandhi was diluting the status of Hindus, whereas many Muslims saw his writings as not especially relevant to Islam. Nevertheless, by emphasizing the negative consequences of British colonialism for members of all castes, regions, and religions, Gandhi drew millions of people into a mass campaign for independence.

Gandhi's strategy of nonviolent noncooperation served to attract the attention of both the rural masses and the international community. This strategy, which was partly replicated by Martin Luther King, Jr., during the U.S. civil rights movement, served two purposes. First, it disrupted British colonial administration and its economic activities, which depended on the cooperation of the native population. Second, it demonstrated to the Indian masses that their strength lay in their numbers and their will rather than in the acquisition of arms. For example, in 1920–1921, Gandhi and the INC orchestrated a major boycott of British cloth; millions of Indians burned cloth manufactured in Britain and began to wear white homespun cotton. In just one year, the value of foreign clothes imported into India was cut nearly in half. Similarly, Gandhi's "salt march" caught the attention of Indians everywhere as he led hundreds of his followers on a two-hundred-mile trek to the sea to make salt on the beaches; this was in defiance of a British law prohibiting Indians from manufacturing salt and requiring them to pay taxes on salt manufactured in factories. One major INC leader, Subhas Chandra Bose, rejected such moves as too passive and quit the INC to organize the Indian National Army to organize a military challenge to British rule in the midst of World War II. However, most INC leaders remained committed to Gandhi's strategy of nonviolence.

It is not clear whether this approach of noncooperation would have put an end to colonial rule when it did absent World War II. What is clear is that the nationalist movement made it increasingly difficult and costly for the British to maintain the existing system of colonial administration. On August 15, 1947, British colonial rule officially ended, giving way to an independent India and Pakistan. Gandhi had hoped for a unified nation encompassing all Hindus and Muslims. Some Muslims supported this view, but many others feared that a Hindu-dominated INC would ignore the interests of the Muslim minority. Mohammad Ali Jinnah, an INC member who helped found the Muslim League in 1920, insisted on a separate Pakistani nation and would become its first leader. At the same time, several Hindu organizations that once supported the INC now devoted themselves to elevating traditional Hindu ideals and symbols that they felt had been diluted by Gandhi's efforts to court Muslims. Fearing civil war, the INC agreed to a plan that would form a separate nation, Pakistan, in parts of the subcontinent where Muslims constituted a majority. During the partition, millions of people set out to find new homes across the new borders, while thousands died in bloody clashes between frustrated Hindus and Muslims. Gandhi himself was assassinated in 1948, but by then the violence had subsided. The leaders of a truncated India set out to draft a new constitution. The Indian constitution, based on principles of democratic federalism and English common law, went into effect on January 26, 1950.

Building a Nation: India's "Third Way"

For the remainder of the twentieth century, the global environment in which independent India emerged helped to shape the nation's self-image, its political system, and its approach to development. Specifically, the Cold War between the United States and the Soviet Union provided India with the opportunity to define itself as a leader in the nonaligned movement. At the same time, India's constitution and political system reflected the influence of Western doctrines and institutions. And, India's "mixed" strategy of economic development combined private entrepreneurship with a broad commitment to social justice and elements of Soviet-style central planning. Collectively, these features added up to a developmental path that Indian leaders proudly embraced as a "third way." Although regional or internal security concerns would make it difficult to maintain strict neutrality, India's generally independent foreign policy and its conscious effort to balance elements of capitalism and socialism made it a model for other postcolonial developing countries while giving Indians a sense of identity and pride in an international order dominated by the Cold War.

Secularism and Parliamentary Democracy

After independence, the Indian National Congress (INC) reconstituted itself as a powerful national political party, the Congress Party (henceforth referred to as simply "Congress"). Although the party inherited the INC's grassroots organization and regional leadership, it had lost many of its distinguished national leaders. Mahatma Gandhi was assassinated in 1948 by a Hindu fanatic. Subhas Bose, who had formed an anticolonial army in seeking to oust the British, is thought to have died in a plane crash shortly after independence. Sardar Patel, who envisioned an industrialized India in which vibrant capitalism would coexist with Hindu traditions, died of natural causes. As a result, Jawaharlal Nehru found himself to be Congress's undisputed leader and the nation's first prime minister (1950–1964). Much more so than Gandhi, Nehru embraced a vision of progress defined by rapid industrialization accompanied by the spread of literacy, science, and technology. More than Patel, Nehru sought to temper capitalism with an egalitarian ethos inspired by socialism. And more than Bose, who was partial to a strong centralized state, Nehru remained firmly committed to democratic principles and institutions. Above all, Nehru envisioned a modern India in which a secular, cosmopolitan citizenry would gradually rise above preexisting divisions based on caste, religion, and language.

"**Secularism**" usually implies that public life should be governed by the rule of law as evident in a written constitution and legal codes (and not by traditional customs, religious texts, or hereditary privileges). In the Indian context, secularism acquired an additional meaning in opposition to "communalism." Indian secularism stresses that public authority must not be identified with a dominant religious or ethnic group, and that members of all caste, religious, and linguistic groups should be treated as equal before the law and as equal stakeholders in the nation. This also implied that religious minorities and previously disadvantaged groups would be entitled to special privileges until the playing field became more level for all citizens. Thus, although the caste system was abolished by law, a system of "**reservations**" (which may be viewed as India's version of affirmative action) was instituted to help members of the lowest caste groups gain entry into educational institutions and employment. Similarly, to offset any advantages enjoyed by Hindus, who constituted 80 percent of India's population, Muslims and other religious minorities were granted special exemptions or privileges, including the right to attend religious schools and observe certain religious laws and practices.

India's political system was adapted from the British Westminster model of parliamentary democracy and has remained more or less unchanged since independence. The legislative branch is bicameral. The lower house of the parliament, the Lok Sabha, is the focus of most crucial legislative battles. Elections for the lower house are held every five years unless early elections are either called by the ruling party or necessitated by a no-confidence motion with defections depriving the ruling coalition of its majority. Of the 545 members in parliament, 543 are candidates winning a plurality of votes in single-member districts as determined by a first-past-the-post system (the candidate receiving a plurality of votes wins the seat of that electoral district). The other two are special members appointed by the president. A governing majority requires control of 272 of the 543 elected members of parliament.

The upper house of the parliament, the Rajya Sabha, consists of 250 members elected for fixed six-year terms, with one-third standing for elections every two years. Most members are elected by the parliamentary assemblies of the states and territories constituting India, but 12 are appointed by the president on the basis of special considerations or expert knowledge. Like the British House of Lords (but not the U.S. Senate), the primary function of the upper house is not to independently make laws but to approve existing laws and provide continuity and stability through changing governments. Given these functions, the Rajya Sabha can never be dissolved. The term "parliament" will be used from here on to refer to the Lok Sabha, which performs the main legislative functions.

The head of government is the prime minister. He or she is the focal point of national politics, responsible for appointing cabinet ministers, launching new initiatives or programs, and making important decisions on key domestic and foreign policy issues. The prime minister is usually the leader of the party or coalition that holds a majority in the lower house of the parliament (although **Sonia Gandhi,** the leader of Congress, opted to nominate **Manmohan Singh** to serve as the prime minister after her party's victory in 2004). The president, the head of state, is usually a nominee of the victorious party in parliament but is formally elected to a five-year term by an electoral college that gives votes to each member of parliament and weighted votes to all members of the state assemblies (to ensure reasonable representation across regions). The president often is not a career politician but an individual with significant personal accomplishments (for example, in science or literature) who is thought to stand above political conflicts as a symbol of unity and order throughout the republic. Often, the president has been drawn from groups that are somehow underrepresented; of the thirteen presidents to date, three were Muslims, three were originally from southern states, one was Sikh, and one was a woman. Table 10.1 lists the prime ministers and presidents of India to date.

The first-past-the-post electoral system is used at both the national and state levels. This means that a larger, better-organized party can convert narrow margins in popular votes nationwide into a disproportionately large share of seats in the parliament or the state assembly. In the course of the system's first four decades, only Congress was sufficiently large and organized to be able to benefit from this. In six of the first eight national elections, Congress managed to capture from about two-thirds to three-quarters of the seats in the national parliament without once gaining a majority of the popular vote (see Table 10.2). During this period, Congress also controlled the state assemblies in most states. This led to the characterization of India's political system as a "**dominant-party system,**" with the Congress Party holding sway over national politics over a period of several decades while several smaller national or regional parties acted as "parties of pressure" to lobby Congress leaders or mobilize public opposition to particular policies.

India's dominant-party system should not be seen as a variant of authoritarianism or semi-authoritarianism. Elections came to be contested by an increasing number of parties; the parties were free to embrace vastly different ideologies and platforms; leadership transitions were generally orderly, with losers willing to accept defeat; and the rule of law was upheld for most of India's existence as an independent republic (with the exception of the eighteen-month "**Emergency**" in 1976–1977, to be discussed later in the chapter). Congress leaders did not undertake any initiatives or institutional reforms that might lock in their hold on power even as more parties began to challenge or pressure them. In addition, many of the smaller national parties and several regional parties eventually became large and organized enough to be able to incrementally weaken Congress's hold on national politics. This process began with the Congress losing control of several state assemblies during the late 1960s and 1970s. Then in 1977, Congress experienced its first defeat in national parliamentary elections at the hands of an unwieldy opposition coalition. By the 1990s, it was clear that Congress could no longer count on its organizational machine to guarantee control of the parliament. Even if it did return to power a number of times, its ability to rule depended increasingly on the formation of alliances and coalitions.

It is worth noting that this shift neither constituted a regime change nor resulted from electoral reforms or institutional transformations. It was simply a function of the steady growth of other parties, some of which became especially powerful in certain states and managed to capture both the state assembly as well as a solid block of seats in the parliament. These eventually reduced Congress's share of seats and its own internal unity, as more and more Congress representatives from different states had to fight off challengers and make locally specific appeals to preserve their core constituencies. These facts suggest that the early dominance of Congress in Indian politics was simply the result of the initial organizational and reputational advantages the party enjoyed as the successor to the mass independence movement once led by Gandhi.

Table 10.1 Leaders of India, 1950–Present

Prime Minister** (Head of Government)	President (Head of State)
1950–1964: Jawaharlal Nehru, Congress [1]	1950–1962: Rajendra Prasad
1964–1966: Lal Bahadur Shastri, Congress [1]	1962–1967: Sarvapalli Radhakrishnan
1967–1977: Mrs. Indira Gandhi, Congress-I [2]	1967–1969: Zakir Hussain [1]
1977–1979: Morarji Desai, Janata Party	1969–1974: Varahagiri Venkata Giri
1979–1980: Charan Singh, Janata Party	1974–1977: Fakhruddin Ali Ahmed [1]
1980–1984: Mrs. Indira Gandhi, Congress-I [3]	1977–1982: Neelam Sanjiva Reddy
1984–1989: Rajiv Gandhi, Congress-I [4]	1982–1987: Giani Zail Singh
1989–1990: V. P. Singh, Janata Dal	1987–1992: Shri R. Venkataraman
1990–1991: Chandra Shekhar, Janata Dal	1992–1997: Shankar Dayal Sharma
1991–1996: N. P. Narasimha Rao, Congress-I	1997–2002: Shri K. R. Narayanan
1996–1997: Deve Gowda, United Front [5]	2002–2007: A. P. J. Abdul Kalam
1997–1998: Inder Gujral, United Front	2007–2012: Pratibha Patil
1998–2004: Atal Behari Vajpayee, BJP/NDA [6]	2012– : Pranab Mukherjee
2004–2014: Manmohan Singh, Congress/UPA [7]	2014– : Nardendra Modi, BJP/NDA

**Prime minister is from the party or coalition holding the majority after parliamentary elections (prime ministers in office for less than one month not included).

[1] Died in office

[2] After splits, most of Congress follows Indira Gandhi, referred to as Congress-I from 1977

[3] Assassinated while in office 1984

[4] Lost bid for re-election in 1989, but later assassinated during campaign for 1991 elections

[5] "United Front" is name taken for Janata Dal and allies in 1996–1998

[6] BJP-led alliance of parties called "National Democratic Alliance" (NDA)

[7] Congress-I renamed Indian National Congress, heads "United Progressive Alliance" (UPA)

India's founders also adopted an independent judiciary headed by a national Supreme Court. This body consists of a chief justice and twenty-five justices who are formally appointed by the president but are usually chosen by the prime minister in consultation with sitting members of the court. As in the United States, the Indian court's main purpose is to interpret the constitution and ensure civil liberties. However, its prerogative of judicial review has been limited in certain areas thanks to constitutional amendments passed by the parliament. Notable among these is Amendment 42 (1976), which prohibits the court from reviewing

Table 10.2   Congress Party's Share of Votes and Seats, 1952–1991 (without coalition partners or allies)

Year	Popular Vote (%)	Seats in Parliament (%)
1951	45	74
1957	48	75
1962	46	73
1967	41	54
1971	44	68
1977*	35	29
1980	43	65
1984	49	76
1989**	39.5	36
1991***	37	45

* 1977 elections held after ending of "emergency rule" declared by Indira Gandhi in 1976; Janata party coalition forms government 1977–1980.

** Congress, led by Rajiv Gandhi, wins more popular votes than any one opposition party, but Janata coalition secures majority to form government.

*** Congress gets even less of the popular vote than it did in 1989, but because of a more fragmented opposition, gains 45 percent of seats and obtains outside support to set up a ruling majority.

changes introduced by other constitutional amendments. The high courts must also fend off pressures from powerful politicians and economic elites, especially at the state level. But, this is also true of courts in other democratic settings. For the most part, compared with courts in other postcolonial settings, India's courts have functioned in a generally fair manner and have managed to safeguard the basic spirit of the constitutional and legal order.

Nehru's Successors and the Fading of Congress Dominance

After Nehru's death in 1964, Lal Bahadur Shastri emerged as the new leader of Congress and served as the next prime minister of India. However, his untimely death in 1966, just two years into his term, left Congress scrambling again to identify a new leader who could lead it to victory in the 1967 elections. That leader turned out to be Indira Gandhi, the Oxford-educated daughter of Nehru (and wife of Feroz Gandhi, who was not directly related to Mahatma Gandhi). As Nehru's daughter, Indira was viewed as an asset to the Congress in new elections scheduled, but the party bosses mainly expected her to behave as a figurehead following the election. In the 1967 elections, although Congress's popular support declined to 41 percent, it was able to gain 54 percent of the seats in the parliament. As leader of the majority party, Indira Gandhi was named prime minister, becoming only the second woman in the world elected to head a national government (after Sri Lankan prime minister, Sirimavo Bandaranaike).

Once in power, Indira Gandhi surprised the party bosses by announcing her own policy agenda and elevating individuals personally loyal to her at the expense of more established party elites. The rift between Indira Gandhi and the old bosses became so deep that Congress split into two distinct parties. The bulk of the party followed Mrs. Gandhi and called itself Congress-I (the "I" stood for Indira, but this party may simply be referred to as Congress). The smaller splinter, formed by the defecting party bosses, was named Congress-O (the "O" stood for the organization), and joined the opposition. Under Nehru, Congress had been able to build on the extensive organizational framework set up during the independence movement across national, state, and local levels. This infrastructure had enabled regional party bosses to deliver large **"vote banks"** (blocs of votes obtained by local party officials as a result of deals with leaders of a local caste or village community) to support Congress's continued dominance. With the departure of many of these bosses, Indira Gandhi now had to find ways to shore up her own base of support.

One strategy was evident in Mrs. Gandhi's distinctive brand of populism. This was an effort to directly appeal to the masses by emphasizing the common economic interests of the impoverished masses throughout the country. This populism took the form of promises that the central government would invest heavily in eradicating poverty on a national scale and boosting agricultural production so as to enable India to achieve self-sufficiency in food. These promises were calculated to construct what was effectively a new, larger vote bank that would rely upon the hundreds of millions of lower-class and lower-caste voters while compensating for the loss of local vote banks that regional party bosses used to deliver through leaders of particular caste or village communities. Mrs. Gandhi's populist appeals initially resonated well with voters and enabled Congress to dramatically increase its share of the popular vote and capture over two-thirds of the seats in Parliament in the 1971 elections. Extending this populism, Mrs. Gandhi would also begin to make direct appeals to Indian national pride. This was evident in the framing of protectionist policies (which targeted foreign multinationals, prompting many to leave the country) and in the cultivation of nationalistic fervor accompanying the 1971 war with Pakistan (in which India provided military support to successfully aid the secession of Bangladesh).

A second strategy Mrs. Gandhi used to shore up her political influence was her own brand of patronage politics. She set out to carefully track and recruit new party activists whose loyalty she could count on in exchange for advancement to higher ranks of the party and to key positions in government. In light of her proven ability to maintain Congress's control of the parliament and her soaring popularity following India's victory over Pakistan, Mrs. Gandhi was successful in attracting new recruits to Congress and even regaining the loyalty of some former politicians who had initially defected to the splinter party, Congress-O. What was strikingly apparent during this process was Mrs. Gandhi's active personal involvement in the appointment and promotion of party leaders. Increasingly, such personnel decisions were based not on demonstrated competence or experience in politics but on *personal* loyalty to Mrs. Gandhi. She and her advisers, including her son Sanjay, regularly reviewed personnel files to identify and reward politicians who were loyal to Mrs. Gandhi, while taking note of those who might challenge her authority within the party. Although patronage politics was nothing new to India, Mrs. Gandhi's emphasis on personal loyalty resulted in a more hierarchical web of patron-client networks centered on the prime minister and her closest advisers.

This latter approach initially worked well to shore up Mrs. Gandhi's base of support. However, it also served to alienate opponents as well as some former supporters who were troubled by her accumulation of personal power through patronage. This fed a political crisis that almost brought down India's constitutional order. In 1974, a number of opposition leaders banded together to accuse Mrs. Gandhi of corruption and campaign violations. One leader, J. P. Narayan, once a devout follower of Mahatma Gandhi, organized massive protests and even called upon the army to oust the prime minister for stepping beyond her constitutional powers. The Indian army, noted for its noninterference in civilian politics, did not see enough of a reason to intervene. But, Mrs. Gandhi felt that her opponents had gone too far, and she responded by declaring a national emergency. The next eighteen months (1976–1977), referred to simply as "the Emergency," represented the only period during which India took on certain characteristics of an authoritarian regime. Some opposition leaders were arrested for their part in the campaign to oust Mrs. Gandhi, selective censorship was introduced, and some parts of the constitution were suspended for a time. Yet, unlike typical dictators in authoritarian regimes, Mrs. Gandhi had come to power via an electoral process rather than a military coup; she did not seek to dismantle opposition parties or rewrite the constitution; and she did convene a new round of national elections as she had promised, stepping aside when her party lost.

In the 1977 election, Mrs. Gandhi had hoped that the voters would understand her actions and that Congress would retain its power by virtue of its sheer size. Instead, the voters turned their back on her while a new government was formed by an unwieldy opposition coalition known as the **Janata Party**. Just as the first-past-the-post electoral system had enabled Congress to convert small pluralities in the popular votes into a larger majority of seats, the Janata Party converted 43 percent of the popular vote into 55 percent of the seats in Parliament. The result demonstrated that Congress's previous electoral dominance was partly a result of a multiparty system in which it was usually difficult to field a unified opposition that could wrest power from Congress. At the same time, the opposition had been fragmented for a reason: its constituent parties did not share an alternative ideology or policy agenda. Some parties were on the Left, others were on the Far Right, and still others were offshoots of the original Congress. In effect, the Janata Party was little more than a loose umbrella organization for parties opposed to Indira Gandhi. This may have been sufficient to mobilize voters to defeat Congress in the specific context following the Emergency. It was not sufficient, however, to promote an alternative program of national development and end Congress electoral dominance for good. As a result, the 1980 elections saw Indira Gandhi stage a spectacular comeback, with Congress capturing 65 percent of the seats in parliament.

Following her return to power, Mrs. Gandhi sought to consolidate her political base by more frequently incorporating Hindu nationalist themes. She was still officially committed to her father's vision of a modern secular India, but she also needed new ways to boost her personal appeal among as large a segment of the Indian population as possible. Wedding familiar Hindu symbols and ideals to Indian nationalism was one way to do this. However, it also triggered fears among India's religious minorities, giving impetus to a militant movement for greater autonomy in the Punjab (where there was a Sikh majority). In her efforts to quell militants seeking an independent "Khalistan," Mrs. Gandhi ordered the army to storm the Sikh Golden Temple at Amritsar (where militants had holed up). This sparked violent Hindu-Sikh riots and provided the main motivation for her assassination at the hands of her own Sikh bodyguards on October 31, 1984.

Following Indira Gandhi's death **Rajiv Gandhi,** her elder son, reluctantly agreed to lead Congress (his younger brother, Sanjay, was being groomed for this role but had died in a plane crash). Rajiv Gandhi led his party to a landslide victory in the 1984 elections as it captured over three-quarters of the seats in Parliament. The results appeared to point to the continuing strength of both Congress dominance and the Nehru dynasty (which had now provided three generations of leaders). At the same time, Congress's electoral landslide in 1984 was partly the result of a massive wave of sympathy following Mrs. Gandhi's death. By 1989, Rajiv's government was undermined by a massive corruption scandal that allegedly reached into the highest levels of his cabinet. Congress's huge parliamentary majority allowed it to serve out its full five-year term, but it was unable to retain power in the 1989 elections. Although no other single party won more seats in those elections, Congress's opponents banded together once more under the rubric of the Janata Party and managed to form a ruling coalition with the backing of several smaller parties. Congress was swept out of power for only the second time since independence. The new Janata coalition, like the one that had come to power in 1977, suffered from too many tensions and was unable to maintain its ruling coalition, resulting in new elections in 1991.

In those elections, Rajiv himself was assassinated while campaigning in the south. He was killed by a suicide-bomber sent by the Tamil Tigers (who were fighting for more autonomy in Sri Lanka, but were angry at India for not backing them). Once again a wave of sympathy helped Congress bolster its appeal. Even so, it captured only 45 percent of the seats in the parliament and required support from other parties to form a ruling majority under Prime Minister **Narasimha Rao**, the first Congress leader in twenty-five years who was not from the Nehru dynasty. Thus, although Congress did regain power in 1991, this election may be regarded as the point at which the dominant-party system came to an end. We shall see in the next section how the basic dynamics of electoral politics in India have shifted since that election.

Indian Federalism and Center-Periphery Relations

Consistent with the views expressed by James Madison and Alexander Hamilton in *The Federalist Papers,* India's founding leaders (most notably, Prime Minister Nehru and B. R. Ambedkar, chair of the committee that drafted India's constitution) opted for a federal structure that balanced states' rights with a strong center that could maintain national unity and promote social change. Unlike the United States, however, state boundaries in India were set up by the 1956 States Reorganization Act to coincide with regions dominated by particular linguistic groups. Nehru viewed this approach as reinforcing the provincial attitudes of Congress's regional bosses, but he went along with the plan because he expected such attitudes to fade as the central government took the lead in modernizing India. Yet, by linking state boundaries to ethno-linguistic identity, the States Reorganization Act also allowed for situations where contending interests of states would be intensified by cleavages based on linguistic identities even as other identities (such as caste) cut across state boundaries. Moreover, new claims would later emerge among smaller ethno-linguistic groups seeking to carve out separate states within some of the original states. This accounts for why the fourteen states and six territories set up in the 1956 States Reorganization Act has now grown to twenty-nine states and seven territories (with the latest state, Telengana, recently carved out of Andhra Pradesh after a fierce, often chaotic political struggle).

At the state level, the main institutions of governance are roughly similar to those at the national level. There is a state high court, a state assembly, a chief minister (head of government and leader of the ruling majority in the assembly), and a governor (the official head of the state). Unlike the nation's president, however, state governors are not nominated by the leading party in the state assembly but are instead appointed by the Indian president (usually following the suggestion of the nation's prime minister). This is done to ensure that public order, the rule of law, and the constitution are upheld at the state level, but this is just one of several measures through which the Indian constitution, more so than the U.S. constitution, seeks to ensure the unity of the nation and the primacy of the central government vis-à-vis states. In part, this emphasis on national unity was understandable in view of the conflicts that were activated throughout India immediately upon independence. For example, Hindu-Muslim riots broke out with the creation of Pakistan; the latter then laid claim to the Muslim-majority province of Kashmir (which India views as an integral part of one of its states, Jammu & Kashmir); and there were nascent secessionist movements and inter-state rivalries to cope with.

Crafted in such an environment, India's constitution formally treats the Union as indestructible. It also gives the national parliament the power to alter the boundaries of its constituent units, a power that would be used to carve out more state and territorial units. Moreover, the constitution allows for "**President's Rule**" (Article 356) when serious disturbances are reported by a state's governor. Since independence, the article has been invoked on dozens of occasions, sometimes for valid reasons but sometimes on shaky grounds for the purpose of ousting uncooperative state legislatures. Also, unlike the federal system in the United States, where residual powers are left to states, India's central government retains the residual powers of legislation and can preempt any state legislation that contradicts a parliamentary act or federal law. Collectively, these provisions aim to ensure the survival of the nation-state as an integral whole.

At the same time, the division of labor between the central and state governments is not very different from federal arrangements in other countries. The central government enjoys certain prerogatives, as specified by the constitution on what is called the "Union List." These include: defense, foreign policy, currency, inter-state commerce, major infrastructure projects, and collection of income taxes along with budget transfers to states. The state government enjoys certain prerogatives, as specified on what is called the "State List." These include the management of law and order, agricultural and land policy, public health, separate state taxes based on wealth, and the administration of local municipalities and districts (this last function would be amended in 1992, as discussed later on in the chapter). There is also a "Concurrent List" that includes educational policy, the coordination of electrical power, and price controls. The latter two lists suggest that, despite the emphasis on preserving the authority of the center, Indian states had more leeway than states in many other federal systems in pursuing their own policies in certain key domains. This resulted in significant variation across states in such areas as the extent of growth rates, land reform, effective tax rates, and educational programs and standards.

India's linguistic state boundaries, local caste and religious identities, and electoral system have combined to produce three broad forms of political mobilization at the subnational level. The most challenging of these are in those few areas where a non-Hindu group constitutes a majority within a state and seeks greater autonomy, if not full independence. This is evident in the state of Punjab (where Punjabi-speaking Sikhs constitute 51 percent of the population); in the state of Jammu and Kashmir (which encompasses the disputed area of Kashmir, where a Muslim majority is split on whether to join Pakistan, seek independence, or secure greater autonomy within India); and in the northeastern region of India (which is economically underdeveloped and inhabited by tribal populations that feel neglected by the center). Since the time of Nehru, the central government has encouraged political parties in these areas in the hopes that they would channel secessionist impulses into organized participation in political institutions and formal bargaining processes. Nevertheless, violence has flared up at different points in time in all of these areas. Conflicts in the Punjab reached a peak during the 1980s but have largely subsided now; conflicts in the northeast have been sporadic in the past but have been gaining in significance; and conflicts in Kashmir have been a persistent problem that has become more complicated by the support some Muslim separatists have received from Pakistan and/or groups linked to Al-Qaeda.

More common in India is a second pattern where regional political parties are formed for the purpose of advancing the distinctive interests of the dominant ethno-linguistic group within a given state. This dynamic is most common in the southern states, where much of the population is identified as Dravidian and where the main state languages (e.g., Tamil and Malayalam) are distinct from those languages with roots in Sanskrit (e.g., Bengali, Gujarati, Marathi). For example, two major parties have dominated politics in the state of Tamil Nadu since the 1960s: the Dravida Munnetra Kazhagam (DMK) and its splinter party, the All-India Anna DMK (AIADMK). These parties can be traced back to a powerful regional movement during the 1940s and 1950s that aimed at reducing the influence of northern (Indo-Aryan) culture in southern India and even called for an autonomous state of "Dravidastan." More recently, the Telegu Desam Party, formed in the early 1980s, has sought to promote the interests and advancement of Telegu-speaking people, mainly in the state of Andhra Pradesh. For the most part these parties, after initially trying to leverage secessionist sentiments, have focused on controlling their respective state assemblies and bargaining with national parties (such as Congress) for more influence and resources for their states.

The third pattern of center-periphery politics involves regional branches of a national party behaving as advocates of groups in a particular state where the party has enjoyed electoral success. One example of this pattern is the **Communist Party of India** (**Marxist**), or CPI-M, which gained a majority in the West Bengal state assembly in 1977 and was able to retain that majority for over three decades. Although the party originally emphasized socialist programs such as land reform and working-class mobilization, the CPI-M's long-term success in the state was made possible in part by its stance as a steadfast defender of Bengali interests within the nation. In addition, as Congress's initial clout declined, regional branches of national parties began to split off to form separate parties aiming to cater to the interests of a large bloc of voters in a particular state. For example, the Samajwadi Party in Uttar Pradesh broke away from the national Congress party and gained influence by forging local alliances and appealing to specific caste constituencies within the state. In sum, India's political institutions, in combination with a wide-ranging set of social identities and political elites' interests, have generated both centrifugal forces (among those trying to resist the authority of the center) and centripetal forces (among those whose attention is focused on the center as they seek to improve the bargaining positions of their states and localities).

Economic Development, 1950s–1990s: From State-Led Industrialization to Economic Liberalization

On the economic front, India's development strategy was set in motion by Nehru in a global context featuring two competing economic systems promoted by the two Cold War adversaries (U.S.-led capitalism and Soviet-led socialism). India's national economic goals and the strategy for pursuing these were shaped by both the achievements of innovative capitalist firms in the West and the dramatic leaps in technology and industrial production engineered by central planners in the USSR. This led to the emergence of what might be termed a "mixed" strategy of state-led development.

As part of this strategy, the principle of private property was respected, and private economic activity was encouraged in some sectors. But, half of the gross domestic product (GDP) was, by design, accounted for by a large public sector managed according to Soviet-style "five-year plans." This public sector, consisting of thousands of large state-owned factories, was mainly concentrated in heavy industry (that is, the large-scale extraction or production of major industrial goods along with massive infrastructure projects such as coal mining, power stations, dams, railroads, and so forth). Private firms were selectively authorized to participate in heavy industrial production, but most tended to be concentrated in the production of agricultural and consumer goods. Moreover, both public and private sectors were protected and regulated by the Indian government so that their activities could be coordinated for broader national objectives while also being shielded from competition with multinational firms from more advanced industrial countries.

This strategy was linked to an assumption about the basic structure of the international economy. The assumption was that, because colonial economies were predicated on the exploitation of cheap labor and primary commodities (rather than efforts to support entre-preneurship and boost industrial manufacturing), it had left behind an economy that was fundamentally incapable of becoming internationally competitive without some degree of state intervention. Even if a laissez-faire approach were desirable over the long-term, the playing field immediately after decolonization was thought to be too uneven to allow India or other postcolonial countries to catch up economically to its former colonizers through free trade. The only possibilities for economic progress depended on state coordination of industrialization coupled with some protection from foreign multinationals. These ideas essentially anticipated the strategy of "import-substitution industrialization" that would proliferate across much of the postcolonial world during the late 1960s and 1970s.

Under Nehru, India's approach to development did enable native industrialization to take off as large industrial houses and state enterprises became well established in a matter of a few years. Yet, in spite of Nehru's personal commitment to improving the lot of the lower classes, the priority given to heavy industry neither helped to reduce poverty and inequality nor brought tangible benefits to the working masses. Even more problematic was the contin-ually low level of investment in the agricultural sector, which left millions of villagers peril-ously close to the threshold of subsistence. As a result, when droughts struck during the early 1960s, there was no mechanism for redirecting surplus grain to rural districts facing mass starvation or even famine. In light of these problems, Nehru's successors were forced to make some adjustments, albeit still within the framework of "mixed development."

First, a new consensus emerged on the imperative of eliminating chronic food scarcity for India's rapidly growing populace. In 1965 the government set up the "**public distribu-tion system**," a network of thousands of shops through which surplus grain from high-yield agricultural regions would be redistributed throughout the country at controlled prices to be monitored by state governments. This system played a major role in alleviating the prob-lem of hunger throughout rural India, and it became an entrenched component of India's agricultural policy over the next three decades. In fact, the program has been credited with ensuring a level of food security that would allow for Indian leaders to later pursue other economic objectives; and the scaling back of this program in recent years is thought to be one reason some of India's poorer farmers have suddenly found themselves in a precarious position even as the country's economy began to grow at an impressive rate.

The other part of the solution was India's "**green revolution.**" Under Indira Gandhi, the government encouraged the use of new varieties of seed, new methods of fertilization, and new techniques of crop rotation. Although the green revolution targeted regions with good soil and irrigation and tended to benefit relatively wealthy farmers, the total increase in agricultural production was dramatic and made India self-sufficient for the first time. Although the green revolution and the public distribution system did not put an end to poverty and malnutrition, the combination of the two measures did help to sharply reduce chronic hunger by greatly raising food production and guaranteeing access to cheap food-stuffs for poorer citizens nationwide. Between 1965–1966 and 1983–1984, India's food pro-duction more than doubled from 72 million tons to over 150 million tons.

A second set of changes was evident in increased state control over the economy, mani-fested in greater protectionism and greater regulation of the private sector. With developing countries becoming a dominant majority in the United Nations by the early 1970s, India joined a group of seventy-seven such countries (G-77) that passed a United Nations resolution calling for a "new international economic order." Although it was not enforceable, the document reflected the proponents' common view that free trade would effectively perpetuate the exploitation of former colonies unless protectionist measures were allowed to boost native manufacturing capabilities and create a level playing field. In keeping with the spirit of this movement, Indian banks and some key firms were nationalized, and new restrictions were imposed on multinational corporations, prompting many to leave. Moreover, the domestic private sector came to be more thoroughly regulated through the expansion of the "**license raj,**" the bureaucratic practice of requiring private firms with assets above a certain threshold to secure a government license to manufacture, export, or import goods in several key sectors. These measures were designed to protect Indian firms from foreign competition and boost native industrial production, but they also increased the government's leverage over large private-sector firms, benefiting some while stifling others.

Between the 1950s and 1980s, India's strategy of mixed development did not generate the sort of rapid growth seen among East Asian newly industrialized countries during the same period. Given its burgeoning population, India's per capita GDP growth rate remained low. With economic pressures mounting, corruption became a more serious problem. Bribery became a part of everyday life, and government funds for special programs often ended up in the pockets of local officials. The license raj also facilitated large-scale corruption, enabling those who were politically connected or willing to offer bribes to obtain licenses more expeditiously, while others faced endless delays caused by bureaucratic red tape. There was little incentive for established firms protected by the government to become more efficient while the high cost of entry stifled the proliferation of newer firms that were potentially more innovative. Among the working class, organized workers in the public sector had secure jobs whereas most other workers continued to toil under poor working conditions for low wages. Poverty was still widespread, with nearly half the rural population officially considered below the poverty level. Sharp differences also emerged between states and regions in levels of growth, poverty, and literacy.

Yet, it is important to bear in mind that the economic legacies of colonialism, the limited pool of entrepreneurs and managers in the early going, and the initial advantages enjoyed by firms from advanced industrial countries, all combined to make it difficult for most postcolonial nations to achieve any dramatic results during the first decades after independence. Against this background, India's mixed economy did make some important strides that should not be ignored, especially as they may have helped provide a platform for subsequent improvements in economic growth.

Between 1950 and 1990, the real gross domestic product (GDP) gradually went up fivefold, and the average annual rate of growth increased with each passing decade. During the 1980s, India's GDP grew at an annual rate averaging 5.5 percent. The industrial sector as a whole grew at a rate of 6.6 percent. In the first four decades since independence, coal production went up fourfold, steel production went up more than six fold, and electricity generation rose more than twentyfold. There were also significant improvements in health and literacy. Average life expectancy rose from under forty years in 1950 to nearly sixty years in 1990. During the same period, the literacy rate rose from 18 percent to over 50 percent. Although India received some foreign aid, the per capita rate of borrowing was much lower than in other developing countries, and foreign debts were generally repaid as scheduled. Given the more rapid growth accompanying liberalization since the 1990s, one might argue that much more could have been achieved during the 1950–1990 period with less government intervention and more open markets. At the same time, this recent period of growth might not have been possible at all without first solving the problem of food scarcity, establishing a secure base for domestic manufacturing, chalking up marked improvements in basic health and literacy, and keeping foreign debt in check.

Nevertheless, by the end of the 1980s, pressures for economic liberalization began to mount as developing countries throughout Asia, Africa, and Latin America scaled back state-led industrialization and opted for market-oriented reforms. The demise of communism in Eastern Europe accelerated the pace of trade liberalization and privatization in many more countries, while increasing the competition for foreign investment. For many heavily indebted countries, cutbacks in government spending and progress on market reforms were conditions for "structural adjustment" loans from the World Bank and the International Monetary Fund. India did not face the same sense of internal crisis or the same level of external pressures as did the more heavily indebted developing countries. As a result, there was neither as much urgency in pushing market reforms nor as much stringency in the conditions established by international financial institutions. Nevertheless, a new consensus began to form among India's economic elites and policy makers that further liberalization was desirable, indeed unavoidable, if India was going to get ahead of, or at least keep up with, the rest of the developing world.

The first signs of this emerging consensus can be traced to changes in the licensing system under Rajiv Gandhi. The government raised the asset threshold that determined whether a company needed a government license, and then permitted companies with licenses to manufacture certain products to produce upgraded versions of those products without having to acquire a new license. In effect, this meant that there were now fewer barriers to entry for new firms and that a wider range of existing companies could now expand their activities without going through the long and corrupt process of obtaining a license. The Janata government of 1989–1991, although an ardent critic of Congress, also contributed to the consensus in favor of liberalization, linking its attack on corruption to a critique of the government's role in the economy. The most decisive turn, however, came when Congress returned to power in 1991 under the leadership of Narasimha Rao. Licensing requirements were further relaxed to allow for the growth of the private sector, and imports were liberalized more significantly. New initiatives were launched to attract more foreign investment to India, particularly in the service sector. Even state governments under leftist parties (for example, West Bengal) had to embrace more business-friendly policies in order to attract investment and compete with neighboring states. These shifts did not constitute a dramatic transformation along the lines of market reforms initiated after the fall of communism in Eastern Europe. However, after four decades of state-guided development, these changes incrementally paved the way for a more sustained period of economic liberalization that has lasted into the twenty-first century.

India in the Twenty-First Century: Stable Institutions, Resilient Identities, Evolving Interests

The end of the Cold War coincided with a marked shift in the development path that India had been following since independence. Heading into the twenty-first century, India's democratic institutions have remained intact, but the dynamics within these institutions have become more fluid the rise of the BJP as a major national party, the devolution of power to the local level, and the formation of shifting alliances and coalitions involving regional parties. Economic liberalization has been accompanied by a relative high rate of growth, turning India into a more significant player in the global economy as one of the "BRIC" countries (alongside Brazil, China, and Russia). Core identities related to caste and religion remain politically salient, but the manner in which these are mobilized for political ends has been more complicated in a new political and economic environment. This environment has also engendered a wider and more diverse range of values and interests in Indian civil society, sparking new social movements and nongovernmental organizations that are making their voices heard more loudly on issues ranging from poverty and corruption to environmental degradation and the social position of women.

The Evolution of the World's Largest Democracy

Heading into the twenty-first century, the core institutions of federalism and democracy have proven to be flexible and stable in the face of new challenges brought on by a changing global environment, a large and growing population, persistent social cleavages, and continuing economic liberalization. In fact, the durability of India's political system stands in stark contrast to the political turmoil seen during the Arab Spring and the more recent crisis in Ukraine. There are, however, changes within the basic institutional framework that have reshaped the *dynamics* of politics in India.

First, there is the devolution of authority within the framework of federalism. There are now many more states within India. Given the establishment of state boundaries along ethno-linguistic lines, the carving of new states out of larger states began to gain momentum after independence. Haryana, for example, was carved out of a region within the original state of Punjab where most people spoke Hindi rather than Punjabi. Several other provinces were granted statehood during the 1970s and 1980s (such as Goa, Himachal Pradesh, and Sikkim). In the twenty-first century, this process has continued and intensified, with three new states being formed out of larger states (Chhatisgarh out of Madhya Pradesh, Uttarakhand out of Uttar Pradesh, and Jharkhand out of Bihar). More proposals are being considered on the heels of a fiercely contested move to create a separate Telengana state out of a part of Andhra Pradesh, which was finally approved by both houses of parliament in February 2014. The creation of more sub-national units (now at twenty-nine states, including Telengana, and seven union territories) has resulted in a more complex set of interactions between center and periphery. The center must now pay more attention to a larger number of actors at the state level; at the same time, some of the larger states initially established by the States Reorganization Act have been broken up into smaller units that individually have less ability to pressure the center.

In addition, *within* each of the states, there has been a more formal effort to devolve power to the local level. The **73rd and 74th constitutional amendments,** adopted in 1992, created standardized administrative divisions and elected assemblies all the way down to rural districts, villages, and municipalities. During the independence movement, Mahatma Gandhi and others had stressed the importance of local governance and self-sufficiency, but these ideas had fallen by the wayside in the process of organizing the boundaries of states within a newly independent republic. A few states had established local administrative units to handle the management of basic public services, but only West Bengal had set up elected assemblies for villages and municipalities. The 73rd and 74th amendments extended and standardized this practice, empowering villages and townships to manage local public services and make policies at the substate level, including budgetary decisions. The amendments also mandated quotas for members of the lower castes and for women in order to ensure that representation in assemblies was proportional to the makeup of the local population. Although some see this shift as a return to the ideals of grassroots participation and rural self-governance emphasized during the independence movement, others see the change in more strategic terms as it is now possible to deflect blame away from the central or state governments for local challenges or problems.

India's Westminster model of parliamentary democracy also remains intact, but the dynamics of party politics has shifted away from Congress's dominance on the national stage and toward the formation of alliances and coalitions that give smaller parties more of a role to play. Congress had twice lost elections in the twentieth century, both times when it received less than 40 percent of the popular vote and when disparate forces joined together to form an unwieldy opposition coalition. Both times (1977–1979 and 1989–1991), the coalition fell apart within two years and Congress was able to return to power relying on its well-organized party machinery. But, during the 1990s, Congress's dominance began to fade for good, and a new political party, the Bharatiya Janata Party (BJP) began to enjoy growing electoral success across several states. The BJP's rise and the politics of identity are examined in more detail later in the chapter. Here, what is significant is the manner in which the competition between Congress and BJP combined with the regional power of several smaller parties to form a new pattern of party politics based on alliances and coalitions.

In 1991, Congress again received less than 40 percent of the vote but this time managed to form the government because, first, the opposition was not as unified and, second, it was able to add the support of outside parties to control a majority of seats in parliament. Leaders of the party may not have realized it at the time, but this election was a watershed in that it marked a decisive shift not only away from the previous pattern of Congress dominance but also away from the general idea that any national party could independently form the government. This became even clearer in the 1996 elections, when neither Congress nor any other national party managed to get over 35 percent of the seats in the parliament. The two parties that sought to unseat Congress were the Janata party (which had led the coalition that briefly unseated Congress in 1977 and 1989) and the increasingly influential Bharatiya Janata Party (BJP), a Hindu nationalist party whose rise is discussed in the next section. In the end,

Table 10.3 Alliances and Ruling Coalitions in India, 1991–2009

Year	Party	Popular Vote (%)	Seats in Parliament (%)
1991	Congress	37	45 (forms government)
	BJP	20	24
	Janata	11	11
	Others	32	20
1996	Congress	29	26
	Janata & allies (UF)*	29	32 (forms government)
	BJP & allies	24	34
	Others	19	8
1998	BJP & allies*	36	46 (forms government)
	Congress & allies*	26	26
	Janata & allies (UF)*	21	18
	Others	17	10
1999	BJP & allies (NDA)*	41	55 (forms government)
	Congress and allies*	34	25
	Others	25	20
2004	Congress-led UPA*	35	40 (forms government)
	BJP-led NDA*	33	33
	Left parties**	8	11
	Others	24	16
2009	Congress-led UPA*	37	48 (forms government)
	BJP-led NDA*	25	29
	Left parties & 3rd Front**	21	15
	Samajwadi & 4th Front**	5	5
	Others	6	3

the government was formed when Congress agreed to offer support to a Janata-led "United Front" coalition so as to keep the Hindu fundamentalists of the BJP out of power. In subsequent elections, the engineering of alliances and coalitions would become a built-in feature of Indian elections (see Table 10.3). In the 2014 elections, although the BJP was able to secure a majority of seats on its own, it still went into an election with a host of alliance partners that gave the BJP much greater control of parliament for the next five years.

An **alliance** refers to a set of parties that act as a coordinated bloc in national elections, often with a candidate from only one of the allied parties running in a given electoral district. For example, if a small party that is an ally of the BJP were to have a strong candidate in a certain electoral district, then the BJP would not run its own candidate in that district and would count on the candidate from its smaller ally to support its legislative agenda. In the 1998 elections, the BJP set up a large, well-organized alliance that was able to form the ruling majority. The alliance was later solidified and formally given the name of "National Democratic Alliance" (NDA). Interestingly, among the BJP's allies were many regional parties, including the Telegu Desam Party, from Andhra Pradesh, which had historically attacked the central government for favoring the interests of northern Hindi belt states but was now backing the BJP, which owed its rise to these same states. Congress, which was a late-mover in the quest for alliances given its past dominance, managed to patch together an alliance that took only 25 percent of the seats in 1998. But, in 2004 and 2009, Congress showed that it had adapted to the new game by putting together a more organized, effective alliance under the rubric of the "United Progressive Alliance" (UPA). The UPA captured 40 percent of the seats in 2004 and 48 percent of the seats in the 2009 elections. The Congress-led UPA and the BJP-led NDA are at present the two major alliances that contend for power, although even smaller parties have begun to form alliances, as in the case of the "Third Front" alliance set up by CPI-M and other Left parties as well as the "Fourth Front" set up by several regional parties, including a few caste-based ones.

A **coalition** refers to an agreement among parties that operate independently during parliamentary elections (possibly in direct competition with each other) but decide to join a leading party's or alliance's efforts to form a ruling majority, often in exchange for cabinet positions or to keep a less desired party out of power. In the six elections since 1991, only

Table 10.3 *(cont.)*

(*) In 1996, Janata formed a "United Front" (UF) alliance in 1996, but both the leading party and the alliance as a whole were too diverse to be able to govern, staying in power for two years thanks to outside support from Congress. The BJP then formed a more successful alliance in 1998, and in the snap election called in 1999, this alliance officially took on the label of "National Democratic Alliance" (NDA). Congress was late to recognize the importance of alliances, but it did begin to seek out allies from the late 1990s onward, managing to establish a more permanent and more successful alliance under the label of "United Progressive Alliance" (UPA).

(**) By 2004, smaller parties, which previously ran independently and often had strengths only in particular states, were also ready to form alliances. Several leftist parties ran as allies in 2004 and later began to refer to their alliance as the "Third Front." The Samajwadi party also put together an alliance of regional parties in 2009 under the label of the "Fourth Front."

once did a leading party and its allies manage to secure a majority of seats (the BJP-led government of 1999); in the other five, the formation of government has only been possible with the establishment of coalitions. For example, the government formed by the Congress-led UPA in 2004, even though it outperformed the BJP-led NDA, captured only 40 percent of the seats and thus still needed the support of several other parties to form a ruling majority. Of course, coalition partners can also pull their support at times over particular issues. This was evident when the communist CPI-M, which had offered support to the Congress-led UPA government of Manmohan Singh in 2004, withdrew this support when the government opted to ratify the Indo-U.S. nuclear treaty. The government did not fall, however, as Congress was able to gain support from other parties to maintain its ruling coalition. In the 2009 elections, the Congress-led UPA managed to get 48 percent of the seats, and so needed far less outside support in order to maintain control of the parliament (see Table 10.3).

The new pattern of party politics based on coalitions and alliances means that larger parties not only have to broaden their appeal but also have to be flexible in terms of letting their local branches craft their electoral strategies based on the interests and identities of local constituencies within particular states. This is not the result of a regime transition or constitutional change. It is the result of the rise of the BJP as a serious national competitor of a Congress Party that is no longer the sole dominant party on the national scene. It is also the function of the growing strength of smaller regional parties within a multiparty parliamentary system based on single-member districts with first-past-the-post electoral rules. In fact, the proliferation of alliances and coalitions is very much intertwined with the regularized competition between two relatively large national parties, each needing a host of smaller parties to support it in order to form the central government.

The new pattern of party politics based on coalitions and alliances means that larger parties have to broaden their appeal and be flexible about working with local parties that speak to the interests and identities of local constituencies within particular states. This is not the result of a regime transition or constitutional change. It is the result of the rise of the BJP as a successful competitor of a Congress Party that is no longer the sole dominant party on the national scene. It is also the function of the growing strength of smaller regional parties within a multiparty parliamentary system based on single-member districts with first-past-the-post electoral rules. In effect, Congress and the BJP remain the two parties that are most capable of mobilizing substantial support across multiple states, whereas regionally influential parties seek to leverage their electoral strength in particular states or regions into cabinet positions.

The 1999 election results revealed that the BJP had already learned to play this new game. The party spearheaded a formal alliance – the National Democratic Alliance (NDA) – that secured control of 55 percent of the seats in parliament, even though the BJP itself only got 33 percent of the seats. In the next two elections, in 2004 and 2009, Congress showed that it had adapted to this game. In 2009, Congress secured less than 30 percent of the seats in parliament, but its own formal alliance – the United Progressive Alliance (UPA) – captured 48 percent of the seats, making it easy to then form a ruling coalition at the center. In the latter election, none of the smaller parties in Congress's UPA or BJP's NDA were able to exceed 5 percent of the parliamentary seats. Yet, the two larger parties needed most of these smaller blocks of seats in order to stake a claim to forming a ruling coalition at the center.

In 2014, frustrations with Congress ran so deep that the BJP would manage to capture a majority of seats on its own. This was the first time any one party had secured a majority of seats by itself in some 30 years. Yet, not being sure of this outcome, the BJP had formed an alliance with regional parties (such as Telegu Desam) that got it an additional block of 50 seats, resulting in control of over 62 percent of the seats in parliament. The BJP's resounding victory over Congress, whose alliance barely managed 10 percent of the parliamentary seats, is leading some to ponder whether Congress can bounce back as a national party. However, it is difficult to tell from just one election whether we are entering a new era of BJP dominance, or whether the 2014 elections reflected a surging tide of discontent that Congress could later exploit if the BJP if it fails to deliver on its many campaign promises, which included commitments to employment (millions of new jobs every year), basic needs (such as toilets in every home), and high-tech infrastructure (such as bullet trains), alongside lean government, lower corruption, and higher growth.

For its part, although Congress saw its share of seats plummet to historic lows, it still got the second largest block of seats secured by any one party, with those seats coming from constituencies in different states. Also, Congress's share of the popular vote in 2014 (19.4 percent) was actually slightly higher than the BJP's share in 2009 (18.8 percent), and the gap between the leading party and its top challenger did not rise by much: in 2014, the BJP secured 12 percent more of the popular vote than Congress, whereas in 2009, Congress received about 10 percent more of the popular vote than BJP. Also worth noting is that, in both elections, the two parties together accounted for half the popular vote, with the rest scattered among smaller national parties or parties that only campaigned in a given state to position themselves as potentially coalition partners. Thus, barring repeated electoral landslides in favor of the BJP or a total dismembering of the Congress apparatus, party politics in India is best characterized as a "bipolar" multiparty system in which many parties exist but only two are strong enough across regions to act as "poles" around which ruling coalitions can be formed.

Economic Liberalization in a Global Age: Growth, Problems, Prospects

The transformation of India's economy has not been as dramatic as that of postcommunist countries in Eastern Europe, and it has not produced growth rates as high as those of China. Nevertheless, India's economic liberalization has proceeded steadily since the early 1990s, and India's GDP as well as the annual rate of economic growth have both increased dramatically (see Table 10.4). India's GDP, measured using the purchasing power parity method (PPP), makes it the world's fourth largest economy, behind the United States, China, and Japan. Between 2005 and 2010, India's annual GDP growth rate exceeded 8 percent in every year except 2008. And, unlike economies that may depend on a single sector to generate growth – as Russia's economy depends on the energy sector – India's GDP growth has come from increases in all of the main sectors, from agriculture to manufacturing and services.

Table 10.4   India's Economic Growth, 1980–2010

Year	GDP – PPP valuation * (million U.S. dollars)	GDP Per Capita – PPP * (current U.S. dollars)
1980	286,100	419.35
1985	475,970	627.10
1990	744,630	883.04
1995	1,072,560	1,150.19
2000	1,571,460	1,534.26
2005	2,431,200	2,190.27
2010	4,069,930	3,418.60

* The data is from the International Monetary Fund's World Economic Outlook (WEO). PPP refers to "Purchasing Power Parity," a system introduced by the World Bank and applied to economic data going back to 1980. GDP data based on current U.S. dollars or national currency units can artificially inflate the gap between richer and poorer countries, exaggerating the extent of poverty in poorer countries by discounting the real cost of living. In contrast, the PPP method allows for more realistic comparisons between countries because it takes into account the actual requirements for acquiring a standardized basket of key products across nations.

At least as significant is the fact that the service sector (not agriculture or industry) now accounts for over half of India's GDP and includes an increasingly significant high-tech component, tied to the proliferation of research and development centers established by such global corporate giants as IBM, Intel, Nokia, and Google.

India's economy did experience a downturn after 2011. In the fiscal years ending in 2013 and 2014, the growth rate fell below 5 percent. This was partly a reflection of the drop in international sales in a global economy that was growing at a much slower rate. At the same time, given the peaks to which the Indian economy had risen in 2010, the recent downturn prompted many to raise questions about the soundness of India's economic policies and the future prospects of the world's fourth largest economy. However, it must be remembered that the global economic crisis of 2008–2009 affected the fortunes of many emerging economies, including the other BRIC countries. Brazil experienced negative economic growth (-0.3 percent) in 2009, before rebounding to 7.5 percent in 2010 and falling again to under 3 percent in 2011. Russia's GDP fell even more sharply in 2009 (-7.8 percent) and then rebounded to around 4 percent in 2010–2011. China is the only BRIC country to have performed better than India throughout the first decade of the twenty-first century, and even China's growth rate declined from a spectacular 14 percent in 2007 to under 8 percent in 2013. Taking these considerations into account (see Table 10.5), India's economy can be considered to be in relatively good shape in spite of frustrations with slower growth rates since 2012.

Table 10.5 Economic Performance of BRIC Countries, 2007–2012

	2007	2008	2009	2010	2011	2012
BRAZIL	6.1	5.2	-0.3	7.5	2.7	0.9
RUSSIA	8.5	5.2	-7.8	4.5	4.3	3.4
INDIA	*9.8*	*3.9*	*8.5*	*10.5*	*6.3*	*3.2*
CHINA	14.2	9.6	9.2	10.4	9.3	7.8

Note: Annual rate of growth of GDP, in percent, calculated on the basis of constant local currency.
Source: World Bank, as available on http://data.worldbank.org

In terms of the general direction of economic policy, India has continued to move steadily down the path of liberalization through the first decade of the twenty-first century. To some extent, this path has been dictated by rapidly changing technologies and dramatic shifts in the international environment since the end of the Cold War. These changes have generated pressures on any country seeking to thrive in an increasingly competitive global economy. At the same time, the push for liberalization in India has been more "home-grown" than in most other developing countries. In contrast to countries where reforms were frequently a response to stringent conditions imposed by the World Bank and the IMF in exchange for much-needed loans, India's central government coordinated with these international financial institutions to design conditions that could work with the policies that it wanted to pursue. This was a way for the central government to resist demands from states seeking more resources from the center while characterizing unpopular policies (such as the privatizing of certain public corporations or the scaling back of key social programs) as unavoidable steps that were necessary to improve India's position in the global economy.

It is worth noting that, despite heated battles between Congress and the BJP, the leaders of the main ruling parties have followed more or less similar policies when they have been in power, with only minor variation in the pace of privatization in certain sectors and in the extent of resources devoted to social protection. The Congress-led government had taken the first major steps toward liberalization in the early 1990s, with a leading role played by Manmohan Singh, then finance minister and later prime minister. Congress subsequently lost power to an alliance led by the BJP, a Hindu nationalist party that held power in 1998–2004. Although often portrayed as a party preoccupied with preserving India's traditions, the BJP showed that it would take the necessary steps to further India's rising stature in the global economy, courting foreign investment, supporting big business, and promoting research and development in the high-tech sector. Subsequently, frustrations among the lower strata of the population over their economic stagnation helped a Congress-led alliance regain a parliamentary majority in 2004, at a time when the GDP had been growing at nearly 8 percent.

Although Manmohan Singh, now as the Congress prime minister, did pay more attention than his predecessors to poverty alleviation and problems with grain distribution, the overall direction of economic policy did not change radically. When the rate of economic growth fell below 6 percent in the first half of 2012, Singh responded not by retreating in the face of criticism from opposition parties but by pushing forward with further liberalization, allowing global retail companies such as Walmart to own majority shares in Indian retail ventures. Although Congress lost the support of some key allies in the process and faced intense criticism from the BJP, it managed to secure additional outside support and win passage of the new bill in Parliament. Although the BJP, as the leading opposition party, criticized the bill, it is not clear that its leaders would have done anything differently had they been in power. For the most part, both parties have continued along the path of liberalization and both have presided over periods of impressive growth and economic downturns during their years in power.

At the same time, in a country like India, politicians must balance the push for liberalization, which foreign investors and international financial institutions like to see, with attention to the situation of the poor, who are ready to vote leaders out of office if their living standards do not improve. Thus, with national elections approaching and food prices rising, the Congress-led government rolled out an expensive food security bill. The **Right to Food Act,** adopted in August 2013, is designed to expand the public distribution system to provide access to heavily subsidized food grains to about two-thirds of India's population (corresponding to those below the national poverty line as well as "priority households" that are just above that line but still vulnerable to rising food prices). This bill was seen by some as a pre-election gimmick and was criticized abroad for being out of step with further liberalization. However, most BJP parliamentarians ultimately supported the Right to Food Act, despite their continued criticism of Congress's leadership style and of the manner in which the bill would be implemented. This episode further affirms that sharp arguments between the two leading national parties should not be mistaken for a battle between fundamentally different economic programs: both Congress and BJP have contributed key pieces of legislation to support economic liberalization, but both realize that there are hundreds of millions of impoverished Indians whose lives revolve more around access to cheap food than GDP growth rates.

For many critics of India's economic policy, the issue is not one of generating higher growth but of dealing with more bread-and-butter issues that affect the everyday lives of the vast majority of India's impoverished masses. Even though the official poverty rate has fallen since 1990, with the growth in population, the absolute number of people living in poverty has actually increased to 380 million people. In addition, income inequality has grown sharply since 1990, with a much greater concentration of national income in the hands of the wealthiest strata of the population. One indicator of this is the fact that the total national wealth of the top 10 percent of all wage earners is now 12 times higher than that of the bottom 10 percent (which is double the ratio during the early 1990s). The income disparities are also startling when we compare median incomes of poorer rural districts with those of wealthier urban neighborhoods. Also problematic is the stark difference between states, especially in per capita GDP (Haryana, for example, has a per capita GDP that is *five* times that of the more densely populated Bihar).

Especially worrisome is the growing vulnerability of some segments of the rural population in the twenty-first century. Prior to the adoption of the Right to Food Act, the public distribution system (discussed previously in relation to the Indian economy of the

1960s–1970s) had been scaled back to offer subsidies only to those at or below the poverty line. This left millions of farmers who were just slightly above the poverty line with no line of defense in the face of sudden price increases or crop failures. It is among this group that we find the first reports of starvation-related deaths in India in nearly two decades. It is also among this group that we find one of the most tragic and shocking stories concerning the unintended consequences of liberalization. This is the story of an epidemic of farmer suicides: between 2002 and 2006, over thousands of farmers reportedly committed suicide each year. The issue became a key challenge for the Congress government that came to power in 2004 and prompted Prime Minister Manmohan Singh to commit millions of dollars in rural credit to alleviate problems of mounting debt in suicide-prone regions. Even then, sporadic reports of farmer suicides continued to emerge out of some states, including Maharashtra and Andhra Pradesh.

How could such an unimaginable thing happen in a high-growth emerging economy? Thanks to the lowering of barriers to foreign direct investment, large numbers of peasants came into direct contact with giant multinationals offering new varieties of genetically modified seeds that were supposed to dramatically increase the yield of particular crops. In order to acquire these new seeds, farmers had to borrow heavily, often from local moneylenders charging high interest rates, thereby taking on large debts they had hoped to repay by selling off their larger surplus grain at market prices. But, the crop yield proved to be less substantial than expected and, according to some sources, reduced the richness of the soil (which hurt future harvests). In the meantime, millions of farmers had given up their previous systems of crop diversification and rotation and now found themselves unable to repay their debts, while their families were close to starvation. Taking their own lives seemed to be one way to escape the crushing burden of unpaid debts while allowing their families to get subsidies. One can hope that the steps taken by the national and state governments, and also by nongovernmental organizations, are adequate to prevent another surge in farmer suicides in the future.

When we consider the broader comparative context, the overall picture in India concerning poverty, inequality, and social development does not seem as bleak as some critics contend. Although poverty has been a sticky problem, with two-thirds of the population living under the World Bank's $2/day poverty line, the percentage of the population living in extreme poverty, as defined by the World Bank's $1.25/day threshold, has declined from nearly 60 percent in 1980 to around 35 percent (the exact figure varies depending on the sources and methods). This is not an insignificant shift considering that the decline in extreme poverty came in a period during which the population of the country grew from 700 million to more than one billion. Inequality is rising, but the overall level remains comparatively low when India is compared to the other three BRIC countries or to the United States. Using the World Bank's gini coefficient (in which 0 represents the absence of inequality and 100 represents maximum inequality), India's figure went up from 31 in 1994 to 33.4 in 2005, but this is still significantly lower than the figures for China, Russia, and the United States (which are all greater than 40), as well as for Brazil (over 55).

Moreover, in two key indicators of human development – life expectancy and literacy – a comparison of Brazil and India reveals that, although India remains behind, it has been steadily catching up (see Table 10.6). India's current life expectancy of sixty-five years

Table 10.6   Social Development in India and Brazil, 1960–2010

	INDIA	BRAZIL	Difference
Life Expectancy			
1960	42 yrs	55 yrs	−13 yrs
2010	65 yrs	73 yrs	−8 yrs
Literacy Rate			
1960	28 %	60 %	−32 %
2010	74 %	90 %	−16 %

(as of 2010) is well below Brazil's and even lower than the world average; but, it represents an increase of twenty-three years compared to the life expectancy of forty-two years in 1960. Over the same time period, Brazil's life expectancy has risen from fifty-five years to seventy-three years, which means that the gap between the two countries has fallen from thirteen years in 1960 to eight years in 2010. Similarly, although India's adult literacy rate of 74 percent (as of 2010) is well below Brazil's rate of 90 percent, it is worth noting that India's rate in 1960 stood at 28 percent whereas Brazil's was already at 60 percent. This means that, in five decades, India's literacy rate has gone up by forty-six percentage points while Brazil's has risen by thirty. Of course, a country with higher literacy cannot rise as fast, but the literacy gap between the two countries has been cut in half from thirty-two percentage points in 1960 to sixteen in 2010. These improvements in basic human development indicators represent important achievements, but it remains to be seen whether even more can be done for a still growing population of over one billion.

The Evolving Significance of Caste and Religion in Politics

Neither the political transformations described previously, nor the growing exposure to the global economy, imply that preexisting identities – such as those based on caste and religion – are fading away in the twenty-first century. Such identities not only remain important in everyday life, but also remain politically salient, especially at election time. In fact, the political mobilization or manipulation of religious and caste identities might have increased thanks to the end of Congress dominance and the corresponding increase in the clout of BJP and a host of regional parties. This section looks briefly at the ways in which Hindu nationalism and caste identities are being mobilized in political contexts.

The main bearer of Hindu nationalism at present is the aforementioned BJP, which has its roots in the **Rashtriya Swayamsevak Sangh (RSS)**, a national volunteer organization created in 1925 to preserve and promote Hindu traditions, values, and interests. Although it had joined the INC's struggle against British colonialism, after India became independent, the RSS steadfastly opposed Congress's secular conception of the Indian nation in favor of the revival of pride in *Hinduttva*, the values and ideals of a centuries-old Hindu civilization. The RSS criticized Congress-led governments for disregarding the values and interests of India's Hindu majority while granting special privileges and considerations to Muslims, Sikhs, and Christians. The RSS became especially active in Hindi-speaking states across northern and western India, cultivating ties to various social and political organizations and holding weekly meetings devoted to discussions of nationalist-religious ideology. While it has a track record of organizing effective relief efforts and social services in many areas, it has also been implicated in organized attacks on minorities during times of communal tension. In the 1970s, the RSS began to coordinate its activities with the **Vishva Hindu Parishad (VHP)**, which promotes the idea of *Hinduttva* on a global scale while seeking financial support among affluent Hindu Indians settled in Europe and North America.

In 1980, the main political party sponsored by the RSS, the Jan Sangh, was reorganized as the BJP, which was supported by the growing financial and organizational resources of the RSS and VHP. Although quite small and insignificant at first, by 1990, the BJP began to attract the attention of a growing number of upper-caste Hindus who not only embraced *Hinduttva* for its own sake but also saw it as a means to preserve their inherited status in the midst of governmental efforts to promote the upward mobility of lower-caste groups. In effect, the BJP benefited from upper-caste groups' anxieties over the **Mandal Commission's** recommendations to expand the system of reservations (quotas) in government jobs and higher education to include a longer list of lower-caste groups. The Mandal Commission's work had been supported by a wide range of leaders, many from Congress and others from opposition parties, including **V. P. Singh,** the Janata party prime minister (1989–1990) and a staunch supporter of programs to boost the position of lower-caste and lower-class communities. The implementation of the Mandal Commission's recommendations would not have disproportionately limited educational or job opportunities among upper-caste Hindus as the latter were a minority and as no more than half the positions were being reserved for lower-caste groups. Yet, as more and more upper-caste Hindus became worried about their own prospects, the BJP increasingly appeared to be a viable alternative. In the 1991 elections, the BJP was able to capture 20 percent of the popular vote, which marked it as a significant national party, albeit not yet popular enough to dethrone Congress.

Throughout the 1990s, the BJP's electoral base expanded, partly as a result of a key event that increased its appeal among a significant number of lower-caste Hindus. In 1990, a top BJP leader, **Lal Krishna Advani,** who was to become the home minister in the BJP-led government of 1998–2004, was arrested for exhorting Hindus to tear down the Babri mosque in the town of Ayodhya in order to rebuild a Hindu temple that had supposedly stood at the same spot to honor the demigod Rama. Advani's arrest sent a strong signal that Congress would defend the rights of religious minorities, but it also had the effect of catapulting the BJP into the national spotlight as many Hindus from all caste groups began to rally around their shared religious identity. The subsequent destruction of the Babri mosque by Hindu activists allowed BJP leaders to deflect attention from caste divisions and to emphasize instead the "injustice" being suffered by the majority Hindus in their own homeland while religious minorities, including Muslims, were granted special privileges and rights in the name of secularism.

This message enabled the BJP to attract more lower-caste voters and make major inroads at the state level, with the party capturing the state assemblies of Gujarat and Maharashtra in 1995. The following year, the BJP managed to get over a third of the seats in the national parliament, and in 1998, the BJP managed to form a powerful alliance that captured nearly half the seats in the parliament. In the latter election, the BJP not only got strong support from upper-caste Hindus, but also received 40 percent of the votes from lower-caste communities while also garnering some support among some urban workers (those linked to its trade union), business communities, student groups, and educated professionals working in high-tech sectors. This cross-caste coalition of Hindus enabled the BJP to form a ruling coalition under Prime Minister **Atal Behari Vajpayee** (1998–2004). Even though it would lose in the 2004 and 2009 elections, the BJP had shown itself to be an enduring force in Indian politics, and it scored its most impressive victory to date in the 2014 elections. At a minimum, it remains the only party other than Congress capable of forging successful cross-regional coalitions and mobilizing electoral constituencies on a national scale (see Table 10.3).

Significantly, despite its ideological commitments and roots, the BJP's national leadership has usually behaved in a pragmatic manner, at least when in power. There was initially some talk of amending the constitution to reflect the influence of Hindu beliefs and ideals. But, the BJP's need for allies and coalition partners (some of whom had no interest in Hindu nationalism) made it impossible to push forward on that front. In terms of economic policies, the BJP rejected the Left's focus on the working class and tended to ally with big business, but its positions on most issues seemed to follow logically from the steps that Congress had been taking since 1991 to advance liberalization. The BJP's decision to launch nuclear tests in May 1998 surprised and worried some in the West, but given that the BJP only came to power that same year, it is clear that much of the planning and preparation for these tests had been set in motion under the previous Congress government. The BJP's decision to join the U.S.-led war on terror in the aftermath of the 9/11 attacks was consistent with past Indian leaders' efforts to secure international backing for the suppression of militants in Kashmir, and the decision *not* to join in the U.S.-led coalition's invasion of Iraq was consistent with India's staunchly independent foreign policy posture since independence. Thus, the BJP's rule at the center did not bring any dramatic shifts either in the political system or on major policy issues.

At the state and local levels, however, BJP politicians' often strident rhetoric of Hindu revivalism has tended to drown out the pragmatic postures adopted by the party's national leadership since 1998. This has contributed to tensions between Hindus and Muslims in some places, occasionally fueling deadly communal violence, as was the case with the **Gujarat riots** of 2002. The latter riots began with a fire that tore through a train carrying hundreds of Hindus who were returning from a trip to Ayodhya (the site where the Babri mosque had been destroyed and where some were pushing for the construction of a Hindu temple). The fire was seen by some as set deliberately by Muslims, which then led to a rampage by Hindus, who spent several days attacking Muslims and burning their homes and shops. When it was over, over a thousand people – 790 Muslims and 250 Hindus – had been killed and another ten thousand people left homeless. The BJP prime minister Vajpayee condemned the violence, but the BJP chief minister of Gujarat, **Narendra Modi,** was seen as failing to act quickly to stop the violence, perhaps to exploit the riots to consolidate BJP support in the 2002 state elections. Yet, within Gujarat, Modi managed to lead the BJP to a decisive victory not only in 2002 but also in the next two state elections. Indeed, Modi's strong victory in 2012 catapulted him into the position of the BJP's national leader. Following the BJP's resounding victory in the 2014 elections, Modi would become India's fifteenth prime minister.

On the whole, neither the BJP's electoral successes nor its defeats should be viewed as indicative of any dramatic shifts with respect to the place of Hindu nationalism in Indian politics. The appeal to *Hinduttva* did turn the BJP into a major player on a national scale, but it was only through alliances and coalitions that the party was able to form a government. And, although Congress took back power in 2004, this was not the death knell of Hindu fundamentalism; in fact, the popular vote won by the BJP-led alliance was almost the same as that won by the Congress's alliance (see Table 10.3). Moreover, some of the parties in the alliances formed by BJP have done so not out of a shared ideological vision but for tactical reasons, namely to improve their influence within particular states or increase their regions' leverage in national politics. For example, the BJP's allies in 2004 included the Akali Dal (Punjab), the Telegu Desam Party (Andhra Pradesh), and the Trinamool Congress (West Bengal). In the 2014 elections, the BJP's triumph was more a massive response to its platform of effective governance and faster development than to its elevation of Hinduttva. Collectively, these electoral dynamics suggest that although BJP and Hindu nationalism are here to stay, the BJP's electoral strength and the relevance of appeals to Hindu themes vary significantly depending on the immediate concerns of voters, the politics of coalitional bargaining, and the local appeal of other parties in a given state.

The story of the BJP is not only one about religious nationalism but also a story about the growing political significance of lower-caste communities. Without the support of a significant minority of lower-caste voters, the BJP would not have been able to ever form a ruling coalition at the center. But, the politics of caste is perhaps even more evident in the growing influence of several caste-based parties and lower-caste politicians who have gained ascendance in states such as Bihar and Uttar Pradesh. That this dynamic is occurring after several decades of economic and social development may be surprising to some, but it is not too difficult to comprehend if we bear in mind the complex interplay of India's political and social environments since independence.

It is true that the traditional connection between caste structures and occupational hierarchies has steadily faded away with industrialization. India's business elites extend beyond the Hindu merchant caste and include members of other caste groups and non-Hindu minorities. Also, India's laboring classes are comprised of members of all caste groups, including Brahmins. India's cultural elites, once dominated by the upper castes, are now from a much more varied background, with several lower-caste writers and musicians rising to national prominence. And, thanks to the system of reservations, there are now more lower-caste groups represented in the civil service and in institutions of higher education. These changes do not, however, mean that caste-based identities and practices have become marginalized. In fact, caste remains relevant in everyday social relations, as is evident in the still high rate of within-caste marriages, the activities of community service associations, and the continuing role of Brahmins in the performance of all kinds of regular Hindu rituals.

Even more interesting, and perhaps a little ironic, is that the government's efforts to diffuse the significance of caste through reservations (quotas) for lower-caste communities has served to strengthen the practical and political salience of caste. Since independence, "scheduled castes" (representing the 20 percent of the population consisting of "untouchables" and several marginalized tribal groups) have been granted reservations for positions in government, higher education, and public-sector employment. In addition, various strata of peasant or artisan caste groups (about 25 percent of the population) are considered "other backward castes" and are eligible for a narrower range of quotas in education and employment. But, as in the case of "affirmative action" in the United States, India's system of reservations has been the subject of much debate. This has been especially true since the government's acceptance of the aforementioned Mandal Commission report, which identified a lengthier list of "other backward caste" groups and set aside half the available positions in government and higher education for lower-caste groups. Even though upper-caste Hindus represent less than one-fifth of the population and remained eligible to apply for the other half of the available positions, the basic principles behind the Mandal Commission report initially triggered some stunning reactions, ranging from the suicide of upper-caste students to large numbers of upper-caste individuals changing their names to acquire lower-caste surnames. Eventually, these reactions gave way to a more sober acceptance of the fact that lower-caste communities would have more opportunities for upward mobility and greater political influence.

This is most evident in the rise of successful regional parties led by lower-caste politicians mobilizing electoral support from their own caste communities. Of course, appeals to caste are not new. In the past, even though Congress's national leadership officially disavowed caste-based politics, local Congress candidates often negotiated for whole blocks of votes from entire caste communities in exchange for promises to advance the interests of these communities. With the end of Congress dominance, however, there are now multiple candidates from multiple parties competing for the votes of caste communities. And, at least in some states, regional and splinter parties, whether or not they publicly claim to stand for particular caste groups, have been successful in capturing power in state assemblies by targeting the support of lower-caste communities that are larger and more numerous. Moreover, many candidates are themselves lower-caste politicians who have enjoyed success by making direct appeals to members of their own caste communities. These appeals have not only led to the capture of certain state assemblies by lower-caste parties, but have catapulted several low-caste leaders into national prominence. One example is Laloo Prasad Yadav who founded the Rashtriya Janata Dal party and reigned as chief minister in the state of Bihar from 1990 to 1997. Yadav's party then became the largest ally of Congress in the 2004–2009 UPA government, and Yadav himself served as railways minister (and is credited by some for bringing about major improvements in the operation of the Indian railroad system).

In sum, caste and religion continue to matter a great deal in everyday life, but their significance for politics is mediated by the nature of India's political institutions and by changing patterns of national and subnational political competition. In relation to religion, although Hindu nationalism has proven to be a strong enough force to turn the BJP into a powerful and enduring contender in national politics, the party's ability to govern at the center remains dependent on alliances and coalitions involving parties that do not care much for *Hinduttva*. In relation to caste, the effort to eradicate caste hierarchies through reservations has ended up making Indians simultaneously more conscious of caste distinctions and more calculating in terms of the impact of caste-related social policies on their individual and group interests. Even though cultural values and social practices have undergone significant change since independence, particularistic identities linked to religion or caste are likely to remain politically salient well into the twenty-first century. Yet, these are also not the only bases for political mobilization, as a wider, more diversified range of values and interests has become increasingly visible throughout civil society.

The Diversification of Interests: New Social Movements and Nongovernmental Organizations

The growing fluidity of electoral politics and the liberalization of the economy have been accompanied by the mobilization of a wider array of groups and organizations that cut across long-standing cleavages based on caste, region, and religion. Several of these groups stand at the forefront of India's integration into the global economy. India's business elites are sophisticated, well educated, attentive to international trends, and strategic in their pursuit of new opportunities both within India and abroad. India's economic reformers rely heavily on the advice of native scholars who are well trained in macroeconomics and thoroughly familiar with the dynamics of international trade and global financial markets. Younger members of the urban middle class are hooked into satellite television, carry smart phones, and regularly surf the Internet, absorbing certain common topics of discussion, lifestyles, and consumption patterns found worldwide. However, these groups, although more visible to outside observers, constitute only a small fraction of India's huge population. A more careful examination of Indian civil society in the twenty-first century suggests that there are now many more groups, interests, and organizations that were once small or invisible but are now more active, more organized, and more politically consequential.

India's working class represents a heterogeneous social category with significant variation across different industries and regions. The most organized means for representing their interests are India's trade unions, established during the period of British colonialism but steadily growing in size since that time. Although 10 percent of the total workforce is unionized, there are several points worth noting. First, the sheer size of India's workforce means that the number of individuals in trade unions is actually quite large even if the percentage of workers in unions is low. Second, and more important, is the fact that India's trade unions are growing in size, with the total membership of different unions quadrupling since 1980. The rate of growth has been even faster since economic liberalization began in earnest during the 1990s, with much of the growth coming from the expansion of the unions into the growing informal sector. This trend is the opposite of what we see in most advanced industrial countries where trade union membership has been declining for over three decades. In this regard, India is more similar to China where total union membership has also increased with the acceleration of market reforms. However, in China, much of the growth in membership is because of the government's efforts to organize workers in the expanding manufacturing sector into a single centralized trade union federation that can be managed more easily by the state; in India, the growth in membership is because of the efforts of unions themselves in extending beyond their core base in state-owned enterprises into the informal sector, which had been ignored during the era of state-led development in the 1950s–1980s.

The other major trend is in the increasing possibilities for coordination among trade union federations that have historically competed with each other for membership and influence. During most of the twentieth century, Indian trade unions were fragmented because they allied with competing political parties and subscribed to different ideologies. The largest trade union federation, accounting for over a third of the total membership, used to be allied with Congress. This federation, however, was challenged by unions backed by the BJP, as well as those unions that supported leftist parties. With the end of Congress dominance, the BJP and other parties increased their efforts to mobilize their trade union membership and contributed to the growth of trade union membership. But, until recently, the party-union linkages interfered with efforts to organize a more unified front for advancing the interests of the working class. As we move further into the twenty-first century, however, the more fluid patterns of party competition, together with the common threat of workforce reductions in the public and private sectors, has given rise to increasing coordination across union bodies and to the growing visibility of other labor organizations that had always resisted political affiliations. This coordination is evident in the role that competing unions have played in jointly supporting strikes and protests to challenge privatization in certain sectors or to preserve job security and social benefits associated with public-sector employment. Although there is little reason to expect that organized labor will be able to generate enough unity and influence to affect key economic policies, the sheer size of India's trade unions and the growing possibilities for expansion and coordination make them a formidable component of civil society.

For the hundreds of millions of laborers in the informal sector who have not been drawn into unions, the challenges are quite different. The informal sector encompasses workers in agriculture, industry, and the service sector who are employed without formal contracts on a casual basis. Although some workers in the informal sector have benefited from opportunities brought by liberalization and the influx of foreign employers, for the majority, the lack of contracts and adequate legal protection has translated into long working hours, low hourly wages, and miserable working conditions. It is among the most impoverished segments of this informal sector that we find the greatest receptiveness to radical social movements. Some of these are organized around revolutionary ideologies, as in the case of the radical Naxalite movement, which is active along the eastern states of

India and pursues the overthrow of the present "bourgeois" government in the name of workers, peasants, and other marginalized groups. In other cases, where extreme poverty is concentrated among members of a particular caste or tribal group in a particular region, frustrations with the status quo have helped to swell movements pursuing the creation of a new state. This is the case with the movement that helped carve a separate Telengana state out of Andhra Pradesh.

The majority of India's women, too, are facing new challenges as a group. India was traditionally a patriarchal society, with men dominating the decision making in most communities and women often confined to the domestic sphere. Today, the gender gap in India, although smaller than before, remains significant. Men continue to be disproportionately represented in higher education, public office, and the organized workforce. Women tend to suffer from low social status, limited opportunities for decent employment, and mistreatment in connection with insufficient dowries in traditional arranged marriages. At the same time, women's participation in the Indian political system has been steadily increasing over the past century. Women's involvement in the nationalist movement, the arrival of universal suffrage in connection with parliamentary democracy, the increase in the literacy rate for women and girls, and the rise of Indira Gandhi and other women to prominence in national and state politics all helped to gradually increase the visibility of women in the public sphere. This is evident in the increasing number of female voters and candidates in electoral politics, in feminist movements spearheaded by urban middle-class women who have set out to challenge patriarchal attitudes, and in the proliferation of nongovernmental organizations (NGOs) that seek to boost women's literacy, health, and capacity to engage in independent economic activities.

In addition, since the 1990s, the aforementioned expansion of the informal sector, within which women constitute a large and growing segment, has given more momentum to movements and organizations that focus on the protection and upward mobility of women seeking employment. Noteworthy among these is the **Self-Employed Women's Association (SEWA).** SEWA began in the 1970s as a small trade union for self-employed women in the state of Gujarat in the 1970s. Since 2002, it has been formally recognized by the Indian government as a national trade union center with nearly one million members (half of whom reside in states other than Gujarat). Yet, SEWA also functions as a NGO and a broader social movement, establishing programs to provide credit and support for poor women who are unable to find decent work but seek to maintain their independence by becoming self-employed or working in self-sufficient cooperatives. Interestingly, the social component of globalization has enabled SEWA to form transnational alliances with organizations in other countries (such as Thailand and Turkey) where efforts have been made to organize and support home-based women workers or street vendors.

Women have also become more active in social movements and spontaneous protests that target violence against women. In 2012, a brutal (and ultimately fatal) gang rape of a female medical student in the Indian capital of New Delhi triggered a massive protest in which thousands of women, accompanied by male students supporting their cause, protested angrily for several days. Among their demands were more stringent penalties for the perpetrators of violence against women along with more personnel and attention devoted to the physical safety of women. Although the problem of rape had been growing more serious for a while, the particularly brutal nature of this crime led to a swelling of the protests to the point that they grabbed international headlines and forced Prime Minister Manmohan Singh to issue a personal plea for calm as the government set out to respond to violence against women. These protests have given fresh impetus to long-standing efforts by some activists to link violence against women to the broader issues of the value placed on women's lives. Although none of these forms of collective action – not the more organized efforts exemplified by SEWA or the more spontaneous protests in defense of women's rights and protection – are necessarily precursors for a Western-style feminist movement, that is not a concern considering the specific cultural, social, and economic contexts within which Indian women are defining their challenges and opportunities. What is more important is that a growing number of Indian women – regardless of their religion, caste, or language – are coming together within and across a growing number of states in order to overturn prejudices and practices that have suppressed their voices, restricted their opportunities, and endangered their physical safety.

Another area where the vibrance of Indian civil society in the twenty-first century has been manifested is in protests and social movements targeting corruption. Although corruption has long been a problem in Indian government and business, and although past governments have been brought down by corruption scandals, the issue had not garnered much attention beyond elite circles during the first fifty years following India's independence. But, in recent years, with the gap between rich and poor growing in the era of economic liberalization, ordinary Indians have become more aware of – and angry about – the illegal or quasi-legal manner in which wealth has been amassed by prominent politicians and businessmen who use their positions to attract massive bribes or share insider information with their personal cronies. Corruption is now the target of a large and growing social movement that has received national and international attention thanks in part to the efforts of **Anna Hazare.** Hazare had long been a social activist, previously known for his campaigns for more local autonomy and self-reliance. In 1992, he had even received an award from the Indian government for establishing a new village in Maharashtra noted as a model of grassroots self-governance and local self-sufficiency. His more recent campaign against corruption was reminiscent of tactics used by Mahatma Gandhi, including hunger strikes and marches. These efforts helped to galvanize millions of people who joined in massive protests to pressure the government to pass more stringent legislation to battle corruption at the highest levels. The Lokpal Bill, passed in 2011, was not everything that Hazare wanted, but it set up a powerful, independent office to investigate and combat corruption in public places. In 2011, the journal *Foreign Policy* included Hazare on a list of the hundred most influential global thinkers. However, some of his colleagues, most notably **Arvind Kejriwal,** felt that the movement was stalling out without having achieved its main goals. Kejriwal believed that the time had come for more direct political action and, in November 2012, established the Aam Aadmi (Common Man) Party, AAP. The party surprised many, including Congress and BJP, by capturing a plurality of seats in the 2013 Delhi local assembly elections and forming the ruling coalition. In the 2014 national elections, however, the party managed only four seats. While this leaves the future of the party very much in doubt, anti-corruption activism is likely to remain a powerful force in Indian society.

Environmental activism also is now more visible in the public sphere, with growing fears that the quest for economic growth will further accelerate environmental degradation. Until the 1990s, environmental movements were mostly made up of relatively poor people focused on the protection of their own communities and habitats. The "Chipko" ("Embrace the Trees") movement, for example, was launched in the early 1970s when a group of poor hill people in northern India stood between trees and loggers' saws in order to prevent the loggers from destroying the forests that constituted their habitats. In the 1980s, several communities in western India banded together to form a campaign to protest against the construction of a massive dam on the Narmada River, which would have meant relocating the tens of thousands of people who lived in these communities. The protests gained enough international attention to get the World Bank to withdraw financial support for the project and led the Indian government to change the original blueprint for the dam.

In the twenty-first century, these movements have evolved into more established NGOs that have been expanding their areas of operation and coordinating with each other on a regular basis. Collectively, these organizations have been attempting to establish linkages between the specific threats faced by various local communities to broader problems of pollution and environmental degradation in the era of increasing globalization. One example is the National Alliance of People's Movement, which strives to organize local communities in different states to promote greater conservation and defend the rights of local communities to have more control over their local natural resources. Another example is the Foundation for Ecological Security, which was set up in 2001 and has operations in more than a half dozen other states, focusing on ecological restoration in places where land and water resources have been becoming increasingly scarce. The growing visibility of such NGOs suggest that the environmental movement in India has evolved from being a collection of uncoordinated community groups dealing solely with local issues into a more organized and enduring network of local, national, and transnational advocacy groups.

In sum, India's civil society has moved well beyond the grassroots nationalist movement once led by Mahatma Gandhi as well as the more particularistic forms of mobilization around caste, language, or religion. This is evident in the growth of trade unions, the expansion of organizations devoted to women's opportunities and independence, the mass campaign against corruption, and the sophisticated networks formed by environmental activists. All of these types of collective action are indications of the vibrant character and growing relevance of India's civil society.

CONCLUSION

Table 10.7 summarizes some of the broader themes of this chapter in the process of laying out key phases in India's development, as represented in the regime; the global context in which this regime operated; the interplay of identities, interests, and institutions; and the overall path of economic development. Under Prime Ministers Nehru and Indira Gandhi,

India's national identity remained secular and tied to its self-conception as a leader of the developing world on the international stage. India's political institutions functioned well compared with those in many other postcolonial developers, but Congress's initial advantages produced a "dominant-party system" in which other parties could not yet compete on the national stage. A "mixed" economy with a large public sector became firmly entrenched. Indira Gandhi introduced her own brand of patronage politics and some new economic initiatives (for example, the green revolution and antipoverty campaigns), but these coexisted within the institutional framework and program of development initiated by Nehru during the 1950s. During this period, even though local politicians often made appeals based on caste during elections, most of India's elites followed Nehru in embracing a secular vision of a modern India.

Since the 1990s, changes in the global order have been accompanied by a fundamental shift in India's developmental path (see Table 10.7). India's political institutions have remained stable, but the increased number of states and the devolution of power to local districts have produced a more complex and fluid process of politics at all levels of government. At the center, with the growth of the BJP, Congress no longer dominates, and both parties depend on alliances or coalitions involving dozens of regional and splinter parties. This has been accompanied by a move away from a mixed economy, with economic liberalization accompanied by greater integration into the global economy. In the evolving political and economic environment, a wider and more diverse array of interests is now in evidence in the form of new social movements and NGOs that are part of a vibrant and energetic civil society. At the same time, preexisting identities linked to caste and religion not only remain relevant in most people's everyday lives but have also been mobilized in more sophisticated ways depending on the political landscape evident in particular states or locales.

These transformations mean that India's leaders in the twenty-first century will have to demonstrate considerable political skill if they wish to maintain the delicate balance between social forces pulling in different directions – between cosmopolitan secularists and those identifying with centuries-old civilizational ideals; between a majority Hindu population and Muslims and other religious minorities; between upwardly mobile lower-caste groups and anxious upper-caste groups fearful of losing access to educational and employment opportunities; between an urban elite that is seizing new opportunities in the information technology sector and a rural population that constitutes over 60 percent of the population but accounts for just one-quarter of India's GDP; and between those trumpeting India's achievements in science, technology, and industry and those concerned with food security, environmental degradation, labor standards, and the gender gap in social status and economic opportunities.

But, perhaps the key to India's past and future stability in the face of these diverse centrifugal forces is not its leaders so much as its institutions. Without minimizing the social problems and conflicts that continue to plague India today, it is necessary to recognize that India's institutions have enjoyed a measure of durability and legitimacy not often seen among postcolonial late-developers. This is most clearly evident in the durability of India's democracy. During the 2014 elections–the world's largest election to date–new records

Table 10.7   Key Phases in India's Political Development

Time Period	Regime	Global Context	Interests/ Identities/ Institutions	Developmental Path
Pre-1757	empires, kingdoms	invasion and settlement	emergence of race, caste, religious, and regional identification; tributary systems, local autonomy, rivalries among local elites	diffusion of some common administrative, social, and cultural practices (most notably caste structures and Hindu rituals)
1757–1947	British colonialism	European imperialism	indirect rule via princely states, with more direct rule from 1857; nascent commercial interests and working class, accompanied by parliament and courts established to stabilize British rule but challenged by nationalist movement led by Indian National Congress	scattered pockets of early industrialization with "misdevelopment" resulting from focus on cash crops, search for raw materials, and limits on opportunities for native entrepreneurship
1947–1990s	Independent nation state with federal system linking linguistically defined states to a center dominated by one party (Congress)	leading role in nonaligned movement in pursuit of "third way" between the two camps led by United States and USSR during the Cold War	caste-based "vote banks" at local level alongside mobilization of peasants and working-class interests, within Westminster-style parliamentary democracy backed by a large, powerful bureaucratic state.	state-led development with "mixed" economy featuring large public sector and national planning (becomes full-scale import-substitution industrialization in 1970s, backed by "green revolution" aimed at self-sufficiency in food.

(continued)

Table 10.7 (*cont.*)

Time Period	Regime	Global Context	Interests/ Identities/ Institutions	Developmental Path
Twenty-first century	federalism with more authority devolved to local level, and with greater space for locally influential parties that join alliances and coalitions led by major national parties (BJP and Congress).	post–Cold War exposure to globalization, with rising influence, enhanced by rapid economic growth and membership in "BRIC" and nuclear clubs	Hindu nationalism more visible with instances of Hindu-Muslim violence; but partly checked by secular and socialist parties at national level and by some lower-caste politicians at state level; business elites' interests backed by secularists *and* Hindu nationalists, but challenged by movements and NGOs focused on corruption, poverty, inequality, womens' rights, and environment	incremental process of liberalization and privatization, with rising exports and foreign investment; service sector now accounts for over half of GDP and includes high-tech industries; improving literacy and life expectancy; but long-term challenges to economic and social security for those below or just above poverty line (especially given population pressures).

were set for the number of votes cast (over 550 million), eligible voters (over 800 million), and voter turnout (over 66 percent). The real test for these institutions, however, may well lie ahead as this nation of over one billion people continues to grow in population while attempting to sustain economic growth, reduce poverty, maintain social peace, and elevate its position in a changing global order.

BIBLIOGRAPHY

Bardhan, Pranab. *Awakening Giants, Feet of Clay: Assessing the Economic Reform in China and India*. Princeton, NJ: Princeton University Press, 2010.

Bhagwati, Jagdish, and Arvind Panagariya, eds. *India's Reforms: How They Produced Inclusive Growth*. New York: Oxford University Press, 2012.

Bose, Sugata, and Ayesha Jalal. *Modern South Asia: History, Culture, Political Economy*. Third edition. London: Routledge, 2011.

Bowen, H. V. *The Business of Empire: The East India Company and Imperial Britain, 1756–1833*. Cambridge: Cambridge University Press, 2006.

Brass, Paul. *The Politics of India since Independence*. Cambridge: Cambridge University Press, 1994.

Carras, Mary C. *Indira Gandhi: In the Crucible of Leadership*. Boston: Beacon, 1979.

Chakraborty, Bidyut. *Forging Power: Coalition Politics in India*. New York: Oxford University Press, 2006.

Chanda, Asok. *Federalism in India*. London: Allen and Unwin, 1965.

Chhibber, Pradeep. *Democracy without Associations: Transformation of the Party System and Social Cleavages in India*. Ann Arbor: University of Michigan Press, 1999.

Chibber, Vivek. *Locked in Place: State Building and Late Industrialization in India*. Princeton, NJ: Princeton University Press, 2003.

Cohen, Stephen. *India: Emerging Power*. Washington, DC: Brookings Institution Press, 2002.

Corbridge, Stuart, John Harriss, and Craig Jeffrey. *India Today: Economics, Politics and Society*. Cambridge: Polity Press, 2013.

Dalton, Denis. *Mahatma Gandhi*. New York: Columbia University Press, 1993.

Das, Gurucharan. *India Unbound: The Social and Economic Revolution from Independence to the Global Information Age*. New York: Anchor Books, 2002.

Dasgupta, Jyotirindra. *Language, Conflict and National Development*. Berkeley: University of California Press, 1970.

Frankel, Francine. *India's Political Economy, 1947–2004: The Gradual Revolution*. New Delhi: Oxford University Press, 2005.

Ganguly, Sumit, ed. *India's Foreign Policy: Retrospect and Prospect*. New York: Oxford University Press, 2010.

Gopal, Sarvepalli. *Jawaharlal Nehru: A Biography*. New Delhi: Oxford University Press, 1984.

Guha, Ramachandra. *India after Gandhi: The History of the World's Largest Democracy*. New York: HarperCollins, 2007.

Gupta, Akhil. *Red Tape: Bureaucracy, Structural Violence, and Poverty in India*. Durham, NC: Duke University Press, 2012.

Handy, Femida, Meenaz Kassam, Suzanne Feeney, and Bhagyashree Ranade. *Grassroots NGOs by Women for Women: The Driving Force of Development in India*. Thousand Oaks, CA: Sage Publications, 2006.

Hasan, Zoya. *Politics of Inclusion: Castes, Minorities, and Affirmative Action*. New Delhi: Oxford University Press, 2012.

Heller, Patrick. *The Labor of Development: Workers and the Transformation of Capitalism in Kerala, India*. Ithaca, NY: Cornell University Press, 2000.

Jaffrelot, Christophe. *Religion, Politics, and Caste in India*. New York: Columbia University Press, 2011.

Jalal, Ayesha. *Democracy and Authoritarianism in South Asia*. Cambridge: Cambridge University Press, 1995.

Jenkins, Rob. *Democratic Politics and Economic Reform in India*. Cambridge: Cambridge University Press, 1999.

Jenkins, Rob, ed. *Regional Reflections: Comparing Politics across India's States*. New York: Oxford University Press, 2004.

Jha, Raghbendra. *Indian Economic Reforms*. New York: Palgrave Macmillan, 2003.

Kapur, Devesh, and Pratab Bhanu Mehta, eds. *Public Institutions in India: Performance and Design*. New York: Oxford University Press, 2006.

Kirk, Jason A. *India and the World Bank: The Politics of Aid and Influence*. London: Anthem Press, 2010.

Kohli, Atul. *Poverty amid Plenty in the New India*. New York: Cambridge University Press, 2012.

Kohli, Atul, ed. *The Success of India's Democracy*. New York: Cambridge University Press, 2001.

Kothari, Rajni. *Politics in India*. Boston: Little, Brown, 1970.

Mahadevan, Prem. *The Politics of Counterterrorism in India*. London: I. B. Tauris, 2012.

Mitchell, Lisa. *Language, Emotion, and Politics in South India: The Making of a Mother Tongue*. Bloomington: Indiana University Press, 2009.

Mohan, C. Raja. *Impossible Allies: Nuclear India, the United States, and the Global Order*. New Delhi: India Research Press, 2006.

Nehru, Jawaharlal. *An Autobiography*. New Delhi: Oxford University Press, 1980.

Pandey, Gyanendra. *Remembering Partition: Violence, Nationalism and History in India*. Cambridge: Cambridge University Press, 2001.

Parekh, Bhikhu. *Gandhi*. New York: Oxford University Press, 1997.

Perkovich, George. *India's Nuclear Bomb*. Berkeley: University of California Press, 2001.

Ray, Raka, and Mary Fainsod Katzenstein. *Social Movements in India: Poverty, Power and Politics*. Lanham, MD: Rowman & Littlefield, 2005.

Robb, Peter. *A History of India*. New York: Palgrave, 2002.

Shah, Alpa. *In the Shadows of the State: Indigenous Politics, Environmentalism, and Insurgency in Jharkhand, India*. Durham, NC: Duke University Press, 2010.

Sinha, Aseema. 2005. *The Regional Roots of Developmental Politics in India: A Divided Leviathan*. Bloomington: Indiana University Press, 2005.

Srinivas, M. N. *The Dominant Caste and Other Essays*. New Delhi: Oxford University Press, 1987.

Talbot, Ian, and Gurharpal Singh. *Region and Partition: Bengal, Punjab and the Partition of the Subcontinent*. New York: Oxford University Press, 1999.

Van der Veer, Peter. *Religious Nationalism: Hindus and Muslims in India*. Berkeley: University of California Press, 1994.

Varshney, Asutosh. *Democracy, Development and the Countryside: Urban-Rural Struggles in India*. Cambridge: Cambridge University Press, 1995.

Varshney, Asutosh. *Ethnic Conflict and Civic Life: Hindus and Muslims in India*. New Haven, CT: Yale University Press, 2003.

Wilkinson, Steven. *Votes and Violence: Electoral Competition and Ethnic Riots in India*. New York: Cambridge University Press, 2006.

Wolpert, Stanley. *A New History of India*. Fifth edition. Oxford: Oxford University Press, 2008.

IMPORTANT TERMS

73rd & 74th constitutional amendments – adopted in 1992, these two amendments combined to establish standardized administrative divisions and elected assemblies within India's states at the level of rural districts, villages, and municipalities. In principle, these were designed to enhance local self-governance.

Aam Aadmi Party (AAP) – "Common Man Party," formed in November 2012 by Arvind Kejriwal who split with the anti-corruption movement of Anna Hazare (see term) to advance the movement's agenda through a new party; surprised many by winning a plurality of seats in the 2013 Delhi legislative assembly elections.

Lal Krishna Advani – leading Hindu nationalist who served as home minister in the 1998–2004 BJP government. Noted for his public advocacy of the destruction of the Babri mosque in Ayodhya, for which he was once arrested.

alliance – refers to a bloc of parties organized by a major national party to compete in national elections, usually with a candidate from only one of the allied parties running in a given electoral district (examples include the Congress-led United Progressive Alliance and the BJP-led National Democratic Alliance).

B. R. Ambedkar – a key national leader and a major social activist, known for his staunch opposition to caste hierarchies, who served as chair of the committee that drafted India's constitution immediately after independence.

Bharatiya Janata Party (BJP, or the Indian People's Party) – a political party that has its roots in past Hindu fundamentalist organizations and gradually became a major political force during the 1990s on the strength of its glorification of *Hinduttva* (see term).

Brahmins – Hindu priests, considered to be the most "pure" of the caste groups and uniquely qualified to read scriptural texts and perform Hindu religious ceremonies.

caste – the generic term employed to mean a fivefold occupational and social hierarchy ranging, in descending order of "purity," from Brahmins (see term) and warriors to merchants/traders, peasants/artisans, and "untouchables." Should be distinguished from the term "jati," which is used to identify groups of families belonging to a subcategory of a caste within a particular region or community.

coalition – a negotiated arrangement whereby parties that are *not* part of an alliance (see term) but decide to offer support to a leading party (and its allies) so that the latter can form a government even without holding a majority of seats.

Communist Party of India – Marxist (CPI-M) – the most significant leftist party in India, notable as a rare case of a communist party that gained power through elections. It maintained continuous control over the state assembly of West Bengal from 1977 to 2011, sometimes behaving as a regional party in bargaining with the center.

Congress Party – referred to simply as "Congress," this party grew out of the Indian National Congress (INC) and held power for most of the first five decades after independence. Identified with Congress-I (for Indira Gandhi), after the 1967 defection of some party bosses who formed the smaller Congress-O (for "organization"). Since the 1990s, the party has been using its original pre-independence appellation (INC).

dominant-party system – a term employed to characterize India's political system as a result of Congress's steady control over Parliament for all but one election between 1952 and 1984. Not an authoritarian system but rather the combined result of India's "first-past-the-post" electoral system and the initial advantages inherited by the party from the independence movement (Indian National Congress).

Emergency – an eighteen-month period from late 1975 to early 1977 when Indira Gandhi suspended parts of the constitution and arrested opposition leaders in response to her opponents' calls for the army to remove her from power for alleged campaign violations.

Indira Gandhi – daughter of Jawaharlal Nehru, and prime minister of India (1967–1977, 1980–1984). Identified with the rise of patronage politics, a populist antipoverty campaign, the "Emergency" (see term), and the assault on Sikh militants in the Punjab. Assassinated by Sikh bodyguards in 1984. No direct relation to Mohandas K. Gandhi.

Mahatma Gandhi – born Mohandas Karamchand Gandhi but later referred to as "Mahatma" (**"Great Soul"**), acquired a law degree in Britain and later organized nonviolent civil-disobedience campaigns and mobilized grassroots support for the independence movement. Opposed the caste system and favored Hindu-Muslim unity. Assassinated in 1948 by a Hindu fanatic.

Rajiv Gandhi – elder son of Indira Gandhi. He became prime minister of India (1984–1989) following Indira's assassination. His administration took the first steps toward economic reform. Following Congress's defeat in 1989, Rajiv was assassinated while campaigning for the 1991 elections.

Sonia Gandhi – Italian-born wife of Rajiv Gandhi. Initially stayed out of politics, but then led the Congress Party to victory in 2004, although declining the post of prime minister in favor of Manmohan Singh (see name).

green revolution – campaign during the early 1970s to promote the use of new seeds and new methods of fertilization and crop rotation in order to boost agricultural production. Helped to make India self-sufficient in food production but did not reduce inequality (except in a few areas that also carried out land reform).

Gujarat riots – a deadly conflict between Hindus and Muslims that broke out in 2002 in the state of Gujarat, killing over a thousand people, the majority of them Muslims; the BJP-led state government was blamed for failing to halt the violence quickly, with some seeing the chief minister Narendra Modi (see person) as exploiting the riots to mobilize Hindu support in advance of the 2002 state assembly elections.

Anna Hazare – social activist who launched several well-publicized hunger strikes in order to promote major anticorruption legislation, the Lokpal Bill (see term), intended to combat corruption in the public realm at the highest levels. Previously, he had set up a village in Maharashtra as a model of local self-governance and self-sufficiency.

Hindi – one of India's most used official languages (along with English), constructed on the basis of commonly spoken Sanskritic languages in northern and central India (sometimes referred to as the Hindi belt). Hindi is less popular in the southern states, where the main local languages are Dravidian, not derived from Sanskrit.

Hinduttva – a term popularized by the BJP and some Hindu nationalist social organizations to emphasize the greatness and distinctiveness of Hindu civilization and to make this civilization the basis for defining India's national identity.

Indian National Congress (INC) – an organization that emerged in 1885 and became the main mass movement for independence from British rule. Turned into the Congress Party (see term) after independence.

Janata Party – also referred to as Janata Dal (in Hindi), an umbrella party for several political groups that claim to share a common vision of reduced planning, local self-reliance, and reduced poverty and equality. In actuality, its affiliates' unity stemmed from the desire to unseat Congress, which it did three times (in 1977, 1989, and 1996), but without being able to develop a common policy or finish out a full term.

Arvind Kejriwal – anti-corruption activist and founder of the Aam Aadmi Party; formerly allied with Anna Hazare, who opposed the formation of a political party as a means to combat corruption.

license raj – an aspect of India's statist economy in which large private-sector firms had to obtain a government license to produce, import, or export goods. Has been steadily scaled back since the late 1980s as part of economic liberalization.

Mandal Commission – an official commission that submitted a report – accepted by the government in 1990 – extending the list of groups that could be labeled as "other backward castes" and could thus qualify for consideration in India's system of "reservations" (see term).

Narendra Modi – prime minister of India following BJP's victory in 2014 elections. Previously, chief minister of Gujarat since 2001, re-elected in three consecutive state elections. Faulted by some for slow response to riots that killed over a thousand people in Gujarat before the 2002 elections.

Jawaharlal Nehru – leading figure in the Indian National Congress and India's first prime minister. He is identified with a "third way" of development that rejected alliances with the superpowers while combining aspects of Western-style capitalism and Soviet-style planning.

public distribution system – a network of thousands of shops that redistributed surplus grain from high-yield agricultural regions to other parts of the country at controlled prices monitored by state governments; previously administered universally, but later transformed into a more targeted system focused on only those below the national poverty level, which led to pressures for those slightly above the threshold and paved the way for the 2013 Right to Food Act (see term).

Narasimha Rao – prime minister of India (1991–1996) who led the Congress Party after Rajiv Gandhi's assassination. His cabinet sped up the pace of economic liberalization.

President's Rule – the rule stipulated in Article 356 of the Indian constitution whereby the president can authorize intervention by the central government in states thought to be experiencing extraordinary political or social unrest. Has sometimes been invoked on shaky grounds to oust uncooperative state assemblies.

Rashtriya Swayamsevak Sangh (RSS) – a Hindu social organization created in 1925 to preserve and promote Hindu traditions, values, and interests. Together with the VHP (see term), it helped mobilize support for the BJP.

reservations – the term used by Indians to refer to India's "affirmative action" system for increasing the representation of lower-caste groups in educational institutions and the public sector.

Right to Food Act – also known as the food security bill, adopted in 2013 to provide heavily subsidized grains to approximately two-thirds of India's population, including many households above the national poverty line but struggling with rising food prices.

Sanskrit – an ancient Indo-Aryan language used by Hindu priests in liturgical services across most of the Indian subcontinent; also the origin of many of India's regional languages (for example, Gujarati, Marathi, Bengali) in the northern and central parts of the subcontinent.

secularism – the principle that the state is not identified with any particular religion and that members of all religious and ethnic groups are to be treated as equal under the law.

Self-employed Women's Association (SEWA) – registered as a trade union organization dating back to 1972, it behaves as a hybrid of a trade union and a nongovernmental organization to offer opportunities and social protection to poor women in the informal workforce.

Sikhs – followers of the Sikh religion, who constitute a narrow majority in the state of Punjab. In the 1980s, Sikh militants waged a struggle for a separate "Khalistan" nation but the conflict has since subsided.

Manmohan Singh – prime minister of India in the Congress-led governments from 2004 to 2014. Previously the finance minister in the Congress government led by Narasimha Rao, 1991–1996.

V. P. Singh – prime minister of India under the Janata government of 1989–1991. Noteworthy for efforts to check corruption and expand system of "reservations" (see term).

Urdu – a language spoken by many of India's Muslims. It combines an Arabic script with a vocabulary that overlaps significantly with that of spoken Hindi.

Atal Behari Vajpayee – BJP leader who served as prime minister of India from 1998 to 2004. Identified with the pragmatic wing of the BJP's national leadership.

Vishva Hindu Parishad (VHP) – a worldwide organization of Hindus committed to promoting *Hinduttva* (see term). Constitutes a major social base and source of funding for the BJP.

vote bank – a bloc of votes for a particular candidate delivered by members of a given community (usually a local caste group or a village) as a result of deals brokered between the candidate and the community's leaders.

STUDY QUESTIONS

1. What were the various sources of collective identity on the Indian subcontinent prior to British colonialism? Why have these cleavages generated less collective violence than in postcolonial Africa?

2. In what ways did British colonial administration affect the prospects for political and economic development in postcolonial India?

3. Why was Mahatma Gandhi's leadership important to the success of the Indian National Congress? What was the rationale behind his strategy of nonviolent noncooperation?

4. What are some of the similarities and differences that emerge when comparing democracy and federalism in India with democracy and federalism in the United States?

5. What accounts for the Congress Party's dominance between the 1950s and 1980s? What accounts for the loss of this dominance since the 1990s? How have the dynamics of electoral competition (at the national and state levels) changed as a result?

6. What, if anything, does the Bharatiya Janata Party's (BJP's) appearance as an alternative national party tell us about the salience of caste and religious identities over time?

7. In what respects did India's development program between the 1950s and 1980s represent a "third way" of economic development? How has this approach been modified in the economic policies introduced since the 1990s?

8. Why might the ruling party lose electoral support at times of high economic growth? What does this tell you about the trade-offs facing leaders pursuing market reforms might in democratic (as opposed to authoritarian) regimes?

9. Have the ideological differences between Congress and the BJP translated into fundamental differences over domestic and foreign policy?

10. What problems gave rise to (a) the suicides of thousands of farmers in some rural districts, (b) the establishment and expansion of SEWA, and (c) the anticorruption movement led by Anna Hazare? What do these phenomena tell us about the long-term stability of India's political institutions?

IRAN

MAP 11.1. Map of Iran.

11 Iran

Vali Nasr

Introduction

At the turn of the twentieth century, Iran embarked on a path to development that was typical of many late developers. Iran's experience, however, has proved to be unique. Development was accompanied by ideological conflicts that culminated in a religiously inspired revolution in 1979. In the process, a modernizing monarchy gave place to the theocratic and revolutionary politics of the Islamic Republic of Iran (the official name of Iran since the revolution). As populism changed the character of the economy and Islamic ideology (a political doctrine based on Islam) transformed Iranian society, its norms, institutions, and, for a time at least, pursuit of its interests were subsumed under preservation of identity. Since the revolution, the nature of development has been complex, revealing modernizing impulses tempered by the pressures of Islamic ideology. Beyond its ideological and institutional particularities, the Islamic Republic shares many of the characteristics and problems of populist authoritarian regimes elsewhere in the developing world: a bloated public sector, mismanagement, and corruption.

There are three distinct and yet interrelated periods in Iran's modern development: the early and later **Pahlavi** (the dynasty that ruled Iran from 1925 to 1979); those of **Reza Shah Pahlavi** (1925–1941) and **Muhammad Reza Shah Pahlavi** (1941–1979); and the Islamic Republic (1979–present). There is greater continuity between the first two periods, under the Pahlavi monarchs, although there are notable differences as well. The Reza Shah period coincided with the rise of the modern Iranian state and started the process of development. The Muhammad Reza Shah period continued in the footsteps of the first period but accelerated the pursuit of modernization. Development under the second Pahlavi monarch was, moreover, conditioned by different global influences and domestic sociopolitical identities and interests. The Islamic Republic has been distinct from the earlier periods in its ideological orientation and in many aspects of its economic policies and political characteristics. Above and beyond their differences in ideological orientation or policy choices, the three periods are similar in the dominant role of the state in development. The basis of Iran's path in the modern world is to be found in the historical circumstances in which Iran first embarked on development.

The Global Context and the Rise of the Modern Iranian State

Iran is among the handful of developing countries to escape direct colonialism but not the impact of imperialism. Throughout the nineteenth century, the ruling Qajar dynasty (1796–1921) was unable to resist Western imperialist penetration; nor could it stave off the gradual loss of territory and control over national assets to foreign powers. This provided the context for the rise of the modern Iranian state and the path to development that it would follow (see Table 11.1 at the end of the chapter).

Also important was the pivotal role of the monarchy during the nineteenth century. The monarchy was important to imperial powers who wished to maintain a captive and weak center in Iran. As a result, imperial powers provided strategic support to the monarchy and helped thwart significant challenges to its authority. The broader powers of the monarchy were rooted in the dominant social position of the feudal aristocracy and tribal leaders, who sustained monarchical authority at the center, even as they resisted taxation and defended their autonomy. Of equal importance was the role of the religious establishment. Throughout the nineteenth century, the clergy resisted domination by the monarchy and defended the rights of the nation before imperialist interests that often worked through the monarchy. Still, at a more fundamental level, the clergy defended the sociopolitical position of the monarchy, just as the monarchy protected the socioeconomic interests of the clergy. The nature of relations among the state, the elite, and the religious establishment would change over time, with important consequences for Iran's pattern of development.

Concentration of power in the monarchy occurred at a time of weakening of the ruling political establishment as a whole, in large part caused by pressures that were brought to bear on Iranian society and Iran's body politic by imperialism. The concentration of power in a decaying central government led to circumstances in which neither the state nor social forces enjoyed countrywide domination. This, in turn, produced a crisis for monarchical absolutism. Eventually the monarchy found itself on the defensive against a strong constitutionalist movement that included the intelligentsia – who were the conduit for European constitutionalist ideals – elements of the religious establishment, the urban poor, and aspiring members of the bureaucracy and the emerging middle classes. The Constitutional Revolution, as this movement and the resultant 1906 constitution came to be known, placed limits on the power of the monarchy and vested much of its authority in a parliament. This would be the first serious attempt to alter the balance of power between the state and society. It produced a period of democratic rule in Iran, which proved to be short-lived. By the end of the first decade of the twentieth century, Iranian democracy had begun to lose ground to authoritarian tendencies.

The rise of democracy did not produce stable governing coalitions or well-organized and effective political parties. Democracy intensified political competition in the central government, just as it weakened the hold of the central government over the country, leading to palpable fears of the country's disintegration. This, along with the collapse of law and order, rampant corruption, and deteriorating economic conditions, limited the prospects for democratic consolidation. Elected governments proved to be just as pliable in the face of imperialist pressure as had absolutist monarchs before 1906. It had further become evident that democracy would not produce rapid modernization. Hence, those social forces that supported the Constitutional Revolution with the hope of bringing both political and economic modernization to Iran were confronted with a zero-sum choice – democracy or socioeconomic modernization. Many opted for the latter, believing that a strong central state would better protect fundamental rights to life and property, the integrity of national borders, and national rights before imperialist demands.

In the meantime, the Anglo-Russian rapprochement of 1907 made the division of Iran between the two world powers a distinct possibility, placing greater pressure on the democratic order. This possibility would continue to haunt Iranians until the Bolshevik revolution of 1917 drove a wedge between Russia and the West. Thenceforth, the British would once again take an interest in strengthening the central government in Iran. However, by then, the democratic order had been seriously damaged. Consequently, the domestic and foreign efforts to shore up the central authority and the increasing demands for effective modernization and development within Iran – which had first been pursued through the Constitutional Revolution – would now lead to a regime change. The result would be a new political order that would draw heavily on the institutional framework of the absolutist era. Iran would thus embark on its path to development by reconstituting the pre-1906 political institutions.

The Reza Shah Period and the Beginnings of Development, 1921–1941

The crisis of democracy ended with a military coup in 1921 that was led by Reza Khan (later Reza Shah Pahlavi) in alliance with dissident civilian politicians and intellectuals. Reza Khan quickly consolidated power and in 1925 ascended the throne. The coup ushered in a new period in Iran's history, during which national boundaries became institutionalized; the country committed itself to development; and its interests, identity, and institutions became defined and entrenched. In many ways, the fundamental characteristics of the modern state and the defining elements of its path to development were outlined during this period.

Reza Shah's monarchy was concerned with two separate but interrelated objectives: first, to assert the power of the central government and limit regional autonomy – that is, to ensure law and order and guarantee the territorial integrity of the country; and second, to develop Iran, understood at the time to mean social modernization and industrialization. The first objective required the establishment of a strong military, and the second required the construction of modern bureaucratic institutions. The realization of both objectives required an increase in state revenue and the mobilization of financial resources through taxation, greater regulation of the economy, and attempts to increase the proceeds from oil production and export. Both objectives would in time broaden the state's ability to formulate and implement coherent policies and to reach into society. The two objectives were the most important examples of the state's provision of "public goods" (that is, things that people want but that no individual or group of individuals can provide) in a society where such a concept was largely absent. The provision of these public goods had popular support and helped the state to expand its role in the society and economy and to organize resources and people effectively. In fact, reshaping identities and value systems in order to better provide those goods became central to the state's conception of its own function.

Reza Shah was largely successful in realizing both objectives. His military campaigns defeated separatist movements and subdued autonomous regions and rebellious warlords. In the process, he asserted the primacy of the central government and laid the foundations for strong centralized control of the country. Still, this did not end the obsession with territorial integrity, which at key junctures would translate into xenophobic nationalism but would otherwise further serve to strengthen state control and nudge Iran in the direction of absolutism. Historically, military-bureaucratic absolutism in Europe had facilitated the mobilization of resources in the face of threats to borders. The same process was evident in Iran as well. Hence, early on, the modern Iranian state developed authoritarian tendencies in response to international and domestic military threats and the need to mobilize resources to respond to them.

The goal of economic development led the state to extend its control over the economy to mobilize resources for industrialization. Following the examples of Germany and Japan during 1921–1941, the state established the first industries; invested in infrastructure; and tightened its hold over customs, banking, and foreign trade. The result was a form of state-led capitalism in which the state would see to industrialization, just as it would manage the day-to-day affairs of the economy, although it would provide a role for the private sector.

The objective of economic development both required and promoted administrative and social reform. Reza Shah supported the rise of modern bureaucratic institutions, a new judiciary, and the reform of public health and education. Students were sent abroad, and modern educational institutions were established in Iran. In addition, new administrative procedures and secular civil and penal codes were adopted.

Reza Shah was convinced that making Iran strong and fostering its economic development would require fundamental changes in the country's identity and social relations – an ambitious project of cultural engineering that required a coherent state ideology. The state secularized the judiciary and the educational system, and it restricted the powers of the clergy. It mandated the change of traditional dress to Western dress and promoted secular values. In so doing, it hoped to make popular culture compatible with the requirements and goals of development. In place of Islam, the state promoted nationalism, defined in terms of pre-Islamic Iranian identity. Such an identity would be secular and would provide an ideological foundation for both monarchical power and rapid development. The change in identity was also intended to inculcate discipline in the population as a prelude to development. It was then believed, largely because of imperialist propaganda, that Iranian cultural beliefs could not promote discipline and the values that are necessary for a modern society. Secular nationalism would remedy that problem. In all of this, Reza Shah was deeply influenced by the examples of Germany and Japan, and of **Kemalism** (a model of development based on secularism, nationalism, and state dominance in socioeconomic matters) in Turkey. Global context thus shaped interests, identities, and the relation between the two.

The concern with identity as a necessary prerequisite for successful development would become a hallmark of state-society relations in Iran. In Iran, the two dominant markers of identity are Islam and Iranian nationalism. The two have at times reinforced one another and at other times have represented different political ideals. Iranians became Muslim pursuant to the Arab invasion of Iran in the seventh century. As such, Islam has always been viewed by Iranian nationalists as the invader's faith. Iranians are unique among the early civilizations that converted to Islam in that they did not adopt the Arabic language and culture. This has created tensions between Iran's nationalism and its faith. Iranian **Shia** Islam is a minority sect in Islam that is distinguished from the majority Sunnis in that it believes that the descendants of the Prophet (whom Shias refer to as Imams) were the legitimate successors to the Prophet and that today the clergy (*ulama*, the highest-ranking among whom the Shias call **ayatollah**) serve as their representatives and as such exercise authority over the Shias. The Shias were always a suppressed community, and they did not exercise power until 1501, when a Shia monarchy made the faith the official religion of Iran. Shias differ from Sunnis in matters of faith much as the Eastern Church differs from the Western Church in Christianity. That Iran became the seat of Shi'ism gave the country its own unique attachment to Islam, which has always distinguished it from the Arab world and as such underscored the uniqueness of Iranian identity – setting it apart from the rest of the Muslim world.

Islam and Shi'ism have always played an important role in defining Iranian identity. However, with the advent of the modern state, emphasis was placed on secularism, which demanded separating Islam from Iranian nationalism. In place of Islam, Iranians were to identify themselves with their ethnicity and language, which as secular concepts were seen to be more compatible with modern nationalism and developmentalism. Iranian nationalism never replaced Islam, nor were the complex relations between the two ever completely resolved. Rather, from Reza Shah's regime to that of the Islamic Republic, identity featured importantly in state policy. The preoccupation with questions of identity – and hence issues such as music, dress, popular beliefs, and the cultural outlook of the individual – became important in defining the public good and setting the agenda for development. The legacy of the state's cultural policies continues to influence state-society relations in Iran to this day, and hence debates about development begin with struggles over identity.

Giving the state the means to govern effectively was expensive. In fact, how it dealt with financial needs shaped, to a significant degree, the nature of state power. Since the beginning of the twentieth century, Iran received royalties from the **Anglo-Iranian Oil Company**, a British company that managed oil production in southern Iran. Efforts to increase royalty payments to the Iranian government proved futile, which forced the state to rely more on tax revenue. Tax farming – a system in which local officials' incomes are tied to the amount of taxes they manage to collect – and other forms of unsystematic revenue collections were replaced with a centralized taxation system. The state also turned to foreign advisers to streamline Iran's financial system. Foreign expertise helped the state to extract resources from society and develop plans for economic development; it did not, however, altogether resolve the financial problems confronting the state. Financial constraints encouraged the state to monopolize power in order to increase its ability to extract resources from society and to negotiate more effectively with foreign commercial interests over royalties.

That a strong state did in fact rise in Iran at this time and that it did so despite significant financial constraints and resistance to central control, and in contravention of foreign interests, is noteworthy. It has been generally accepted that the rise of states is directly correlated with war making, and that societies that experience wars or significant social dislocation are more prone to produce strong states. The rise of the modern Iranian state during the 1920s was closely tied to the military campaigns that consolidated the central government's hold over the country and occurred amid the significant hardships – for example, economic hardship, famine, disease, social strife, and civil war – that Iranians endured during the first two decades of the twentieth century. The campaign to centralize power and defend the territorial integrity of the country had broad support among many social groups, notably those who had also been the main support for democracy. This allowed Reza Shah to tie the defense of the integrity of state borders to his own consolidation of power. It also allowed his regime to avoid compromises with various social actors – the feudal elite, tribal leaders, and merchants – in order to mobilize resources for the military campaigns.

During the 1920s, local power in Iran was strong but unorganized. It was, moreover, dissociated from politics at the center, and in some cases was supported by, and integrated with, foreign interests. It therefore did not serve as a source of support for the Parliament during the turbulent years of the democratic period or during the period of regime change in the 1920s. The subsequent weakening of democratic institutions such as the Parliament during the period of regime change meant minimal oversight by the Parliament of the administrative and financial activities of state leaders. Consequently, power accumulated at the center, and absolutist tendencies grew unbridled.

The growing dominance of the monarch combined with the social changes that development entailed created tensions in Iranian politics. In the first place, Reza Shah had been prevailed upon by the clergy to become a monarch, whereas in reality his regime was a "republican monarchy." No sooner had Reza Shah become king than he embarked on secularization and modernization and also abolished the hereditary titles of the aristocracy. In addition, his campaign to assert centralized control over the country pitted the state against local leaders. He thus moved away from those elite groups and social classes that had until then served as the pillars of the monarchy – the elite, the religious establishment, and the tribal leaders – and was looking instead to the new middle classes to bolster his regime. The Reza Shah period thus changed the social base of the ruling order. In the economic arena, the same trend was evident. Traditional tradesmen and commercial interests became alienated from the state as it extended its control over the economy. The change in the social base of the monarchy would prove consequential. Disenchanted elite groups, the religious establishment, and small merchants and traders would form the basis of the anti-Pahlavi oppositional coalition. This coalition would eventually serve as the backbone of the revolution of 1979.

Initially, Reza Shah allied himself with the new middle classes to take on the elite, local leaders, and the clergy. The new middle classes were then receptive to modernization, secularization, and the nationalist identity that Reza Shah promoted in lieu of Islam. The alliance between the new middle classes and the monarchy, however, failed to provide the state with a countervailing base of support because these classes were not ideologically committed to the monarchy. As the pace of modernization increased, tensions in the monarchy's relations with the new middle classes grew. By the 1930s, many in these classes were joining pro-democracy and various leftist organizations.

Development spearheaded the rise of modern bureaucratic agencies. At the outset, the bureaucracy supported Reza Shah. Over time, however, he became wary of the rising power of the bureaucracy and purged it of its principal leaders. By exercising more control over the bureaucracy, Reza Shah precluded the possibility that the bureaucracy would develop as a legal-rational institution independent of the control of the monarchy. The Iranian state from this point forward would display many characteristics of what comparativists sometimes term *patrimonialism*, in which power is concentrated in the ruler, whose exercise of authority is only partially influenced by legal and administrative procedures.

In sum, during this period, the global context – in the form of imperialism and the German-Japanese model – combined with the state's need to safeguard territorial integrity and pursue development to shape interests, identity, and institutions in a manner that empowered the state and hence ensured its domination over Iranian politics.

The Democratic Interregnum, 1941–1954

The pattern of development that began in 1921 was interrupted by World War II. The Reza Shah state fell victim to changes in the broader international environment. The western Allies were keen to use Iranian territory for supplying the Soviet Union against Germany, and for this it was imperative that they maintain control over Iran. Reza Shah's constant bickering with British oil companies, combined with Iran's reliance on Germany for a number of public projects, had made the British wary of him. The Allies demanded that Iran declare neutrality and expel all German citizens, that Reza Shah abdicate, and that the Iranian military disarm. In 1941, Reza Shah was replaced on the throne by his son, Muhammad Reza Pahlavi (known in the West as "the Shah"). Foreign intervention thus ushered in a new era in Iranian politics that was characterized by greater openness and new possibilities for state-society relations. Still, foreign intervention did not decisively reshape Iranian politics – rearranging its institutions and altering the balance of power among them – in the manner that the United States would do in Germany and Japan after the war. The British retained the monarchy and did not change the country's constitution or the balance of power among the various social and political actors. That the monarchy would in later years emerge once again as a dominant force in an all-powerful state was therefore not very surprising.

Still, Reza Shah's departure opened the political process and created alternate developmental paths. During the war, political groups that had been suppressed by Reza Shah – liberals, leftists, and the clergy – organized and established a place for themselves in the political arena. The Parliament, which since 1921 had steadily lost ground to the monarchy, was empowered and once again occupied center stage. The political opening suggested that Iran could develop along democratic lines and that power might permanently shift from the monarchy to the parliament, devolving in the process from state institutions to a broader spectrum of social and political actors. By 1954, however, domestic problems combined with changes in the global context to end the democratic opening.

The 1941–1954 period witnessed an intense struggle over the definition of political identity in Iran. The outcome of that struggle would be important for the fate of democracy. Some of the political forces that became dominant during the 1941–1954 period were illiberal. Communist, fascist, and religious groups and parties operated in the open political process but were not committed to democracy. In fact, their activities would serve as the pretext for once again vesting the state – and the institution of the monarchy – with greater powers.

Most important in this regard was the communist Tudeh (Masses) Party. Closely allied with the Soviet Union, the Tudeh Party posed a strong challenge to the ruling order and Western interests in Iran. The party was active among the middle classes, labor, intellectuals, and students, mobilizing these social groups in defense of social justice. It subscribed to the cult of Stalin and did not favor democracy. The Tudeh Party's ambiguous role in the Soviet Union's attempt to separate two provinces in northern Iran after World War II helped create both popular and Western support for strengthening the political center, which ultimately weakened the Tudeh Party and, in the process, the budding democracy.

The resurgence of religion in politics was equally significant. Religious forces were keen to roll back the secular policies of the Pahlavi state and to institutionalize their role in society and politics. To this end, they became active in the political arena, but not with the aim of strengthening democracy. Both the communists and religious forces weakened democracy by engaging in agitational politics: demonstrations, strikes, and sit-ins in the case of the Tudeh Party, and political assassinations in the case of religious activists. By creating political uncertainty, disruptions, and social tensions, the two groups made the task of democratic consolidation difficult and helped the monarchy enlist foreign support for its campaign to consolidate power.

Most damaging to democracy was the oil crisis of 1951–1953 and its link with Cold War politics. The dispute over royalties with the Anglo-Iranian Oil Company, which had begun during the 1930s, eventually culminated in an impasse during 1951–1953. As the British company refused to accommodate Iran's demands for higher royalties, nationalist feelings were aroused and they dominated Iranian politics. The monarchy, the military, and some in the business community favored a low-key approach, believing that a confrontational attitude would not favor Iran. Because of British intransigence, however, Iranians demanded more. The popularly elected nationalist prime minister, **Mohammad Mossadeq**, and his National Front Party capitalized on the public mood and nationalized the assets of the Anglo-Iranian Oil Company in Iran in 1953. The decision was widely popular within Iran and was supported by the Tudeh Party and religious activists as well.

Britain responded by cutting Iran out of the oil market. The Iranian economy collapsed, causing social tension and political radicalism. The palpable fear of a communist takeover changed the political alignment that had dominated Iranian politics. The clergy, worried about communism, switched sides, as did key segments of the middle classes, commercial interests, and elements of the nationalist elite. This political realignment facilitated concerted action between the monarchy and the Iranian military in close cooperation with the United States and Britain. The result was a military coup that toppled the National Front government, ending the democratic interregnum and restoring the monarchy to power. The 1941–1954 period had seen the possibility of alternate identities – Islamic, secular, democratic – shaping state-society relations and Iranian politics developing along a different path. By 1954, however, those possibilities were no longer present. Foreign intervention first interrupted and then led to the resumption of the state's development in the direction first instituted by Reza Shah. Interests, identities, and ultimately institutions were reshaped by the changing global context.

Resurrection of the Pahlavi State, 1954–1963

The 1954–1963 period was one of consolidation of monarchical power. Relying on the military, and with crucial financial and technical assistance from the United States, the monarchy went on the offensive against its opponents. The National Front Party and the Tudeh Party were banned. The military and bureaucracy were purged of their sympathizers. The campaign also weakened the institutions of civil society and ultimately the Parliament, dimming the prospects for democracy. Cold War considerations led the United States to support these developments in Iran and to help train Iranian military and intelligence agencies to protect the state, which was viewed as a bulwark against communism and the southward expansion of the Soviet Union. Financial aid helped buoy Iran's economy and generated support for the ruling order. The consolidation of power under the monarchy would commit the state to a largely economic vision of development. The spirit of this posture was captured in the Shah's statement: "When the Iranians learn to behave like Swedes, I will behave like the king of Sweden."

The single-minded pursuit of development – the public good whose provision would justify state authority from this point forward – required further streamlining the organization of resources and people, the imperatives that had also propelled the expansion of state authority under Reza Shah. This led the state to reformulate its relations with agrarian elites, who had to this point remained close to the monarchy; the religious establishment, with which the monarchy had only a tenuous alliance; and the middle classes, which were the main agents and beneficiaries of development, although they were not committed to the monarchy. The consequences of these reformulations would determine the course of Iran's subsequent development.

Economic Growth and Authoritarianism, 1963–1979

Between 1959 and 1963, the Pahlavi state had to weather a number of challenges, the resolution of which both necessitated redoubling its commitment to development and created greater room for pursuing it. The political rumblings occurred at a time when the United States began to waver in its unconditional support of the Pahlavi state and viewed some form of reform in Iran as necessary to limit communist influence in the country. The change in the U.S. attitude was parlayed into momentum for wide-scale reform.

In the meantime, an austerity package prescribed by the International Monetary Fund, which included a cut in government spending and devaluation of the currency to discourage imports, brought on a severe recession during the 1960–1962 period. The perceived threat to the ruling order convinced state leaders that they could not afford prolonged economic crises. Oil revenue, even despite modest increases ($555 million in 1963–1964, comprising 12 percent of the GNP), would not remedy the crisis or satisfy development needs. Hence, reform would have to go hand in hand with, as well as help spur, economic growth. The state began to see its objective of development as integral to sociopolitical reform. This vision culminated in the "White Revolution" of 1963, the term coined to upstage the Left and its promise of "Red" revolution.

The White Revolution was a package of sweeping reforms that aimed to change the structure of societal relations in Iran and to enable more effective resource mobilization in the service of development. The most important initiatives were land reform, the enfranchisement of women, and the provision of greater rights and a greater share of industrial profits to industrial labor.

Through the White Revolution, the state was hoping to institutionalize its hold over the middle classes and among those social groups that might serve as the base of support for an effective communist movement, including the poor, the peasantry, and industrial labor. These reforms, so the argument ran, were necessary for effective development. They would modernize Iranian society, changing it in ways that would help industrialization.

The White Revolution was a risky venture because the principal losers in the reforms – the landed elite and the clergy – had in the past served as sources of support for the monarchy, whereas the support of the modern middle classes for monarchy had at best been tenuous. The Shah was falling into the same trap that his father had, vesting his political fortunes in a social class whose loyalties ultimately would not rest with the monarchy. In addition, given the Pahlavi state's pro-industry bias, it did not cultivate a base of support among the peasantry that it was enfranchising. Industrial labor, meanwhile, did not as yet possess sufficient power to act as a significant source of support for the monarchy; and if they were to become a force, the monarchy was unlikely to claim their allegiance for long. More immediately, however, the state would rely on the rising power of the bureaucracy, which itself was being modernized from within. The bureaucracy was committed to development, and to that end joined in a ruling alliance with the monarchy. In effect, the state reformulated its links with society and also defined the shape of its opposition. The landed elite, the clergy, and the "liberal Left," all of whom opposed the White Revolution or viewed it as the means through which the state might devour their base of support, gravitated toward a united antistate stance. The restoration of power to the monarchy thus reconstituted the oppositional alliance that had first surfaced during the earlier Reza Shah period.

The first expression of this opposition was the protest movement led by the cleric **Ayatollah Ruhollah Khomeini** in 1964. The protest was strongly antistate, but its immediate concern was with the White Revolution. Khomeini characterized the enfranchisement of women as "un-Islamic." He also rejected land reform as a violation of Islamic protection of property rights. The protest movement brought together the landed elite, the religious establishment, and the liberal Left. The first two groups opposed specific points of the White Revolution, whereas the liberal Left viewed the entire reform package as a threat to its political position and had a vested interest in its failure. The White Revolution sought to change the social structure, in opposition to which the liberal Left had mobilized support, and to render the Left's political programs obsolete.

The protest movement failed. The state's agenda of social reform and rapid economic development thus unfolded unencumbered. Still, the protest movement had the effect of committing the state to a greater use of force in contending with the opposition. This in turn led to the consolidation of the anti-Pahlavi forces into a more coherent alliance under the unified leadership of the clergy and the liberal Left. Such thinkers as **Ali Shariati** actually began to formulate a socially conscious religio-ideological perspective that could consolidate an anti-Shah alliance. This opposition would in time become increasingly violent and would, in turn, face greater violence from the state. From this point forward, the security apparatuses of the state, most notably the secret police, **SAVAK**, would use repressive measures, including detentions and torture, to subdue the opposition. The opposition produced radical communist and Islamist urban-guerrilla organizations, escalating antistate activities to the level of armed conflict and acts of terror. The radicalization of the opposition and the state's use of violence in suppressing it polarized Iranian politics and gradually concentrated power in a limited number of state institutions – most notably its security apparatuses – and in the monarchy.

Economically, however, the 1960s was a period of relative success. Land reform, the overhaul of the bureaucracy, and the weakening of the Parliament allowed economic managers to pursue growth aggressively and with greater freedom from outside influence. The result was an industrial transformation, producing growth rates that were unmatched in Iran's history. The gross domestic product (GDP) for this period grew at an average of 9.2 percent per year, and industrial growth rates averaging 15 percent per year were among the highest in the developing world. At the same time, the central characteristics of the economy changed as it acquired medium and heavy industries and a modern private sector.

Economic development in Iran during the 1960s was based largely on **import-substitution industrialization (ISI)**. Although ISI produces rapid growth rates early on and helps kick-start industrialization, it also poses political and economic challenges down the road. As we saw in the chapters on Mexico and India, ISI places emphasis on capital-intensive industries and hence leads to the neglect of small-scale production and the agricultural sector. It can lead to uneven development, overurbanization, and income inequality. It also puts pressure on government finances and the balance of trade, just as it augments state control of the economy. It was partly to address problems born of ISI that Iran decided to support the oil-price hikes of **OPEC** (the Organization of Petroleum Exporting Countries) during the 1970s.

The rise in oil prices ($958 million in 1968–1969, comprising 18 percent of Iran's GNP, in contrast with $20 billion in 1975–1976, representing 35 percent of the GNP) removed financial pressures from the state and allowed it to spend more freely on various industrial and social projects. It is interesting to note, however, that higher oil prices augmented the challenges before the Shah. They adversely affected the pattern of economic development as the state deepened ISI, but did so with decreasing efficiency. Although the Iranian economy performed well during the 1970s, it veered off the path toward viable industrialization and market development and eventually faced serious crises.

The oil boom created bottlenecks in the economy and led to wasteful spending on grandiose projects. Iran spent billions of dollars on infrastructure and industrial projects. It also spent huge sums on war material and public enterprises of questionable economic value. All of this eroded trust in the management of the economy. The rapid pace of growth also created social dislocation, cultural confusion, and new political demands with which the state was unequipped to contend. In addition, the newfound wealth encouraged corruption and speculative financial activities. This adversely affected public morale and skewed popular perception about the meaning and intent of entrepreneurial activity. The oil wealth also raised expectations – so much so that the state not only was unable to gain political support for acquiring the new wealth but also found itself falling short of fulfilling growing expectations.

The Iranian state began to face political problems associated with "**rentier states**," that is, states in which income that is external to the productive capacity of the economy accounts for the lion's share of state revenue. Rentier states are generally politically weak because the state derives little if any of its income from the population and, as a result, does not devise ways to increase revenues through taxation. Nor does it negotiate with the population in order to increase society's contribution to state revenue. Instead, rentier states invest in distributive mechanisms and, having developed a relationship of distribution and patronage with their populations, do not develop meaningful links with society. The population does not credit the government for the generation of wealth, although it expects more from the government in terms of distribution of wealth. Popular support remains contingent on a continued flow of "rent."

As oil income came to dominate the Iranian economy, the Pahlavi state began to face a serious political crisis. On the one hand, its developmental agenda had concentrated power in the state and the monarchy and isolated both from other social groups. On the other hand, the state justified its course of action in terms of provision of a public good: development. Between 1946 and 1979, the state had changed the character of the economy in a fundamental fashion from agriculture to industry. Public planning, urbanization, industrialization, diversification, and infrastructural and human capital investments had produced sustained change and growth. The increase in oil wealth, however, denied the state the ability to claim credit for its economic achievements. It undermined the state's developmentalist claims as it depicted development as synonymous with oil revenue, rendering redundant the political apparatuses that the Pahlavi monarchs had argued were necessary for realizing development. All of this pushed an already narrowly based state to the brink of collapse. The resultant political tensions erupted in 1977, culminating in the Islamic Revolution of 1979 that toppled the Pahlavi state.

The global context proved important at this juncture as well. The revolution unfolded at a time of change in Iran's relations with the United States. Jimmy Carter, the U.S. president, was unwilling to provide unconditional support to the Shah's regime and instead strongly advocated political reform in Iran. The new U.S. approach created confusion in the Iranian state and emboldened the opposition.

The opposition to the Pahlavi state consisted of liberal and pro-democracy forces, the Left, and religious activists, but it increasingly adopted a strongly Islamic character, especially after Ayatollah Khomeini – then in exile in Iraq – assumed its leadership. Khomeini used his position of authority to put forward a particularly revolutionary and antistate reading of Islam and used its symbols to mobilize the masses. Khomeini also built on the traditional role of Shia clerics, arguing that given their knowledge of religion, they must rule politically if the society was to be Islamic, just, and prosperous. His religio-political crusade was therefore directed at constructing a theocratic form of government.

Khomeini's arguments – which were published as *Islamic Government* – were part of a broader movement of revolt against secularism, and the state institutions that represented and promoted it, that was defining politics in the Muslim world at the time. Across the Muslim world, thinkers such as Khomeini were rejecting the modern state as a failure. They argued that it had failed to bring about genuine development or resolve regional crises such as the Arab-Israeli conflict, and most importantly it had failed to reverse the palpable decline of Muslim worldly power before that of the West. These thinkers captured the frustration of those whom development had left behind and those who lamented the weakness of Muslim states on the world stage when they argued that, rather than empower Muslims, the modern state had merely trampled on their culture by promoting secularism and marginalizing Islam in public life. These thinkers contended that the problem in the Muslim world was secularism and its protector and promoter, the modern state. Far from being the solution to sociopolitical problems and agents of positive change, the modern state had cut Muslims off from the roots of their power – their religion. Therefore, it would be by dismantling the secular state and erecting in its place an Islamic state that Muslims would find the path to development. For these thinkers and activists, Islam provided the blueprint for a perfect government that would be built on Islamic law and the model of the Prophet of Islam's rule during the religion's early years in the seventh century. Their vision of the Islamic state was revolutionary and utopian, rejecting the existing social and political systems and promising a perfect order in their place. Their challenge to the state was not only socioeconomic – as was the case with the Left –but also cultural. The Shah's regime –with its pro-Western secularism – and Khomeini's challenge to it in many regards epitomized the politics of Islamic activism and served as the opening battle between Islamic activism and the secular state, which has defined Muslim politics since 1979.

The success of Islamic activism in Iran was not entirely a matter of ideology. In promoting his cause, Khomeini strengthened the alliance between the religious establishment and the Left that had been in place since 1964. Khomeini successfully managed to keep the opposition focused on overthrowing the Shah, while postponing the resolution of ideological disagreements and cultural tensions between the religious and secular opposition to the Shah to the postrevolutionary period. His presence on the political scene, however, made religious identity central to politics. In so doing, Khomeini and the revolutionary forces rejected the developmentalist secularism of the Pahlavi state. The revolution owed its success, in large part, to the fact that this stance did not create tensions in the ranks of revolutionary forces, segments of which were politically at odds with the Pahlavi state but shared in its secularism and were themselves products of the Pahlavi state's social engineering. As a result, the revolutionary movement in Iran in 1979 was politically uniform but culturally and socially eclectic in that it had both Islamist and secular-liberal and leftist elements in it.

The revolution itself unfolded rather rapidly over the course of a mere eighteen months. It fed on a set of cascading events that converged to overwhelm the Shah's regime, which failed to react adroitly to the challenge before it. These events were: wide-scale street demonstrations, the mobilization of religious institutions and activists, labor strikes, the disappearance of the democratic middle, and the collapse of the military. The first three events had the effect of including larger numbers of people in the revolution, producing a degree of popular mobilization that overwhelmed state institutions. The latter two events ensured that the state would not respond effectively to the mobilization, guaranteeing the success of the revolution.

Throughout 1977 and 1978, a growing number of Iranians joined street demonstrations to ask first for political reform and later for regime change. The Shah's government proved unable to contend with the demonstrations either through a show of force in the streets or by giving in to demands for reform. The growing religious tenor of the demonstrations that was facilitated by the growing political importance of a network of mosques, seminaries, and religious organizations soon provided a backbone to the demonstrators and helped tie their demands to the larger ideological arguments that were put forth by Khomeini. The popular mobilization reached a critical stage when it led to labor strikes, which included not only government workers but also employees of critical industrial sectors such as oil and electricity, whose walkouts were of more than symbolic importance and impacted the economy directly.

There were then two forces capable of dealing with the mobilization: the first were the pro-democracy politicians who were associated with the National Front Party of the 1950s, and the second was the military. The first could contain and manage the mobilized social force, and the second could have suppressed them. The democratic middle failed to play its historic role, partly because it would not reach an agreement with the Shah on how to deal with the mobilization and partly because it decided not to challenge Khomeini or the Left. The military was not deployed in an effective way during the early months of the agitations when it could have changed the outcome. It was not until the Shah had left Iran in February 1979 that the military decided to flex its muscles, only to find that its window of opportunity had already been closed.

In the end, the Shah's failure to divide the opposition along ideological and cultural lines precluded the possibility of negotiations between the monarchy and the liberal Left over a transfer of power. The result was that the political situation continued to radicalize in favor of the religious element in the revolutionary coalition. This did not bode well for democratic development in Iran in 1979. In the end, the Pahlavi state collapsed because of the Shah's inability to contend with political challenges at a critical juncture. The Pahlavi state had in effect become reduced to the Shah, and his inaction meant that despite the broad coercive power available to the state, it would not survive.

With the fall of the Shah in 1979, the evolution of state authority and function took a new turn. However, despite significant changes in the way in which the state and the economy work in the Islamic Republic, the balance of power between state and society, and the role of the state in socioeconomic change, cannot be understood separately from what occurred during the Pahlavi period. Despite the regime change, ideological shift, and radical social transformation, the path down which the Pahlavi period set Iran continued to shape its subsequent development.

The Revolutionary Era, 1979–1988

The collapse of the monarchy in February 1979 ushered in a new era in Iranian politics. The ideological force of the revolution suggested that the working of the state, the role of interests, and the centrality of identity in development were all likely to change. The revolution promised an axial shift in Iranian politics that would occur in a changing global context.

The immediate aftermath of the revolution was a period of great fluidity during which the old order was dismantled and revolutionary forces began to leave their imprint on the state and society. Revolutions destroy certain social classes and alter state bureaucracies, and thus make other paths of development possible. In Iran, however, the revolution did not produce a strong state but took over an existing one and adapted it to its ideology. The central role of the state in development thus remained unaffected. As a result, the postrevolutionary state displayed continuity with the past as well as change from it.

Revolutionary forces purged supporters of the old order from various state institutions, public and private organizations, and economic enterprises, and the revolution quickly produced institutions of its own. Revolutionary courts and committees and the **Revolutionary Guards** were organized to serve the functions of the judiciary, the police, and the military. Just as the rise of the Pahlavi state had been closely associated with the creation of the Iranian military, the rise of the new revolutionary state was closely tied to the emergence of these new institutions. Although initially formless and disorganized, the new institutions wielded a great deal of power. In time, their presence would create confusion in the state, as the purview of activities of the old military, police, and judiciary would overlap with those of the newly formed revolutionary committees, guards, and courts.

The liquidation of the old order, however, was only a prelude to larger struggles over defining the new order. With the success of the revolution, Ayatollah Khomeini became the undisputed leader of Iran. His supremacy only thinly disguised the intense conflict that was being waged over the definition of the new order. With the triumph of the revolution, the political concord of the disparate groups in opposition to the Shah began to unravel. The liberals, the Left, and the clergy now competed to determine Iran's future.

In March 1979, Iranians voted in a referendum to replace the monarchy with an "Islamic Republic." The term was coined by Khomeini, but it symbolized the struggle among the various factions of the revolutionary alliance over the identity of the regime that was to rule Iran. Throughout 1979, the struggle became more pronounced in the debates over the new constitution. The resulting document envisioned the Islamic Republic as a modern state with all of the constitutional and organizational features of such a state. It provided for a parliament, a judiciary, and an executive branch. It delineated the powers of each through a system of checks and balances. But the constitution also made Islamic law supreme. It furthermore recognized Khomeini's position as that of the supreme leader of the revolution (office of *Vali-e Faqih*, or "supreme guardian-jurisconsult"), an office whose occupant would not be elected, would not be accountable to any authority, and would have total veto power over all government decisions and policy making. This arrangement subjugated the political to the religious in state affairs. It also made identity central to the question of state authority, above and beyond economic and social interests.

The outcome of the constitutional process suggested that the religious element, led by Khomeini, had gained the upper hand. His domination became more apparent as the revolutionary regime demanded greater popular observation of Islamic strictures, especially those concerning women's dress. Religious elites also mobilized support among the lower middle classes and the poor – groups with close ties to the religious establishment – to marginalize the modern middle classes, who served as the social base of the liberal Left. With the victory of the religious hard-liners in this conflict, the number of clerics in high political offices grew dramatically.

The final consolidation of power in the hands of the religious element came in 1981–1982. Although Islamic activists had already gained the upper hand, it was the global context in the form of the **hostage crisis** in 1979–1980 (when a group of militant "students" took over the U.S. embassy in Tehran and held its American personnel hostage for months on end) and the **Iran-Iraq War** (1980–1988) that facilitated their complete domination. These events diverted popular attention in Iran, and international attention abroad, from domestic power struggles. In addition, both events created a siege mentality that bolstered the popularity of the religious leadership, who could claim to be defending Iran from American and Iraqi aggression. In this climate, the liberal Left was portrayed as U.S. stooges, and resistance to a greater role for Islam in society was depicted as a Western ploy to destabilize the revolution.

With the purge of the liberal Left, the revolution became a distinctly Islamic affair. Revolutionary zeal and concern with identity would henceforth define the nature and function of the state. As in the formation of the Pahlavi state under Reza Shah, the Islamic Republic likewise justified its power in terms of the provision of a public good, except that the public good presented by the Islamic Republic was to be greater Islamization of society and politics rather than economic development. The Islamic Republic was not interested in rolling back the state's control over society or its ability to penetrate and control it. It, too, believed in a domineering state. In fact, the leadership of the Islamic Republic aimed at expanding rather than contracting the state's control of society.

As in the early Pahlavi state, the Islamic Republic engaged in social engineering as a prerequisite for the realization of its public-policy agenda. It, too, became directly concerned with the dress, music, and cultural outlook of Iranians. It instituted tight control of both the public and private arenas, and viewed social engineering as central to successful policy formulation and implementation. The state's understanding of its function and powers, in some respects, reflected significant continuities with the Pahlavi period.

The centrality of Islamic ideology to state policy made identity and revolutionary fervor central to the flow of politics and the relations between the state and society. That fervor, in turn, continued to unfold in the context of the Iran-Iraq War during the 1980s. The war, caused by border disputes and Iraqi leader Saddam Hussein's expansionism, was one of the most costly and devastating of the latter part of the twentieth century. During the course of the eight-year war, some one million Iranians lost their lives. Iran temporarily lost control of parts of its oil-rich province of Khuzestan and incurred significant damage to its urban centers, agriculture, and industrial infrastructure. It was able to turn the tide of the war only at a tremendous human cost. The need to mobilize support and resources for the war pushed the state to emphasize ideology and the revolutionary values that are associated with it. The successful use of ideology in mobilization for war helped entrench revolutionary zeal and identity in lieu of socioeconomic interests in Iranian politics. Consequently, throughout the 1980–1988 period, the workings of the state remained closely tied to the pursuit of Islamization. This, in turn, committed Iran to a confrontational foreign policy and shifted power to the more radical elements in the state leadership. Khomeini supported this trend because it bolstered his power in Iran and served his ambitions to influence regional and international politics.

Ideological zeal also shaped politics and economics in the Islamic Republic. The Islamic Republic has been different from the Pahlavi state in that despite greater state domination of society, it has avoided personalized rule. Even when Khomeini was at the helm, power was spread among the clerical leaders, who were unified through a patronage network that connected the religious leadership at the center to clerical power brokers. The clerical establishment was committed to the Islamic Republic and to Khomeini's leadership. In fact, Khomeini quickly inculcated group interest in a politically active clergy, thus tying their political ambitions and social position to the fortunes of the Islamic Republic. The clerical leadership ruled collectively – acting as a dominant class – distinguished from the general population by dress and education. The uniform commitment to the Islamic Republic and Khomeini's ideology, however, did not eliminate struggles for power, differences over policy, and disagreements over ideological interpretation among the religious activists and the clerical leadership.

The clerical leadership did not produce a satisfactory way of managing these political debates and conflicts. Before the revolution, there had existed no dominant revolutionary party, as had been the case in Russia or China before their communist revolutions. Iran's revolutionary movement was not ideologically and culturally uniform, further limiting the development of a dominant revolutionary organization either before or immediately after the revolution. This revolution, then, turned out to be the first modern revolution to lack a "**vanguard**" **party**.

In the absence of a formal organization to manage struggles of power and debates over policy among state leaders, factional politics came out into the open. In the 1980s, three notable factions emerged within the Islamic Republic. The first favored a relaxation of revolutionary vigilance and stabilization of economic relations. Its members came to be known as the "moderates." Those identified with the second faction favored a continuation of revolutionary fervor but at the same time wished to promote a mercantile economy and the right to private property. They came to be known as the "conservatives." The third faction favored a strong anti-Western policy and the export of the revolution, as well as state control of the economy and limited rights to private property. It came to be known as the "radical" or "hard-line" faction and was responsible for much of the excesses of the Islamic Republic in foreign policy and for the expropriation of private property during the first decade of the Islamic Republic. The Iran-Iraq War and Iran's confrontational foreign policy helped the radical faction, whose members were closely allied with the Revolutionary Guards and oversaw Iran's support for revolutionary activism in the Muslim world. The revolutionary fervor espoused by this faction served the aims of mobilizational politics. Although the hard-liners had only a small base of support, mainly in the Revolutionary Guards and in the lower-middle and lower classes, they wielded much power in the government and were supported by Ayatollah Khomeini throughout the 1980–1988 period. The hard-line faction owed its power to its role in mobilizing support for the war and for the Islamic Republic's foreign policy. That power, derived from the global context in which Iran found itself, worked to increase state domination of the economy and promoted centralized economic planning.

The three factions existed only informally. There has been no actual organization, charter, rules, or platforms to define membership; nor are there any grassroots movements or party structures. The factions have functioned as informal circles within the revolutionary elite, with ill-defined and often changing boundaries. The factions have, however, become proto-party structures, especially because they have shaped electoral results directly.

Struggles for power among these factions occurred for the most part in the Parliament, in various consultative forums, in government agencies, in **Friday Prayer** sermons, and in the media. Whereas debates over foreign policy were restrained, in economic matters the differences were pronounced and the debates were acrimonious. Most notably, the radical faction clashed with the two other factions over the right to property and the legal protection of mercantile activities, both of which were eventually accepted by the revolutionary government.

Factionalism dominated politics in Iran throughout the 1980s. It greatly influenced the distribution of power between the president and prime minister on one side and the Parliament on the other. It also influenced the state's relations with society. More important, it influenced the working of the economy and determined the extent to which interest or identity would shape the state and its policies.

The revolution changed the course of economic development in Iran significantly. The political turmoil of the revolution (1977–1979), subsequent domestic political crises, legal uncertainties following the collapse of law and order, the meting out of revolutionary justice, debates over property rights, the "brain drain" (the exodus of educated people), the war with Iraq, and international isolation after the hostage crisis all acted to retard the rate of growth. The revolution also radically altered the perceptions of socioeconomic interest and the nature of development. The leftist elements in the revolution viewed economic development under the Pahlavi state as misguided, capitalistic, and, hence, doomed to failure. The religious element was uninterested in development as such and favored replacing it as a national goal with Islamization. Khomeini set the tone in this regard when he commented that "economics is for donkeys" – that is, only Islamization matters. The pursuit of interest, he maintained, should be made subservient to identity.

After 1979, therefore, economic development occupied a less prominent place in the priorities of state leaders. To the extent that there was an economic policy in the early years, it was heavily influenced by Marxist models that had been tried in a number of developing countries. Hence, soon after the revolution, the government nationalized the financial institutions, major industries, and business ventures of those who had been close to the Pahlavi state. By 1998–1999, the state owned 80 percent of the Iranian economy, relegating the private sector to small-scale economic activities.

The expansion of the state's control of the economy in time served political ends because the state could distribute jobs to its most ardent supporters. The growth of the public sector also produced new avenues for corruption in the bureaucracy and the political leadership. The net result of this was significantly reduced efficiency. Between 1978 and 1988, the GDP fell by 1.5 percent per year. Put differently, in 1988, the GDP stood at 1974 levels. Industry experienced six years of negative growth. Rapid population growth produced high levels of unemployment, which in 1988 exceeded 30 percent. The weak private sector was unable to create enough jobs to absorb the surplus labor. The government throughout the 1980s addressed the problem by providing employment in the public sector, which by 1988 accounted for one-third of all jobs. In the meantime, oil income fell. The share of oil revenue as a percentage of GDP fell from 30–40 percent in the 1970s to 9–17 percent in the 1980s as production levels fell from 5.6 million barrels per day to between 2.2 and 2.9 million. The government increased the rate and scope of taxation, but the economy depended on oil revenues, which continued to account for 85 percent of hard-currency earnings.

By 1988, the economic impact of the war with Iraq, international isolation and economic sanctions, and a growing population and declining production presented the Iranian economy with a serious crisis. Shortages in consumer goods had produced a thriving black market that skewed economic interests and the distribution of resources, further reducing efficiency. In addition, the growth of the public sector did not eradicate poverty. By weakening the private sector, it did reduce income inequality. But standards of living, especially of the urban poor, did not improve substantially. Inflation and unemployment had effectively undermined the radicals' populism.

Although during the 1980–1988 period economic hardships could be blamed on the Iran-Iraq War, the conclusion of the war denied the state that excuse. The scope of the economic crisis facing the state now posed serious political challenges. Interests could no longer be easily made subordinate to ideological concerns and the rhetoric of identity politics. Change thus became imperative.

The Post-Khomeini Era, 1988–Present

In 1988, the Iran-Iraq War ended with Iraq's unequivocal victory. The following year, Ayatollah Khomeini died. These two events had a profound effect on politics in the Islamic Republic. The defeat in the war was a psychological blow to the revolutionary elite. It diminished their legitimacy and reduced the utility of their ideological politics. The population became less tolerant of sacrifices demanded of them, especially because eight years of such sacrifices had ended in an ignoble military defeat. Khomeini's passing from the scene made it more difficult for the ruling order to resist change. As the state began to yield to pressure for change, its policy making became more pragmatic, reflecting a greater concern for interests over identity.

After Khomeini died, the president, **Ayatollah Ali Khamenei** (a member of the conservative faction), became supreme leader, and the speaker of the Parliament, **Ayatollah Ali Akbar Hashemi-Rafsanjani** (a member of the moderate faction), became president (1988–1997). The ascendance of the two suggested an alliance between the conservative and moderate factions to marginalize the radical faction. The immediate consequence of Khamenei's and Rafsanjani's assumption of power was the streamlining of the workings of the offices of supreme leader and president. These changes were followed by constitutional reforms that, among other things, integrated revolutionary committees and courts and the Revolutionary Guards with the police, judiciary, and the military, respectively. The Rafsanjani administration also vested greater powers in the bureaucracy and reduced the influence of ideological politics in its day-to-day work. These efforts once again made economic development a central concern of the state and a justification for its power. The post-Khomeini era thus saw the revival of the Pahlavi conception of the state. These changes did not, however, altogether resolve problems of governance in the Islamic Republic. Most important, the position of the supreme leader limited the power of the president and continued to tie the political system to ideological politics.

The Iranian legislature wields extensive power and limits the scope of the presidency. This is because of the complexities of the political relations of the ruling elite. From the outset, the Islamic Republic did not have the institutional means to distribute power among its various elements and factions. The function that should have been performed by internal party elections was thus performed by general elections. As such, the Islamic Republic itself functions as a party with regular and free elections among "Islamic" candidates. The ruling order has viewed the voters as party members, mobilized through mosque networks and ideological propagation, and the Parliament as a "**Central Committee**" of sorts. Still, the regularity of general elections has helped institutionalize the place of the Parliament, the Islamic Consultative Assembly, in the Islamic Republic. Hence, the requirement of deciding over the distribution of power within the ruling regime, and the absence of institutional mechanisms to do so outside of the public arena, by default introduced electoral politics and parliamentary behavior to Iran.

General elections and parliamentary practices, despite all their limitations, have brought about a certain degree of pluralism in the essentially theocratic structure of the Islamic Republic. This means that although Iran is an authoritarian state, far more of its political offices are distributed on the basis of elections – albeit limited elections – and its Parliament wields far more effective power than comparable bodies in the Arab world. In fact, one observes two contradictory tendencies working themselves out in the Islamic Republic: on the one hand, the concentration of supreme power in an ideological state; and on the other, democratic practices that are being given significant, if limited, scope for expression within a power structure governed at its apex by a clerical leadership.

It is important to note that elections in the Islamic Republic have not been entirely open in that there are strict limits on which candidates are allowed to participate. However, once the list of candidates has been set, the elections have been generally free. This has to do with the combination of the institutional restriction and procedural freedom that characterizes the structure of the Islamic Republic. The state possesses an authoritarian control over society, but the state itself is complex and made up of powerful factions that continuously vie with one another for control. Although the state has been successful in eliminating from the electoral process all those who challenge its fundamental ideological vision, it has not been able to eliminate those who, while sharing this vision, nonetheless challenge various aspects of policy making. Elections are therefore real insofar as they determine the relative influence of the various power centers at the top. They are less than real, however, in that they do not allow for any genuine change in the distribution of power within society nor do they alter the composition of the leadership of the state.

The importance of the elections and the Parliament increased in the post-Khomeini era because Khomeini's passing from the scene intensified factional rivalries. Khomeini's death also increased interest in electoral politics, which reached its climax in the presidential elections of 1997. The intensification of the factional rivalries has in effect nudged the Islamic Republic in the direction of electoral politics and vested greater powers in its representative institutions.

Also important in this regard has been the growing role of economic considerations and, more generally, interests in policy making. Rafsanjani assumed his presidency at a time of economic crisis in Iran. He proposed to reform the Iranian economy and also change the policy-making environment to better reflect economic interests and pragmatic considerations. His government proposed an extensive privatization program, investment in infrastructure, introduction of free-trade zones, relaxation of currency restrictions, and the attraction of expatriate entrepreneurial talent. The proposals were designed to generate growth through effective state management of the economy, an interesting return to the Pahlavi state's developmentalist approach.

The reform initiative enjoyed some success. Investment in infrastructure increased, management became more efficient, and as a result the economy began to grow again. In this regard, the institutional and industrial developments of the Pahlavi period were extremely useful to the economic policies of the Islamic Republic. Nevertheless, more fundamental reforms proved difficult. The government faced stiff resistance to privatization from the bureaucrats and the myriad quasi-private foundations that manage state-owned enterprises, as well as from labor – and the power brokers who had used public-sector jobs for patronage – who feared the loss of jobs. As a result, privatization meant the transference of the ownership of public-sector industries to state-controlled foundations and cronies of the regime. In this way, the state retained control of the industries, even though technically it had privatized them.

The bureaucracy's attempt to assert its autonomy in economic policy making also faced resistance, as it would have reduced kickbacks and patronage, along with profits made by merchants and black marketers. This resistance translated into support for the conservative faction in subsequent elections and pressure to prevent Rafsanjani from running for a third term in 1997.

In the end, Rafsanjani's economic initiative suffered as a consequence of the tightening of Western sanctions against Iran. New efforts to isolate Iran internationally and stop its support of terrorism during the 1990s led to a collapse of the Iranian currency and a decline in the rate of economic growth. The consequence of change in the global context was a heightened debate over Iran's future. Should economic interests continue to be sacrificed in the pursuit of ideological goals, or should Iran subordinate its commitment to identity politics in favor of economic growth? Although there is strong support for continuing Iran's commitment to Islam and the values of the revolution, the scope of economic crises facing the state has prevented complacency in the economic policy-making arena. By 1998, 65 percent of Iran's population was under twenty-one years of age, the unemployment rate stood at 40 percent, inflation was at 300 percent, and the GDP growth rate lagged behind the population growth rate. Without ending Iran's international isolation as well as undertaking domestic economic reform, Iran could face a political crisis, which could threaten the ruling order and its revolutionary values more seriously than would pragmatism.

By the mid-1990s, revolutionary values and ideological politics came under attack from an unexpected quarter – a resurgence of the secular values of the Pahlavi period. The Islamic Republic has enforced a strict cultural code in Iran. The "Islamization" of society has extended beyond the public sphere and has sought to transform the private lives of Iranians as well. Women's dress; music; public programs; school texts; publications; and all manners of cultural, social, and educational activities have been subject to state control. This state policy has generated unhappiness and opposition.

The Pahlavi state, too, had sought to transform its citizens, secularizing as well as modernizing them as a prelude to development. Its collapse in 1979, however, has diverted scholarly attention from the extent to which it was successful in transforming Iranian society. In 1979, there existed a peculiar circumstance wherein the Pahlavi state was weak politically but quite strong culturally. The fact that its secular subjects did not have the same political outlook as the rulers weakened the state. The new Islamic Republic, on the other hand, enjoyed far more political appeal among the middle classes than it did cultural support. The Islamic movement in Iran triumphed politically in large measure because it was able to divide secular Iranians along political lines. The Pahlavi state's political failure, however, should not be read as evidence of its cultural irrelevance because the underlying cultural impact of Pahlavi policies continues to be a major force in Iranian society. Its continued salience is attested to by the inability of the Islamic Republic to establish uncontested cultural hegemony in Iran two decades after the revolution and also by the fact that pre-revolutionary cultural attitudes have increasingly served as the starting point of important dissenting tendencies in the political arena. Those social groups that continue to live by the norms of the past may be out of power but they remain nonetheless potential contenders for power.

The Islamic Republic was never able to win over the secular social stratum or eliminate it. It could merely suppress it. Islamic clerics imposed new laws and regulations on the population, largely by force. For instance, new attire for women was imposed after several large demonstrations, one of which drew more than a million woman protesters into the streets in 1979. Since then, the strict women's dress code has been enforced brutally by the Revolutionary Guards.

The "**Cultural Revolution**" in 1980 "cleansed" educational institutions of all those who did not subscribe to Islamic ideology. As far as the liberal Left element within the revolutionary movement itself was concerned, the Islamic Republic eventually resolved that inherent anomaly in the alliance that brought it to power. After an open struggle for power in 1979–1981, the Islamist element in the revolutionary alliance purged the secular liberal Left element.

Secular Iranians, among them prominent professionals and intellectuals, were forcibly marginalized, but they remained important as they shifted their activities to the private arena and the important sphere of civil society. In fact, this social stratum has acted in a fashion similar to those groups who spearheaded the uprising in the name of civil society against Eastern European communist states. The refusal to abide by state ideology at the popular and even personal levels has challenged the domination of Islamic ideology and is forcing changes on the ruling regime. The cultural influence of the Pahlavi era has continued and remains dominant at the personal level among the middle classes. Since the early 1990s, economic crises and problems of isolation have constricted the ruling regime and weakened its hold over society. Creeping pragmatism in policy making has, moreover, made the secular middle classes and the values they espouse the vanguard force for a decisive movement of political resistance. That economic growth both needs and will empower this social stratum has made it difficult for the Islamic Republic to resist its influence.

The Presidential Elections of 1997

All of these factors coalesced to determine the outcome of the presidential elections of 1997. These elections were the first to involve a transfer of power at the level of the presidency during the post-Khomeini era. Given the debates over the relative importance of identity and interests in state policy, the elections were viewed as decisive. Early on in the election campaign, the nominee of the conservative faction emerged as the front-runner. The faction had a strong base of support among small businessmen and in the political apparatus of the Islamic Republic, and it also had the backing of Ayatollah Khamenei. In addition, the conservatives posed as a force for continuity, and to some extent retrenchment, of the values and norms of the Islamic Republic. They held to a conservative line on social and cultural issues and supported the thrust of Iran's anti-Western foreign policy. In this way, they differed from President Rafsanjani, who had favored easing the strictures that govern social and cultural practices, and who had tried – albeit with little success – to reduce tensions between Iran and the Western powers.

What appeared to be the conservatives' unchallenged march to the presidency, however, soon became a closely contested race with **Ayatollah Mohammad Khatami.** Khatami did not represent any of the rival factions but appealed to the moderate faction and its followers. In addition, his promise of relaxing the state's ideological vigilance also gained him a following among women, youth, and the secular elements. In many regards, Khatami's platform and following greatly resemble those of Gorbachev in the Soviet Union. Khatami, too, believes in the promise of the revolutionary ideology and hopes that once that ideology is freed from the authoritarian control of the state through reform measures, it will fulfill its promise of progress and prosperity. Many who followed Khatami (again, similar to Gorbachev in Russia) did not share his belief in the promise of revolutionary ideology but liked the implications of his reform proposals.

The intensity of the factional rivalry guaranteed the openness of the elections and paved the way for greater freedom of expression in the media. The election itself, held in May 1997, proved to be nothing short of an earthquake in Iranian politics. Most observers had expected Khatami to do well but thought that in the end the conservatives would win. This did not come to pass. Khatami won the elections with an overwhelming majority of the vote – 70 percent (some twenty million votes). The defeat of the conservative faction was total and humiliating. Iranians had taken the elections seriously and had voted convincingly in favor of fundamental changes in the nature, structure, and workings of the Islamic Republic. Many saw the elections as a referendum on the Islamic Republic and, at the very least, as a referendum on how its existing leadership ought to understand its mission and relations with society. The vote was also one for interests over identity in the workings of the state.

The election results had important implications. First, this was a unique case in the Middle East: a head of state stepped down from power at the end of his term of office and peacefully handed over power to a successor elected through constitutional means. The transition of power from Rafsanjani to Khatami has therefore been of tremendous significance in itself. Second, the large turnout – some thirty million, an overwhelming majority of the eligible voters – meant that Iranians of all political persuasions had taken the elections seriously and decided to voice their views and demands within the political process rather than outside of it. This means that the electoral process has become institutionalized in the Islamic Republic and has become the most important means of integrating various social groups into the political system. It is no longer an artificial appendage to the Islamic state but rather is very much part of the fabric of its politics.

Khatami's campaign speeches were peppered with references to "democracy," "civil society," "women's status," "rule of law," and "dialogue between civilizations." He in particular emphasized "civil society" and championed the cultural freedoms and legal protections that empower it. As such, Khatami gave new direction and energy to the demand for reform. The decision by so many to use the ballot box to promote change has also strengthened the

Islamic Republic, as those who have been unhappy with its achievements have chosen to participate in it rather than opt out of it. The elections and the transition of power have the potential to include greater numbers of Iranians within the Islamic Republic. However, to do so successfully, the Islamic Republic must accommodate a broader set of sociopolitical demands, and most notably move farther away from ideological politics and the values of the revolution. This generated democratic expectations on which Khatami now had to deliver.

The elections of 1997 had caught the leadership of the Islamic Republic off guard. This led to a short-lived "Prague Spring" in Iran during which significant freedom of expression in the press and certain relaxations in control of social behavior gave new impetus to demands for change. These demands began to take an increasingly secular orientation as the new cultural opening mobilized the Iranian middle class, which now became a new force in Iranian politics. This new political constituency was no longer merely satisfied with debating Islam and began to demand fundamental political reforms.

Khatami's campaign promised to address those demands and by so doing create a bridge between reformers inside the regime – who were attached to its ideological foundations – and the larger constituency for reform. His ideal of "Islamic civil society" captured this objective. His success in this endeavor would have transformed the Islamic Republic but would have kept it in control of the process of change. However, his failure has instead created a rift between reformers within the Islamic Republic's ideological fold and political reformers in the larger society, and clearly pitted the latter against the Islamic Republic.

Within a year after Khatami assumed office, the supreme leader, Ayatollah Ali Khamenei, began to use the judiciary and the Council of Guardians (a watchdog institution that is dedicated to protecting the ideological foundations of the Islamic Republic), and his allies in the media, the Parliament, and various government agencies, to stifle reform. Khatami repeatedly lost ground to these conservative forces in showdowns over legislation, freedom of the press, the rule of law, and individual rights. His more reform-minded ministers were pushed out of government, and some were tried and incarcerated. From the time that Khatami assumed office in 1997 until January 2004, the Council of Guardians vetoed 111 of his 297 legislations. Faced with strong resistance to change, Khatami and his lieutenants and supporters began to speak about instituting limits to theocracy and advocated the rule of law and the protection of individual rights.

These developments shifted the focus from calls for rational government to demands for democratization. However, Khatami shied away from openly breaking with the theocratic core of the Islamic Republic. He would not endorse fundamental constitutional changes and proved unwilling to openly challenge Khamenei's authority. On a number of occasions, he threatened the supreme leader with resigning, and on one occasion with not running for re-election in 2001, but each time he backed away from an open breach with Khamanei and his conservative allies.

More important, Khatami continued to declare fealty to the theocratic constitution of the Islamic Republic, which runs counter to his support for "civil society" and the "rule of law." As such, at the end of the day, Khatami's rhetoric went no further than advocating better management of government. Khatami's capitulations to Khamanei have attested to his reluctance to step beyond the bounds of the constitution of the Islamic Republic. This in turn has severely limited his ability to continue to lead the popular demand for democracy that his own electoral success had unleashed.

Khatami's dilemma has, however, had a cathartic effect on the democracy debate. By failing to reconcile the demands for change with the reality of the Islamic Republic, Khatami relinquished control of the democracy debate to voices outside the regime. The debate moved to the streets, where, for instance, student demonstrations became a leading voice in demanding fundamental changes to the structure of the Islamic Republic. Student demonstrations during the summer of 1999 to protest the closure of some reformist newspapers, in November 2002 to protest against a death sentence for alleged blasphemy imposed on a university lecturer, and in 2003 to demand greater political rights have not only posed direct challenges to theocracy but also confirmed the shift in focus of the struggle for reform from the high circles of power to the society and to those who want constitutional change and secular democracy. Popular demands for change have further mobilized secular intellectuals and activists associated with civil-society institutions and universities as well as journalists, who initially rallied in support of Islamic reform.

The ideal of the reformists is not Islamic democracy but secular democracy. This involves placing limits on the exercise of state power and creating legal institutions and a system of checks and balances that guarantee individual and social rights. This trend found greater impetus when the 2003 Nobel Peace Prize was awarded to a leading advocate of individual rights, Shirin Ebadi. However, the democracy movement in Iran today lacks clear leadership. The Khatami presidency has failed to provide that leadership, and secular political activists and the students have yet to fill the void.

In the meantime, the ruling establishment has a different path of development in mind. The supreme leader and the conservative leadership look to the Chinese model of reform: economic change and opening to the world with little or no political reforms. They believe that the Soviet transition to democracy under Gorbachev was not a success; rather, it is the Chinese path to change that holds true promise. The conservative leadership is now looking to roll back gains made by pro-democracy forces under Khatami – following a "Putin" strategy, referring to the creeping authoritarianism in Russia under Vladimir Putin. With that aim in mind, the conservative Council of Guardians prevented many pro-reform candidates from participating in the parliamentary elections of 2004, producing a conservative Parliament ahead of the presidential elections of 2005, in which a conservative victory gave the conservatives complete domination over the political power structure as well as the scope and extent of political reforms.

The Presidential Election of 2005

In June 2005 Iranians went to the polls to choose Mahmoud Ahmadinejad as the country's sixth president – the first since 1981 not to hail from the ranks of the clergy. The election marked the second transfer of presidency in the post-Khomeini period. It proved to be the most intensely contested since the 1979 revolution, and the first to go to a second round of voting. Close to 30 million (62 percent of the electorate of 47 million) voted in the first round on June 17, and over 27 million (60 percent of the electorate) voted in the second round on June 24.

The election produced dramatic results. It brought to power a hard-line conservative populist whose election confirmed the conservative consolidation of power, and stood in marked contrast to the popular choice in 1997. The election also marked a shift away from the middle class and its youth culture, which had become increasingly important since 1997, to the lower class and its grievances. The presidential campaign was one of the most dynamic and innovative in Iran's history. It brought to the fore intense debates over various conceptions of government and social organization, economic development, and foreign policy. The campaign witnessed experimentation with new language and styles of politics, using methods that were openly borrowed from campaigns in the West. The election result, however, opened new fissures in Iranian politics and raised new questions about the pursuit of development and the prospects of democracy.

The impact of privatization and the extent of private-sector growth in Iran in the 1990s had largely been absent in political discussions. However, in Iran, as was also the case in Eastern Europe or Latin America, privatization had led to economic disparities that translated into support for populist platforms at the polls. In 2005 the demand for reform was upstaged by the lower-class revolt at the ballot box. In the campaign hard-line candidates adopted a populist platform directed at the urban poor and disadvantaged areas of the country.

The reformist platform continued to promise political change, cultural freedoms, civil society activism, and improvement in the status of women. It targeted the urban middle class, virtually ignoring the poor. It argued that participation in the elections was the only way to prevent a reversal of gains made during the Khatami period and to sustain the momentum for reform.

Reformist candidates did not, however, provide a compelling argument for why they would fare better than Khatami in achieving these goals, in particular because conservatives were now far more powerful and better organized than they had been in 1997. As such, reformist candidates faced difficulty in attracting disillusioned pro-democracy forces that had called for a boycott of the elections to join the process.

The reformists did not initially have to compete with hard-line conservatives. Far more important were pragmatic conservatives, such as the former president Rafsanjani, who to varying degrees straddled the boundaries between reformism and conservatism, and who put forward new political programs that confounded the reformist platform.

Expectation of victory after the parliamentary elections of 2004 had intensified competition among conservative candidates – hailing from various conservative factions and the Revolutionary Guard – to differentiate their respective positions, and also to broaden their appeal to the conservative vote bank, as well as to other voters. The competition led to divergent political paths. Whereas hard-liners turned to the poor for support, pragmatic conservatives looked to the middle class. It was pragmatic conservatives who were targeting the reformist constituency that captured the most attention early on and looked most promising in the opinion polls. Conservative pragmatists presented new ideas, and more significant, introduced a new style to politics that used secular and youthful themes, pop music, and stylish dress along with colorful advertising. The pragmatists did not reject reform, but rather redefined it. They did not advocate a return to theocracy, revolutionary values, or militant foreign policy – in fact their campaigns were largely secular in tone and notably silent on Islamic issues – but rather pragmatic domestic and foreign policies that although lacking in democratic intent nevertheless promised change. They combined the promise of economic growth, better living standards, accountable and strong government, and engagement with the outside world with a strong appeal to Iranian nationalism. The central theme in pragmatists' arguments was the promise of a "strong government" that would solve social problems, bring about development, and maintain order. Strong government was defined in terms of competence and the capability to get things done. More important, it meant a government that would be able to work with the Supreme Leader and hence avoid the kind of gridlock that characterized the standoff between Khatami's reformist administration and the conservative leadership. This was an argument that also favored Ahmadinejad, who was expected to fare well with the hard-line conservative Parliament. The pragmatic conservatives in effect promised government reform rather than political reform, arguing that this approach would more quickly and directly impact economic problems.

The intense rivalry of conservatives showed that despite their opposition to reform they have nevertheless internalized certain democratic forms, and in particular looked to public opinion and elections to settle struggles of power. Absence of a democratic state therefore has not precluded contestation of power.

In the first round the pragmatic conservative Rafsanjani won 21.2 percent of the vote, followed by hard-line conservative Ahmadinejad with 19.2 percent. The reformists garnered most votes, but those votes were divided among several candidates – and some went to pragmatic conservatives – denying reformists a place in the runoff election. The outcome of the first round quickly changed the tenor of the campaign and its central issues. Rafsanjani's campaign continued to reflect middle-class demands for cultural opening and political reform. He was endorsed by reformist intellectuals and politicians in an effort to prevent an Ahmadinejad victory, which was seen by them as a return to war fundamentalism and the militancy of the early years of the revolution – characterized by reformists as the "Talibanization" of Iran – and also a turning back on the economic reforms, which since 1989 had restructured the economy but had benefited the private sector and the middle class. Shocked by the emergence of class politics, the reformist-pragmatic conservative alliance put forth a defensive campaign, hoping to rally the middle class to stop Ahmadinejad, thus underscoring the ideological and class divisions that had surfaced in the first round of voting. The dilemma facing reformists and pragmatic conservatives was that in an election now focused on socioeconomic grievances their candidate epitomized the wealth and corruption that the lower class was mobilizing against.

Ahmadinejad's stealth campaign now came into the open. Posing as an outsider and a man of the people, he promised to fight corruption and the political and economic domination of the clerical leadership – the first generation of the revolution – and to redistribute wealth to the poor. He touted his record as mayor of Tehran, promising effective, accountable, and transparent government. To his detractors he promised a future that was modeled on Iran's past: militant Islamic socialism and a Third Worldist foreign policy. His platform appealed to the urban poor and the disadvantaged provinces, who had gained little from privatization strategies and look nostalgically to state control of the economy in the 1980s. He subsumed his hard-line ideological position under a populist platform, and as such created a popular base of support for conservative rule. After he became president he outlined a strident anti-Western foreign policy built around a defiant rejection of Western demands that Iran curb its nuclear program, and virulent attacks against Israel. Using populist rhetoric at home and anti-Westernism abroad Ahmadinejad sought to consolidate power in the presidency – hoping that hard-line conservatives equipped with populist rhetoric could accomplish what reformists failed to do. Beyond populism, nationalism, and anti-Westernism, Ahmadinejad's presidency is likely to serve as another chapter in the power struggle between the Iranian presidency and the Supreme Leader.

The 2005 presidential elections entrenched competitive politics in conservative ranks, and compelled them to fight for control of the middle in Iranian politics. These were the most closely fought presidential elections in Iran's history, which were taken particularly seriously by conservatives and their constituency. These were also the first presidential elections in which the candidates' image and message were shaped by the need to garner votes and the realization that to do so politicians must reflect the demands of their constituencies.

During his first term as president, between 2005 and 2009, Mahmoud Ahmadinejad sought to entrench conservative control of politics and adopted economic populism. The state distributed significant resources to the poorer segments of society, took over new economic spheres, and weakened the private sector. Ahmadinejad cultivated a base of support among the poor through a combination of economic populism and appealing to populist religious sentiments. The president was particularly keen on harping on messianism. That caused worry in the international community, and earned him scorn of many senior clerics and politicians, but resonated with many among the religious masses.

Ahmadinejad's hope was that populism would strengthen the state, and his mix of populism and messianism would confirm the conservatives' control of the more powerful state through elections. In effect, he hoped to create a permanent conservative electoral majority that would rule the growing state. During his tenure the Iranian economy reverted to greater state control, but the conservative domination of politics remained tenuous – in part because many conservatives and even the country's Supreme Leader were suspicious of Ahmadinejad's power grab.

The 2005 election had not been a complete rout of reformism, but rather had showed the growing importance of socioeconomic issues – enough to overshadow political issues. These issues divided the electorate along ideological and class lines, and also brought home the complex question concerning the role of elections in promotion of democracy. The conservatives themselves became divided over these issues as was evident in the turn of some to populist politics and others to pragmatism and courting reformists.

The outcome also compelled reformists to regroup and reformulate their position to reflect changes that the election has brought about. The reformists were blindsided by the depth of socioeconomic disgruntlements. Lacking a united platform or a strong candidate, they failed to mount an effective campaign and to adequately organize the electorate. They expected to win – a high turnout would favor them – but the election denied them that advantage. In this election, in the words of one prominent reformist editor, "reformism lost to democracy." The challenge before pro-democracy forces now is to build a cohesive movement, and relate the demand for change to socioeconomic grievances – building bridges between middle and lower classes.

These developments set the stage for a decisive showdown between conservatives in power and resurgent reformism in the elections of 2009. Conservatives were banking on Ahmadinejad's populism to carry the elections, but reformists who were dejected in 2005 mounted an effective electoral campaign around Mir Hossein Mousavi, a one-time prime minister. The pro-Moussavi faction adopted the color green as its emblem, and so the battle cry for reform and democracy became known as the **Green Movement**.

The popular support for Moussavi was so strong that most observers thought that he would surely win the election. But the results gave a clear first-round victory to Ahmadinejad. The incredulous masses poured into the streets asking "where is my vote?" For a time it looked like the Islamic Republic might fall as rapidly as had the Berlin Wall in 1989. The ruling regime resorted to violence, deploying paramilitary and irregular forces on the streets, arresting thousands, and intimidating protesters to abandon the streets. The outcome looked like Tiananmen Square in China in 1989. The state successfully defended its position against a direct pro-democracy challenge. The brutality of the suppression left little room for doubt that Iran remained an authoritarian state; but one that could no longer manage political participation through elections. The conservative elite had come to believe that in Ahmadinejad and populism they had found a winning formula that could beat reformists at the polls, hence, preserving authoritarianism through elections. But reformists had proved that formula to be a failure.

In the aftermath of the June 2009 uprising the Islamic Republic resorted to greater oppression. It intimidated opponents, silenced criticism, censored the press, and purged universities of freethinkers and dissidents. Ahmadinejad tried to revive his political fortunes by challenging the authority of the Supreme Leader, weakening theocracy in favor of political institutions of the Islamic Republic. That he hoped would appeal to the anticlerical sentiments of the reformists who had supported the Green Movement. The Supreme Leader reacted swiftly, beating back Ahmadinejad's challenge with the backing of senior clerics and the middle class whom Ahmadinejad had alienated during elections. The popular base of the Islamic Republic was initially divided but ultimately took the side of the Supreme Leader. Ahmadinejad ended his term isolated atop a weakened presidency. His legacy is one of authoritarian populism first reversing reformist gains, and then collapsing before reformist protests and a sagging economy.

Equally important to the changing direction of development was a shift in the international context. Frustrated with Iran's expanding nuclear program, the United States and its allies in the international community in 2010 imposed crippling sanctions on Iran that drastically reduced Iran's ability to conduct trade. That plunged the Iranian economy into crisis. Inflation soared and shortages led to closure of industries and unemployment.

Popular disgruntlement grew, but the sense of siege and fear that war might break out also diverted popular attention from domestic political struggle against the ruling regime to the international debate over Iran's nuclear program. A national security crisis did not help reform and democratization, and so the more the international community put pressure on Iran, the more the ruling regime clamped down on the population in the name of protecting the country against outside aggression.

However, with political dissent under control, economic pressure persuaded the clerical leadership to allow for a more open presidential election in 2013. This they hoped would increase popular participation and strengthen the Islamic Republic as it contemplated entering into serious nuclear negotiations with the international community. The opening allowed a pragmatic moderate, **Hassan Rouhani**, to win the presidency with an outright majority in the first round of voting.

Rouhani's victory revived hope for both political and economic reform. Rouhani freed political prisoners, relaxed control of the press and social media, moved away from Ahmadinejad's populism, and reached out to the United States. But his priority is to resolve the nuclear impasse and end Iran's isolation. Domestically he chose to serve as a bridge between conservatives and reformists rather than as a challenger to the ruling order. The fate of reformism now is tied to Iran's foreign policy prerogatives. Success in resolving the nuclear issue could give Rouhani the power to bring about real change.

Looking back at developments since 1988, one can conclude that greater pragmatism restored the state to its central role in the management of society, politics, and the economy in the name of economic development, as in the earlier Pahlavi era. Nevertheless, the possibility of greater democratization of politics suggested that beyond restoration of power to the state and greater attention to the pursuit of economic growth and development, Iranian politics may be developing along a new trajectory. Whether elections could have evolved beyond settling struggles for power among ruling factions into a broad-based democratic system or whether the state will be able to regain control depended on changes in the relative power of the state and society as well as the relative importance of interests and identity in shaping institutions and, ultimately, Iran's developmental path. The pace and scope of economic reform influenced those changes in turn. But then just when the process seemed to be at a tipping point, the authoritarian state reasserted its primacy. That was a risky gambit and could have failed, but for the intrusion of international forces in the form of sanctions and threat of war to stop Iran's nuclear program. That foreign policy challenge at first diverted attention from the democracy debate, but then necessitated bringing it back in.

CONCLUSION

At the beginning of the twentieth century, there existed little in the form of interests, identity, or institutions in the Iranian polity to provide an impetus for development or to chart a path for that process. It was the global context at the time that imbued the Iranian political process with interests and set the country on its path to development. Those interests, in turn, influenced identity and shaped institutions to give form to the modern Iranian state. Iran looked to Germany and Japan – and also Turkey – as models to follow, and so invested in strong state institutions and promoted a secular national identity. As state institutions expanded, they defined interests and identity in order to serve the state's objectives in the economic and the political arenas. Thus, early on in the process of development, the global context and interests that emerged from it shaped Iran's identity and institutions, guaranteeing the central role of the state in that process.

A changing global context in subsequent years, along with crises that are inherent in development, altered the state in important ways but would not change the state's dominant role in society and politics. Even the Iranian Revolution did not reverse this trend. The revolution placed more importance on identity – articulated in Islamic terms – in charting the country's developmental path. It changed some old institutions and produced some new ones, but it did not change the role of the state in economic development. Ultimately, at the turn of the twenty-first century, these tensions led to a breakdown in the pattern of development in the form of the June 2009 uprising demanding much more rapid reform and opening of the political process, and the state's decision to roll back change and reassert authoritarian control of society and the economy. The case of Iran shows that the interaction among interests, identities, and institutions – as militated by changes in the global contexts and imperatives of the domestic scene – is more fluid early on in the development process but becomes increasingly less so over time. As institutions grow in size and reach, they become more rigid. Although institutions continue to respond to the global context and reflect the influence of interests and identity, they do so with greater infrequency, and seldom in major ways. The size and power of the state thus become more important in determining the course of development than do interests and identity, the impact of which must now happen through institutions rather than separate from them.

In many ways, the domination of institutions that emerged through Iran's experiment with development – producing a strong and centralized state – accounts for the fact that Iran has been unable to achieve the end goal of democratic capitalism. Still, in major and minor ways, the global context has shaped interests and states' responses to them, and through them identity and institutions, to present Iran with new development possibilities. At the dawn of the twenty-first century, Iran has yet to arrive at democratic capitalism, and in fact now looks like it is drifting farther away from that goal. However, history has shown that even strong institutions – such as the eighteenth-century French monarchy, nineteenth-century Meiji Japanese feudalism, and twentieth-century Soviet Union – change in response to global pressures. Those pressures are intensifying in Iran's case. Global economic change is straining Iranian economy's ability to compete and sustain development, but more important, economic consequences of international pressure on Iran to abandon its nuclear program is making Iran more vulnerable to change. Given the changes in economic and political life in Iran during the early years of the twenty-first century, the possibility of realizing that goal is not as remote as it may have been only a short while ago.

Table 11.1   Key Phases in Iran's Political Development

Time period	Regime	Global context	Interests/identities/institutions	Developmental path
1921–1941	autocratic monarchy foreign occupation	European imperialism World War II	authoritarian institutions landed and tribal elite, ethnic and regional forces, and authoritarian forces	state-building state collapse
1941–1954	constitutional monarchy and parliamentary democracy	European imperialism	democratic, Islamic, and communist force and authoritarian institutions	democratic institution- building
1954–1963	autocratic monarchy	Cold War	landed elite, authoritarian institutions	state-building
1964–1979	autocratic monarchy	Cold War	bureaucratic and industrial elite; authoritarian institutions	state-building and centralized economic development
1979–1988	revolutionary theocracy	Cold War	lower classes and revolutionary institutions	state important
1988–1997	autocratic republican and theocracy	globalization	revolutionary institutions, mercantile and bureaucratic forces	state-building and economic development
1997–2009	autocratic theocracy and reformist presidency	globalization/war on terror	authoritarian institutions, civil society, mercantile forces	state-building, economic development, and democratic institution-building
2009–2013	autocratic theocracy and presidency	economic isolation/nuclear crisis	authoritarian institutions/security state, populism	state-building, economic populism, authoritarian reversal
2013-present	autocratic theocracy and presidency	Ending economic isolation/nuclear negotiations	authoritarian institutions/security state, reform	state-building, economic and political reform

BIBLIOGRAPHY

Abrahamian, Ervand. *Iran between Two Revolutions*. Princeton, NJ: Princeton University Press, 1982.

Abrahamian, Ervand. *A History of Modern Iran*. New York: Cambridge University Press, 2008.

Akhavi, Shahrough. *Religion and Politics in Contemporary Iran: Clergy-State Relations in the Pahlavi Period*. Albany: SUNY Press, 1980.

Amuzegar, Jahangir. *Iran's Economy under the Islamic Republic*. London: I. B. Tauris, 1993.

Arjomand, Said A. *The Turban for the Crown: The Islamic Revolution in Iran*. New York: Oxford University Press, 1988.

Arjomand, Said A. *After Khomeini: Iran under His Successors*. New York: Oxford University Press, 2009.

Azimi, F. *Iran: The Crisis of Democracy*. New York: St. Martin's Press, 1989.

Bakash, Shaul. *The Reign of the Ayatollahs: Iran and the Islamic Revolution*. New York: Basic Books, 1984.

Bakhtiari, Bahman. *Parliamentary Politics in Revolutionary Iran: The Institutional-ization of Factional Politics*. Gainesville: University Press of Florida, 1996.

Dabashi, Hamid. *Theology of Discontent: The Ideological Foundation of the Islamic Revolution in Iran*. New York: New York University Press, 1993.

Ehteshami, Anoushiravan. *After Khomeini: The Iranian Second Republic*. New York: Routledge, 1995.

Elm, Mostafa. *Oil, Power, and Principle: Iran's Oil Nationalization and Its Aftermath*. Syracuse, NY: Syracuse University Press, 1992.

Ertman, Thomas. *Birth of Leviathan: Building States and Regimes in Medieval and Early Modern Europe*. Cambridge: Cambridge University Press, 1997.

Ghani, Cyrus. *Iran and the Rise of Reza Shah: From Qajar Collapse to Pahlavi Rule*. London: I. B. Tauris, 1998.

Gheissari, Ali, and Vali Nasr, *Democracy in Iran: History and the Quest for Liberty*. New York: Oxford University Press, 2006.

Karshenas, Massoud. *Oil, State and Industrialization in Iran*. Cambridge: Cambridge University Press, 1990.

Katouzian, Homa. *The Political Economy of Modern Iran, 1926–79*. New York: New York University Press, 1981.

Kurzman, Charles. *The Unthinkable Revolution in Iran*. Cambridge, MA: Harvard University Press, 2004.

Looney, Robert. *Economic Origins of the Iranian Revolution*. New York: Pergamon Press, 1982.

Migdal, Joel S., Atul Kohli, and Vivienne Shue, eds. *State Power and Social Forces: Domination and Transformation in the Third World*. Cambridge: Cambridge University Press, 1994.

Schirazi, Asghar. *The Constitution of Iran: Politics and the State in the Islamic Republic*. London: I. B. Tauris, 1997.

Skocpol, Theda. "Rentier State and Shi'a Islam in the Iranian Revolution." *Theory and Society* 11, no. 3 (May 1982): 265–283.

Takeyh, Ray. *Guardians of the Revolution: Iran and the World in the Age of Ayatollahs*. New York: Oxford University Press, 2009.

IMPORTANT TERMS

Mahmoud Ahmadinejad – Iran's president from 2005 to 2013.

Anglo-Iranian Oil Company – the British company that owned the concession to excavate, process, and export Iran's oil until 1954.

ayatollah – literally meaning "sign of God," the title of the highest-ranking religious leader in Shia Islam. He has the authority to interpret religious law and to prescribe proper personal, social, and political behavior.

Central Committee – the central decision-making body in a communist party structure.

Cultural Revolution – attack by the revolutionary forces on Iranian universities and intellectuals in 1980 in order to purge them of liberal and leftist elements and to force conformity with revolutionary values. This term originated in China during the purges of the 1960s.

Friday Prayer – congregational Muslim prayer on Fridays. In the Islamic Republic, it has been used as a political forum to propagate government views and mobilize the masses in support of government policies.

Green Movement of 2009 – marked the high point of reformist challenge to the state. Supporters of the reformist presidential candidate Mir-Hossein Moussavi launched a massive protest when his conservative rival President Ahmadinejad was declared the winner of the 2009 elections. The movement was eventually suppressed by brute force.

Ayatollah Ali Akbar Hashemi-Rafsanjani – revolutionary leader, speaker of the Parliament, and president between 1988 and 1997. He introduced the first efforts to reform the Islamic Republic.

hostage crisis – the crisis initiated in November 1979 when radical students took U.S. diplomatic personnel hostage at the U.S. embassy in Tehran, demanding the handover of the Shah to Iran and recognition of Iran's grievances against the United States for its role in the 1953 coup and support of the Shah. The hostages were released in January 1981 after 444 days.

import-substitution industrialization (ISI) – a strategy for industrialization that became popular in the developing world after World War II. It advocates beginning industrialization by producing finished goods and then expanding the scope of the process by moving to intermediary and primary industrial goods and using protectionism to favor the young industries. It has been associated with several economic and political problems.

Iran-Iraq War – an intense war between Iran and Iraq between 1980 and 1988 during which Iraq first occupied parts of Iran but then was compelled to defend its own territory against Iranian offensives. The most bloody and costly war since World War II, it ended with Iran's defeat.

Islam – a monotheistic religion and the world's second-largest faith, with more than one billion followers.

Islamic ideology – a political doctrine with views on society and government that are drawn from a puritanical understanding of Islam. Advocating that politics should be subservient to religion, it was the guiding ideology of the religious faction of the revolution.

Islamic Republic of Iran – the official name of Iran after the revolution. It attests to the centrality of Islam to statecraft since 1979.

Kemalism – a model of development that emerged in Turkey during the 1920s. Named after the Turkish president Mustafa Kemal, its most important features were secularism, nationalism, and a domineering role for the state in socioeconomic change.

Ayatollah Ali Khamenei – revolutionary leader, president, and currently supreme leader of Iran. He has been associated with the antireform faction since 1997.

Ayatollah Mohammad Khatami – Iran's president from 1997 to 2005. He spearheaded efforts to liberalize the Islamic Republic.

Ayatollah Ruhollah Khomeini – the chief architect and leader of the revolution of 1979, who ruled Iran as supreme leader between 1979 and 1988.

Mohammad Mossadeq – the nationalist prime minister at the time of the 1953 coup. He nationalized Iran's oil industry and led the drive for limiting foreign influence in Iran and for instituting democracy in the country.

Mir-Hossein Mousavi – Iran's prime minister, 1981–1989, and presidential candidate and leader of the Green Movement of 2009.

OPEC – Organization of Petroleum Exporting Countries, a cartel formed in the late 1960s to strengthen the position of oil producers in the international market. It pushed for higher oil prices during the 1970s.

Pahlavi – the name of the dynasty that ruled Iran between 1921 and 1979.

Muhammad Reza Shah Pahlavi – the second Pahlavi monarch, who ruled between 1941 and 1979.

Ayatollah Hassan Rouhani – Iran's president since 2013.

Reza Shah Pahlavi – the founder of the Pahlavi monarchy and the initiator of Iran's development during the twentieth century. He ruled between 1921 and 1941.

rentier state – a state that earns an overwhelming proportion of its income from sources outside of its domestic economic activity. Such states become autonomous from the society and rely on distributive mechanisms to assert authority. That, in time, will erode their legitimacy.

Revolutionary Guards – an ideologically committed militia that was formed after the revolution to perform the functions of the police and the military.

SAVAK – Iran's intelligence agency between 1954 and 1979. It was responsible for contending with the opposition and was associated with the Pahlavi monarchy's human-rights violations.

shah – "king" in Persian.

Ali Shariati – an intellectual who blended Marxist ideology with Islamic teachings to produce a potent ideology of revolutionary change in Iran during the 1970s.

Shia – a branch of Islam that is dominant in Iran. It places great authority in its religious leaders and values sacrifice in the path of justice.

Vali-e Faqih – literally meaning the "supreme guardian-jurisconsult," it is a position that was put forward by Ayatollah Khomeini to embody his belief that it is religiously mandated for Shia clerics to rule in the political arena. This view justified the religious nature of the revolution and the constitutional setup of the Islamic Republic.

vanguard party – a party that spearheads a revolution.

STUDY QUESTIONS

1. How has change in identity influenced Iran's development?
2. How has the revolution altered prospects for democratic capitalism?
3. What are the most important turning points in Iran's development?
4. Was there a greater chance for democratic development in 1977 or in 1997?
5. Has identity been important in Iranian institutional change? If so, how?
6. Does the pursuit of interests produce a more sustainable development path than pursuit of identity?
7. Can religious identity sustain secular state institutions and serve developmental goals?
8. How important is the location of Iran to its path of development?
9. Which factors decided positive development toward economic and political freedoms, and which caused development reversals?
10. In what ways can the global context influence Iran's development from this point forward?

SOUTH AFRICA

MAP 12.1. Map of South Africa.

12 South Africa

Antoinette Handley

Introduction

Much of what is commonly known about South Africa centers on a single reality: this is probably one of the most racialized societies on earth. South African society is notorious for how, over the course of a century and a half, its economic, social, and political system systematically structured identities, interests, and institutions in that country on an explicitly racialized basis. The country is also rightly famous however for the courageous, multifaceted, and long-standing attempts to oppose that system, for the struggle to build a more just and free society, and for its apparently miraculous transition to a multiracial democracy in the mid 1990s. This struggle in turn has constructed an alternate set of identities, interests, and institutions. More recently, South Africa has continued to capture headlines for the challenges and difficulties associated with the attempts to consolidate democracy in a society that remains, socially and economically speaking, radically unequal – albeit now increasingly in terms of class rather than, as it was previously, in terms of race.

For much of the country's history, the dominant rules of the game that governed both political and economic life were built around the deliberate construction of race – or attempts to erode and challenge it. From at least the 1700s until 1994, those rules overwhelmingly favored white settlers and their descendants while other South Africans were systematically excluded from access to political and economic power. Throughout, this exclusion was most forcefully directed at Africans. Racialized identities shaped how most South Africans came to identify their interests, often overriding (if never quite eliminating) the importance of other identities such as class and gender; they structured also the society's key institutions, both formal and informal, political and economic. In particular, the racialization of politics built a very particular kind of state – one of the strongest and richest on the continent, but one that explicitly sought to meet the needs only of a small fraction of the society. This was especially true under the **National Party** (NP) government.

From the beginning, these attempts to exclude black South Africans from meaningful participation in the country's economic and political life met various forms of resistance, including early forms of armed resistance as well as increasingly sophisticated and radicalized forms of political organization. The **African National Congress** (ANC) and the debate about organizing the resistance to apartheid on a non-racial basis are two of the best known of these responses.

That it is necessary at the outset to define the racialized terminology employed in this chapter is an indication of the powerful valence of racialized identities for much of the country's recent history. While recognizing that race is meaningless as a biological marker but nonetheless immensely powerful and consequential, this chapter employs racial categories as they have tended to be deployed in South Africa itself. The term "African" is used to describe those whose ancestral lineage is indigenous or African in origin, now comprising close to 80 percent of the contemporary population. "White" describes those South Africans whose ancestors originated in Europe and, as a category, can be subdivided into those who identify as English-speaking (often but not always the descendants of British settlers) and **Afrikaners** with a more hybrid ancestry including Dutch. Taken together, white South Africans total 9 percent of the population. South Africans use the term "Colored" to describe those of mixed racial origin, many of whom reside in the Western Cape and whose heritage may include Malay slaves and the Khoi/San peoples, and they comprise around 9 percent of the total population. Finally, South Africans describe their citizens of South Asian origin as "Indians"; this population tends to be clustered principally in kwaZuluNatal and totals almost 3 percent of the total population. "Black" has historically meant all non-whites (i.e., Africans, Coloreds, and Indians) although it is now often used to denote only "Africans."

The conflict over political power in South Africa then was shaped by at least two contending identities – both a sort of nationalism. Afrikaner nationalism sought to construct apartheid (literally "separateness") in order to secure political and economic opportunities for all Afrikaners including the indigent and working class. Black or African nationalism sought to oppose that vision and the dehumanizing racism associated with it. This stark dichotomy of two opposing nationalisms is of course a vast oversimplification of a much messier set of contestations. For a start, each of these nationalisms was contested both from within and without, the NP's version of Afrikaner nationalism principally by more conservative and more liberal while the ANC's brand of non-racial African nationalism was contested from the Left by its more radical socialist or communist allies, as well as by more assertive/Africanist strains of black consciousness.

This is not to argue that apartheid was simply an expression of racism (although those sentiments were a large part of it). Rather apartheid emerged and took hold so powerfully because it served the key interests of the dominant elites of the time. Structuring and systematizing race into the very fabric of the society served a larger economic set of interests, namely those of agriculture and mining, not merely the prejudices of bigots.

This was not simply a struggle of competing identities, but also of competing interests too, again within both the black and white communities. Many of the core practices and institutions of apartheid significantly predate 1948, emerging out of the country's colonial context and out of a bloody conflict between English-speaking whites and Afrikaners. Divergent economic interests arguably lay at the heart of this conflict: Afrikaners had historically been associated primarily with various forms of agriculture whereas the more monied settlers with access to British capital effectively seized control of the country's emerging mining and business interests in the late nineteenth century. Indeed, part of the power of racialized politics in South Africa has been precisely the way in which those struggles have amplified other fissures, in some instances reinforcing and in others occluding class or material interests.

Although these two communities – Afrikaner and English-speaking – regarded each other with some suspicion and hostility, they both agreed on the need to secure white dominance. This resulted, early in the twentieth century, in an effective parceling out of economic power on the one hand to the English-speaking community and political power on the other hand to the Afrikaans community. This arrangement of course almost entirely excluded all other South Africans – especially black South Africans – from meaningful access to either. Afrikaner nationalists effectively won control of the state with the electoral victory of the National Party in 1948, control that was ever more brutally secured all the way up until the country's first non-racial elections in 1994.

Race has thus been cultivated and constructed as the signal political identifier in South Africa, although ethnicity and class have been important too. Apartheid was perhaps the most dramatic institutional expression of these competing interests and identities. This chapter tells the story of the emergence of the system of apartheid, the struggles that ended it, and the challenges for the democratically elected post-apartheid government of building a just and equitable society on such unpromising foundations. We turn now to examine the local and international conditions that facilitated the construction of apartheid.

Laying the Foundations for Apartheid

South Africa's early history was shaped by the fact that it was not just a colonized society but a settler society, that is, Europeans sought not only to colonize South Africa, but large numbers of whites sought also to settle themselves there permanently, to make the country their new home. As opposed to much smaller numbers of colonial officials who, at the end of their tour of duty would likely return home to the metropole, the large numbers of white settlers sought to secure political and economic rights for themselves and their children. This provided the impetus for a much more thoroughgoing transformation of existing land ownership and tenancy arrangements as well as of existing political and governance systems. The settlers sought to restructure all of these in their own interests, and those did not always coincide with those of the colonizers – the British. The early history of South Africa then was characterized by a series of violent struggles for control over the country's key resources – labor and land – both within white society (for example the Anglo-Boer South African war, fought principally between the English and Afrikaans-speaking Boers) and between whites and the indigenous peoples they sought to subdue (for example the Anglo-Zulu war).

Even by contrast with other settler societies in Africa (such as Zambia, Mozambique, or even Kenya), the numbers of white settlers in South Africa was large, certainly in proportion to the indigenous population. Many of these settlers were drawn by the promise of the immense riches associated with the country's diamond and gold mines. The almost complete elimination of precolonial economic and political institutions in South Africa therefore would more closely come to resemble that which occurred in other British dominions such as Australia or Canada than it would other British colonies in Africa where much more minimal restructuring took place, such as Nigeria.

In particular, the underlying class structure of South Africa was almost completely transformed. The basis for the indigenous peasantry in South Africa was much more thoroughly destroyed than in other African continents, not merely by pushing large numbers of Africans off the land in order to secure land for white farmers, but also by the unfolding capitalist transformation of both agriculture and of the broader economy, driven by the discovery of gold and diamonds. The political and legislative institutions that were developed – both by the settlers and British colonialists respectively – bore the very strong imprint of white settlers who intended to make this land a permanent and secure home for themselves.

Under both British colonialism, which governed the Cape and Natal territories, and in the two Boer (Afrikaner) republics of the Transvaal and the Orange Free State, Africans in the late 1800s were increasingly denied access to land, to broader economic opportunity, and to political rights, as white settlers came to successfully monopolize both political and economic power. There was of course, as already indicated, important variation within the white community: generally speaking, Afrikaners tended to be dominant in the agricultural sphere, whereas the often more recent settlers, principally those of British descent (including some Americans) and those who enjoyed access to capital and some technical mining skills, came quickly to dominate ownership and management of the new mining sector.

To understand the structure of the mining-dominated economy that was being built in South Africa, one must first understand something about the geological structure of the country's mineral wealth. South African gold is, for the most part, embedded in quartz and buried in extraordinarily deep reefs. To access these considerable riches then required the construction and maintenance of some of the world's deepest gold mines, making mining an investment-, capital-, and skills-intensive undertaking. There were not many pockets deep enough to fund such a proposition. This fact not only advantaged those with ready access to capital and skills but also quickly fostered a centralization of mine ownership into the hands of an ever smaller number of ever larger firms – laying the basis for what would come to be a highly oligopolistic economy. Finally, if South Africa's mines were to be profitably worked, these firms needed to keep all of their other costs as low as possible, especially labor, which comprised a large proportion of their total costs. The structure of the mining industry in South Africa thus created an economically powerful constituency whose economic interests lay in securing a ready supply of politically compliant, cheap, and unskilled labor to perform the dirty and dangerous manual work of extracting the ore. The mineing industry on its own, of course, could not create such an economy, but it could – and did – lobby the government of the day to do so. Moreover, it was not only mineowners who sought the ear of government. White mineworkers also sought to secure their interests, for example by lobbying for the imposition of a color bar in the mines that would render the more skilled and better paying jobs in the mines off-limits to non-whites and hence would protect the wages and status of white miners.

This set of mining-based incentives intersected neatly with the needs of an emerging white-dominated agricultural economy. The struggle for control of South Africa's best agricultural land had fostered a series of wars between almost every group in the country: between early white settlers and the Xhosa, between the British and the Boers (as the Afrikaners came to be called), between the British and the Zulu kingdoms, and more besides. White settlers managed to grab a good share of the best farming land in the territory – and all of the land with the precious minerals. This laid the beginnings of an economy built on "maize and gold," and of a political system that could provide the labor that that economy needed (like mining, settler agriculture required large numbers of unskilled black laborers to be economically viable).

The question that then arises is why Africans would provide their labor under such obviously disadvantageous terms. Indeed, why would anyone agree to go and work in often terrible conditions on white farms or in the mines when they perfectly well make a living for themselves and their families on the land? The answer of course was that they would not. However, access to superior military firepower allied with the introduction of various hut and poll taxes in the late 1800s and early 1900s created the means to force people off the land to provide that labor and to earn the wages that would pay those taxes. We see here then the coercive and bureaucratic power of the state being yoked to the creation and defense of white privilege.

For the most part, both English-speakers and Afrikaners, colonialists and settlers, agreed that black South Africans ought to occupy a subordinate position in the society. Racist attitudes at this time were widely held, and racism was far from being the exclusive purview of Afrikaners. Consider the following view expressed by the arch British imperialist and mining magnate, Cecil John Rhodes: "I contend that we are the finest race in the world and that the more of the world we inhabit, the better it is for the human race. Just fancy, those parts that are at present inhabited by the most despicable specimens of human beings, what an alteration there would be if they were brought under Anglo-Saxon influence." Structural expressions of racism were also evident in a number of key measures that were put in place well before the formal adoption of a system called **apartheid**.

In 1910, the Union of South Africa was created as a unitary state, bringing together what had previously been four disparate territories (the two Afrikaner republics of the Orange Free State and the Transvaal, and the British colonies of Natal and the Cape) as provinces under a single government. The new Union of South Africa granted political representation only to its white male citizens; white women would follow some decades later, but meaningful representation for any of the country's remaining citizens was simply not countenanced. Economically too, it was evident that this was a system intended to serve the interests of whites first and foremost. The 1913 **Natives Land Act** secured white control of the majority of the country's arable land, severely restricting the ability of black South Africans to acquire land outside of designated areas (which for Africans comprised just over 7 percent of South Africa's total territory). It was not that the new national government was oblivious to questions of poverty – but that it only responded to white poverty.

The Carnegie Commission report of the late 1920s for example highlighted the poverty experienced by many poor whites, mostly Afrikaners. It provided an increasingly potent focus for building Afrikaner nationalism as a rallying force around which Afrikaners were eager to organize.

The new South African government, although remaining within the orbit of the British empire, grew increasingly autonomous and representative of local interests. Nonetheless, despite often heated opposition by Afrikaner nationalist elements, the South African government committed troops to the British cause in both world wars. For many Afrikaners, this was both a humiliation and an insult: to have to watch "their" government side with a government (the British) that many Afrikaners still regarded as the enemy. The official allegiance of the country was a critical source of tension within the governments in office at the outbreak of both the First and Second World Wars. During both wars, significant sections of the Afrikaner community had bitterly opposed the entry of South Africa into war on the side of the British, and a few even expressed their opposition in acts of sabotage. In the Second World War, this was not just about anti-British sentiment; some Afrikaners were actively pro-Germany and pro-Nazi. Many resolved that what was required was for a stronger and more assertive brand of Afrikaner nationalism to win control of the South African state.

In the interwar period, South Africa had not been spared the impact of the Great Depression although its mineral wealth (and gold exports in particular) and distance from the worst-affected markets may have mitigated this impact. These economic strains and tensions were expressed via significant labor unrest on the Rand in the 1920s, which saw the government of the day deploy the police and significant military force against white striking miners, many of whom were Afrikaners. The violent clashes between strikers and the country's security forces shocked many unused to seeing white men as the target of repression by the state and strongly suggested that the interests of the government lay closer to those of the country's (English-speaking) mining magnates that to those of the working class Afrikaners who labored in the mines (scant attention was paid to African miners). These events too then galvanized a political constituency that stridently argued for the need for a political party that would explicitly protect the interests of white working class Afrikaners.

To be fair, the government of the day had not seemed to be overly concerned with the fate of indigent or working class Afrikaners. Rather the focus of economic policy was on growth, diversifying the economy and facilitating industrialization; South Africa was at the beginnings of an ongoing process of urbanization that would transform the lives of most of its citizens. The government of the day was also deeply involved in international affairs at this time, especially via Premier Jan Smuts's involvement in the 1919 Paris Peace Conference and later in the establishment of the League of Nations. The leading role played by Smuts and thus South Africa in establishing the central international institution of the time is clear evidence that the actions of the South African government at home were not regarded as being wildly out of touch with global norms. Far from being the pariah it would later become, at this time South Africa was regarded as a state whose leadership was integral to the construction of a stable international world order. After all, the League of Nations represented an international order dominated by imperial European states.

To point out that there were racist extremists in South Africa at this time is not to suggest that the Union's governments prior to 1948 were free of racism. Far from it. Although white women were added to the ballot in 1930, what limited political rights had been enjoyed by non-white South Africans were demolished in 1936 with the misnamed Representation of Natives Act. This government was however also regarded as insufficiently attentive to the defense of Afrikaner interests. During the 1930s, probably at least in part in response to the nature of South Africa's participation in the Second World War, a "purified National Party" under the leadership of D. F. Malan was formed, the party that would go on to become the country's ruling party for some fifty years. As its name suggests, the new NP represented a more stridently Afrikaner nationalist party than its predecessor with the same name. Its success provided evidence that increasingly, English-speaking South Africans were ceding the active pursuit of political power to Afrikaners and were instead focusing their energies on business and the accumulation of economic power.

For all the devastation that it wrought in terms of lives lost, the Second World War also contributed decisively to the economic development of South Africa, as the country was called on to contribute its impressive mineral resources as well as other goods and services to the allied war effort. Moreover, because of the dangers to shipping internationally, South African producers were effectively protected from competition with producers in more advanced industrialized economies. This was a boost in particular to the country's manufacturing and services sectors, as well as for mining. The economy grew strongly in the 1940s and 1950s but the benefits of that economic growth were unevenly experienced among the population, many of the benefits falling disproportionately to the English-speaking elites who dominated the country's business sector, while agriculture – where Afrikaners had historically dominated – occupied a dwindling share of GDP. Competing strands of Afrikaner nationalism contested the political terrain including both more *verlig* ("enlightened"/liberal) traditions associated with the western Cape and with a more classically liberal approach to trade and the market, and a more (*verkramp*) conservative and more fervently nationalist tradition rooted in the Transvaal. Both strands contested the politics of the new NP although the latter was probably dominant at this period, and the party effectively mobilized sufficient numbers of votes to win political power in the 1948 elections.

Building the Apartheid State

It was only after 1948 that the term "apartheid" began to be used to describe the kind of society that the NP government would try to build in South Africa. It is really at this time that South Africa began to split out from other states and colonies in the systematic, comprehensive, and thoroughly legislated nature of its discriminatory treatment of black people and Africans in particular.

Party planners and ideologues developed an increasingly elaborate ideological framework justifying white economic and political domination. This would motivate the attempt to implement a much more thorough elaboration and implementation of "grand apartheid," along with a massive legislative and state-building process that sought to force South African society to conform to that vision; in addition, the NP was increasingly willing and able to use the state and its economic power to systematically advance the position of Afrikaners. Afrikaners made canny use of their control of the state not only to roll out a rigid and ever more formalized system of racial discrimination – "apartheid' – but also to secure and advance a place for Afrikaners in all of the key state institutions (notably the state's coercive apparatus, including the military and police forces, as well as crucial economic institutions, including parastatals such as the railways, the post office, and the iron and steel corporation, and those in the public transport sector).

Apart from the organization of race – in terms of which South Africa diverged increasingly from new global norms of human rights, the right to self-determination, and belief in the fundamental equality of all human beings – many of the other policies adopted by the South African state were relatively conventional for the time. In keeping with broader international trends, the South African government pursued a form of import substitution industrialization (ISI) – albeit in a highly racialized form that denied ownership and management opportunities to black South Africans, restricting their role to the provision of basic and poorly paid unskilled labor. For all its limitations however, the South African economy continued to enjoy robust growth in the 1960s and early 1970s, fostering the emergence of a powerful and highly diversified economy that included increasingly important new sectors such as manufacturing and services. Economic policy sought to favor industrialization and assumed a significant and guiding role for the state in the overall model of economic development. Under the firm hand of the NP, state power continued to be centralized and institutionalized, significantly bolstering the capacity of the South African state, albeit to serve only a very limited proportion of the population.

Two acts laid the basis for the elaboration of grand apartheid, both of which formalized a set of previous practices. The **Population Registration Act** of 1950 in many ways served as the very foundation of the system. It enshrined race as central to a person's legal personhood in a way that was rigid, inescapable, and tremendously consequential. Apartheid sought to classify every South African as the member of a distinct racial category. This of course does not accord with the meaninglessness of race as a biological category; even if one somehow accepted the broad racial categories that apartheid sought to reify, many South Africans and their families did not fit easily or cleanly into a single category. Despite this – or perhaps because of it – the process of assigning racialized identities and then following through in terms of what that identity permitted was a central preoccupation of apartheid's planners. The necessary first step of systematizing a race-based society was to assign each and every South African a racial identity and to have that persist in a non-discretionary way. This single Act therefore made possible the further enactment of the hundreds of pieces of legislation that would make apartheid an ever more ruthless and deeply penetrating feature of South African life. Citizens' racial identities were recorded at birth and in the assignment of a single, lifelong identity number, recorded in the document that was supposed to be carried on one's person at all times and could be demanded at will by any passing police officer. This document established one's right – or not – to be in a particular place at a certain time.

Every fact of a South African's life henceforth would follow from the designation of that person's racial identity, from the trivial (which entrance one could use to enter the post office, which bars one could drink at, and which public toilets one could use) to the profound (where and how one would be educated; the location and quality of health care one would receive; one's capacity to obtain a certain kind of job and hence to earn a certain kind of salary; one's ability to vote, or to organize a trade union; where one could live and whether one could own one's home – in effect, the person's likely per capita income and life expectancy). Even the most intimate parts of people's lives were affected as legislation barred marriage and sexual intercourse between interracial couples.

The second foundational act of grand apartheid was the **Group Areas Act** of 1950, focused on the enforcement of complete residential segregation. Group Areas built on the foundations of what was first laid out in the 1913 Natives Land Act and 1936 Native Land and Trust Act respectively, which by most estimates effectively restricted Africans (comprising then over 70 percent of the total population) to just 13 percent of the country's land, depriving most of any meaningful kind of land ownership and herding them onto overcrowded and economically marginal "native reserves." Group Areas extended this logic to the urban areas and to Colored and Indian communities, seeking to segregate the country's vital residential, commercial, and industrial zones too. It was promulgated as a series of three successive legislative actions and confirmed the ambition to physically separate South Africa's now racialized populations, carving both the countryside and urban areas up into what the planners hoped would be racially pristine, segregated zones. It sought to move large numbers of South Africans far from where they lived and worked. Because of this, the ruthless implementation of the Group Areas Act, often exercised with due assistance from the police, caused enormous economic and social distress. Established communities were ripped apart as families were separated from their homes and livelihoods and relocated at best to the poorly serviced dormitory townships designated for their group, miles from any opportunities for work or from the provision of goods or services, or even worse to areas newly designated as their "traditional" areas – dusty, overcrowded rural reserves on which many of them had never set foot before. Within the apartheid framework, there was no recognition of any forms of permanent land tenure or ownership for Africans outside of these small labor reserves. Effectively, black South Africans had been stripped of their citizenship and rendered, at best, as "guestworkers" in the country of their birth.

Crucially, however, apartheid's planners did not seek to completely exclude black South Africans from "white" cities, towns, and farms. On the contrary, apartheid required their labor – but sought to extract that labor under very particular conditions. It therefore sought to regulate the movement and living conditions of black South Africans in a way that would secure their labor supply but grant them few other privileges or rights.

In particular, grand apartheid sought to control the movement of Africans from the reserves and into "white" land and cities. This motivated the consolidation and elaboration of the notorious pass laws that required all Africans who sought to venture outside of the reserves to carry in their identity documents a "pass," signed by their employer, testifying that they were employed and therefore justifying their (temporary) presence in a designated "white" area. Even those in possession of the requisite pass, indicating that they were employed and hence could legally enter the "white" cities and towns, were often housed at some distance from those towns in dormitory townships. This built the distinctive and racialized geography of modern South Africa: a well-developed, well-serviced core that was relatively well-supplied with infrastructure and amenities, surrounded by a bleak periphery.

In this way, the South African landscape was not only racialized, it was also ethnicized and gendered. Which particular reserve Africans were assigned to depended on which "tribe" or ethnic group they were designated as belonging to. As part of the attempt to divide and rule, apartheid sought to justify the denial of citizenship to Africans by arguing that as members of a distinct ethnic group, they enjoyed citizenship, belonging, and rights within the purview of their "traditional" homeland. Tswanas then, were relocated "back" to the tiny and fragmented territories of the Bophuthatswana homeland and were supposed to obtain services and political representation from the political and bureaucratic institutions set up for that homeland. Those Tswana, men who were lucky enough to obtain employment on the mines were often housed in ethnically distinct, same-sex hostels (although township life was often much more mixed). The same pertained for Sotho, Zulu, and so on.

As for gender, initially at least it was predominantly male labor that was required by the apartheid economy, while women, children, and old people were left to scratch out an existence via subsistence farming in the reserve. The movement of women too was brought increasingly under the control of the state with the extension of the pass system to African women in the 1950s. Over time, larger numbers of black women were allowed into the "white" cities to serve in a range of distinct occupations including as household help and later in such industries as the rapidly growing textile and clothing sector. The ruthless enforcement of the pass system and the difficulty of obtaining passes in the same neighborhoods effectively destroyed and rewrote the nature of family life in South Africa as couples were often forced to spend most of their working years apart from each other and from their children. Low salaries and onerous working hours meant that many children were raised by grandparents.

The post 1948-period saw also the rigidification and intensification of the employment color bar that denied Africans entry into skilled and better paying jobs, reserving these for white South Africans. Colored and Indian South Africans were often granted access only to an intermediate level occupation, requiring slightly more skills and paying more than those for Africans, but less than those for whites. Such measures, implemented alongside racially preferential hiring and employment practices in the state and in the growing numbers of state-owned enterprises, effectively wiped out the problem of white poverty within a few decades as larger numbers of Afrikaners were effectively incorporated into the heart of a flourishing and prosperous economy. Job reservation, protected employment, and secure access to a much higher quality of education provided the basis for the resilient economic power of the white minority.

Over time, the ideology of apartheid was increasingly elaborated to provide a set of justifications for the system. The public defense of the system shifted away from crude racism to the elaborate fiction that each of the country's ten African groups ought to be autonomous and ultimately self-governing and that this was part of the God-given nature of things. The population of South Africa was not simply divided into racial categories but black South Africans were also further subdivided into separate ethnicized groups based on their "tribe." (It is striking that white South Africans were not considered to be ethnically divided or diverse or to require separate **homelands** or governing systems.) As intimated above, each "tribe" was designated as having a "traditional homeland": tiny, often quite disparate pieces of land that were patched together from the reserves system and not necessarily even contiguous, with an often quite hastily invented structure of so-called traditional governance; separate government departments; and in some cases a nascent legislature, police force, and army. The result was an enormous duplication of bureaucracies and severe inequalities in the funding and quality of government institutions and the services they delivered. In the field of education, for example, there were some nineteen separate and supposedly ethnically and racially distinct departments of educations. In addition to being extraordinarily expensive, the system also fostered corruption: as one might imagine, the kind of people willing to be associated with these homeland institutions were not public-minded civil servants who had the best interests of their people at heart but those who sought to access economic opportunities ahead of all else.

For much of the twentieth century, most South African businesses were happy to go along with this political situation. Indeed business owners, who were overwhelmingly white, benefited from the healthy growth experienced by the South African economy from the 1950s through to the mid-1970s. Mining and other labor intensive industries benefited from conducive conditions in the international economy and the abundance of cheap labor at home.

This growth drove tremendously consequential long-term shifts in the nature of the South African economy. The slow but steady structural transformation of the South African economy away from being a primary product producer (previously overwhelmingly reliant on agriculture and mining) to being a more diversified economy (where services and manufactured and processed products were comprising an ever larger share of that economy) contributed to higher salaries and better lifestyles for skilled (white) workers. The apartheid state continued to pursue a kind of affirmative action for poor white Afrikaners (by providing them with secure jobs in the civil service and the state) and for Afrikaner firms by granting them preferential access to lucrative government contracts. Over time a community that had previously seen itself as based in farming came to look increasingly urban and white collar, closely resembling their English-speaking counterparts. Indeed in terms of class profile, English-speaking and Afrikaans communities grew increasingly indistinguishable, as did their interests. Racialized inequalities, however, were stark.

Resistance to Apartheid

As one might imagine, black South Africans at the receiving end of these measures were not inclined to passively accept them. Within every community there were those opposed to the broad direction in which the society was moving and who organized in myriad ways to oppose or confound those developments. There is only time and space to review select examples.

Perhaps the most high profile anti-apartheid organization is also one of the oldest liberation movements on the continent. The ANC was founded in 1912 as the South African Native National Congress "to unite tribes and races in defence of their rights." It began life, as did so many of the national liberation movements in Africa, as a thoroughly moderate, middle-class movement. In its initial decades, it was far from a mass-based or popular movement but its relatively conservative membership was drawn instead from the ranks of black school teachers, preachers, chiefs, and professionals. Accordingly its politics and processes were correspondingly mannered and middle-of-the-road. As one might anticipate, these early efforts did not make much impact, and by the 1930s, the Congress appeared to be in decline because its strategies had achieved so little.

The ANC was significantly reinvigorated in the 1950s, however. The ANC Youth League played a key role in energizing the "mother" organization; inspired by the U.S. civil rights movement, its program urged black South Africans to defy unjust and discriminatory laws, thus launching what would become the Defiance Campaign, a new era of electrifying mass mobilization. The leaders of the Youth League, including **Nelson Mandela**, Walter Sisulu, and Oliver Tambo, would go on to play a critical role in the Congress's – and the country's – future.

After some initial internal debates between those who were more Africanist in inclination and those who prioritized non-racialism, the ANC self-consciously developed what would become a formal and long-standing set of alliances with white, Indian, and Colored activists working in fraternal organizations in 1955. The disproportionate impact of activists situated in the tiny but formidably well-organized South African Communist Party was crucial here in establishing non-racialism as a central precept, practice, and principle of the alliance. The adoption of the **Freedom Charter** in 1955 gave coherence to the organization and its allies, providing an inspiring vision of the kind of South Africa for which they pledged to strive, a vision generic enough that it could motivate both die-hard communists and those more inclined toward market-based policies. The Charter explicitly articulated a firmly non-racial vision of the country's future, as encapsulated in the phrase "South Africa belongs to all who live in her, black and white," thus succinctly articulating the ideal of a non-racial future, and implying the need, in the present, to work non-racially to oppose a racist state.

These developments resulted in many of the Africanists within the ANC peeling away to found an alternate movement, the **Pan African Congress** (PAC), in the late 1950s. Although the PAC's influence and popularity has waned more recently, at key moments in the country's history, it loomed at least as large as the ANC. In fact, in the 1960s, it may well have been the more prominent and powerful of the two. Whereas the ANC organized on a non-racial basis, the ideological underpinnings of the PAC were much more explicitly informed by the ideas of black consciousness thinkers and writers. Many in the PAC (and at least some in the ANC) were strongly influenced by a long-standing tradition of ideas articulated in international struggles against racism, including the writings of Marcus Garvey and W. E. B. Du Bois. For those who aligned themselves with the PAC and to some extent its smaller cousin AZAPO, although the ultimate goal was a non-racial society, blacks and only blacks would play the critical role in the process of liberation. However well-meaning, they argued, liberal whites were not integral to that process, which required first and foremost for black South Africans to liberate themselves from the mentality of subservience, inferiority – the "slave" mentality – that apartheid had sought to inculcate.

Both the ANC and the PAC attracted powerful allies in the student movement; indeed it was out of the South African Students Organization that Steve Biko emerged as one of the most prominent and influential voices for black consciousness in South Africa, before he was fatally beaten by policemen in his jail cell. Both movements also sought to organize and mobilize widespread anger at the apartheid regime with a series of mass campaigns in the 1950s inspired by ideas of passive and non-violent resistance. The launch of these campaigns and the way in which they caught both the popular imagination and headlines around the world mark the beginnings of mass politics in South Africa. A number of demonstrations and marches focused in particular on the hated pass system – and many of these were met with repression and violence by the police.

Thus ensued a vicious cycle that was to characterize South African politics for the next twenty years or so, in which a violent reaction by the state to campaigns by the black opposition in turn produced a radicalization of that opposition and further protest from black communities, and hence engendered even more concerted and repressive reactions from the state. These rhythms of resistance and repression ebbed and flowed somewhat over the decades that followed, now surging, now waning, but the overall trend was one of a strong and growing level of civil society organization and the growing securitization and militarization of the South African state.

This cycle was dramatically demonstrated in March 1960 in the small township of Sharpeville where the PAC had launched a campaign against pass laws. The police opened fire on unarmed protesters, killing 69 people and wounding close to 200. The massacre made international headlines and galvanized international revulsion against apartheid. Internally too, some of those who had long benefited from the economic structure of apartheid began to have qualms about the system. In the immediate aftermath of Sharpeville, a range of South African business associations (including Afrikaner business) began to argue the need for political reforms. This did not last long however. They slumped into complacency again with the eerie political calm of the latter half of the 1960s. This "calm" was in fact the result of ruthless repression, the state's reaction to these non-violent campaigns. The NP government moved swiftly to ban the major liberation movements, including the ANC, and to imprison key leadership figures – at least, all of those who had not already fled into exile.

For both the ANC and PAC, this series of events prompted their separate decisions to embark on armed struggle in the 1960s. As they had to move their leadership and headquarters into exile, the focus of both organizations necessarily shifted away from popular mobilization within South Africa to the new imperatives of adapting to life in exile and establishing the strategic capacity to take on one of the most effective militaries on the continent. The ANC's military wing would be named Umkhonto we Sizwe (meaning Spear of the Nation), and the armed wing of the PAC was named Poqo (whose meaning is variously interpreted as "go it alone" or "pure" or "authentic").

The leadership of both movements was either forced underground or fled into exile to avoid arrest – but not everyone managed to escape the attentions of the police. The result was a series of high profile political trials including at Rivonia where Nelson Mandela was tried for treason and used his public testimony to make a riveting statement of political principle: "During my lifetime," he argued, "I have dedicated myself to this struggle of the African people. I have fought against white domination, and I have fought against black domination. I have cherished the ideal of a democratic and free society in which all persons live together in harmony and with equal opportunities. It is an ideal which I hope to live for and to achieve. But if needs be, it is an ideal for which I am prepared to die." The judge was however unmoved and sentenced Mandela to life in prison. He would serve twenty-seven years of that sentence, many of those years in the notorious political prison on Robben Island along with many other key leadership figures of the anti-apartheid struggle.

The state's reaction effectively pushed both organizations out of South African public life. Both movements sought to set up new headquarters in exile in one of the neighboring states, beginning also to try to build some kind of "underground" presence and organizational structure inside the country. As argued previously, they also had to establish some meaningful military capacity, to channel and focus the anger and militancy of the youth who fled across the border to take up arms against apartheid. These were tough times. Both movements at this point were struggling to survive internationally, to find a secure physical base outside of the country but not completely lose touch with their popular constituencies inside South Africa. The fact that the ANC secured Soviet financial and military support was crucial to its subsequent political fortunes. Less important here than the actual prosecution of the armed struggle was instead the success of the ANC's quiet, patient international campaign to win recognition as the only legitimate voice of black South Africans. The ANC effectively beat out other black organizations and liberation movements, especially the PAC, to become the single most prominent voice in the international anti-apartheid campaign.

The international context was shifting in vitally important ways as decolonization was won across the continent and, globally, the tolerance for white supremacist views declined. As larger numbers of African states in particular achieved independence, the balance of power within the UN General Council tipped in favor of the numerically preponderant Third World states, and fora such as the Organization of African Unity became extremely hostile to the few surviving white minority regimes in Africa, pledging instead support for and solidarity with the liberation movements fighting those regimes.

The international environment was of course also increasingly characterized by Cold War–related tensions, and these fed directly into both unfolding domestic politics within South Africa and the broader set of military conflicts and political antagonisms playing out in the neighboring states. The NP government felt increasingly embattled and isolated as, one after another, its neighbors achieved majority rule. Apartheid's ideologues described their country as subject to a "total onslaught" by its black and communist neighbors, and hence justified the development of a "total strategy" to combat this. This strategy involved not only domestic repression but also the military and economic destabilization of neighboring states that were prepared to provide succor to the liberation movements.

The result was a growing role for the military and security services, both as a share of the government budget and in terms of the political significance of these sectors in broader government policymaking. The conscription of young white men into the **South African Defence Force (SADF)** was stepped up, and many of these young men were deployed in cross-border raids into neighboring states such as Angola, Namibia, and Zambia. Other tactics were also unleashed against the movements in exile, including letter bombs and the use of double-agents to collect intelligence, all of which, over time, began to foster more centralizing, secretive, and occasionally paranoid modes of organization within the liberation movements.

The 1970s also began to see a growing rift between what had previously been friendly or even fraternal black organizations, such as the Inkatha Freedom Party, a Zulu nationalist party based in Natal, and the ANC. As the stakes increased, tensions within the black community grew about how best to oppose apartheid.

The South African economy was also changing. It seemed by the early 1970s that ISI had to some extent succeeded: the South African economy had effectively diversified its economy with flourishing manufacturing, industry, and services sectors, and although mining continued to be important, this traditional mainstay of the economy, along with agriculture, contributed a far smaller share of GDP than previously. The economy was about to hit a decidedly rough patch, however, in part the result of the international slowdown following the oil shocks of 1973 and 1979, but also related to domestic developments. The limitations of the early apartheid model for this new economy became increasingly evident from the early 1970s. For example, although it had once seemed an advantage to business not to have to worry about African trade unions, a series of "wildcat" strikes in Durban in 1973 demonstrated the real dangers of the lack of institutionalized mechanisms for conflict resolution. Rather than being able to sit down at a table with their trade union representatives, some employers had to literally pick up a loudspeaker at the factory gate and attempt to communicate with a fractious mob of hundreds of angry workers. All of this led sections of business to support a series of reforms to legalize African trade unions. This process that would ultimately enable the emergence of the **Congress of South African Trade Unions (COSATU)**, an immensely powerful trade union federation that organizes and speaks on behalf of the vast majority of those formally employed in unionized workplaces in South Africa today and remains a key political broker in the country. Although most of COSATU's members were and are African, the union confederation is aligned with the values of non-racialism. When this nascent trade union federation made the decision to align itself with Congress politics (in the mid 1980s), this was an immense shot in the arm for the ANC in its struggle to be recognized as the preeminent liberation movement in South Africa.

The final trend that exploded into prominence in the late 1970s was the growing politicization of black South African youth and their increasing impatience with the gradualism and reformism of their elders. From the late 1970s and into the 1980s, African schoolchildren come to be at the forefront of many of the most prominent political struggles. Their politics began with a clear rejection of the tenets and foundations of what was called "Bantu" education, a highly ideological and directive form of education that was intended to drill into black students just enough of the most basic levels of numeracy and literacy to equip them to be the economy's unskilled labor supply ("hewers of wood and bearers of water" in the notorious words of one NP Minister of Education). In an echo of the tragedy of Sharpeville some sixteen years previously, peaceful protests (this time against the compulsory use of Afrikaans in black schools) turned deadly. On June 16, 1976, in Soweto, police opened fire on protesting schoolchildren. Hector Peterson, just thirteen years old, was one of the first people to be killed on that day. Horrifying images were splashed on the front pages of the world's newspapers and, once more, the world recoiled.

The repressive machinery of the apartheid state was deployed yet again with the imposition of a state of emergency and another round of arrests, detentions, and bannings; once again, a period of eerie political quiescence followed. This time, the next eruption of protest would not take more than a decade. However, the world had begun to pay closer and more critical attention to events in South Africa.

When this racialized system was initially being constructed, it had not been grossly at odds with the norms of a global society dominated by imperialism and its attendant ideologies, including "scientific" racism. Over time however, the system of apartheid (as it came to be formalized) diverged increasingly from emerging norms elsewhere: on the continent, former colonies won the right to independence and majority rule, and internationally, human rights norms became increasingly prominent. Successive apartheid governments after the 1950s were nonetheless able to play quite effectively into the tensions associated with the Cold War. By depicting itself as a strategically crucial bastion of pro-Western, pro-market, and anti-communist values, the apartheid regime won some protection from international pressures for reform of its political system. From the 1970s on (as noted previously), the state increasingly militarized itself in an attempt to deal with ever sharper political opposition to the system. In addition to imposing increasingly repressive laws and responses at home, the regime intervened extensively, both militarily and economically, in the affairs of other states in the region in an attempt to secure a *cordon sanitaire* around its borders of regimes that would not be overtly hostile to the apartheid project. In turn, activists both within South Africa and abroad continued to campaign tirelessly to expose the brutal and exclusionary nature of the regime and to push the South African state to reform. These efforts included the beginnings of a campaign to enforce international sanctions against South Africa and to isolate the regime diplomatically.

Reforming Apartheid

In 1983, the apartheid government introduced what was supposed to be a set of constitutional reforms that would break the political logjam. The government proposed to create a tricameral parliament, with elections and representation for white, Indian, and Colored South Africans respectively in three separate legislative chambers, and with the size and power of each chamber carefully calibrated to ensure continued white dominance of the government. The NP argued that this represented a legitimate widening of political representation in South Africa for which it should be lauded (indeed, extremists split away from the NP in protest to form an even more right-wing party). Many anti-apartheid campaigners however saw this as a thinly veiled attempt to divide the non-white opposition and co-opt Indians and coloreds into collaborating with a system that continued to exclude the majority – Africans – from any meaningful political power. Most black South Africans reacted with fury. The result was a torrent of internal mobilization against apartheid, much of it bubbling from the ground up via an array of civic and community organizations.

The **United Democratic Front (UDF)** was the most high profile and successful organizational response to these developments: a large internally based opposition that took the form of a front loosely affiliated with Charterist traditions (i.e., with the ideas of the Freedom Charter and hence of the ANC) but which provided an umbrella under which an astonishingly wide range of civil society organizations could be accommodated, coordinated, and deployed against apartheid. The significance of the UDF lay in its wide reach and deep roots inside South Africa. The civic organizations, students councils, and church groups that made up the UDF were born in local neighborhoods, led by those the community recognized and saw on the streets every day – and were therefore superbly well-placed to connect local struggles (for example over access to local government services such as water or transport) to the big national political issues of the day. This was in striking contrast to the ANC in exile, which could at times seem very remote from the everyday lives of those remaining inside South Africa. Indeed, for much of the 1980s, the ANC appeared to be trying to play catch-up with very rapidly unfolding political developments inside the country, slow to grasp the extent of what was happening in South Africa's townships and what this meant for the broader anti-apartheid struggle.

In their speeches to the country's white citizens and the international community, the government maintained that the country's internal turmoil was the work of a conspiracy hatched by the ANC in alliance with its international communist ally, the Soviet Unioni. Contrary to the assertions of apartheid's propagandists, however, the township activists were in most instances very far from being easily manipulated lackeys. Many of these organizations were sympathetic to the ANC and identified with the tradition of struggle that it represented, but it rapidly became clear that the popular anger being expressed on township streets was growing beyond the control of any one organization or individual.

Nonetheless, the notion that the country was the object of an onslaught by a ruthless, communist-backed foe was used to justify the increasing militarization of the institutions of the state. Successive new states of emergency were declared, along with the passage of more legislation to provide for the detention and prosecution of anti-apartheid activists and for new restrictions on freedom of the press and the freedom to organize.

Once again, the SADF and its capacities were further expanded. Since 1967 all white men of school-leaving age had been conscripted for training and a tour of duty in the SADF; over the course of the 1970s, these tours of duty had become ever longer. By the 1980s, conscripts were deployed not merely on (or indeed beyond) the country's borders but also *inside* the country, against other South Africans. An insidious militarization was occurring inside the polity with the development of a "shadow state": the notorious Bureau of State Security gave way to the technocratically named National Security Management System, a set of governing structures operating behind closed doors, parallel to every level of public and elected government, which saw security personnel being drawn increasingly into everyday governance. Alongside these domestic developments was an intensification of military conflicts and engagements with the ANC and with pro-ANC movements in neighboring states.

The new forms of anti-apartheid resistance took myriad forms. The repertoire of protest actions included bus boycotts by commuters, protests by journalists and others over the threats to press freedom, school boycotts by students and in some instances unionized teachers, and even resistance by a small number of progressive white conscripts to being compelled to serve in the apartheid army. Chillingly, many of these protests also included vigilante action against those within the black community suspected of in some way collaborating with the apartheid system. What was striking was the relative youth of those at the forefront of many of these actions. The "young lions" of the UDF (as they came to be called) vowed to make apartheid South Africa effectively ungovernable – by for example refusing to pay rates to black township councils or pay taxes on government-owned houses. They proposed to dismantle the governing structures of the apartheid state, rejecting the authority of the police and judicial system and seeking instead to replace these with local forms of what was termed "people's power:" block defense committees, and people's courts. In many places the attempt to make apartheid effectively ungovernable succeeded as South Africa's townships were plunged into an era of almost constant protest and bloody conflict with the authorities. Ugly excesses, including attacks on suspected "collaborators and spies" on occasion, accompanied this turmoil. When they were allowed to report on these events, the media broadcast images of running battles between youth and police in the streets and burning barricades that effectively restricted the access of the authorities to what had effectively become battle zones; it became a common sight to see armored vehicles patrolling black residential neighborhoods.

Not only black neighborhoods were affected, however. Walkouts and strikes on the factory floor took the struggle into the heart of the "white" economy as COSATU, the newly consolidated and increasingly powerful trade union movement, began to flex its considerable muscle in the workplace. This imposed real costs on businesses as the number of workdays lost to political protest and industrial action soared. Once again, sections of the business community began to wonder if the costs associated with the defense and maintenance of apartheid were worth it. Behind these second thoughts lay important long-term shifts in the nature of the South African economy. The now thoroughly diversified economy not only looked very different than previously, but needed very different things from country's labor and consumer markets. Whereas early mining and agriculture had lobbied principally for a system that produced an abundant supply of politically quiescent and cheap black labor, this was not what a thriving manufacturing or services sector needed in the 1980s. Instead, what these sectors increasingly required were skilled employees with advanced levels of education who could produce higher-order consumer goods and large numbers of prosperous local customers who could buy those goods. Apartheid was not well equipped to deliver either one of these.

Moreover, the political opposition to apartheid was beginning to significantly damage the overall environment within which business operated. A militant and organized trade union sector embarking on politically motivated strikes bit deeply into the productivity and profitability of factory floors across the country. The increasingly turbulent state of the country's politics, along with the impact of trade sanctions and restrictions on foreign exchange movements, worried investors, who grew increasingly nervous about South Africa's long-term prospects. Important sections of business began to see that apartheid no longer served their interests. Afrikaner businesses joined English-speaking businesses in calling for political reform.

The state, however, did not seem especially inclined to listen. Successive states of emergency facilitated the adoption of increasingly repressive measures, and each new move on the side of the state was met with anger and defiance by the opposition. The result was a growing number of arrests and the widespread use of detention without trial. Many of these measures occurred within a legislative framework, something that had long been a feature of apartheid, which was to a large extent effected via constitutional and legalized institutions. However over the course of the 1980s, observers began to note increasing lawlessness on the part of the state itself. Detainees reported the widespread use of torture in detention, and analysts began to discern the workings of a mysterious "Third Force" (made up, many assumed, of "rogue" elements of the intelligence and security services) behind the extrajudicial killings and disappearances of anti-apartheid activists. In a number of places, an increasingly politicized police force began to arm conservative factions within black communities that were inclined to be hostile or unsympathetic to the ANC or its ally, the UDF, and hence to foster internecine conflict within black communities. In Natal and on the East Rand townships this resulted in a virtual small-scale civil war between those groups sympathetic to the Inkatha Freedom Party and those aligned with the ANC.

All of this upheaval further interfered with the conduct of business. Over the course of the 1980s and into the early 1990s, economic growth dropped off precipitously. Alarmed by this volatility, investors fled and the level of international trade dropped further. The effects were compounded by growing international support for the campaign to isolate apartheid South Africa. Trade sanctions sought to strangle the export-oriented South African economy by effectively depriving it of access to lucrative overseas markets. At the same time, the tightening of the cultural and sporting boycott sought to drive the message home to white South Africans that the policies that many of them supported were regarded with opprobrium in other parts of the world. The U.S. divestment campaign led to the erasure of such big brand names as Apple, Pepsi, and Kodak from South Africa. In many cases, it was not clear whether these decisions to withdraw from South Africa were purely business decisions, motivated by falling profits and growing political uncertainty, or evidence that these firms were taking the moral high ground, part of the international campaign to isolate the South African regime.

Initially the U.S. government maintained a policy of "constructive engagement" vis-à-vis apartheid South Africa. Ultimately however as the international anti-apartheid campaign grew in strength and numbers and became an electoral issue in the United States, even the conservative Reagan government was forced to announce limited sanctions against the country. The British government under Margaret Thatcher was similarly reluctant to adopt measures against the South African regime but also found its position increasingly untenable as it was progressively isolated in such fora as the European Economic Community (forerunner of the European Union) and the Commonwealth. Ultimately the British government too passed sanctions against South Africa. The costs of apartheid were being raised on every front – including in the Southern African region more broadly.

The extensive involvement of the SADF in a series of regional conflicts over the course of the 1980s grew increasingly expensive for the South African state as its army was forced to fight or to fund surrogates on a very wide front along its extensive borders. In an attempt to contain those conflicts by diplomatic means, South Africa under the leadership of P.W. Botha effectively coerced neighboring Mozambique into a series of accords, signed at Nkomati, in which the Mozambican government pledged to cease providing shelter or assistance to the anti-apartheid guerrillas.

It was however the end of the Cold War that probably had the biggest pacifying impact. The entire regional balance of power shifted in response to the collapse of the Soviet Union and the West's triumph in the Cold War, unraveling a series of international conflicts that ultimately would lead to the resolution of South Africa's own internal political conflict. This series of events began with an international settlement brokered by the U.S. Department of State under the leadership of Chester Crocker that secured the mutual withdrawal from Angola of both Cuban and South African troops. This agreement paved the way for the granting of independence – and hence majority rule – to South West Africa (which would later name itself Namibia) and the withdrawal of South African troops from that country too.

The dawning of the 1990s saw the region in a state of profound flux associated with the end of the Cold War. This had at least two profound implications for both those who sought to defend apartheid and those who struggled to end it. First, it signaled the end of South Africa's strategic importance to Western governments – which arguably weakened the apartheid government's ability to resist calls for political reform. Second, however, the end of Soviet ability and willingness to support guerrilla movements in the South unquestionably weakened the strategic position of the ANC too. Both parties then faced a new and urgent set of incentives to reach a political solution to their conflict.

The 1990s also witnessed a wave of democratizations across the continent and, as argued previously, the conclusion of a number of regional settlements that eroded both international tolerance for the white minority regime and perceptions by the white South African government that it needed to protect itself against a regionalized "communist" onslaught.

The End of Formal Apartheid

The fall of the Berlin Wall thus had momentous implications for South Africa's domestic politics. The collapse of the Soviet Union and the progressive withdrawal of its financial and military support for liberation movements around the world, including in Southern Africa, meant that strategically speaking, the ANC was now weaker than it had been in decades, as its single largest international backer withdrew almost completely from its international obligations. Moreover, the ideological victory of the market and the West would further undermine the appeal and cohesiveness of the ANC and its ability to effectively pursue a radical agenda. From the NP's point of view, if there was any time to engage in negotiations with The ANC, this was it.

However, as much as the ANC was in a weakened position, the NP government was too. Although the trade sanctions and international cultural and sporting boycotts had been damaging, a series of new international financial sanctions really hit the apartheid regime hard. Analysts point in particular to the refusal in 1985 by Chase Manhattan Bank of New York – soon followed by other commercial banks – to roll over their loans to the South African government. Suddenly Pretoria was staring a real credit crunch in the face. In the view of many analysts, this was what finally ended apartheid: it could no longer pay its bills.

Accordingly, on February 2, 1990, South Africa's then President F. W. de Klerk, who had until then given little indication of being particularly reform-minded, stunned the world by announcing the unbanning of key anti-apartheid organizations including the ANC and SACP, alongside the release of a number of high profile political prisoners including Nelson Mandela. This dramatic announcement would ultimately pave the way for the beginning of political negotiations between these two parties. Exiles began returning home and the ANC set up its new headquarters in downtown Johannesburg. The Conference for a Democratic South Africa, the forum that brought all the major parties together to negotiate the transition, met inside South Africa amid escalating violence as the right wing sought to block the transition; indeed, as various parties sought to shape the nature of the transition, the level of political violence grew to horrific new heights.

The negotiations were thus far from trouble-free or entirely pacific. Ultimately, however, the parties were able to agree on a process that would produce a remarkable new constitution for the country as well as the hosting of its first ever truly democratic and non-racial elections. Despite apparently impossible deadlines and attempts to derail the process with a bombing campaign, the elections proceeded amidst remarkable calm in April of 1994. In no great surprise to anyone, the ANC was duly elected by over 60 percent of the popular vote as South Africa's first post-apartheid government. Four years after he had walked out of jail as a free man, Nelson Mandela was inaugurated as the country's first black president. The ANC has governed the country since, winning every national election by a comfortable margin despite some considerable ructions and leadership struggles within its own ranks, which will be discussed later in the chapter.

The Challenges of the New South Africa: Institutional Legacies and Changing Identities

There is no question that the newly elected government inherited a formidable set of challenges, many of which continue to consume the attention of the country's policymakers. Responses to these challenges were profoundly shaped by the regional and international context of the time: first, neither the ANC nor the NP had scored a decisive battlefield victory. Rather, they were both forced to compromise with each other in important ways. Second, and at least as important, was the advent of what political scientist Francis Fukuyama described as "the end of history": viz. the international triumph of liberal democracy on the political front and neo-liberalism on the economic front. These realities would seriously constrain the policy options that any new democratically elected government could adopt.

Inherent to the political transition was the question of how South Africans were going to deal with the political legacy of their troubled past. This was a particularly urgent question because how it was answered was crucial in determining the extent to which the country's security forces – deeply implicated in human rights abuses – supported or opposed the process of political transition.

All hopes were vested in a single institution: The **Truth and Reconciliation Commission (TRC)** was established in 1996 with the highly respected Archbishop Desmond Tutu at its head. As a leading Anglican cleric, Tutu had long been a prominent and esteemed figure in the anti-apartheid struggle but was not regarded as a partisan of the ANC and hence had the credibility to head up an institution whose brief was to consider the behavior of all parties to the South African conflict. At the heart of this institution and the process it set down was a Faustian-type bargain that would effectively trade justice for access to the truth. The terms of the Commission were that, if those who had committed gross abuses of human rights for a political end, as part of a political organization, pledged to tell the complete truth about those events, they would be granted amnesty and spared from prosecution for those crimes. There is no doubt that this bargain represented a significant compromise and did not satisfy those who sought justice for the many victims of human rights abuses. It was a clear indication that the liberation of South Africa had not been the result of a decisive and overwhelming victory on the part of the anti-apartheid forces; they were therefore not able to unilaterally dictate the terms of a post-apartheid settlement or to simply try and jail apartheid's henchmen. Rather the country's transition process epitomized a reluctant compromise on all sides, built on the understanding that it would be fatal to construct a process that gave the men with guns – principally those in the apartheid security services – any incentive to fear the transition to democracy. Instead, they had to be reconciled to the new South Africa and the end of white rule, given a reason to go along with the process rather than to oppose it.

Although the achievements and goals of the Commission were modest, they were not inconsequential. The TRC mattered in at least two, closely related senses: first, it gave the victims of human rights abuses a voice and a respectful hearing, a public acknowledgement of what they had suffered. In turn what this made possible, perhaps for the first time in South African history, was the construction of a common narrative that all South Africans could share, a single telling of their past. One of the many tragedies of apartheid had been not only how it physically separated black and white South Africans but how it had enabled groups to construct very different and often wildly contradictory versions of the reality of both their history and of contemporary South Africa. As the hearings of the TRC were broadcast daily via a range of media, they reached a very large number of people. It was, for some white South Africans, the first time that they were directly confronted with the brutalities that had been committed to secure their privileges.

It is important to understand the imperative that drove much of the new ANC government's decision-making in the first few years of democracy: how to safeguard the fragile transition. And here, securing the effective assent of white South Africans to the end of their monopoly on political power, and hence securing the capital and economic assets that they controlled, was paramount. The new South Africa was acutely aware of how the rapid and embittered departure of white settlers from other liberated colonies had hamstrung economic development elsewhere in Africa, as crucial skills and large amounts of capital had fled with those communities. The new ANC government was at pains to reassure white South Africans that their economic interests would not be threatened. In addition to making De Klerk one of two vice presidents in a Government of National Unity, key ministries such as Minerals and Energy, and Finance were left in white hands – the latter in the hands of the very same minister who had served the NP government. The country's new president, Nelson Mandela, played a crucial role in giving whites a sense that they could live with the new political order – indeed that they were welcome and valued members of the new democracy. His stress on reconciliation and understanding white fear defused what could have been a potent source of instability within and opposition to the new regime.

Although Mandela was an incredibly effective figurehead for the new democracy, the real architect of the post-apartheid economic order was probably his other vice president, **Thabo Mbeki**. As Mandela's deputy, Mbeki was responsible for overseeing key aspects of South Africa's foreign and economic policy. Once the political crisis had been stabilized, it became clear that the economy presented, if anything, an even larger set of challenges.

Although the elections of April 1994 effected a dramatic shift in political power, they did not impact the underlying features of the country's socio-economy. The day after the elections, black South Africans woke up in the same ramshackle houses, attended the same weak schools, and faced the same dismal job and economic prospects as they had before, and white South Africans continued to enjoy the economic security that their superior education and hence access to higher-paying skilled employment could ensure. The persistence of radical socio-economic inequality may have made the transition easier for whites to accept, but for a majority government it was to prove one of the toughest legacies of the apartheid era and a potential threat to securing the consolidation of democracy in the medium and long term.

After all, the ANC was elected to power with a mandate to represent the interests of the majority of South Africans, those who had been neglected and marginalized by the apartheid state for decades. It therefore faced immense pressure to begin to address the social welfare inequalities that had come to define South African society. However, there were some sharp constraints on what could be achieved – or even attempted. As argued previously, the ANC won political power in the midst of the neo-liberal era when it would have been suicide for any African government to embark on radical, redistributionist politics. Indeed, conservative international bankers and financiers watched warily for signs of imprudence or heterodoxy on the part of the new government. The country's first black finance minister, Trevor Manuel, was rudely reminded of this when the value of the currency plunged in response to relatively anodyne remarks he made about the "amorphous" nature of the markets. Fully aware of the pressing need for the new government to demonstrate that it was fiscally responsible and could be trusted with the curatorship of the economy, the new ANC government unilaterally adopted a relatively conservative macroeconomic policy strategy called GEAR, designed to please and reassure the business community.

The third pressing challenge went to the heart of the state: how to extend the provision of state services and the authority of government to the whole population – all the while having to work with the personnel and structures inherited from the apartheid state. As argued earlier in the chapter, the bureaucracy of the apartheid state had previously only really served about 20 percent of the population – and, to be fair, it had been relatively effective at that. Now, however, it was being called upon to provide goods and services to 100 percent of the population. Moreover, the civil service continued to be staffed largely with white, Afrikaner, and often conservative bureaucrats who were not particularly sympathetic to the priorities of their new political masters.

There was therefore a pressing need for the new government to restructure key state institutions. This was a massive undertaking that included setting up a new constitution and supreme court to serve as the apex of a new South African legal order, alongside a broader attempt to rebuild, integrate, and reform the numerous formerly divided and racialized civil services into a single coherent bureaucracy. The new government was also keen to see the face of the civil service transformed: to have it more closely reflect the country's ethnic and racial diversity as well as to weed out those conservatives who might be inclined to sabotage the efforts of the country's new political leadership. This was effected via a series of "sunset clauses" and generous early retirement packages for those who did not wish to serve the new government. The problem with this solution was that although it defused a potentially tricky political issue, some of the country's most effective and efficient civil servants left the employ of the state while much of the "dead wood" remained. Moreover, it turned out to be tougher than expected for the public sector to recruit skilled black labor – mostly because the private sector could often significantly outcompete the state on salary. The reform of state institutions would prove to be a slow and frustrating process. The police force in particular struggled to adapt to the challenges of becoming a non-racialized, de-politicized crime fighting force and seemed overwhelmed in the face of an ominous crime wave in the immediate post-democracy era. A much smoother process of integration occurred in a most unexpected place: the military. The new South African National Defence Force was created by merging the old SADF with the military wings of the ANC and PAC.

In terms of the provision of services, then, it took much longer than anyone had imagined, but there were some areas in which the new government slowly began to make headway. These included broadening access to housing, clean water, health care, and electricity as well as a significant expansion in social security payments. There has however been much less progress on job creation. In many ways, job creation is a much harder problem for a government to solve than, say, providing access to clean drinking water or staffing a health clinic. Job creation is rather about the broad nature and functioning of the economy.

So the new government recorded important improvements in at least some of the indicators of unequal access to government services. It was slow going, however, and in some instances things have gotten worse rather than improving since 1994. In particular, stark inequalities remain and some have grown worse: inequality within the black community has spiked as a small number of black South Africans have, in a very short space of time, amassed fortunes while the great majority continues to struggle to secure even a very basic standard of living. The legacies of apartheid here are crucial – the very poor quality of education that many South Africans continue to receive (concentrated in the rural areas and the poorer urban communities) condemns many to a fate of long-term unemployment in a society with a massive excess of unskilled workers. Unemployment numbers are disputed but almost everyone agrees that they are extremely high – indeed among the highest in the world; for narrow measures of unemployment, figures are in the 20 percent range, while for broader or more expansive definitions of unemployment the percentages are in the 30 percent range. Crucially, inequality post-apartheid has declined between race groups but grown within race groups, suggesting that class is replacing race as the key marker of inequality in the new South Africa.

All of this reflects the stark reality that the morning after the country's first non-racial election in 1994, South Africans woke up to a situation in which some things – mostly to do with the country's political institutions – had changed, and others – mostly to do with the key social and economic institutions – had stayed the same. There had unquestionably been a dramatic transfer of political power but the economy has proven much tougher to transform. As we are now into the second decade post-apartheid, it is natural for the majority of black South Africans to begin to reflect a little more critically on what it is that has not changed – or at least, not for the better. It is also not entirely surprising that we have started to see an increase in expressions of discontent with the pace and nature of the delivery of government services. At least at the level of rhetoric, it seemed that government policy might be taking a populist turn, if not a turn to the left, with the victory of **Jacob Zuma** over Thabo Mbeki in the late 2000s in the contest for the presidency first of the ANC and then the country. However, since his having been in office, it is not clear that Zuma's major economic policy direction looks dramatically different from the broad outlines of the policies that Mbeki adopted. The international constraints within which the South African government is attempting to maneuver remain difficult to ignore.

South Africa's domestic and international challenges were compounded by the emergence of the devastating HIV/AIDS epidemic. HIV prevalence in the country's general population passed the crucial 5 percent point just around the time of the political transition. Focused as they were on preventing a catastrophic political meltdown, few of the key political decision-makers were able to grapple with the implications of the epidemic. AIDS was simply not at the top of the list of priorities. However it has since emerged as a very serious issue indeed, not least because of the curious stance adopted by then President Thabo Mbeki in his response to the epidemic, which was to entertain denialist interpretations of it, muzzling the ability of the country's health department to respond effectively to the epidemic. A Harvard study has estimated that conservatively put, his government's lack of action on this issue between 2000 and 2005 and the extent to which denialism delayed in particular the rolling out of effective anti-retroviral treatments has cost the lives of 333,000 South Africans. This policy has happily since been reversed, not because of a change of heart by Mbeki or an institutional challenge to his policies, but because of his loss of the presidency and replacement by his former deputy, Zuma. South Africa has the dubious distinction of being the country with the largest number of HIV-positive citizens in the world. However, under Zuma's presidency, at least the ability of the country's health department to respond to the crisis has been restored and the country has belatedly rolled out one of the world's largest publicly funded ARV programs.

Domestically speaking, the politics of South Africa in post-2000 increasingly became concerned with personalistic struggles for power within the new ruling party. Given the huge electoral support for the ANC and hence the strong probability that the ANC will be the country's government for some time to come, differences over policy directions and struggles for access to office and power have focused on factional struggles internal to the ANC. In particular, these struggles have centered on the influence of Congress's key allies – the SACP and the unions – on party policy. Publicly, these struggles were expressed in a contest between then President Mbeki and his then-deputy, Jacob Zuma, for leadership of the party and country. There are, as yet, few signs of an opposition outside of the party with the capacity to defeat the ANC in a national election. At a local and regional level the Democratic Alliance has impressed voters with superior service delivery and responsiveness but it may be some time before they present an urgent threat to the ANC's hold on power at the national level. Nonetheless, ANC policy direction is being fiercely contested both from within and without.

Given these many challenges, one might ask about what benefits, if any, accrued to South Africa as a result of its apparently miraculous transition to democracy in 1994. The death of Nelson Mandela in late 2013, coming as it did just before the country celebrated twenty years of democracy, provided the country with an important opportunity for assessing what had and had not been achieved over that period. It is easy now to lose sight of just how remarkable and unexpected the transition to democracy and its persistence since was: most observers had expected the struggle over political power in South Africa to end in a devastating racialized civil war, or to drag on interminably, driving the country's economy into ever greater crisis and all of its peoples into poverty. The settlement of 1994 and the country's rapid transition into a "normal" democracy was regarded then as extraordinary and, for a time, generated something of a mini international growth industry for key South African leadership figures, who flew around the world advising others in conflict situations how the South Africans did it. From one perspective then, the mere fact of two decades of democracy is itself cause for celebration.

Closer to home, the new South African government sought to establish an authoritative and influential presence in African affairs, with much less success than many expected. The new South Africa has often failed to exercise the leading role on the continent that the country's international and home-grown admirers hoped it would after apartheid despite – or perhaps because of – its economic stature on the continent. The country's early diplomatic efforts were often clumsy and ill-judged, and elicited resentment and suspicion about the extent to which the new South Africa understood the nuances and specificities of Africa's international relations. This is despite the fact that Thabo Mbeki articulated the very powerful idea of an African renaissance long before most international observers had begun to notice the resumption of growth, cessation of conflict, and flowering of democracy that began across the continent some fifteen to twenty years ago. South Africa's relations with neighboring Zimbabwe in particular have been ambiguous and much criticized.

Two decades old now, the "new" South Africa is widely accepted as a key member of the G20 and the BRICS group of nations. The resumption of growth that has been seen since the mid-1990s across much of Africa presents tremendous new challenges and opportunities for South Africa as one of the continent's largest economies. Some have argued that South African investment into those economies has driven a small share of that economic growth; certainly the opportunities for increased investment and trading ties with other African states are immense (and here South Africa may be competing with the growing influence of China), but so too are the potential pitfalls. The challenge for South Africans will be to find a model of growth and redistribution for their own economy that is both congruent with these rapidly shifting international developments and capable of producing thousands of jobs for South Africans at home. Here the country's achievements are mixed. The economy has delivered sharply better economic rewards for a few, but very large numbers of South Africans continue to face dismal prospects. There are also growing expressions of dissatisfaction with the failures especially of local government to deliver crucial services, as is manifest in an upturn in local service delivery protests. While the central government has presided over an impressive expansion in infrastructure and public goods provision, serious unevenness in the quality of state services persists along with evidence of some fraying of the country's much vaunted political institutions. The deaths of forty-four people at the Marikana mine in 2012 raised a number of disturbing questions about the extent to which the country had shaken off its past: it pointed to the persistence of a culture of brutality, coercion and the use of extra-legal strategies within the very police force charged to uphold the law. Working South Africans were increasingly coming to regard even the organized trade union movement as out of touch, elite-driven and no longer representing their real interests. The same charges are increasingly leveled at the ruling party. As South Africa enters its third decade of democracy, then, a key question will concern the ability of South Africans to craft new political institutions – or amend the old – to better represent and address their interests.

Table 12.1.   Key Phases in South Africa's Political Development

Time Period	Regime	Global Context	Interests/ Identities/ Institutions	Developmental Path
Up to mid 1600s	Diverse forms of autonomous governance.	International trade.	Multiple; not racialized; few contacts between Europeans and Khoisan at the Cape.	Fragmented; hunter-gathering, pastorialism, agriculture, and trade.
mid 1600s– 1910	Creation of settler-dominated states (two British colonies and two Boer republics).	Imperial; trade with the region is dominated by the UK.	Series of violent political and racial conflicts fought to secure key economic resources (esp. land, and labor).	Natural resources-based economy: agriculture and then mining (a.k.a. "maize and gold").
1910– 1948	Union of South Africa.	Two world wars; SA fights in both on the side of the UK and her allies.	Unitary state dominated by coalition of English and Afrikaner interests; oligopolistic economic institutions; white control over majority of arable land.	Growing dominance of mining-based economy.
1948– 1960s	National Party builds the apartheid state; republic declared in 1961.	Wave of independence across Africa and growing prominence of the developing world in international fora.	Formal institutionalization of race and ethnicity in every sphere of society and economy; triumph of Afrikaner nationalism. Rise of black consciousness and non-racialism as key oppositional ideologies.	State-led development to advance Afrikaner economic interests and foster ISI.

Time Period	Regime	Global Context	Interests/ Identities/ Institutions	Developmental Path
1960s–1990	Repression and reform; National Party still in power.	Cold War; global economic slowdown in the 1970s; tightening economic and political sanctions against apartheid government.	Growing militancy in resistance by black South Africans; successive states of emergency and range of repressive measures directed at opposition. Afrikaner and English interests become more or less indistinguishable as "white" interests.	Growing prominence of manufacturing and services; growth slows and economy moves into recession.
1990–1994	Transition; National Party still officially in power but increasingly unable to govern on its own.	Post Cold War and the "End of History."	Political negotiations; establishment of Constitutional Assembly and preparations for country's first democratic elections.	Tentative liberalization of the economy.
1994–present	Democratic South Africa with new constitution; government led by ANC.	Post-Washington consensus; regionalized AIDS pandemic.	Consolidation of the ANC as a dominant party. Growing inequality within the black community; rise in protests re lack of local service delivery.	Adoption of relatively conservative / orthodox macroeconomic strategy.

BIBLIOGRAPHY

Chigwedere, Pride, George R. Seages, Sofia Gruskin, Tun-Hou Lee, and M Essex. "Estimating the Lost Benefits of Antiretroviral Drug Use in South Africa." *Journal of Acquired Immune Deficiency Syndrome* 49, no. 4 (2008): 410–415.

Clark, Nancy L. *Manufacturing Apartheid: State Corporations in South Africa*. New Haven, CT: Yale University Press, 1994.

Davenport, T. R. H, and Christopher Saunders. *South Africa: A Modern History*. Fifth edition. London: Macmillan Press Ltd., 2000.

Gevisser, Mark. *Thabo Mbeki: The Dream Deferred*. Johannesburg, South Africa: Jonathan Ball, 2007.

Giliomee, Hermann. *The Afrikaners: Biography of a People*. Charlottesville: University of Virginia Press, 2003.

Gumede, William Mervin. *Thabo Mbeki and the Battle for the Soul of the A.N.C.* Cape Town, South Africa: Zebra Press, 2005.

Keegan, Timothy J. *Colonial South Africa and the Origins of the Racial Order*. Cape Town, South Africa: David Philip, 1996.

Krog, Antjie. *Country of My Skull*. Johannesburg, South Africa: Random House, 1998.

Lipton, Merle. *Capitalism and Apartheid: South Africa, 1910–1986*. Aldershot, UK: Wildwood House, 1986.

Marais, Hein. *South Africa Limits to Change: The Political Economy of Transition*. London: Zed Books Limited, 2001.

O'Meara, Dan. *Forty Lost Years: The Apartheid State and the Politics of the National Party 1948–1994*. Athens: Ohio University Press, 1996.

Posel, Deborah. *The Making of Apartheid 1948–1961: Conflict and Compromise*. Oxford: Clarendon Press, 1991.

Sampson, Anthony. *Mandela: The Authorised Biography*. London: Harper Collins Publishers, 1999.

Seegers, Annette. *The Military and the Making of Modern South Africa*. New York: St Martin's Press, 1996.

Sparks, Allister. *The Mind of South Africa*. London: Heinemann, 1990.

Thompson, Leonard. *A History of South Africa*. Revised edition. Binghamton, NY: Yale University Press, 1995.

IMPORTANT TERMS

African National Congress (ANC) – now the ruling party in South Africa; one of the key organizations in the struggle to end apartheid, the ANC is also Africa's oldest liberation movement.

Afrikaners – subset of the white community, Afrikaners are the descendants of mainly Dutch forebears, who speak Afrikaans as their mother tongue.

Apartheid – literally means "separateness"; the system of rule that was introduced after the election of the National Party to power in 1948 and which formalized and legislated race as the key determinant of access to political and economic rights and resources; institutions were structured and organized in accordance with the view that different races and ethnic groups ought to develop separately, which effectively positioned whites as the top of a strictly racialized hierarchy and excluded blacks from meaningful access to political and economic power.

Congress of South African Trade Unions (COSATU) – formed in 1985 as a confederation of trade unions affiliated with the Charterists; subsequently entered into a formal alliance with the ANC and the South African Communist Party.

Freedom Charter – a vision of what a post-apartheid South Africa should look like adopted by "The Congress of the People" at Kliptown in 1955; formed the ideological heart of the ANC-led alliance.

Group Areas Act – legislated systematic and wide-reaching attempt to completely racialize access to land in South Africa, by physically separating the living and working spaces of all race groups.

Homelands – ethnically defined territories that Africans were confined to if they did not have a work permit that enabled them to live and work elsewhere.

Nelson Mandela – South Africa's first black president in the post 1994 era. He rose to prominence as a leader in the ANC Youth League in the 1950s. He was imprisoned in 1964 Rivonia Treason trial and only released in 1990; while in prison came to be widely regarded as the leader and face of the global anti-apartheid movement.

Thabo Mbeki – served as Mandela's deputy president and then as the country's second president. His term as president was prematurely ended in a fierce political contest with his then-deputy, Jacob Zuma.

National Party – formed in 1914 as a vehicle for Afrikaner nationalism; won the 1948 election and then served uninterruptedly as the ruling party in apartheid South Africa till 1994.

Natives Land Act 1913 – a piece of colonial-era legislation that laid the groundwork for the racialized and highly unequal parceling out of land in South Africa.

Pan African Congress (PAC) – a rival liberation movement to the ANC; built around an Africanist ideology.

Population Registration Act – foundational act of apartheid, this piece of legislation created the machinery to allocate every South African a particular and permanent racial identity.

South African Defence Force (SADF) – the combined military forces (including army, navy and airforce) of the apartheid state; after 1994, the military wings of the ANC and PAC were merged with the old SADF to form the new South African National Defence Force.

Truth and Reconciliation Commission (TRC) – the institution charged with confronting and dealing with the political legacy of apartheid; the Commission was empowered to grant the perpetrators of politically motivated human rights abuses amnesty for those acts in return for a full and truthful accounting of their deeds.

United Democratic Front (UDF) – a broad front of anti-apartheid organizations, formed in response to the Tri-cameral Constitution of 1983 and loosely affiliated with the ANC/Charterist tradition.

Verlig – the so-called enlightened/more liberal strand of Afrikaner nationalism.

Verkramp – the more conservative brand of Afrikaner nationalism.

Jacob Zuma – the third president of a democratic South Africa.

STUDY QUESTIONS

1. How important was South Africa's colonial history to the unfolding of minority rule under apartheid?

2. Can the story of modern South Africa be told purely as a story of competing nationalisms (Afrikaner nationalism versus African nationalism)? Why or why not?

3. Compare and contrast the role of ideas (principally racism) and economic interests respectively in motivating the elaboration of the system of apartheid.

4. Did the process of industrialization principally bolster or undermine systematized racial discrimination in South Africa?

5. Assess the role of domestic and international forces respectively in South Africa's transition to democracy.

6. Discuss the following statement: "The Faustian bargain struck by the Truth and Reconciliation Commission was critical to South Africa's peaceful transition to majority rule."

7. How significant is it that racism and racial discrimination in South Africa were not simply limited to social attitudes or implicit inequality in economic opportunities but were instead legislated into the very fabric of the state? Put another way, how (if at all) is South Africa different from other deeply racist or unequal societies?

8. How has inequality in South Africa changed over time and what has driven these changes?

9. The death of Nelson Mandela has been regarded by some as foreshadowing the death also of hopes for a prosperous, peaceful and non-racial future for South Africa. Critically assess this view.

EUROPEAN UNION

MAP 13.1. Map of the European Union.

13 The European Union
Paulette Kurzer

Introduction

Students of comparative politics readily admit that the European Union is an implausible construct. As a rule, sovereign states guard their government authority and national independence zealously. So why would mature democracies agree to effectively reduce their policy independence and compromise their national sovereignty by transferring many areas of decision making to a supranational organization?

The answer goes back to the impact of international economic and security arrangements on European countries, many of which are small and trade-dependent. European heads of government agreed to an expansion of supranational European decision making in order to compete in the postwar world economy and cope with the post-1945 security dilemmas.

The story begins at the end of World War Two. In 1951, France and Germany – with the blessing of the United States – agreed to an economic, political, and trade partnership that also included Italy and three small export-dependent economies: Belgium, Luxemburg, and the Netherlands (Benelux). The first agreement sought to address the threat of communism and Soviet aggression while at the same time finding a politically palatable way to incorporate the new Federal Republic of Germany into the Atlantic alliance.

In 1957, the same six countries entered into another agreement, which committed the participating countries (France, Germany, Italy, and the Benelux) to an ambitious agenda that consisted of removing trade barriers among the member states (free trade area), the formulation of joint external commercial policy (customs union), and the pooling of sovereignty to implement a supranational agricultural policy (common market). Thus, the solution to the problem of how to contain Soviet aggression, while incorporating Germany into Western Europe and the American-led security alliance, was to sign the Treaty of Paris in 1951 and the Treaty of Rome in 1957. The Treaty of Paris established a common market in coal and steel, which promoted the European reconstruction of coal and steel production under the supervision of a supranational agency, representing the six participating countries.

The Treaty of Rome took off from the Treaty of Paris and extended the principle of a common market to manufactured goods and agriculture and created the European Economic Community alongside the European Coal and Steel Community and the European Atomic Energy Community.

In the early 1970s, heads of governments and other political forces turned away from European integration and increasingly adopted more inward-looking policies. The economic crisis of the 1970s, caused by the sudden increase of oil prices and by the decline in expansion of international trade, prompted protectionist policies among European governments seeking to shelter their labor and product markets from international turmoil. However, by the mid-1980s, the European Community was poised to introduce an ambitious program to revive European integration by enacting the single European market and by ratifying the Single European Act. The revival of European integration in the mid-1980s was spurred by at least two separate international developments. First, shifts in the international economy in the 1970s contributed to the painful economic syndrome of both high inflation and high unemployment. Increasingly, European leaders sought a solution by distancing themselves from national interpretations of Keynesianism and by embracing neoliberal economic thinking advocated by policy think tanks, international organizations (IMF), and British and American political leaders. The new approach to macroeconomic management involved state retrenchment, deregulation, and liberalization.

Second, European leaders and corporate businesses expressed concern about the rise of Japan and its global dominance in cars, electronics, and consumer durables. To compete with Japanese and American advances in information technology, computer, electronics, and biotechnology, European politicians argued that European corporations were at a disadvantage so long as they were limited to national markets. They lacked the economies of scale and access to large consumer markets that both American and Japanese companies enjoy.

With a new understanding of the role of the state in markets coupled with heightened anxiety about losing out against Japan and the United States, political leaders revived European integration. The single European market (1992 project) led to an ambitious program to create a European market in goods, services, labor, and capital in order to stem the decline in European competitiveness, generate more jobs, and promote investments in capital-intensive new technologies. Under the aegis of the single market, the European Union called for the wholesale eradication of all physical (border control, customs), technical (divergent standards and rules), and fiscal (divergent taxes) barriers. The single market was accompanied by a treaty amendment (Single European Act), which changed voting procedures, improved political cooperation, and strengthened the role of the European parliament (EP). Therefore a confluence of international economic challenges brought about a revival of European integration after 1985: the end of the domestic Keynesian model and shifts in international markets.

In the early 1990s, unexpected external events prompted further commitments to increase European integration and strengthen European institutions. The collapse of the Soviet Union and German unification brought about two new opportunities. First, it pushed the boundaries of the European Union eastward as many new democracies became eligible to join. In 1994, the European Union had twelve member states. Ten years later, in 2004, it counted twenty-five member states.

In addition, the end of the Cold War signified by the unification of Germany and the reemergence of Central and Eastern Europe, prompted European leaders to establish stronger pan-European security institutions. In December 1991, European leaders decided to expand the scope of European activities to include areas of cooperation outside the field of economic integration. A complex structure was formed whereby the heads of governments agreed to cooperate in foreign and security policy as well as justice and internal security. At the same time, the supranational institutions were strengthened and the EP received more powers. The Treaty of European Union/Treaty of Maastricht (1993) also introduced the concept of EU citizenship, and all citizens of the European Union could travel with a common passport and new rights to work and vote throughout the EU.

Moreover, during that same summit meeting, in December 1991, governments also reached an agreement on economic and monetary union (EMU). Separate from the treaty itself, EMU was not mandatory and was open to member states who wanted and who could join. The agreement laid out a blueprint for creating a single currency that involved increased economic convergence and a detailed timetable.

In short, between 1957 and 1986 there were no new treaties. Since 1986 there have been six treaties. All the treaties, including the founding treaties, can be viewed as a specific European reaction to global events and developments. The large number of treaties after 1986 mirrored the end of the postwar economic model of Keynesian interventionism and the disappearance of the bipolar international system. In the early 1990s, the implosion of the Soviet Union; German unification; and the reemergence of Central Eastern Europe, the Baltic states, and Balkan countries spurred further integration, more intergovernmental cooperation in military security and defense, and a strengthening of the supranational institutions of the European Union. Over time, the purpose of the new treaties or treaty amendments was to sort out how to maintain political, geographic, demographic, and economic balance in a European Union consisting of twenty-eight member states. The Treaty of Lisbon in force since December 2009 is the most ambitious attempt to improve the operation of the European Union while also strengthening democracy, accountability, and efficiency.

The first part of this chapter explores the issues briefly noted previously. The second half of this chapter looks at the EU institutions, interests, and identity.

The Origins of Regional Integration

A few years after the end of World War II, toward the late 1940s, European leaders faced a "trilemma," namely: (1) how to keep Communism and Soviet power at bay, (2) how to expedite economic recovery and secure political and social stability, and (3) how to handle the reemergence of an economically vibrant Federal Republic of Germany.

After the disasters of the Great Depression and World War II, a consensus emerged among Western leaders that economic prosperity was a powerful weapon against undemocratic movements. Moreover, economic prosperity would also beef up the state capacity of West European countries, which was necessary to withstand the threat of Soviet aggression. Thus, economic growth and then redistribution were high on the agenda. The question was what to do about Germany, which occupied a central position in Europe, was its largest country, and had its most important economy. The leadership in many European countries, and in France in particular, felt decidedly ambivalent about a strong, dynamic Germany, which could pose a threat to their own security.

Against this background, European integration emerged as a plausible solution. Here was a way to restrain both German nationalistic/authoritarian tendencies while promoting economic growth and bolstering Europe's military defense simultaneously. Regional integration presented itself as the most convenient strategy to accelerate economic growth as well as supervise the economic revival of Germany. Economic integration accompanied trade liberalization while expansion of export markets would bolster economic growth and manufacturing capacity. Second, regional integration would divert unpleasant forms of nationalism that had been so central in the emergence of the Nazi regime. It was thought that if regional integration turned out to be a real success, citizens' allegiance would shift from the nation-state to European supranational institutions, and ferocious militarism would be a thing of the past.

The architects of European integration relied on to the idea of spillover. Although the thrust of integration focused on economics, eventually officials and politicians would have to cooperate politically to address new economic or technical challenges. Market integration would lead to pressures to seek greater political coordination and elites would be forced to venture beyond economics into politics. In the end, at some future date, increased political cooperation would spur the creation of a federation of European states.

Americans pushed for the full rehabilitation of Germany so that it could be part of the Western defense alliance. France would have preferred a weak, fragmented Germany, which would pose no threat to its own existence. Yet an economically self-sufficient Germany was a strategic necessity to ward off Soviet aggression and create a West European defense system. To placate the concerns of French leaders, European integration was proffered as a solution to manage conflict in the European heartland and to promote economic growth and thereby political and social stability.

Looking back, therefore, there were compelling reasons that six nations ratified a treaty that transferred limited competences to a supranational organization. The original six countries were France, West Germany, Italy, Belgium, the Netherlands, and Luxembourg (Benelux), and they signed a treaty establishing the European Coal and Steel Community (ECSC) in 1951, which laid out provisions for a single market for coal and steel through the gradual elimination of tariffs and other barriers to trade. Britain was invited to participate but the Labour government had ambitious plans to nationalize British coal and steel industries while the British foreign policy establishment preferred to preserve its ties with the Commonwealth and the United States.

The ECSC was a success, and government leaders decided in 1955 to explore further options by creating a common market for other industries and atomic energy. This exploration culminated in the Treaty of Rome, signed in 1957 by the original six governments. The treaty established two bodies: the European Economic Community (EEC) and the European Atomic Energy Commission (Euratom). It called for the elimination of all internal tariffs and the creation of common external tariffs over a period of twelve to fifteen years. In 1967, the EEC and Euratom were merged and formed the European Community (EC).

The founders of European integration speculated that economic integration would bring the people of Europe to "ever closer union." The Treaty of Rome left many details blank and unspecified. Yet the assumption of many of its early promoters was that this was the first step toward a federal or federated Europe.

Evolution of the European Union

France and Germany constituted the twin engines of integration because once they agreed on an issue or project, other countries usually came around and accepted the compromise. France and Germany held divergent ideas about regional integration, each representing an approach or opinion prevalent in the rest of Europe. If they were able to reconcile their differences, other countries felt assured that their interests would be protected as well.

The Treaty of Rome was based on such a bargain. By the mid-1950s, Germany had emerged as an economic powerhouse with a highly competitive export sector. German leaders were eager to export to the rest of Europe, and for this reason were keen to push for trade liberalization. The French preferred to protect their agricultural sector and nurture their ties to former colonies by giving them access to the European market. The French were less enthusiastic about trade liberalization. The agreement they struck consisted therefore of opening the European/French market to German manufactured goods while the EEC market became accessible to French agricultural products and those of its former colonies. The economic bargain was underpinned by specific political calculations as well. The French political elite hoped to use the EEC to pursue ambitious foreign policy goals for France and Europe. The German leadership sought to rehabilitate and normalize the Federal Republic of Germany by participating in an international venue. The Italians hoped to check the influence and appeal of the Left and to modernize backward regions. The small states felt vulnerable surrounded by much larger economies and preferred to deal with their powerful neighbors in a multilateral context.

Nevertheless, it was the deal struck between Germany and France that made it possible to proceed with a common market. Germany obtained free access to neighboring markets while France received support for a declining yet oversized agricultural sector. As part of the bargain, the heads of state agreed to create a Common Agricultural Policy (CAP), which opened trade to agricultural goods while simultaneously designing a price support program to ensure a decent standard of living for its farmers (of which France had many). In return, tariffs on manufactured goods were abolished.

In January 1974, after difficult negotiations, the United Kingdom, Ireland, and Denmark joined the EC. The enlargement, however, was plagued by rancor. By the time Britain joined it was desperate to share the economic benefits of European integration. Alas, this scenario did not play out in the ways in which the British had envisioned membership in the

EC. By 1974, the world economy was absorbing the first shock of steeply rising oil prices while the immediate economic advantages of trade liberation had been exhausted. Growth rates shrunk virtually everywhere. As the 1970s unfolded, advanced industrialized countries increasingly struggled with large trade deficits, growing budget deficit, and a chaotic international economy.

From the beginning, therefore, the British harbored resentments against European institutions. Since the British had been in a rush to accede, they had failed to strike a very hard bargain and became, ironically, a large "net contributor" to the EC budget. In their haste to accept the conditions of membership, they did not pay much attention to the funding of the common agricultural policy, which absorbed a huge slice of the EC budget. Because of its colonial history, Britain had always imported foodstuff from its dependent territories. Its own agricultural sector was minimal and barely benefited from the generous payments made by the EC. Thus, Britain was one of the poorer countries, yet it paid more into the EC budget than it received back in terms of subsidies, financial aid, or regional development.

The first enlargement was therefore an unhappy experience and reflected challenging external conditions and uncertain internal policies. The squabbles about the EC budget and agricultural subsidies undermined European integration, and European institutions showed little life in the late 1970s and early 1980s.

Out of this bleak period grew one of the most innovative and dynamic initiatives. The best way to understand the extraordinary turnaround was the depth of the budget and economic crisis and the growing alarm expressed by observers and politicians alike that in the absence of bold thinking, the EC might disappear. In the 1970s, national governments had pursued their own solutions to bring down high inflation, high unemployment, and growing budget deficits, with little success. The export prowess of Japan, which threatened the car industry and electronics sector in Europe (and the United States) brought home that Europe was falling behind and did not keep up with the newest designs and innovative technologies. As national approaches had not yielded much improvement, the realization dawned that a collective response might be more effective than divergent and competing national strategies.

Originally, the Treaty of Rome had called for the free movement of goods, services, people, and capital. In the mid-1980s, heads of state agreed to move forward with this program and approved in 1985 the White Paper on Completing the Internal Market, which listed more than three hundred measures to meet the original goals outlined in the Treaty of Rome, namely the creation of a genuine single market. The measures would result in the free movement of goods, persons, services, and capital, and give birth to an area without internal boundaries. Such a project would bolster European competitiveness, provide new opportunities to European business, and benefit consumers by lowering prices and increasing choice.

In short, the single European market and the Single European Act arose in response to the second wave of enlargement, which brought Greece, Spain, and Portugal on board, as well as the rise of Japan and other Asian exporting countries. Confronting internal and external pressures meant strengthening the European economy by pooling the combined resources of the member states. The White Paper of the Commission laid out a timetable of six years to achieve the end goal of a stronger, more competitive European economy (1986–1992).

What were these measures? Of the three hundred, the bulk concentrated on physically removing cross-border formalities, of developing common European standards and norms, and of harmonizing value added and excise taxes. In sum, it amounted to a very ambitious scheme to liberalize and deregulate different aspects of the European economy.

Because this grand program was to be completed in a relatively short period of time, it included amendments to the Treaty of Rome. The Single European Act (in force since 1987) introduced qualified majority voting in the Council in order to expedite the implementation of single market measures. Prior, member states enjoyed veto power to block any piece of legislation. As the need for unanimity would obviously greatly slow down the single market project, the member states agreed to accept a qualified majority vote for matters considered not too sensitive. Unanimity would continue to govern fiscal policy, border controls, workers' rights, and the movement of people. Because member states could be outvoted, the Single European Act (SEA) extended the powers of the EP in order to broaden the democratic accountability of the EC.

As officials in Brussels and the state capitals worked feverishly on meeting the deadlines of the single European market, momentous geopolitical shifts transformed the very foundation on which the EC has been built. The withdrawal of the Soviet Union from Central-Eastern Europe put both German unification and further enlargement on the agenda. The Treaty of Rome specified that a country eligible for membership should fulfill two minimum requirements: be part of the European continent while embracing liberal democracy and market capitalism. The redrawing of the European map and the possibility of ten or more additional member states led to another intergovernmental conference to revisit the amended Treaty of Rome and account for the changes taking place right there and then. The Treaty on European Union (TEU) was negotiated in 1991 and was ratified by all member states in 1993. The summit took place in Maastricht (the Treaty is also called the Maastricht Treaty).

The TEU formally designated the EC as the European Union and introduced a new structure of three pillars with different levels of integration. The first and largest pillar consisted of single market legislation, CAP, and Community (EU) legislation (external commercial policy, single currency, environmental protection, development aid, consumer protection). Legislative proposals would be decided by mostly qualified majority voting. The second pillar contained common foreign and security policy and remained under the purview of national leaders. The third pillar housed cooperation in justice and internal affairs (policing, transnational crime) and also remained under the control of national elected leaders. The most surprising outcome of the summit meeting was the agreement to go ahead with the single currency. Again, a Franco-German bargain explains why European leaders agreed to monetary integration: France insisted on more control over monetary policy by handing it over to a European central bank and away from German monetary authorities, while Germany insisted on more political integration. The result was the increased cooperation of the member states on internal and external security in return for a European monetary policy.

In the wake of the collapse of the Soviet Union, three small and prosperous countries joined the European Union in 1995: Austria, Finland, and Sweden. Norway held a hardly fought referendum and a slim majority voted against membership. Switzerland preferred to preserve its neutral status and declined membership application.

At a summit meeting in Copenhagen in 1993 the heads of state of the member states issued a statement that the European Union would be willing to accept new applications from candidate states if they met four criteria: they need stable political and legal institutions, they must have a functioning market economy, they have to accept and adopt the body of legislation produced by the European Union, and they can join only if their accession does not destabilize the EU. In 1994, Hungary and Poland had applied for membership, and by 1997 all eight Central-East European countries plus Malta and Cyprus had expressed interest.

Realizing that it was just a matter of time before the EU-15 would become EU-28, the member states convened another intergovernmental conference in 1997 to address future enlargements. But this summit was highly contentious and did not produce any serious amendments and reforms. It was decided to postpone any hard decisions to a later summit scheduled for 2000 in Nice. The Treaty of Nice, however, was another fiasco and plagued by quarrels. However, it finalized the accession of the candidate members and it outlined provisional plans for reforms of institutions so they could function more effectively with as many as thirty members.

The Treaty of Nice was much criticized. It failed to produce a solution to the prospect of enlarged membership. It also did little in furthering the goal of "ever closer union." There was therefore pressure to continue the debate in order to define the exact limits of powers between the European Union and its member states, to incorporate the Charter of Fundamental Rights into EU treaties, to define the role of national parliaments, and to bring the European Union closer to the people. Subsequently, political leaders decided to launch a debate on the Future of Europe. This debate was more like a convention, and societal groups, national parliaments, the EP, and the twelve candidate countries all participated in the convention that would lead to a European constitution, strengthen foreign policy, and simplify decision- making procedures, and that would democratize the internal organization of the Commission and hold European elections to select a Commission president. The result was a new treaty that addressed many of the demands for more transparency, for clarification of rights of member states and the European Union, and for a more people-friendly EU. The Constitutional treaty was signed in Rome in October 2004. However, the treaty was rejected in a referendum in France in May 2005 and in the Netherlands in June 2005. After all these lengthy and elaborate efforts, the Constitutional treaty was defunct and finished.

A year earlier, in 2004, a large group of new members acceded to the European Union. In January 2007, Romania and Bulgaria joined. The last major expansion added 30 percent to the population but only 9 percent in GDP because most of the new member states were substantially poorer than the EU average. Table 13.1 shows that many of the new member states are small in size because six out of the twelve have a population of less than four million. And all of them have a GDP per person less than the average of EU-28.

Table 13.1   Economic and Demographic Statistics for EU28 (selected years)

Member State	Population (millions)[a]	GDP per Person (EU-28 = 100)[b]
EU-28	507	100
Austria	85	129
Belgium	11.2	120
Bulgaria	7.3	47
Croatia	4.2	61
Czech Republic	10.5	81
Cyprus	0.86	94
Denmark	5.6	126
Estonia	1.3	69
Finland	5.4	116
France	65.5	109
Germany	80.5.	123
Greece	11.0	80
Hungary	10.0	67
Ireland	4.6	129
Italy	60.0	102
Latvia	2.0	60
Lithuania	3.1	68
Luxembourg	0.54	266
Malta	0.42	86
Netherlands	16.7	129
Poland	38.5	65
Portugal	10.5	77
Romania	20.0	48

(*continued*)

Table 13.1   (*cont.*)

Member State	Population (millions)[a]	GDP per Person (EU-28 = 100)[b]
Slovakia	5.4	75
Slovenia	2.1	84
Spain	46.7	96
Sweden	9.6	125
United Kingdom	63.9	105

[a] Figures are from 2013.

[b] GDP is measured in Purchasing Power Parities. EU28=100. Commission of the European Union. Eurostat: GDP per Capita in PPS for. 2012. http://epp.eurostat.ec.europa.eu/tgm/table.do?tab=table&plugin=1&language=en&pcode=tec00114

The inevitable burden of absorbing so many small and poor member states put pressure on the political leadership to resurrect the defunct Constitutional treaty and to continue the process of recalibrating the EU institutions and procedures while cementing closer ties between the European Union and the people of Europe. The end result was the Treaty of Lisbon, in effect since December 2009, which is supposed to prepare Europe to face the challenges of the twenty-first century such as sustainable energy, demographic shifts, climate change, and a more effective and open mode of operation. Interestingly, it has taken European leaders eight years since the failed Nice summit to make the make the European Union "more democratic, more transparent and more efficient."

The Institutions

European integration is shaped by two conflicting forces, each of which negotiates and maneuvers to gain the upper hand. At one end of the integration pole stands the European Commission, the engine of European integration. At the other end are the nation-states represented by heads of governments, national cabinet officials, and civil servants. The history of European integration can be captured by a tug-of-war between the supranational complex of organizations (the European Commission and the EP) fighting against the natural instincts of the EU Council to retain as much autonomy and authority under national control as possible. At various times, the Commission gains the upper hand over the Council, whereas at other times the heads of state successfully put a brake on further supranational institution building. Mediating the triangular relationship among Commission, Council, and Parliament is the EU court system, which interprets and defends European law. What often prompts a shift in the balance is some kind of external crisis. Thus, the economic pressures to improve the overall competitiveness of the economies of the European Union resulted in a stronger mandate for the Commission and a slight loss of national sovereignty of the member states. The crisis and corresponding opportunities caused by the end of the Cold War and German unification produced the political agreement to create a single currency to anchor Germany to the European Union and to preserve the gains of the single market.

The Commission

The European Commission located in Brussels is the executive center of the European Union and has four tasks: first, it has the exclusive right to propose legislation. This legislation comes in two forms: directives and regulations. A directive is a collective legislative act of the European Union that requires member states to achieve a particular result without dictating the means of achieving that result. European regulations apply to all member states and are automatically in effect because they do not require any implementing measures. Directives normally leave member states with a certain amount of leeway as to the exact rules to be adopted, and they are only binding in those member states to whom they are addressed. In practice, directives are usually addressed to all member states. Regulations become European law without requiring adoption by national legislatures.

Second, the Commission oversees the adoption of Community law and policy into national law. For this, it relies greatly on national agencies to report back on the execution of EU directives and regulations. As it is the guardian of the treaties, it can bring noncompliant member states and private actors before the EU courts. Its third task is to guarantee administration and implementation of European law. Finally, the staff of the Commission represents the European Union in international venues and is the public face of Europe.

It employs approximately twenty thousand people. Of these, around six thousand are the real Eurocrats who draft recommendations, rules, and laws. Another several thousand work in the language/translation services because every piece of major legislation must be translated in twenty-four original languages. At the head of each service or department (directorate general – DG) stands a commissioner. This person is nominated by the home government and is approved by a qualified majority vote in the Council. They serve renewable five-year terms. Once they are approved, they swear an oath of allegiance to the European Union and are not supposed to take instructions from the home governments.

The commissioners form a college and they meet regularly to deliberate on key decisions. The college is led by a president who is appointed by the heads of state. The president is the public face of the European Union and he or she presides over Commission meetings, coordinates, sets the agenda, and provides leadership and moral support to the vast multilingual staff. All commissioners serve what are currently five-year renewable terms, coinciding with the electoral cycle of the EP. The previous president of the Commission was the center-left Italian politician Romano Prodi (2000–2004). The current president is José ManuelBarroso (2004–2014) who is a center-right politician from Portugal.

Once the Commission is in place and the president and commissioners are nominated and approved, the real work begins. The Commission works on the principle of collegiality, and the agenda of each DG is a collective decision taken by the entire college. Each commissioner is expected to participate in general affairs and events of the Commission. Commissioners are assisted by a cabinet or personal staff who do most of the legwork and prepare the commissioner for weekly meetings with the college of commissioners and with the administrative staff of bureaucrats. Cabinets play an important role and exercise considerable influence. Supporting the appointed commissioners are the "services" consisting of administrative civil servants recruited from the member states through competitive exams. The Commission employs approximately 24,000 officials in addition to around 6,000 people on temporary contracts.

There are twenty-eight commissioners, one for each member state. Commissioners can design legislative proposals only in areas set aside for supranational decision making. The Commission's prerogatives have gradually expanded from agriculture, competition law, and common external trade policy to the single market, regional development aid, environmental policy, research and development, social funds for disadvantaged regions, food safety, public health, and consumer protection. The Lisbon treaty of 2009 clarified exactly when or how the Commission can draft legislative proposals. The first principle is subsidiarity, which declares that Community action is justified only in areas where the objectives could not be achieved by the member states themselves. A further guiding principle is that of proportionality, which says that the European Union may do only what is necessary and no more, in order to achieve its objectives. In many areas, therefore, the Commission shares competences with the member states. It has sole and exclusive competences in the customs union (guaranteeing the same treatment of trade coming from third countries into the European Union), monetary policy, competition law (antitrust law), international trade policy (negotiations with World Trade Organization), and conservation of marine biological resources (part of the common fisheries policy between EU states). It has shared competences in a vast array of policies where both member states and the EU have the power to make laws. Shared competences cover anything from food, its safety and its sources, to passenger flying rights, film and television, aid to Africa, the environment, energy, agriculture, fishing, transport, and human rights. There are also areas that are explicitly excluded from European legislation such as K-12 education, national citizenship, housing, the funding of public television, social security, hospitals and the health service, corporate tax rates, and any policy that requires large commitments of public money, as well as common foreign and security policy and police and judicial cooperation in criminal matters.

Council

The Council of the European Union and its more prestigious format, the European Council, are often in competition with the European Commission. The Council represents the national interests of the member states and constitutes the intergovernmental part of the European Union. Formally, the Council has four responsibilities. It develops large strategic visions set out during European summits or intergovernmental conferences (IGC) held at least twice a year in December and June. These visions often shape the agenda for years to come. The Commission tends to frame legislation to meet the goals of the broad agenda outlined during the intergovernmental conference.

The Council also signs all international agreements and formulates defense and security policies while it signs off on all accession agreements. It also meets to discuss world affairs of political and strategic importance to the EU. The Mideast may be on the agenda, or relations with the United States. The Council also decides the budget and major legislation. It selects the president of the Commission, which is an arduous and difficult process in which the interests of small and large member states are balanced against the need to have ideological representation of the main political trends in European politics. Finally, its responsibilities include matters related to criminal judicial affairs, which fall outside the first Community pillar and have remained under the control of national governments.

The Council actually consists of two institutions. When the heads of state gather to discuss major themes during an IGC, we speak of the European Council. The European Council deliberates on larger issues, including the budget and the geopolitical situation, and determines the appointment of a new president of the Commission. The meetings of the European Council are grand affairs often held in fancy resort towns with fine scenery, good food, and plenty of expensive alcohol. The IGC meeting is held in the country that holds the presidency of the council, which rotates every six months. The presidency of the council is organized as a trio of presidencies to guarantee continuity over a period of eighteen months. The 2012–2013 trio consisted of Ireland (January to June 2013), Lithuania (July to December 2013) and Greece (January to June 2014). The next presidency trio will be Italy, Latvia, and Luxembourg.

The EU Council (Council of the European Union) deals with the more mundane day-to-day issues that face the European Union, and is the "legislative" branch of the European Union. Its composition varies with the policy terrain or issue. Frequency of meetings also varies in relation to the salience of a policy issue. Ministers of tourism may meet three times a year to discuss areas of importance related to tourism. By contrast, ministers of the environment may meet monthly to strategize how to discuss global climate change. Each meeting is chaired by the relevant cabinet minister of the presiding member state. The council also implements and executes EU policy. The Commission does not have the administrative staff to oversee EU directives and regulations. This is delegated to the national capitals. Members of the Council usually head a ministry or department that is in charge of implementing laws and regulations. The Council administers both the implementation of rules and the disbursement of funds.

The Council demonstrates the continued power of the national governments. However, national governments have witnessed a decline in power starting with the ratification of the Single European Act in 1987. All Commission proposals become law only after they have been passed by the Council. Until 1987, most decisions had to be unanimous, giving each member state veto power. The unanimity rule repeatedly paralyzed the decision-making process, and it would have buried single market legislation. At an

Table 13.2 Seats in Parliament and Votes in the European Council

	Seats in EP	Votes in Council	Population (in millions)	% of Population in EU
Belgium	21	12	10.4	2.15
Bulgaria	17	10	7.3	1.52
Croatia	11	7	4.3	0.8
Czech R.	21	12	10.2	2.09
Denmark	13	7	5.4	1.10
Germany	96	29	82.5	16.41
Estonia	6	4	1.4	0.27
Greece	21	12	11.0	2.25
Spain	54	27	40.7	9.17
France	74	29	59.6	12.88
Ireland	11	7	4.0	0.8
Italy	73	29	57.3	12.02
Cyprus	6	4	0.7	0.16
Latvia	8	4	2.3	0.45
Lithuania	11	7	3.5	0.67
Luxembourg	6	4	0.4	0.10
Hungary	21	12	10.1	2.01
Malta	6	3	0.4	0.08
Netherlands	26	13	16.2	3.30
Austria	18	10	8.1	1.67
Poland	51	27	38.2	7.63
Portugal	21	12	10.4	2.13
Romania	32	14	22.3	4.30
Slovenia	8	4	2.0	0.41

	Seats in EP	Votes in Council	Population (in millions)	% of Population in EU
Slovakia	13	7	5.4	1.08
Finland	13	7	5.2	1.07
Sweden	20	10	8.9	1.85
United Kingdom	73	29	59.3	12.33

Note: Countries are arranged according to their formal name in the original language.
From: http://en.euabc.com/

IGC in 1985, the European Council introduced treaty amendments by permitting qualified majority voting for all proposals except the most dramatic and sensitive initiatives. Table 13.2 tallies the votes assigned to each country roughly in correspondence with its population size. As attention must be paid to the fact that laws cannot defy the wishes of a sizable minority of member states and cannot be imposed against the expressed will of the majority of EU citizens, the current formula therefore speaks of a qualified majority vote.

The Lisbon treaty extended qualified majority voting to more areas and also introduced a new voting system that is based on the concept of a double majority. From 2014, a qualified majority will imply that 55 percent of member states agree, and those member states supporting the decision account for 65 percent of the EU population. A decision cannot be blocked by fewer than four member states irrespective of the size of the population of the member states.

In the early years of the European Union, many decisions required unanimity through which a member state could block a proposal with a no vote. However, after 1986, more and more policy areas are being decided through a qualified majority vote. All the legislation that comes under the single market – free movement of goods, services, labor, and capital – are subject to qualified majority voting. In addition, consumer protection, public health, and environmental regulations fall under a qualified majority vote. The Treaty of Lisbon mandates that energy, asylum, humanitarian aid, funding for common foreign and security policy, and immigration should also be decided by qualified majority voting. The only areas still governed by unanimous voting are accession, taxation, judicial cooperation in criminal affairs, security and defense policy, and institutional reform.

Some of the most heated political fights concerned the introduction of new voting procedures. Yet in truth, it is rare for the EU council to vote. Typically, the president chairs a discussion and announces that a sufficient majority has been reached, or asks if anyone remains opposed. The culture is to seek consensus, and there is great reluctance to "push for a vote" when national representatives indicate their objections. Rather, most of the voting takes place on smaller issues in subcommittees.

Court of Justice of the European Union

The Court of Justice of the European Union consists of three courts: Court of Justice, the General Court (previously called Court of First Instance), and the European Union Civil Service Tribunal (for personnel issues). All the courts are located in Luxembourg, and the most important is the Court of Justice of the three judicial bodies.

Legal integration has greatly contributed to the metamorphosis of the modest EEC to a state-like European Union. The Court of Justice and the General Court each have twenty-eight judges, appointed by the member state for renewable six-year terms. The Court of Justice is supported by nine advocates-general, also appointed by the member states for a six-year term. For the most part, the judges meet in separate and smaller chambers of three or five judges unless a case intersects with a significant treaty issue, in which case the full court of twenty-eight judges assembles. Advocate-generals review cases and provide legal opinion to the judges, who usually adopt the recommendations of the advocate-general.

The Court has the right of judicial review over the interpretation of the EU treaties and over the secondary legislation (directives and regulations) issued by the Commission and approved by the Council. Legal cases arrive at the court through two different procedures. Direct actions relate to EU law and actions taken by member states and EU institutions. The judges can rule on whether the actions of national governments, private actors, and EU institutions are consistent with the obligations set out by treaties and EU secondary law. Usually, a direct action case involves an infringement proceeding brought by the Commission or a member state against another member state for noncompliance. Direct action is supposed to ensure enforcement of EU law although member states routinely ignore direct action rulings as the political and economic consequences of noncompliance are minimal.

The second procedure is called preliminary reference. National courts submit queries on how an EU law applies. The EU court responds without giving detailed instructions on how to implement the EU law, directive, or regulation, although it elaborates on the legal principles behind its reasoning. Local or national judges decide on how to proceed once the ruling is published. Originally, preliminary reference was meant to provide private individuals with access to the Court of Justice to challenge the actions of EU institutions. Over time, it has grown into a powerful tool for the Court to expound on the legal principles of EU treaties and legislation.

Preliminary references account for the majority of cases, and national governments find it much harder to ignore a ruling based on a preliminary reference than a direct action. The reason is that national courts are in charge of enforcing decisions stemming from preliminary references as they ultimately use the rulings of the Court to decide how to resolve the legal conflict that prompted the preliminary ruling in the first case. Under preliminary reference, national judges decide whether national law or action is compatible with EU law once they obtain a judgment from the EU court. Politicians face high political costs if they do not comply with informed decisions of their national court. Thus the preliminary ruling has a broader reach because it ties national courts to the EU courts and constrains national governments.

The Court has gradually expanded its role, although it was mostly dormant during its first five years of existence. In 1963, in a landmark case (Case 26/62, Gend en Loos v. Nederlandse Administratie der Belastingen), the Court was asked to rule on the question of whether individuals or firms could invoke rights based on EEC law even if the national government had not adopted such a law. Thus the question was whether European law vested corporate entities and private citizens with rights not recognized by national law. The six judges at that time responded that EEC law was autonomous and carried a "direct effect" on individuals and corporate entities. Because of that, EU law governed citizens through national courts.

In 1964, a second landmark case (Case 6/64, Costa v. ENEL) arrived when the arbitration court in Milan (Italy) submitted a query on how to resolve a direct conflict between national/Italian law and treaty obligations. The judges in this case replied that member states willingly accepted the constraints imposed by European law and transferred a limited amount of sovereignty to EEC institutions, with the result that EEC law should be granted primacy over national law. This ruling established the doctrine of supremacy in that European law takes precedence over national law.

Both rulings were controversial, and member states challenged them. However, over time the rulings produced other rulings with similar implications and contributed to the emergence of a legal order that is closer to the U.S. federal system than centralized state systems of France or the United Kingdom.

National courts became important allies of the Court of Justice, enabling it to construct a legal space. Thanks to their queries under the procedure of preliminary reference, the judges were able to render important judgments on general principles. The Court could also rely on national courts to enforce the interpretation of EU law stemming from the preliminary reference. In the beginning, national judges were reluctant to adopt the role of "enforcer or guardian" of EU law but eventually they saw some real benefits in aligning themselves with the ECJ. Ironically, preliminary reference enlarged their independence because it permitted national courts to exercise judicial review over national policy, an option that many national judiciaries missed in centralized state systems.

For national governments, the costs and consequences of ignoring directives, regulations, and legal rulings are minimal. Ultimately, neither the Commission nor the Court can oblige national courts and governments to adopt European law. The Commission maintains a list of violators and hopes to name and shame them, but there are modest political costs and hardly any economic ramifications if national authorities disregard infringement procedures. The Court is aware that its reach is limited, and it restrains itself when it senses that the mood is frosty and governments are unlikely to agree with its judgments. Like the Commission, its political influence fluctuates in accordance with the overall integrationist ambiance in the European Union and its capitals.

European Parliament

During the first two decades of its existence, the EP was a docile extension of national governments. In 1979, the first direct elections were held to the EP although it continued to play a subordinate role in EU institution building and policy expansion. Once the SEA went into effect, the EP increased its powers. Elections are held every five years during the same week in June. The current parliamentary session lasts until the next election in 2014.

The Treaty of Lisbon (2009) capped the size of the EP to 751, although the heads of government afterwards decided that Germany would get three additional seats. The treaty also stipulates that the minimum number of seats per member state should be six to ensure that all major political trends will have a chance of gaining representation in the small member states while the maximum will be set at ninety-six (Germany). Whereas the Lisbon Treaty imposed a limit of 751 seats, the accession of Croatia added another twelve seats (Croatian MEPs were "observers" until its accession in July 2013) and pushed up the total number of MEPs to 766. In March 2013, the EP voted on a resolution that would reduce the number of seats by one for twelve member states – Austria, Belgium, Bulgaria, Croatia, Czech Republic, Greece, Hungary, Ireland, Latvia, Lithuania, Portugal and Romania –while Germany would return three seats and would be left with 96, the maximum allowed by the Lisbon Treaty. That way, the parliament would be brought back to 751 seats. This new allocation of seats will be in force in the 2014–2019 parliamentary term. Table 13.2 shows the number of seats allocated to each member state based on its population size and in accordance with the Lisbon Treaty requirements.

Parliamentary candidates run in the member state on a national party ticket. There are no pan-European political parties that field candidates across different political jurisdictions. However, once elected, MEPs become affiliated with political families or groups and seek out the group to which they belong ideologically. MEPs from all the different social democratic parties belong to the Progressive Alliance of Socialists and Democrats Socialists (184 seats/25 percent of seats). The Christian democratic parties are grouped in the European People's party and are the largest family with 265 members (36 percent of the seats). The third important group – Alliance for Liberals and Democrats for Europe – brings liberal, free market parties together (84 seats/11.4 percent of the vote). Finally, another sizable political family is the Greens/European Free Alliance with 55 seats and 7.5 percent of the vote. In the 2009 election turnout was 43 percent, which is low and much lower than the rate in national elections.

All tasks and functions are distributed according to the size of the party groupings. The political groups negotiate and bargain about committee assignments, office staff, office space, agenda lists, and so forth. The leaders of the political groups guarantee party discipline and a party vote. Because political affiliation outweighs nationality, the political blocs form a cohesive voting bloc.

Members of the EP serve in committees, which produce reports and position papers, and prepare the vote on the relevant issues. The EP has around twenty-four committees covering relevant policy and political issues. Thus, there is a committee for the Environment, Public Health and Food Safety, which has sixty-three members and a staff of ten. Its main counterparts in the European Commission are DG Environment and DG Health and Consumer Protection. Because committees have large membership, they often create subcommittees.

The EP has come a long way from a forum for discussion by national delegates appointed by national parliaments. In the original conception of the Treaty of Rome, the EP was divested of any real power and influence. It had only consultative powers, and the Council would take into consideration Parliament's opinion. Europe's legislative body had no legislative power. In the 1970s, it received the right to deliberate on the Community's annual budget. As the European Union took over more and more policy areas, it became increasingly obvious that the institution suffered from a "democratic deficit." To remedy this, the SEA (1987) introduced cooperation procedures so that the EP could propose amendments to single market legislation.

The architects of the SEA realized that the powers of the EP had to be increased after the Commission received greater responsibilities and many decisions would be taken by qualified majority voting in the Council. The legitimacy of the European Union was literally at stake. Nevertheless, the reforms contained in the SEA were far too thin to redress the deficit. Therefore, in 2001 and 2004, the powers of the EP were expanded and streamlined with the result that ordinary legislative procedure now prevails. The Commission must submit a proposal to the EP and Council for consideration. Under ordinary legislative procedure, the EP has the right to approve or reject the proposal. It co-decides with the Council, literally. If it rejects the proposal, it can suggest amendments or announce its intention to reject the measure altogether. If Parliament proposes amendments, and the Council disagrees, it must negotiate with the EP to hammer out a common position via a special conciliation committee. If members of the EP and Council can find a common ground, the joint text is submitted to Parliament where it can be approved or rejected by an absolute majority. The text also passes if Parliament fails to vote on it or fails to vote it down within six weeks. The Council and Parliament each receive the right to read and discuss a proposal twice.

Nevertheless, although the EP has steadily acquired more powers, its standing is low. On the one hand, its formal powers are more limited because MEPs approve legislation only in areas designated as falling under the EP's treaty base. On the other hand, because MEPs are not beholden to a government or cabinet, they can exploit all available powers to the fullest. Therefore, to some extent, one can make the argument that the EP is more powerful than its national counterparts. Yet the EP is unloved and underappreciated.

Some of the factors that have contributed to its lowly status are beyond its control. Unfortunately, a deal struck among heads of state has meant that its plenary meeting hall is located in a post-modern building in Strasbourg whose offices and meeting rooms appear to be empty and devoid of activity as most of the action takes place in Brussels where the MEPs hold committee meetings and hearings, and interact with other European institutions. Its administrative staff is housed in Luxembourg. MEPs travel back and forth from Brussels to Strasbourg, which is both a waste of time and funds.

Second, its organization is extremely complex as it brings together over a hundred separate national parties from twenty-eight member states. Turnover at each election is very high, and many MEPs have had no previous European political experiences. Debates are held in the native language with the result that nearly everything needs to be translated. When it involves an obscure language such as Latvian, the speech is first translated into

English and French and then retranslated into the twenty other official languages. Obviously much gets lost in translation!

Third, it covers mostly technical regulations, and it skirts highly emotional debates. The discussions are dull and avoid the kind of parliamentary debate arising from clashing ideological perspectives. Moreover, the EP cannot initiate its own legislation. It responds to legislation drafted by the Commission.

Fourth, because the candidates of the political parties run their campaigns for EP elections on national issues, voters do not learn how the EP or European Union works and why it matters. Therefore, voters regard European elections as second order national elections, and the outcome often says more about domestic politics than events in the European Union. European political life and decisions are subordinate to the concerns of the voters at home, and voters routinely vote for candidates from opposition parties in order to express dissatisfaction with the incumbent government. In the meantime, citizens spend little time following and understanding European parliamentary debates. Accordingly, voter turnout is low as many voters stay home during elections. Remarkably, voter apathy is especially strong in the twelve new member states where less than 40 percent of the electorate bothered to vote in 2009. The low turnout is surprising because the new member states had to wait years before they received the green light and were admitted to the European Union. For them, accession represented a major milestone, signifying their arrival as democratic and advanced European countries. EU membership constitutes the final rupture with their Communist past and authoritarian legacy. Yet interest in the workings of the EU is clearly minimal!

Finally, proportional representation and voter apathy have long made European elections a prime target for fringe parties, and the June 2014 elections taking place after five years of stagnant economic growth and rising unemployment sowed fertile soil for right-wing anti-EU politicians. Anti-EU parties are popular in Finland, France, United Kingdom, the Netherlands, Greece, Poland, Hungary, and Slovakia. They share two commonalities: a deep distaste for Brussels and EU elites as well as a rejection of poor immigrants who are viewed as taking advantage of the welfare state to pocket undeserved social benefits. Nationally, these parties are expected to win a fair share of the vote, which will increase their representation in the European parliament. Such a development arouses fear in Brussels (the headquarters of the EU) because it would give these parties an official platform to lambast and criticize European integration and institutions. Having anti-EU parties in the European parliament could make a mockery of the EU democratic process by legitimizing their anti-EU rhetoric in the single institution that actually represents the voice of the European people.

Of course, another way of viewing the presence of rightwing anti-EU parties in the EP is that their election validates the EU democratic process. It shows that the EU represents a great diversity of opinion and preferences. That is to say, these parties are gaining votes because voters believe that these parties represent their opinion, views, and priorities. Instead of viewing the European parliament as an elite institution speaking on behalf of the establishment, the election of rightwing anti-EU parties proves that European institutions are transparent, open, and welcomes all kinds of political movements and trends. Still, it does not much good for the EP to be the target of political parties that openly proclaim their disgust with the EU and its policy procedures.

In short, the EP has acquired greater influence and importance. Treaty amendments have sought to close the gap between the extensive policy authority granted to the unelected Commission and the democratic principles of participation and accountability characteristic of the political system of EU member states. But the institutional standing of the EP is low. At the core of the dilemma is of course the absence of a European political culture, sustained by pan-European political parties to foster a European political discourse. Ironically, while its institutional status is low, voter apathy and indifference offers fringe parties a good chance of capturing seats in the EP. As the economic crisis of 2008 simmers on, many voters gravitate to political parties promising easy solutions such as pulling out of the Euro or throwing up tariff barriers to protect industries or returning non-Western immigrants to their country of origin.

Interests

From the previous discussion, the obvious conclusion to be reached is that the European Union is neither a nation-state nor an international organization such as the United Nations. It is more than an international organization because European rules, regulations, and laws supersede national law while European institutions acquired many of the trappings and features of an administrative bureaucracy. At the same time, it is not a nation-state as much of political life unfolds in the national arena; key areas remain beyond its control; and heads of state, representing the national interests of the member states, shape many of its policies.

By far the most underdeveloped area is electoral politics and civic participation. Political and economic elites struck complex bargains that gradually expanded policy competencies from national to European institutions. Yet the public has been absent in the building of European institutions. However, as the Commission and Parliament have become more involved in market regulations, environmental and consumer protection, technical standards, and opening of protected firms and industry sectors, interest groups and lobbyists have proliferated and become entrenched in the EU policy process.

At the EU level, interests do not organize around class (labor unions), ethnicity (disadvantaged minorities), or religion (Catholic church, Muslim organizations). At the EU level, such new social movements are absent because the European Union does not define family law or civil partnerships, which remain safely lodged in the hands of national governments. The European Union regulates and reshapes market relations so interest groups reflect that particular focus. The dominant type of interest group that has emerged in the wake of Europeanization of legislation mirrors the functional specialization of the Commission. Producer groups are prominent players, and scores of industry sectors, firms, and business groups rushed to establish a European presence in Brussels to defend their interests, to influence the outcome of the deliberations, and to inform group members of future EU developments.

The target of all this lobbying energy is both Commission officials and EP committee members. Many business groups and professional associations recognize that so many rules and regulations are decided in Brussels that they need to be there. They often design a three-pronged strategy. They consult with national civil servants who assist the Commission with the drafting of legislative proposals, they approach sympathetic members of the EP serving on relevant committees or subcommittees, and they knock on the doors of Commission officials to gain access to information and influence. What makes this process slightly different from similar activities in the national theater is that many officials and EP politicians welcome the lobbying efforts of private sector agents. In fact, they rely on the feedback and input of stakeholders, as they are called in Brussels parlance, to grasp the limits of what can be achieved, and to determine how to calculate the varied costs of different proposals and to assess the depth of resistance to certain initiatives. Interest groups are a key part in the process of legislation and EU institution building.

The staff size of the Commission is modest considering the complexity of the drafting legislation applicable across twenty-eight distinct national jurisdictions. For the Commission, it does not make sense to squander time on futile proposals so it seems most efficient to invite feedback, advice, or information from umbrella organizations. Interest groups are therefore partners of the Commission although often adversarial partners as they are not necessarily on the same wavelength and may seek to obstruct European regulations or impose their version of the rules. Likewise, MEPs rely on lobbyists and associations to understand the trade-offs of competing initiatives and proposals.

Most of this lobbying is performed by professionals who speak for economic or producer interests. The Commission and Council, committed to bridging the "democratic deficit" expressed concern about the lopsided influence peddling in Brussels. Producers possessed ample representation. Consumers were barely visible.

To shed the impression that economic integration is all about nurturing the competitive advantages of big business, both the Council and Commission actively encourage civic organizations to become pan-European federations and participate in the policy deliberation process. With the help of funding and subsidies, hundreds of nongovernmental organizations (NGOs) have appeared in Brussels and lobbied the Commission and EP. Even more so than the economic interests, NGOs occupy a contradictory space as both partner and adversary of the Commission and EP. They are partners because they provide input on suggestions for measures and initiatives. By the same token, they are adversaries in that they criticize the Commission on matters where the European process fails, misses, or goes too far.

In short, over time, the Commission and EP have attracted the attention of many business groups, firm associations, professional federations, civic action groups, and NGOs. There are thousands of registered lobby and interest groups in Brussels. The Commission (with the approval of the Council) releases funding to encourage the formation of consumer groups or civic organizations to balance the dense representation of producer interests. But many NGOs are small outfits with only a small staff and limited funding. Producer interests tend to be overrepresented while environmental, consumer, and health tend to be underrepresented.

Identity

The first question is: What do we mean by European identity? Are we referring to people's identification with the European Union and EU institutions? Or do we mean self-identification of individuals with the norms and values represented by Europe (which means all of Europe, including Switzerland and Norway)?

In this chapter, we are looking at EU political identity, examining whether the people of Europe perceive themselves as being citizens of the European Union and recognize a relationship between themselves and EU institutions and processes. We would expect that EU institutions engage EU citizens through policies (some of which are described later in the chapter) and problem-solving tasks of the EU institutions. The EU institutions also express their objectives and decisions on a set of pan-European integrationist values and norms. In short, during the course of more than fifty years of European integration, we should expect European citizens to possess traces of an EU identity.

However, many studies show that in fact EU identity is thin. There is a small minority of people who identify themselves as European, but for the majority of EU citizens, political identification with the European Union is weak.

What explains this relatively weak identification with the European project? There are different explanations offered in the literature, but we should mention at least three.

First, there are the European elections, which would appear to be a good exercise to confirm EU political identity and foster identification with the institutions of the European Union. However, as mentioned earlier, EU issues do not feature much in electoral campaigns, and European elections are not fought by pan-European parties representing European policy preferences. Rather, European elections tend to be ignored by a large part of the electorate and are contested by national parties on national issues. European elections have not produced European political parties, which would articulate European preferences and worldviews. Rather, as mentioned earlier, European elections are an opportunity to mobilize against the EU and rail against EU technocrats and policies.

Second, the European political elite from the start suspected that the "people" were not ready for European institution building and should therefore not be consulted and engaged. Possibly, in 1957 when the Treaty of Rome was signed, Europeans were strongly wedded to their national identity, culture, norms, and values, and were unlikely to endorse "ever closer union" among the peoples of Europe. Since then, especially since 1991, the people of Europe may in fact be more interested and concerned about the European Union. However, as governments got into the habit of not consulting their voters, political leaders concluded far-reaching agreements without involving the public. Subsequently, people began to harbor suspicions of "Brussels" and EU institutions, which exerted considerable influence over their lives. Once political leaders decided to consult the people by organizing an EU referendum, they received some nasty surprises in the form of rejections. In Denmark and Sweden, where the people were asked to vote on the euro, the people voted no. In 2005, both France and the Netherlands when they were able to cast a vote on the Constitutional treaty, rejected the treaty. In 1992, 2001, and 2008, the no votes in Denmark, Ireland, and Ireland delayed the ratification of important treaties (Maastricht, Nice, and Lisbon). In response, political leaders have decided to avoid mobilizing public opinion and to rely on the "permissive consensus," so-called because citizens for many years did not object to major EU initiatives. Obviously, this lack of engagement has not had a positive impact on European political identities while it may have sharpened cynicism about the European Union. Some voters would argue that the EU is run by an opaque and seemingly unaccountable technocracy.

Third, insofar as national elites have touted the EU project, it is in terms of economic benefits. In the past, Europeans appreciated the European Union for bringing peace and prosperity, and generally believed that membership benefited their country. However, the economic benefits of EU membership have become more diffuse and fragmented, with the result that support for EU membership has stagnated in many countries. For many citizens, what matters now are the sacrifices they are supposed to make to comply with euro-zone requirements of limited budget deficits, modest public debt, and sound fiscal policy. People blame the European Union for austerity measures and cutbacks in social entitlements. Therefore, since the mid-1990s, public opinion has become ambivalent about the benefits of membership. At the very least, people's attitudes toward the European Union are split as the advantages of the single market are negated by the disadvantages of having to compete in a larger economic space. These three factors account for why EU political identity is underdeveloped and stunted. It also explains why the economic crisis has stirred growing resentment against the EU. Political identification with the EU was weak to begin with, but now, as the economic crisis has brought about high unemployment, massive youth unemployment, and a loss of social benefits and programs, some people are increasingly advocating diluting ties with the EU, exiting the Eurozone, or sidestepping previous EU treaties and agreements.

What Has Been Accomplished

Over the decades, the European Union has become involved in an ever-larger circle of policy activities. A recent count claims that EU institutions have issued more than 90,000 binding acts, broken down into 30,000 legal acts issued by the Commission, 11,000 Court verdicts, and 44,000 international standards set by Codex Alimentarius (WHO & FAO food standards system) and other international agencies.

The output of the Commission comes in the form of directives, regulations, and decisions. Directives oblige member states to implement their content, leaving it to national agencies to decide how they will incorporate the new legal act. Regulation is directly binding on all member states throughout the European Union, without the need for approval by governments or parliaments. A regulation goes into effect as soon as it is listed in the EU law register. Decisions are binding on those entities (member state, corporation, local authority) to whom they are specifically addressed.

However, this still leaves open the question of what exactly is decided and legislated in the European Union. The European Union is a bit like a federal system except that the split is between national and Euro/supranational. The organization of the European Union reflects that division of authority. The Commission has exclusive decision-making power on external commercial policy, single currency, and competition policy. National governments control social welfare programs, tax policy, health care, and education. Then, there is a third set of policies in which responsibility is shared. Aspects of internal security (asylum, immigration, policing), agriculture, food safety, climate change, international development, foreign aid, consumer protection, and public health are supposed to be coordinated by both levels. In 1991 (during the TEU negotiations), it was decided that the lowest level of government is always the appropriate decision-making level. Only areas of policy intervention that involve a fair amount of international coordination and oversight should be delegated to the European Commission (i.e., subsidiarity). The first successful Euro-policy was the Common Agricultural Policy (CAP), which underpinned the original pact to ratify the Treaty of Rome.

Common Agricultural Policy

The structure of the CAP is very complex and has been a major source of global trade disputes. Its twin goals are to support the livelihood of farmers and protect the European economy from cheaper agricultural commodities grown in countries with more suitable climate, better soil conditions, and more land, such as the United States, Brazil, and Argentina. The Commission guarantees prices by promising to buy products that do not sell on the open market. Prices are set to reflect the cost of living of farmers in different regions in the European Union and are set relatively high to provide adequate income for farmers. Food prices in Europe are therefore higher than what they could have been if there had been no CAP. The Commission often ends up having to fulfill its pledge and buy up surplus foodstuff, which it has to transport and store. It then tries to sell surplus grain, milk, or wine abroad at lower prices in order to rid itself of inventory. The dumping of agricultural commodities has been an enormous source of aggravation for more efficient exporting countries such as the United States and Canada because the dumping lowers the price for these products on the global market and cuts into the profit margins of foreign farmers.

In the 1990s, under international and fiscal pressure, the Commission extracted concessions from member states with sizable farming/food sectors to reduce the income support scheme to minimize its disruptive impact on global agricultural trade. Over the years, reforms have indeed decreased the surpluses and reduced the CAP's share in the total EU/ budget from three-quarters to half. Price guarantees have been lowered to discourage overproduction, which not only led to huge surpluses but also hurt local ecology and caused pollution of groundwater and soil. Currently, the CAP supplies direct payments to farmers if they produce less or reduce their herds or convert part of their holdings into an eco-habitat for tourism or wildlife. Nevertheless, it is the largest funding program of the European Union.

The Single European Market

Regional integration is best understood as a lengthy attempt to achieve market integration. The Treaty of Rome called for the removal of barriers against the free movement of goods, labor, capital, and services, which necessitated the adoption of a common external commercial policy and a watchdog to guarantee that the member states would play fair and square by introducing competition policy (antitrust). By the 1960s, most member states had removed tariffs on industrial goods and opened their markets to foreign trade. However, the lifting of tariffs on goods faltered in the 1970s when international economic conditions deteriorated and governments increasingly revived semi-protectionist measures to protect struggling manufacturing firms and industrial sectors.

In the 1970s, as economic growth decreased, unemployment increased, and budget deficits exploded, many governments became ever more creative in finding ways to protect domestic actors from international trade. The removal of tariffs on manufactured goods simply generated a whole new system of protectionism that was more insidious and harmful.

The Single European Act and Single European Market (SEM) grew out of concern for the future of the European Union and the weaknesses of the European economy in light of the emergence of Japan and newly industrialized countries (South Korea). The Commission's 1985 White Paper set out new goals and priorities. It emphasized market liberalization and deregulation. The objective was to give firms greater room to innovate, grow, develop and become global competitors. Alongside the transparent economic aims of the White Paper, the Commission also called for European institution building so that it would possess additional powers to issue complementary legislation in competition, consumer protection, food safety, and research and development, which meant that national governments had to transfer some powers to European institutions.

The Commission relied on the principle of "mutual recognition" to open the European market. The principle implies that any national law with reasonable policy goals, such as environmental conservation, health, and so on, should be tolerated within the European Union. Rather than imposing common rules for determining whether a product complies with the descriptive characteristics and norms of each individual member state, the Commission freed itself from this impossible task and declared that products approved by a regulatory agency of one member state can be legally marketed throughout the Community. The only task of the Commission was to determine minimum standards across a wide range of similar products. Earlier, the Commission had sought harmonization, which was extremely controversial and provoked much resistance from national governments. Mutual recognition was simpler because the free movement of goods and services did not require harmonization but rather recognition by national authorities.

The single market has not been the final answer to slow growth and lagging international competitiveness. But it has certainly addressed the fragmented nature of the European economy and the tendency to coddle selected firms and industries. Compared to two decades ago, European firms have become more competitive and the European Union has become an attractive destination for foreign direct investments. European consumers pay lower prices on a range of products and services thanks to liberalization of previously protected industries and sectors. Many European firms have become serious global players.

However, as in any process of rationalization and liberalization, the creation of the single market also created winners and losers. Furthermore, many of the economic regulatory adjustments were taken without the active participation of political parties or interest groups, with the result that the changes wrought by increased openness to markets and global competition has left deep dissatisfaction and insecurity. European economies have undergone an amazing transformation, yet it was without open debate and mostly achieved through technical regulations bypassing parliamentary debate. The impact of liberalization and deregulation has also varied as some economies were more adept at absorbing the challenges than others. Countries with a more liberal version of market structures dealt with the demands of liberalization more easily than tightly organized economies with comparatively large state intervention. Thus, the United Kingdom was well positioned to take advantage of the new regulatory standards. But France and Italy have struggled and have not fully come to terms with the economic changes.

A Single Currency

For the Commission, it was a truism that the single market project was not complete without a single currency. How can we speak of a single market if goods are priced in fifteen or twenty-eight different currencies? The SEM concluded its list of measures with a reference to the creation of a single currency. Commission officials made it clear that currency differences concealed inefficiencies, undermined the ability of the consumer to compare prices, and hampered the free movement of goods and services. However, a single currency challenges the core definition of what it means to be a sovereign nation state. The main task of governments is to spend money that they collect in taxes. Politics is about the distribution of resources. Governments would not be in a position of authority if they did not control the national purse. Voters elect politicians who in turn determine macroeconomic policy together with central banks, which are independent from the political system. They set interest rates and thus determine the price of money. In turn, interest rates determine the cost of borrowing capital and influence how much governments spend on public programs. If interest rates are low, governments can borrow more. If interest rates are high, it is more costly to borrow both for governments and private agents.

The question therefore is: Why would national governments ever agree to the idea of a single currency, considering the resulting loss in monetary autonomy and policy independence? The short and simple answer is that national governments had already lost their ability to set policy independently from the strongest, most stable economy in the European Union, namely Germany. Central bankers followed the decisions made by their German counterpart and set interest rates according to what was best for the German economy. They no longer were able to fine-tune monetary policy in response to the particular needs of the domestic economy.

This situation emerged in the wake of the success of the European Monetary System. In 1978 most of the EU-9 (Benelux, Denmark, France, Italy, Germany, Ireland, United Kingdom) agreed to form a zone of monetary stability in a world of fluctuating exchange rates and decided to fix their exchange bilaterally. The European Monetary System (EMS) had two remarkable features. It came with a "fake" currency, the ECU, which was used as an accounting unit to enable companies and public agencies to avoid exchange-rate costs.

More important, each EMS-member government was obliged to stabilize its currency value with respect to the value of a basket of EMS-member currencies, namely the ECU. Each country's currency had a weight in the ECU that was proportional to that country's trade within the EC. An autonomous shift in the external value of any EMS-member currency changed the value of the ECU and therefore imposed exchange-rate adjustment obligations on all members of the system. However, the burden of adjustment fell mostly on the currencies of smaller or weaker economies. By definition, the system was asymmetrical in its operation. A shift in the external value of the currency of a major member of the EMS (such as the German mark) had a greater effect on the external value of the ECU than had the same percentage disturbance to the external value of the currency of a less important member (for example the Belgian franc). It therefore imposed greater exchange-rate adjustment responsibilities on the smaller members. Many of the EMS countries welcomed this asymmetrical burden because it was the price they paid for exchange-rate stability with their main trading partners (including France and the German Federal Republic).

Eventually, small EU member states decided to shadow German fiscal and monetary policies as that would minimize the need for exchange-rate adjustments. By the mid-1980s, virtually all EMS currencies were following German monetary policy to avoid inflation rates higher than that of Germany and unwanted, although needed, exchange-rate realignments. Eventually, all the EMS currencies shadowed the German mark and national monetary authorities followed the lead of the German central bank. Of course, the latter made policy based on West German economic conditions, and often the decisions taken by the German authorities did not suit the needs of other EMS countries.

Thus, when the Commission revived the idea of creating a common currency, by the early 1990s, quite a few countries were ready for that momentous change. There was plenty of resentment of having to follow in the footsteps of German macroeconomic policy, and a single currency would greatly dilute the weight and influence of the German central bank, which would be one of many participating central banks.

During the TEU negotiations in 1991, EMU was incorporated into the amended treaty. Countries received an opt-out clause if they did not want to participate, and Britain and Denmark decided to withdraw from the negotiations. The heads of state adopted the Commission guideline to demand strict convergence criteria so that unstable financial countries would not be eligible. Participants were supposed to record modest budget deficits (3 percent of GDP), manageable public debt (60 percent of GDP), and inflation and interest rates within the average of the three best performing economies. The Commission report also set out the blueprint for the new European central bank, which would be independent from the political class and would be endowed with a strong commitment to price stability. The time line designated January 1997 as the date on which the member states and Commission would determine who is eligible, and January 1999 would be the start of EMU.

The single market and single currency have been the European Union's most significant achievements. The euro symbolizes the crowning achievement of regional integration at the expense of national sovereignty. Its adoption grew out of several developments and calculations. First of all, most of the European countries were no longer in control of their "monetary destiny" that was decided in Frankfurt. Second, they strongly felt it was better to have a European central bank in control of their monetary destiny than German officials at the German central bank. Finally, the single currency accompanied the success of the single market project.

Nevertheless, why would Germany ever have agreed to EMU when it ran Europe's monetary regime? Here, political factors played a major role. German unification after the fall of the Wall stirred all kinds of worries about a resurgent strong Germany more interested in its Eastern borderlands than the European Union. Germany was the largest net contributor to the European Union, it possessed the largest economy, and it played an active role in European integration. What if its attention and interests wandered eastward and it lost interest in the European Union? Its partners expressed their concerns in many different ways, and the German federal government acquiesced to these concerns by demonstrating that it would never abandon European integration and would always remain committed to its Western allies (and especially France). Former chancellor Kohl therefore agreed to the creation of a single currency. The Germans sacrificed a treasured symbol of their postwar rehabilitation to reassure their European partners that Germany would remain committed to the European Union. As the EMS did not constrain German monetary policy, the German authorities had to make the largest sacrifices. They did so for the sake of the future of the Franco-German partnership.

Cohesion Policy and Structural Funds

Most of the activities of the EU institutions fall under the label of regulations because they aim to create a uniform economic space in which people, goods, services, and capital move freely. Much of the legislative activities go into creating technical standards such as the size of strawberries that can be sold to the consumer or additives in milk or toxins in drinking water. However, cohesion policy is an example of redistribution in that it transfers money from the EU budget to the poorer regions in the European Union. At this point, cohesion and structural funds account for 35 percent of the total EU budget, which is more or less equivalent to €300 billion or $400b during the 2007–2013 budget cycle. Before enlargement in 2004, the main beneficiaries were regions in Greece, Portugal, Ireland, the new East German "Länder," Southern Italy, and Spain. With enlargement, many of the former poor member states are now part of the wealthier group, and the Commission and Council have rechanneled funds to the new member states since 2007.

The European Union employs a special formula to transfer funds to regions whose per capita GDP is less than 75 percent of the average EU GDP per capita, making them eligible, which in practice includes most of the new member states and accounts for over 80 percent of all spending under the label of cohesion policy. As richer member states may also have regions that are struggling economically, another objective is to assist member states if they cope with economic and social change, which accounts for 16 percent of all cohesion spending. A modest sum of money (2.5 percent of the total) is available to stimulate cross-border cooperation in order to find joint solutions to shared problems.

The EU budget is tightly controlled, and the European Union cannot run a deficit. Guidelines for annual spending are laid down during multi-annual planning years, covering a budget cycle of seven years. Nevertheless, it is important to remember that the European Union's budget is relatively modest and represents only 1.2 percent of the total GDP of twenty-eight member states and 2.5 percent of the total EU public spending. The EU budget is small because the bulk of the spending programs – retirement, health care, social benefits – are managed by central governments of the member states. In turn, this makes cohesion and structural funds, although modest, nonetheless extremely significant. The determination of budget and its allocation of funds tend to provoke heated debates because it divides the European Union into net payers (Austria, Germany, the Netherlands, Sweden – and minor net payers Denmark, France, Finland, and Italy) and net recipients. In short, Cohesion and Structural Funds are based on the principle of solidarity in that citizens in the richest member states contribute to the development of the poorer member states. As many rich member states suffer economic austerity and high unemployment, even small amounts of money become a source of contestation.

Challenges: The Euro Crisis

In 2009, the European Union celebrated ten years of the euro. The celebrations started in 2008 and led to many triumphant reviews of EMU. Numerous observers spoke highly of the achievements of EMU and dismissed the erstwhile naysayers who had fretted about the inconsistency of a single monetary policy and divergent national fiscal policies.

In retrospect, the laudatory celebrations of EMU were premature while the worries about its long-term sustainability in light of the tensions between a single European monetary policy and divergent national fiscal policies were justified. A handful of Eurozone countries had pursued loose fiscal policies in the years preceding 2008, and their economies were fueled by excessive consumer spending and public sector debt. The same forces that contributed to the housing bubble in the United States resulted in a spending bubble in some Mediterranean countries, Ireland, and Slovenia.

Concurrently with the founding of the euro, a period of historic low interest rates emerged across the world. Investors looking for "safe" yet profitable (high yield) investments gravitated toward mortgage-backed securities (contributing to the American housing bubble) and they sought out government bonds of Eurozone members with large borrowing needs (resulting in a spending bubble in Greece, Portugal, Spain, Ireland, and some other Eurozone countries). In the EU, the subsequent fallout from years of debt-driven spending has not yet been resolved. Some countries have experienced more than four years of economic recession and their GDP has shrunk by 25 percent, which is reminiscent of the Great Depression of the 1930s.

Fundamentally, the Eurozone crisis is a tale of divergent adjustments to the introduction of the euro in Northern and Southern Europe. All Eurozone countries fixed their national exchange rates by adopting the euro. Nonetheless, labor costs and productivity in the Eurozone continued to diverge and created two distinct economic groups. One group of

Eurozone countries, led by Germany, kept labor costs in check and recorded low growth and low inflation. In these economies, the introduction of the euro spurred a surge in exports in part to compensate for the sluggish growth at home and in part to take advantage of rising demand in faster growing countries in the Mediterranean periphery. By contrast, the second group consisted of countries in southern Europe with initially high growth rate and higher inflation rates. The elimination of exchange rate volatility in these countries opened up opportunities to catch up with the richer north. Greece, Portugal, Spain, and also Cyprus and Slovenia enjoyed interest rates lower than what they would have been if they still possessed their own currency. Low interest rates spurred a construction, private consumption, and public sector boom while a rise in private and public spending also pushed up inflation and growth rates. As inflation rose, labor costs went up as well. As these countries acquired more disposable income (in the form of higher pay, more generous social benefits, and capital gains from assets such as housing and stocks) they consumed more goods, many of which were imported from the slower growing northern Eurozone countries. Spotting opportunities, German, Austrian, Finnish, and Dutch firms exported to the faster growing southern periphery of the Eurozone. These countries recorded large surpluses on their trade balance. The southern countries recorded large deficits on their trade balances because they bought large volumes of imported goods. To cover the gap in imports and exports (the trade deficit), the southern Eurozone countries borrowed money in Euros from European financial institutions. Eventually, striking imbalances emerged. Financial institutions in northern countries held an enormous pool of IOUs issued by Greek, Portuguese, Spanish, and Irish institutions.

By late 2009, the party was over and the creditor countries refused to lend more money to the southern periphery, thereby ejecting them from the capital markets. In the absence of access to capital market, governments in Greece, Portugal, Spain, and Ireland could no longer service their current loans and interest payments.

European and international financial officials prescribed a painful regime of internal deflation to those countries needing a "bailout." Such a course of action relied on many rounds of fiscal retrenchment, layoffs, cutbacks in social benefits, and lower public sector wages. The successive measures to shrink public debts and deficits by cutting back on social services and benefits, in addition to the layoffs in the public sector, depressed domestic consumer demand and caused a recession. The recession in turn dampened private business and consumer confidence. While governments reduced budget deficits, the private sector also retrenched in light of depressed consumer demand. In response, the chorus of international and European financial agencies convinced the Eurozone countries in trouble to seek salvation by improving their export competitiveness, and thus to rely on European and global markets to compensate for the recession at home.

In theory, this sounds like a great idea. In reality, the export strategy has not worked. To improve export competitiveness, many firms in southern Europe slimmed down their total wage bill and managed to lower the prices of goods and services. Yet the export competitive strategy has not brought much relief

One problem is that the entire Eurozone/EU has witnessed stagnant growth. All Eurozone governments and private sector agents are deleveraging and holding down spending. If there had been no single currency, then Greece, Spain and Portugal could have devalued their currency and Germany, the Netherlands and Finland, for example, would have witnessed an appreciation of their currencies. That would have meant that goods from Greece would have been cheaper in Germany, and more importantly German exports to Greece would have been more expensive. Thus, if these countries could have devalued their currencies, they would have benefited from an automatic adjustment. Instead, the member states in trouble must seek to achieve the same effect by lowering costs at home, pursuing a policy of internal deflation.

Budget austerity and economic adjustment have taken an enormous human toll. Unemployment rose from 2.8 million in 2008 to 4.6 million in 2012 in the EU. Unemployment is especially high among young workers up to the age of twenty-five. In countries like Spain, Greece, and Portugal, the youth unemployment rate has approached 50 percent. For many young people, there is literally no future at home and those who can have left and moved to northern EU member states.

Predictably, the Eurozone crisis has had a devastating impact on popular attitudes to the European Union. The collapse of confidence in the EU is not limited purely to countries that have been required to slash wages and benefits in return for international financial aid. Support has also declined in member states in relatively good shape such as Germany and Austria. The northern group of Eurozone countries is frustrated with the slow financial and economic recovery and disturbed by the idea that their tax money is used to bailout southern Eurozone countries. European-wide solidarity appears to be missing.

At the EU level, some progress has been made in strengthening the European-wide response in case of a new major financial crisis. I will mention a few examples. When Greece required an immediate rescue in May 2010, the efforts were improvised and relied on the contribution of Eurozone participants and the International Monetary Fund. Governments negotiated through the night and many of the decisions were hasty and makeshift. Soon it appeared that Greece was not the only member state in financial trouble, so the first major bailout loan was replaced with the temporary European Financial Stability Facility (EFSF). The EFSF was used for the second Greek bailout and contributed toward the Irish and Portuguese rescues. These commitments came to €192 billion and again involved a direct contribution by all EU member states, backed by the credit ratings of their sovereign debt. But the EFSF had a weak spot. Its borrowing was backed by guarantees from the euro-zone states, some of which were in no condition to honor their pledges because their credit rating dove into "junk bond" territory.

After that, the Commission pushed hard for a more permanent fund that would rescue stricken countries if they were willing to accept strict reforms of their budget policies and spending programs. That new fund is called the European Stability Mechanism (ESM) and it is located in Luxembourg. Along with the ESM's ability to collect financial contributions from Eurozone members, it can also borrow money in capital markets. Its total capital is €500billion, some of which has been used to bailout Greece for a third time, Portugal for a second time, and Slovenia for the first time. The board of the ESM makes decisions on who receives what and under which conditions. The board members are required by law to impose conditions that the recipients of rescue funds must accept in order to be eligible for financial assistance. Thus, once a government seeks financial assistance it also revokes its right to decide on how to manage its financial and fiscal affairs. Such an arrangement cuts right into the fiscal accountability of elected governments, which must prioritize the demands of the ESM board above the needs and interests of voters.

In late 2013, the Council and the European parliament agreed on reforms to establish uniform deposit guarantee schemes in the EU. Together with the insured deposit scheme, the member states also agreed on national rules to rescue failed banks, which will mean that governments impose fees on banks equivalent to 1 percent of insured deposits to cover the costs of rescuing banks.

Furthermore, at the same time, negotiations have taken place to create a banking union. Such a union would be the largest surrender of national sovereignty since the creation of the euro. A Single Supervisory Mechanism (SSM) will oversee the 6,000-odd banks scattered across the EU. The new regulator will employ a stress test and in-depth probe into the balance sheets of Eurozone banks and will prevent local regulators from sheltering national banking champions. A single regulator does not yet amount to a full-fledged banking union, but it is a major step toward establishing a European-wide framework to assess the health of national banking corporations and of laying down a blueprint of how to intervene if a bank is in trouble.

The banking union with its resolution system will only go into force in 2015 and it includes many national safeguards to enable governments to weigh in when an emergency situation occurs. Although there will be a resolution mechanism and a common fund, national leaders will be able to decide how these funds will be distributed and when banks need to be rescued. Nevertheless, the new institutional features accompanying EMU point to a further deepening of EU cooperation and legislation, constraining the decision-making authority of national governments.

CONCLUSION

The founding father of the European Union, Jean Monnet, many decades ago observed that "Europe will be forged in crises, and will be the sum of the solutions adopted for those crises." This chapter has linked many of the major European integration initiatives to international security challenges, international economic pressures, and European institutional and political crises. The institutions of the European Union were originally meant to support the Atlantic alliance and to endow small-to medium-sized countries with additional tools to compete in global markets. The founding treaty (Treaty of Rome) resolved the issues of how to strengthen the economic self-sufficiency of Western Europe so that it could withstand Soviet aggression and how to assuage concerns expressed by France and other Western countries about the revival of the German economy. The single market and the Single European Act (1986) remedied the shortcomings of fragmented European producer markets and also paved the way for wider European political cooperation. The Treaty of European Union (1991) contained new articles to take advantage of the end of the Cold War, opening of Central Eastern Europe, and German unification. The Lisbon treaty (2009) grew out of the defunct Constitutional treaty, which in turn sought to reform the European Union in light of enlargement and the accession of a dozen new member states.

If European integration arose from the remains of successive security and economic crises, it could be that the global economic crisis of 2008 may occasion another round of treaty negotiations to strengthen fiscal coordination in order to offset European monetary integration. With that, the "economic" component of EMU would finally emerge.

Member states have made progress, to some extent, in filling in the EU's regulatory and policy voids by establishing the ESM and by crawling toward a banking union. But trust in the EU has continuously eroded. Economic insecurity has weakened support for Brussels and EU institutions among Europeans since 2008. Disapproval is strongest in the bailout countries where the EU has imposed austerity policies, compounding the economic hardships individuals were already experiencing from the financial and economic crisis. But the problem is not merely economic. Individuals' sense of disconnect from the institutions and processes of the EU is clear from the dwindling turnouts in EU elections, the rise in popularity of radical right-wing parties and movements in Austria, France, Greece, Hungary, Italy, and the Netherlands, and the critical tone take by mainstream politicians in connection with the crisis and austerity measures. All of these trends indicate that a sizable segment of the public sees the EU as unable to provide satisfactory responses to their concerns.

Moreover, the alienation from EU institutions and decision-making processes will not be alleviated by constructing another elite mechanism to impose fiscal discipline from above. As politicians already like to blame the European Union for painful spending cuts, it stands to reason that European fiscal coordination will further reinforce resentment against the European Union. Thus, it is difficult to predict whether the crisis in the euro-zone will strengthen European integration or not. Eventually, political leaders will have to find a solution to the debt crisis, but whether this solution will yield some sort of fiscal union or provoke a destabilizing crisis of confidence and electoral backlash remains to be seen. One thing is certain, however: voters in the weaker Eurozone face years of economic and social challenges that do not auger well for the general well-being of the EU.

BIBLIOGRAPHY

Bache, Ian. *Europeanization and Multilevel Governance: Cohesion Policy in the European Union and Britain*. Lanham: Rowman & Littlefield, 2008.

Bilbao-Ubillos, Javier, ed. *The Economic Crisis and Governance in the European Union: A Critical Assessment*. New York: Routledge, 2013.

Bulmer, Simon, and Christian Lequesne. eds. *The Member States of the European Union*. New York: Oxford University Press, 2005.

Bermeo, Nancy and Jonas Pontusson, eds. *Coping with Crisis: Government Reactions to the Great Recession*. New York: Russell Sage Foundation, 2012.

Chiva, Cristina, and David Phinnemore. *The European Union's 2007 Enlargement*. New York: Routledge, 2011.

Coen, David, and Jeremy Richardson, eds. *Lobbying the European Union: Institutions, Actors, and Issues*. New York: Oxford University Press, 2009.

Corbett, Richard, Francis Jacobs, and Michael Shackleton. *The European Parliament*. London: John Harper, 2007.

Dedman, Martin. *The Origins and Development of the European Union, 1945–2008*. New York: Routledge, 2010.

Dehousse, Renaud. *The European Court of Justice: The Politics of Judicial Integration*. St. Martin's Press, 1998.

Falkner, Gerda. *Complying with Europe: EU Harmonisation and Soft Law in the Member States*. New York: Cambridge University Press, 2005.

Fligstein, Neil. *Euroclash: The EU, European Identity, and the Future of Europe*. New York: Oxford University Press, 2008.

Greenwood, Justin. *Interest Representation in the European Union*. Second edition. New York: Palgrave MacMillan, 2007.

Hayes-Renshaw, Fiona, and Helen Wallace. *The Council of Ministers*. New York: Palgrave Macmillan, 2006.

Hix, Simon. *The Political System of the European Union*. New York: Palgrave Macmillan, 2005.

Hösli, Madeleine. *The Euro: A Concise Introduction to European Monetary Integration*. Boulder, CO: Lynne Rienner Publishers, 2005.

Kenneth, Dyson, ed. *The Euro at 10: Europeanization, Convergence and Power*. New York: Oxford University Press, 2008.

Kurzer, Paulette. *Markets and Moral Regulation: Cultural Change in the European Union*. New York: Cambridge University Press, 2001.

Laffan, Brigid. *The European Union and Its Member States*. New York: Palgrave Macmillan, 2011.

Laursen, Finn, ed. *The EU and the Eurozone Crisis: Policy Challenges and Strategic Choices*. Farnham, Surrey: Ashgate, 2013.

Leonardi, Robert. *Cohesion Policy in the European Union: The Building of Europe*. New York: Palgrave Macmillan, 2005.

Marsh, David. *Europe's deadlock: How the Euro Crisis Could Be Solved – And Why It Won't Happen*. New Haven, CT: Yale University Press, 2013.

Mérand, Frédéric. *European Defence Policy: Beyond the Nation State*. & New York: Oxford University Press, 2008.

Phinnemore, David, and Alex Warleigh-Lack, eds. *Reflections on European Integration: 50 Years of the Treaty of Rome*. New York: McMillan Palgrave, 2009.

Princen, Sebastiaan. *Agenda-Setting in the European Union*. New York: Palgrave Macmillan 2009.

Risse, Thomas. *A Community of Europeans? Transnational Identities and Public Spheres*. Ithaca, NY: Cornell University Press, 2010.

Sanders, David, Paolo Bellucci, Gábor Tóka, and Mariano Torcal. Eds. *The Europeanization of National Polities?: Citizenship and Support in a Post-Enlargement Union*. New York: Oxford University Press, 2012.

Schulz-Forberg, Hagen, and Bo Stråth. *The Political History of European Integration: The Hypocrisy of Democracy-through-Market*. New York: Routledge, 2011.

Van Munster, Rens. *Securitizing Immigration: The Politics of Risk in the EU*. New York: Palgrave Macmillan, 2009.

IMPORTANT TERMS

Common Agricultural Policy – a system of agricultural subsidies and programs. It represents about 30 percent of the European Union's budget in 2011. These subsidies work by guaranteeing a minimum price to producers and by direct payment of a subsidy for crops planted. It formed the basis for a Franco-German agreement to establish the EEC.

Barroso José – president of the Commission (2004–2014)

Commissioner – serves in the Commission and heads a department or division called directorate general. Commissioners are appointed by home governments but swear allegiance to the European Union. There are twenty-eight commissioners.

Common Foreign and Security Policy – the second area of policy making in the European Union, referring to foreign policy and military matters. Most decisions require Council unanimity vote, and the involvement of the Commission and Parliament is limited. Decisions are based on intergovernmental cooperation.

Community Pillar – the first and largest policy area of the European Union, it includes economic, social and, environmental policies. All decisions are taken by qualified majority vote in the Council of Ministers. Decisions are based on supranational principles.

Constitutional Treaty – was signed by the member states in late 2004 and was in the process of ratification until French and Dutch voters rejected the treaty in June 2005 in referenda. It was reborn as the Lisbon Treaty.

Council of the European Union – is a governing body that forms, along with the European Parliament, the legislative arm of the European Union. It contains ministers of the governments of each of the member states.

Court of Justice – previously the European Court of Justice, it ensures that the law is observed in the interpretation and application of the Treaties and of the decisions laid down by Community institutions. It rules on applications for annulment or actions for failure to act brought by a member state or an institution and on actions against member states for failure to fulfill obligations, and answers queries through preliminary reference.

"Democratic Deficit" – refers to the perceived democratic shortcomings of the European Union because of the shift of policy making to the Commission and Council and away from national parliaments. First used in the 1980s, it now mostly concerns questions on how to increase the limited powers of the parliament and civic participation.

Direct Effect – the doctrine developed by the ECJ where unimplemented directives in conflict with national law nonetheless carry direct legal force.

Directive – a collective legislative act of the European Union, which requires member states to achieve a particular result without dictating the means of achieving that result.

Directorates-General – the Commission is organized into over 30 distinct departments, each of which is responsible for specific tasks (collecting statistics) or policy areas (employment, environment, internal market, regional policy). Some commissioners lead more than one DG, especially if the DG is small and closely related to another task or policy area such as taxation, customs, statistics, audit and anti-fraud.

Economic and Monetary Union – part of the Treaty of European Union (1993), it committed countries to abolish national currencies and adopt a European currency (euro). It also created the European Central Bank, which is responsible for monetary policy within the euro-zone.

ECU – key feature of the EMS; it was a "fake" currency representing the basket of currencies of EC member states, which had to prevent movements above 2.25 percent around parity in bilateral exchange rates with other member countries.

Euro – launched in 1998 with eleven member states, which had met the convergence criteria. Physical coins and banknotes were introduced on January 1 2002. Latvia joined in January 2014, bringing the total Eurozone membership to over 330 million people and eighteen member states.

European Central Bank – responsible for monetary policy covering the eighteen member countries of the euro-zone. It also prints and mints all notes and coins. It was established in 1998, and its headquarters are located in Frankfurt.

European Coal and Steel Community – founded in 1951 (Treaty of Paris), by France, West Germany, Italy, Belgium, Luxembourg, and the Netherlands to pool the steel and coal resources of its member states. It was also strongly supported by the United States.

European Commission – formally the Commission of the European Communities, it is the executive body of the European Union. It is located in Brussels and has a staff of 20,000.

European Council – refers to the European summit meeting of the heads of state and the president of the European Union, which are held at least twice a year and are chaired by the country that holds the Council Presidency (different from the European Union Council of national cabinet members).

European Monetary System (EMS) – established in 1979 when most nations of the EC linked their currencies to prevent large fluctuations relative to one another. It is the precursor to EMU because it led to a loss of monetary autonomy and increased willingness to phase out national currencies.

European Parliament – directly elected by EU citizens once every five years. Together with the Council of Ministers, it composes the legislative branch of the institutions of the Union. It meets in two locations: Strasbourg and Brussels. It has only restricted legislative power because it cannot initiate legislation, but it can amend or veto it in many policy areas.

European Stability Mechanism – a permanent crisis resolution mechanism for the countries of the Eurozone. The ESM issues debt instruments in order to finance loans and other forms of financial assistance to Eurozone members states. It went into force in late 2012.

Intergovernmental Conference – the formal procedure for negotiating amendments to the founding treaties. Under the treaties, an IGC is called by the European Council, and is composed of heads of state, with the Commission, and to a lesser degree the Parliament.

"Mutual Recognition" – important breakthrough in the creation of the Single Market. According to this principle, promulgated first by the ECJ in 1979, a product or a service is allowed access to the markets of other member states if it has been approved or legalized by authorities in the country of origin. Barriers to free movement of goods and services will be illegal unless justified by a set of specifically provided rules in the EC Treaty. It alleviated the need to establish uniform standards for each and every product or service.

Ordinary Legislative Procedure – formerly co-decision; Parliament can amend and block legislation in those policy areas that fall under its mandate, which currently make up about three-quarters of EU legislative acts.

Police and Judicial Co-operation in Criminal Matters – third area of policy making in the European Union, it concerns cooperation in the fight against crime. This pillar was originally named Justice and Home Affairs but since 1997, asylum, migration, and judicial cooperation in civil matters have been transferred to the Community pillar.

Preliminary Reference – is specific to EU law because the ECJ is not the only judicial body empowered to apply EU law. National courts retain jurisdiction to review the implementation of EU law and they also guarantee that rights conferred to EU citizens through regulations and directives are upheld. National courts turn to the ECJ to seek clarification of a judicial issue concerning the interpretation of Community law to ascertain whether their national legislation complies with that law.

President of the European Commission – the highest-ranking unelected official within the EU bureaucracy, appointed by heads of state, both leads the Commission and is the public face of the European Union.

Proportionality – says that the European Union may do only what is necessary, and no more, in order to achieve its objectives.

Qualified Majority Voting – a voting procedure employed in the Council of Ministers for all decisions coming from the Community pillar. Each member state has a fixed number of votes, which is roughly determined by its population, but progressively weighted in favor of smaller countries.

Regulation – a legislative act of the European Union that does not require any implementing measures.

Single European Act – entered into force in July 1987 and introduced the first wave of institutional reforms to prepare the institutions for completing the Single Market. It introduced Qualified Majority Voting to areas related to the Single Market and granted more decision-making powers to the EP.

Single European Market – agreed upon in 1986, it involved a huge program of removing barriers to the free movement of all the four factors of production (goods, services, capital, and labor). The ultimate aim was to increase the international competitiveness of European economies.

Spillover – the idea that intense cooperation in economics will eventually spill over into more sensitive high political arenas and thus lay the foundation for political integration.

Subsidiarity – the principle that the European Union should act only where separate national legislation would be insufficient. It was proposed during the negotiations for the TEU.

Treaties of the EU – the basic constitutional texts of the European Union because they set out the objectives of the European Union and establish various institutions that are intended to achieve those aims. There have been four additional treaties since the ratification of the Treaty of Rome in 1957.

Treaty of Amsterdam – entered into force in 1999 and made substantial changes to the **Treaty on European Union** (1993) by increasing the powers for the European Parliament, adding a social dimension to the European Union, and introducing a Community area of freedom, security, and justice; it began the reform of the institutions in the run-up to enlargement.

Treaty of European Union – entered into force in November 1993 and changed the name of the European Community to European Union. It also introduced a new structure to the European Union by dividing policy areas into three areas or pillars. It added two new policy areas that remained under the auspices of member governments: foreign and defense policies, as well as internal security.

Treaty of Lisbon – went into force December 2009 and defines what the European Union can and cannot do, and what means it can use. It also restructured EU institutions to take into account a large and heterogeneous organization, which needs to be transparent and accountable to EU citizens.

Treaty of Maastricht – see Treaty of the European Union.

Treaty of Nice – entered into force in February 2003 and readied the European Union for further enlargement by putting a ceiling on the number of MEPs and the European Commission.

Treaty of Paris – was signed in Paris in 1951 and brought France, Germany, Italy, and the Benelux countries together with the aim of organizing free movement of coal and steel and free access to sources of production. This treaty is the origin of the EU institutions.

Treaty of Rome – established the European Economic Community; it was signed in March 1957. Six countries joined: France, Italy, Germany, and Benelux. It had two major components, the European Economic Community and Euratom.

STUDY QUESTIONS

1. What lessons does European integration hold for other regions in the world?
2. Why is/was the Franco-German partnership a key feature of European institution building?
3. What were the main objectives of the Single European Market and Single European Act?
4. How would you describe the balance of power among the various components of the European Union: Commission, Council, Parliament, and Court?
5. How are the policy responsibilities between the Commission and Council determined?
6. What led to the increase of power of the European parliament, and how has it influenced the policy process and regional integration?
7. What are some of the contributing factors that account for the stunted development of a European identity and Euro-level public participation?
8. How do we begin to understand why European countries agreed to abolish their currencies and adopt a brand new untested currency, the euro? Will the Eurozone crisis serve to reinforce or to undermine European integration in the long run?
9. How would you compare the development of interests, identities, and institutions in the European Union to that of any of the country studies examined in this volume?
10. How would you assess the impact of the "international environment" in the formation of the European Union and in the launching of various ambitious programs and objectives?

ABBREVIATIONS

Benelux	Belgium, Netherlands, Luxembourg
CAP	Common Agricultural Policy
DG	Directorate General
EEC	European Economic Community (1957)
EC	European Communities encompassing the EEC, ECSC, and European Atomic Energy Community
ECB	European Central Bank
ECSC	European Coal and Steel Community (1950)
ECU	European Currency Unit
EMS	European Monetary System (1979)
EMU	European and Monetary Union (1993)
EP	European parliament
ESM	European Stability Mechanism (2012)
IGC	Intergovernmental Conference
MEP	Member of European parliament

NGO	Nongovernmental Organization
SEA	Single European Act (1987)
SEM	Single European Market (1987)
TEU	Treaty of European Union (1993)

THE EU: THE BASICS

Country	Date of Accession
Belgium, France, Germany, Italy, Luxembourg, Netherlands	1957
Denmark, Great Britain, Ireland	1973
Greece	1981
Portugal, Spain	1986
Austria, Finland, Sweden	1995
Cyprus, Czech Republic, Estonia, Hungary, Latvia, Lithuania, Malta, Poland, Slovakia, Slovenia	2004
Bulgaria, Romania	2007
Croatia	2013

KEY EVENTS: EVOLUTION OF THE EUROPEAN UNION

Year	Event
1951	Creation of the ECSC
1957	Treaty of Rome signed
1967	Creation of EC
1972	First enlargement concluded
1981	Greece admitted
1985	Single European Act passed
1986	Portugal and Spain admitted
1991	Treaty of Maastricht signed

(continued)

Year	Event
1995	Austria Finland Sweden admitted
1997	Treaty of Amsterdam signed
1998	Benelux, France Germany, Italy, Spain Portugal Greece, Ireland, Austria, Finland form EMU
2001	Treaty of Nice signed
2002	Euro launched
2004	Ten new members join
2007	Bulgaria, Romania admitted
2008	Slovenia, Cyprus, Malta, and Slovakia joined EMU
2009	Lisbon Treaty
2011	Estonia joined EMU
2012	European Stability Mechanism
2013	Croatia admitted
2014	Latvia joined EMU

WEB SITES

EUABC – A dictionary on words related to the European Union: http://en.euabc.com/
EUObserver – latest news in the European Union: http://euobserver.com/
EUactiv – EU information Web site: http://www.euractiv.com/
Delegation of the European Union to the United States: http://www.eurunion.org/eu/

NIGERIA

MAP 14.1. Map of Nigeria.

14 Nigeria

Okechukwu C. Iheduru

Introduction

January 1, 2014 marked the centenary of the founding of Nigeria as a country. Competing interests, identities, and institutions have all played a central role in shaping the country's developmental path from the precolonial through the colonial to the postcolonial era. In each of these historical periods, Nigeria's material interests, identities, and institutions have in turn been shaped by the international environment in which its roughly 174 million people and over 250 ethno-linguistic groups have interacted among themselves and with the outside world in their quest for modernity. What makes Nigerian politics interesting is the constant changes in and interactions of these material interests, identities, and institutions – often arising from domestic, regional, and global pressures – and the myriad ways in which they have either been accommodated or rejected by the given political order.

The combination of these four mutually interacting variables – interests, identities, institutions, and the global context – provides a robust framework for analyzing the events that have shaped the political life of this fascinating country. We will situate Nigerian politics within the global context by answering the following set of questions: What are the global and domestic factors that have shaped Nigeria's development path, from the precolonial through colonial and post-independence eras? How have these factors shaped the interests, identities, and institutions that, in turn, have shaped these development paths? We will also weave into the narrative the local and domestic political and economic threats Nigeria has faced as it navigates its way through the modern world. As the story moves along, we will evaluate the principles and values upheld by the Nigerian government in terms of whether they are considered legitimate by people in other countries, or are shunned as immoral or outmoded. The second set of questions that will be woven into the story concerns how Nigerian politicians and ordinary citizens have adopted domestic interests, identities, and institutions in response to the global challenges they face. The "interests" of Nigerian peoples can be assessed by asking the following questions: What are the major goals of politicians, businesses, civil associations, and ordinary citizens, and what strategies have they adopted to achieve them? The identities of Nigerians can be assessed by exploring the values, norms, ideological beliefs, and emotions that shape their worldviews most profoundly. Finally, we will analyze the institutions that have co-shaped the country's developmental path toward modernity by focusing on the authoritative rules of the political order, whether written or informal, and how they reward or punish particular sorts of behavior.

We then explore how particular configurations of interests, identities, and institutions have produced the various developmental paths by which Nigeria has tried to maintain its political, economic, military, and cultural standing within an ever-more technologically advanced and interconnected world. Have these developmental paths allowed the country to achieve significant power over rival nations in Africa, or have they led to outright failure or momentary success that later fell apart? The fourth section evaluates the "feedback effects" of these developmental paths on Nigeria's domestic interests, identities, and institutions. The analysis will explore whether the outcome has been positive or negative; who were the beneficiaries and challengers; and whether there has been radical change or maintenance of the status quo, and why. Finally, the chapter will evaluate the feedback effects on Nigeria's domestic politics, as well as on the global context of the country's developmental paths to the modern world. To what extent have Nigeria's international trade goods, its relations with its neighbors, or its overall behavior as an international actor shaped – positively or negatively – the environment in which other countries seek to advance their own interests, identities, and institutions?

We will utilize this framework to make sense of the historical and social origins of Nigeria today, beginning first with events that took place in the colonial period (1914–1960), in the period from independence to the fall of the First Republic and the Biafran war (1960–1970), and during the rise of "military federalism" and the petroleum economy – also known as the "curse of black gold" (1970–1979). The second set of events comprises developments that occurred during the Second Republic (1979–1983) and the era of military dictatorships, as well as a stillborn Third Republic (1983–1998) that followed the collapse of the Second Republic. The final set of events centers around the return to democracy since 1999, or what Nigerians call "The Fourth Republic." The chapter ends by exploring what became of these material interests, identities, and institutions during the unprecedented, unbroken fourteen years of electoral democracy that began in 1999, and how they have been affected by global developments.

The Global Context of Nigerian Politics and Government

Conquest and Colonialism: The Sources of Identity and Unity in Nigeria

In 2012, the National Population Commission estimated Nigeria's population at about 174 million people. One in five Africans is Nigerian; Nigerians speak more than 250 mutually unintelligible languages. Three of these ethno-linguistic groups, namely the Hausa-Fulani in the north, the Yoruba in the southwest, and the Igbo in the southeast, have dominated much of the country's political and economic life. Following the British abolition in 1807 of the transatlantic slave trade – the areas that form modern Nigeria supplied a substantial proportion of the estimated fifteen million Africans sold into slavery – their ancestors were brought under British colonial rule between 1861 and 1902. Colonialism was instituted through a combination of wars of conquest, treaties of "protection" between the British and besieged rulers and communities, and Christian missionary activities that sowed discord among the people. There were also conquest and control by British trading companies, especially the Royal Niger Company, which was granted a charter by the British Crown to administer the areas along the River Niger as its colony from 1886 until 1900. No matter how each community was brought under British rule, the process was driven by – and the state tradition that developed operated for – a mixture of commercial interests and booty seekers, as well as local participants and imperial interests in London who were also competing with their counterparts in other European countries. The colonial history of state-society relations that developed in response to these global and local forces has continued to shape political life in postcolonial Nigeria.

At the turn of the twentieth century, two separate colonies, the Colony of Lagos and Protectorate of Southern Nigeria (administered from Lagos) and the Protectorate of Northern Nigeria (administered from Kaduna) were firmly established. In 1914, the British brought the two colonies under one entity ruled by one governor (based in Lagos) in what is now known as the **"amalgamation"** of Northern and Southern Nigeria. These disparate ethnic groups and cultures were given the name "Nigeria" by an English woman, Flora Shaw, who later married the British officer, **Sir Frederick Lugard,** who supervised this amalgamation. Whereas most parts of the south had been under colonial rule only for barely a decade before this forced merger, thus lacking any sense of common political identity, much of the north had been ruled as a single colonial political entity for more than forty years – generating a high degree of political identity built upon the century-old **emirate political system**. Even then, the two colonies, now called provinces, each under a lieutenant governor, continued life as two separate administrative entities until 1947, thus ensuring that their historical, cultural, linguistic, and religious differences – mediated by colonial institutions and local and foreign interests – would play a pivotal (mostly negative) role in what would later become contemporary Nigeria. Not surprisingly, some Nigerians in frustration have continued to blame the "**mistake of 1914**" enforced by "the first evil genius," Lugard, for much of the country's checkered political history.

Another "mistake" introduced in 1903 was the **indirect rule system**, whereby the British ruled conquered territories through existing "traditional" or "natural" political institutions and sought to disrupt the extant local institutions as little as possible. Northern Nigeria was suited to this system of rule because of the centralized political system on which the emirates in the precolonial era had been based since 1804. The people, now British colonial subjects, hardly noticed any change, while the emirs and their palace officials and tributary chiefs continued with their daily functions except that they henceforth had to take instructions from the district officer – known as "the Crown on the ground" – and his handful of police, military officers, and court officials. Although this policy was successful in the north, quite a number of emirs refused to cooperate with Lugard's proclamation subjecting them under his rule, and they were promptly deposed and exiled from their territories. Indirect rule was also fairly successful in western Nigeria, where a variety of centralized monarchical political systems also predated colonial rule.

The east and southeast of Nigeria, the homeland of the Igbo and other minority ethnic groups, were more challenging because precolonial society in these areas was characterized by ritualized decentralized segmented political systems, often described erroneously by anthropologists as "stateless" or "acephalous" societies. These are the societies masterfully described in Chinua Achebe's classic novels, *Things Fall Apart* and *Arrow of God,* where there were generally no kings or chiefs with political authority and the all-male village assembly was the highest form of political organization. Consequently, the British imposed "**warrant chiefs**" in these areas to conform to the indirect-rule policies largely informed by their colonial experience in northern Nigeria, Uganda and India.

Colonial Legacies: Emerging Interests, Identities, and Institutions

The whole system of indirect rule quickly turned many of the new rulers – British and African – into tyrants acting on behalf of the colonial government and the emerging colonial economy. The colonial economy was export oriented, requiring immediate integration of peasants and the precolonial subsistence economy into the modern capitalist system through taxation and the commodification of land. This was accompanied by the development of modern systems of transportation and communication, especially railways and roads, to convey agricultural and mineral produce to the newly developed seaports at the coast for shipment to European factories. Inevitably, this gave rise to budding urban centers, largely segregated according to race in the south, but also divided along ethno-religious groups in the north.

Not only did **urbanization** create new interests and institutions, it also created cleavages between rural areas controlled by the "natural rulers" and the newly mobilized urban dwellers. Urbanization also brought Africans, who continued to retain links to their birth villages, into constant friction with entrenched European, Lebanese, and Indian commercial interests. The latter two groups had accompanied European colonialism to Africa as service providers and/or indentured servants, but never returned to their homelands, and were placed a notch above Africans in the colonial racial pecking order. Although their populations have gradually diminished over the years, more than a hundred years later the Lebanese and Indian populations have still not fully integrated into Nigerian society.

Perhaps the most lasting legacy of British colonialism in Nigeria was the introduction of an anomalous federal system of government in 1954 comprising the government at the center based in Lagos and three regional governments: Eastern, Northern, and Western. Not only was the Northern Region geographically larger than the two other regions combined, each region was also dominated economically and politically by one of the three largest ethnic groups – the Igbo in the east, the Hausa-Fulani in the north, and the Yoruba in the west. Each region was also identified with the three export products that became the mainstay of the Nigerian economy at the time: coal in the east, cocoa in the west, and peanuts (groundnuts) in the north. Most accounts of ethnicity have, for good reason, tended to focus on competition (often a divide-and-rule strategy instigated by the British) and cooperation among the trio of Hausa-Fulani, Yoruba, and Igbo. The heart of ethnicization of Nigerian politics, however, lies with the numerous minority groups in each region who since 1954 have continued to agitate against their "marginalization" and consequently for further state creation as a solution to their perceived right of self-determination. We shall return to this issue later in this chapter, but suffice to say that ethnicity or "tribalism" is a quintessential example of the interplay of global and domestic interests, identities, and institutions in the shaping of politics in contemporary Nigeria.

Nationalism and the Anticolonial Movement

British colonialism in Nigeria lasted anywhere from 60 to 100 years, depending on the date of each community's conquest and/or incorporation into the British Empire. Agitation against colonial rule, however, began in one form or another almost as soon as incorporation took place. The earlier forms of resistance, often referred to as "proto-nationalism," ranged from scattered peasant revolts to devastating wars, including the Benin massacre of 1897, and agitation by newly educated Nigerians for inclusion in the colonial governing structures and to be treated like the "civilized" Europeans. Some African merchants also protested against colonial laws and policies that discriminated against "natives" or that outlawed competition with European merchants. The colonial government and other European interests, however, undermined these putative nationalist risings through violence and time-tested divide-and-rule tactics that pitted one "tribal" or ethno-religious interest against the others – further setting the stage for the political salience of ethnic and religious identities in the country's later political development.

The relatively peaceful era of colonialism in Nigeria was jolted out of its slumber in the mid-1940s by the rise of militant anticolonial nationalism. The rise of urban centers attracted large numbers of migrants who, while retaining their ethno-religious identities, had begun to develop a common identity, especially against the racially discriminatory Europeans. This putative "national" identity was further sharpened by the founding of newspapers by indigenous Nigerians, especially the American-educated **Dr. Benjamin Nnamdi Azikiwe,** whose chain of newspapers became the mouthpiece of the movement. Dissatisfied with the "gentleman" politics of the extant elite and urban-based political parties in Lagos, Dr. Azikiwe in 1944 founded Nigeria's first truly national political party, the National Council of Nigeria and the Cameroons (NCNC).

The rise of labor unions in urban centers added more fodder to the anticolonial movement, particularly after the three-month civil service strike in 1945 that almost crippled the colonial government. As higher-educational opportunities widened and reached the urban and rural areas, Nigerian student unions and fledgling professional associations, both at home and overseas, provided additional pressure on the colonial government to quit. The return of hundreds of thousands of Nigerian ex-servicemen, many of whom had fought more gallantly in World War II than their white comrades in Europe, Africa, and Asia, further eroded the myth of white supremacy and the white man's entitlement to rule over the native. Internationally, the 1945 Pan-African Congress in Manchester, England, which was attended by many home-based Nigerian politicians and students, called on Africans to go back to their respective countries and demand "independence now." The independence of India and Pakistan from Britain in 1947 further whetted the appetite of the agitators and made them more impatient with British rule.

Britain, now severely weakened by World War II, responded by investing the huge reserves accumulated by colonial Nigeria during the war into public infrastructure, social welfare, and education. A new constitution, which created the three regions, was introduced in 1947, but was denounced by the nationalists almost immediately. It was replaced by another one in 1951, which for the first time created a federal structure of government in Nigeria, ostensibly to allow each region to develop politically and economically at its own pace. This arrangement would later not only exacerbate the differential impact of modernization in the north and the south, but also lay the foundation for the creation of new ethno-geographic identities, which have since become overlaid with preexisting ones. The nationalists pushed ahead with their demand for an end to British rule, making often damaging compromises along the way to ensure that the ultimate end was achieved – especially after Dr. Kwame Nkrumah's Ghana upstaged Nigeria in 1957 to become sub-Saharan Africa's first country to become independent.

As part of its colonial disengagement plans, the British granted self-government to the Eastern and Western Nigerian regions in 1957, with the Northern Region following in 1959. On October 1, 1960, Nigeria became an independent country, with a central government that was structurally and administratively weaker than the three regional governments, saddled with the task of building a new nation in an increasingly complex and diverse society. The 1960 constitution created a legal system that conferred all residual legislative powers to the regions and put twenty-eight items of governance on the concurrent list, subject only to the paramount rule of federal law in case of any conflict of interest with regional law. The federal government had exclusive competence in a very restricted list of forty-four subjects of a fiscal or semi-technical nature, including the politically sensitive areas of defense, emergency powers over regions, and foreign relations.

It is worth noting also that, unlike other countries at independence, Nigeria's most powerful and experienced indigenous politicians and administrators either preferred to remain as premiers in the regions – for example, Chief **Obafemi Awolowo**, the leader of the **Action Group** (AG) party in the west and Sir **Ahmadu Bello**, the leader of the **Northern People's Congress** (NPC) in the north – or were prevented from doing otherwise, while the central government machinery was led by less competent subordinates and officials. The only exception was Dr. Azikiwe, arguably the foremost nationalist and the founder of the NCNC, who gave up the premier's position in the east to one of his subordinates in order to take up the ceremonial post of governor-general and, ironically, representative of the British Crown in Nigeria. When Nigeria became a republic in 1963, Dr. Azikiwe became president of the Federal Republic of Nigeria, but his functions remained unchanged. This institutional arrangement became a source of friction a few years later between Azikiwe and the prime minister, Sir Abubakar Tafawa Balewa– a northerner and NPC lieutenant, and the actual power holder.

From Independence to the Fall of the First Republic

Federalism and the Quest for Unity in Diversity

Nigeria entered postcolonial life with an explicitly federal constitution accepted by the political class as the only guarantee of "unity in diversity." However, there was little agreement among the founding fathers of modern Nigeria on what exactly they were founding. At the 1958 constitutional conference in London, the leader of the NCNC, Dr. Azikiwe, reportedly called on the delegates to "forget our differences" and focus on the issues that would help forge a common identity for a future Nigeria. In reply, Ahmadu Bello, the NPC leader, contended that it was dangerous to forget Nigerians' differences; instead, the conference should highlight these different identities as the foundation for forging an independent multinational Nigerian state. In fact, until the military intervention that proscribed all political parties in 1966, the NPC made no pretentions to represent any other interests beyond those of the Northern Region. It was simply a "northern" peoples' party. Until his death in 1986, the leader of the AG and premier of the Western Region in the First Republic, Dr. Awolowo, unabashedly stated in his autobiography and elsewhere that he was "first a Yoruba before being a Nigerian" and that Nigeria was "a mere geographical expression." Not surprisingly, the quest for a social consensus on what constitutes the Nigerian nation and what form its statehood should take has continued to be ever more elusive for subsequent generations of Nigerians.

Although **federalism** resolved many of the political questions arising from the country's competing ethno-religious and economic interests and identities, it created many more and even exacerbated existing ones. On the positive side, by allowing considerable devolution of power to the three regions (increased to four in 1963), the three major ethnic groups and their various minority compatriots were not only able to manage their differences, but also actually engaged in a healthy competition that led to real accomplishments in agriculture, education, social development, and public infrastructure. The availability of more lucrative opportunities in the regions also restrained the ambitions of many local politicians and led to a rapid growth in the number of professional and technocratic cadres of managers and administrators, more than in any other African country in the first few years of independence. Since then, each major constitutional revision (in 1963, 1979, 1989, 1999, and the ongoing national constitutional conference of 2014) has maintained the sanctity of this power-sharing arrangement.

Ethnicity, Patronage Politics, and Party Politics

The federal imperative arises from the fact that Nigeria's 250–350 ethnic groups, with their distinct cultural characteristics and largely mutually unintelligible languages, are geographically separated. Almost anyone with a passing knowledge of Nigeria would be familiar with the main "tripod" – Hausa-Fulani, Igbo, and Yoruba – which are unquestionably the most numerous and most influential groups in the country's politics. There are, however, several politically and economically powerful smaller ethnic groups, as well as national-level minorities who constitute dominant ethnic groups in their own states.

Until 1947, the colonial government and the colonial economy had unwittingly encouraged the migration of southern Nigerians into other parts of the country through the expansion of roads, railways, the colonial civil service, and the rise of urban centers. Migrants into these new urban centers formed numerous cultural and "hometown" associations that helped them maintain ties to their "traditional" ethnic group's homeland, and also provided an anchor and source of help to newly arrived co-ethnics. Yet, despite the continuing separation of ethnic groups, some sense of "one Nigeria" was actually developing, as evidenced by the election of a Hausa mayor for Enugu in the Igbo east, the Igbo Azikiwe's political successes in the Yoruba west, the large and influential Yoruba residents in Kaduna in the Hausa-Fulani north, and the prominent role of some northerners such as Said Zungur in the Igbo-dominated Zikist Movement (youth arm of the NCNC). However, the trend toward a politically homogeneous country and common citizenship was halted with the introduction of the **Richards Constitution** in 1948 (named after Sir Arthur Richards, Lord Milverton, the colonial governor). This constitution split the country into three regions – the Northern Region, dominated by the Hausa-Fulani; the Western Region, dominated by the Yoruba; and the Eastern Region, dominated by the Igbo – even as the country continued to operate a unitary system of government.

The Richards Constitution also introduced a legislative council for the "natives" in Lagos in which representation was to be based on political parties. The previous all-white legislative council had been gradually opened up earlier to a few "civilized natives," giving rise to Nigeria's first political party: the Nigerian Democratic Party, founded by Herbert Macaulay, who often competes for the title of "father of Nigerian nationalism" with Dr. Azikiwe. The imperatives of nationwide party representation in the new council quickly led to the transformation of some of the larger cultural associations into mass political parties. With the exception of Azikiwe's NCNC, formed in 1944 with a multiethnic membership and hence more fully "nationalistic," the other parties that emerged were largely ethnic-based mass movements led by charismatic ethnic identity brokers. The Action Group (AG), which would later dominate politics in the west, emerged from the Yoruba cultural association *Egbe Omo Oduduwa*. The Northern People's Congress (NPC), the regional and exclusionist outlook of which could not be mistaken, simply mutated from *Jamiyaa Mutanem Arewa*, the cultural association dominated by the Hausa-Fulani and especially by the princes of the emirates conquered by Captain Lugard in 1886. Minority groups similarly formed their own political parties, such as the radical Northern Elements Progressive Union (NEPU) representing the indigenous minority groups in the north; the United Middle Belt Congress in the central Benue-Plateau region; and the Independent Party and Mid-West Union representing minority groups in the east and west, respectively.

This more divisive form of ethnic identity mobilization spilled over into economic and social life as Nigerians sought and competed for opportunities in education, employment in the civil service and the fledgling private sector, and even residential sites. The Yoruba were initially most favored to compete in the emerging economic and political order, given their longer experience with Westernization (especially in the educational sphere) dating back to 1861, when the Crown Colony of Lagos was formally incorporated into the British Empire. Within a few decades, the Igbo, who were formally conquered in 1902, quickly caught up with the Yoruba, igniting an often vicious interethnic competition involving stereotypes and mutual suspicions between the two groups that persist to this day. The north, which had agreed with Lugard to bar the entry of Christian missionaries into the region – ostensibly to minimize what the Hausa-Fulani elites considered the corrupting influence of the West – continued to lag behind other regions, further triggering a northern fear and resentment about "southern domination" that has continued to define north-south relations for most of the country's history. Ethnic considerations also influenced recruitment into the armed and security forces as well as the bureaucracy, as the country pursued an "Africanization" policy to fast-track Nigerians into positions of authority vacated by the departing colonialists.

The introduction of a federal constitution and granting of executive and legislative powers to regions dominated by the three major ethnic groups in 1954 further cemented this geographical separation in the ethnic identity of Nigerians. Ethnicity finally crept into the anticolonial movement, splitting northern and southern leaders. The north, fearing complete domination by the south in an independent Nigeria, wanted a slower process of decolonization, while the west and the east wanted "independence now" as recommended by the 1945 Pan-African Congress in Manchester, England. A "premature" motion for independence by southern politicians in the colonial legislature led to the infamous Kano Riots of 1954, in which hundreds of southerners (mostly Igbo) were killed and "stranger" properties were burned and looted.

At independence, therefore, Nigeria was a deeply divided country that truly needed "unity in diversity" if the entity described by the leader of the Action Group as "a mere geographical expression" were to survive at all. The Northern Region's main political party, the NPC, made little effort to expand its reach into other regions – not surprisingly, given its exclusivist self-definition. In order to govern, however, the NPC needed the support of the dominant party in either the west or the east. Meanwhile, instead of uniting to defeat the NPC (which would probably have ended the federation), the NCNC and the AG focused primarily on exploiting ethnic minority resentment in each other's regions to enable them to acquire enough political power to form a government with the NPC – which enjoyed a solid power base that was hardly dented by the north's much weaker ethnic minority parties.

In 1960, the NCNC, with its predominantly Igbo leadership but also a multiethnic following, allied with the NPC, shutting out the Yoruba from the new government and further exacerbating Igbo-Yoruba rivalry and mutual suspicion. Alhaji Abubakar Tafawa Balewa of the NPC became the federal prime minister, while NCNC's Dr. Azikiwe settled for the ceremonial office of governor-general – formally representing the British monarch, which was a very odd irony for the acclaimed "father of Nigerian nationalism." Azikiwe's title was later changed to "president" when Nigeria became a republic in 1963. The exclusion of the AG – and hence, of the Yoruba ethnic group – from the new national government led to an AG revolt. This was eagerly exploited by the NPC-NCNC alliance, who quickly declared a state of emergency in the Western Region that removed Awolowo and the AG from power.

By 1964, the "marriage of convenience" between the Igbo-dominated NCNC and the NPC had collapsed, with the latter engineering a split in the AG and forming a new governing alliance with an AG splinter group called the Nigerian National Democratic Party (NNDP). Meanwhile, a disputed national census conducted in 1963 that estimated the Northern Region at more than half of the country's population had raised ethnic tensions to the boiling point, while massive rigging of the 1965 federal elections, especially in the Western Region, resulted in protracted violence. An aloof NPC/NNDP federal government ignored calls to declare emergency rule in the west and stem the tide of violence gripping the country; instead, it focused its attention on hosting a Commonwealth Heads of Government summit that year. Elite compromises to capture political power had also left wide gaps in political authority, encouraging massive corruption and misuse of public funds by politicians. Government corruption became so blatant that the name of the federal finance minister at the time, Chief Festus Okotie-Eboh, became synonymous with financial corruption in Nigeria. Corruption was also common at the regional level.

Military Intervention and the Biafran War of Secession

The single most important institution that has co-shaped Nigeria's developmental path to the modern world is the Nigerian military, especially the Nigerian Army, through a range of formal and informal authoritative rules of the political order they created, and how these rules rewarded or punished particular sorts of behavior. This process began on January 15, 1966 when Nigeria's First Republic was ended by a military coup d'état– coincidentally a mere few weeks following the publication of Chinua Achebe's third novel, *A Man of the People,* in December 1965, in which an irredeemably corrupt African regime was sacked by the military. The real coup, led by five army majors, all but one of whom was Igbo, resulted in the death of the federal prime minister (a northerner), the Northern Region premier, the federal finance minister, and a number of senior army officers of northern and western origin, and only two Igbo army officers. No Igbo or eastern senior politician was killed or arrested, while the president, Dr. Azikiwe (an Igbo) had left the country for a medical checkup overseas shortly before the coup. The indiscipline among the coup-plotters, especially those assigned to carry out the operation in the Eastern Region and in the west, caused it to quickly collapse. The general officer commanding (GOC) the Nigerian Army, **Major General Aguiyi-Ironsi**, an Igbo who himself had been targeted for elimination, was able to mobilize troops and negotiate an end to the coup with the leader of the group, Major Chukwuma Kaduna Nzeogwu, after three days.

Instead of reconstituting the shattered civilian government, General Ironsi and his advisers, motivated by the need to first "restore order within the shortest possible time," went ahead and established a military government led by a Supreme Military Council (SMC), supported by a Federal Executive Council of military and civilian appointees and military governors for each of the four regions. Another similarity with *A Man of the People* was the wild celebration and dancing in the streets all over the country by Nigerians, relieved that Major Nzeogwu and his coconspirators – who had become instant national heroes, although less so in the north – had ended the menacing rule of the corrupt and insensitive politicians who had seemed untouchable before the coup. The celebration quickly turned into a nightmare, as the military stayed in power for the next twenty-nine years – interrupted only briefly by the Second Republic from 1979 to 1983 – thus turning Nigeria into a coup-prone, politically unstable country.

Contrary to the assertion that the first coup was an "Igbo coup" intended to allegedly foist Igbo domination on the rest of the country, the putschists claimed to have been motivated purely by patriotism to end corruption, restore integrity to government, and maintain national stability. Recent accounts by one of the surviving perpetrators and by their military contemporaries have lent credence to this claim. In 2007, the private secretary to Chief Awolowo, jailed leader of the AG, made the startling revelation that the coup plotters had intended to release Awolowo from prison and make him prime minister, whether or not he liked it, as he had seemed amenable to their inchoate socialist rhetoric. However, in the ethnically poisoned atmosphere of the early 1960s, the plotters' motives were overshadowed by the deep cleavages among the political class at the time. The suspicion that the coup was simply an Igbo plot to dominate the country was compounded by the ethnic composition of the coup-plot victims and by the fact that General Ironsi, the head of the SMC, himself was Igbo. Ironsi's government did not help matters either when it enacted **Decree no. 34 of 1966,** unifying the federal bureaucracy and police forces and providing further ammunition to those alleging an Igbo conspiracy.

The unification decree, more than the coup itself, undermined the most important elite pact, federalism, which had managed to keep the country together even as it had militated against genuine nation building. On July 29, 1966, General Ironsi and several Igbo army officers were killed in a countercoup led by officers of northern origin, who installed Lt. Col. Yakubu Gowon – General Ironsi's Chief of Staff, who had several times denied rumors of the coup to his principal – as the head of the SMC and commander in chief of the Armed Forces of Nigeria. After initially flirting with the idea of supporting the Northern Region's secession from the federation, Gowon quickly retraced his steps at the urging of the British High Commissioner in Lagos, and declared his commitment to "one Nigeria."

The countercoup was followed by a **pogrom** that resulted in the deaths of more than 10,000 eastern civilians, mostly Igbos living in northern Nigeria. Scores of Igbo army officers were also killed by their military colleagues, who had joined or led hordes of cheering northerners as they went on a house-to-house hunt for their innocent victims. Another even more deadly pogrom occurred three months later – despite assurances by the federal government about the safety of all Nigerians in all parts of the country, which had encouraged many easterners to return to their places of residence in other parts of the country. This put the total number of deaths in what amounted to genocide against Igbo civilians that year at more than 100,000, including more than 200 Igbo army officers. There were also numerous reports of rape of Igbo women and the looting and destruction of Igbo property. The Eastern Region government subsequently asked all easterners living in other parts of Nigeria to return to the east, as the federal and other regional governments could no longer guarantee their safety. Other Nigerians also now left the Eastern Region, but the effects of this migration paled in significance compared to the misery and political tension generated by the mass exodus of Igbos to the east.

Tensions flared further as the Igbo military governor of Eastern Nigeria, Lt. Col. Chukwuemeka Odumegwu Ojukwu, refused to accept the legitimacy of Lt. Col. Gowon and the government that replaced General Ironsi, arguing that Gowon was not the most senior officer in rank to replace the slain head of state. Negotiations by military and civilian leaders of all the regions and mediation efforts by foreigners failed to produce an acceptable elite pact to reunify the country.

On May 27, 1967, the federal government – now led by Yoruba, Hausa-Fulani, and Middle Belt elites who were determined to finally end Igbo domination of politics in the east and to preempt a rumored secession by the Eastern Region – divided the country into twelve states, three of which emerged from the old Eastern Region, and confining the Igbo to just one landlocked state. The Eastern regional government responded on May 30, 1967, by declaring its territory "**the Sovereign Independent Republic of Biafra.**" The following week, Gowon ordered federal forces to initiate "police action" in the breakaway region. This quickly escalated into a thirty-month civil war, pitting ill-equipped but determined Biafrans against better-trained and well-equipped federal forces, internationally supported by the United Kingdom and the USSR. Only four mostly inconsequential countries – Côte d'Ivoire, Haiti, Tanzania, and Trinidad and Tobago – recognized the Biafran state. The war, which ended on January 12, 1970, with the Biafran surrender, is generally acclaimed to be one of the most devastating civil wars of the twentieth century. It caused more than two million Biafran deaths – mostly children – from starvation, because the Nigerian government refused to lift its embargo on relief materials supplies getting to rebel-held territories. It is worth noting that even if one assumes (without necessarily conceding) that the first coup was indeed an Igbo coup, none of the subsequent coups, attempted coups, and even transitions from military to civilian regimes were undertaken for "national" reasons. Instead, as the remainder of this chapter will show, sectional forces simply took over and foisted their narrow interests upon the rest of the country, while claiming that these were "national" interests.

Military Rule, Prebendalism, and the "Curse of Black Gold" (1970–1979)

One of the themes this chapter seeks to explore is the mainstay of Nigeria's economy, whether its economy is globally competitive and self-sufficient, and the extent to which the political order, interacting with the global order, has shaped the economy and vice versa. The contradictions of the colonial economy were complicated by a military regime that further entrenched a corrupt political culture fuelled by easy money from petroleum. Starting from 1966, the new military regime sacked the legislature and abolished the 1963 constitution and began ruling by decree. The political instability and the Biafran civil war quickly led to a militarization of the economy, as much of the national effort was devoted to prosecuting the war. Following the Biafran surrender in 1970, the government declared an official policy of "no victor, no vanquished" and embarked on a policy of "reconciliation, reconstruction, and rehabilitation" – the three *R*s, as they came to be called. Its haphazard and sometimes insincere implementation notwithstanding, the military government's three *R*s policy largely succeeded, with the east (now broken up into three states) quickly recovering. The government adopted a number of measures to encourage civic education and the absorption of some Igbo and other easterners who had been dislocated by the civil war.

Given that all policies emanated from the SMC in Lagos, and state governors were appointees and lower-ranking officers of the regime, it was inevitable that centralization would undermine the federal foundation of the country. Thus the irony of military rule in Nigeria was that the Gowon regime in essence did implement Decree no. 34 of 1966, for which General Ironsi had been deposed and assassinated and over 100,000 Igbos slaughtered in the infamous pogroms that followed. Schools, universities, and budgets were increasingly centralized. Civil service rules also became centralized, while regional police forces were abolished. Consequently, large numbers of bureaucrats in the regional and state governments joined the federal civil service, which had grown tremendously.

The mainstay of what some observers have termed Nigeria's "military federalism" was the sudden infusion of oil money – otherwise known as the "oil boom" – which had become the source of approximately 90 percent of national revenue by 1979. Although petroleum was first discovered in Oloibiri in the Niger Delta in 1958, it was not a prominent feature of the economy during the First Republic. Moreover, the civil war from 1967 to 1970 had stopped all exports. The war's end, however, coincided with a number of developments in the international arena – especially the 1973 Yom Kippur war between Israel and its Arab neighbors and the Iranian Revolution of 1979 – that drove the price of oil to as high as $39 per barrel. Consequently, the revenue accruing to the Nigerian government grew so dramatically that the head of state, General Gowon, actually claimed that Nigeria's biggest problem was what to do with its money. The oil boom triggered a spending spree that saw Nigerians importing all manner of goods from all over the world, in addition to launching several capital projects back home. The oil boom, with its massive infusion of wealth in the cities, also accelerated population migration from rural to the urban areas, increasing the country's rate of urbanization from 20 percent of the population in 1970 to 39 percent by the end of the 1980s.

With the oil boom also came massive corruption, complacency, and a further decline of political legitimacy. The military regime that had prosecuted the war and had initially done a laudable job of reintegrating the country now lost its focus and reneged on its promise to hand over power to civilians in 1976. Nigeria seemed to have caught the bug of frequent military incursions into politics found in many other African countries, with most of the military rulers either declaring themselves "presidents for life" or changing into civilian garb and legitimizing their authoritarian rule through sham elections. The oil bonanza, which might have accelerated sustainable economic development under more effective management, instead became a "resource curse."

We asked at the beginning of the chapter whether Nigeria's developmental path has allowed the country to achieve significant power over rival nations in Africa, or whether it has led to outright failure or momentary success that later fell apart. With lots of petrodollars at its disposal, the military regime threw its weight around as the "big brother" in Africa and even challenged great powers and the superpowers on African issues such as the independence of Angola in 1975, the apartheid regime in South Africa, and the white minority regime in Rhodesia (now Zimbabwe). Several African countries benefited from Nigeria's concessional oil supplies; anticolonial liberation movements received financial and diplomatic support; and the military regimes often bankrolled regional integration initiatives such as the Economic Community of West African States (ECOWAS), founded in 1975. Through these activist foreign policy measures, the military was able to rekindle a high degree of self-confidence and patriotism – and sometimes arrogance – in most Nigerians of that generation. Yet the national planners and the military regime during this period failed not only to invest in productive activities but also to anticipate the impending collapse of the world price of oil as they prepared to exit the political scene in 1979. Even in the field of education, where they initially achieved tremendous successes, a lack of resources, infrastructure, and instructors at all levels nearly crippled the educational system, and the government had little choice but to massively import personnel from anywhere in the world to enable it to implement a hastily introduced Universal Primary Education (UPE) program.

The Mixed Economy

Emboldened nationalism and patriotism also manifested in the domestic economy as Nigeria's post–civil war rulers sought to minimize the vestiges of neocolonialism and the dependence of the Nigerian economy on the multinational corporations (MNCs) and other businesses that were part of the colonial system. The Second National Development Plan (1972–1975) was based on the import-substitution industrialization model; this sought to create a mixed economy whereby the private sector would exist side by side with government control over the "commanding heights of the economy." The indigenous private sector was considered either too weak to engage the MNCs, or too profit driven to lead the nationalist quest for rapid economic development, without state support.

By the late 1970s, several capital projects such as the Ajaokuta Steel Mill and four other steel rolling mills were planned or constructed. The government created, single-handedly or in joint ventures with MNCs, scores of state-owned enterprises (SOEs) in the banking, insurance, transportation, manufacturing, and construction sectors. Massive sums were invested in creating fifteen River Basin Development Authorities as the foundation for the takeoff of mechanized agriculture. Investments in the national electricity grid, telephone and telegraph systems, and seaport development increased. Symbols and trappings of nationhood such as Nigeria Airways, the Nigerian National Shipping Lines, the Nigerian National Petroleum Corporation (NNPC), new national producers of fertilizer and newsprint, and even manufactured food distribution outlets constituted part of the "commanding heights" of the economy – now under complete government control or indirectly controlled through joint ventures.

The government also tried to foster the rise of an indigenous entrepreneurial class, which had been hindered during and after colonial rule by the activities of MNCs and Lebanese, Syrian, and Indian businesses. In 1972, the government introduced the **Nigerian Indigenization Policy Decree,** reserving certain sectors of the economy for local businesses, whereas other enterprises had to be joint ventures either with local businesses or the government. Foreign-owned banks, insurance companies, manufacturing concerns, and retail companies in all sectors were compelled to sell their shares to Nigerians, while the government provided investment loans to enable indigenous Nigerians to purchase such shares.

Perhaps the most enduring consequence of the indigenization policy was the politicization of Nigerian capitalism, in that one section of the country, the Yoruba, benefited the most from corporate divestiture and government loan programs. The Hausa-Fulani had political power and controlled the military, but still lacked economic power, having yet to recover from the impact of differential economic development related to the historical north-south divide. The worst hit were the Igbos, many of whom were still recovering from the aftermath of the civil war.

By the time the military retreated to their barracks temporarily in 1979, the southwest of Nigeria was so firmly in control of the Nigerian economy that one northern sociologist contended that about 80 percent of the amount of any contract awarded anywhere in Nigeria would be circulating between Ibadan and Lagos within two weeks of its signing. Although some aspects of the mixed-economy policy did expand the level of industrialization in the country, the strategy actually crowded out the indigenous private sector and largely became a conduit for capital accumulation by the political elite. The resulting state-society relations have been described as **prebendalism,** defined as a form of corruption whereby state offices are regarded as a form of patronage given by an official or a ruler to individual clients in return for their loyalty, and used to generate material benefits for the officeholders, their constituents, and kin. Overall, such prebendalism has created a sense of entitlement in many people in Nigeria. Elected officials, government workers, and members of the ethnic and religious groups to which they belong all feel they have a right to a share of government revenues.

The Second Republic (1979–1983)

A combination of global and domestic forces continued to shape Nigeria's development path and its relations with its neighbors and the rest of the world in the Second Republic, which was inaugurated when the military returned to the barracks in 1979. A new U.S.-style presidential constitution was drawn up, ostensibly to avoid the "mistakes of the past." The Westminster parliamentary system of government and its winner-take-all nature was said to be unsuitable for a divided society such as Nigeria, where no political party was capable of winning a majority and where ruling coalitions were largely unstable. The 1979 constitution enshrined complete separation of powers among the three arms of government: a strong executive headed by a popularly elected president, who was limited to only two terms; a dual chamber legislature made up of the Senate (representing the states) and House of Representatives, both popularly elected; and the judiciary, which would be appointed by state or federal chief executives and approved by the legislature.

In striving to create "genuine and truly national political parties," as opposed to the regional and culturally based parties in the First Republic, the new constitution stipulated that support for candidates for president must reflect the "federal character" of Nigeria.

Specifically, candidates for president must win a majority of the total votes plus at least 25 percent of the votes cast in each of at least two-thirds of the now nineteen states of the federation. Elections became a national function implemented by a Federal Election Commission (FEDECO), which also was given the authority to register only those political parties that meet the "federal character" test, that is, two-thirds of the states must be represented in the party leadership and membership. Governments at the state level would be led by elected governors, single chamber legislatures known as Houses of Assembly, and a judiciary appointed by the governor with legislative approval. Local government councils were recognized in the constitution as "the third tier" of governmental power, with guaranteed revenue but still subject to supervision by the state governments.

Political parties were again made legal in 1978. Nigeria's political class responded like hungry lions and founded about 150 political parties, but in the end, the military regime registered only five of them. Yet the ghost of the First Republic hung over the transition and re-created old problems in new guises. The National Party of Nigeria (NPN) was led by Alhaji Shehu Shagari and scions of the NPC, supported by leaders of the United Middle Belt Congress founded in the First Republic to resist Hausa-Fulani internal colonialism over non-Muslim parts of the northern Nigeria. The Nigerian People's Party (NPP) was led by Azikiwe and his former NCNC stalwarts, along with a section of the anti–Hausa-Fulani middle belt. The Unity Party of Nigeria (UPN) simply reconstructed Awolowo's Action Group. The Great Nigeria People's Party (GNPP) was a breakaway faction from NPP. Finally, the People's Redemption Party (PRP) brought together radicals from the banned Northern Elements Political Union, led by the highly revered and indomitable Mallam Aminu Kano, which had traditionally represented the poor indigenous communities against the NPC elite. An additional grouping, the Nigerian Advance Party (NAP), was a later addition led by an alliance of labor and pseudo-socialist activists, perhaps to play the old game of countering the influence of Chief Awolowo in the west.

In the presidential elections of 1979, the NPN's Shagari emerged as the victor, barely winning at least 25 percent of the votes in twelve of the states. Despite the controversy over the meaning of "two-thirds of 19 states" (eventually resolved by the Supreme Court) and allegations that it was favored by the departing military regime, the NPN was the only true "national" party among the five that were officially registered, winning five states in the north and three in the southeast – and thereby complicating the ethno-religious formations that reemerged in the Second Republic. The UPN dominated five states (all in the Yoruba southwest and the old Midwest Region); NPP carried the two Igbo states and one in the central-middle belt; Aminu Kano's PRP won Kano (his home state), while a PRP governor won in an NPN-dominated legislature in neighboring Kaduna state; the GNPP won two, while the NAP failed to win any states. At the national level, the NPN – which failed to win a majority in the National Assembly – formed a governing alliance with the NPP that, as in the First Republic, broke down very quickly.

Despite early warnings about the country's dwindling revenue from oil, the civilian leadership of the Second Republic behaved as if they had learned nothing from the country's tragic past and continued the departing military regime's profligate spending and lack of proper economic planning. With declining oil output and revenues, the Shagari administration was forced to borrow about $2.8 billion from the IMF to cover the country's foreign debt, followed by halfhearted **austerity measures** to curtail public spending. Even these measures were undone by the 1983 general elections, in which the NPN-led government did everything it could to win, especially in NPP and UPN strongholds in the east and west, respectively. There were accusations of massive vote-rigging and election violence, even as corruption and brazen flaunting of ill-gotten wealth became the hallmark of the regime.

President Shagari was generally perceived as inept and incapable of controlling the excesses of his subordinates. The old demons of ethnic and sectarian violence reappeared, while the powerful influence of patron-client networks characterized daily political life, making it extremely difficult for the government to address the urgent issues that faced the country.

The Return of Military Dictatorships and "Transition without End" (1983–1998)

President Shagari's 1983 re-election victory was short-lived. On December 31 of that year, the government was deposed in a coup led by Major General Muhammadu Buhari, a Northern Fulani infantry officer, launching the country into another round of military dictatorship that ended only sixteen years later in 1999. General Buhari and his deputy, Major General Tunde Idiagbon – also a Muslim from north-central Nigeria – rode on the crest of nationalist resentments against Nigeria's acceptance of the structural adjustment program (SAP) imposed on Nigeria by the IMF, and they promptly broke off negotiations with the organization. Like previous military regimes, Buhari sacked the civilian government and legislature and incarcerated many politicians accused of corruption and ruining the economy.

In 1985, General Ibrahim Babangida, Buhari's chief of army staff, deposed him in a palace coup, purportedly for Buhari's "high-handedness" and human rights violations, but actually to forestall Babangida's forced retirement by Buhari. Babangida, who took on the title of president, moved quickly to allow Nigerians to "democratically" decide whether to accept further loans – and therefore continued structural adjustment – from the IMF. More important, Babangida promised a quick return to civilian rule, an issue on which General Buhari had been noncommittal. A national "great debate" soon ensued over the IMF structural adjustment program, and in the end Babangida declared that Nigerians had decided to implement SAP without recourse to IMF loans. This set Nigeria on an ill-conceived economic reform program characterized by public-sector layoffs, privatization of state-owned enterprises, and a massive devaluation of the local currency that impoverished millions of Nigerians overnight.

In 1992, the regime created and funded two political parties to which all politicians were compelled to belong. One of them, the Social Democratic Party (SDP), was supposedly "a little to the Left" while the other, the National Republican Convention (NRC) was "a little to the Right." The forced two-party system was an ill-conceived contraption devised by Babangida to use nonexistent ideological or class identities to defuse the ethnic and sectarian forms of political mobilization that Nigerian politicians had allegedly failed to eschew. The NRC selected as its presidential candidate Chief Moshood K. Abiola, a Yoruba multibillionaire business mogul and friend of various military officers and regimes, while SDP selected another Muslim, Alhaji Ibrahim Tofa from Kano State in the north, as its flag-bearer.

Babangida's two-party system seemed at first to have succeeded. The June 12, 1993, election (**June 12** hereafter) fought by the two parties sanctioned by the Babangida regime was judged to be the fairest and freest in the history of Nigeria. The 1993 elections demonstrated the capacity of the Nigerian voter to rise above ethnic and religious identities. The two presidential candidates were both Muslims, and Chief Abiola won across ethnic, religious, gender, and class lines in all zones – even beating his opponent in his own ward in Kano. Press reports even claimed that a majority of junior military officers had voted for the Yoruba politician in the election. However, after several days of delay in announcing the results and heightened apprehension across the country, the military government annulled the result, popularly believed to have been won by Abiola.

Following the annulment, Babangida "stepped aside" in August 1993 and appointed an Interim National Government led by Chief Ernest Shonekan, a Yoruba businessman, although power actually lay with **General Sani Abacha**, the chief of defense staff. Shonekan was not only shunned by his Yoruba co-ethnics, he also had virtually no support across the country, let alone from the rest of the world. It was therefore relatively easy for General Abacha to push him out in November 1993, and thus began the story of the most brutal and brazenly corrupt military dictatorship Nigerians had yet experienced. On June 12, 1994, the anniversary of the annulled 1993 election, Chief Abiola declared himself president, having exhausted his patience waiting for Abacha's duplicitous promise to grant Abiola the presidency; it was on the basis of that promise that Abiola and several Yoruba pro-democracy activists had allegedly supported Shonekan's removal from office. On June 23, Abacha arrested Abiola, charged him with three counts of treason, and placed him in prison, where he died in 1998.

With the presumed winner of the 1993 elections out of the way, General Abacha, who had been central to the two preceding military regimes, took Babangida's political trickery and Machiavellian tactics to unprecedented levels. The regime was, however, now buffeted by a more vocal civil society, mobilized to pressure the government to restore the June 12 mandate to Abiola. In July 1994, the National Union of Petroleum and Gas Workers (NUPENG) and the Petroleum and Natural Gas Senior Staff Association (PENGASSAN) embarked on strike actions that paralyzed the country. Abacha promptly arrested Frank Kokori, secretary of NUPENG, and forced most members of the two associations back to work. University faculty, staff, and students became more vocal, and many campuses were shut down for months, with armored personnel carriers guarding every entrance point to the most riot-prone campuses. The Nigerian Labor Congress and its seventeen affiliates, including local government employee unions and the Nigerian Association of Resident Doctors, all had running battles with the military during this period. General Abacha's biggest headache, however, was human rights and pro-democracy groups, such as the National Democratic Coalition (NADECO), the Campaign for Democracy (CD), and the Constitutional Rights Project. Their international connections and affiliations with global civil society groups rankled the regime, but their effectiveness was limited because of their unrepresentative ethnic, urban-based, and middle- and upper-class composition and, ironically, their nondemocratic and often authoritarian leadership – a contradiction that the regime eagerly exploited to the fullest.

The single most important action that sealed Abacha's reign in infamy was his execution of writer and environmental activist Ken Saro-Wiwa and eight other Ogoni activists in November 1995, for allegedly ordering the murder of four Ogoni chiefs in 1994. Saro-Wiwa was the founder of the **Movement for the Survival of Ogoni People (MOSOP)**, which campaigned against the environmental degradation caused by oil drilling by Shell Petroleum Development Corporation (SPDC), from which the 500,000 Ogoni people had derived few economic benefits. Saro-Wiwa and eight other Ogoni activists were convicted by a kangaroo military court in October 1995, and despite last minute pleas for clemency by world leaders, including South Africa's Nelson Mandela, Abacha had them hanged in November of that year. Not only would Abacha never recover from the international opprobrium this action earned him, but the killing of the Ogoni Nine in turn galvanized other Niger Delta communities to rise up against the government and oil companies – and at times against one another – making this the most intractable ethnic mobilization problem Nigeria had faced since independence.

Moreover, by the time he died in 1998, Abacha had joined the league of Africa's most kleptocratic dictators, having stolen more than $6 billion from the national treasury, which he stashed away in banks in Switzerland, France, the United Kingdom, and the United States. His family's business empire reached into every sector of the Nigerian economy, from petroleum and banks to construction companies and choice government real estate.

Ironically, the most enduring legacy of the Abacha dictatorship is the strong endorsement given to the concept of "zoning" of political offices at all levels of government by his carefully selected Constitutional Conference in 1995. The idea of zoning was to divide up the country's states and political offices by six geographic zones that did not coincide with ethnic groups, thereby strengthening federalism and weakening ethnicity as a factor in politics.

For Abacha, the seemingly intractable nature of Nigeria's ethnic divisions and the added mistrust injected into the polity by the June 12 saga – along with new speculations of secession by the Yoruba ethnic group – highlighted the need to assure every major group of a turn at the presidency and other top posts. States had become too weak compared to the center, and some would not be financially viable without financial allocations from the center. Zoning was therefore seen as an alternative to the call by some for a return to the federal structure of the First Republic, where stronger regions had reduced the political significance of capturing power at the center. As we will see later in this chapter, zoning, which is not officially recognized in the constitution, has become an important basis for political identities and resource allocation in the Fourth Republic.

Despite projecting the outward appearance of a tough infantry officer without whom Nigeria would supposedly fall apart, General Abacha was in fact deeply paranoid. He rarely attended public functions, let alone traveled out of the country. Abacha retired or reassigned "problem" military officers frequently and unleashed his security apparatus, including death squads – a first in the history of Nigeria – on perceived and real opponents of the regime.

Alleged coup plots in 1995 and 1997, which resulted in death sentences being imposed on a large number of officers and civilians (including General Oladapo Diya, Abacha's Yoruba deputy, in 1977) could not be carried out because of disagreements within the now hopelessly fractured and seriously de-professionalized military.

Nonetheless, Abacha remained enigmatically vague about his vaunted transition plans until 1997, when he allowed the creation of seven political parties that contested local and state elections. Critics referred to them as "the seven dwarfs" because they not only agreed to Abacha's demand that they refrain from criticizing the regime, but also "adopted" Abacha as their "consensus candidate" for the upcoming presidential election in 1998. Like Babangida, Abacha also funded the creation of several civil society organizations (most notably, Youths Earnestly Ask for Abacha, or YEAA). He co-opted several academics, religious leaders, and traditional rulers who were "settled" with money and/or plum appointments; they became vocal supporters of the regime's self-succession transition plans, which they tried to sell to the international community as the only antidote to the alleged imminent collapse of the Nigerian state. Abacha's sudden death in June 1998 abruptly ended "the game of the seven dwarfs" – the closest Nigeria had come to a military dictator exchanging his khaki military uniform for the *agbada*, the flowing, colorful, and ridiculously expensive gown that has now become the trademark of most Nigerian politicians.

The Return to Democracy and the Fourth Republic

Institutions and Elite Coalition Politics

Nigerians and students of Nigerian politics both agree that military rule is an aberration, while its dictatorial variant is generally considered illegitimate or shunned as immoral or outmoded. By 1998, the military itself seemed to agree because it had become weary of ruling the country for twenty-nine years, as it was being blamed by all and sundry for every political, economic, and social problem in the country. The military as an institution had become a mere shadow of its former self, lacking in basic equipment, wracked by factionalism; undermined by a loss of professionalism, esprit de corps and sense of mission; and hijacked by rapacious politicians in military uniform. For much of this period, enlisted officers and soldiers of lower ranks saw little direct benefit from military rule, and preferred a return to rule by civilian politicians who would not dare to offend the military too much for fear of coups. Feverish deliberations about what to do with Chief Abiola, the presumed winner of the 1993 election, were still going on when Abiola suddenly died in his prison guesthouse in the presence of visiting American diplomats in 1998. Under such circumstances, Abacha's equally rapacious successor, General Abdusalami Abubakar, had little choice but to quickly cobble together a transition program, which eventually returned the country to elected civilian government on May 29, 1999. Marginal changes were made to the 1979 constitution, but the presidential system of government and the principles of federalism with Nigerian peculiarities were retained in the 1999 constitution.

The transition process started with local council elections. Three of the nine major political parties that had received the most votes in the December 1998 elections in the country's 774 local councils were subsequently allowed to contest the presidential and general elections in 1999. These were the People's Democratic Party (PDP), the All People's Party (APP) which had won 182; and the Alliance for Democracy (AD) with 100; other parties won the remaining 103 local council seats. Unofficially, the presidency was "zoned" to the Yoruba southwest, ostensibly to assuage the injustice of the June 12 debacle and Abiola's subsequent death, and to blunt mooted secessionist moves by the Yoruba. Retired general Obasanjo, who had relinquished power to civilians in 1979 and who had just been released from prison (for alleged involvement in an anti-Abacha coup in 1995) following Abacha's demise, was "invited" by the PDP to be their candidate, while Chief Olu Falae, also a Yoruba and a Yale University–trained economist, former finance minister, and former secretary to the federal government under Babangida, became the joint flag-bearer of the AD and ANPP. Obasanjo won the presidential election with 62.8 percent of the votes, while Falae received a mere 37.2 percent. Obasanjo's PDP also won a majority of the parliamentary seats in both the Senate and the federal House of Representatives.

Like all previous Nigerian elections, the 1999 elections were characterized by reports and allegations of vote-rigging and other electoral irregularities, most of them stemming from the limited time the Abubakar regime had to organize the polls. Indeed, Falae's unexpectedly poor showing was attributed to the strong backing given to Obasanjo by retired and departing military officers, who allegedly could not trust civilians to protect their interests. Another interesting feature of the transition process was the virtual eclipse of pro-democracy and human rights movements in the post-military elite pacts and power-sharing arrangements that followed. Some have speculated that the unofficial zoning of the presidency to the southwest by the departing military and the emergence of two prominent Yoruba presidential candidates in 1999 simply pulled the rug out from under the feet of ethnic Yoruba-dominated pro-democracy movements. This result may also have to do with the authoritarian leadership and the democracy deficit of many of the civil society associations, which caused them to fragment into various factions – some of which could not count more than the founder and his or her spouse, plus their fax machine, as members.

President Obasanjo's international connections, good reputation (including positions as vice president of Transparency International and founder of the Africa Leadership Forum), and post-military service rhetoric captured the imagination and hopes of Nigerians and the world. Indeed, no Nigerian government had ever come to power with such domestic and international legitimacy as the Obasanjo administration in 1999. The president even whetted the appetite of Nigerians hoping for an end to political corruption and militarization of Nigerian politics by dismissing, a day after his inauguration, ninety senior military officers who had political ambitions or were tainted by their involvement in previous military regimes. He also quickly embarked on a program of reprofessionalization of the armed forces, especially to institutionalize civilian control of the military.

Indeed, most Nigerians genuinely expected President Obasanjo to borrow a leaf from South Africa's Nelson Mandela and serve only one term, during which he was expected to stabilize the polity and use his post-military national and international goodwill to extricate Nigeria from its Abacha-era pariah status and reintegrate the country into the world community. Ironically, Obasanjo who claimed to have become a born-again Christian while

Table 14.1 Nigeria: Federal Election Results of 2003

Type of Vote	PDP	ANPP	AD	Others
Presidential election	61.9%	32.2%	no candidate	5.9%
House of Rep. (seats)	54.5% (213)	27.4% (95)	9.3% (31)	8.8% (7)
Senate (seats)	53.7% (73)	27.9% (28)	9.7% (6)	8.7% (0)

Source: The Independent National Election Commission, 2003.

in jail, seemed to have learned from his nemesis Abacha by keeping mum about his future political intentions, saying only that God would determine whether he would be a candidate for the 2003 election. By 2002, most PDP governors had fallen out with the president due to his autocratic and brusque governing style and were urging his vice president, **Alhaji Abubakar Atiku** – who had been instrumental to the PDP adopting Obasanjo in 1998 – to run against Obasanjo in the party primaries, which Atiku declined to do. In the end, Obasanjo did run, beating his closest opponent, General Muhammadu Buhari of the All Nigeria People's Party (formerly the APP), a tough-talking dictator in the 1980s with a reputation for unflinching patriotism and zero tolerance for corruption. In addition to the landslide electoral victory shown in Table 14.1, the PDP, now in charge of the state machinery including the electoral commission, also won twenty-eight out of thirty-six governorships, and began to refer to itself as "Africa's biggest political party."

Whereas Obasanjo had been shunned by significant percentages of his southwest Yoruba people in 1999 – including a humiliating loss in his village ward – the PDP in 2003 captured five governorship positions from the AD in the Yoruba southwest. The disunity among the thirty registered political parties (twenty-six of which fielded presidential candidates) may have split the opposition vote, while General Buhari was unable to erase his record of brutal dictatorship and human rights abuses when he was military ruler. Additionally, the Yoruba-dominated AD was so fractured that it was unable officially to agree on a presidential candidate, perhaps unofficially adopting Obasanjo as its candidate for the presidential vote. Nonetheless, the 2003 election must rank as among the most rigged in the history of Nigeria. Indeed, General Buhari spent vast sums of money and twenty-three months seeking to overturn the elections in the courts, which eventually sustained most of the rigging claims, but ruled that the fraud was not sufficient to have produced a different electoral outcome. The appeals court even agreed – although this finding was later reversed by the Supreme Court – that in the president's home state of Ogun, the number of votes reported for the PDP governorship candidate who purportedly won the election was far greater than the total number of votes actually cast in the general elections in that region.

The Politics of "Resource Control" and the "Resource Curse"

One of the most divisive issues in the Fourth Republic has been – and will continue to be – increased agitation for more local control over resources generated in each group's homeland.

Return to civilian rule created new opportunities to challenge the 1992 revenue allocation formula decreed by the military as follows: 48.5 percent for the federal government; 24 percent for the states; 20 percent for local governments; and 7.5 percent for the so-called Special Fund, made up of 1 percent for the Federal Capital Territory Abuja, 2 percent for the Ecological Fund, 1.5 percent for Economic Stabilization, and 3 percent for Natural Resources.

Obasanjo's proposal to increase the Special Fund's allocation to 11.7 percent resulted in the infamous "Resource Control" suit in the Supreme Court by oil-producing coastal states seeking clarification about which tier of government was entitled to revenue from offshore oil. In April 2002, the Supreme Court declared the Special Fund unconstitutional and ordered the following revenue allocations: 56 percent for the federal government; 24 percent for the states; and 20 percent for local governments. In March 2003, after a series of disputes among the three levels of government, the president by executive order allocated 52.68 percent to the federal government, 26.72 percent to states, and 20.6 percent to local governments. By creating the perception that lopsided revenue allocation was to blame for the underdevelopment, lack of public infrastructure, and massive poverty and unemployment of their regions, oil-producing state governors added fuel to the festering "youth restiveness" or militancy in the Niger Delta, whose goal was to retain greater control of oil revenue where oil is produced. This set the governors on a collision course with President Obasanjo, who in 2007 controversially indicted some of these "resource control agitators" for corruption.

In the post-Obasanjo era (2007–present), the resource control issue has assumed wider dimensions and greater salience, as it has come to symbolize the problem with the Nigerian state and its federal arrangement. A 2012 report claimed that about 80 percent of oil blocs within the Niger Delta littoral were awarded to several former generals, state elites, and their private sector counterparts from the north and southwest from which they have made great fortunes, further agitating Niger Delta resource control politicians and their foot soldiers who were passed over. Although oil-producing states and their resource control activists are demanding 25–50 percent of oil revenue, however, even the current "paltry" 13 percent derivation revenue makes these states disproportionately richer than some African countries.

Resource control has also been a sticking point in the various attempts since 2002 by the National Assembly to amend the 1999 constitution, explaining the vehement opposition of the north against the strident calls by southern politicians and activists for either a "National Constitutional Conference" or a "Sovereign National Constitutional Conference." At the same time, these resource control debates mask the **"resource curse"** – poverty and underdevelopment amid great wealth – that has become the lot of Nigeria's oil-producing communities. Many incurably corrupt Niger Delta politicians, especially state governors, have latched onto ethnic solidarity to defend and rationalize barefaced theft by public officials in the name of resource control amid shockingly awful developmental reports on the region. Available data show a remarkable wealth disparity between the oil-rich South-South/Niger Delta states and other states, in stark contrast to the widespread poverty and lack of public infrastructure in the zone, which are the purported reasons for resource control mobilization. In 2006 the United Nations *Human Development Report* described the Niger Delta as "a region suffering from administrative neglect, crumbling social infrastructure and services, high unemployment, social deprivation, abject poverty, filth and squalor, and endemic conflict." The report went on to say that "for most people of the Delta, progress and hope, much less prosperity, remain out of reach. If unaddressed, these do not bode well for the future of Nigeria or an oil hungry world." The "paradox of plenty" in the Niger Delta has begun to attract the scrutiny of anticorruption civil society organizations and individuals. For instance, the Niger Delta Budget Monitoring Group, an NGO, claimed that as of 2009 oil had generated about $600 billion in revenue since the 1960s, and that not less than ₦7.282 trillion (about $46 billion) of derivation money had been squandered by the governors since the 13 percent policy became operational. In its "Analyses of the 2013 Budget Proposal of the Ministry of Niger Delta Affairs and Related Matters," the group claimed that the decline in the Human Development Index had been steeper for the Niger Delta than for the rest of Nigeria. Similarly, Chief Edwin Clark, a prominent Ijaw leader, claimed that instead of the derivation policy bringing faster development to the people of the host communities, they have continued to wallow in abject poverty while "politicians from the area, especially the governors, bask in obscene affluence," embarking on self-aggrandizing projects such as the purchase of private jets. James Ibori, a former governor of Delta State (1999–2007) who was jailed in Britain in 2011 for money laundering and looting his state's treasury – charges that a Nigerian court had earlier thrown out – has nevertheless continued to draw his pension from the state government. Bayelsa state, Nigeria's second-richest state and one of Nigeria's less populated with less than three million people, has the second highest payroll bill after the federal government, yet its citizens are among the poorest in Nigeria. In response to such examples, Nigeria's former central bank governor Sanusi Lamido Sanusi, a prince of the northern Kano emirate, controversially claimed in 2012 that the huge derivation revenue being pumped into the Niger Delta states was responsible for the poverty in Nigeria's northern states. The Northern Governors' Forum and a powerful northern sociocultural group, Arewa Consultative Forum, have also called for a reduction in the amount of oil revenue going to the Niger Delta.

Population Counts, Ethnic Mobilization, and Insurgency Movements

No set of variables better demonstrates the "feedback effects" of Nigeria's developmental path since 1914 than population counts, ethnic mobilization, and the rise of numerous insurgency movements. In the Fourth Republic (since 1999), these challenges to the Nigerian state have become more pervasive, further sharpening the country's more notorious ethno-religious and class cleavages. The national population census has been highly politicized in Nigeria, beginning with the introduction of limited representative government in 1948. Since then every head count has either been rejected outright (1958 and 1973) or been a source of controversy (1963, 1992, and 2006) for the simple reason that population is also a basis for federal revenue allocation, political representation, and state creation – as well as an important marker of identity. As of 2005, the most populous and politically influential of Nigeria's 250 ethnic groups were the Hausa and Fulani at 29 percent, Yoruba at 21 percent, Igbo at 18 percent, Ijaw at 10 percent, Kanuri at 4 percent, Ibibio at 3.5 percent, and Tiv at 2.5 percent. In terms of religion, those identified as Muslim were 50 percent, Christians 40 percent, and adherents of indigenous beliefs 10 percent of the population. Notably, almost every head count in the country since the 1930s has given the north a majority. Most southerners reject this, arguing that it is very odd that Nigeria is the only country where the farther away one moves from the coast the larger the population, instead of the typical experience of population concentration in coastal areas. In 2006, the federal government decided to expunge religious and ethnic identities from the head count, ostensibly to blunt the saliency of these factors in national politics.

The 2006 population totals by geographic zones gave the three zones in the old Northern Region a combined 52.6 percent of Nigeria's population. One controversial surprise from census data was that Kano State had 9.3 million people, surpassing Lagos – one of Africa's most notorious megacities – at 9.01 million. Indeed, the government of Lagos State was so dissatisfied with the results that it actually published its own population estimate, giving the state about 12 million people. The southeast (Igbo) states – now clearly a national minority – also argued that because most Igbos actually lived outside the five states in the zone, the exclusion of ethnic and religious information from the census was intended to deliberately undercount them. By July 2012, Nigeria's population was estimated at 170,123,740, with a 2.6 percent growth rate. Nigeria had a median age of 19.2 years, a fertility rate of 5.38 children born per woman; life expectancy of 52.05 years for the total population (male: 48.95 years and female: 55.33 years), infant mortality rate of 74.36 deaths/1,000 live births (male: 79.44 deaths/1,000 live births; female: 68.97 deaths/1,000 live births), and 50 percent of the total population lived in urban areas. More important, the demographic dominance of the north was unchanged, if not increased. The sensitivity of population figures in Nigeria was further demonstrated in 2013 when the chairman of the National Population Commission, Festus Odimegwu, an Igbo, was dismissed for publicly stating that the 2006 census was as inaccurate and manipulated like all previous headcounts.

Related to demographic politics is ethnic mobilization, which continued to grow during the twenty-nine years of military dictatorship and has actually escalated during the Fourth Republic, especially in the Niger Delta and Middle Belt and central Nigeria. Since the return of civilian rule there has been bloody anarchy in the Niger Delta, which by 2012 produced most of Nigeria's 2.7 million barrels per day of oil and increasing volumes of gas. At least 1,000 people a year were killed in battles on land and sea between the 50-odd militia groups, including the MOSOP, the **Movement for the Emancipation of the Niger Delta** (MEND), the **Niger Delta Peoples' Volunteer Force** (NDPVF), the **Egbesu Boys of Africa**, the **Ijaw Youth Council**, and other such groupings, who fight against marginalization by the central government and despoliation of their environment by oil companies, as well as against each other for opportunities to steal oil. More than 1,000 Nigerians and foreigners – most, but not all of them, connected to the oil industry – were kidnapped for ransom since 1999, with about 80 percent abducted between 2006 and 2010. By some accounts, every year between 2003 and 2010, more than 300,000 barrels of oil, or more than $1.5 billion – as much as 20 percent of Nigeria's oil exports – were stolen or disrupted by the insurgency. Although some of the militants genuinely wanted the government to cede control of the oil industry to Niger Delta states, where the crude is pumped, most of them were simply criminal gangs and thugs trained and equipped by rival corrupt politicians – including oil-state governors – who use them for their political purposes, including vote-rigging, intimidation of opponents, and extortion of money from oil companies and the various levels of government.

In the first of a series of actions taken by the federal government to forestall any threats to its oil revenue, the government of Obasanjo sent in the army to level the **village of Odi,** Bayelsa state in 1999, in what some human rights groups consider an act of genocide. This was in retaliation for the killing of policemen by youth gangs opposed to oil exploration in the area. The government followed this up with the setting up of a **Joint Task Force (JTF)** of all security agencies, whose initially small-scale campaigns later escalated to include the complete destruction of fishing villages accused of harboring the militants. The JTF itself lost scores of personnel, materiel, and equipment. Allegations of connivance with militants and personal enrichment by some elements of the JTF became so widespread that security personnel reportedly lobbied to be posted to the Niger Delta for JTF internal security operations. For its part, the federal government's strategy of divide-and-rule through coercion and lucrative payoffs in its engagements with Niger Delta governors, militant leaders, environmental and human rights NGOs, and local politicians only further exacerbated the insurgency.

The government's efforts at full militarization of the creeks and mangrove swamps occupied by the Niger Delta militants failed, sparking fears of more deadly violence as the militants' criminal activities – including the kidnapping of school children, aged parents, and other relatives of politicians and prominent citizens – spread to the southeast and other parts of Nigeria. Meanwhile, Nigeria's "restive youth" population climbed to about 70 million; even more troubling was the fact that more than 75 percent of the youth remained unemployed, making them easy prey and fodder for elites and ethnic identity entrepreneurs bent on using the youth to achieve their selfish political ends. By mid-2009, the militancy and oil theft – known in Nigeria as "**illegal bunkering**" – continued unabated, reducing Nigeria's total crude oil production from 2.5 million barrels per day to about 1.9 million barrels per day.

Under pressure by the United States, which received 10 percent of its crude oil needs from Nigeria, and fearful of further erosion of its revenue base at the height of the global financial crisis and recession, President Umaru Musa Yar'Adua (who succeeded Obasanjo in May 2007) on June 25, 2009 initiated an "**amnesty policy**" for all Niger Delta militants who agreed to surrender their weapons. Yar'Adua also created a **Ministry of the Niger Delta** to funnel additional billions of dollars into the region to address the infrastructure deficit and neglect of the oil- and gas-producing communities. When Yar'Adua died in May 2010, his successor, President **Goodluck Jonathan** from a former governor of the Niger Delta state of Bayelsa, continued and implemented the amnesty policy while also expanding the JTF campaigns against Niger Delta militants. At least 30,000 former militants who gave up arms have been "rehabilitated" through salaries and stipends. Most of them have been offered further education and skills training in entrepreneurship, crafts, technical trades, and even airplane pilot training – at a cost of over $1 billion (the budget for 2011 alone was about $635 million). In addition, some of the repentant militant leaders were further "empowered" as custodians for the security of the nation's oil and gas pipelines through lucrative contracts.

By early 2014, relative peace had returned to the Niger Delta region even though oil theft, sabotage of oil pipelines and flow stations and kidnapping of oil workers continues (especially by MEND whose leader, Henry Okah, was convicted of gun-running and jailed in South Africa), albeit on a lower scale than in 2009. Nigeria's daily crude oil production climbed back up to about 2.7 million mb/d instead of the 1.9 mb/d at the height of the insurgency in 2010 and declined to about 2.2 mb/d in early 2014 as more than six hundred mb/d were stolen or lost as a result of renewed sabotage of oil flow stations and pipelines.

Critics of the amnesty program are legion, given the admission of the JTF commanders of corruption within their ranks. Moreover, oil industry pollution and environmental damage continue to have a serious impact on people's lives and livelihoods. Affected communities still lack access to vital information about the oil industry's local impact. Environmental laws and regulations continue to be poorly enforced, partly because of government agencies being compromised by conflicts of interest. Yet a critical appraisal suggests that the program, like other post-conflict mediation efforts in areas of the world wracked by civil war, has had some real success. Experiments such as the Niger Delta Amnesty program are works in progress; taken together, they offer not only alternative approaches to sustainable development, but also a fascinating new research agenda for those interested in post-conflict security promotion.

Ethnic mobilization and fragmentation have similarly occurred among the larger ethnic groups. Competition has emerged between the Yoruba Afenifere and the Yoruba Council of Elders; among the Hausa-Fulani Arewa Consultative Forum, the Northern Governors Forum, and the Northern Elders Forum; and between the Igbo Ohanaeze and southeast governors. The Ijaw National Council, meanwhile, competes for support in the Niger Delta with various splinter groups that seem to spring up on a daily basis. Often these elite groups are upstaged by their more militant competitors, such as the O'dua Peoples' Congress (OPC) in the southwest, the Movement for the Actualization of the Sovereign State of Biafra (MASSOB) in the southeast, and Islamist vigilantes such as the Yandaba and ethno-religious groups such as the Ombatse religious cult in Nasarawa state in the north. Occasionally, some of these violent groups are either co-opted by governments and rival groups, or subdued by arrests, the indefinite imprisonment of their leaders, and intragroup factionalism and dissidence. As Nigeria prepares for a pivotal election in 2015, many of these groups have become more active, even as new insurgent groups have joined their ranks, further heightening the country's political risk profile.

One important negative "feedback effect" of Nigeria's development path can be inferred from several human rights groups' reports showing that more than 20,000 people have died in more than 20 instances of intercommunal violence during the Fourth Republic. These have occurred between the Tiv and the Jukun in Zaki Biam in the middle belt; between the so-called indigenous populations and Fulani "settlers" and herdsmen in Jos, Yola, Zangon Kataf, and many other parts of northern Nigeria; among supposedly homogenous Yoruba communities as in the case of the perennial Ife-Modakeke wars in Oyo State; and among the Igbo communities of the Umuleri and the Agulueri in communal clashes in Anambra State. The failure of the authorities to punish the perpetrators of past abuses, along with the ineptitude and ethnic biases of the security forces, often caused the violence to escalate. More than 800 people were also killed in politically motivated violence across Nigeria before, during, and after the national parliamentary, presidential, and state elections in April 2011, especially in the Kaduna and Plateau states.

As long-standing conflicts within and among ethnic groups continue to be unresolved, and citizenship for many Nigerians remains incomplete or unequal, new conflicts are likely to emerge, further complicating the politics of ethnic mobilization and insurgency in Nigeria. For example, in August 2012 a faction of MOSOP declared Ogoni self-government under the "Ogoni Central Indigenous Authority," or OCIA. Earlier the same month, a group under the name "Bakassi Freedom Fighters" threatened to seek independence if Nigeria renounced sovereignty over the Bakassi Peninsula, which Nigeria lost to the Republic of Cameroon following an International Court of Justice decision in 2002. The group even hoisted the Bakassi flag of the rising sun in Abana, the Bakassi headquarters now officially located in Cameroon. The failure of the two countries to properly implement the United Nations–brokered Green Tree Agreement of 2006, which guaranteed the right of Bakassi citizenship and resettlement in Nigeria, has been the basis for the emergence of this latest insurgency.

Fiscal Federalism, "Federal Character," and the Politics of Zoning

As noted previously, Nigeria entered postcolonial life with an explicitly federal constitution accepted by the founding fathers as the only guarantee for "unity in diversity," even though there was little else they agreed to about the nature of the new state they were founding. Paradoxically or consequently, the logic of federalism has also exacerbated the perpetual quest for a further devolution of powers, especially the creation of more states. Every new region or state created to assuage the agitation of minorities for self-determination, however, immediately spawned new "minorities" – sparking a new cycle of devolution that has seen the number of the federating units grow from three in 1960 to thirty-six in 1995. Although that number has remained unchanged since the Fourth Republic, from 1999 to 2014 there were no fewer than twenty-five active movements for state creation, with varying degrees of cohesion and rationality. State creation is a volatile issue with serious consequences for the equally hotly contested issues of population and resource control. Hence, with the exception of the creation of Midwest Region out of the old Western Region in 1963 under a state of emergency, subsequent state creation – from twelve states in 1967, to nineteen in 1975, to the thirty-six in 1995 – has only been done by military rulers. And unlike many federal systems, the 1979, 1989, and 1999 constitutions in Nigeria went a step further by enshrining a three-tier federal structure, with local government councils (now 774 in all) having constitutionally guaranteed political and fiscal authority with minimal control by state governments – although the other two tiers have yet to learn to respect this constitutional guarantee.

Behind these demands for state creation lie the politics of **fiscal federalism** by which all the federating units theoretically contribute to, and derive allocations from, federally collected revenue equitably. In the First Republic, revenue distribution was based on the formula of "derivation," allocating 51 percent of the revenue back to where it was collected. This revenue-sharing formula made the regions more powerful and more attractive than the government at the center, even as it tended to widen the gap between the relatively better endowed Eastern region (relying on palm oil and coal) and Western region (relying on cocoa) and their poorer northern neighbors, whose revenue came mainly from peanuts. Although various military regimes since 1966 retained the federal principle, the twenty-nine years of military dictatorship actually resulted in more centralization of both state power and revenue – producing an oxymoronic **"military federalism"** that has seen only marginal changes under the Fourth Republic.

The rise in the financial power of the federal government has also been accompanied by a corresponding expansion of its powers to the detriment of the federating units, further exacerbating demands for more devolution of powers. The fact that military rule was dominated by northern military officers who were seen by southern activists as bent on perpetuating northern domination of Nigerian politics, financed by wealth increasingly derived from the south, did not help matters either. The choice of "Born to Rule" as a state motto by Sokoto state, the spiritual headquarters of establishment Islam in northern Nigeria, further inflamed southern distrust.

Since 1979, military and civilian regimes have implemented the principle of "**federal character**," Nigeria's version of affirmative action, which seeks to guarantee a proportionate share of federal positions – including recruitment into educational institutions, military academies, and the civil service – to all states, in a process increasingly based on ethnic group identification. A **Federal Character Commission** (FCC) that is constitutionally charged with enforcing this policy has, however, only placed additional burdens on an already inefficient state bureaucracy. For instance, recruitment into several agencies had to be cancelled by the government in late 2012 because their heads had allegedly selected more than 50 percent of their new employees from their home states. Meanwhile, certain agencies, such as Nigerian Customs Service and the armed forces, continue to be northern-dominated. In reality, the federal character policy was introduced to ensure against southern domination of public life, given the wide economic gap that continues to exist between the north and the south, even though the north has controlled political power for much of the country's history. While the military and security agencies remain overwhelmingly dominated by northerners, especially among the officer corps, southerners continue to dominate the economy, academia, and the state-managed organizations known as parastatals.

The zoning policy institutionalized under General Abacha as a further entrenchment of the "federal character" principle is becoming a crucial basis for interest aggregation, allocation of the spoils of office, and elite identity politics. In the preceding section, we noted how the departing northern military and the political cabal that ruled the country from 1984 to 1998 zoned the presidency in the upcoming Fourth Republic in 1999 to the Yoruba. The president chose a vice president from the north-east zone, while the position of senate president – third in the line of succession – went to the Igbo. The position of Supreme Court chief justice was zoned to the north-central zone, while chief of the armed forces and deputy senate president were from the central Benue-Plateau zone. In a classic balancing act, all the military service chiefs were chosen from ethnic minority groups that did not occupy top positions in the government. Similarly, legislative leadership and committee assignments, ministerial appointments, as well as capital projects, were allocated along zonal lines. Ideally, the presidency would eventually rotate to the other zones, namely the south-south and the south-east, before returning to the north again.

The 2007 elections, however, seemed to have confirmed speculations in 1999 that President Obasanjo at the time may have struck a deal to return the presidency to the north after eight years. In 2007, Obasanjo handed over power to Alhaji Umaru Musa Yar'Adua, the governor of Katsina state in the north-west zone, who in turn chose as his vice president Goodluck Jonathan, Bayelsa state governor from the Ijaw minority ethnic group in the south-south zone. When Jonathan became president in 2010 following Yar'Adua's death, he chose the Kaduna state governor in the north-central zone as his vice president. The zoning logic has also been applied to the allocation of political party positions as well as promotions and appointments at the top-level civil service, armed forces, and diplomatic corps positions.

Zoning, rotation, "state character," and even "local government character" have become the mantra, and often the source, of serious protracted political contestation and violence whenever politicians have attempted to ignore these arrangements. Contrary to the expectation of many northerners that Jonathan would only serve out Yar'Adua's term so that the north would complete its eight-year turn at the presidency like the southwest, Jonathan sought and won the presidency in 2011, seemingly throwing the ruling PDP's "gentleman's" zoning arrangement out of kilter. Some northern politicians had threatened to make the country "ungovernable" should Jonathan win, hence they were blamed for the postelection violence and the upsurge in sectarian violence that has escalated since 2011. As Nigeria gears up for another presidential election in 2015, the north has continued to mobilize to deny Jonathan a second-term run, just as his south-south kin insist on the "sanctity" of their turn. The south-east Igbo, meanwhile, are demanding a power shift to them "by right" – just like the other two major ethnic groups.

Critics point to the deficiencies and perversions of this system of managing **reinforcing cleavages** whereby individuals are appointed or selected as representatives of their zones, states, or local councils, and not because of their competence or integrity. Yet the system seems to have served the country well in terms of political stability, in the sense that it gives hope to the political class from all zones that they might one day have their turn at ruling the country – a scenario that is highly unlikely under any other "democratic" power-sharing arrangement. For instance, it would have been extremely difficult for an Ijaw person to have become Nigeria's president without the ruling party's "turn-by-turn" zoning policy, which Jonathan is accused of violating.

Economic Reforms and the Politics of Development

On April 7, 2014, Nigeria recalculated the value of its gross domestic product (GDP) to include previously uncounted industries like telecoms, information technology, music, online sales, airlines, and its famous film production industry called Nollywood. The new GDP for 2013 totaled N80.3 trillion ($509.9 billion; compared with the World Bank's 2012 GDP figures of

$262.6 billion), pushing Nigeria above South Africa (with a 2013 GDP of $370.3 billion) as the continent's biggest economy. The revised figure makes Nigeria the 26th biggest economy in the world, but the country lags in income per capita, ranking 121 with $2,688 for each citizen. Based on the new data, Nigeria's economy grew at 12.7 percent between 2012 and 2013. Oil and gas, however, are by far the biggest source of government revenue.

Since its discovery in 1956, oil has played an ever greater and now all-consuming role in Nigeria's economy, politics, and society. Petroleum's share of GDP rose from 1 percent in 1960 to 26 percent in 1970, and its share of total export revenue grew to 94 percent by 1976, gradually falling to about 83 percent in 2013. High government revenue derived from easily controllable petroleum created a classic **"rentier" state,** with the government receiving revenue streams independent of broadly based taxation and the electorate, and hence the state became largely unaccountable to its people. The reforms discussed in the remainder of this section were therefore initiated to reverse the radical transformation of the material base of Nigerian society caused by oil dependency. Long-term macroeconomic reforms under the Obasanjo administration (1999–2007) were anchored on a **National Economic Empowerment and Development** (NEEDS) program setting measurable benchmarks for federal and state governments. The program itself was designed to facilitate the achievement of the country's *Vision 20: 2020* document, which captures Nigeria's aspiration to become one of the top twenty global economies by 2020. The government also introduced open bidding for oil and gas exploration blocks, instituted a relatively stable exchange rate and more prudent financial management and much greater budgetary transparency, having subjected the country to the discipline and monitoring that comes with membership of the Extractive Industries Transparency Initiative (EITI). Other significant reforms implemented by Obasanjo include the consolidation of the nation's banking and insurance sectors (pruning the banks from 93 to 25 in 2005), privatization of state assets and corporations, and elimination of archaic laws that crowded out the private sector. A highlight of the reforms (especially under Obasanjo) was the reduction of the country's foreign debt, down from a high of $36 billion in 1999 to $3 billion in 2006, earning the country debt relief of $18 billion from the London and Paris Clubs of international creditors.

Although the NEEDS program no longer exists, its basic tenets became the building blocks of macroeconomic reforms of the successor Yar'Adua and Jonathan administrations. Following his inauguration in May 2007, Yar'Adua enunciated a "Seven Plus Two Point Agenda to Transform Nigeria," focusing on energy, food security and agriculture, wealth creation and employment, mass transportation, land reform, security, and education, plus an ambitious development master plan for the Niger Delta and plans to empower disadvantaged groups. This program sounded all the right notes and had the potential to consolidate the erratically executed reforms initiated by Obasanjo. Yar'Adua also streamlined revenue allocation and reiterated his government's respect for the federal principle. But debilitating illness, including frequent medical trips and long hospital stays abroad, stymied the administration and prevented him from implementing most of the above agenda. The regime – which Nigerians dubbed "Go-Slow" – came to an end on March 5, 2010, when Yar'Adua died in Abuja, having been brought back home a few weeks earlier from a Saudi hospital where he had been undergoing treatment since September 2009.

Yar'Adua's successor, Goodluck Jonathan, soon launched his *Transformation Agenda* which covers the period 2011–2015 and centered on entrenching a sound macroeconomic framework in the key thematic areas such as infrastructure, human capital development, and the cultivation of private investment. The Transformation Agenda also seeks to promote effective monitoring and evaluation to ensure that Nigeria did not fall back into its notorious pattern of development efforts lacking in continuity, consistency, and commitment and the absence of a long-term perspective.

Following his inauguration in May 2011, the Jonathan administration adopted various measures to maintain macroeconomic stability, such as intensified efforts to bring the fiscal deficit down from 2.96 percent in 2011 to 2.17 percent in 2013 in compliance with the Fiscal Responsibility Act. On balance, the result of these economic reforms has been a mixed bag. Nigeria's economic reforms have been hampered by the haphazardness and inconsistency of the vital ingredient for success – good governance – and exacerbated by corruption, rent-seeking, and more brazen forms of prebendalism and assaults on the rule of law. Bank reforms and financial liberalization, for instance, spawned a rush of "easy money" that caused a 50 percent collapse of the stock market. The Jonathan administration's reform credentials were further damaged following its 2014 suspension of the central bank governor, Sanusi Lamido Sanusi, for "financial recklessness"–shortly after Sanusi had alleged that about $40 billion from the Nigerian National Petroleum Corporation was missing from the treasury. The Fourth Republic has yet to resolve perennial shortages of gasoline and to end the black market for gasoline, as none of the country's three refineries have worked properly in ten years. Thus, despite huge sums thrown at the problem, the world's seventh largest oil exporter continued to import refined petroleum for domestic use. Some officials of the three administrations since 1999 are allegedly part of a "mafia" that made billions of dollars from the importing of refined oil for huge legal and illegal payments from the petroleum subsidy funds at $4.2 billion in 2012, compared to $1.6 billion in 2006. Such individuals therefore had every reason to thwart efforts to refine petroleum locally. Jonathan's attempt to scrap in part the gasoline subsidy on January 1, 2012, without prior warning, sparked an eight-day nationwide strike and revolt led by organized labor and civil society, which became known as the "Occupy Nigeria" movement. In the end, these protests forced the government to rescind the decision.

The most glaring example of reform failure is the power sector, where despite repeated promises of "regular, uninterrupted power supply," most Nigerians have to live with an average of three hours of electricity daily. Frustrated with persistent interruptions of power supplies by the National Electric Power Authority (NEPA), Nigerians refer to NEPA as "Never Expect Power Always." Between 1999 and 2012, over $26 billion was spent and seven successive ministers appointed for the sector; meanwhile NEPA was broken up into eighteen (later reduced to ten) separate companies and renamed the Power Holding Company of Nigeria. Several well-known Nigerian investors reportedly began migrating to neighboring countries to escape the destructive effects of the power sector crisis and other unfriendly policies. The change in name from NEPA to PHCN was more noticeable in the continued deterioration of the power sector; hence, Nigerians now refer to the new entity as "Problem Has Changed Name." In December 2013, the government finally handed over the ten companies to private operators for a $2.5 billion acquisition fee from which it paid off electricity workers whose resistance had threatened to derail the power sector reforms.

Notwithstanding the reform challenges noted in the preceding paragraphs, and in spite of the global economic slowdown starting in 2008, the Nigerian economy has exhibited robust growth, with GDP growing by 7.6 percent from 2002 to 2013 (compared to 1 percent from 1980 to 1999) – a pace of growth that is expected to be maintained in 2014 and beyond. In 2011, Nigeria ranked first in the top five host economies for FDI in Africa at $8.91 billion (dropped to $7 billion in 2012), followed by South Africa with $5.9 billion and Ghana with $3.2 billion. Nigeria also accounted for over one-sixth of flows into Africa, as well as for 41.6 percent of FDI flow to West Africa; indeed, only Nigeria, South Africa, and Ghana attracted FDI inflows above $3 billion in 2011. Although FDI inflow to Nigeria dropped to $7 billion in 2012, Nigeria still controls 27.6 percent of the GDP and 24 percent of the gross fixed capital formation in Africa in 2012. In 2012, U.S. President Barack Obama proclaimed Nigeria as "the world's next economic giant", a prediction supported by the 2014 recalculation of the country's GDP noted earlier. Under Jonathan, the Nigerian economy has been growing consistently by nearly seven percent per annum, one of the highest growth rates in the world. Yet, Jonathan must be the most vilified president in the history of Nigeria, even though his record in office, suggests he may indeed be the best president Nigeria has ever had. His supporters counter that whereas he has not been able to address the age-old problem of corruption, much of these attacks have little to do with Jonathan's competence (given the giant strides Nigeria has been making under his administration), but because he comes from the minority South-South zone of Nigeria.

Agriculture and food production, which suffered under Obasanjo and Yar'Adua, –and indeed since 1960–has recently registered commendable successes. Despite huge subsidies to farmers, especially fertilizer (totaling about $722 million from 2002 to 2007), Nigeria remained a net food importer as more and more people left the farms to swell the population of urban areas. Between 2011 and 2013, an estimated 4.2 million farmers received subsidized inputs via the government's growth enhancement scheme. Nigeria produced an unprecedented 1.1 million metric tons of "dry season" rice in 2013. In order to make these achievements sustainable, the government launched a program to attract 750,000 young Nigerians to become agricultural entrepreneurs, or what the Minister of Agriculture calls *Nagropreneurs* who will embrace agriculture as a business and help the country become self-sufficient in food production by 2025. The government also initiated a plan to distribute 10 million mobile phones to farmers (at an estimated cost of $384 million) so as to reach them in their local languages and to use the phones "to trigger an information revolution which will drive an agricultural revolution." In 2012 alone, the banking sector guaranteed billions of naira in loans for agricultural financing, with the prospect of further expansion and wealth creation. Johnathan has so transformed Nigerian agriculture that the minister, Akinwunmi Adesina, was named Forbes magazin's African of the Year 2013. (Italicize Forbes and African of the Year 2013)

Yet recent reversals of important privatization efforts by courts and successor governments raise doubts about the sincerity and capacity of the government to seriously implement its otherwise unassailable "transformation" agenda. For many local and foreign private sector operators, therefore, risk from physical insecurity or terrorism pales in comparison with that of government interference and other political impediments such as corrupt officials, an onerous bureaucracy, and continuous policy somersaults. In 2012, one private sector executive quipped that port delays in Lagos alone were actually a bigger investor concern than the bomb blasts or plane crashes that have become common in Nigeria.

Corruption: Fighting the Cankerworm in the Social Fabric

Although Nigeria is becoming an attractive FDI destination being Africa's biggest economy since April 2014, its notoriously corrupt public and private sectors have continued to delegitimize – as immoral or outmoded – the principles and values articulated by Nigeria's leaders. Historically, several measures have been taken by successive governments in Nigeria to fight corruption and money laundering. During military rule, these included the War Against Indiscipline (WAI), Mass Mobilization for Social Justice, Self-Reliance and Economic Recovery (MAMSER), and the War Against Indiscipline and Corruption (WAI-C), all of which eventually morphed into the National Orientation Agency (NOA). Since the return of civilian rule in 1999, corruption has become more widespread in Nigeria. Under Obasanjo (who was ironically the world vice president of Transparency International until 1999), the country ranked 152nd out of 158 countries in Transparency International's *Corruption Perception Index* in 2005. This actually marked an improvement from being the second most corrupt country in 1999. In 2012, Nigeria continued to rise in the Transparency International ranking, becoming the 124th most corrupt among the 170 countries included in that year's study. In 2013, however, Nigeria dropped again to the rank of 144th most corrupt among 177 countries.

Although recent revelations allege that Obasanjo, who was declared bankrupt prior to his election in 1999, has become one of the richest Nigerians, his was nevertheless the first administration to seriously embark on an anticorruption war by establishing institutions with the legal authority to go after the big fish and sacred cows of Nigeria's corruption industry. In 2002, Obasanjo set up the **Economic and Financial Crimes Commission (EFCC)** as the lead agency in the anticorruption war; Mallam Nuhu Ribadu became the first chairman of the EFCC. Ironically, Obasanjo's regime was itself deeply implicated in serious and blatant cases of public corruption, beginning with the first speaker of the House of Representatives, who was found guilty of certificate forgery in 1999 and left office. There were also numerous allegations of and indictments for bribery and corruption leveled against many legislators and twenty-six of the country's immensely powerful thirty-six state governors. Three successive senate presidents and several ministers were removed from office for corruption and embezzlement of public funds and abuse of office, while the EFCC described the country's 774 local councils as "stealing factories."

Most Nigerians believed the EFCC under Obasanjo had granted immunity to many "big men" and godfathers of the ruling PDP, citing its reluctance to probe the president's alleged self-enrichment, particularly the latter's willingness to accept billions of naira from individuals as well as corporate entities in the name of fund-raising for his presidential library in 2005. The top donors to the library fund were beneficiaries of Obasanjo's huge transfers of public assets to private hands – especially through the notorious Transnational Corporation (Transcorp), a megacorporation put together in 2005 by the private sector at the behest of the president, who also bought about ₦200 million Transcorp shares through his Obasanjo Farms Holding Company. In the same vein, while the president's friends had rescued his Temperance Farms from a court-ordered bankruptcy that would have derailed his election in 1999, his personal assistants claimed in 2005 that the same farm had been earning profits of $300,000 per year since Obasanjo assumed office. The EFCC allowed itself to be used by Obasanjo to attack Vice President Atiku with a view to preventing him from running for president in 2007. The agency also engineered a rash of impeachments of governors who, although clearly corrupt, were known to have lost favor with the presidency. Four of those impeachments were later voided by the Supreme Court – and the impeached governors reinstated – because the affected state legislatures, under tremendous pressure from the EFCC, had failed to follow constitutionally mandated procedures.

Ribadu was unceremoniously removed by Yar'Adua in 2008, under pressure from some ex-governors who had bankrolled the 2007 presidential election and who had been indicted by the EFCC. Ribadu's replacement with the more pliant Mrs. Farida Waziri, who was similarly removed in 2011, signaled the reluctance of the ruling class to empower an agency that could eventually consume them. As Nigeria entered 2014, the war against corruption continued to rage with the anti-graft body clearly not having the upper hand. Yet the commission had recorded significant achievements, namely the conviction of more than 500 persons out of 700 prosecutions since its founding in 2003. In 2010, the EFCC claimed to have recovered $6.5 billion of stolen assets between 2007 and 2010, even as it developed *Eagle Claw* and *Eagle-Eye* software to fight cybercrime and tax evasion. The commission also claimed that it secured 117 convictions out of the 533 corruption suspects charged in 2013 alone, and was optimistic about higher conviction figures in 2014, especially given the new practice directive issued by Nigeria's first female chief justice on the expeditious handling of corruption cases in the courts.

The EFCC's published prosecution list includes ex-governors, former and serving ministers, ex-bank chiefs, top government officials, clergymen, some foreign and local business men and women, and "high value" con artists. Under Ribadu's watch (2002–2008), the EFCC convicted more than 150 persons involved in economic and financial crimes. Some of the most prominent cases include the trial and conviction of Emmanuel Nwude and others in one of the biggest bank frauds in history. Perhaps the most infamous of these cases involved Tafa Balogun, the inspector-general of police, who escaped with only six months of jail time after he was convicted by a magistrate's court for diverting to private use ₦17 billion (about $150 million) meant for his poorly paid and unconscionably ill-equipped police force. So far, Lucky Igbinedion is the only former governor (of Edo State) who has paid back part of his loot. In 2008, facing a 191-count charge of money laundering, Igbinedion opted for a plea bargain and paid back ₦4.3 billion. Another ex-governor, James Ibori, who reportedly bankrolled Yar'Adua's presidential election in 2007, was discharged by a Nigerian court of a seventy-two count arraignment for corruption, embezzlement, and money laundering, only to be convicted and jailed for three years by a court in the United Kingdom for the same charges from which the Nigerian government shielded him. Bode George, a former deputy national chairman of PDP and retired navy commodore and former military governor, was convicted and jailed for two years for fraud while he was board chairman of the Nigerian Ports Authority. His conviction was unanimously overturned by the Supreme Court in 2013, two years after he had completed his jail sentence, because the procurement law under which he was convicted had not been enacted when the alleged fraud was committed.

The most awaited prosecutions in 2014 involve suspects, including at least 151 individuals and companies with connections to the presidency and the ruling PDP, who have been indicted for over ₦1.4 trillion in fraudulent claims in the chaotic refined petroleum subsidy program that were uncovered by various investigation panels in 2012. Preliminary arraignments began precisely ninety-seven days after the submission of the report of the investigation, but as of May 2014, the trials were yet to commence, raising suspicions that these massive fraud cases might be swept under the rug like others before them. Similarly, sixteen foreign multinational corporations – including household names such as Halliburton, Kellogg Brown & Root LLC, Technip SA, Snamprogetti Netherlands BV, ENI SpA/Saipem, Royal Dutch Shell Plc, Tidewater Inc, Transocean Inc, Shell Nigerian Exploration and Production Co. Ltd, and Siemens AG – who were convicted or paid fines to avoid prosecution in the United States and Europe for bribing Nigerian officials for lucrative contracts are yet to be tried in Nigeria almost two decades after their indictment, ostensibly because the bribery allegations run through the top echelons of Nigerian society from 1993 to the present. Some of these companies later paid fines of up to $100 million to the Nigerian government in lieu of prosecution.

Critics contend that President Jonathan's apparent lip service to the anti-corruption campaign may have to do with his background as part of the regime of corruption in the country. In 2006 when Jonathan was governor of Bayelsa State, he was indicted for false declaration of assets and for acquiring expensive cars and extensive real estate holdings beyond his legitimate income. He was subsequently recommended for prosecution by the Code of Conduct Bureau, but a year later, he became vice president and went on to become president. To many critics, therefore, the EFCC over the years has simply been playing to the gallery as it continued to drag people to court, and the number of convictions obtained did not show that the commission was indeed winning the war against graft. The commission, however, blames the Federal Government for not allowing it to function without undue interference by the office of the Attorney-General of the Federation, such as securing bails for suspects and providing protection for known corrupt individuals, unless they have fallen out of favor with the government. The commission also blames the broader Nigerian elite; defense attorneys who employ all forms of trickery to frustrate the prosecution by delaying trial of especially bad cases; and, as Farida Waziri put it, "the masses who rather than take up the fight against graft … choose to adore those that we should all join hands to condemn for looting our commonwealth." Successive EFCC leaders have called for the passage of the Asset Forfeiture bill aimed at tackling the menace of illegally acquired assets, which continues to languish in the National Assembly, to enhance crime-fighting efforts.

Despite some successes under very difficult circumstances, the inescapable conclusion has to be that Nigeria's anticorruption war at times amounts to a game of deception. Although the law provides criminal penalties for official corruption, the government does not implement the law effectively. Public officials (including both political appointees and civil servants) and private sector managers frequently engage in corrupt practices with impunity. Massive, widespread and pervasive corruption has affected all levels of government and the security forces. The constitution provides immunity from civil and criminal prosecution to the president, vice president, governors, and deputy governors while in office. No matter who is to blame for the mixed bag that is Nigeria's anticorruption regime, the cost of corruption to the country is staggering. According to a 2006 estimate by the International Monetary Fund, as much as $384.6 billion – revised upward in 2007 to $600 billion by Nigeria's Central Bank – in ill-gotten gains are sitting in foreign bank accounts while about 71 percent of the population lives on less than a dollar a day.

Poverty, Unemployment, and Widening Social Inequality

Although Nigeria is rich in both human and material resources and is now Africa's biggest economy, it has paradoxically experienced the worst forms of poverty since the return to civilian rule in 1999, further exacerbating its status as a "resource-cursed" nation. According to the National Bureau of Statistics (NBS), Nigeria recorded an average growth rate of over 6 percent between 2005 and 2011, but this growth did not translate into improvement in the standard of living, as the percentage of Nigerians living in absolute poverty rose to 60.9 percent in 2010, compared with 54.7 percent in 2004. Poverty levels rose to about 71.5 percent in 2011, which amounted to about 112.52 million Nigerians. The proportions of extremely poor, moderately poor, and non-poor Nigerians in 2011 were 38.7 percent, 30.3 percent, and 31 percent respectively. The gender and generational dimensions of these inequalities are also quite revealing for a country with the aspiration to become a top-twenty world economy. A United Nations report titled *Trends in Maternal Mortality: 1990 to 2010* released on May 16, 2013 showed that 14 percent of the world's deaths related to childbearing occur in Nigeria. While maternal death rates around the world have been cut almost in half over the past two decades, according to the UN report, Nigeria's rate – 630 deaths for every 100,000 live births – is the world's tenth highest, behind nine other sub-Saharan African countries led by Chad and Somalia. Statistics from Save the Children, an international nonprofit group, revealed that almost 800,000 Nigerian children die every year before their fifth birthday, making Nigeria the country with the highest number of newborn deaths in Africa.

A regional analysis further revealed the seriousness of poverty as a trigger for all of the other cleavages in the country. The NBS reported that the North West and North East zones accounted for the highest poverty rates, with 77.7 percent and 76.3 percent of their populations living in poverty, respectively. The South West, with 59.1 percent, recorded the lowest poverty rate in the country. Unemployment in the rural areas could be as high as 60 percent, while the youth jobless rate is as high as 72 percent. The government's own commitment to "downsizing" the public sector to the tune of more than 100,000 jobs, as well as its failure to reach its job creation targets have further compounded the unemployment situation. The United Nations Human Development Index (HDI) report of 2011 ranked Nigeria 156th out of the 177 countries surveyed, with an index of .459, based on 51.9 years of life expectancy at birth; a mean of five years of schooling (compared to 8.9 expected years of schooling); Although the recalculated GDP per capita rose to $2,688 in 2013, Nigeria still remains one of the most unequal societies in the world today.

The Wave of Insecurity, Sectarian Violence, and the Boko Haram Insurgency

Nigeria has consequently reaped a harvest of rampant insecurity, as youths roam the streets without jobs or hope for the future. One commentator puts it starkly: "Where there were few thieves in the past, Nigeria now boasts an empire of armed gangs on a rampage." There is hardly any part of the country today that is safe from the menace of resurgence of armed robberies. Many robbers often outgun and outman the police, wasting lives and property and paralyzing economic activity. Kidnappings, assassinations, communal and inter-communal violence resulting in painful loss of life, massive social displacement, injurious interruptions of productive activities, acute food shortages, destruction of property in excess of billions of naira, and capital flight have become common experiences for many Nigerians. Piracy off the West African coastline also remains a threat to the shipping sector – although the Nigerian government seems intent on addressing the situation, evidenced by the recent military linkup with neighboring Benin.

Sectarian violence, often depicted as "religious riots," continued to occur in hotbeds of violence, such as Jos in Plateau State (which witnessed battles between the "indigenous" Berom and "settler" Hausa-Fulani), Kaduna in the North Central zone and Maiduguri in the North East. The death toll from sectarian violence – generally triggered by many of the socioeconomic and political factors adumbrated earlier – between 1999 and 2013 was over 50,000, with more than 250,000 internal displacements, while property damage, including over 5,000 churches and mosques, run in the millions of dollars.

Yet the most serious internal threat the country has seen after the Nigeria-Biafra war must be the emergence of Boko Haram, which can be roughly translated as "Western education is sinful." The group was founded in 2002 by a pious and charismatic cleric known as Mohammed Yusuf, one of the new-generation Muslim intellectuals and activists who came of age during the era of economic and political liberalization in one of the poor neighborhoods of Maiduguri, the capital of Borno State, northeastern Nigeria. Yusuf's critique of state governors in the Muslim north and his challenge to the religious authority of mainstream Muslim scholars – the *ulama*, whom he accused of collaborating with a Western educated elite who profess Islam but are the biggest beneficiaries of an exploitative secular Nigerian state and economy – attracted a strong following among the area's impoverished youth. Yusuf, however, saw the imposition of strict Islamic law across Nigeria, and not only in the north, as the best solution to the collapse of the social bond between the poor and the ruling elite.

Ironically, many Nigerians truly share the contempt that the Boko Haram terrorists have for their country's corrupt social and political order. The major factor that unites them and many other angry activists is the changing nature and perceptions of wealth, now overwhelmingly concentrated in the hands of a tiny group of Western-educated elites, and its interface with politics. What the elite do with unchecked power is what the Boko Haram detests, not Western education per se. Mindless elite-led economic reforms have gutted the ideological consensus on which an independent Nigeria was founded. The Western-educated elite would rule with greater legitimacy provided a modicum of social welfare and minimum living standards of human decency were provided for the poor. This concept of "mixed economy" is actually enshrined in the 1999 constitution. Although the erosion of the social bond between rich and poor began immediately after independence, it accelerated in the 1980s and 1990s and created an economic and political environment that is generally unpredictable.

In the absence of either the social welfare state or frayed traditional social support networks that held Nigerians together, a theology of prosperity and miracles stepped in, promising to rescue the nation from the traumas of neoliberal reforms and nineteen years of military dictatorships. Mosques and new Islamic educational institutions (often funded by the Wahhabi Islamists from Saudi Arabia and Iranian Shi'ites) proliferated, accompanied by more visible and audible expressions of traditionalist public piety. New religious associations for marginalized social groups such as women, youths, and students became vehicles for expressing religiosity and sociality in response to a growing "demand for religion" as well as a way to participate in political debates. The resulting social transformation has generated a massive out-migration of Nigerians from rural areas to urban centers and out of the country, creating a huge market for recruits for new religious movements. This is the historical basis for the introduction of *Shar'ia* in twelve northern states between 1999 and 2000, based on democracy and its foundational principle, majority rule. Predictably, sharia in the north has been manipulated by the Western-educated and "establishment" religious elite to maintain their power, further escalating the demand for real political Islam in northern Nigeria.

Yusuf was murdered in controversial circumstances while in police custody in 2009, and was replaced by a more radical lieutenant called Abubakar Shekau. Critics claim that, tactically, Yusuf's Boko Haram has been hijacked by a murderous and confused bunch, now being manipulated by the very elite that created the problem Yusuf set out to correct. The group dishes out generalized rationalizations for its activities and makes inchoate demands, dreaming of instigating interfaith violence to drive Christians out of the north. Human Rights Watch reports that by December 2013, the Islamist insurgency had killed more than 5,000 people, mostly poor Muslims and southern Christians who reside in the targeted areas, in what has become a daily orgy of bloodletting. According to the Christian Association of Nigeria, out of the 137 religiously motivated violent incidents they tracked in 2012, 88.3 percent were attacks on Christians, 2.9 percent were attacks on Muslims, 4.4 percent were attacks on security agents, 2.2 percent were sectarian clashes, and 2.1 percent were extrajudicial killings. The 2011 United States Terrorism Report estimates a total of 136 terrorist attacks in Nigeria. By August 10, 2012, about 80 percent of the forty-nine incidents reported that year targeted Christians.

Among the worst crimes committed by Boko Haram terrorists through the end of 2013 were the suicide-bombing of a UN building in Abuja, which killed at least twenty-four people in August 2011, the coordinated attacks on Christmas Day in 2011 that killed dozens of people, including thirty-seven at a Catholic church in Madalla, Niger state, near Abuja; the 2012 attacks at the Armed Forces Command and Staff College, Jaji near Zaria; the night-time attacks and murder of more than 100 students in a high school and in a polytechnic in Yobe state in 2013; and the multiple bomb attacks at a bus station in Nyanya on the outskirts of Abuja that killed at least 100 people and injured over 200 others on April 14, 2014. They have also escalated the abduction of young women used as human shields and sex slaves; the most dramatic and abhorrent being the April 14, 2014 abduction of over 270 mostly Christian teenage girls from a secondary school in Chibok, Borno State whom the Boko Haram leader **Abubakar Shekau** threatened to sell into slavery.

The Nigerian government's perceived continuous display of incapacity to confront the Boko Haram terrorist insurgency and other manifestations of insecurity have eroded the confidence of the citizenry in the state's ability to protect them, leading to general panic – to the extent that many Nigerians, locally and abroad, are seriously questioning the continued existence of Nigeria as one country. On January 16, 2014, President Jonathan fired and replaced his service chiefs, ostensibly to reinvigorate the government's counterterrorism and counterinsurgency efforts. Yet attacks by Boko Haram continued unabated, further undermining the legitimacy of the government and sapping the morale of the security forces. Following worldwide condemnation and social media mobilization through the **#BringBackOurGirls** campaign, the Nigerian government accepted assistance from the United States, the United Kingdom, France, and Israel to help find the girls and possibly eliminate the Islamist insurgency that now threatens to spread to some of Nigeria's neighbors.

Some observers reject explanations of the Boko Haram insurgency based on social factors such as poverty, lack of education, unemployment, and ideological and religious fundamentalism as untenable and hypocritical, claiming that none of these reasons is strong enough to warrant the wanton destruction being perpetrated by the dreaded sect. Instead, they see the insurgency as an attempt by some northern politicians to destabilize President Jonathan's government. Some of them had publicly declared in 2010 that they would make Nigeria ungovernable should Jonathan win the election. Many northerners had expected that Muhammadu Buhari, a former military dictator and presidential candidate of the opposition and largely northern-based Congress for Progressive Change (CPC), to win the 2011 election and return power to the region, since Yar'Adua had not completed his tenure by the time he died in 2010. There is therefore speculation that one of the ways these northern agitators sought to achieve their "ungovernability" objective was to instigate attacks on security agents and Christians so as to ignite a full-scale religious war in the country. To that extent, Boko Haram could be interpreted as a political (not religious) strategy to scare Jonathan from running for a second term and to capture executive power and ensure a power shift to the north in 2015.

Irrespective of how one interprets the Boko Haram insurgency, there is no doubt that it has become "a manifestation of a virulent religious backwardness," according to Nigeria's Nobel Laureate, Professor Wole Soyinka. The insurgency has become a self-inflicted wound that could exacerbate Nigeria's history of severe north-south cleavages. Already, the north is far behind the south in every aspect of development, be it education, business, health, or employment, and this insurgency will only widen the gap. Long after the insanity of the alleged terror sponsors is over, northern children yet unborn will continue to suffer for what their leaders have planted, all in the name of politics.

Elections and Nigerian Democracy after a Pivotal Election

Interests, Institutions, the Failed Third Term Plot, and the 2007 Elections

We have seen in the preceding sections that Nigeria has had more than five general elections since its independence on October 1, 1960, two of them conducted by military regimes preparatory to their disengagement from formal politics. These elections did not lead to peaceful transfer of power from one administration to another. The only exception was the 1983 general election that saw the then incumbent, Alhaji Shehu Shagari, succeeding himself. However, the events that led to his overthrow by the military in December 1983, three months after the election testified to the shaky credibility of that exercise. The 2007 presidential election was therefore more than just another election. Indeed, it was billed as a pivotal one that would permanently redefine Nigerian politics and give a mighty boost to the democratic project in Africa in the twenty-first century.

Nigeria's opportunity to experience genuine democratic regime change was almost ruined by Obasanjo's political ambitions. His efforts to institutionalize needed reforms for political and economic development were matched or surpassed by actions or policies that undermined the regime's legitimacy and public trust in institutions of government. The most baffling and contentious example was his ill-fated plot to change the constitution to allow him to run for a third term as president. The **"third-term" plot** was disguised in a bill that included 103 other legally unassailable amendments aimed at smoothing the rough edges of the 1999 constitution imposed by the military, which the president and the ruling PDP wanted to ram through the legislature. The plot was eventually stopped by both chambers of the National Assembly in one of those rare moments when the legislature truly asserted its independence as a coequal arm of government. The collapse of the third-term plot plunged Nigeria into a crisis that mortally undermined the presidency and other institutions of government more than any of the other maladies discussed in this chapter. It set the stage for the present-day leadership selection process and the quality of leaders that emerged in the ruling PDP for all levels of government.

A humiliated Obasanjo utilized a number of state agencies officially intended to curb the crimes of corruption and electoral malfeasance (for example, the EFCC, the Independent

Corrupt Practices Bureau, and the Code of Conduct Bureau) to attack anyone who may have disagreed with him, especially on his desire to extend his tenure. Meanwhile, several notoriously corrupt prominent politicians and godfathers around the president were spared from prosecution, even after some of these agencies had submitted damning indictments against them. The biggest fallout from this failed plot was an open fight between Obasanjo and his vice president, Abubakar Atiku, which publicly tarnished Nigeria's image and scandalized the citizenry. Atiku had openly opposed the third-term agenda from the very moment the idea was floated in 2003. As we noted earlier, in 2003 Atiku had managed to convince the PDP, especially the party's state governors, to allow Obasanjo to run for a second term with the understanding that he, Atiku, would "naturally" be the party's presidential flag-bearer in the 2007 presidential elections. Obasanjo, however, vowed not to allow Atiku to run for president, accusing him of disloyalty, corruption, and misuse of public funds belonging to the Petroleum Development Trust Fund (PTDF), of which Atiku was in charge as vice president – a charge that the vice president flatly denied. Instead, in December 2006, Obasanjo midwifed a seriously flawed PDP primary that anointed Umaru Musa Yar'Adua, a quiet former chemistry lecturer and sickly incumbent governor of the northern sharia state of Katsina, as his successor. Atiku eventually contested the election on the platform of a new party, the Action Congress, and lost woefully.

In 2007, there were fifty-five registered political parties, but only twenty-five fielded candidates for president. A total of 61,567,036 Nigerians were registered by the Independent National Election (INEC) for the vote, compared to the 60,823,022 registered in 2003. At least 120,000 polling stations were designated, while local and international election observers numbered more than 100,000 and covered almost every part of the country. With a population of about 150 million people, this meant that less than 40 percent of Nigerians supposedly decided who would run the affairs of the nation for the next four years.

Unfortunately, this unprecedented transfer of power from one elected president to another was not executed cleanly at all, largely because of the disruptive effects of Obasanjo's botched third term plot that resulted in last-minute arrangements for almost everything related to the poll. Although a new president was sworn in on May 29, 2007, the process was marred by unprecedented and embarrassing widespread organizational flaws, fraud and violence. The 2007 polls, like all previous elections, unleashed the worst aspects of a political system run by godfathers – state governors, political contractors, Western powers, and local and foreign multinational corporations – who forge deals and alliances to support candidates. Depending on whose figures one chooses, anywhere from 100 to 300 people were killed or died in political clashes or related events between November 2006 and April 2007, a figure that grew following bouts of predicted postelection violence.

The Alliance for Credible Elections and the Transition Monitoring Group called the elections a "charade," while international observer groups such as the International Republican Institute, the National Democratic Institute, the ECOWAS Election Observer Mission, the European Union, and the Commonwealth Observer Group concluded that the elections "failed to meet acceptable minimum standards." Specifically, there was colossal rigging, falsification of results, rampant cases of ballot-bag snatching at gunpoint, under-age voting, a shortage of voting materials, and a general intimidation of the electorate and opposition party agents during the elections.

Compounding the problem was INEC, whose credibility took a nosedive following its disastrous voter registration exercise in 2006. This saw the number of eligible voters mirac-ulously leap from 50 million to 61 million, while hundreds of thousands of people were clearly unable to register because of the chaos emanating from the Electronic Data Capture machines used in the exercise. INEC's partisan pronouncements and actions, for which its chairman, Professor Maurice Iwu, was severely chastised by the high courts, and its sheer ineptitude in conducting the state and federal elections, badly tarnished Nigeria's efforts to establish genuinely democratic electoral politics. In Anambra State, a notoriously rancor-ous bastion of thuggish politics in the southeast, the commission was forced to adjust the votes of the declared winner from 1.9 million to 1 million – after discovering that the total number of registered voters was 1.7 million. In Rivers State, where the 2006 census gave the adult population as 2 million, or about 45 percent of the total population of 5.1 million, INEC curiously awarded 1.9 million votes to the winner of the governorship election. The implication is that each member of the adult population registered and voted for the PDP when there were forty-nine other political parties and this made the commission's claims seriously suspect. By the time Yar'Adua was inaugurated, there were election petitions in all states for almost every seat, including about five seeking to invalidate the presidential election. As in previous Nigerian history, archaic court rules and corruption within the judiciary and electoral commissions once again made it extremely difficult to overturn even clear cases of irregularities, including the presidential election.

Despite these monumental failures, the significance of the 2007 election and the civil-ian-to-civilian transition still should not be underestimated. Since independence, Nigeria had not had this kind of election, in which twenty-six out of thirty-six state governors were virtually in transition and the president himself agreed (although reluctantly) to leave office at the expiration of his term and to hand over power to another person. Moreover, this was the first time voter registration and general elections were conducted electronically. Perhaps most important, Nigerians strongly diminished the likelihood of any future incum-bent fighting to retain the presidency by mobilizing to stop President Obasanjo's third-term plot. That "emperor" Obasanjo stepped down involuntarily after eight years in power says something for the strength of Nigeria's fledgling parliament, which derailed the third-term plot. While a number of parliaments in Africa have yet to evolve beyond rubber stamp status, Nigeria's parliament, especially between 2005 and 2007, demonstrated remarkable political will to restore the integrity of the legislature.

The 2011 Elections: Free and Fair, Yet Still Unconsolidated Democracy

As 2014 was dawning, Nigerians were celebrating fifteen years of uninterrupted civilian democracy since 1999 (the longest in the country's history) with a bicameral National Assembly. Total voter registration in 2011 was 74 million, with 40 million valid votes and

1.3 million invalid votes. In the presidential election the Peoples' Democratic Party (PDP) emerged as the winning party for the third time, with 58.89 percent of the votes, followed by the Congress for Progressive Change (CPC) with 31.98 percent, and the Action Congress of Nigeria (ACN) with 5.41 percent. The south-west zone had the lowest voter turnout for the presidential election while the south-south had the highest turnout – perhaps because there was no Yoruba presidential candidate for any of the major political parties. The PDP led in the three south zones, except in Osun state, which supported ACN, while CPC was predominant in the Northern zone except in the north-central states and Taraba state of the northeast.

Although the number of registered political parties was still fifty-five in 2011, the PDP remained the leading political party in Nigeria with a majority of the state governors and members of the National Assembly and state assemblies. The party's majority diminished after the 2011 general elections, mainly because of dissatisfaction with the party's nomination process in which many presidential contenders, especially those from the north who had hoped for the chance to shift power once more to the zone, were cleverly maneuvered out of the contest in favor of President Jonathan, who was serving out the late Yar'Adua's truncated term. This was the basis for the threat by these northern politicians to make the country ungovernable should Jonathan be elected president. The balance of power did not change in the National Assembly, even though only six out of the fifty-five political parties are represented in the Senate and/or House of Representatives. Nigerian political parties get funding mainly from their members and from INEC, but the Electoral Act's stipulations about how much individuals or organizations can contribute to a political party are hardly enforced.

Contrary to earlier predictions of impending implosion, Nigeria's 2011 elections ushered in quite a number of unprecedented changes. First, Jonathan's resounding, if controversial, victory over veteran opposition leader retired general Muhammadu Buhari, along with the earlier defeat of the former dictator, retired general Ibrahim Babangida, in the PDP primaries, has probably precluded the chance that any of the dictators who plundered the country during twenty-nine years of military rule will ever come back to rule the country again A more revolutionary change is the fact that Jonathan is the first southern minority leader to win the presidency, having become the incumbent by his predecessor's death in office. Third, although PDP retained its majority in the National Assembly, 72 of 109 senators lost their seats to new members, while 260 of the 360 members of the current House of Representatives were newly elected. Also important considering the authoritarian temptations of **one-party dominant democracies** is the fact that President Jonathan's PDP lost its two-thirds majority in the Senate and held the governorship in only twenty-three of the thirty-six states, compared to twenty-seven after the 2007 elections.

The blend of cautious optimism and foreboding on the eve of the 2011 polls deserves elaboration because it highlights the challenges of managing the differential impacts of Nigeria's development paths and the difficult choice the state elite, citizens and other social forces have to make between radical change or maintenance of the status quo. The appointment as chairman of a respected university vice chancellor and former leader of the university teachers' union, Professor Attahiru Jega, restored credibility to INEC, whose image was not helped by the combative persona of the previous chairman. Jega and his INEC team quickly instituted important reforms, such as the voting procedure; the introduction of the idea of community mandate protection to prevent malpractice; the deployment of hundreds of National Youth Service Corps (NYSC) members as poll unit staff; and the prosecution and sentencing of officials, including the electoral body's own staff, for electoral offenses. At the same time, there were several red flags that indicated all might not be well with the polls: the upsurge of violence in several states, encouraged by politicians and their supporters who feared defeat; the Electoral Act, an ambiguous and confusing legal framework for the elections; and a flawed voter registration exercise, with poorly functioning biometric scans, that resulted in an inflated voters roll.

Many observers, however, could not have predicted the violent orgy of destruction and bloodletting that erupted in some northern states following the announcement of the presidential results. More than 800 people were killed (compared to 300 in 2007), making an otherwise free and fair elections one of the bloodiest ever in Nigeria. It would not have been Nigeria if there had not been cases of malpractice, logistical deficiencies, and procedural inconsistencies. One of the biggest puzzles was why the reported voter turnout of about 78 percent in the South-South and the South-East during the presidential elections exceeded the national average by at least 50 percent, suggesting electoral fraud. Cumulatively, however, these irregularities were not strong enough to undermine the credibility of the polls. Domestic and international observers commended INEC for improved logistics and a smooth voting process, and agreed that the strength of the electoral process appeared mostly to have trumped its weaknesses across the country.

Yet, Nigeria's democracy will not be consolidated until truly free and fair elections become routinized in the country. Although the country may have taken steps in 2011 toward reversing the degeneration of its previous elections, that election and follow-up gubernatorial and by-elections in some states since then suggest that Nigeria's culture of flawed elections persists. The current INEC chairman, Professor Jega, was appointed barely a year before the election, unlike in neighboring Ghana or South Africa where the same individuals were in charge of the electoral body for over a decade. Intensive preparations for the balloting did not start until a few months into the process. Consequently, the usual fire brigade culture led to the midmorning cancellation of the first poll even after many people (including President Jonathan) had voted. That the Nigerian president was not consulted in the cancellation, however, showed the extent of independence allowed the INEC by the government.

Opposition Politics, Power Shifts, the Judiciary and the Legacies of One-Party Dominance

In 2008, the national chairman of the PDP boasted that the party would rule Nigeria for at least sixty years before losing power. As preparations moved into top gear in May 2014 for the 2015 elections, speculations about a serious challenge to the continued dominance and complacency, if not outright defeat, of the ruling PDP were rife. A similar, though less optimistic, speculations in 2011 failed to materialize. One of the major winners in the mobilization of opposition to PDP in that election was the Action Congress of Nigeria (ACN), whose success in the South-West returned that region to its tradition of being in opposition to the ruling party at the center. Mohammadu Buhari's CPC (founded in 2009) came third in both the Senate and House of Representatives with 6 senators and 21 house members, respectively. In the Senate, the PDP won 53 of the 109 seats, followed by the ACN's 13, 4 for ANPP and another 4 shared by other minor parties. In the House of Representatives, the PDP gained 123 seats, the ACN 45, the CPC 21, the ANPP 11 and other parties 18 seats. Although Buhari lost the presidential election, he came second with 12,214,853 votes, compared to Jonathan's 22,495,187 winning votes. Buhari also won in all the northern states, while Jonathan won in all middle-belt and southern states apart from Osun State in the southwest. Another winner, though on a lesser scale, was the All-Progressive Grand Alliance (APGA)–led by former Biafran leader, Ojukwu–, which wrested control of Imo state from the PDP; along with Anambra state, which it won in 2007 to hold two core South-East states and a senatorial seat. PDP's predicted 60-year rule seemed to be a done deal.

By late 2013, however, the political power equations were thrown into a state of flux. First, the PDP's loss of its near invincibility in the 2011 elections created an opening for aggrieved members to challenge the party's culture of leadership impunity and lack of internal democracy. Between 2011 and 2012, the most serious opposition to both the Jonathan presidency and PDP leadership emanated from among PDP governors and National Assembly members, starting with the election of Aminu Tambuwal of Sokoto state as Speaker of the House in June 2011, instead of a South-West candidate preferred by both the president and the party. Deep-seated divisions and resentment against the culture of stage-managing primaries and subverting the rule of law was blamed for PDP's defeat in governorship elections in Osun, Edo, and Anambra states in 2012 and 2013. A May 2013 attempt by the PDP and President Jonathan to annul the election of the Chairman of the National Governors Forum caused five PDP governors to leave the party, while a botched election for the national working committee of the party in July 2013 led to the emergence of a splinter group called New PDP, led by former Vice President Abubakar Atiku who had re-joined the party in 2009. Most observers blame the current governance crisis and insecurity in the country on the corruption and dysfunction in the ruling PDP. In 2014, Kashim Shettima, ANPP governor of Borno State captured these sentiments when he quipped that: "apart from colonialism and the slave trade, nothing so terrible has befallen Nigerians in the last 14 years more than the emergence of PDP rule at the national level."

As the crises in the PDP deepened, Nigeria's opposition parties, themselves embedded in much deeper governance crises, began to conspire to dislodge "Africa's biggest political party." In February 2013, the CPC, ACN, ANPP, and a faction of APGA merged to form the All Progressives Congress (APC) in preparation for the 2015 elections. For a brief period in January-February 2014, the APC gained a majority in the House of Representative when 77 PDP members crossed over to the new party. The APC has succeeded in wooing into its fold many disaffected PDP members, including the Atiku-led

New PDP faction. A taste of the challenge a united opposition might pose to the PDP occurred in January 2014 when the APC leadership instructed its parliamentary delegation to block passage of President Jonathan's 2014 budget and screening of newly appointed service chiefs. It remains to be seen whether this latest round of mergers by opposition parties will stick and finally challenge the hegemony of the PDP. Indeed, by mid-February 2014 five APC members had re-joined PDP thereby reinstating its majority. Doubts also abound regarding the sustainability of ongoing party realignments because most politicians crossing over to the APC (including Atiku and Buhari) are clearly driven by personal interests, especially the failure of PDP to guarantee them automatic slots on the ballot for 2015. The merger could also unravel before the elections if the leadership fails to fairly and democratically manage the division of party offices and primaries in the run-up to the elections. A more worrisome concern, however, is the ability of the APC to guarantee political order, should it try to oust the PDP from power in 2015 and discover that the PDP is not willing to relinquish it. Despite its flaws, the PDP remains the first Nigerian post-independence political party to successfully transcend Nigeria's overwhelming ethnic, religious, cultural, geographical/geo-political diversity and cleavages. For these reasons, its disintegration amidst rising levels of domestic insecurity would be a cause for alarm. The APC would need to advance beyond its current reliance on popular dislike for the PDP and President Jonathan as the basis for forging a national consensus for a united, democratic Nigeria.

The exploration of the institutions that have shaped Nigeria's developmental path would not be complete without at least a brief analysis of the judiciary in Nigeria. Like other Nigerian political institutions, the judiciary has also had mixed experiences during the Fourth Republic. During Obasanjo's first four years, the judiciary had a somewhat timid relationship with the executive. A number of judges were removed from office by the National Judicial Council for various offenses that demonstrated the extent of bribery and corruption in the judiciary. The Supreme Court also alienated minority groups by siding with the federal government in its effort to quash minority efforts to exercise greater control over mineral resources in their regions. Even more damaging for the judiciary's legitimacy, the government frequently ignored or selectively implemented judicial decisions against it.

It was only in the last two years of Obasanjo's administration that the judiciary began to assert its authority, thereby regaining some of the credibility it had lost over the previous three decades. Perhaps the most audacious assertion of judicial independence occurred in the context of the face-off between Obasanjo and his vice president. Three days prior to the presidential election in 2004, the Supreme Court ruled clearly that the INEC did not have the power to disqualify candidates for election and should therefore not have excluded Atiku's name from the list of presidential candidates. The judiciary followed up on its landmark ruling by voiding the 2007 gubernatorial election in Anambra state, in which Obasanjo's former valet was foisted on the state, and reinstating former governor Peter Obi of the All People's Grand Alliance (APGA). The judiciary also gets credit, especially since the appointment of Justice Mariam Aloma Muktar as Nigeria's first female Chief Justice of the Supreme Court in 2011, for taking steps to modernize archaic court rules and procedures, and to launch investigations into corruption involving at least twenty-three judges at various levels of the judiciary. Unfortunately, the judiciary still suffers serious erosion of talent as more experienced jurists refuse appointments to the bench; courts are generally understaffed and face years of case backlogs; it is rare to find computers in courts, while judges still record most proceedings by hand. Access to lawyers and justice thus remains a pipe dream for most Nigerians.

Old and New Media and Democracy in the Fourth Republic

The most effective means of assessing the feedback effects of any national development path is the media. In this regard, Nigeria continues to be awash with a vibrant, if not noisy, media culture, especially with the rise of many private TV and FM radio stations (including many community radio stations), and the explosion in the availability and use of new social media. Since the return of the country to democracy in 1999, quite a lot has changed in terms of freedom for journalists. With the expansion of information and computer technology, the Nigerian media has blossomed, even as traditional print and electronic media, like their counterparts around the world, have had to adapt to the challenges and opportunities of new media and the "liberation technologies," such as Facebook, Twitter, Instagram, blogosphere, cyber-citizen journalism, and so on. The most famous example of the impact of new social media on governance in Nigeria is the #BringBackOur Girls campaign mentioned earlier. The campaign was started on April 23, 2014 by a Nigerian lawyer, Ibrahim Abdullahi, when he tweeted the hashtag off a speech by Mrs. Oby Ezekwesili, ex-minister for education and ex-World Bank Vice-President at the Port Harcourt (Nigeria) World Book Capital 2014 event. The tweet quickly snowballed into a national trend and within two weeks over three million people worldwide had tweeted it, with heads of state (and their spouses), Amnesty International and UNICEF, movie and pop music stars and women's rights leaders, all joining in to highlight the plight of the more than 270 school girls and their hapless families.

In terms of the safety of journalists, however, there has not really been any marked departure from the past. The only difference is that journalists are now more prone to die in crisis/conflict zone (e.g., from Boko Haram attacks) or killed by "freelance assassins" – unlike during the military era when they were directly targeted by the state. The Freedom of Information (FOI) Act, which was signed into law in May 2012, not only guarantees the right of access of individuals and groups to information held by public institutions, but it also challenges the media to be more accurate or risk severe punishment and/or loss of reputation for flouting any provision of the Act.

Where the media has failed (except the cyber-media) is in their role as "the fifth estate of the realm" and the watchdog over the state and society. For instance, most observers agree that the media that ought to be in the forefront of the campaign against corruption is mired in corruption itself. The ownership and the general climate of corruption in Nigeria are often to blame. A lot of the media outfits in Nigeria are owned by politicians or those close to them, a relationship that makes it difficult for journalists not to pander to the whims of their employers. In a way, media censorship has ceased being an exclusive preserve of the state, and is now exercised by a diverse group of perpetrators. A number of online news outlets (some based outside Nigeria) such as *Saharareportersonline* and *Premiumtimesonline* have become major outlets for investigative journalism, especially about public mismanagement, producing stories which are often republished in mainstream media outlets. Critics, however, accuse them of being not only opposition mouthpieces, but also increasinlgy dangerous platforms for whipping up or exacerbating Nigeria's tinderbox of **reinforcing cleavages**.

What Future for a "Crippled Giant" at the Century Mark?

On January 1 2014, Captain (later Lord) Fredrick Lugard's "mistake" of 1914, through which Nigeria was created as a modern state, turned 100 years old. The following year, 2015, will witness pivotal general elections that could either finally undo Lugard's "evil genius" – or at last convince Nigerians about the need to preserve and strengthen their common national identity and citizenship. At times, it is frustrating that the century-old history and the recent history of Nigeria's corrupt leadership give little hope that this enigmatic but fascinating country will ever evolve those institutions, interests, identities, and global connections capable of enabling its political class to replace bribes, vote-rigging, and intimidation of rivals with genuine electoral franchise and consolidated democracy. As the elections closed in both 2007 and 2011, Nigeria resounded with prophecies of clashes and chaos, including civil war or the military intruding yet again into politics. In the case of the 2011 elections, this was sadly not just prediction; more than 800 people died in post-election violence and millions of dollars in property damage further sharpened Nigeria's ever-present cleavages.

Nigeria, which has been described as a "crippled giant", has had similar political crises in the past as detailed earlier in this chapter. Remarkably, this national tendency to predict disaster and head for the precipice has historically always ended with remarkable swerves to avoid it at the last second. As noted by Richard Dowden, director of the Royal African Society in London, the trouble in the twenty-first century is that this tendency to head for disaster and then pull back is a terrifying nightmare for Nigeria's neighbors on the road they hope will lead to mutual prosperity and stability. As one Ghanaian minister said in 2007, "Please beg those Nigerians for all our sakes to stay cool and calm. We don't want a disaster that will damage us, too." Yet such fears may have underestimated the possibility of some order emerging in the midst of seemingly impossible options – as demonstrated in the 2007 civilian-to-civilian transition, President Jonathan's accession to the presidency in 2010, and his overwhelming victory at the polls in 2011 in all but a few states of the federation and across all lines of cleavage and inherited, socially constructed identities.

Yet if President Jonathan's January 2013 claim that "Nigeria is too old to break up" will stand the test of time, there is an urgent need to address the persistent problems that have retarded its political and economic development. This will not be an easy task. Hortatory statements alone are not strategies for the serious, sustainable nation-building that needs to be done. If the founding fathers of modern Nigeria could not agree on what exactly they were founding, the quest for a consensus on what constitutes the Nigerian nation and what form its statehood should take has continued to be ever more elusive for subsequent generations of Nigerian peoples and their leaders. Figuratively speaking, while the original architects built a huge Nigerian mansion without prior agreement on what the design plan should be, subsequent occupants of the mansion have found it even harder to decide what to do with the edifice – including whether even to live in it. Attempts to patch up leaks or cracks in the structure have been equally contentious and haphazard, up to the point of almost pulling down what has been built on a structurally flawed foundation. If this house survives past its predicted collapse in 2015, it will certainly still be sitting on a dangerous edge of the precipice. Nigeria's serious cleavages may ultimately be incompatible with a twenty-first-century global economy that has little use for potential that cannot be turned into reality.

One of the most difficult and most urgent issues that must finally be resolved as Nigeria looks toward the next century is the **national question**. This refers to the tensions and contradictions of the Nigerian federalism and inter-group relations pivoting around issues of marginalization, domination, inequality and injustice in the distribution of resources, citizenship rights, and differential representation and access to political offices. These potential triggers of conflict are a major preoccupation of the ongoing constitutional review exercise convened in April 2014, which already faces a complex agenda of potentially explosive issues including indigeneship, federal character and citizenship; the creation of new states, fiscal federalism and the devolution of power; the review of local government administration and judicial reforms, including a review of the laws on terrorism with a view to giving more powers to security agencies fighting the menace; regional cooperation and autonomy, devolution of powers from the center, and community policing; and the fate of the National Youth Service Corps (NYSC) scheme. These unresolved national questions are the reason for the flawed federal arrangement and the difficulties of managing it, no matter how theoretically unassailable the formal institutions adopted for this purpose. Nigeria's unresolved national identity is at the root of persistent and increasingly more deadly ethno-religious cleavages, economic retardation, mind-boggling and pervasive corruption and pillaging of the country, youth restiveness, and the unprecedented wave of insecurity. It is also the cause of the most pressing problem of Nigeria today: how to get credible people well-prepared ahead of time and eventually elected and/or appointed into leadership positions. The suggestion that the unity of the Nigerian state is a "no-go area" for any constitution review may in the end be a self-defeating delusion because it will not go away until it is resolved.

Although history might judge the first fifteen years of the Fourth Republic and the three civilian presidents (Obasanjo, Yar'Adua, and Jonathan) harshly for the way they pursued personal power and their halfhearted anticorruption crusades, these leaders must be given credit for their apparent ability to permanently exclude the military from government and seemingly subject it to civilian control. The process began with Obasanjo's dismissal in 1999 of about ninety senior military officers tainted by their involvement in politics under military rule who might have the potential to nurse political ambitions. Both Yar'Adua and Jonathan also caged the military through generous budgetary allocations and by substantially improving the material conditions of the senior officer corps, dangling the possibility of promotion to the military's top echelons through frequent reshuffling of the service chiefs. The military has also been engaged in – and benefited materially from seemingly unregulated millions of dollars poured into – the various "Joint Task Forces" created to tackle the wave of insecurity discussed earlier. Many Nigerians today believe that civilian control of the military is so entrenched that they do not envisage gunmen in uniform again holding the population hostage while pillaging the state treasury. Indeed, during the constitutional crises sparked by Yar'Adua's six-month absence because of ill health in 2009–2010, junior, middle, and senior-level officers reportedly refused entreaties by some local and international interests to intervene and stabilize the polity. The civilian presidents (especially Obasanjo) may have looked the other way as many of their PDP party men robbed the country blind, but they have been quite decisive about the military and what its role should be in their government. The ease with which they frequently changed or eased out insubordinate or potentially troublesome service chiefs and generals could not even be contemplated under military rule.

Nonetheless, it is a sad commentary that Presidents Obasanjo, Jonathan, and their teams, who were expected to use the tremendous goodwill and support poured out to them upon their assumption of office to steer the country away from its chaotic past, will likely go down in history as a mixed bag, if not as outright failures. Their failure would not necessarily be because there was anything wrong with them or that they failed to build institutions; it may be because there is everything wrong with Nigeria – its structure and terms of existence, its interests, identities, and institutions, and the vexing problem of the "national question." One may even be tempted to come to the conclusion that the country's founding fathers and mothers, by their actions, choices, or omissions, inadvertently created a country where mediocrity is celebrated and where people limit themselves to personal gain, as did the booty hunters that created, more than three decades before Lugard, the rudiments of commercial enclaves governed by royal charters that eventually became Nigeria. In this respect, the Fourth Republic has been both remarkably similar to, and is an extension of, its predecessors. The post-military political class has only reinforced the unfortunate history of postcolonial Nigeria – one of perpetual struggle by the people against bad leadership.

Breaking this jinx in order to free the people from the tyranny of a few self-righteous individuals, however, depends on the outcome of a number of struggles that have always underlain Nigerian politics. These are the struggle between dictatorial temptations of one or a few individuals and irrepressible popular demand for democracy, arbitrariness versus the rule of law, an entrenched culture of impunity versus due process, and the booty-hunter mentality and selfish interests of a few individuals versus the national interest. Nothing short of a complete break from the chaotic history highlighted in this chapter can fix Nigeria's problems while tapping into its immense potential. A combination of electoral, constitutional, and economic reforms is needed to make the 2015 polls truly free and fair and to ensure they are not tainted by blood as in 2011. Genuine and comprehensive electoral reforms should be implemented. to make the system more inclusive; economic reforms should be introduced to reduce poverty and create jobs for restive young school-leavers and graduates. Constitutional reform – which should benefit from the 2014 constitutional conference – should be done with a more holistic, less piecemeal approach, and with the full involvement of the Nigerian people, who have long been demanding it. There is a limit to how long a small cadre of elites – whether based on ethnicity or class – can continue to delay action on these issues without bringing the predicted disintegration of the Nigerian state by 2015 to fruition.

The Goodluck Jonathan administration has a chance to make a clean break with the past. Some aspects of his Transformation Agenda have already begun to dismantle some of very same interests, institutions, and competing identities that stopped previous administrations from fulfilling their promises to Nigerians. As already noted, the deadly post-presidential election violence in the north in 2011 and the long-drawn and escalating violent threat from the Islamist terror group, Boko Haram since 2009 amplify the link between broad-based economic development and democratic consolidation in Nigeria. An integrated program of economic reconstruction and development, drawing from the Transformation Agenda, would be necessary to address chronic poverty all over the country, but especially in the north, as part of a strategy to contain the wave of violence and insecurity engulfing the country. Even if the Boko Haram insurgency is not caused by chronic poverty and underdevelopment in the north, such a strategy would at least undermine the legitimacy of the political sponsors of the terrorist group.

At the same time, there are still many self-inflicted wounds, including the seeming inability of the government to tackle the general wave of insecurity; to finally fix the energy and petroleum sector; and to rein in corruption in the ruling PDP, the government, the civil service, and increasingly in the private sector. Jonathan pledged during his 2011 campaign to transform the country. Yet, his various cabinets, a hodgepodge of recycled, failed, and controversial ministers; party stalwarts indicted in the past; a few possible reformers; and some technocrats, inspire little confidence among Nigerians. Many of them have further undermined the credibility of the government by their ineptitude and personal aggrandizement; yet the president kept them for too long. Time may not be on his side to bring about the changes he has been promising since 2010, even as his mixed-bag record could be a much harder obstacle than a seemingly united opposition, should he decide to run for a second term in 2015.

Once again, where Nigeria goes from here after a century of existence will be a function of the mutual interactions among those interests, institutions, and identities the state and society have developed over the years, which have in turn been mediated by global forces.

Table 14.2   Key Phases in Nigeria's Political Development

Period	Regime	Global Context	Interests/ Identities/ Institutions	Developmental Path
Until nineteenth century	empires, kingdoms, emirates, and hundreds of village-level councils; company rule	trans-Atlantic slave trade	African chiefs and kings; Islamic revolutionaries and state-makers; emergent trading city-states; European merchants and booty hunters; missionaries; returnee slaves	unequal exchange; imperialism and mercantilism; trade in human, natural, and agricultural resources
1860–1914	Crown Colony of Lagos; Protectorate of Northern Nigeria; Oil Rivers Protectorate; Protectorate of Southern Nigeria; amalgamation	renewed European mercantilism, industrialization, rise of new states; World War I	indirect rule with emirs, obas, and warrant chiefs; European trading firms; competition among various communities	promotion of cash-crop economy; monetization of the economy
1914–1945	Colonialism (authoritarian)	European imperialism; World War II	native authority (indirect rule); newly educated class; nascent urban commercial interests; missionary and European merchants; nascent political parties; national identity began to clash with ethnic/ tribal cultures and identities	amalgamation of Northern and Southern Nigeria; infrastructural development to promote cash-crop economy; disarticulation of indigenous economies

(continued)

Table 14.2 (*cont.*)

Period	Regime	Global Context	Interests/ Identities/ Institutions	Developmental Path
1945–1960	colonialism; local/regional autonomy/ self-government;	Cold War and trend toward decolonization	militant nationalist movement; nascent trade unions; mass-based cultural organizations and political parties; print media; local and Asian, Levant and European merchants; marginalized women	infrastructural development; mining; cash-crop economy; poll tax and self-financing colonial administration
1960–1966	First Republic; Northern People's Congress dominance and alliance with either Igbo or Yoruba parties	Cold War and nonaligned movement	Weak central government and powerful regions; religious and ethnic diversity; parliament and judiciary; Hausa-Fulani, Igbo, and Yoruba dominance and minority rights agitations; peasant and working-class interests	State-dominated import-substitution industrialization; planned development
1966–1979	Military rule (authoritarian) and civil war	Cold War; nonaligned movement; oil and rise of OPEC	secession and Biafran civil war; state-creation; "military federalism"; labor unions, students; multinational oil companies;	state-dominated import-substitution industrialization; indigenization/ economic nationalism

Period	Regime	Global Context	Interests/ Identities/ Institutions	Developmental Path
1979–1983	Second Republic; National Party of Nigeria dominance and alliance with Igbo-led Nigerian People's Party	Cold War; nonaligned movement; collapse of oil price and reduced impact of OPEC	military disengagement; federalism and "federal character" principle; nineteen states, parliaments; courts; organized labor and students; state-dependent foreign and local capital; prebendalism and corruption	state-dominated import-substitution industrialization; indigenization; first phase of structural economic adjustment
1983–1999	military (authoritarian); stillborn Third Republic	late Cold War; end of Cold War, globalization	return of the military; minority rights agitation and thirty-six state structure; revenue allocation; religious and ethnic conflicts; organized labor and mobilized pro-democracy civil society; ethnic militias and youth insurgency in the Niger Delta; corruption	neoliberal economic reforms and structural adjustment; quest for export-led growth

(continued)

Table 14.2   (*cont.*)

Period	Regime	Global Context	Interests/ Identities/ Institutions	Developmental Path
1999–Present	Fourth Republic; People's Democratic Party dominance	post–Cold War globalization	federalism, zoning and revenue allocation and "resource control" politics; political parties, organized labor, civil society; religious and ethnic mobilization and increased youth and militia insurgency; Boko Haram Islamsit terrorism oil multinationals	neoliberal economic reforms and structural adjustment; export-led growth and privatization

BIBLIOGRAPHY

Achebe, Chinua. *A Man of the People*. New York: Anchor Books, 1966.

Achebe, Chinua. *There Was A Country: A Personal History of Biafra*. New York: Penguin Press, 2012.

Achebe, Chinua. *The Trouble with Nigeria*. London and Exeter, NH: Heinemann Educational Books, 1983.

Adebanwi, Wale and Ebenezer Obadare. *Democracy and Prebendalism in Nigeria: Critical Interpretations*. New York: Palgrave Macmillan, 2012.

Ajayi, Gboyega I. *The Military and the Nigerian State, 1966–1993: A Study of the Strategies of Political Power Control*. Trenton, NJ: Africa World Press, 2007.

Ake, Claude. *Political Economy of Nigeria*. London and New York: Longman, 1985.

Ayoade, John A. and Adeoye A. Akinsanya, eds. *Nigeria's Critical Election, 2011*. Lexington Books, 2012.

Beckett, Paul, and Crawford Young, eds. *Dilemmas of Democracy in Nigeria*. Rochester, NY: University of Rochester Press, 1997.

Campbell, John. *Nigeria: Dancing on the Brink*. Lanham, MD: Rowman & Littlefield.

Coleman, James S. *Nigeria: Background to Nationalism*. Berkeley: University of California Press, 1958.

Diamond, Larry. *Class, Ethnicity and Democracy in Nigeria: The Failure of the First Republic*. Basingstoke, UK: Macmillan, 1988.

Diamond, Larry, Anthony Kirk-Greene, and Oyeleye Oyediran, eds. *Transition without End: Nigerian Politics and Civil Society under Babangida*. Boulder, CO: Lynne Rienner Publishers, 1997.

Elaigwu J. Isawa. *The Politics of Federalism in Nigeria*. London: Adonis & Abbey, 2007.

Falola, Toyin and Michael M. Heaton. *A History of Nigeria*. Cambridge University Press, 2008.

Falola, Toyin, and Julius Ihonvbere, eds. *The Rise and Fall of Nigeria's Second Republic, 1979–84*. London: Zed Books, 1985.

Forrest, Tom G. *Politics and Economic Development in Nigeria*. Boulder, CO: Westview Press, 1995.

Ihonvbere, Julius O. *Nigeria: The Politics of Adjustment and Democracy*. New Brunswick, NJ: Transaction Publishers, 1994.

Ilesanmi, Simeon O. *Religious Pluralism and Nigerian State*. Athens.: Ohio University Press, 1997.

Joseph, Richard A. *Democracy and Prebendal Politics in Nigeria: The Rise and Fall of the Second Republic*. New York: Cambridge University Press, 1987.

Kuka, Matthew H. *Religion, Politics and Power in Northern Nigeria*. Ibadan: Spectrum Press, 1994.

Maier, Karl. *This House Has Fallen: Midnight in Nigeria*. New York: Public Affairs Press, 2000.

Nnoli, Okwudiba. *Ethnicity and Development in Nigeria*. Aldershot, UK, and Brookfield, VT: Avebury, 1995.

Odetola, Theophus. *Military Politics in Nigeria: Economic Development and Political Stability*. New Brunswick, NJ: Transaction Books, 1978.

Okonjo, Isaac M. *British Administration in Nigeria 1900–1950: A Nigerian View*. New York: NOK Publishers, 1974.

Okonjo-Iweala, Ngozi. *Reforming the Unreformable: Lessons from Nigeria*. Cambridge, MA: MIT Press, 2012.

Okonta, Ike, and Oronto Douglas. *Where Vultures Feast: Shell, Human Rights, and Oil*. London: Verso, 2003.

Okpaku, Joseph, ed. *Nigeria: Dilemma of Nationhood: An African Analysis of the Biafran Conflict*. New York, Third Press, 1972.

Osaghae, Eghosa. *Crippled Giant: Nigeria since Independence*. Bloomington, IN: University Press, 1998.

Rotberg, Robert, ed. *Crafting the New Nigeria: Confronting the Challenges*. Boulder, CO: Lynne Rienner Publishers, 2004.

Schwarz, Frederick O. *Nigeria: The Tribes, the Nation, or the Race: The Politics of Independence*. Cambridge, MA: MIT Press, 1965.

Sklar, Richard. *Nigerian Political Parties: Power in an Emergent African Nation*. Princeton, NJ: Princeton University Press, 1963.

Smith, Daniel J. A. *Culture of Corruption: Everyday Deception and Popular Discontent in Nigeria*. Baltimore, MD: Johns Hopkins University Press, 2008.

Soyinka, Wole. *The Open Sore of a Continent: A Personal Narrative of the Nigerian Crisis*. New York: Oxford University Press, 1996.

Suberu, Rotimi T. *Federalism and Ethnic Conflict in Nigeria*. Washington, DC: United States Institute of Peace Press, 2001.

IMPORTANT TERMS

Aba Women's war of 1929 – grassroots mobilization by Igbo women against British colonial rule, especially the rumored imposition of a poll tax on women following the introduction of a similar tax for men two years earlier.

Sani Abacha – Nigeria's brutal dictator from 1993 to 1998, infamous for corruption and for stashing up to $6 billion in foreign accounts, who died before actualizing plans to transform himself into a civilian president.

Johnson Thomas Umunnakwe Aguiyi-Ironsi – a major-general and general officer commanding Nigerian Armed Forces during the first military coup in 1966; became Nigeria's first military ruler and was killed in the July 29, 1966, anti-Igbo countercoup.

amalgamation – the merging of previously separate administrative units into one for ease of administration. For example, the amalgamation of the protectorates of Northern and Southern Nigeria into one British Colony of Nigeria in 1914 by Sir Frederick Lugard.

Amnesty Program – a program of forgiveness and rehabilitation (including salaries and stipends, skills acquistion in crafts, entrepreneurship, technidcal trades, and professional and further education domestically and abroad) implemented by the Nigerian government since 2009 for over 30,000 Niger Delta who agreed to surrender their weapons.

austerity measures – structural adjustment program (SAP) to curtail public spending, especially on social services and subsidies.

Obafemi Awolowo (1906–1987) – often called the father of opposition politics in Nigeria; leader and founder of the Action Group; premier of the then Western Region, later imprisoned for sedition, and presidential candidate of the Unity Party of Nigeria (UPN) in the Second Republic.

Benjamin Nnamdi Azikiwe (1904–1986) – often called the father of the Nigerian nationalist movement; leader and founder of the National Council of Nigerian Citizens (NCNC); premier of the then Eastern Region, president of the First Republic of Nigeria, and presidential candidate of the Nigerian People's Party (NPP) in the Second Republic.

Ahmadu Bello (Sadauna of Sokoto) – leader and founder of the Northern People's Congress and premier of the then Northern Region, killed in the 1966 coup.

Sovereign Independent Republic of Biafra – the ill-fated breakaway Eastern Region dominated by the Igbo ethnic group; collapsed on January 12, 1970.

coinciding cleavages – these are cross-cutting cleavages (difference, elg.; class dived across ethnic or religiosu groups) that tend to contribute to social stability because even the most committed demagogue would have difficulty pitting one group against the other. Cross-cutting cleavages tend to lead to political cultures of coalition-building and compromise.

Boko Haram – violent Islamist group that first emerged in 2002 demanding "full sharia" in twelve northern states but which became increasingly disillusioned with these governments for compromising the movement through corruption and materialism. The group has killed over 5,000 people, razed hundreds of churches and mosques, and escalated kidnappings and abductions, especially of female school children most of whom are sold into sex slaveryl.

Decree no. 34 of 1966 – introduced by General Ironsi's regime to unify the federal bureaucracy and police forces; undermined national consensus on federalism.

Economic and Financial Crimes Commission (EFCC) – Nigeria's anticorruption watchdog, which convicted over 500 persons from 2002 to 2013, but whose effectiveness has been weakened by corruption within the organization and by political interference.

emirate political system – the Islamic political system in the emirates defeated by the British in 1886, which became the model of British colonial administration in Nigeria – successful in the north, fairly successful in the west, but a colossal failure in the east.

federalism – a power-sharing arrangement between the central government and the federating units; Nigeria is unusual in that the constitution includes local councils as a coequal third tier of power.

federal character – Nigeria's version of affirmative action, seeking to guarantee a proportionate share of federal positions for all states, especially to protect "educationally backward areas."

fiscal federalism – an arrangement by which all the federating units theoretically contribute to, and derive allocations from, federally collected revenue.

Hausa-Fulani – the ethno-linguistic group that has historically dominated the politics and economy of northern Nigeria; also dominant in Nigeria's politics and the armed forces since independence in contention with the Igbo and Yoruba, Nigeria's two other major ethnic groups.

Hisbah – a form of religious police (initially recruited from youth gangs) that enforces dress codes, a ban on the sale of alcohol, and male-driven motor bike taxis carrying women in the twelve sharia states in Northern Nigeria.

Igbo – the ethno-linguistic group that has historically dominated the politics and economy of eastern Nigeria; the nucleus of the ill-fated breakaway Republic of Biafra; often in contention with the Hausa-Fulani and Yoruba, Nigeria's two other major ethnic groups; also can refer to the language spoken by the Igbo.

Indigenization Policy Degree – sought to restrict ownership and management of 40–60 percent of the national (especially "the commanding heights") economy to Nigerian nationals.

indirect rule system – a system of rule by which the British governed conquered territories through existing "traditional" or "natural" political institutions and sought to disrupt the extant local institutions as little as possible.

Joint Task Force (JTF) – a joint security force made up of the armed forces, state security services, civil defense, and police engaged in internal security operations (e.g., Operation Pulo Shield against the Niger Delta militants and Operation Restore Order against Boko Haram terrorists.

June 12 – refers to the June 12, 1993, presidential election won by Yoruba business mogul Moshood K. Abiola but which was annulled by the military.

Sir Frederick Lugard – British colonial officer (initially a captain) who conquered and ruled northern Nigeria from 1900 to 1914, the year he effected the amalgamation of the two protectorates of Northern and Southern Nigeria. Lugard (referred to as Nigeria's first "evil genius") then became governor of colonial Nigeria, a policy still regarded by Nigerians today as "the mistake of 1914."

"mistake of 1914" – the British policy that merged or "amalgamated" the two protectorates of Northern and Southern Nigeria in 1914 under the governorship of Sir Frederick Lugard.

Movement for the Survival of Ogoni People (MOSOP) – founded by writer Ken Saro-Wiwa, who was hanged in 1995 (with eight others) for campaigning against the environmental degradation caused by oil drilling by Shell.

Nagropreneurs – a term describing about 750,000 young Nigerians who are expected to embrace agriculture as a business and help the country become self-sufficient in food production by 2025.

National You Service Corps (NYSC) – compulsory one-year national integration program to acquaint graduates of tertiary institutions with the immense diversity of their country as they prepare to assume national leadership positions.

NEEDS – National Economic Empowerment, Development and Sustainability program initiated under President Olusegun Obasanjo in 2002 but subsequently absorbed into the Transformation Agenda of the president Goodluck Jonathan administration in 2011.

Olusegun Obasanjo – military ruler from 1976 to 1979, when he handed power back to a civilian regime; ruled again from 1999 to 2007 as elected civilian president.

pogrom – massacre of more than a hundred thousand innocent civilians and more than two hundred army officers of Igbo origin in various parts of (especially northern) Nigeria, following the January 15, 1966, and July 29, 1966, military coups against the Igbo; sometimes referred to as genocide.

prebendalism – a form of corruption whereby state offices are appropriated by officeholders who use them to generate material benefits for themselves and their constituents and kin groups.

protectorate – a colonial territory acquired through the signing (often under duress) of a "treaty of protection" between a European power and an African ruler or community.

reinforcing cleavages – serious class, racial, ethnic, or religious divisions that feed on or reinforce one another. Reinforcing cleavages, even in healthy democracies, tend to lead to much more competitive politics where every election necessarily means one social group wins at the expense of the others.

resource control – a continuation of the politics of revenue allocation whereby oil-producing states seek more local control of the revenue derived from the resource instead of the current lopsided control by the federal government.

Royal Niger Company – British trading company granted a royal charter to administer areas along the River Niger, 1886–1900.

Sabon Gari – "stranger quarters" or residential enclaves for non-Muslim migrants from southern Nigeria found in many cities in northern Nigeria.

Abubakar Shekau – leader of the Boko Haram Islamist terrorist group operating in northern Nigeria. He replaced Mohammed Yusuf, a more moderate leader of the group who was killed in police custody in 2009.

third-term plot – a plot by President Obasanjo to amend the constitution so as to allow him to seek a third term as civilian president, which was defeated by Parliament in response to domestic and external pressure.

warrant chiefs – local rulers whose authority was modeled on the emirate system in northern Nigeria and imposed by the British on southeastern Nigeria, especially among the Igbo, who did not have a widespread tradition of kingship.

Yoruba – the ethno-linguistic group that has historically dominated the politics and economy of western Nigeria; also dominant in Nigeria's economy since independence; and often in contention with the Igbo and Hausa-Fulani, Nigeria's two other major ethnic groups; language spoken by the Yoruba.

STUDY QUESTIONS

1. Compare and contrast civilian and military governments in Nigeria in terms of how they have dealt with the problems of corruption, minority interests groups, and overall economic development. What accounts for their differences and/or similarities?

2. Compare and contrast the institutional arrangements to share power among the various tiers of government in India, Nigeria, and the United States. Which country has done a better job at protecting the interest of minorities?

3. What are the costs and benefits associated with the federal and presidential systems of government adopted by Nigeria since 1979? Is "zoning" of political offices an improvement over earlier problems associated with the dilemma of implementing the "federal character" principle and running an efficient and effective government?

4. What are the immediate causes of the Biafran war (1966–1970)? In what ways does that war differ from the ongoing insurgency in the Niger Delta?

5. What do Nigerians mean by "the mistake of 1914"? To what extent have those "mistakes" shaped the politics of ethnicity and "resource control" since independence in Nigeria?

6.   What lessons can we take from the 2007 general and presidential elections in Nigeria in terms of democracy promotion and the consolidation of democratic regimes?

7.   In what ways did the legacies of British colonial rule shape the institutions, material interests, and identities that have structured the nature of interactions among Nigerians and postcolonial politics? How have these institutions, material interests, and identities been affected by global economic, social, and political processes?

8.   If you were a Nigerian voter and a member of civil society groups, what would you do regarding the government of President Umaru Yar'Adua, which succeeded the Obasanjo administration in May 2007, given the verdict by local and international election observers that the poll failed to meet acceptable minimal standards of fairness?

9.   Religious fundamentalism – both Islamic and Christian – and the recourse to African traditional religions have been on the rise as Nigeria's economic fortunes have declined and poverty become more pervasive over the past two decades. In what ways have these movements affected political development in Nigeria?

Early Developers, Middle Developers, Late Developers, and Experimental Developers

Taken together, the chapters you have just read underscore the importance of domestic political responses to international political challenges. In fact, a different title for the book might well have been "Liberal Democracy and Its Challengers." As we have seen, Britain and France developed first, each with its own institutional variation on the liberal democratic theme. This development, as positively as we may now evaluate it from our own perspective, made these two states powerful and ultimately threatening to Europe and the rest of the world.

Still, because of British and French successes, other countries sought to emulate the experience of the initial developers. In terms of our five-step framework: (1) Although middle developers Germany and Japan reacted to British and French development, devising variations on the initial British and French innovations, they were never actually able to replicate them for the simple reason that they were trying to catch up from behind. (2) In middle developers, middle-class interests were weaker, nationalist identity more pronounced, and bureaucratic state-institutions stronger and democracy weaker. (3) These different circumstances of development ultimately weakened liberalism in Germany and Japan, which paved the way for the Nazi and fascist responses. It makes sense therefore to speak of a fascist path to the modern world. (4) The Nazis and the Japanese launched World War II, which ultimately led to occupation by the core liberal powers and a recasting of domestic identities, interests, and institutions. (5) In contemporary democratic Germany and Japan interests, identities, and institutions grapple with the economic and political legacies of their distinctive authoritarian path to the modern world.

The late developers in this book are the (post) communist giants Russia and China. In terms of our five-step framework: (1) Both tried to industrialize their societies in a global order dominated by liberal democratic and fascist capitalist states. (2) In late developers, middle-class interests were even weaker, nationalist identity more pronounced, bureaucratic state-institutions even stronger, and democracy even weaker. (3) These different circumstances of development cut off both the liberal democratic and fascist paths and paved the way for communism – the twentieth century's third main contender for a path to the modern world. (4) After an initial flirtation with global dominance, both the Soviet Union and China settled into an effort to legitimate their specific response to liberalism with superior economic performance under communist economic institutions. (5) Both failed. After desperately trying to repair a basically unworkable communist economic and political model in the decades after Stalin's death, the Russian response was to give up communism and introduce democracy and markets in the hope of rejoining the democratic capitalist world system. Neither democracy nor markets were terribly successful in Russia after communism. Under President Putin's strong hand and buoyed by high energy prices, Russia reverted to a relatively stable form of authoritarian-led market development. China, on the other hand, shed its communist economy but not its communist party. Under the influence of the other successful semi-authoritarian capitalist states in East Asia, the Chinese response was to introduce markets into society, while attempting to maintain communist party dominance. Whether either country is able to succeed in its newfound flirtation with a complete or partial reintegration with the international liberal order remains to be seen.

Experimental Developers: Mexico, India, Iran, South Africa, The European Union, and Nigeria

Our final group of countries embodies a distinctive global historical heritage and shares common links. Most often, this commonality is colonial. Mexico, India, Iran, South Africa, and Nigeria experienced the impact of European colonial power. All now confront the cultural, institutional, and economic pressures of the global economy. Despite these similarities, each of these countries has distinctive, if modal, kinds of political problems that are of great interest to comparativists.

South Africa and India respectively conduct democratic politics in countries with very high levels of ethnic and racial diversity. Both have developed an innovative set of institutional arrangements for adjudicating conflicting ethnic and racial interests and identities within the parameters of what we normally think of as democratic institutions. Their experiments with multicultural democracy may even provide lessons, both positive and negative, for more industrialized Western societies. Furthermore, both confront the problem of sustaining democracy in environments of economic scarcity.

Nigeria also has attempted to structure democratic politics in a highly diverse society. Before independence the British colonial authorities encouraged and even strengthened ethnic fragmentation as a tool of colonial rule. After independence, the demands of so many competing ethnic groups in an environment of economic scarcity put tremendous strain on the country's institutions and has not made for stable democratic politics. Nigeria is also in many ways cursed with having so much oil. The rich countries of the world are interested in this country primarily for its oil, and Nigeria's elites have frequently misused and even stolen the country's wealth rather than cobble together a set of economic policies that would enable high energy prices to foster sustained economic growth.

Iran experienced decades of steady Westernization under a dictator, the Shah. After an Islamic revolution in 1980, it sought to reshape its society and live under the rules of political Islam. It thus stands as a fascinating case of the religious reaction to global cultural, economic competition, and political pressure. The recent on-again, off-again turn to more moderate leadership in Iran illustrates vividly just how powerful are the homogenizing forces of global liberalism. It remains unclear whether these latest developments signal a gradual return to the modernizing path taken before the Islamic revolution or whether it is a sign that the Islamic revolution is now institutionally stable and has indeed carved out a viable alternative to the liberal democratic and global capitalist order that it consciously rejected.

Finally, Mexico has taken precisely the opposite route from Iran, choosing economically to integrate itself as closely with the United States as it can. Integration into the global trading system, however, has created both new political elites that are supportive of this move and new social movements that oppose it. Until the year 2000 Mexico was steadily (if corruptly) ruled by one party (the PRI). The election of Vincente Fox in 2000, however, turned a new and important page in Mexican history. Whether the new political elites and social movements that have emerged as a result of rapid economic change will contribute to the consolidation of liberal democracy remains an open question.

Perhaps the most challenging experiment of all has been the European Union. In some ways, this case does not neatly fit into our framework of analysis. The European Union is not a country and of course it has never been colonized. Instead, the European Union is an experiment that challenges one of the key assumptions of comparative politics – that the world is divided into relatively independent states. The entire purpose of the European Union has been to secure peace and prosperity for the multiple peoples of Europe by pooling the one resource that is normally guarded by national elites: sovereignty. Rather than figuring out ways to prevent the powerful currents of international markets and the rise of new powers from undermining national authority, the members of the European Union have embraced economic and political integration on a regional level. The intention is to build and preserve something that is distinctly European and banish war from the European landmass forever. The question remains, however, what the final destination of integration will be. What began as a trade organization has developed into something much more serious and complex with its own set of interests, identities, and institutions. Europeans disagree about whether the purpose of the European Union is to promote trade or to create a new overarching European identity. They disagree about how much sovereignty should be ceded to Brussels and where the member states should pursue their own interests and strengthen their own identities. Finally, they also disagree about the limits on enlargement and where Europe's "borders" lie. Which countries should be admitted and which excluded? How these disagreements are resolved will determine whether the European Union becomes a model for other regions of the world or remains an entity particular to the European experience.

In sum: six cases, six experiments. Mexico's grand experiment is independence: Is it possible for a country to be autonomous when its northern neighbor happens to be the most powerful nation in the world? Iran's grand experiment is Islamic governance: Is it possible for a country to be economically and politically powerful in the modern era when it has had an Islamic revolution that creates an Islamic state? India's grand experiment is nonrevolutionary democracy: Is it possible for a large postcolonial country to be a democracy when it has had a major independence movement but not a social revolution? South Africa's grand experiment is interracial democracy. Is it possible for ethnoconstitutional democracy and markets to survive in a country that made a relatively peaceful transition from colonialism and apartheid? Nigeria's experiment combines the challenges of all of these: the diversity and nonrevolutionary colonial heritage of India, the difficulties of democracy amid tribal fragmentation of South Africa, and the dependence on oil revenues of Mexico and Iran – all in an environment of dire scarcity. What is the long-run fate of democratic rule with such unfavorable initial conditions? Our final experiment, the European Union, is not a country but a new form of political organization that raises the crucial question of whether states and societies are willing to give up their sovereignty in pursuit of peace and prosperity. Will the European experience be exportable to other regions of the world?

More generally: twelve cases, twelve experiments. The closer we look the more we discover that there have been twelve developmental paths to the modern world. States made their own development choices and evolved local institutional variations of globally dominant political economies. In the words of our framework: (1) the constant of global context influences (2) the types of domestic interests, identities, and institutions that produce (3) the variables of developmental paths to the modern world, which, in turn, generate (4) international-relations feedback effects on the global context and (5) comparative-politics feedback effects on domestic interests, identities, and institutions.

Index